DŌGEN'S EXTENSIVE RECORD:
A TRANSLATION OF THE EIHEI KŌROKU

DŌGEN'S EXTENSIVE RECORD

A TRANSLATION OF THE
EIHEI KŌROKU

TRANSLATED BY
TAIGEN DAN LEIGHTON &
SHOHAKU OKUMURA

EDITED & INTRODUCED BY
TAIGEN DAN LEIGHTON

FOREWORD BY **TENSHIN REB ANDERSON** WITH INTRODUCTORY
ESSAYS BY **STEVEN HEINE** AND **JOHN DAIDO LOORI**

Wisdom Publications • Boston

Wisdom Publications
199 Elm Street
Somerville, MA 02144 USA
www.wisdompubs.org

Library of Congress Cataloging-in-Publication Data
Dōgen, 1200-1253.
 [Eihei kōroku. English]
 Dogen's extensive record : a translation of the Eihei kōroku / translated by Taigen Dan Leighton & Shohaku Okumura.
  p. cm.
 Includes bibliographical references and indexes.
 ISBN 0-86171-305-2 (hardcover : alk. paper)
 1. Sōtōshū—Doctrines—Early works to 1800. I. Leighton, Taigen Dan. II. Okumura, Shohaku, 1948– III. Title.
 BQ9449.D653E13 2004
 294.3'927--dc22

                                                2004011571

Cover design by Rick Snizik
Interior design by Gopa&Ted2, Inc. Set in Adobe Garamond 11/13.

Printed in Canada

Hōkyōji portrait
(see page 602, verse 3)

Eiheiji portrait
(see page 605, verse 10)

PUBLISHER'S ACKNOWLEDGMENT

THE PUBLISHER GRATEFULLY ACKNOWLEDGES the kind help of the Hershey Family Foundation in sponsoring the publication of this book.

CONTENTS

The Significance of Eihei Kōroku and Its Translation *by Steven Heine* 51

Dōgen and Kōans *by John Daido Loori* 61

"On Reading Eihei Kōroku" *by Ryōkan (1758–1831)* 69

Eihei Kōroku

Indexes

FOREWORD

THERE IS A PRINCIPLE in Zen Buddhism that for our practice to be alive and relevant to the actual problems of our current suffering as sentient beings, we must go beyond the previous ways the tradition has gone beyond itself. Here in this wonderful translation of the Extensive Record, we have a separate transmission that goes beyond the Zen tradition of separate transmissions beyond the Buddhist scriptures. Now, thanks to the great and loving efforts of two devoted students of Eihei Dōgen, we are challenged by this vast pile of precious records from our brilliant ancestor. These are records of his repeated attempts to free his self-expression from the Chinese Zen tradition of trying to leap free of the Buddhist tradition. In the face of this tradition, how are we going to study this oceanic record without damaging the living spirit that brings us to this text in the first place? One possibility would be to close the book now. But if we avoid reading it, how will we develop our skill as escape artists? On the other hand, if we do read and study these dusty old records, how will we avoid becoming like Huangbo's "dreg slurpers"?[1]

In reading this text, we can see how our Lofty Ancestor ingested, transformed, and became a new expression of his own Dharma nourishment. We can observe how his study chews up the records of his own ancestors and completely or incompletely digests them. We can see how his process of meditative digestion turns the old stories of the tradition into warmth, Dharma protein, and waste products. Or do we suppose

1 See Dharma hall discourse 125.—*Ed.*

that the Ancestor is so great that he completely burns up the tradition, with no waste products?

If we just sit by and watch while not participating in the dynamic way that Dōgen leaves the tradition behind in the dust, the dust will engulf our present generation. We must gratefully receive these records into the furnace of the ancestors' samādhi and let them be completely burned up, thus giving off their great sweetness and light.

The cooking of the ancestors' samādhi is demonstrated on every page of the Vast Record of Eihei. For example, in Dharma hall discourse 503 of this marvelous translation, we hear that a monk asked the great Chinese master Yunmen, "What is Buddha?" Yunmen then stands on the Buddha's shoulders, leaps, and says, "A dried piece of shit." Then Dōgen's master, Tiantong Rujing, going beyond Yunmen, composed a verse saying:

> Yunmen took a shit from the opposite end,
> Upsetting Gautama, like an acupuncture needle in a painful
>   spot.
> We need to see the ocean dried up clear to the bottom,
> To know the person dead, without remaining mind.

Then our great Japanese ancestor, going beyond his master, says:

> Today, I, Eihei, would like to continue this rhyme:
> How could myriad activities lead to this careless nature?
> When Buddha was sick, Jīvaka offered a needle.
> Even if we see the ocean dried up without any bottom,
> Who can clarify the person dead, without a mind remaining?

Now it's our turn. Do we have a fresh needle to offer? Are we in the West ready to enter this process and make our contribution to this tradition of transcendence of tradition?

Out of deep gratitude for our living tradition, I am not going to study this text any further without wholeheartedly vowing with each reading to express myself in such a way as to stand on the shoulders of this record and leap beyond it, thereby beginning to repay the boundless kindness and compassion that has gone into its creation, preservation, and new translation. How about you? Will you join me in this vow to thoroughly study and continuously refresh this tradition of endless transcendence?

Nine bows,

TENSHIN ZENKI REB ANDERSON
Senior Dharma Teacher and former Abbot
of San Francisco Zen Center

INTRODUCTION

TAIGEN DAN LEIGHTON

Overview of Dōgen's Teaching Career

IN 1227 the Japanese monk Dōgen (1200–1253) returned to Japan from four years of study in China. During his remaining twenty-five years he composed an extraordinary volume of writings, now widely prized for their philosophical profundity, poetic virtuosity, and subtle, evocative wordplay. Dōgen is remembered as the founder of the Sōtō branch of Japanese Zen. But he disdained sectarian labels, saying that "Zen" was "an extremely foolish name" and that "if you use the name Zen School you are not descendants of buddha ancestors, and also have poisonous views."[1] Nevertheless, in the long history of what is now considered the Zen tradition, no master has left a legacy of writings as voluminous and comprehensive, in so many aspects of teaching and practice, as Eihei Dōgen. Although he was a medieval monk born eight centuries ago, his writings about time, space, Buddha nature, and the subtle character of spiritual pursuit and realization are now widely esteemed by contemporary philosophers, physicists, poets, environmentalists, and religious thinkers and practitioners. His writings can be baffling and intensely challenging but also inspiring and deeply comforting. This work of Dōgen's, Eihei Kōroku, or *Dōgen's Extensive Record,* is one of his great collections of wisdom and insight, but it also reveals the unique kindness, authority, wit, and personality he displayed while training his disciples, who successfully sustained his teaching and practice.

Dōgen's earliest writing, his first declaration of awakening, was Fukan-zazengi (Universally Recommended Instructions for Zazen), written after

---

1 See Dharma hall discourse 491 in volume 7 below.

he returned from China to the Kenninji monastery in Kyoto in 1227.[2] It proclaims the value, power, wonder, and accessibility of zazen, or seated meditation, the primary practice that Dōgen advocated throughout his life. The earliest version of this text is no longer extant, but a later version is included at the end of volume 8 in this book.

Aside from the substantial legacy of Dōgen's own writings, much remains uncertain about the historical facts of his life. The first substantial biography of Dōgen, titled Kenzeiki, was not written until the fifteenth century and remained unpublished for another couple of centuries. Much of it might well be considered sectarian hagiography.[3] But we know that Dōgen was born into high aristocracy in the ancient capital of Kyoto and that he was a precocious, highly intelligent child. According to the legendary account, he first decided to enter the spiritual life at the age of seven, after experiencing a deep realization of impermanence while watching the incense smoke rising at his mother's funeral. Five years later he became a monk in the Tendai school, one of the two dominant branches of Japanese Buddhism at the time, which had its headquarters, Enryakuji temple, on Mount Hiei on the northeast edge of Kyoto. Sometime between the age of fourteen and seventeen, for unclear reasons, Dōgen left Mount Hiei and went to practice at Kenninji, the first Zen monastery in Japan.

In 1223 Dōgen traveled to China with his teacher from Kenninji, Butsuju Myōzen, who was a successor of the Kenninji founder Myōan

2 For a full discussion of Fukanzazengi, including its various versions and its sources in Chinese meditation manuals, see Carl Bielefeldt, *Dōgen's Manuals of Zen Meditation* (Berkeley: University of California Press, 1988).

3 A thorough discussion of Dōgen's early life before his trip to China, complete with bibliography on the available Japanese biographical sources, is in Takashi James Kodera, *Dōgen's Formative Years in China: An Historical Study and Annotated Translation of the "Hōkyō-ki"* (Boulder: Prajñā Press, 1980), pp. 7–35. Other useful sources for Dōgen's biography, consulted for this introduction, include William M. Bodiford, *Sōtō Zen in Medieval Japan* (Honolulu: Kuroda Institute, University of Hawai'i Press, 1993), pp. 22–36; Carl Bielefeldt, "Recarving the Dragon," in William LaFleur, ed., *Dōgen Studies* (Honolulu: Kuroda Institute, University of Hawai'i Press, 1985), pp. 21–53; Heinrich Dumoulin, *Zen Buddhism: A History*, vol. 2, *Japan*, trans. James W. Heisig and Paul Knitter (New York: Macmillan, 1990), pp. 51–72; and Daigan Matsunaga and Alicia Matsunaga, *Foundation of Japanese Buddhism*, vol. 2 (Los Angeles: Buddhist Books International, 1976), pp. 233–243.

Eisai (or Yōsai). Eisai, who had also studied in China, was a successor in the Linji (Jap.: Rinzai) lineage and was later considered the founder of the Japanese Rinzai school (although it is a different branch of the school that survived in Japan). We do not know if Dōgen actually met Eisai, who died in 1215. But certainly Dōgen highly esteemed Myōzen, who died at age forty-one in 1225 while practicing together with Dōgen at the Tiantong monastery in China. It was shortly before Myōzen's death that Dōgen met his Chinese teacher Tiantong Rujing, who was a master in the Caodong (Jap.: Sōtō) lineage.

After Dōgen's return from China he was highly dissatisfied with the quality of the practice at Kenninji, as he describes in detail in his essay "Instructions for the Tenzo" in Eihei Shingi. He derides the laxity of the *tenzo* (chief cook) there, who "never went to see whether things were done correctly or not." Instead of exemplifying the appropriate sincere attention and care for the monks and their practice, the Kenninji *tenzo* "was a person without Way-seeking mind who never had the chance to see anyone with the virtue of the Way."[4] In 1230 Dōgen left Kenninji and moved south to Fukakusa, then a suburb of Kyoto, where he lived alone and wrote Bendōwa (Talk on Wholehearted Practice of the Way).[5] In 1233 in Fukakusa he founded the Kannon Dōri Kōshō Hōrin Zenji temple, known as Kōshōji for short.[6]

At Kōshōji, where he resided from 1233 to 1243, Dōgen taught zazen to many students, both laypeople and monks. He also began writing essays, most of them based on talks, though some were apparently drawn from letters to students. During this period Dōgen's teaching emphasized the universal applicability of zazen and its inner meaning. But from early on, while still in Kyoto, he also wrote about monastic community practice and the virtues of practicing in remote mountains. He touched on a variety of

4 Taigen Dan Leighton and Shohaku Okumura, trans., *Dōgen's Pure Standards for the Zen Community: A Translation of Eihei Shingi* (Albany: State University of New York Press, 1996), pp. 45–46.

5 Shohaku Okumura and Taigen Dan Leighton, *The Wholehearted Way: A Translation of Eihei Dōgen's Bendōwa with Commentary by Kōshō Uchiyama Roshi* (Boston: Tuttle, 1997).

6 "Kannon Dōri Kōshō Hōrin Zenji temple" can be literally translated as "Kannon Bodhisattva Beneficially Guides the Sacred to Flourish in Jeweled Woods Zen temple," and the usually abbreviated form "Kōshōji" as "Make the Sacred Flourish Temple."

themes, many from traditional East Asian Buddhist teachings, including the universality of Buddha nature, the teaching and practice of suchness, the richness and multidimensionality of time, and the way to read, and practice with, traditional Buddhist scriptures and Zen dialogue encounters, or kōans. But although his writings are now praised as a high point of East Asian Buddhist philosophy, Dōgen was not writing to expound abstract philosophical doctrines or positions. Rather, his writings are spiritual teachings addressed to the practice of particular students.

Among Dōgen's many writings, most famed is his Shōbōgenzō (True Dharma Eye Treasury). The name comes from the Zen legend about Śākyamuni Buddha's Dharma transmission to his disciple Mahākāśyapa, when the Buddha said that he was transmitting the "true Dharma eye treasury, wondrous mind of nirvāṇa." The same title, "True Dharma Eye Treasury," had earlier been given to his own collection of six hundred kōans by Dahui, a Song dynasty Linji lineage master whom Dōgen would severely criticize at times.

The essays in Dōgen's Shōbōgenzō each elaborate on specific themes, motifs, kōans, or other traditional teachings. The modern collection designated as Shōbōgenzō, first compiled in 1695, includes all ninety-five of the essays found in earlier Shōbōgenzō collections, arranged chronologically. Historically a number of different collections of Dōgen's writings have borne the name Shōbōgenzō: a seventy-five-essay and a twelve-essay version, both probably arranged by Dōgen himself, as well as historically important sixty-, eighty-four-, and twenty-eight-essay editions. Dōgen apparently had the intention late in his life to produce a one-hundred-essay version and rewrote some of the essays to this end, but he did not live to accomplish it. The Shōbōgenzō essays were the first Japanese religious or philosophical writings written in Japanese, using the Japanese syllabary alphabet along with Chinese characters. Previous religious or philosophical writings in Japan were written strictly in Chinese, analogous to the use of Latin for religious works in medieval Europe.

Among Dōgen's other works are two from the early Kōshōji period that also include the name Shōbōgenzō. One is the Shōbōgenzō Zuimonki, a collection of informal talks given to students at Kōshōji between 1235 and 1238.[7] Another work, Mana Shōbōgenzō or Shinji Shōbōgenzō,

7 See Shohaku Okumura, trans., *"Shōbōgenzō-Zuimonki," Sayings of Eihei Dōgen Zenji*

both of which mean "Chinese Shōbōgenzō," is a collection of three hundred kōans selected and arranged by Dōgen without commentary. This seems to have been Dōgen's workbook collection of these Chinese stories drawn from a wide range of sources, many now obscure. Dōgen may have used it as the source for his renowned "Kana" (Japanese) Shōbōgenzō essays, many of which focus on kōans. This Mana Shōbōgenzō was dismissed as inauthentic until recently because the only extant version was from a commentary by a Tokugawa period teacher (after the sixteenth century), and the text has no commentary by Dōgen himself. Also, the (erroneous) modern Sōtō stereotype that Dōgen did not use kōans was influential. But recently discovered versions of the Mana Shōbōgenzō text prove that it was indeed created by Dōgen. (In this book, "Shōbōgenzō" will refer to the Japanese text with longer essays. The Chinese text with three hundred kōans is specified as Mana Shōbōgenzō.)

Another separate work of Dōgen's is Hōkyō-ki, a journal of his studies in China found after Dōgen's death by his successor, Koun Ejō.[8] Scholars now are uncertain whether it was written while Dōgen was actually in China or in later years while Dōgen was reflecting on his time there.

Dōgen's Eihei Shingi (Pure Standards) is a compilation of his writings in Chinese about monastic community practice. The first known compilation was made in 1502 and first published in its entirety in 1667.[9] It includes the much acclaimed and discussed Tenzokyōkun (Instructions for the Tenzo), written in 1237. The other five essays were written after Dōgen left Kōshōji and Kyoto and moved far north to the Echizen Mountains in 1243. Dealing with the specific procedures of monastic life, Dōgen's own emphasis in this material is to offer beneficial attitudinal postures and instructions. Thus this work is relevant to the application of meditative awareness to everyday activity. This practical relevance can be

---

Recorded by Koun Ejō (Kyoto: Kyoto Sōtō Zen Center, 1987); Thomas Cleary, trans., Record of Things Heard: The "Shōbōgenzō Zuimonki," Talks of Zen Master Dōgen as Recorded by Zen Master Ejō (Boulder, Colo.: Prajñā Press, 1980); and Reihō Masunaga, A Primer of Sōtō Zen: A Translation of Dōgen's Shōbōgenzō Zuimonki (Honolulu: University of Hawai'i Press, 1978).

8 See Kodera, Dōgen's Formative Years in China.

9 For a complete translation of Eihei Shingi, see Leighton and Okumura, Dōgen's Pure Standards for the Zen Community. For a discussion of its textual history see pp. 21–22 of that volume.

seen as extending to modern Western Zen with its predominantly lay practitioners.

The work translated in this book, Eihei Kōroku, Dōgen's Extensive Record, is almost as lengthy and substantial as the Shōbōgenzō, which has overshadowed Dōgen's other works in modern times. Eihei Kōroku consists of ten volumes. A more detailed account of each element or genre included follows later in this introduction, but a brief overview is helpful here to start. The first seven volumes are roughly chronological records of Dōgen's *jōdō*, or Dharma hall discourses, formal talks given to his assembly of students (mostly monks). These seven volumes comprise 531 numbered Dharma hall discourses. Only the 126 discourses in the first volume were given at Kōshōji, between 1236 and the seventh month of 1243, just before Dōgen left with his students for the remote northern province of Echizen. The Dharma hall discourses in volume 2 do not resume until the fourth month of 1245, after he had established his new temple there.

The eighth volume contains a variety of material. It includes twenty *shōsan*, or "informal meetings," longer talks given to his students in the abbot's quarters after Dōgen settled at Eiheiji. These are followed by material mostly from the Kōshōji period, fourteen *hōgo*, or "Dharma words," also lengthier writings probably based on Dōgen's letters to individual students, sometimes named in the selections. Volume 8 concludes with the popular version of Fukanzazengi (Universally Recommended Instructions for Zazen). This is a revision that Dōgen made at Kōshōji, around 1242, of writings composed upon his return from China in 1227, which he had also revised in 1233. A copy of this 1233 version (called the Tenpukubon), calligraphed by Dōgen himself, is still stored at Eiheiji.

Volume 9 of Eihei Kōroku consists of a collection of ninety kōans with Dōgen's own verse commentaries, also from the Kōshōji period. Some of these kōans are included in the three-hundred-kōan collection of Mana Shōbōgenzō, and many are discussed elsewhere in the Eihei Kōroku Dharma hall discourses or in the longer essays of Shōbōgenzō.

Volume 10 consists of Dōgen's poetry written in Chinese, 150 poems composed from 1223, while he was in China, up to 1252 at Eiheiji, before his death in 1253.

The Move to Echizen

In the seventh month of 1243 Dōgen left Kōshōji and, apparently fairly abruptly, moved most of his community north to the rugged mountains of Echizen (modern Fukui Prefecture) near the Japan Sea coast, remote from the capital of Kyoto. Speculations about this move are diverse, and none can be clearly validated.

Much of the speculation presumes pressures on Dōgen, or even active harassment, from the Kyoto Buddhist establishment, especially the nearby Tendai headquarters of Enryakuji up on Mount Hiei. In 1243, not far from Kōshōji, construction was begun on the Rinzai lineage Zen temple Tōfukuji, where the noted teacher Enni Bennen (1201–1280) became abbot. Enni had himself returned in 1241 from six years of study in China with one of the leading Linji (Rinzai) masters. Some have speculated that Dōgen moved either out of a desire to avoid competition with this nearby Zen temple, or out of disappointment at not having received such patronage himself. Furthermore, Tōfukuji was officially a Tendai temple initially, and Dōgen's relative independence from the establishment sects may have exacerbated tensions.

But there might have also been positive reasons for Dōgen's wanting to move away from the capital to the remote mountains. In his early writings at Kōshōji in Kyoto, Dōgen refers to himself very frequently with the common Zen term "mountain monk," and he extols the virtues of practicing in the mountains. For example, in his 1240 "Mountains and Water Sutra" essay in Shōbōgenzō, Dōgen states that "mountains have been the abode of great sages from the limitless past to the limitless present.... A virtuous sage or wise person enters the mountains."[10] In Dharma hall discourse 41, below, given in 1241, Dōgen refers to the love of mountains by all buddha ancestors. "With the aspiration to love mountains established, although each mountain is different, thirty-one people [probably the number of monks in the Kōshōji assembly then] are on the same single mountain." Later that year, in Dharma hall discourse 65, Dōgen says, "Although the white clouds [sometimes symbolizing pure monks] have no mind, wherever they go they seem to be attracted to the old mountains."

10 Kazuaki Tanahashi, ed., *Moon in a Dewdrop: Writings of Zen Master Dōgen* (San Francisco: North Point Press, 1985), p. 105.

Dōgen also may have moved after receiving the encouragement of significant patronage and support to build a traditional training monastery in Echizen. Dōgen's main patron from at least 1242 on was Hatano Yoshishige (d. 1258), a politically powerful samurai who had land in the Echizen area, some of which he donated for Dōgen's temple. Yoshishige's influence further assured Dōgen and his monastery in Echizen long-term support and protection.[11]

Imaeda Aishin and others have speculated that Dōgen may have moved to Echizen in alliance with the Hakusan movement within the Tendai school, which included Hajakuji temple, near Eiheiji.[12] Hakusan Tendai opposed the Enryakuji branch of Tendai on Mount Hiei and was affiliated with Shugendō, the Japanese mountain ascetic practice, and with the Onjōji Tendai branch. Since the eleventh century an occasionally violent split persisted within the Tendai school between the Enryakuji branch on Mount Hiei and the branch based at Onjōji temple (also known as Miidera) to the south.[13] Although Dōgen had left Enryakuji before he went to China, perhaps he had maintained good relationships with the Onjōji branch. He had studied briefly at Onjōji with the teacher Kōin (1145–1216) before moving to Kenninji, possibly at Kōin's suggestion. Perhaps Dōgen's move to Echizen might have even been sponsored by some Tendai source.

Another source of support for Dōgen in the Echizen area was Kakuzen Ekan (d. 1251) of the Daruma shū, an immature Japanese Zen movement that predated Dōgen. In 1241 Ekan and many of his students had joined Dōgen at Kōshōji. Ekan's students included future key disciples of Dōgen such as Tettsū Gikai, Gien, and Kangan Giin. Kakuzen Ekan had been abbot of Hajakuji, the Hakusan Tendai temple in Echizen, and some of his disciples who joined Dōgen had various other connections in the area that may have been very supportive.

When he arrived in the Echizen area, Dōgen first stayed at Yoshimine

---

11 See Bodiford, *Sōtō Zen in Medieval Japan,* pp. 27, 30.

12 See Steven Heine, "The Dōgen Canon: Dōgen's Pre-Shōbōgenzō Writings and the Question of Change in His Later Works," *Japanese Journal of Religious Studies* 24, nos. 1–2 (spring 1997): 66–69.

13 See Kazuo Kasahara, ed., *A History of Japanese Religion* (Tokyo: Kōsei, 2001), pp. 80–90, 126–127.

temple while awaiting completion of construction nearby of his monastery, initially known as Daibutsuji, or Great Buddha Temple. Dōgen occupied Daibutsuji in the fall of 1244 and then renamed it Eiheiji, or Eternal Peace Temple, in the sixth month of 1246. The name Eihei was taken from the name of the period in China (57–75 C.E.) when it is said that a Buddhist sutra was first brought to China.

Once Dōgen settled at Eiheiji he remained there, with the exception of a seven-month trip east to the new capital, Kamakura, in 1247. He was probably summoned to Kamakura by his patron Hatano Yoshishige, who was in residence there at the time. Some speculation suggests that Dōgen, or perhaps Yoshishige, was seeking new support in Kamakura for Dōgen's teaching. When he returned to Eiheiji in the third month of 1248, as recounted in Dharma hall discourse 251, Dōgen assured his monks that he had not taught the samurai rulers anything that they had not themselves heard, and he seems to acknowledge that he had made a mistake by leaving the monastery for so long. William Bodiford infers from this Dharma hall discourse that Dōgen's disciples were furious about his trip to Kamakura.[14] Dōgen concludes the discourse: "This mountain monk has been gone for more than half a year. I was like a solitary wheel placed in vast space. Today, I have returned to the mountains, and the clouds are feeling joyful. My great love for the mountains has magnified since before."

In late 1252 Dōgen's health began to decline rapidly. His last Dharma hall discourses in Eihei Kōroku were in the tenth month or so of 1252. In the first month of 1253 he composed his last substantial writing, Shōbōgenzō Hachidainingaku (The Eight Awakenings of Great People), based on Buddha's final discourse. In the eighth month of 1253 he left Eiheiji to seek medical care in Kyoto, where he passed away only a few weeks later.

The Significance of Eihei Kōroku in Dōgen's Writings

The time shortly before the move to Echizen in 1243, and also during the construction of Eiheiji, was a peak period of Dōgen's writing creativity, if one measures solely by his output of Shōbōgenzō essays. Of the eighty-

14 Bodiford, *Sōtō Zen in Medieval Japan*, pp. 30–31.

four essays that bear dates in the inclusive, modern, ninety-five essay version of Shōbōgenzō, a full sixty-three were written between the beginning of 1241 and the third month of 1244, when Dōgen finally moved into the completed Daibutsuji temple. The *jōdō,* or Dharma hall discourses, at the beginning of volume 2 of Eihei Kōroku resumed in the fourth month of 1245. Only seven of the dated Shōbōgenzō essays were written after the *jōdō* resumed in 1245, three of them dating from that year.[15] As Steven Heine has suggested, we might easily infer from this that Dōgen actually came to prefer, as a teaching vehicle, the generally briefer *jōdō* to the *jishu* essay style used in Shōbōgenzō.[16]

The dated essays in Shōbōgenzō do not include most of the essays in the twelve-volume version collected by Dōgen's successor, Koun Ejō, two or three years after Dōgen's death. Supposedly these were from Dōgen's undated writings of his last two or three years, although two of the twelve are dated from before he settled at Eiheiji, and some are reworkings of earlier essays. Nevertheless, it does seem apparent that once Dōgen settled at Eiheiji with appropriate monastic facilities, he mostly discarded the more elaborated *jishu* form used in the Shōbōgenzō essays, preferring to teach his monks with *jōdō.* The latter may likely have appealed to Dōgen as the form most used by the classic Chan masters in their traditional "recorded sayings" genre (Ch.: *yulu;* Jap.: *goroku*).

To consider Dōgen's writings and teaching only through the Shōbōgenzō is to ignore the quality and deep significance of the bulk of Eihei Kōroku, and all that he accomplished in his last decade of his teaching at Eiheiji. Some recent commentators have indeed written off Dōgen's last ten years of teaching. Reflecting lack of appropriate appreciation for Eihei Kōroku, Heinrich Dumoulin says of Dōgen's move to Echizen, "He fell into a depression that had been building up through the external pressures and animosities of the dark times he was going through.... It is not that there are no valuable passages in the late books of the Shōbōgenzō, but the downturn is undeniable.... Dōgen's depression vented itself in a surfeit of

15 These accountings are based on the dating of the ninety-five essays given in the translations in Gudo Wafu Nishijima and Chodo Cross, *Master Dogen's Shobogenzo,* 4 books (Woods Hole, Mass.: Windbell Publications, 1994–99); and also Hee Jin Kim, *Dōgen Kigen—Mystical Realist* (Tucson: University of Arizona Press, 1975), pp. 232–233.

16 See Heine, "Dōgen Canon," pp. 61–63, 70–71.

literary productions."[17] But as Bodiford says in his excellent landmark text on medieval Sōtō Zen, "Dōgen's [Eihei] Kōroku has not attracted the attention it deserves.... His Kōroku reveals an invaluable portrait of Dōgen as a Zen master, presenting a living example for his disciples."[18] The 405 Dharma hall discourses in volumes 2–7 of Eihei Kōroku must be included in any understanding of Dōgen and his teaching career. They demonstrate Dōgen's mature teaching in his last decade, as he trained his core group of monks.

Although these shorter talks were considered more formal in the tradition, they paradoxically are much more revealing than Shōbōgenzō of Dōgen's human qualities and personality. In them we can see more fully his training techniques and probing manner. But also revealed are Dōgen's literary wit, his sense of humor and spontaneous playfulness, as well as his occasional sadness and deep sentiment. As for Dōgen's humor, he prods his monks with playful questions and ironic answers, responds with put-downs and wordplay to the masters in the classic dialogues he cites, or demonstrates his teachings with nonverbal performances. Unlike the more philosophical essays in Shōbōgenzō, in Eihei Kōroku we find Dōgen clarifying points by drawing circles in the air with his whisk, or tossing it down, or pounding his staff emphatically on the wooden platform, or simply descending from his seat.

In one theatrical example, Dharma hall discourse 123, Dōgen relates to his monks a meditative vision—or is it a dream?—from the night before. He says that during the night he punched out the empty sky, or emptiness itself. "My fist didn't hurt," he boasts, "but the empty sky knew pain." Thereupon, he relates, sesame cakes fell from the sky, suddenly turning into the faces and eyes of the world. Then the bodhisattva of compassion, Avalokiteśvara, showed up, seeking to purchase these faces and eyes to equip his many-armed, many-faced form, although he had arrived without any money. Dōgen concludes even such a playful fantasy with deep, encouraging Dharma: "When Avalokiteśvara Bodhisattva

---

17 Dumoulin, *Zen Buddhism*, p. 62.

18 Bodiford, *Sōtō Zen in Medieval Japan*, p. 30. Among various sources, I depended primarily on Bodiford's text for the historical information in this introduction, especially on the major disciples of Dōgen, below.

makes an appearance, mountains and rivers on the great earth are not dead ashes. You should always remember that in the third month the partridges sing and the flowers open."

It is highly ironic that Dōgen's writings (especially Shōbōgenzō) have been so influential in the importation of Zen, and even of Buddhism generally, to the West, since they were of minor significance to the early spread and success of Sōtō Zen in Japan. From Dōgen's time until the 1920s, Shōbōgenzō was not studied widely. Beginning in the mid-sixteenth century, however, it was studied by Sōtō scholars and by the few monks who were educated (10 percent at most).[19] Disparate collections of essays with widely variant versions, all designated as Shōbōgenzō, proliferated until the eighteenth century. This led some leaders of the Sōtō sect to doubt whether Shōbōgenzō was in fact written by Dōgen. Sōtō monks began to actually read Dōgen when new editions were published, and especially during the early eighteenth century when there was a revival in Dōgen studies within the Sōtō school. This renewal was initiated in 1700 by Manzan Dōhaku (1636–1714) when he cited Dōgen in his campaign to restore transmission lineages based on direct relationship with teachers rather than on temple abbacy lineages, as was then the norm. The ensuing debate, with both sides citing Dōgen, culminated in 1722 when the Sōtō hierarchy arranged for the government to ban publication of any version of Shōbōgenzō for a century.[20] Later in the eighteenth century, study of Dōgen was inspired by commentaries on Shōbōgenzō by Tenkei Denson (1648–1735), a brilliant monk who often criticized and frequently "corrected" Dōgen's writings based on his own views and promotion of *kenshō* as a standard for zazen. Slightly later, the influential commentaries in response to Tenkei by Menzan Zuihō (1683–1769), based on the

---

19 The Sōtō college Sendanrin in Edo (modern Tokyo) was founded in the mid-sixteenth century. It eventually became the modern Komazawa University. From its founding, Sōtō monks there studied Shōbōgenzō and Dōgen's other writings. After Manzan Dōhaku became head of that school in the late seventeenth century, for about two hundred years it housed fifteen hundred to two thousand monk scholars. Zengaku Daijiten Hensansho, *Zengaku Daijiten* (Tokyo: Daishūkan Shoten, 1978), p. 695.

20 Bodiford, *Sōtō Zen in Medieval Japan,* pp. 48–50.

reliable commentaries of Dōgen's students Senne and Kyōgō, established new standard versions of Dōgen's writings.

Dōgen generally was revered throughout Sōtō Zen history as the founder figure, but at least until the seventeenth century his reputation was mostly based on his image as a meditator and charismatic miracle worker, rather than on his writings.[21] Ryōkan, the great early nineteenth-century Sōtō monk, famed and still much beloved by the Japanese for his exceptional poetry, delicate calligraphy, and sweetly foolish, colorful character, was among the Sōtō clerics who studied Dōgen's writings in the intervening centuries. But Ryōkan could read Dōgen only after receiving permission from his teacher. At the end of the introductory essays of this book is a long poem by Ryōkan from the 1790s in which he tearfully laments that none of his contemporaries, or anyone since Dōgen's time, had deeply studied or understood Eihei Kōroku, the work translated here. Ryōkan wonders at its neglect: "For five hundred years it's been covered with dust / Just because no one has had an eye for recognizing Dharma. / For whom was all his eloquence expounded?"[22]

It was not until 1815 that Dōgen's collected essays became popularly available through a woodblock edition.[23] And it is only in the last century that Dōgen's writings have been generally read by people outside the Sōtō establishment. Dōgen was first presented as an important Japanese philosopher, apart from the Sōtō sect, in essays by the philosopher Tetsurō Watsuji in the early 1920s.[24] Gradually since then, interest in Shōbōgenzō and in Dōgen's image as a philosophical writer has grown in Japan, and internationally in the past few decades.

21 Ibid., p. 32.

22 Ryōkan actually identifies the text he was reading as Eihei Roku, which might perhaps be the abbreviated Eihei Goroku text compiled in China and brought back by Dōgen's disciple Kangan Giin. But there is some evidence that Ryōkan actually studied the entire Eihei Kōroku. The founder of his temple, Entsūji, where Ryōkan had studied, was a dharma brother of Manzan, compiler of one version of Eihei Kōroku, and a copy of the whole text with notes, perhaps by Ryōkan, has been found. See Ryūichi Abé and Peter Haskell, trans. with essays, *Great Fool; Zen Master Ryōkan: Poems, Letters and Other Writings* (Honolulu: University of Hawai'i Press, 1996), p. 280 n. 67.

23 Ibid., p. 267 n. III.

24 Tanahashi, *Moon in a Dewdrop*, p. 24.

As the founder, Dōgen's actual and significant contributions to the historical establishment and spread of Sōtō Zen in Japan were based not on his writings but rather on his training of capable successors and his initiation of lay precept ceremonies. Sōtō Zen survived thanks to Dōgen's training of a dedicated cadre of monks at Eiheiji. Along with their successors in the next few generations, these talented disciples were able to establish Sōtō Zen as a strong network of vibrant and vital religious communities in the Japanese countryside. Eihei Kōroku, and especially its Dharma hall discourses, are the only real source for understanding the nature of the training Dōgen presented to his highly productive successors during his last decade of mature teaching.

Often through this text we can see Dōgen training his disciples, offering them his image of the Chan tradition he had received in China, and providing his successors with a vision of practice-realization and a model for its application. Sometimes in Eihei Kōroku he explicitly discusses his approach to training monks. For example, in Dharma hall discourse 266, dating from 1248, Dōgen specifies four of his approaches and their intent. He states that sometimes he enters the ultimate state and offers profound comments, so that his students may be "steadily intimate in [their] mind field." Sometimes, while walking around the monastery grounds, he provides "practical instruction, simply wishing you all to disport and play freely with spiritual penetration." Sometimes, he says, "I spring quickly leaving no trace, simply wishing you all to drop off body and mind." Sometimes, finally, Dōgen "enters the samādhi of self-fulfillment, simply wishing you all to trust what your hands can hold." These four approaches indicate Dōgen's subtle awareness of his conduct and impact as a Dharma master. But, characteristically, Dōgen concludes this discourse by expressing the ungraspable true quality of his teaching, beyond any techniques or categories. He poetically describes that which goes beyond all of these teaching approaches as, "Scrubbed clean by the dawn wind, the night mist clears. Dimly seen, the blue mountains form a single line."

A few generations after Dōgen, during the time of Keizan Jōkin (1264–1325) and his successors, the practice of lay ordination and initiation cemented the widening popularity of Sōtō Zen amid the rural populace. Through this precept-taking ceremony for laypeople, many common people could feel connected to the Zen lineage. The strict monastic training and zazen practice of local priests were highly respected. But through these ceremonies, people who had no opportunity for such rigorous practice learned how to apply the Sōtō teachings in their everyday activities. This precept initiation practice continues to be important in Sōtō Zen, even in its modern spread in the West. The impetus for this practice, with its emphasis on bodhisattva precepts, can be traced back to the teachings of Dōgen in his later years in Eihei Kōroku, which emphasized the place of ethical conduct, not ignoring cause and effect, and the importance of attention to the concrete details of ordinary daily affairs. Dōgen himself conducted highly impressive precept recitation ceremonies for many laypeople at Eiheiji.[25]

In many of the teachings in Eihei Kōroku, Dōgen stresses the importance of attention to karma. For example, in Dharma hall discourse 485, given in 1252, Dōgen cites a saying attributed to an ancestral Indian teacher: "Even after a hundred thousand kalpas have passed, [the shadow and echo of conduct] have not been erased." Dōgen adds, "The way of the buddha ancestors is like this. Descendants of buddha ancestors should carve this in their bones and etch it in their skins." For another example, Dharma hall discourse 510 begins with "Students of the way cannot dismiss cause and effect. If you discard cause and effect, you will ultimately deviate from practice-realization." For more on Dōgen's wrestling with the centrality of ethical conduct in his final years, see also note 83 to volume 7.

Thus the teachings of Dōgen, and especially their true role in the successful establishment of Sōtō Zen in Japan, cannot be fully understood without significant attention to Eihei Kōroku, with its demonstrations of Dōgen's training of his successors, and his emphasis on ethical application of the teaching to everyday activity. For more on the crucial role of Eihei Kōroku in the full range of Dōgen's work, in the context of the academic field of Dōgen studies, see the additional introductory essay by eminent Dōgen scholar Steven Heine that follows this introduction.

The Question of Shifts in Dōgen's Teachings

Related to the quality of Eihei Kōroku, and the move from Kyoto to Echizen, is one of the prominent issues in modern Dōgen studies, a

25 Bodiford, *Sōtō Zen in Medieval Japan*, p. 32.

supposed shift between Dōgen's early and late teachings.[26] Some commentators, such as Dumoulin, have claimed that Dōgen's teachings declined severely after moving to Eiheiji, or even that Dōgen had become senile, although he died only in his early fifties. A recent contrary view is that *only* the very late teachings, after his return to Eiheiji from Kamakura in 1248, with their strict emphasis on karma, are in accord with early, supposedly "orthodox" Buddhism, and that Dōgen intended to renounce all of his earlier writings. Both of these extreme views are untenable, for they ignore the nuances and subtlety of Dōgen's shifting emphases during his career and also the basic consistency underlying his teaching. Moreover, these modern views about a fundamental shift in Dōgen's doctrinal position are based primarily on his Shōbōgenzō essays, not the mature teachings presented in Eihei Kōroku.

Briefly, one of the main concerns has been that Dōgen's early writings at Kōshōji in Kyoto generally celebrate the universal applicability of zazen, emphatically including the possibility of awakening for laypeople and women. However, Dōgen's later teachings, including some of Eihei Kōroku, generally emphasize the efficacy and importance of monastic practice, and a few Shōbōgenzō essays even say that full enlightenment is possible only for monks. This is stated in a couple of Shōbōgenzō essays from early on at Eiheiji, when Dōgen was first establishing his mountain monastery. These are "The Thirty-Seven Elements of Enlightenment," from 1244, and "Home-Leaving," from 1246, in which Dōgen says, "Someone who has not left family life is never a Buddhist patriarch."[27] This might be interpreted as a simple acknowledgment that the Zen lineage had been transmitted by ordained monks through Dōgen's time, which remained the case until the twentieth century. But in a later version of this essay, "The Merit of Home-Leaving," in the late twelve-volume Shōbōgenzō, Dōgen states it more strongly: "Within the sacred teaching

---

26 For an excellent, detailed treatment of the issues of the relation between Dōgen's early and late teachings, and a clear description of the complexity of nuances in these shiftings, as opposed to the over simplified views of changes in doctrine, see Heine, "Dōgen Canon," pp. 39–85.

27 Nishijima and Cross, *Master Dogen's Shobogenzo,* book 4, p. 112. For "The Thirty-Seven Elements of Enlightenment," see Nishijima and Cross, *Master Dogen's Shobogenzo,* book 4, pp. 1–25.

there is explanation of lay realization of Buddha, but it is not the authentic tradition. There is explanation of the female body realizing Buddha, but this also is not the authentic tradition. What the Buddhist patriarchs authentically transmit is to leave family life and realize Buddha."[28] This might reasonably be interpreted as indicating that buddhahood is beyond all gender discriminations, and requires renunciation of personal attachments. But such interpretation might seem forced or excusatory to modern Western Buddhists informed by feminist and nonhierarchical perspectives.

However, one of Dōgen's Shōbōgenzō essays from 1240—a few years before his departure from Kyoto—Raihai Tokuzui (Making Prostrations and Attaining the Marrow), includes one of the strongest statements for the equality of women in Asian Buddhist history. The long essay states, for example:

> Nowadays extremely stupid people look at women without having corrected the prejudice that women are objects of sexual greed. Disciples of the Buddha must not be like this. If whatever may become the object of sexual greed is to be hated, do not all men deserve to be hated too?... What wrong is there in a woman? What virtue is there in a man? Among bad people there are men who are bad people. Among good people there are women who are good people. Wanting to hear the Dharma, and wanting to get liberation, never depend on whether we are a man or a woman.[29]

Nothing later in Shōbōgenzō or in Eihei Kōroku gives any indication of a significant alteration of such thoroughly articulated avowals of gender equality.

There is no question that Dōgen's later teachings, including Eihei Kōroku, often emphasize monastic practice, for his focus was the training

28 Ibid., book 4, pp. 145–146.

29 Ibid., book 1, pp. 78–79. See also Francis Cook, *How to Raise an Ox: Zen Practice as Taught in Zen Master Dōgen's Shōbōgenzō* (Boston: Wisdom Publications, 2002), pp. 104–105.

of his monk disciples at Eiheiji. This included an emphasis on precepts, moral conduct, and the attentive care of everyday activities and their karmic consequences. But even in Bendōwa, a very early writing from 1231, even before establishing Kōshōji, Dōgen had already expressed his deep concern with monastic practice and standards. "I do not have a chance now to also present the standards for monasteries or regulations for temples, especially as they should not be treated carelessly."[30] Moreover, even at his later teachings at Eiheiji there were laypeople, including women, who frequently attended the Dharma hall discourses along with the monks.[31]

Another frequently cited concern about Dōgen's later teachings is the increase in his apparently sectarian critiques and even occasionally vitriolic attacks directed against other schools or teachers. But the few writings in Shōbōgenzō in which these appear are not actually from his late period writings, and throughout the Dharma hall discourses in Eihei Kōroku, Dōgen praises Linji and other figures from diverse lineages that he had previously criticized. "The period of Dōgen's intense criticism of rivals was short-lived and did not occur again."[32]

We must once more bear in mind that Dōgen is not seeking to promulgate some philosophical doctrine. He is simply expressing his own understanding and deep personal experience of the Buddha way to encourage and develop the practice of an audience of particular students. Many of his later emphases can be clearly viewed as responses to his many monk disciples formerly of the Daruma shū, or Bodhidharma sect.

The importance of the Daruma shū as the background of many of Dōgen's disciples is quite significant. The Daruma shū was an early Zen group in Japan founded by Dainichi Nōnin, active in the late twelfth century.[33] Nōnin developed his teaching from Chan writings without personal guidance of a teacher. Two disciples whom he sent to China found a Chinese master who authorized Nōnin's teaching without meeting him.

---

30 Okumura and Leighton, *Wholehearted Way,* p. 41.

31 See Heine, "Dōgen Canon," p. 70.

32 Ibid.

33 See Bernard Faure, "The Daruma shū, Dōgen, and Sōtō Zen," *Monumenta Nipponica* 42, no. 1 (spring 1987), along with historical texts already cited.

Nōnin's main disciple, Bucchi Kakuan (n.d.) was the teacher of both Koun Ejō and Kakuzen Ekan, who both later became important disciples of Dōgen.

The Daruma shū is universally accused by later Zen people, including by Dōgen, of severely misguided teachings, especially their purported antinomian view that one's understanding of the omnipresence of Buddha nature is sufficient, with no further practice thereafter required. Many scholars believe that Dōgen's later teachings were strongly affected by these disciples' Daruma shū background, as Dōgen's later emphases—for example, on the necessity of diligent practice and of attending to causality and ethical conduct in daily life—are thought to have been specific antidotes to Daruma shū teachings.

Throughout Dōgen's writings, he persistently assigns a central place to zazen practice, and continually offers commentaries on the kōans from the Chan sources. While there may be shifts in emphasis, these are not substantial changes in doctrine, but rather in teaching style and audience. As Steven Heine indicates, the change in teaching genre from the Shōbō-genzō essay style to the Dharma hall discourses is the most identifiable difference in Dōgen's later teaching. "Yet even this change indicates that Dōgen never abandoned but continued to transform and adapt the roots of his religiosity, especially commentaries on kōans…. The main changes his writings underwent were not so much a matter of either a drastic reversal or a rebirth of ideology as of attempts to work out various literary styles appropriate to the needs of diverse audience sectors, including [both] monks and laypeople."[34]

Dōgen's Great Disciples and the Spread of Sōtō Zen in Japan

We can identify seven great, influential disciples of Dōgen, all of whom were present for many of the Dharma hall discourses and other teachings in Eihei Kōroku. We can envision them as present in the assembly during these teachings, which must have been deeply formative to their training. Thus modern readers may appreciate Eihei Kōroku, not as a compilation of abstract dissertations, but as teachings addressed directly

34 See Heine, "Dōgen Canon," p. 81.

to an assembly whose exact size we do not know but which included these seven individuals: Koun Ejō, Senne, Senne's disciple Kyōgō, Tettsū Gikai, Gien, Kangan Giin, and Jakuen.

Among these foremost disciples, Koun Ejō, Tettsū Gikai, Gien, and Kangan Giin had been part of the Daruma shū before joining Dōgen's assembly. Tettsū Gikai, Gien, and Kangan Giin had all been disciples of Kakuzen Ekan, the Daruma shū teacher mentioned above, and they all joined Dōgen's assembly together with Ekan when he became a student of Dōgen. Their generation of disciples in that school were all given names beginning with *Gi,* meaning "dignity" or "bearing." So of the following seven disciples of Dōgen, all of whom were trained with the Eihei Kōroku teachings at Eiheiji, only Senne, Kyōgō, and Jakuen had not been Daruma shū monks.

Koun Ejō (1198–1280) was Dōgen's personal attendant *(jisha)* and main successor, and he became abbot of Eiheiji after Dōgen. He compiled many of Dōgen's writings, including much of Shōbōgenzō and volumes 2–4 and the informal meetings in volume 8 of Eihei Kōroku. Initially a Tendai monk, Koun Ejō had studied with many of the contemporary Japanese Buddhist movements, including Pure Land, before he met Dōgen in 1227 and then became one of his first students in 1234. It is thought that Ejō's inquiries may have been the model for the questions in Dōgen's early writing Bendōwa (Talk on Wholehearted Practice of the Way).[35] Dōgen's early death prevented him from giving Dharma transmission to the rest of the seven (except probably for Senne, as described below). But Koun Ejō ended up giving transmission to the others. Thus all later successors in Dōgen's lineage officially trace their lineage through Koun Ejō.

Senne (n.d.) and his eventual successor Kyōgō (n.d.) were both present as disciples in the assembly for at least some of Dōgen's teachings at Eiheiji, and Senne from early on at Kōshōji. According to early biographies of Dōgen, beginning with Sanso Gōgyōki, Senne was one of three Dharma successors of Dōgen along with Koun Ejō and Sōkai (see below), who all received transmission at Kōshōji (although some modern scholars have

---

35 See Okumura and Leighton, *Wholehearted Way,* pp. 24–41.

questioned the transmissions of Senne and Sōkai). Senne was Dōgen's personal attendant at Kōshōji. He was the compiler of volume 1 of Eihei Kōroku and the Dharma words in volume 8, and the primary compiler of the kōans in volume 9 and the poetry in volume 10.

After Dōgen's death Senne and Kyōgō left Eiheiji and founded Yōkōji in Kyoto, near the site where Dōgen was cremated. Their lineage survived for only a few generations after Kyōgō, so they are not so important in medieval Sōtō history. But what did survive are their extensive commentaries on Shōbōgenzō, called Goshō, including writings by both Senne and Kyōgō. These writings are vital to our modern understanding of Dōgen. Since Senne and Kyōgō were both personal students of Dōgen and heard him expound these teachings, their commentaries are reliable records of Dōgen's own interpretations and ways of reading his complex, often ambiguous essays in Shōbōgenzō. This is especially crucial for the many instances in which Dōgen intentionally misread passages from old sutras and kōans to render deeper meanings, but in ways that were doubted by later generations without the clarifications of Senne and Kyōgō. First used by Menzan in the eighteenth century, these commentaries have shaped all modern readings of Dōgen. Kyōgō must have been still quite young when Dōgen died in 1253, as Kyōgō's own commentary on Shōbōgenzō was written fifty years later, between 1303 and 1308, and he wrote another important commentary on Dōgen's writing about precepts in 1309.

Tettsū Gikai (1219–1309) was Koun Ejō's main successor and followed him as abbot of Eiheiji from 1267 to 1273 and perhaps again from 1280 to 1293. Like Koun Ejō, Gikai had been a Tendai and Daruma shū monk before he came with Kakuzen Ekan to study with Dōgen in 1241. Gikai was from Echizen, where he had significant noble family contacts, which may have contributed to Dōgen's move there. Clearly a leading disciple, Gikai was the *tenzo* (chief cook) for Dōgen's assembly during the first harsh winter after the move to Echizen. According to Gikai's main successor, Keizan, Gikai had realized his first experience of awakening upon hearing a Dharma hall discourse at Kōshōji in which Dōgen grounded a statement of the ultimate with its concrete expression. This was apparently in Dharma hall discourse 91: "All dharmas dwell in their dharma positions; forms in the world are always present. Wild geese return to the woods, and orioles appear in early spring." However, Keizan's account cited as the second part a similar phrase from Dharma hall discourse 73: "Partridges sing and a hundred blossoms open."[36] This is a specific dramatic example of the impact Dōgen's teachings in Eihei Kōroku had upon his disciples.

According to a work written by Gikai himself, Eihei Kaisan Gōyuigon Kiroku (Record of the Final Sayings of the Founder Eihei), Koun Ejō and Tettsū Gikai nursed Dōgen during his final illness. Dōgen considered giving transmission to Gikai, who was very capable and diligent, but Dōgen told Gikai a few times that he did not yet have sufficient compassionate "grandmotherly mind." After Dōgen's passing, Koun Ejō did eventually give transmission to Gikai in 1255 after Gikai finally declared his realization of the truth of Dōgen's teaching that "the manners and dignified conduct in the monastery are exactly the true Buddha Dharma."[37] Dōgen's emphasis on attentive conduct in everyday activities is frequently expressed in his teachings to the monks in Eihei Kōroku. Apparently Gikai's "grandmotherly mind" could not be activated until he had thoroughly accepted the necessity for this attention to responsible conduct, superseding his previous Daruma shū understanding of all activity as already inherently Dharma.[38]

Gikai traveled to China from 1259 to 1262 to study Chan monastic practices and architecture so as to more fully develop the Eiheiji monastic standards. Koun Ejō retired as abbot in 1267 and appointed Gikai. Gikai retired as abbot in 1273 and lived in a hermitage nearby caring for his aged mother. Although the history of this period is very murky, Koun Ejō likely returned as abbot then. In 1280 Gikai returned to Eiheiji to nurse Ejō before his death, and may have become abbot again, but left around 1292 and became abbot of Daijōji temple. He turned over that temple to his successor Keizan in 1298.

---

36 Bodiford, *Sōtō Zen in Medieval Japan*, p. 52.

37 Ikkō Narasaki, foreword to Leighton and Okumura, *Dōgen's Pure Standards for the Zen Community*, p. x.

38 See Bodiford, *Sōtō Zen in Medieval Japan*, pp. 53–59. Bodiford details how the Eihei Kaisan Gōyuigon Kiroku text was emended in later editions, but he observes that its authorship by Gikai is legitimate and that the stories about Gikai's transmission from Ejō rather than Dōgen are authentic. See also Shunmyo Sato, *Two Moons: Short Zen Stories*, trans. Rev. and Mrs. Shugen Komagata and Daniel Itto Bailey (Honolulu: The Hawai'i Hochi, 1981), pp. 54–56.

Gien (d. 1314) was one of the Daruma shū monks who had joined Dōgen in 1241. From 1249 to 1252, while he was Dōgen's attendant, Gien compiled volumes 5–7 of Eihei Kōroku (Dōgen's final Dharma hall discourses) and also some of the later Shōbōgenzō essays. Gien became abbot of Eiheiji after Tettsū Gikai left, sometime before 1287, and probably remained abbot until his death in 1314. Gien's own lineage did not survive into the fifteenth century. But Gien was highly revered by Gikai's formal successor Keizan, who also studied with Gien, from whom he received transmission of the precepts before Tettsū Gikai. Keizan saw Gien as embodying strict dedication to practice, and he later dreamed of Gie stating that he would never leave Eiheiji.[39]

Jakuen (1207–1299) was a Chinese disciple of Dōgen's teacher, Tiantong Rujing. He had met Dōgen at the Tiantong monastery and, after Rujing's death, traveled to Japan and became Dōgen's student at Kōshōji around 1230. Jakuen served as manager of the memorial hall at both Kōshōji and Eiheiji. A while after Dōgen's passing, in 1261, Jakuen left Eiheiji and founded Hōkyōji monastery in the same region. Hōkyōji continues today as a Sōtō training monastery, and there are still some surviving members of the lineage founded by Jakuen.

Jakuen's disciple Giun (1253–1333) succeeded Gien as Eiheiji abbot from 1314 to 1333. Before coming to study with Jakuen, Giun had helped Koun Ejō edit parts of Shōbōgenzō, and Giun later composed short verse commentaries to the sixty-essay version of Shōbōgenzō. Giun's later teachings comment more on the Chinese Sōtō (Caodong) teacher Hongzhi Zhengjue than on Dōgen, who also frequently cites Hongzhi in Eihei Kōroku. Giun also focused on Chinese Sōtō teachings such as the five ranks. The Jakuen-Giun line dominated Eiheiji until the early seventeenth century.

Starting in the mid-fifteenth century, Jakuen-lineage Sōtō historians claimed that a dispute had arisen between Gien and Gikai or their imme-

---

39 See Bernard Faure, *Visions of Power: Imagining Medieval Japanese Buddhism* (Princeton: Princeton University Press, 1996), p. 53; and Bodiford, *Sōtō Zen in Medieval Japan*, p. 62.

diate disciples. But this is highly dubious, and not verified in any earlier records, although there was certainly rivalry between these various lineages for some time from the fifteenth century on. Many later and some modern historians have made much of the so-called "third generation conflict," including the theory that Gien, Jakuen, and Giun sought to return to a "pure" Zen of Dōgen, while Tettsū Gikai, Keizan, and their successors favored a more eclectic, popular version of Sōtō Zen. The actual evidence of the teachings and range of practices of all involved, and their ongoing cooperation through at least Keizan's generation, call into strong question the notion of an active or ideological conflict.[40] The returns and departures of Tettsū Gikai to and from Eiheiji, which may have given rise to speculations about conflict, easily could have been due to personal issues, rather than any supposed ideological dispute.

The lineage of Kangan Giin (1217–1300), based in the Southern Japanese island of Kyushu, became so strong from the fourteenth to seventeenth centuries as to vie with Eiheiji in prominence. The exaggerated biographies produced during that period make accurate knowledge about many details of Giin's life uncertain. Before joining Dōgen, Giin had been a Tendai monk and was connected with the Daruma shū. He is said to have joined Dōgen at Kōshōji in 1241, although it is possible that he arrived at Eiheiji only several years before Dōgen's death. Giin eventually received Dharma transmission from Koun Ejō. He traveled to China from 1264 to 1267, although some records claim that he also had visited China from 1253 to 1254, after Dōgen's death. In the 1260s Giin showed a copy of Eihei Kōroku to Wuwai Iyuan (n.d.), one of the main disciples of Dōgen's teacher Tiantong Rujing. Wuwai selected less than 10 percent of Eihei Kōroku for an abridged version, Eihei Dōgen Zenji Goroku, which was published at Eiheiji in 1358. (Here *goroku* means "recorded sayings," as opposed to *kōroku*, "extensive record.")

After his return from China in 1267, Kangan Giin founded a Sōtō lineage in Kyushu, based at the temple Daijiji. His disciples, prominently including many nuns, engaged in a range of traditional Japanese Buddhist practices along with zazen. Giin gained popularity and strong patronage

40 Bodiford, *Sōtō Zen in Medieval Japan*, pp. 70–80.

in part for sponsoring and arranging various public works projects, including a bridge over the dangerous Midori River.[41] Giin's lineage flourished late into the seventeenth century and still has some successors today.

Keizan Jōkin (1264 or 1268–1325), sometimes considered the second founder of Sōtō Zen after Dōgen, was officially Tettsū Gikai's successor, but he also had studied with Koun Ejō, Gien, and Jakuen, further demonstrating the quality and impact of the range of Dōgen's trainees, and the compatibility of their teachings. Keizan founded Sōjiji, still considered the second headquarters temple of Sōtō along with Eiheiji. His successors popularized Sōtō Zen throughout northern and central Japan, and the vast majority of the current Sōtō school is from Keizan's line.

This brief survey of the later accomplishments of influential disciples of Dōgen highlights the importance of Dōgen's training, which can best be discerned through study of the teachings of Eihei Kōroku that they all received. But a few other disciples of Dōgen mentioned in Eihei Kōroku are worth mentioning.

Other Disciples

Among other disciples mentioned in Eihei Kōroku, most noteworthy is Sōkai (1216–1242), who is said to have received Dharma transmission from Dōgen at Kōshōji as well as from Koun Ejō and Senne. Dharma hall discourses 111 and 112 are Dōgen's laments after Sōkai's early death at Kōshōji. Sōkai must have been greatly beloved among the assembly, as Dōgen notes their profuse weeping, and also says of himself that "tears fill my breast like an overflowing lake."

Another prominent disciple of Dōgen who died before him was Kakuzen Ekan, already mentioned as having brought his students Gikai, Gien, and Giin when he began study with Dōgen in 1241. In his last illness, Ekan regretted that he would not be able to receive transmission from Dōgen, but encouraged his disciples (then also studying with Dōgen) to do so.[42] Dōgen's memorial Dharma hall discourse for Ekan is discourse 507 in volume 7.

41 Ibid., pp. 38–41.

42 Ibid., p. 53.

Among the *hōgo* (Dharma words) in volume 8, letters by Dōgen to disciples from the Kōshōji period in Kyoto, are three (*hōgo* 4, 9, and 12) addressed to the nun Ryōnen. Not much is known about her, although she was older than Dōgen and died before him, and may not have gone to Echizen. In these dharma words, Dōgen says that Ryōnen has had the seeds of prajñā (wisdom) from youth, and that she is a woman with "strong, robust aspiration." He also says, "Regarding the sincerity of the aspiration for the way of wayfarer Ryōnen, I see that other people cannot match her." Ryōnen is named after Moshan Laoran (Ryōnen in Japanese), the Chinese teacher whom Dōgen praises in his strong defense of women's enlightening capacities in Shōbōgenzō Raihai Tokuzui (Making Prostrations and Attaining the Marrow).[43]

Dharma word 5 and poem 62 in volume 10 are addressed to Yakō, a layperson and official of the imperial office in Kyushu. Dōgen's famous essay Genjōkōan, usually considered part of Shōbōgenzō, was also originally a letter, or dharma word, sent to a Kyushu official named Yō Kōshū. It is possible that Yakō and Yō Kōshū were different names for the same person; if not, the two worked in the same office. It has been speculated that Dōgen met these persons upon his departure to, or return from, China when he embarked via the southern island of Kyushu. Dharma word 5 mentions that Dōgen met with Yakō at Kōshōji in 1234 and again in 1235. Dōgen identifies him as a student of Confucianism, but one who has "kept his mind on the ancestral way [of Zen] for a long time through many years." This individual may not himself be an especially significant student of Dōgen. But he represents an example of the many sincere laypeople who came, sometimes from great distances, to study with Dōgen, especially while Dōgen was still at Kōshōji, although we know that lay students also traveled to Eiheiji.

Perhaps Dōgen's great patron Hatano Yoshishige should also be mentioned as a lay student of Dōgen, judging by the strong encouragements to diligent practice with a teacher probably addressed to him in dharma word 14. Yoshishige also donated the land for Eiheiji and presented a complete copy of the Tripitika to Eiheiji in 1249 (see Dharma hall discourses 361 and 362).

---

43 See Cook, *How to Raise an Ox*, pp. 99–100; and Nishijima and Cross, *Master Dogen's Shobogenzo*, book 1, pp. 72–73.

A number of other people are mentioned, both monks and laypeople, in the Dharma hall discourses and in the dharma words of volume 8. Although not much is known about them, their presence in Dōgen's discourses and dharma words provide some context for seeing these students with whom Dōgen was relating.

Dōgen's Use of Kōans

Although Dōgen claimed in Dharma hall discourse 48 that he returned from China to Japan "with empty hands," he brought with him an extraordinary mastery of the extensive Chinese Chan kōan literature. A popular stereotype is that Japanese Rinzai Zen emphasizes kōan practice whereas Sōtō Zen emphasizes just sitting meditation, or zazen, and even disdains kōans. However, even a cursory reading of Dōgen demonstrates his frequent use of a very wide range of kōans. Contrary to the stereotype, as amply proved in Eihei Kōroku along with his other writings, Dōgen is clearly responsible for introducing the kōan literature to Japan, and in his teaching he demonstrates how to bring this material alive.[44]

One legend about Dōgen is that on the night before he left China to return home, with the help of a guardian deity he copied in one night the entire Hekiganroku, or Blue Cliff Record, still one of the most important kōan anthologies, including one hundred cases with extensive commentary. Whether or not he accomplished such a supernormal feat, Dōgen certainly brought to Japan not only that text but also an amazing encyclopedic knowledge of the contents of many other such collections.

In the centuries after Dōgen, kōan study was often prominent in Sōtō Zen history.[45] But the modes of kōan practice and study promoted by Dōgen, and in much of Sōtō Zen until the present, differ distinctly from the modern Rinzai kōan curriculum study, which emphasizes frequent student interviews with the teacher after intent focus on the kōan as an object of formal meditation. This Rinzai kōan system had its roots in the teachings of Dahui, a Chinese Linji/Rinzai master in the century before

44 For elaboration, see Steven Heine, "Kōans in the Dōgen Tradition: How Dōgen Does What He Does with Kōans," *Philosophy East and West* 52, no. 2 (2004).

45 For discussions of the use of kōans in Medieval Sōtō Zen, see Bodiford, *Sōtō Zen in Medieval Japan*, p. 143–162.

Dōgen. The development of this kōan system, especially as it was informed by the great seventeenth-century Rinzai master Hakuin, has often been seen in the West today, mistakenly, as the definition and limit of "kōan practice." This has led to the erroneous belief that Dōgen, or Sōtō generally, does not use kōan practice. Steven Heine's excellent detailed study, *Dōgen and the Kōan Tradition,* clearly elaborates the varying modes of kōan study and praxis employed by Dōgen, as opposed to the Rinzai approach.[46]

Generally a kōan—the word means "public case"—is a teaching story primarily based on a dialogue or some other encounter between a teacher and a student. The classic kōan stories go back to the genres of the lamp transmission anthology and the recorded sayings (Ch.: *yulu;* Jap.: *goroku*), mostly from the great masters of the Chinese Tang dynasty (608–907). Many of these recorded sayings of individual masters were not actually compiled until early in the Song dynasty (960–1278), which has led many modern scholars to question their historical reliability. However, given the strong monastic culture of memorization and oral transmission, we cannot say definitively whether or not these stories are historically reliable. But they have unquestionably served as useful tools for the realization of awakening truth and spiritual development by generations of monks and seekers throughout the past millennium.

In the development of the kōan literature, the fuller records of individual masters would seem to have preceded the lamp transmission anthologies, but historically they actually often followed them. These lamp anthologies consist of briefer excerpts from many masters descended from the various Chinese lineages, arranged together in the same generation, with each generation included in sequence. The most noted and comprehensive of these is the "Jingde Transmission of the Lamp" (Ch.: Jingde Chuandenglu; Jap.: Keitoku Dentōroku), some sections of which have been translated. But Dōgen cites many other lamp transmission texts as well. One collection that Dōgen quotes very frequently in Eihei Kōroku is the "Collection of the Essence of the Continuous Dharma Lamp" (Ch.: Zongmen Liandeng Huiyao; Jap.: Shūmon Rentō Eyō), published in 1189,

---

46 Steven Heine, *Dōgen and the Kōan Tradition: A Tale of Two Shōbōgenzō Texts* (Albany: State University of New York Press, 1994).

not yet available in English translation. This is the third of the five major dharma lamp transmission anthologies collected in the important compilation Five Lamps Merged in the Source (Ch.: Wudeng Huiyuan; Jap.: Gotō Egen), which also includes the Jingde Transmission of the Lamp. Also among the five is the Jiatai Record of the Universal Lamp (Ch.: Jiatai Pudenglu; Jap.: Katai Futōroku), compiled in 1204, and also often cited by Dōgen.

Finally, in the last stage of creating the classic kōan genre, the stories from the collected records and the lamp transmission texts were excerpted, often in highly abbreviated form, in the great Song dynasty kōan anthologies, which then included many layers of added commentary by later masters. Although there were a great many such anthologies, among the most prominent are the Blue Cliff Record (Ch.: Biyanlu; Jap.: Hekiganroku) and the Book of Serenity (Ch.: Congronglu; Jap.: Shōyōroku), two collections still important today, together with the Gateless Gate (Ch.: Wumenguan; Jap.: Mumonkan), which was compiled in China during Dōgen's life, and which he never saw in that form.

In Eihei Kōroku, Dōgen follows and expands upon many traditional modes of kōan commentary. Volume 9, ninety kōans selected by Dōgen with his own added verse comments, usually only four lines, features a traditional poetic mode of commentary, patterned after the core of the Blue Cliff Record and also followed in the Book of Serenity anthology. This collection in Eihei Kōroku, volume 9, is one of Dōgen's important early efforts at kōan commentary. Of course the many essays in Shōbōgenzō, often with elaborated thematic responses to specific kōans, display one of Dōgen's distinctive approaches and major contributions to kōan commentary. The Dharma words (hōgo), letters to individual students in volume 8 of Eihei Kōroku, are from the earlier period in Kōshōji. They might be seen as a bridge between the longer, more philosophical Shōbōgenzō essay form and the Dharma hall discourses of volumes 1–7 in Eihei Kōroku. The shōsan (informal meetings) in volume 8 are from the Eiheiji period and, though often somewhat longer, are closer to the Dharma hall discourses in their approaches to kōan commentary.

Informal meeting 9 features line-by-line interjected brief responses by Dōgen on Zhaozhou's kōan "The cypress tree in the garden." This was Zhaozhou's response to a monk who asked what Buddha is. This case is

also cited by Dōgen in his Dharma hall discourses 433 and 488. Such inter-
linear commentary is a mode Dōgen here adopts from similar responses
to the cases and primary verse commentaries in the Blue Cliff Record. In
the Dharma hall discourses, Dōgen uses various other modes of comment
on this kōan. In discourse 433 he praises Zhaozhou and questions his own
monks' understanding; then, after a pause, he gives a poetic "capping
phrase," another traditional mode of response to kōans. In discourse 488
Dōgen takes the same story and sharply criticizes common misunder-
standings of it, then offers the responses that he, Dōgen, would give at
each part of the dialogue were he in the story, another traditional mode
of kōan response from the Chinese Dharma hall discourses. This ends
with Dōgen giving his own final response in the form of a four-line verse
comment, thereby mixing modes of commentary. In all these ways and
more, Dōgen plays with these traditional Zen stories to bring forth fresh
teaching and enlivening awareness for his students.

One difference between Dōgen's use of kōan study and a stereotypical
modern view of kōan practice can be found in his critique of *kenshō* as a
goal. This term, which means "seeing the nature," has been understood
at times to refer to an opening experience of attainment of realization,
going beyond conceptual thinking. Dōgen believes that this is a dualistic
misunderstanding and such experiences are not to be emphasized. For
Dōgen, Buddha nature is not an object to merely see or acquire, but a
mode of being that must be actually lived and expressed. All realizations
or understandings, even those from Dōgen's own comments, must be let
go, as he stresses to a student in dharma word 4: "If you hold on to a single word or half a phrase of the buddha ancestors' sayings or of the kōans
from the ancestral gate, they will become dangerous poisons. If you want
to understand this mountain monk's activity, do not remember these
comments. Truly avoid being caught up in thinking."

Unlike in the formal Rinzai curriculum, or the kōan study of Dahui,
Dōgen does not explicitly recommend the kōan stories as objects of formal meditation, but offers them for general contemplation and intent
study. For example, in the last Dharma word, 14, Dōgen says: "When
you meet a teacher, first ask for one case of a [kōan] story, and just keep
it in mind and study it diligently.... Now I see worldly people who visit
and practice with teachers, and before clarifying one question, assertively

enjoy bringing up other stories. They withdraw from the discussion as if they understand, but are close-mouthed and cannot speak. They have not yet explained one third of the story, so how will we see a complete saying?"

In addition to study of the traditional kōan stories, in Eihei Kōroku Dōgen also emphasizes the approach of *genjōkōan,* "full manifestation of ultimate reality," or attention to the kōans manifesting in everyday activity. In this approach, each everyday phenomenon or challenge arising before us can be intently engaged, to be realized and fully expressed. "Genjōkōan" is the name of one of Dōgen's most famous essays, now thought of as part of Shōbōgenzō. But he uses this term and expresses this approach elsewhere in his writings, including in Eihei Kōroku. For example, in Dharma hall discourse 60 Dōgen says: "Everybody should just wholeheartedly engage in this genjōkōan. What is this genjōkōan? It is just all buddhas in the ten directions and all ancestors, ancient and present, and it is fully manifesting right now. Do you all see it? It is just our...getting up and getting down from the sitting platform."

The footnotes throughout our translation of the Eihei Kōroku text offer references to some of the available English sources for other versions and uses of these kōans, as well as other places where they are cited in Eihei Kōroku and in Dōgen's other writings. Checking other uses of the stories may give a fuller context for understanding Dōgen's commentaries. However, we have not attempted to provide a full concordance of every place in the Chinese literature or in Dōgen where each of these stories can be found, a massive project far beyond the scope of this translation.

The prominent contemporary American Zen teacher John Daido Loori offers another useful view of Dōgen's relationship to kōan practice in his essay following this introduction. In his essay, Daido describes the influence of Dōgen's approach and writings in Daido's own contemporary kōan training program for his students. Daido's systematic approach to a curriculum of kōan training is widely divergent from my own way of using kōans in practice and in teaching students, and also from Dōgen's own approach. However, Daido's program is deeply informed by his study of Dōgen's writings, and it exemplifies how Dōgen continues to influence modern innovations in kōan training. Daido's teaching has made excellent use of the three hundred kōans of Dōgen's Mana Shōbōgenzō, which was the immediate basis for much of Dōgen's ninety cases in Eihei Kōroku, volume 9. Daido Loori and Kazuaki Tanahashi have recently completed a reliable, useful, and very welcome translation of the three hundred cases of Mana Shōbōgenzō with Daido's commentary.

The Eihei Kōroku Text and Translation Notes

The present translation is based on the Monkaku version of Eihei Kōroku, copied in 1598 from earlier sources. This version is also called the Sozan-bon or Honzan-bon, or "Main Temple Edition," after its source at Eiheiji. Other extant versions are the Kōshōji-bon, Shingetsuji-bon, and Rinnōji-bon, all later copies of the Monkaku version. A later version (called the Rufu-bon), edited by Manzan Dōhaku in 1672, differs somewhat from the four earlier ones. Manzan sometimes amended the text when it seemed incomprehensible. Manzan viewed such difficulties as indications that copiers' errors had likely entered the text. In some cases when we agree with Manzan, we have used his suggestions, as noted. In some instances we have also mentioned Manzan's alternative readings in the footnotes.

We have often been guided in our translation by the readings in the invaluable edition of the text by the late Genryū Kagamishima, Komazawa University professor and the leading scholar of Dōgen studies in the postwar period. We also often have been guided by Kagamishima as to when to adopt Manzan's readings. However, we have not in every instance agreed with the interpretations of Professor Kagamishima. We have also at times consulted with editions of the text by Tetsuo Ōtani, Hisao Shinohara, and Tōru Terada. All of these editions, listed in the bibliography, include Japanese readings, of necessity implying some interpretation, as well as the original Chinese. Our translations have been primarily from the original Chinese text, but with consideration of the Japanese readings. We have also benefited from the collections of commentaries and studies edited by Shunkō Itō and Seijun Ishii.

We have included the very useful numbers added to the text in the twentieth century, from 1 to 531 for the Dharma hall discourses in volumes 1–7; from 1 to 20 for *shōsan*, and 1 to 14 for *hōgo*, in volume 8; from 1 to 90 for the kōans in volume 9; and 1 to 5 for *shinsan*, 1 to 20 for *jisan*, and 1 to 125 for the rest of the verses in volume 10. We have used these numbers to identify particular passages when they are referred to in the introduction, the footnotes, and the indexes.

At the beginning of each Dharma hall discourse in volumes 1–7, each *shōsan* and *hōgo* in volume 8, and each kōan in volume 9, we have added our own title for each piece. These titles, which serve as a means of identification along with the numbers, should be understood as reflecting only the translators' original interpretations and suggested focus. We have not given names for the verses in volume 10, which are mostly very brief, but many of which include headings in the text from Dōgen himself, or perhaps from their compiler, usually Senne.

In the footnotes we also have tried to clarify references to Buddhist and Zen doctrine and lore. As we wish this work to be accessible to English readers, we have focused on citing sources available in English translation. However, where we know of no English translations, names of Sanskrit, Chinese, or Japanese works referred to by Dōgen are given in the footnotes, with the relevant section of those works. We also offer English-language sources for other examples of stories or teachings cited by Dōgen, but we have not attempted to give every available source and site for such references, as already noted for the kōans. When citing English translations of such references, from Dōgen or elsewhere, we have generally tried to include the best available renditions, but in many cases we have given several options, and these citations should not necessarily be taken as endorsements of these translations, or as criticisms of those not mentioned.

When passages seemed problematic, we have at times offered alternative readings in the footnotes. We have also occasionally offered our own brief interpretive suggestions when these would help the reader.

Throughout the text, phrases or words in brackets are our own additions, not literally present in the text, which we deemed necessary to comprehension. These include implied pronouns and subjects (often fairly clear in context), since personal pronouns in the Chinese used by Dōgen in Eihei Kōroku (as well as in Japanese) are often unstated. Ambiguities in the original or in Dōgen's source texts can be intentional, but coherent English translations usually require choosing between possible meanings. I rejoiced in the instances when we could accurately convey in English a similar range of ambiguities as the original. Of course in some cases the phrases in brackets indicate our own interpretations of Dōgen's meaning. The occasional parentheses in the text indicate our brief clarifying or informative interjections, as opposed to the bracketed interpolations suggested as implied parts of Dogen's text.

Translating Dōgen provides a range of challenges. He is well known for his complex use of language and intricate twisting of conventional grammar and syntax. Even without such wordplay, Dōgen's Japanese, when compared to modern Japanese, is analogous to Chaucerian English compared to modern English. He also employs many technical Buddhist and Zen terms and allusions that need to be clarified. Dōgen especially works to express the inner meanings of Buddhist teaching and expose the limitations of conventional thought patterns. He thereby dramatizes the deeper, radical nondualism of developed Mahāyāna insight, often by overturning standard subject-object grammatical constructions. Through elaborate wordplay and puns, Dōgen often reinterprets traditional readings of sutra passages or kōans.

Many times we felt perplexed by obstacles to understanding particular passages in Eihei Kōroku. Sometimes several hours of consideration were required, puzzling about what point Dōgen was striving to make. In such instances the meaning would usually become apparent, or at least imaginable, when we eventually returned to a literal reading of Dōgen's original. Through our long collaborations on Dōgen, on this and two previous books, Shohaku Okumura and I have become increasingly confirmed in our view that faithful and felicitous renderings of Dōgen can best be achieved though as literal as possible a reading of his wordplay.

Appended to the Eihei Kōroku text is a chronological index of Dharma hall discourses that include their dates, followed by an index and glossary of names, an index of the translators' names for the Dharma hall discourses, and a bibliography. The name index provides dates and some brief biographical information about all historical persons mentioned in the text, along with a list of places where they appear in Eihei Kōroku or the notes. People Dōgen quotes are identified when possible in the footnotes, if they are not named in the text.

As to conventions for this translation, we are using standard diacritical marks on Japanese and Sanskrit words. For readers unfamiliar with these, they need not impinge on readability. Briefly, macron lines over vowels in Japanese words, such as in "Dōgen," indicate a longer vowel sound. For Sanskrit names, the most significant pronunciation issue is that a mark over an *s* indicates a *sh* sound; "Śākyamuni" is thus pronounced "Shakyamuni." For Chinese names we are using the pinyin system of transliteration, although the older Wade-Giles transliteration equivalents are given in the appended index and glossary of names. The main pronunciation issues in pinyin are as follows: *X* as in "Xuefeng" is pronounced with a soft *sh,* like the *s* in "sugar"; *C* as in "Caoshan" is pronounced like the *ts* in "tsetse fly"; *Q* as in "Qingyuan" is pronounced like the *ch* in "chuckle"; and *Zh* as in "Zhaozhou" is pronounced like the *dg* in "judging."

Throughout the Eihei Kōroku text, except for our own headings to sections, the only use of italics is for the places in the Dharma hall discourses where the text itself includes "stage directions" referring to Dōgen as if in third person (although his name is not mentioned explicitly in the original). For example, the text to volumes 1–7 frequently records such features of the Dharma hall discourses as *"After a pause Dōgen said,"* or *"Then Dōgen descended from his seat,"* or *"Dōgen threw down his whisk."* These are all given in italics to clarify where Dōgen is not himself speaking. Japanese terms are given in italics in the footnotes, and defined at least in their initial use, but are not italicized in the text.

In the footnotes, names of books published in English are in italics, but names of works in Sanskrit, Chinese, or Japanese are not italicized, nor are they italicized when referred to by the English translation of their names, except when citing specific published translations. Thus, for example, references to Hekiganroku, or Blue Cliff Record, are not italicized, but the translation by Thomas Cleary and J. C. Cleary, *The Blue Cliff Record,* published by Shambhala, is cited in italics.

The Jōdō (Dharma Hall Discourses), Volumes 1–7

The recorded Dharma hall discourses, Dōgen's formal talks to his assembly, are called *jōdō* in Japanese, literally "ascending in the hall." As mentioned above in the comparison with the longer Shōbōgenzō writings, or *jishu,* the *jōdō* is the form often used by Chan teachers in China in the traditional recorded sayings. The Dharma hall discourses are often very brief. After leaving the monks' hall—where they meditated, took meals in formal ceremony, and slept, each in his assigned place—the monks would come to the Dharma hall. After entering, they stood in lines and listened to the teacher, who was seated high on the altar. Disciples were not seated, as in our modern custom of dharma talks.[47]

Contemporary Sōtō scholars believe that after the recorded Dharma hall discourses in Eihei Kōroku there might perhaps have been either ceremonies or some exchange or discussion between Dōgen and his monks. Such dialogue is often recorded in the Chinese recorded sayings. If this occurred in Dōgen's assembly, it is almost never recorded in Eihei Kōroku, with the unique exceptions of Dharma hall discourses 72 and 243, in which there are dialogues between Dōgen and unnamed monks. In a few other places in Eihei Kōroku, the compiler mentions in a note that there was further discussion by Dōgen and perhaps others (in Dharma hall discourses 88, 105, and 358), but any dialogue is omitted, with only the words of Dōgen himself recorded.

In general, as can be seen from those that are dated, the 531 Dharma hall discourses in Eihei Kōroku are listed in chronological order from the year 1236 at Kōshōji to 1252 in Eiheiji. But there are some exceptions to strict chronology, usually mentioned in the footnotes. One noteworthy example is a sequence in volume 5. Discourse 360 is from the twelfth month in 1249. But discourse 362 was given in the autumn, and discourse 363 is from the second day of the ninth month of 1249, probably before 362. Chronologically, discourse 360 should immediately precede discourses 364, 365, and 367, all from the second month of 1250. But such irregularities are rare exceptions; the Dharma hall discourses present a mostly chronological account of the development and rhythms of Dōgen's teachings. Since most of them are undated, we do not know their exact frequency, or the time lapses between these discourses. But we can often glimpse threads of ongoing themes, or of stories about particular Zen personages, spanning several Dharma hall discourses.

Dōgen's Dharma hall discourses should be read in part for their theatricality, as performative expressions of the teaching. Many aspects of these usually brief performance pieces, including the nonverbal, draw heavily on the Dharma hall discourses in the traditional Chan recorded

47 This is described in the section of the Jingde Transmission of the Lamp on Baizhang, in the Monastic Rules attributed to him. See Steven Heine, *Shifting Shape, Shaping Text: Philosophy and Folklore in the Fox Kōan* (Honolulu: University of Hawai'i Press, 1999), pp. 219–221.

sayings. Frequently Dōgen asks his monks a question and then answers himself, a traditional mode much employed by Yunmen, for example.[48] Dōgen's ending of these discourses by abruptly stepping down from his seat also echoes Yunmen and Linji.[49] Other frequent gestures employed by Dōgen (also drawn from Chinese tradition) include pounding his staff, holding up or throwing down his whisk, or drawing a circle in the air with his whisk.

Another mode very frequently evident in Dōgen's Dharma hall discourses is pausing before giving a response to his own questions to the assembly. This certainly highlights the sense of drama in these events (although during these pauses perhaps there might occasionally have been some unrecorded discussion). But we might imagine the monks, including those already mentioned who would later become prominent teachers themselves, standing and reflecting on a question during one of these silent pauses in the music of Dōgen's teaching. We might also consider Mark Twain's reflection: "The Pause—that impressive silence, that eloquent silence, that geometrically progressive silence, which often achieves a desired effect where no combination of words, howsoever felicitous, could accomplish it."[50]

The Dharma hall discourses featured in Eihei Kōroku, as well as the informal meetings from Eiheiji, discussed next, were primarily addressed to monks. However, according to contemporary accounts, laypeople also regularly attended these events. Drawings included in Teiho Kenzeiki, Menzan's important seventeenth-century biography of Dōgen, also depict laypeople listening to these talks in sections of the hall behind the monks.

Aside from the ritual aspect of these Dharma hall discourses, they seem to include a number of specific functions. Many were given on particular ceremonial days, including New Year's Day; Buddha's parinirvāṇa day; Buddha's birthday; the beginning and end of the summer practice period;

48 See Urs App, *Master Yunmen: From the Record of the Chan Teacher "Gate of the Clouds"* (New York: Kodansha International, 1994), pp. 197–211.

49 See ibid., pp. 153–155, or Burton Watson, *The Zen Teachings of Master Lin-Chi* (Boston: Shambhala, 1993), pp. 18–19, for examples.

50 Mark Twain, *The Autobiography of Mark Twain,* ed. Charles Neider (New York: Harper and Brothers Publishers, 1959), p. 181.

the opening and closing of the fireplace in the monks' hall; and Buddha's enlightenment day. Some were given on memorial days—for example, for Dōgen's teacher Tiantong Rujing. Others were given to mark the beginning or end of a particular monk's term in one of the monastic positions. A very great many of the Dharma hall discourses, including those on ceremonial days, are commentaries by Dōgen on traditional kōans. In these commentaries Dōgen regularly prods the monks, asking them to thoroughly study and penetrate the meanings of these teachings. Evidently this exhaustive study was to include awareness and consideration, not only during the Dharma hall events themselves, but also during their formal meditation periods, as well as throughout their daily responsibilities in the monastery.

Generally, many of the Dharma hall discourses are practice encouragements to the monks to bring their aware and insightful presence into all their everyday activities. Sometimes these encouragements are stern admonishments. Sometimes they are warm and tinged with humor. In one example, Dharma hall discourse 239, Dōgen mentions the courage of a hunter facing tigers or other fierce beasts, or the courage of a warrior facing death in battle. Then Dōgen asks, "What is the courage of patch-robed monks?" After one of his characteristic pregnant pauses, Dōgen suggests, "Spread out your bedding and sleep; set out your bowls and eat rice; exhale through your nostrils; radiate light from your eyes. Do you know there is something that goes beyond? With vitality, eat lots of rice and then use the toilet. Transcend your personal prediction of future buddhahood from Gautama." Dōgen is constantly encouraging the monks to express their awakening in all their activities, not to look to some other, future time or Buddha realm for the fulfillment of their practice.

The Shōsan (Informal Meetings) and
Hōgo (Dharma Words), Volume 8

The *shōsan*, or informal meetings, are informal only when compared to the Dharma hall discourses. They were also a traditional genre of teaching, usually given to smaller groups of monks by the abbot in the abbot's quarters, and significantly longer than the brief Dharma hall discourses. Traditionally these informal meetings were given on days ending with 3 or 8 in the calendar, preceding the days ending with 4 or 9 characterized by a somewhat more relaxed schedule. But the twenty "informal meeting" teachings by Dōgen presented herein were instead given at four special occasions, all on precise dates. These were New Year's Eve (informal meetings 2, 5, 10, 14, and 18); the beginning of the summer practice period (6, 8, 11, 15, and 19); the end of the summer practice period (1, 3, 7, 12, 16, and 20); and the winter solstice (4, 9, 13, and 17). These informal meetings in Eihei Kōroku were all given at Eiheiji after 1245 and are presented in at least roughly chronological order, but the years are not recorded and can only be inferred very inexactly from internal evidence.

In modern Japanese Sōtō Zen, a *shōsan* occurs in the Dharma hall rather than the abbot's quarters. In this event, also used in Western Sōtō Zen, a *shōsan* is a somewhat formal event in which, after a statement by the teacher, students will take turns coming forward to ask the teacher a question, perhaps with a brief follow-up exchange.

The *hōgo*, or Dharma words, are another traditional genre, consisting mostly of letters of practice instructions to specific students. The fourteen dharma words in volume 8 are probably all from Dōgen's earlier, Kōshōji period. Many of the students addressed in these letters are indicated in the texts. Three of them, dharma words 4, 9, and 12, are apparently to the nun Ryōnen, mentioned above. Dharma word 2, probably from 1231, is an encouragement to practice given to a monk named Enchi, who came to visit Dōgen at Kōshōji at least a few times from his temple in the Shizuoka area of eastern Japan. Dharma word 5, probably from 1235, was written to Yakō, the lay student of Dōgen's from Kyushu mentioned above. One of Dōgen's most famous writings, Genjōkōan, usually included among the essays in Shōbōgenzō, was probably written as a letter to this or another fellow official from Kyushu.

Dharma word 6, from late 1240, was written to E'un, a monk in Dōgen's assembly who had exhibited extraordinary diligence and dedication as work leader. Dharma word 7, from 1241, praises Ken'e, the monk then in charge of caring for the monastery toilets. Dharma word 10 was for Futō, the government official in charge of overseeing monasteries. From its content, he may have also been a physician as well as a lay practitioner of Zen. Dharma word 13 was written to encourage a young monk in Dōgen's assembly, Gyōgen, who had become a monk just the year before at age thirteen.

Dharma word 14 is probably to Dōgen's great patron, Hatano Yoshishige, and emphasizes the importance for lay practitioners of finding a good teacher and offers a lengthy encouragement of diligent practice.

Kōans and Juko (Verse Comments), Volume 9

The ninety kōans of volume 9 with Dōgen's verse comments in Chinese, compiled mostly by Senne, were apparently finished before the move to Echizen. Case 10 mentions Sōkai, Dōgen's disciple who died at Kōshōji in 1242. The selection and ordering of the stories in the collection was almost certainly made by Dōgen himself. However, modern scholars speculate that Senne might have divided some of the cases with verse comments, to make an even ninety, and perhaps slightly altered their order.

Many of these ninety cases are frequently cited in the classic kōan literature, although some are fairly obscure, exemplifying Dōgen's encyclopedic knowledge of this literature. But Dōgen idiosyncratically chooses as his entire second case the scriptural dictum "The triple world is mind only," and for cases 58, 85, and 86 he selects sayings of his own teacher, Tiantong Rujing.

Many of the ninety cases in volume 9 also appear in the Eihei Kōroku Dharma hall discourses. A full fifty-two of the ninety are used as well, without comment, in Dōgen's three-hundred-case Mana Shōbōgenzō (as footnoted in volume 9). While the Mana Shōbōgenzō may be seen as Dōgen's early collection of cases to use as a workbook for his future writings on kōans, volume 9 of Eihei Kōroku is one of his early systematic kōan commentaries. One of the riches of Dōgen's writings is his subtle intertextuality, with references to the same stories in his other writings, along with the range of their references in various traditional Zen sources. The footnotes in volume 9 include references not only to the same stories in Dōgen's longer Shōbōgenzō essays, but also to their other uses in the Eihei Kōroku Dharma hall discourses. According to Kagamishima, 298 kōan cases appear in these Dharma hall discourses. These can be traced and compared through the index and glossary of names.[51]

The juko, or verse comments, on each case by Dōgen in volume 9 are

51 See Heine, "Dōgen Canon," p. 75.

in the traditional mode of kōan commentary. Most of these are four-line Chinese verses, although some are longer, and in some cases two or even three such verses are included. The collection in volume 9 follows the pattern of the classic collection of one hundred cases by Xuedou with his verse comments, and the similar collection with verses by Hongzhi. Both collections were well known and cited by Dōgen, who uses a saying and anecdote from Hongzhi for his cases 25 and 88.

These two earlier collections were expanded with extensive prose comments by Yuanwu and Wansong, respectively, to form the classic Hekiganroku (Blue Cliff Record), and Shōyōroku (Book of Serenity). Dōgen was very familiar with the Hekiganroku. But he did not know the Shōyōroku in that form, as Wansong's comments were written contemporaneously with Dōgen, although Dōgen frequently references Hongzhi's cases and verses that are its foundation. Dōgen's commentaries in volume 9, as well as throughout the Shōbōgenzō essays, can thus be seen as part of the contemporary Song Chinese kōan anthology movement that produced the Shōyōroku and Mumonkan collections.

The Poems, Volume 10

Dōgen's Chinese verses in volume 10 were written throughout his life, from some composed as early as 1226, while he was studying in China, up to poems from 1252, in his final illness. The verses are divided into three sections. First are the five *shinsan,* or comments to be inscribed on portraits of great ancient masters, for Śākyamuni, Bodhidharma, Ānanda, and Dōgen's Japanese teacher Butsuju Myōzen.

Next come twenty *jisan,* verses to be inscribed on portraits of Dōgen himself. This was a standard Zen poetic form for verses, often ironic or self-deprecating, to be inscribed on one's own portrait. We are uncertain how many of these might have actually been inscribed by Dōgen himself on such portraits. Apparently Dōgen wrote a number of these verses for portraits that might be done in the future.

Only one portrait probably from Dōgen's own lifetime survives, now enshrined at Hōkyōji monastery, founded by Dōgen's Chinese disciple Jakuen. *Jisan* 3 is inscribed on this Hōkyōji portrait. According to Ōkubo Dōshū the verse was copied onto the portrait by Giun, but perhaps the calligraphy is actually by Dōgen. *Jisan* 10 is on a picture of Dōgen now at

Eiheiji, painted in the fourteenth century, according to Ōkubo Dōshū. These pictures appear at the front of this book.

Jisan 18 is on a portrait of Dōgen now at Honmyōji in Kumamoto in Kyushu. The portrait was supposedly painted by Dōgen himself and inscribed in 1227 upon his return from China, although scholars speculate that it was likely done much later. Honmyōji is now a Rinzai school temple. When I was in residence at a monastery in the area in 1992, I had the unusual opportunity to view this picture. It indeed looks like a young Dōgen, a bit more round-faced than the later portraits, but recognizably the same monk.

The remainder of volume 10 consists of 125 verses on different topics. According to the compiler, Senne, the first fifty verses were written from 1226, while Dōgen was in China at Tiantong monastery, until his departure in 1227. Verses 51–76 were written after his return to Japan but probably before his departure to Echizen, although some of the later ones may have been written at Eiheiji. Verse 77 was written during his visit to Kamakura in 1248. And verses 78–125 were written in Echizen.

In general, the meanings of the poems are often problematic and subject to diverse interpretations. Manzan changed the poems frequently, more than in the Dharma hall discourses, reflecting his own difficulty with comprehending Dōgen's intention. Unlike the previous volumes of Eihei Kōroku (with interpretive headings by ourselves as translators), the headings in volume 10 before many of the verses, or groups of verses, are by Dōgen himself.

While Eihei Kōroku as a whole may be most illuminating as a window on Dōgen's mature teaching at Eiheiji, the early poems in volume 10, composed while Dōgen was still a monk in training in China, provide an intriguing view of the young Dōgen. Some of these verses seem formal or stiff, and many of them were occasional, written for Chinese lay patrons or other monks who visited the monastery where Dōgen was staying. One even suspects that Dōgen might be showing off his literary ability with Chinese verse, as some of these early poems seem notably less profound than his later writings. And yet among these are also many that are striking or moving, such as verse 32, given to a Zen person whose child had died, or the series of verses 19–23, written to a visiting Chinese nun. Another example is verse 26, for a fellow Japanese pilgrim monk who had died in China:

Vast emptiness, nothing holy is as hard as iron.
But placing him into the red furnace, he melts like snow.
And now I ask, to where have you returned?
With the green waves deep, what moon do you see?

The later verses, and especially those written in Echizen from verse 78 on, are often less didactic. Of all Dōgen's writings, they are perhaps the most revealing of his own personal feelings. Many speak of Dōgen's long nights in meditation, his deep love of nature, the beauty of mountains, but also of the severe snows and cold of winter. He often reflects, somewhat whimsically, on his own life of practice, as in verse 90:

In our lifetime, false and true, good and bad are confused.
While playing with the moon, scorning the wind, and
    listening to birds,
For many years I merely saw that mountains had snow.
This winter, suddenly I realize that snow makes the
    mountains.

While the Dharma hall discourses often reflect the strictness of his teaching, in his verses on dwelling in the mountains he sometimes expresses satisfaction with the inner progress of his disciples, as in verse 110:

The evening bell rings in moonlight and lanterns are raised.
Training monks sit in the hall and quietly observe emptiness.
Having fortunately attained the three robes, now they plant
    seeds.
How heartwarming; their ripening liberation in the one
    mind.

Using Eihei Kōroku as a Practice Tool

Although some no doubt will do so, we hardly expect most readers to go through this massive record of Dōgen's teachings from beginning to end in order, as we in fact have translated it. Because this record is made up of small sections, sometimes as brief as a mere sentence, practitioners can digest it in small bites. Some may want to open at random and enjoy

Dōgen's teachings out of sequence—although at times the sequence is not insignificant. Practicing with this material, we may remember that Dōgen's students themselves never heard more than one Dharma hall discourse or informal meeting in any given day, or sometimes even in one week. Indeed, during the Eiheiji period, the Dharma hall discourses seem to have averaged about one a week. So in addition to just reading through this material, the student of Zen may likely want to chew slowly at times, find pieces that are especially provocative, stimulating, or unsettlingly challenging, and take a while to consider, reflect, and digest.

Again, Dōgen's intent is not to present doctrines or philosophical positions, but to encourage deepening religious practice. Much of Eihei Kōroku is dedicated to instructions for zazen, or upright seated meditation, whether in the Fukanzazengi (Universally Recommended Instructions for Zazen), or in the many Dharma hall discourses that mention just sitting or dropping off body-mind. But Dōgen is clearly not recommending zazen as mere blank, mindless sitting. Although he frequently criticizes practice concerned with achievement, or with reaching for particular schematized stages of development, Dōgen regularly asks his monks if they thoroughly understand. He is suggesting a practice that is informed by intense inquiry into the ancient teachings, sayings, and dialogues, as well as into our present immediate experience. Throughout formal meditation as well as in our everyday activity, Dōgen encourages vivid attention and awareness. Modern practitioners may also take the stories and encouragements offered by Dōgen and investigate them thoroughly through daily practice. But clearly Dōgen is suggesting such intensive inquiry also be brought to our daily relationships and conduct.

Dōgen's spirit of inquiry, his realm of intense questioning, is captured in these lines by the great American poet-songwriter Bob Dylan: "A question in your nerves is lit, yet you know there is no answer fit to satisfy, ensure you not to quit, to keep it in your mind and not forget, that it is not he or she or them or it that you belong to."[52] Again and again before his pauses in the Dharma hall discourses, Dōgen questions his monks, asking, "Great assembly, do you completely understand this or not?" He

52 Bob Dylan, "It's Alright Ma, I'm Only Bleeding," in Lyrics, 1962–1985 (New York: Alfred A. Knopf, 1985), p. 177.

insistently demands, "At this very time, what can you say?" (Dharma hall discourse 486). Dōgen persists in lighting a question in the nerves of his students and turning up the heat. For example: "Immediately you should energetically extinguish the flames on your head, and courageously make undaunted effort. At just such a time, how do you practice? Do you want to clearly understand this?" (Dharma hall discourse 497). This questioning is not a matter of mere intellection or discriminating consciousness, but questioning that pervades nerves, sinew, muscle, and spine. And the point is the questioning itself, not some quick answer. As Dylan says, "There is no answer fit." Dōgen crushes all complacency in the practice of his monks, even though they are involved in the deep, calm settling-in of the monastic schedule and immersion in zazen.

The modern reader may want to take one brief selection from this material, one that is found striking or somehow engaging, and consider it closely, and perhaps even consult an experienced Zen teacher when one is available. And in our time many Zen centers and trained teachers are available in the Western world to work with in chewing these teachings. But the teacher is not there to feed you some answer. At best the teacher can only point you toward deepening your own investigation. With each brief teaching from Dōgen, you may consider: What does Dōgen mean here? Why would he say that? What is he encouraging me to consider in this story? What traditional Buddhist teachings are involved here? What might Dōgen have been concerned with or pointing out to his own particular students? And how does this relate to my situation today?

Reading one of Dōgen's Dharma hall discourses in which he comments on a traditional dialogue or kōan, the reader would do well to envision the whole scene. First, imagine Dōgen sitting up on the seat on the altar in the Dharma hall, looking down at Jakuen, Senne, Koun Ejō, Tettsū Gikai, and the other monks standing in the chill mountain air of Eiheiji. Then, before even considering Dōgen's often pithy comments, envision the scene in the story Dōgen is relating. Perhaps it is Zhaozhou, Mazu, Yunmen, or one of the other great masters Dōgen frequently cites, face to face with one of those nameless Chinese monks who wandered around questioning these masters and eliciting great Dharma. See the situation in the story as a theatrical performance. See it from every viewpoint you might imagine. What is going on for the monk? What is the concern of the teacher? How is it for any bystanders who may have been present, mentioned or unmentioned in the original story? What is the issue or concern? What is at stake? If there seems to be a winner or loser, or praise or criticism, check that this is not ironic. These stories should not always be taken at face value. Only after such considerations, check what Dōgen is doing to turn the story. How do his comments change the meaning as you had seen it? What part of the story is Dōgen emphasizing to his monks? Is he simply commending the teaching of the ancient master in question, as is often the case, or is he transforming the original story to make some deeper point?

Deeply considering these nuggets from Dōgen, feel these questions, not only with your conceptual thinking, but physically, with upright attentive posture. Allow the situation in the text and your own questioning to penetrate your present experience, including your breathing and all your senses. With this awareness you may bring the teachings of his Extensive Record to bear in your own life. This was surely his intention.

Wallace Stevens in his poem "Questions Are Remarks" says about the pure questioning of his two-year-old grandson, "In the weed of summer comes this green sprout why." The question that sprouts up from such total innocent immersion "sees it as it is." Reading and practicing with *Dōgen's Extensive Record,* allow your own questioning to shoot up. Stevens's "weeds of summer" may be seen as the meditative awareness and settled concentration developed from ongoing, everyday zazen practice, as engaged in by Dōgen and his assembly. Such practice is still ever available today, nourishing this "green sprout why." Continuing, Stevens proclaims about the child, "His question is complete because it contains / His utmost statement. It is his own array, / His own pageant and procession and display / As far as nothingness permits...Hear him."[53] The questioning by Dōgen, and by the teachers and monks in the old stories, may be complete just as they are. Such childlike questioning may be the total utterances of mature spiritual life, "utmost statements." In this material, questions may be statements, and statements are often questions, inciting further questions. Questions that are such total utterances are nourishing spiritual food to digest and absorb.

53 Wallace Stevens, *The Collected Poems* (New York: Vintage Books, 1990), pp. 462–463.

You can encounter the questions Dōgen offers with your own investigations into the issues posed by Dōgen, as well as into the situations you meet in this present world around you. It is not that such practice of open hearted questioning will yield some final answer or solution. But such questioning may offer the possibility to live authentically, even amid the difficulties and cold winters you may face.

In addition to using this work as a field for probing and deepening insight, modern readers may also appreciate and benefit from Dōgen's encouragements for ongoing practice, and even his warm consolations for the difficulties of such effort. Modern practitioners may also accept Dōgen's reminder to his students, "Don't forget that we are transmitting the Dharma and saving deluded beings" (Dharma hall discourse 505). Dōgen repeatedly returns to the illuminating value of our own zazen, raw and ever fresh. "Although the sitting cushions are old, they show new impressions" (Dharma hall discourse 523).

Acknowledgments

We are very grateful to Professor Seijun Ishii of Komazawa University, who patiently responded to many questions about the text, offered helpful comments on some of our translations, and kindly shared his notes from his study of Eihei Kōroku with Genryū Kagamishima. We are also grateful to Ryūtarō Suzuki and to Jikisai Minami, who each provided source material and commentary texts that aided our translations.

We would like to thank the three writers of introductory material for this book. Tenshin Reb Anderson, my root dharma teacher to whom my personal gratitude is immeasurable, has long brought forth with subtle insight the vital practice dimensions of Dōgen's teachings. His luminous foreword provides a living context for digesting and lovingly engaging with Dōgen's Eihei Kōroku. The work of Steven Heine, Professor at Florida International University, is certainly unsurpassed among American academic scholars of Dōgen. Heine's many fine writings about Dōgen are a valuable resource for all students of Zen. His introductory essay highlights the importance of Eihei Kōroku to modern Dōgen studies, and the timeliness of this present volume to contemporary understandings of Dōgen, and of the Zen tradition generally. John Daido Loori, a prominent American Zen teacher in the lineage of Taizan Maezumi Roshi and

Abbot of Zen Mountain Monastery in New York, has produced a fresh integration of Dōgen and kōan teachings to offer to a new generation of Zen students. Daido's essay situates Dōgen's writings in one innovative example of modern kōan practice, and illustrates how Dōgen's approach can be included in a formal kōan training program. Thanks also to my friend Kaz Tanahashi for his permission to include the poem by Ryōkan lamenting the neglect of Eihei Kōroku, which we translated together and was previously published in *Moon in a Dewdrop*.

Thanks to Wisdom Publications, especially to Josh Bartok for long-time support in bringing forth this teaching of Dōgen, as well as for the helpful suggestions of copy editor John LeRoy. Thanks to the San Francisco Zen Center for cosponsoring this translation project, and especially to Blanche Hartman, Shosan Austin, and Michael Wenger for help arranging this support and our use of Zen Center facilities to do part of the translation work. Thanks also to Sokoji temple in San Francisco's Japantown, and to Taiken Yokoyama, Ikki Nambara, Gengo Akiba Roshi, and the Sōtō Zen Buddhism International Center, whose facilities we also used for our translation work. We thank Beverly Ewing for extensive, and very helpful, proofreading assistance. We especially deeply thank the kind benefactor and donor who wishes to remain anonymous, without whose support this work would not have been even remotely conceivable.

Our gratitude goes to Shinkai Tanaka Roshi, currently the abbot of Hōkyōji, the monastery established by Dōgen's disciple Jakuen. I had the extraordinary privilege of practicing for several sesshins with Shinkai Roshi in the early 1990s when he was the abbot of Saikōji temple outside Kyoto. He has kindly provided for this book a photograph of the painting of Dōgen now enshrined at Hōkyōji, with the inscribed verse given in volume 10, *jisan* verse 3. Thanks also to Daihonzanji Eiheiji, to Dōnin Minamisawa Roshi (General Director of Daihonzanji Eiheiji), and to Rev. Hakujin Kuroyanagi for providing and giving special permission to reproduce the portrait of Dōgen that has inscribed on it *jisan* verse 10 from volume 10. Eiheiji also generously provided Dōgen's calligraphy from Fukanzazengi (whose text is at the end of volume 8), a sampling of which appears on the cover of this book.

Thanks to all the students who have made helpful comments in many classes and workshops that both Shohaku Okumura and I have given on the materials from Eihei Kōroku during the translation process. Thanks also for encouragement and suggestions from various Zen colleagues, teachers, and scholars who have read portions of the text in process, including Tom Kirchner, Steven Heine, Dosho Mike Port, Enkyo O'Hara, Katherine Thanas, Shosan Austin, Gaelyn Godwin, Myo Lahey, Susan Postal, Kimberly Johnson, and Britt Pyland. The white lotus is blossoming, smiling above a sea of clouds.

We would like to acknowledge the efforts of Yuhō Yokoi, who published a rendition of Eihei Kōroku in Tokyo in 1987, based on the Manzan version. Unfortunately, difficulties with English coherency, unclear or questionable interpretations, and omissions from the original text significantly limit the usefulness of that volume. Nevertheless, we did occasionally consult it, and sometimes were grateful to find interpretations that were helpfully suggestive.

I would like to express my great appreciation to Shohaku Okumura. Together we shared the adventure of wrestling with Dōgen, earnestly seeking to convey his ancient words and fresh spirit to contemporary English readers. I have thought of this translation work as ongoing dokusan with Dōgen, deeply investigating each passage of text to penetrate his Dharma, wit, and spiritual depths. At times we have found ourselves with a dismayed "What could he possibly mean here?" Only after sustained mutual reflection and questioning have Shohaku and I been able to bring forth responses that we feel do some justice to Dōgen's insights and playful challenges. Still, after his many years of study and translation of Dōgen, on his own and in collaboration with myself and others, Shohaku Okumura insists that he does not understand Dōgen at all. I can only say that it has been a great privilege and joy to share with Shohaku this study and work.

Finally, we are immeasurably grateful to Eihei Dōgen for his strenuous efforts to convey his profound, simple, and creative teaching and allow it to take root in Japan. Equally, we are deeply grateful to the many generations of Japanese masters who have kept this practice tradition alive, and especially, here, for those such as Manzan Dōhaku who helped preserve

Dōgen's Extensive Record. May Dōgen's teachings, and our efforts to present them in English in this book, now inform and illuminate our lives in this contemporary Western world. It is truly wondrous how much Dōgen's ancient teachings can give us, considering that our modern technological world would surely seem far more alien to him than the most bizarre imaginable science fiction realm could ever appear to us.

TAIGEN DAN LEIGHTON
Fall 2004

THE SIGNIFICANCE OF EIHEI KŌROKU
AND ITS TRANSLATION[1]

STEVEN HEINE

THE PUBLICATION of the long-awaited complete translation of the Eihei Kōroku by Taigen Dan Leighton and Shohaku Okumura, which is thoroughly researched, thoughtfully conceived, and accompanied by detailed annotations, is a major event in the field of Dōgen studies that is bound to have a long-lasting influence. The growing community of scholars, practitioners, and intellectuals ever intrigued by Dōgen's writings will greatly enjoy and benefit from such a precise and clear rendering of this crucial text. The significance of the translation derives from two interrelated factors: one is the overwhelming importance of the text for understanding Dōgen's life and thought, especially in his later period; and the other is the "underwhelming" way the Eihei Kōroku has been received, particularly in Western works about Dōgen that have focused almost exclusively on the Shōbōgenzō and other writings, thereby neglecting an equally important and representative record of his life, thought, and practice.

Main Work of Later Period

The Eihei Kōroku is one of the two main texts produced by Dōgen (1200–1253), the founder of the Sōtō Zen sect in thirteenth century Japan, and the primary work representing the later period of Dōgen's career.

---

1 Some of this material is included in Steven Heine, "The *Eihei Kōroku:* The Record of Dōgen's Later Period at Eihei-ji Temple," in Steven Heine and Dale S. Wright, eds., *The Zen Canon: Classic Texts in the Zen Tradition* (New York: Oxford University Press, forthcoming).

The later period covered the last decade of his life (1244–1253), when Dōgen served as abbot of Eiheiji temple in the remote Echizen mountains, far removed from the capital and the center of Japanese Buddhism in Kyoto. The Eihei Kōroku is a collection of various kinds of verses and discourses, especially formal sermons composed in Chinese *(kanbun)* that are contained in the first seven of ten volumes. It was compiled by Dōgen's disciples according to the model of the "recorded sayings" *(yulu* or *guanglu;* Jap.: *goroku* or *kōroku)* genre, or collected records of the great Chinese Chan masters of the Song dynasty. The Eihei Kōroku is probably the first main example of this genre produced in Japan, and was particularly influenced by the record of Hongzhi, a leading Caodong school master in China from the generation prior to Dōgen's mentor, Rujing.

Until recently, the Eihei Kōroku has received far less attention in Dōgen studies than his other main text, the Shōbōgenzō.[2] The Shōbōgenzō, a collection of informal sermons, is generally considered the first writing on Buddhism in the Japanese vernacular; it was the primary work of Dōgen's earlier period, the ten years (1233–1243) he spent as abbot of Kōshōji temple in the town of Fukakusa on the outskirts of Kyoto. The composition of the Shōbōgenzō was almost entirely completed by the time of the move to Echizen (currently Fukui) Province. Therefore, this work does not reveal Dōgen's teachings or training style from the later period, although Dōgen apparently continued to edit some of the Shōbōgenzō fascicles. It is ironic that Dōgen is best known as abbot of Eiheiji but the most revered text is not the text from the time he was abbot there. During this period he also composed additional fascicles that are included in a special edition known as the twelve-fascicle Shōbōgenzō, in contrast to the better known collection from the earlier period known as the seventy-five-fascicle Shōbōgenzō.

---

2 From the Kamakura period till the revival of Sōtō scholarship in the seventeenth century, both texts were largely ignored, although an abbreviated version of the Eihei Kōroku known as the Eihei Goroku received much attention. During and since the Tokugawa era, the Shōbōgenzō has been seen as Dōgen's magnum opus.

Current Status

Why and to what extent has the Eihei Kōroku been overlooked? The boom in interest in Dōgen began in the 1970s with the translations of Shōbōgenzō Zuimonki by Reihō Masunaga and of major portions of the Shōbōgenzō by Norman Waddell and Masao Abe published in *The Eastern Buddhist*.[3] By the end of the decade, Takeshi James Kodera translated the Hōkyōki, and a number of scholarly studies became available. Following the lead of Japanese scholars who highly valued the Shōbōgenzō, which was receiving enormous attention, at almost no time was the role of Eihei Kōroku mentioned. In fact, the main work of the formative period of Western Dōgen studies, Hee-Jin Kim's *Dōgen Kigen—Mystical Realist*, does not contain even a single reference to the Eihei Kōroku in the index. However, this was not entirely due to a failure to recognize the importance of the work. In an appendix dealing with an overview of each of Dōgen's major writings Kim remarks, "An increasing number of students of Dōgen in the post-war period feel that the work is comparable in its import to Shōbōgenzō and hence must be investigated thoroughly. Research in this regard has been progressing very vigorously in recent years."[4]

In the nearly thirty years since Kim, Dōgen studies have progressed in piecemeal fashion with the publication of numerous complete translations of the Shōbōgenzō and additional specialized studies and translations of other works such as the meditation manual Fukanzazengi, the Japanese waka poetry collection Sanshōdōei, the monastic rules collected in the Eihei Shingi, and the collection of three hundred kōans, Shōbōgenzō Sanbyakusoku (also known as the Mana Shōbōgenzō). Yet, the Eihei Kōroku remained untouched, with the exception of two translations that were either incomplete or inadequate.[5] By contrast, the approach of Leighton

---

3 Much of this material was recently reprinted in Norman Waddell and Masao Abe, *The Heart of Dōgen's Shōbōgenzō* (Albany: State University of New York Press, 2002).

4 Hee-Jin Kim, *Dōgen Kigen—Mystical Realist* (Tucson: University of Arizona Press, 1975), p. 314. Available as *Eihei Dōgen: Mystical Realist* (Boston: Wisdom Publications, 2004).

5 The first of these is a complete rendering that is useful but of limited value by Yūhō Yokoi, *Eihei Kōroku* (Tokyo: Sankibō, 1987), and the translation of some small portions that are not clearly labeled is by Thomas Cleary, *Rational Zen: The Mind of Dōgen Zenji*

and Okumura follows what I consider the central law of translating Dōgen, which is that the more precise and accurate the rendering, the more smooth and easy both the readability and the reliability. Nevertheless, Dōgen's verbal prowess is so profoundly creative and ambiguous that there are many possible interpretations of many passages, and the annotations in this volume try to guide the reader through this.

For my part, I began to realize the crucial role of the Eihei Kōroku several years ago while doing research on the new methodological movement known as "Critical Buddhism" (Hihan Bukkyō), which stresses the theory that Dōgen's creative peak came in the later period. Yet Critical Buddhism puts its focus on the twelve-fascicle Shōbōgenzō, which was produced around the same time and expresses a philosophy emphasizing the role of karmic causality that is quite similar to many passages in the Eihei Kōroku.[6] In an article published in 1997, I tried to highlight that the relationship between the Shōbōgenzō and the Eihei Kōroku needed to be revisited: "But the probable reason the [Eihei Kōroku] has not generated the kind of scholarly attention that the Shōbōgenzō has received is the brief but opaque and complex structure of the sermons…. Therefore, an emphasis on the historical role of the [Eihei Kōroku] may ironically lead us back to an appreciation of the intellectual role of the [Shōbōgenzō]. But the [Shōbōgenzō] must be seen in a new way, through lenses cut by encountering the question of why Dōgen at the peak of composing it abandoned this work."[7]

Comparison of Shōbōgenzō and Eihei Kōroku

Both the Shōbōgenzō and the Eihei Kōroku consist primarily of collections of sermons delivered by Dōgen to his assembly of disciples. However, they

---

(Boulder: Shambhala, 1992). At worst, both translations contain passages that are nearly unreadable because of confusing syntax and misleading renderings.

6 For a work on this phenomenon in English see Jamie Hubbard and Paul Swanson, eds., *Pruning the Bodhi Tree: The Storm over Critical Buddhism* (Honolulu: University of Hawai'i Press, 1997).

7 Steven Heine, "The Dōgen Canon: Dōgen's Pre-Shōbōgenzō Writings and the Question of Change in His Later Work," *Japanese Journal of Religious Studies* 24, nos. 1–2 (1997): 39–85.

represent two very different styles of sermonizing, as shown in table 1 below. The Shōbōgenzō, composed in Japanese, contains *jishu*-style, or informal, sermons with lengthy discussions of specific doctrines and citations of passages from Mahāyāna sutras in addition to many different examples of Zen kōans. The *jishu* sermons were delivered at different times of the day, including late at night, mainly as a special instruction for those who requested or required it, in the abbot's quarters *(hōjō)* or some other setting in the monastic compound. They were often written out prior to delivery, and then recorded and subsequently edited by Dōgen's main disciple, Ejō. Several of these sermons were delivered on more than one occasion or were apparently rewritten and reedited several times over the years.

The Eihei Kōroku, composed in Chinese, contains records of *jōdō*-style, or formal, sermons, which were delivered exclusively in the Dharma hall *(hattō)*, generally according to a set schedule and at a fixed time of the day, often for a ceremonial or memorial occasion. Although this style is considered formal, the *jōdō* was an oral manner of teaching recorded by disciples that contains many examples of spontaneous gestures and utterances.[8] Like the Shōbōgenzō, the *jōdō* sermons often cite kōan cases, and also cite or allude to a multitude of passages from the recorded sayings of Zen masters as well as from the transmission of the lamp histories collected when Zen was the dominant form of Buddhism in Song China during the eleventh and twelfth centuries. Therefore, both texts are characterized by a remarkably extensive intertextuality, in that they achieve a great degree of originality and creativity through the process of citing and commenting on a wide variety of earlier Chan/Zen texts.

Structure and Genres

There are two main editions of the Eihei Kōroku, the Monkaku (also known as the Sōzan) edition from 1598, generally considered more authentic, and the Manzan (also known as the Rufu-bon or "popular") edition from 1672. Despite numerous and at times significant discrepancies

---

8 Dōgen may have written some of the sermons out first, as they reveal a subtle use of rhyme and rhythmic patterns. An interesting question is, to what extent did Dōgen's disciples know enough Sino-Japanese to be able to follow the sermons at the time of their delivery?

TABLE 1. THE TWO DIFFERENT STYLES OF SERMONS
COLLECTED IN THE EIHEI KŌROKU AND THE SHŌBŌGENZŌ

	Eihei Kōroku	Shōbōgenzō
Text	7 volumes	up to 95 fascicles
Period	late	early
Language	Chinese *(kanbun)*	Japanese
Sermon Type	*Jōdō*	*Jishu*
Where	Dharma hall *(hattō)*	Abbot's quarters *(hōjō)*
When	day	evening
Style	formal	informal
Expression	demonstrative	rhetorical
Length	brief and allusive	extended, with details and citations
Audience	monks, with general guests	diverse, those requesting instruction
Atmosphere	public, communal	private, individual

between them, especially in the numbering of the passages particularly in volume 1 and in the exact wording of various passages particularly in volume 10, the contents of all Eihei Kōroku editions follow the same basic structure:

The first seven volumes can be subdivided in two ways. One way is by the three locations for the sermons: Kōshōji temple (volume 1); Daibutsuji temple, the original name of Eiheiji when Dōgen first moved to Echizen in 1244 until it was changed in 1246 (volume 2); and Eiheiji temple proper (volumes 3–7). The other way of subdividing the text is by the three prominent assistants *(jisha)* to Dōgen who served as recorders or editors of the sermons: Senne (recorder of volume 1, in addition to volumes 9 and 10); Ejō (volumes 2–4 and 8); and Gien (volumes 5–7).

The transition from Ejō's editorship to Gien's, which occurred around the first day of the ninth month of 1249, is a significant turning

TABLE 2. CONTENTS AND DATES OF COMPOSITION
FOR THE EIHEI KŌROKU

Vol.			Years	Recorder
1	Kōshōji goroku	*jōdō* 1–126	1236–43	Senne

*Two-year hiatus during transition
from Fukakusa to Echizen with no Dharma hall.*

Vol.			Years	Recorder
2	Daibutsuji goroku	*jōdō* 127–184	1245–46	Ejō
3	Eiheiji goroku	*jōdō* 185–257	1246–48	Ejō
4	Eiheiji goroku	*jōdō* 258–345	1248–49	Ejō
5	Eiheiji goroku	*jōdō* 346–413	1249–51	Gien
6	Eiheiji goroku	*jōdō* 414–470	1251	Gien
7	Eiheiji goroku	*jōdō* 471–531	1251–52	Gien
8	Miscellaneous	20 *shōsan* from Daibutsuji/ Eiheiji 14 *hōgo* from Kōshōji Fukanzazengi		Ejō et al.
9	Kōshōji collection	90 kōan cases with *juko* comment	1236 et al.	Senne
10	Kanbun poetry collections	5 *shinsan* 20 *jisan* 125 *geju*	1223–53	Senne et al.

point according to some scholars. This is because this period also marked another important shift for Dōgen, who had completed work on the seventy-five-fascicle Shōbōgenzō several years before and now began writing and collecting the new collection known as the twelve-fascicle Shōbōgenzō. It is particularly notable that there are some basic correspondences between the sermons of the Gien volumes and the twelve-fascicle Shōbōgenzō, particularly in an emphasis on the doctrines of karmic causality and moral ret-ribution. This seems to mark an important and dramatic intellectual shift or "change" *(henka)* in Dōgen's approach to Buddhist doctrine.[9]

On the one hand, there is a basic consistency of style and content that runs throughout the seven volumes of *jōdō* sermons. For example, many of the sermons were delivered for ceremonial occasions. These range from Buddhist events, such as memorials for the birth and enlightenment anniversaries of the Buddha, to seasonal and secular festivities. Also, a majority of sermons were based on the citations of kōans and other ear-lier Zen writings from China, as well as the demonstrative use of staffs and fly whisks as symbols of the master's authority and transcendent power.

There are some basic themes and approaches that are consistently employed throughout the text. These include the frequent use of the imagery of plum blossoms as a symbol of renewal and awakening; an emphasis on the role of the continuous practice of zazen as an essential component of the religious quest; the demonstrative use of the Zen staff and fly whisk as indicators of the master's authority; and Dōgen's eager-ness to critique the eminent Chinese Chan predecessors whose records he frequently cites. For example, *jōdō* 135, a sermon for the winter solstice at Daibutsuji temple, evokes a combination of these images, symbols, and attitudes in citing and revising a passage from the record of Hongzhi.

Life and Teachings

One of the most intriguing and important aspects of the Eihei Kōroku is the way so many passages reveal key aspects of Dōgen's life that are not disclosed in other sources, as well as the way he presented his doctrines in the later period. The Chinese verses in volume 10 are just about the only way of learning about Dōgen's experiences in China, as the Hōkyōki is a record of his conversations with Rujing that were recorded some time after returning to Japan.

The *jōdō* records contain Dōgen's first sermons at Kōshōji after that temple was established, including famous references to his returning

---

9 The notion of change in the late Dōgen is crucial to the theory of Critical Buddhism. See Heine, "Critical Buddhism and Dōgen's *Shōbōgenzō*: The Debate over the 75-Fasci-cle and 12-Fascicle Texts," in Swanson, *Pruning the Bodhi Tree*, pp. 251–285.

"empty-handed" from China and to his receiving Rujing's recorded sayings, as well as reminiscences explaining why Dōgen considered him such a great teacher. Also included in the *jōdō* are Dōgen's views of his early Japanese teachers Eisai and Myōzen, whom he begins memorializing rather late in his career; his return to Eiheiji from a journey to Kamakura at the behest of the shōgun in 1247; and his receiving the Tripitaka at Eiheiji. Other revelations in Eihei Kōroku include Chinese verses anticipating the experience of death.

The formal sermons also reveal key aspects of Dōgen's strict adherence to the liturgy and ritual of monastic routine following the model of the Chinese patriarchs. Many of the sermons were delivered in a rather mechanical fashion for ceremonial occasions and memorials, although they still often express a sense of spontaneity, especially through the use of verse commentary or demonstrative gestures near the conclusion of the discourse.

According to the pattern prescribed in the Chanyuan Qingguei (Jap.: Zen'en shingi) of 1103, the seminal text containing Chinese Chan monastic rules, the *jōdō* sermons were to be delivered at least five or six times a month, on the first, fifth, tenth, fifteenth, twentieth, and twenty-fifth days of the month, in addition to other special occasions.[10] Dōgen apparently adjusted the prescribed schedule that was implemented in China to fit the needs of his development of Zen monasticism at Eiheiji temple in Japan. It is clear that the Buddha's birth, death, and enlightenment anniversaries, in addition to memorials for his Japanese teacher Eisai and Chinese mentor Rujing, were favorite events in the yearly cycle. Dōgen also consistently presented sermons for seasonal celebrations, especially in the fall (new and full moons in the eighth, ninth, and tenth months).

It is interesting that the most frequently cited Chinese patriarch is not Rujing, whose recorded sayings are cited ten times, but Hongzhi, whose record is cited forty-five times. Dōgen cited Hongzhi three or four times on the occasion of the Buddha's birthday between 1246 and 1249, and also on other occasions during these years, such as New Year's, the beginning of the summer retreat, the Boys' Festival, and the winter solstice,

10 See Yifa, *The Origins of Buddhist Monastic Codes in China* (Honolulu: University of Hawai'i Press, 2002).

often employing the same strategy of combining citation with criticism. These passages are from the section of the Eihei Kōroku *jōdō* sermons edited by Ejō, and this trend of a reliance on the Hongzhi text did not continue for the most part in the later sections edited by Gien. Yet, Dōgen is also quite critical of all the patriarchs, and he frequently rewrites their sayings and gives classic Zen words his unique interpretive stamp.

Finally, the Eihei Kōroku expresses fundamental doctrinal themes regarding the role of zazen meditation, the experience of *shinjin datsuraku* (casting off body-mind), and the philosophy of karmic causality that is consistent with the twelve-fascicle Shōbōgenzō. Some of the doctrines dealt with extensively in Shōbōgenzō fascicles also are treated more briefly or elliptically in *jōdō* sermons. These include Zenki (in Dharma hall discourse 52), Genjōkōan (in 51), Immo (in 38), Kattō (in 46), Ikkya myōjū (in 107), Kūge (in 162), Ōsakusendaba (in 254), and Udonge (in 308). Dharma hall discourse 205 comments ironically on the "Baizhang and the wild fox" kōan that is the main theme of the Daishugyō and Jinshin inga fascicles and is also discussed in Dharma hall discourse 62 and kōan 77 in volume 9, among other passages.

The current translation by Leighton and Okumura carefully and beautifully reveals the thought and style of Dōgen's Eiheiji period, particularly in the *jōdō* sermons in the first seven volumes, as well as key aspects of his earlier days (especially the poems written in China in the mid-1220s included in volume 10, and the kōan collection compiled in the mid-1230s at Kōshōji temple in volume 9). Reading this work should be an eye-opener for all those interested in understanding and penetrating to the depths of Dōgen's approach to Zen theory and practice.

DŌGEN AND KŌANS

JOHN DAIDO LOORI

THE PREVAILING HISTORICAL PERSPECTIVE in the literature on Zen regards Master Dōgen as an opponent of kōan introspection. Nothing could be further from the truth. Dōgen not only used kōans as an integral part of his teachings but commented on them extensively, in a unique and innovative way. In fact, he might have been one of the key contributors in introducing kōans to medieval Japan.

Shortly after his return from China and then settling at Kōshōji temple, in 1235, Dōgen compiled his Mana Shōbōgenzō (Chinese Shōbōgenzō), also referred to as the Shōbōgenzō Sanbyakusoku (Shōbōgenzō of Three Hundred Kōans). This was a collection of three hundred kōan cases, written in Chinese, that he gathered from Song kōan sources during his trip to the mainland. These kōans "seeded" his subsequent teachings, beginning with Eihei Kōroku, volume 9, written in 1236 at Kōshōji. This volume contained verse commentaries on ninety kōans of which fifty-two are from his Mana Shōbōgenzō. Dōgen's compilation was followed by the gradual development of his *jōdō,* brief formal presentations in the Dharma hall often built around one or more kōans from his own Mana Shōbōgenzō or from the classical collections. It is estimated that Dōgen employed over 290 kōan cases in the first seven volumes of Eihei Kōroku as part of his *jōdō.*

Dōgen's allusive teaching style in these brief *jōdō* was demonstrative and poetic, and used many of the techniques of wordplay and multiple meaning that has come to characterize his Dharma. These brief comments in the Eihei Kōroku contain a unique treasure trove of information on many of the kōan cases and are an invaluable source of insight for students of kōan introspection.

Dōgen's most extensive and subtle use of the Mana Shōbōgenzō kōans was in his Kana Shōbōgenzō (Japanese Shōbōgenzō). Here, Dōgen takes up 172 of the 300 cases, using them in different ways in the ninety-five chapters. In some instances the kōans are employed as simple examples, clarifying a point in the teachings. In other cases the entire chapter is built around a kōan, as in Shōbōgenzō Kannon (the Bodhisattva of Compassion), where case 105 (of the Chinese Shōbōgenzō), "The Hands and Eyes of Great Compassion," is the starting point; or Shōbōgenzō Hakujushi (Cypress Tree), built around case 119, "Cypress Tree in the Garden."

Because Dōgen appeared, on the surface, as an outspoken critic of kōan study, many scholars concluded that he would never have collected or used kōans. What seems closer to the truth is that he opposed the superficial treatment of kōans, not kōan introspection itself. Dōgen is likely to have trained with kōans when he studied with Master Myōzen. He must have been familiar with the kōan literature that was accessible at that time. Several of the major Chinese kōan collections were available in Japan. It is almost certain that Dōgen also trained his students in systematic kōan study, since his teachings require a solid understanding of Chinese kōan literature. As scholar William Bodiford points out in his *Sōtō Zen in Medieval Japan,* Dōgen used "more than 580 kōans" in his teachings. They are peppered throughout all his works and are used to point out how the teachings are embedded in every aspect of practice.

Temples of the Five Mountain system of early medieval Rinzai Zen in Japan imitated the Chinese style of kōan study, which required a sophisticated understanding and mastery of Chinese language and the ability to compose Chinese verse. Monks less inclined toward scholarly pursuits trained in other monasteries, outside the Five Mountains system, where kōan study was simplified and standardized. There were answers to be memorized and prescribed methods for guiding students. This form of kōan study was practiced by both Sōtō and Rinzai lineages.

The use of Dahui's "short cut," or *huatou* (literally, head word), method of working with kōans was also known in Japan at this time. This emphasized concentrating on the principle point or critical phrase of a kōan in order to minimize unnecessary distractions or misleading discursive thoughts that might arise from studying the entire exchange.

In contrast to these formulized views, Dōgen's approach to kōans was wide ranging. He addressed key points of each case, as well as minor secondary points. He frequently examined the kōans from the perspective of the "Five Ranks of the Universal and Particular" of Dongshan. He also pointed out the questions that should be addressed, challenging the practitioner to examine them and sometimes also providing his responses.

Dōgen was a master of language. It is impossible to study his writings and not be moved by the poetry and creativity of his words. His way with language was so unusual that it has earned the appellation "Dōgenese" among modern scholars. He brought to the kōans this sophistication of language, familiarity with Buddhism, and perhaps an unparalleled understanding of the Dharma. To help communicate his appreciation of the teaching, Dōgen used not only ordinary language but also what he referred to as *mitsugo*, "intimate words." These are direct and immediate words that are grasped intuitively in an instant, not understood in a linear, sequential way. Dōgen used both methods freely to transmit his understanding. His teachings had the "lips and mouth" quality found in the Zen of Masters Zhaozhou and Yunmen, who were famous for their live and turning phrases, pointers that went immediately to the heart of the matter, to help practitioners see into their own nature.

Dōgen's apparent criticism of kōans ran parallel to his condemnation of the Five Ranks of Dongshan. And it had a similar purpose. Dōgen was not opposed to the principles conveyed by the Five Ranks. He was critical of the very intellectual, stylized, and inconsequential way that they came to be used in his time. Extending this argument even further, we could say that his teachings in Eihei Shingi on cleaning the teeth, using the lavatory, preparing and eating a meal, or washing the face were responses to the superficiality and self-consciousness that had invaded the Buddhist liturgy of thirteenth-century Japan.

As a Zen teacher, my main interest in Dōgen's treatment of kōans has little to do with the nature or reasons of Dōgen's critique and everything to do with his creative way of commenting on the kōans in both the Kana Shōbōgenzō and the Eihei Kōroku.

Commentaries on many of the kōans in Dōgen's collection of three hundred kōans can be found in classic Song collections such as Hekiganroku, Shōyōroku, and Mumonkan. A careful comparison of these texts with the commentaries offered by Dōgen in the Kana Shōbōgenzō shows no substantial differences in the expression of the Dharma truth of the kōan. Further, there does not appear to be any discrepancy whatsoever between the commentaries by Dōgen, the commentators in the classical collections, and the truth of these kōans as transmitted face-to-face in traditional kōan introspection practice. In other words, what the masters are expressing, whether it is in the Blue Cliff Record, the Book of Serenity, the Gateless Gate, or Dōgen's Shōbōgenzō, is identical in principle but radically different in style and depth.

Both the classic commentaries and those of Dōgen are perfectly consistent with the traditional Mahāyāna teachings found in the sutras and sutra commentaries, with no departures from traditional understanding. None of the teachers presenting the kōans invented a new Dharma. Everything they said always reflected the historical teachings of the Buddha, particularly as understood in the Mahāyāna tradition, although they may have said it in new and perhaps dramatically different ways. There is, however, something especially fresh in how Dōgen expressed the Zen truth of the traditional kōans that sets the Kana Shōbōgenzō in a class by itself. What are the unique characteristics that placed Dōgen's treatment of the kōans apart from the traditional commentaries?

One unusual aspect of Dōgen's treatment of kōans is his use of the Five Ranks and, more than likely, the Fourfold Dharmadhātu teaching of Huayan. He never explicitly talked about either system, except to summarily dismiss the Five Ranks, but he definitely engaged them in a way that reflected a profound understanding and appreciation for their method. In Shōbōgenzō Sansuikyō (The Mountains and Waters Sutra), for example, Dōgen wrote: "Since ancient times wise ones and sages have also lived by the water. When they live by the water they catch fish or they catch humans or they catch the Way. These are traditional water styles. Further, they must be catching the self, catching the hook, being caught by the hook, and being caught by the Way." Then he introduced case 90 of the Mana Shōbōgenzō (Jiashan Sees the Ferryman) and commented on it, saying, "In ancient times, when Chuanzi Dechung suddenly left Yaoshan and went to live on the river, he got the sage Jiashan at the Flower Inn River. Isn't this catching fish, catching humans, catching water? Isn't this catching himself? The fact that Jiashan could see Dechung is because he is Dechung. Dechung teaching Jiashan is Dechung meeting himself."

Even a cursory examination of these teachings reveals elements of Dongshan's Five Ranks. The phrase "When Jiashan sees Dechung, he is Dechung" is the particular within the universal (or the universal containing the particular), the First Rank. The phrase "Dechung teaching Jiashan is Dechung meeting himself" (in other words, the teacher teaching the student is the teacher meeting himself) is the universal within the particular, the Second Rank. "Catching the self, catching the hook, being caught by the hook, being caught by the way"—these are all expressions of the interplay of apparent opposites.

It is clear that though Dōgen was cautionary about the Five Ranks, it was not because he did not find them true, but rather that he did not want them to become a mere abstraction. He did not use them in the way they were taught classically, but more so in the manner where they would be realized face-to-face in the kōan study between teacher and student.

Again, in the Kana Shōbōgenzō, in the fascicle Kattō (Twining Vines), where Dōgen wrote about Bodhidharma's transmission of the marrow to Dazu Huike, he said, "You should be aware of the phrases *You attain me; I attain you; attaining both me and you; and attaining both you and me.* In personally viewing the ancestors' body/mind, if we speak of there being no oneness of internal and external or if we speak of the whole body not being completely penetrated, then we have not yet seen the realm of the ancestors' present."

For Dōgen the relationship of a teacher and student is *kattō,* spiritual entanglement, which from his perspective is a process of using entanglements to transmit entanglements. "Entanglements entwining entanglements is the buddhas and ancestors interpenetrating buddhas and ancestors."

This is the same statement made previously about the teacher–student relationship. All of it expresses the merging of dualities as treated in the Five Ranks of Dongshan or the Fourfold Dharmadhātu, or for that matter in the Sandōkai (the Harmony of Difference and Sameness) by Shitou: "Within light there is darkness but do not try to understand that darkness; within darkness there is light but do not look for that light. Light and darkness are a pair like the foot before and the foot behind in walking. Each thing has its own intrinsic value and is related to everything else in function and position." This was the relationship between Jiashan and Dechung. This was the relationship between Bodhidharma and Huike. This was the relationship that Dōgen referred to when he expounded the nondual Dharma in the kōans used in the Kana Shōbō-genzō.

We live in a country and in a period of time in which the different schools and sects of Buddhism are not so widely separated as they have been historically in their native regions. This situation affords us the unique opportunity to learn from all of the schools and not be bound and limited by sectarianism. The use of a systematic kōan introspection curriculum has been a central part of training at the monastery where I teach, Zen Mountain Monastery, but the teachings of Master Dōgen have also played a pivotal role here. We have found that using Master Dōgen's 300 Kōan Shōbōgenzō (the Mana Shōbōgenzō), many cases from which he comments on in his (Kana) Shōbōgenzō and Eihei Kōroku, has added another dimension to our appreciation of Dōgen's incredible Buddha Dharma. My late teacher Hakuyu Taizan Maezumi Roshi always encouraged his successors to "create an American Shōbōgenzō." For me, this means melding the spirit of Dōgen's work with kōans and a treatment of kōans informed by the classic kōan tradition.

Zen centers from Japanese lineages in the West fall in to three basic groups with regard to kōan study. First is the Sōtō school, which traditionally does not include systematic kōan introspection as part of their curriculum, although the study of kōans is included, as, of course, is the teaching of Dōgen. A second group consists of the Inzan and Takujū lineages of the Rinzai school, both of which have a curriculum of systematic kōan introspection. The third group consists of Sōtō/Rinzai hybrids, which include the teachings of Dōgen as well as some system of kōan introspection. In many cases, systematic curriculums in Western kōan study employ Dahui's *huatou* or "turning word" method of working with kōans.

My own formal training included elements of the Sōtō line as well as some experience of the two Rinzai lines of Inzan and Takujū. This incorporated a traditional collection of miscellaneous kōans, the Gateless Gate, Blue Cliff Record, Book of Serenity, Transmission of the Lamp, kōans on Dongshan's Five Ranks, and 120 precept kōans. The approach was essentially *huatou*-style with some attention to the verses as well as the use of capping phrases. In training my own students with kōans, I found early on that there were gaps in their understanding and clarity. Inspired by Dōgen's comprehensive approach to working with a kōan, we abandoned *huatou* approaches and instead worked with the main case and verse line-by-line with testing questions for each line, another traditional mode. In most cases, I now require my students to present a rounded out understanding with a capping verse.

The ultimate point of passing through a kōan, however, is being able to present not just one's understanding but rather a whole-body-and-mind embodiment of the truth of the kōan, its manifestation in the practitioner's everyday behavior.

As part of bringing more of Dōgen's influence into the way we do kōan study, I have created a collection of 108 kōans along with commentary and verse, many of which are selected from the Mana Shōbōgenzō cases that were used by Dōgen in his Kana Shōbōgenzō and Eihei Kōroku. This kōan introspection requires that the student present line-by-line understanding of the main case, commentary, and the verse. In this process, the Kana Shōbōgenzō and Eihei Kōroku become valuable source material and a useful perspective for understanding the kōan.

This approach to kōan introspection, fusing Dōgen's vision with the traditional ways of working with kōans, has opened up new possibilities in my training of Western students in kōan study. I have found that it addresses Western students' natural philosophical and psychological inclinations, and also allows them to further appreciate the endless depth of the incredible teaching of Master Dōgen.

"On Reading Eihei Kōroku"

RYŌKAN

RYŌKAN *(1758–1831) was a Sōtō Zen monk who is still revered in Japan as a saintly "fool" figure. After finishing his monastic training, Ryōkan returned to his hometown and lived humbly in a hut where he meditated, supporting himself by doing the traditional begging rounds. Along with writing a large collection of truly exceptional spiritual poetry, Ryōkan was famed in his own lifetime as an elegant master calligrapher. But he is most beloved for the many stories of his foolish simplicity, his sweet loving-kindness, and the joy he found in playing with village children. He gave himself the spiritual name Daigu, "Great Fool." The following poem describes his love of Dōgen's writing, Eihei Kōroku in particular, and his deep regret that the material translated in this book was not more fully appreciated and studied.*[1]

On a somber spring evening around midnight,
Rain mixed with snow sprinkled on the bamboos in the garden.
I wanted to ease my loneliness but it was quite impossible.
My hand reached behind me for the Record of Eihei Dōgen.
Beneath the open window at my desk,
I offered incense, lit a lamp, and quietly read.
Body and mind dropped away is simply the upright truth.

1 For more on Ryōkan, see Ryūichi Abé and Peter Haskell, trans., *Great Fool: Zen Master Ryōkan: Poems, Letters and Other Writings* (Honolulu: University of Hawai'i Press, 1996); Burton Watson, trans., *Ryōkan: Zen Monk-Poet of Japan* (New York: Columbia University Press, 1977); John Stevens, *Three Zen Masters: Ikkyū, Hakuin, Ryōkan* (Tokyo: Kodansha International, 1993).

In one thousand postures, ten thousand appearances,
   a dragon toys with the jewel.
His understanding beyond conditioned patterns cleans up
   the current corruptions;
The ancient great master's style reflects the image of India.

I remember the old days when I lived at Entsū monastery
And my late teacher lectured on the True Dharma Eye.
At that time there was an occasion to turn myself around,
So I requested permission to read it,
   and studied it intimately.
I keenly felt that until then I had depended merely
   on my ability.
After that I left my teacher and wandered all over.
Between Dōgen and myself what relationship is there?
Everywhere I went I devotedly practiced
   the True Dharma Eye.
Arriving at the depths and arriving at the vehicle—
   how many times?
Inside this teaching, there's never any shortcoming,
Thus I thoroughly studied the master of all things.

Now when I take the Record of Eihei Dōgen and examine it,
The tone does not harmonize well with usual beliefs.
Nobody has asked whether it is a jewel or a pebble.
For five hundred years it's been covered with dust
Just because no one has had an eye for recognizing Dharma.
For whom was all his eloquence expounded?
Longing for ancient times and grieving for the present,
   my heart is exhausted.

One evening sitting by the lamp my tears wouldn't stop,
And soaked into the records of the ancient Buddha Eihei.
In the morning the old man next door came
   to my thatched hut.
He asked me why the book was damp.
I wanted to speak but didn't, as I was deeply embarrassed;

My mind deeply distressed, it was impossible
   to give an explanation.
I dropped my head for a while, then found some words.
"Last night's rain leaked in and drenched my bookcase."[2]

---

2 Translated by Taigen Dan Leighton and Kazuaki Tanahashi, first published in *Moon in a Dewdrop: Writings of Zen Master Dōgen*, edited by Kazuaki Tanahashi (San Francisco: North Point Press, 1985).

E K
I Ō
H R
E O
I K
U

DŌGEN'S EXTENSIVE RECORD

TRANSLATED BY

TAIGEN DAN LEIGHTON AND SHOHAKU OKUMURA

KŌSHŌJI GOROKU

RECORDED SAYINGS OF THE FOUNDER OF KŌSHŌJI
ZEN TEMPLE IN KYOTO, UJI PREFECTURE

COLLECTED BY SENNE, ATTENDANT OF DŌGEN ZENJI

E K
I Ō
H R
E O
I K
  U

THE EXTENSIVE RECORD OF EIHEI DŌGEN, VOLUME ONE

The master gathered the assembly and expounded the Dharma for the
first time at this temple on the fifteenth day of the tenth month of the second year of Katei (1236 C.E.).

The Family Style in the Golden Country

1. Dharma Hall Discourse[1]

For [following] the family style of relying on grasses, and the mind of
grasping trees, the best practice place is the monastery.[2] One rap on the
sitting platform and three hits on the drum expound and transmit the
subtle, wondrous sounds of the Tathāgata. At this very time, what do you
Kōshōji students say?

After a pause, Dōgen said: South of the Xiang River and north of the
Tan, there is a golden country where the countless common people sink
into the ground.[3]

---

1 "Dharma hall discourse" is *jōdō,* a formal talk given in the Dharma hall by abbots, speaking from a seat set up on the main altar.

2 "Relying on grasses" and "grasping at trees" are usually Zen expressions for ghosts taking form in the world—for example, as tree spirits—and also for relying on mere intellectual understanding. Here Dōgen uses grasses and trees positively as the forms and
lifestyle that monks use for practice in the monastery. "Monastery" is *sōrin,* literally "shrubs
and woods," referring to a gathering place of monks or a residential practice place. The
temple in this case, Kōshōji, was on the outskirts of Kyoto and accessible to lay students.

3 "South of the Xiang River and north of the Tan, there is a golden country" is from a

Dropping Off Old Sandals

2. Dharma Hall Discourse

Even if your speech penetrates the whole universe, you are still not free from discussing the good or bad fortune [predicted] from a spring dream. Even if your speech can enter and leave the inside of an atom, you are still not free from creating a beautiful woman out of cosmetics. If you truly see into one atom, and if you intimately see as many worlds as the sands of the Ganges River, suddenly you will realize that up until now you have been employing your efforts in vain.[4] How can we consider the universe of many worlds large; how can we consider an atom small? Both are not true. How can you get it right with a single phrase? Smashing our old nest [of views held] of the whole universe until now, dropping off our old sandals [worn to enter and leave] an atom until now, how will you speak of it? A frog on the ocean bottom eats porridge; the jeweled rabbit in the heaven washes the bowl.[5]

Not Negating the False; Not Hiding the Straight

3. Dharma Hall Discourse

Seeing an opportunity and then taking action is not skillful. Manifesting a body and plotting some stance is not accepting the situation. So it is said,

---

poem by Danyuan Yingzhen describing the style of his master, the national teacher Nanyang Huizhong, himself a disciple of the sixth ancestor. It is used in Shōyōroku (Book of Serenity), case 85, and in Hekiganroku (Blue Cliff Record), case 18. This is an expression that means wherever you are can be a golden country. See Thomas Cleary, trans., Book of Serenity (Hudson, N.Y.: Lindisfarne Press, 1990; Boston: Shambhala, 1998), pp. 361–366. See Thomas Cleary and J. C. Cleary, trans., The Blue Cliff Record (Boulder: Prajñā Press, 1978), pp. 115–122. Note: Page citations in the notes are from this first edition in one volume, which has the same pagination as the Shambhala 1977 edition in 3 volumes. A later one-volume edition from Shambhala, 1992, differs in pagination. The case numbers in the citations do not vary between editions.

4 In Bendōwa (Talk on Wholehearted Practice of the Way), Dōgen says that when we sit the entire universe becomes enlightenment and that in each atom there are buddhas freely expounding the Dharma. The Dharma reaches from the inside of atoms to the entire universe. See Shohaku Okumura and Taigen Leighton, trans., The Wholehearted Way: A Translation of Eihei Dōgen's Bendōwa with Commentary by Kōshō Uchiyama Roshi (Boston: Tuttle, 1996), pp. 22–23.

5 In Asia a jeweled rabbit is said to be in the moon, like the man in the moon seen in the West. This rabbit is said to derive from the Jataka story about the Buddha's past life in which he was a rabbit who gave himself as food to save a starving old man.

"What is this that thus comes?"[6] What is the principle of "What is this that thus comes?"

After a pause Dōgen said: Truth does not negate the false. The crooked does not hide the straight.

The Wondrous Essence Beyond Assessments

4. Dharma Hall Discourse

When we lift up the wondrous essence, the standing pillars [in the hall] furrow their brows. When we depart from conventional patterns with profound conversation, a tortoise approaches fire [rather than water]. Plain reality is nothing special. How can praising or criticizing ancient or modern masters save your selves? Moreover, how could we then save others? All of you, apart from this [plain reality], are there any other special assessments to make? Apart from this, how do you assess it? Every four years we encounter leap year, in the ninth month is the double yang day. Long months have thirty-one days, short months have thirty days.[7] Kōshōji students, anyone with such opinions [as praising or criticizing ancient or modern masters] should just be called a donkey in front with a horse's behind, or a dragon head with only a snake's tail.[8]

---

6 "What is this that thus comes?" was a question by the sixth Chinese ancestor, Dajian Huineng, to his student Nanyue Huairang when the latter first arrived. After eight years of consideration, Nanyue responded, "The moment I said it was 'this' I'd miss the mark." Huineng said, "Then should one engage in practice-realization or not?" Nanyue replied, "It is not that there is no practice and realization, only that they cannot be defiled." Huineng approved, saying, "Just this non-defiling is what all buddhas keep in mind." This dialogue is discussed by Dōgen in Dharma hall discourse 374, and in kōan case 59 in volume 9 below. It also is cited in Dōgen's important essay "Buddha Nature" in Shōbō-genzō. See Norman Waddell and Masao Abe, trans., *The Heart of Dōgen's Shōbōgenzō* (Albany: State University of New York Press, 2002), p. 61.

7 In East Asia (and in Dōgen's Japanese text) a leap year occurs every third year when an extra month is added to the lunar calendar. "Double yang day" is the ninth day of the ninth lunar month, a festival day during which people go to hilltops and drink sake while viewing chrysanthemums for good health. In the lunar calendar (and again in Dōgen's Japanese text) long months actually have thirty days, short months twenty-nine days. Dōgen cites these common calendar occurrences as examples of ordinary events that would be familiar to his audience.

8 The phrase we translate as "a donkey in front with a horse's behind" has also been interpreted as a servant who "walks in front of a donkey and behind a horse," or any person who stupidly does so. It also could be read as "ahead of an ass but behind a horse." In any

The Range of Pilgrimage
5. Dharma Hall Discourse
Upholding [Dharma] within Guanyin temple, upholding [Dharma] within Shanglan temple, are both pilgrimage.⁹ Fully pervading mountains, fully surveying rivers, wearing through straw sandals, is also pilgrimage.¹⁰

What Is the Sutra
6. Dharma Hall Discourse
Even practicing for three great kalpas, your effort is not yet complete. Attaining realization in a single moment cannot be defiled. An ancient said, "Relying on the sutras, understanding their meaning, is the enemy of the buddhas in the three times. Departing from the sutras by one word is the same as demons' speech."¹¹ Without relying on the sutras, and without departing from the sutras, how could we ever function? Would all of you like to see the sutra?

Dōgen held up his whisk and said: This is my, Kōshō's, whisk.¹² What is the sutra?¹³

---

case it refers to incomplete understanding and faulty practice. The bracketed material is our interpretation of what Dōgen is criticizing here, since Dōgen considers ordinary reality as positive. "A dragon head with a snake's tail" refers to something that begins impressively and fades in the end. It also implies the strong beginning of a dialogue fading to something inconsistent or trivial.

9 Guanyin temple (Jap.: Kannon-in) was the temple where Zhaozhou taught. Shanglan temple (Jap.: Jōran-in) was the temple where Shanglan shun taught and Mazu Dao-i had previously lived.

10 "Penetrating mountains and rivers" is a phrase used for traveling to visit and study with various teachers. In Manzan's later version of the text (see the introduction on Manzan's revisions) two more sentences are added at the end: "What is the matter of pilgrimage? Body-mind dropped off."

11 This statement is attributed to Baizhang Huaihai in volume 6 of the Jingde Transmission of the Lamp (Ch.: Jingde Chuandenglu; Jap.: Keitoku Dentōroku). See Sohaku Ogata, trans. *The Transmission of the Lamp: Early Masters; Compiled by Tao Yuan, a Ch'an Monk of the Sung Dynasty* (Durango, Colo.: Longwood Academic, 1990), p. 213.

12 "Whisk" is *hossu*, a fly whisk made of horsehair used as a traditional emblem for a Buddhist teacher. At this time, "Kōshō" would also be a name used by Dōgen as the teacher at the Kōshōji temple, where this first volume of Eihei Kōroku was delivered.

13 "This" and "what" in "This is the whisk; what is the sutra?" refer to "this" as concrete phenomenal reality and to "what" as ultimate reality.

Following a pause Dōgen added: After that is a long sentence; I will leave it for later.[14]

Dragon Howls and Tiger Roars

7. Dharma Hall Discourse

A dragon howls in a dark cave; the whole universe quiets. A tiger roars at the edge of a cliff; the cold valley becomes warm. Kaaa![15]

A Plum's Ripening

8. Dharma Hall Discourse

Here is a story. Mazu said, "This mind itself is Buddha." Damei ("Great Plum") studied this more than thirty years, dwelling on his mountaintop, hiding his traces in the sounds of the valley and the colors of the mountain. The ancestor Mazu finally sent a monk to visit and say to Damei, "Mazu's Buddha Dharma is different these days."

Damei responded, "How is it different?"

The monk said, "No mind, no Buddha."

Damei said, "Even if he says 'No mind, no Buddha,' I just follow 'This mind itself is Buddha.'"

The monk returned and told the ancestor.

Mazu said, "That plum is ripe."[16]

Dōgen said: "This mind itself is Buddha" is most intimate. Year after year Damei ripened in the middle of summer.

---

14 Ciming (Shishuang) Quyuan held up his staff and said, "This is the staff; what is the sutra? After that is a long sentence; I will leave it for later." The last sentence, "After that is a long sentence; I will leave it for later," is also quoted from Ciming Quyuan by Hongzhi Zhengjue in volume 1 of his Extensive Records. The "long sentence" might refer to the vastness of ultimate reality itself as a sutra that clarifies the relationship of the ultimate to concrete phenomena. This sentence is so long that it can never be spoken. By "leaving it to later," Dōgen is emphasizing the necessity to continuously put this into practice.

15 "Kaaa!" is an exclamatory shout known as *katsu,* literally, "to yell," used especially in the Rinzai tradition to induce or express awakening. This passage refers to the resonance of zazen in the world.

16 This story appears later in Eihei Kōroku in Dharma hall discourse 319, and in Dharma words 9 in volume 8. It is recounted elsewhere in the Mumonkan (Gateless Barrier), cases 30 and 33. Damei Fachang is considered a Dharma successor of Mazu Dao-i. See Robert Aitken, trans., *The Gateless Barrier: The Wu-men Kuan (Mumonkan)* (San Francisco:

A Phrase of Bright Clarity
9. Dharma Hall Discourse

With one phrase [that expresses the essence], a block of ice melts and a tile breaks. With one phrase, a ditch is filled and a valley is dammed. Within this one phrase, all the buddhas of the three times and the six generations of [Chinese] ancestors are born in heaven and descend from heaven, enter a womb and emerge from a womb, accomplish the way, and turn the Dharma wheel. Therefore it is said, "The bright clarity of the ancestral teacher's mind is the bright clarity of the hundred grasstips."[17] Although it is like this, today in the Kōshōji assembly I have one phrase that has never been presented by buddhas or ancestors. Do you want to thoroughly discern it?

After a pause Dōgen said: The bright clarity of the ancestral teacher's mind is the bright clarity of the hundred grasstips.

Expounding and Practicing atop a Hundred-Foot Pole
10. Dharma Hall Discourse

Taking a step forward or backward at the top of a hundred-jo pole, with a single mind, turn your face and transform your self.[18] This mountain monk [Dōgen] will allow the pillars and lanterns to expound this principle for everyone.[19] Have they finished expounding it yet or not? They

---

North Point Press, 1990), pp. 189–194, 204–207; and Thomas Cleary, trans. and commentary, *Unlocking the Zen Kōan: A New Translation of the Wumenguan* (Berkeley: North Atlantic Books, 1997), pp. 144–145, 155–157; originally published as *No Barrier: Unlocking the Zen Kōan, a New Translation of the Wumenguan* (New York: Bantam Books, 1993). The story also appears in the Jingde Transmission of the Lamp; see Ogata, *Transmission of the Lamp,* p. 240.

17 "The bright clarity of the ancestral teacher's mind is the bright clarity of the hundred grasstips," is a saying cited by the famed eighth-century Chan adept Layman Pang to his daughter Lingzhao, herself an adept. "The ancestral teacher" here refers to Bodhidharma. See Ruth Fuller Sasaki, Yoshitaka Iriya, and Dana R. Fraser, trans., *The Recorded Sayings of Layman P'ang: A Ninth-Century Zen Classic* (New York: Weatherhill, 1971), p. 75; and Chang Chung-yuan, trans., *Original Teachings of Ch'an Buddhism* (New York: Vintage Books, 1968), pp. 145–146.

18 The usual Zen saying about stepping from a hundred-foot pole is literally "a hundred-*shaku* pole," a *shaku* being approximately one American foot. Here Dōgen says "a hundred-*jo* pole." One *jo* is approximately three yards.

19 The word "expound" (Jap.: *setsu*), repeated frequently in this passage, might also be

expounded it last night, and also the night before. Tomorrow they will expound it, and also the day after tomorrow. If they have finished expounding it, has everyone heard it or not? If you have not yet heard it, the pillars and lanterns have grown lazy and have not yet expounded it. So this mountain monk [Dōgen] will allow the whole great earth and all people to expound it. Have the whole great earth and all people finished expounding it yet or not? If they have not yet expounded it, then they also have grown lazy. Expounding and practicing this principle are both the ultimate way.

Therefore among the ancients, Daci said, "Expounding one yard does not equal practicing one foot. Expounding one foot does not equal practicing one inch."[20]

Dongshan said, "Practice that which cannot be expounded. Expound that which cannot be practiced."[21]

Yunju said, "When expounding there is no path of practice. When practicing there is no path of expounding. When neither expounding or practicing, what kind of path is that?"[22]

Luopu said, "If both practice and expounding arrive, there is no original matter. If neither practice or expounding arrive, the original matter exists."[23]

The teacher Dōgen said: For Daci, expounding one yard cannot be done without practicing one yard; expounding one foot cannot be done without practicing one foot.

---

translated as "express" or "explain" and may also imply these meanings here depending on context.

20 Daci Huanzhong was a disciple of Baizhang Huaihai. "One yard" is literally one *jo* (see previous note), so the actual length is three yards. We have translated it as "one yard" in the text to maintain the feeling of the original. These four quotations appear together in volume 3 of Hongzhi's Extensive Record (Jap.: Wanshi Kōroku); and in the section on Daci from the Keitoku Dentōroku. See also Dharma hall discourses 498.

21 Dongshan Liangjie is the founder of the Caodong (Sōtō) lineage that Dōgen inherited and brought to Japan.

22 Yunju Daoying was Dongshan's disciple.

23 Luopu Yuanan was a disciple of Jiashan Shanhui. The "original matter" might refer to reality prior to conceptualization or to the one great cause for buddhas' manifesting, to lead all beings into the path of awakening.

For Dongshan, [one should] practice that which cannot be practiced, and expound what cannot be expounded.

For Yunju, there is both practice and expounding, letting go and grasping.

For Luopu, if both practice and expounding arrive, the country prospers, if neither practice or expounding arrive, buddhas and ancestors confirm [you].

Studying Together without Lack
11. Dharma Hall Discourse

Taking down the pole in front of the temple gate is just the transmigration of birth and death.[24] Giving out the tree at the center [of the garden] is still an upside-down illusion.[25] Having studied as such is study together with all the buddhas and ancestors. Not having studied as such is study together with the self. All buddhas study together, the self does not study together. There is a difference between speaking of yards and speaking of feet, between saying ten and saying nine. What is not studying together, that is self. What is studying together, that is all buddhas.

Here is a story about Nanyue: Great teacher Mazu had been teaching at Jiangxi Province. [Mazu's teacher] Nanyue asked his assembly, "Does [Mazu] Dao-I expound the Dharma for his assembly or not?"

A monk said, "Already he has been expounding Dharma for his assembly."

Nanyue said, "Nobody has brought any reports at all." The monks did not respond. Because of this he sent one monk and said, "Wait for him to give a discourse, and just ask, 'How is it?' Remember what he says and tell me."

The monk went and did what his teacher asked. He returned and told

24 "Taking down the pole in front of the temple gate" is a reference to the story that also appears in case 22 of the Mumonkan in which Mahākāśyapa asked Ānanda to take down the banner signaling Dharma debate (but in this case also symbolizing Ānanda's ego) from in front of the temple. Thereupon Ānanda awakened. See Aitken, *Gateless Barrier*, pp. 142–146; and Cleary, *Unlocking the Zen Kōan*, pp. 106–109.

25 "Giving out the tree at the center" refers to a saying by Xuansha Shibei in Keitoku Dentōroku, vol. 16: trying to gain understanding is like trying to sell a garden while still retaining the tree in the center of it.

Nanyue, "Master Mazu said, 'Since I left confusion behind thirty years ago, I have never lacked for salt or sauce to eat.'"[26]

After the story the teacher Dōgen said: Out of the causes and conditions in this story, make one round dumpling and offer it to the buddhas and ancestors. There are three people who confirm this. The first person says, "I offer heavenly māndārava and mañjūṣaka flowers." Another person says, "I offer four grams of precious incense from the seashore." A third person says, "I offer my head, eyes, marrow, and brain." Put aside these three people's confirmations for a while. The present great assembly before me provides confirmation, and allows the third son of Zhou and the fourth son of Li (i.e., the common people) to express it. What do they say? "After departing from confusion for a million years, no lack of salt and vinegar."[27]

Remain atop a Hundred-Foot Pole with Each Step
12. Dharma Hall Discourse
Time does not wait for people, so we should value our days and nights. Since ancient times, people of the way do not value the nation's powers, societal hierarchies, the seven treasures, or the hundred things, but only

---

26 This story appears in Mazu's completed record, which adds that Nanyue approved it when he heard Mazu's response. See Cheng Chien Bhikshu, *Sun Face Buddha: The Teachings of Ma-tsu and the Hung-chou School of Ch'an* (Berkeley: Asian Humanities Press, 1992), p. 61.

27 The offerings of heavenly flowers, precious incense, and finally one's own body were offerings that, according to chapter 23 of the Lotus Sutra, were given by a bodhisattva named "Seen with Joy by All Living Beings" during a past life of the Bodhisattva Medicine King. The tiny amount of the incense from the seashore that is offered is described as having equal value to the entire world. See Leon Hurvitz, trans., *Scripture of the Lotus Blossom of the Fine Dharma* (New York: Columbia University Press, 1976), pp. 294–295. Manzan has a different interpretation of the line "After departing from confusion for a million years, no lack of salt and vinegar." His version—presumably changed from the earlier editions (see the introduction)—reads something like "How will the present great assembly before me provide confirmation, and cause the third son of Zhou and the fourth son of Li to express it by themselves saying, 'After departing from confusion for a million years, no lack of salt and vinegar'?" The interpretation in the Monkaku version, used in our translation, implies that the ultimate reality of all people is that they are already fed, and fundamentally already departed from confusion. The Manzan version implies the sangha's responsibility to help the common people to realize this.

value the passing time.[28] It is said that practice of the way proceeds together with the passing of time. Therefore all people take one step forward and one step back from the top of a hundred-jo pole and attain practice of the way.[29] One third of this summer [practice period] has already passed. Have you been able to say a phrase or not? An ancient person said, "Take one step forward from a hundred-foot pole."[30] It has also been said, "Take one step backward from a hundred-foot pole." From ancient times it has never before been said to remain with each step on the top of a hundred-foot pole. When practicing, move forward one step, move backward one step, abide with each step. This top of the pole is exactly where all people settle the body and establish their life, and exactly the seat of realization where all buddhas attain unsurpassed complete awakening.[31]

I remember that Huangbo said to his assembly, "Every senior master in all directions exists on the top of a monk's staff." A monk departed after making prostrations and went to Dashu, where he repeated this saying.[32]

Dashu said, "Huangbo speaks thus, but has he already seen in all directions or not?"

Langye Huijue said, "Dashu speaks thus, but although he has eyes he seems blind. Even if everyone under heaven bites through the one staff of Huangbo, it will not break."[33]

---

28 "Societal hierarchies" is literally "men and women" but also refers to all attachments from societally imposed distinctions. The "seven treasures" are gold, silver, lapis lazuli, crystal, agate, ruby, and carnelian (though in some lists the last two are replaced with coral and amber). The "hundred things" refers to the whole phenomenal world.

29 For the "hundred-jo pole" see note 18 above.

30 This famous statement is by Changsha Jingcen, a disciple of Nanquan and Dharma brother of Zhaozhou.

31 "Settle the body and establish their life" is *anshin ritusmei,* a common Japanese expression derived from Confucianism, which usually uses the character *shin* for mind. Dōgen replaces it with the character *shin* for body to emphasize the physical practice of enacting awakening.

32 Master Dashu (Jap.: Daiju) is unknown aside from this story.

33 Langye Huijue was a disciple of Fenyang Shanzhao. This entire exchange is taken from the Recorded Sayings of Langye.

The teacher Dōgen said: Langye spoke thus, and although his statement says quite a lot, he was only able to say eighty or ninety percent. How could he have failed to say that when everyone under heaven bites through, it immediately breaks? If you are able to see this, what have you got? Have you completely understood?

After a pause Dōgen said: The senior masters in all directions exist on the top of Huangbo's single mountain staff. If it suddenly toppled, the wide heavens would fall. Unknowingly, I so far have been discussing the long and short of it.

Completing a Full Moon

13. Full Moon Evening Dharma Hall Discourse [1240][34]
Unsurpassed bodhi (awakening) is just seven upsets, eight tumbles; turning the wondrous Dharma wheel is falling into three or falling into two.

I remember when Mazu viewed the moon on this occasion. Nanquan Puyuan, Xitang Zhizang, and Baizhang Huaihai were in attendance.[35] Mazu said, "Right at this very time, how is it?"

Xitang said, "Just right to make offerings."

Baizhang said, "Just right to cultivate practice."

Nanquan flapped his sleeves and left.

Mazu said, "The sutras enter the Treasury (Zang); Zen returns to the Ocean (Hai); only Universal Vow (Puyuan) transcends beyond things."[36]

The teacher Dōgen said: Making offerings, cultivating practice, flapping his sleeves and leaving, these three people are just right to complete one full moon. Enjoying the moon at Jiangxi (where Mazu taught) is like this.

---

34 "Full Moon Evening" refers specifically to the full moon in the eighth month of the lunar calendar, a traditional occasion in East Asia for moon viewing and creating poetry about the moon. All dates will be given by the number of the lunar month as used traditionally in China and Japan, which do not coincide with January, February, and so forth of our modern calendars.

35 Nanquan Puyuan, Xitang Zhizang, and Baizhang Huaihai were all famous Dharma successors of Mazu Dao-i. This story is mentioned in the commentary to case 6 of Shōyōroku. See Cleary, *Book of Serenity,* p. 25.

36 In his final statement here Mazu is playing with the meanings of his disciples' names: Xitang Zhizang means "Western Hall Wisdom Treasury"; Baizhang Huaihai means "A Hundred-Jo Cherishing Ocean"; Nanquan Puyuan means "South Spring Universal Vow."

The rabbit and toad [in the moon] in front of the Milky Way fully confirm it.

Refined Daily in the Open Furnace
14. Opening the Fireplace Dharma Hall Discourse [1240][37]
We have opened the furnace and bellows of our own house. Buddha ancestors of the past refined [their disciples and themselves]. If someone questions the significance of this activity, this morning is the first day of the tenth month.

Igniting Practice
15. Dharma Hall Discourse
The seed of buddhas arises from conditions, Buddha Dharma arises from the outset. When you encounter good conditions, do not stumble but just practice. Within practice there are both subduing and surrender. Staying here [at Kōshōji], do not stumble, but just wholeheartedly engage the way. Within wholehearted engaging of the way there is both practice and effort. With one morning of thoroughness, ten thousand dharmas become complete. If you are not yet thorough, ten thousand dharmas stumble.

Now Zen Master [Bao'en] Xuanze had affinity with Fayan.[38] Once Xuanze was appointed as director in the assembly of Fayan. One day Fayan said, "How many years have you been here?"

Xuanze replied, "I have already been in the teacher's assembly for three years."

Fayan said, "You are a student, so why don't you ever ask me about Dharma?"

---

37 "Opening the Fireplace" happened at the beginning of the tenth (lunar) month. At this time of year the large metal container behind the altar in the monks' hall was first used to burn charcoal and give heat.

38 Bao'en Xuanze became a Dharma successor of Fayan Wenyi, founder of one of the Chinese five houses of Chan/Zen. "Affinity" here is the same character translated in the previous paragraph as "conditions." Dōgen repeats this story in a number of places, for example in the Chiji Shingi (Pure Standards for Temple Administrators). See Taigen Dan Leighton and Shohaku Okumura, trans., *Dōgen's Pure Standards for the Zen Community: A Translation of Dōgen's Eihei Shingi* (Albany: State University of New York Press, 1996), pp. 132–133. Dōgen also repeats it in Bendōwa (Talk on Wholehearted Practice of the Way). See Okumura and Leighton, *The Wholehearted Way*, pp. 37–38.

Xuanze said, "I dare not deceive the teacher. When I was at Qingfeng's place, I realized peace and joy."[39]

Fayan asked, "Through which words were you able to enter?"

Xuanze responded, "I once asked Qingfeng, 'What is the self of the student [i.e., my own self]?' Qingfeng said, 'The fire boy comes seeking fire.'"[40]

Fayan said, "Good words, only I am afraid that you did not understand them."

Xuanze said, "The fire boy belongs to fire. Already fire but still seeking fire is just like being self and still seeking self."

Fayan exclaimed, "Now I really know that you do not understand. If Buddha Dharma was like that it would not have lasted till today."

Xuanze was overwrought and jumped up. Out on the path he thought, "He is the guiding teacher of five hundred people. His pointing out my error must have some good reason."

He returned to Fayan's place and did prostrations in repentance. Fayan said, "You should ask the question."

Xuanze asked, "What is the self of the student?"

Fayan said, "The fire boy comes seeking fire." Xuanze was greatly enlightened.[41]

The teacher Dōgen said: Previously the fire boy came seeking fire. Afterwards again the fire boy came seeking fire. Previously, why was he not enlightened, but flowed down into the path of intellection? Afterwards, why was he greatly enlightened and cast away the old nest? Do you want to understand?

---

39 Qingfeng Zhuanchu is cited as Xuanze's former teacher in the version of this story in the commentary for case 17 of Shōyōroku. See Cleary, *Book of Serenity,* p. 72. However, in the Jingde Transmission of the Lamp (Keitoku Dentōroku) a dialogue similar to this had occurred between Xuanze and Baizhao Zhiyuan. See volume 17 of Keitoku Dentōroku in *Taishō Shinshū Daizōkyō,* vol. 51 (Tokyo: Taishō Issaikyō Kankokai, 1924–33), pp. 196–467.

40 "Fire boy" is *byojōdōji,* or *heiteidōji,* which also could be read "fire-spirit's apprentice," referring to fire as one of the five elements in Chinese cosmology. The *byojōdōji* was the novice in the monastery who attended to the lamps.

41 Xuanze had only realized that the fire boy belongs to fire, not the necessity for him to actualize "comes seeking."

After a pause Dōgen said: The fire boy comes seeking fire. How much do the pillars and lanterns care about the brightness? The fire is covered with cold ashes and while searching we don't see it.[42] Lighting it and blowing it out again gives birth to practice.[43]

Healing the Separation between Blades of Grass
16. Dharma Hall Discourse

Here is a story. Sudhana studied with Mañjuśrī.[44] Mañjuśrī said, "Go out and bring back one stalk of medicinal herb." Sudhana left and looked throughout the entire earth, but there was nothing that was not medicine.

He came back to Mañjuśrī and said, "The whole great earth is medicine. Which one should I pick and bring you?"

Mañjuśrī said, "Bring back one stalk of medicinal herb." Sudhana plucked one blade of grass and gave it to Mañjuśrī.

Mañjuśrī held up the single blade, showed it to the assembly and said, "This one blade of grass both can kill a person and can give them life."

The teacher Dōgen said: Previously one blade of grass, afterward also

---

42 This sentence is a reference to the story about Guishan studying under Baizhang. When Guishan could not find any fire in the ashes, Baizhang dug in the fireplace and pulled out an ember. See Leighton and Okumura, *Dōgen's Pure Standards for the Zen Community*, p. 136.

43 "Lighting it and blowing it out" refers to the story of Deshan Xuanjian studying under Longtan Chongxin. Deshan asked Longtan for a lantern as he left Longtan's room on a dark night. Longtan lit a lamp but after handing it to Deshan, Longtan blew it out. Deshan awakened. The story appears in the commentary to case 4 of Hekiganroku. See Cleary and Cleary, *Blue Cliff Record*, pp. 24–25.

44 Sudhana (Jap.: Zenzai; Virtuous Treasure) is the pilgrim protagonist of the Gaṇḍavyūha Sūtra, which is the last chapter of the vast Avataṃsaka Sūtra (Flower Ornament Sutra). In this sutra Mañjuśrī, the bodhisattva of wisdom, sends Sudhana off on a pilgrimage in which he ends up studying with fifty-two teachers in succession, with Mañjuśrī reappearing as the penultimate teacher at the end of the journey. See Thomas Cleary, trans., *Entry into the Realm of Reality: A Translation of the Gandavyuha, the Final Book of the Avatamsaka Sutra* (Boston: Shambhala, 1987). However, this story about medicinal herbs does not appear in the version of the Gaṇḍavyūha translated by Cleary, which is the translation into Chinese by Śikṣānada in 699 C.E., and it does not appear in any of the versions translated into Chinese of any portions of the Avataṃsaka Sūtra. Presumably this is an old legend, or a story invented in early Chinese Buddhism. A version of this dialogue is cited in the commentary to Hekiganroku, case 87. See Cleary and Cleary, *Blue Cliff Record*, p. 560.

one blade of grass, how much separation is there between the former and the latter?

After a pause Dōgen said: The separation is only one blade of grass.

The Simplicity of True Spiritual Power

17. Dharma Hall Discourse

Consider the story about National Teacher [Nanyang] Huizhong examining Tripitaka Master Da'er's penetration of others' minds, and also consider the commentaries by Yangshan Huiji, Xuansha Shibei, Yongjia Xuanjie, and Zhaozhou Congshen.[45]

The teacher Dōgen said: Why didn't the national teacher say to the tripitaka master in the beginning, "How much penetration of others' minds have you attained? Have you only attained penetration of others' minds,

---

45 National Teacher Huizhong was a successor of Huineng. This dialogue with Da'er (Daiji in Japanese, meaning "Big Ears") is discussed in the Shōbōgenzō essay Tashintsū (Penetration of Others' Minds), although that essay was written from a Dharma talk in 1245, long after this Dharma hall discourse in volume 1 of Eihei Kōroku. The word *tashintsū* implies spiritual or supernatural powers that may develop in meditation and are used to read others' minds. For further discussion of this story, see Dharma hall discourse 196.

To recount the basic story briefly, in the eighth century Tripitaka Master Da'er arrived from India to the Tang dynasty capital, claiming that he had the wisdom eye which has the power to know others' minds. National Teacher Nanyang Huizhong tested him and asked Da'er where the national teacher was now (in his thoughts). Da'er responded that, though he was teacher of the nation, Huizhong was watching boat races. Nanyang Huizhong asked a second time, and the tripitaka master replied that the national teacher was on a famous bridge, watching monkeys playing. But when Nanyang Huizhong asked a third time, the tripitaka master could say nothing, and Nanyang Huizhong called him a fox spirit and said, "Where is his power to see others' minds now?"

As for the other masters who are mentioned as giving later commentaries: A monk said that Da'er did not see the national teacher the third time and asked Zhaozhou where the national teacher had been. Zhaozhou said that the national teacher was on Da'er's nose. Later a monk asked Xuansha why, if the national teacher was on Da'er's nose, Da'er did not see him. Xuansha said it was simply because he was so very close. Another time a monk asked Yangshan why Da'er did not see the national teacher the third time. Yangshan said that the first two times the national teacher's mind was concerned with external circumstances, but the third time he had entered the samādhi of self-fulfillment, in Japanese the *jijuyu zanmai*, which Dōgen often discusses. In the Shōbōgenzō essay, Dōgen does not mention Yongjia Xuanjie, but instead has Haihui Baiyun Shouduan say that no one had recognized that the national teacher was inside Da'er's eyeballs.

For Shōbōgenzō (Penetration of Others' Minds), see Gudo Wafu Nishijima and Chodo Cross, *Master Dogen's Shobogenzo,* book 4 (Woods Hole, Mass.: Windbell Publications, 1999), pp. 89–99.

or have you also attained penetration of your self's minds?" If he had said this, wouldn't the tripitaka master have been speechless? All of the four venerable ones [whose comments are referred to] thought it was [only] the third time that he didn't see [the national teacher's thoughts].[46] Especially they didn't know that [the tripitaka master] couldn't see [the national teacher's thoughts] the first two times also. If they considered that the tripitaka master's penetration of the two vehicles was the buddha ancestors' penetration of others' minds, then these four venerable ones have still not escaped from the cave of the two vehicles.[47] They still stay in the one-sidedness of the tripitaka master.

Do you want to understand the buddha ancestors' supernatural penetrations? Self mind and other mind completely kill and completely give birth. The [wondrous] transformations of spiritual powers are [simply bringing] a basin of water and making tea.[48]

The Practice of Thusness
18. Dharma Hall Discourse

Before the fifteenth day [when the moon is full], the wind is high and the moon is cool. After the fifteenth day, the ocean is peaceful and the river

46 Manzan mentions five venerable ones here, including Haihui Baiyun Shouduan and Xuedou Chongxian and leaves out Yongjia Xuanjie. These five are the ones cited by Dōgen later in the Shōbōgenzō essay Tashintsū, which may be why Manzan amended his version of the Eihei Kōroku text.

47 The "two vehicles" here refers to the paths of the śrāvakas and pratyekabuddhas as opposed to the bodhisattva vehicle. The śrāvakas are disciples who only listen to the teaching, and pratyekabuddhas are self-enlightened but don't teach others. This "two vehicles" is also distinguished from the One Vehicle (Ekayāna) of buddhas, as described in the Lotus Sutra.

48 "A basin of water and making tea" refers to a story also mentioned by Dōgen in the Shōbōgenzō essay Jinzū (Spiritual Powers). Guishan awoke and asked his disciple Yangshan to interpret his dream. Yangshan went and brought Guishan a basin of water. After Guishan washed his face, his disciple Xiangyan Zhixian arrived and Guishan told him that Guishan and Yangshan had just demonstrated spiritual power. Xiangyan said that he had witnessed it. Guishan asked Xiangyan what he had seen. Xiangyan just made a cup of tea and brought it to Guishan. Guishan praised both of them and said that their spiritual powers and wisdom were superior to that of Śāriputra and Maudgalyāyana (great disciples of Śākyamuni Buddha). For Shōbōgenzō Jinzū, see Kazuaki Tanahashi, ed., *Enlightenment Unfolds: The Essential Teachings of Zen Master Dōgen* (Boston: Shambhala, 1999), pp. 104–115.

is clear. Right on the fifteenth day, the sky is everlasting and the earth is forever. Already having attained thusness, you should be thus. Taking one step forward, buddhas and ancestors come. Taking one step backward, expose every bit of your heart. Not stepping forward or backward, don't say this mountain monk [Dōgen] doesn't give a hand for the sake of others.[49] Don't say that all [you] people don't have a realm that matches enlightenment. Having already heard thusness, do you want to practice thusness or not?

After a pause Dōgen said: Without turning your back on a thousand people or ten thousand people, drop off body and mind, go to the hall, and sit zazen. *Dōgen got down from his seat.*

A Phrase for Manifesting Form
19. Dharma Hall Discourse

There is one phrase that encompasses the eight directions. There is one phrase that is crystal clear on all eight sides. If you can say it you are not fettered. If you cannot say it, you are a fettered person. An ancient Buddha said, "Buddha's true Dharma body is like the empty sky. According with things, it manifests form like the moon in water."[50] The ancestral teachers in each generation could only express the principle of accord, but could not express the manifesting form of the Buddha body. Therefore, they expressed half and did not express [the other] half, manifested half and did not manifest half. Kōshōji monks, how do you express it? Buddha's true Dharma body is like the empty sky. Buddha's true Dharma body is just Buddha's body. According with things and manifesting form like the moon in water, accord with things and manifest form in the monks' hall and the Buddha hall.

Inhaling and Exhaling Sutras
20. Dharma Hall Discourse

Here is a story. A king in eastern India invited Venerable Prajñātāra for a

---

49 "Expose every bit of your heart" is literally "red heart (or mind), pieces of heart." A similar phrase, together with "for the sake of others," is part of the commentary to the main verse of Hekiganroku, case 1, about Bodhidharma departing from Emperor Wu. See Cleary and Cleary, *Blue Cliff Record,* p. 8.

50 This statement is from the Suvarṇaprabhāsa Sūtra (Golden Splendor Sutra), vol. 24.

feast. Then the king asked, "All people are reciting sutras. Venerable one, why don't you recite them?"

Venerable Prajñātāra said, "This humble person while exhaling does not follow the various conditions, while inhaling does not dwell in mental or physical realms. Continuously I recite a hundred, a thousand, ten thousand, a billion volumes of such a sutra, not only one or two volumes."[51]

Dōgen said: Thus I have heard, and faithfully receive and respectfully practice it.

Practice Together with a Single Person
21. Dharma Hall Discourse
Dongshan [Liangjie] said to the assembly, "Who is this person who, even when among a thousand or ten thousand people, does not face a single person and does not turn his back on a single person?"

Yunju left the assembly saying, "This person is going to the hall to practice."

When you can see like such [a person], then all the buddhas appear in the world, and this person goes to the hall; and then also eating gruel and rice, speaking one phrase, and coming from within the universal and particular are all this person going to the hall; and that you should be like such [a person] is also this person going to the hall.[52] How could you say a phrase that is not practicing together with Yunju?

After a pause Dōgen said: All of you monks, go to the hall and practice.

---

51 Another version of this story about Prajñātāra is case 3 of Shōyōroku. See Cleary, *Book of Serenity,* pp. 11–16. "Mental or physical realms" refers to the skandhas, or the accumulated aspects of which a person is composed.

52 Dōgen's statement here is a reference to a later utterance by Dongshan's successor Yunju. Yunju once said to his assembly, "If you want to attain such a thing you should be such a person. You are already such a person, why do you worry about such a thing." See the Shōbōgenzō essay Immo (Suchness), in Thomas Cleary, *Shōbōgenzō: Zen Essays by Dōgen* (Honolulu: University of Hawai'i Press, 1986), pp. 49–55. "Coming from within the universal and particular" is a reference to the Chinese Soto lineage teaching of the five ranks initiated by Dongshan. "Universal and particular" could also be translated as "true and partial"; "upright and inclined"; or "ultimate and phenomenal." See Taigen Daniel Leighton with Yi Wu, trans., *Cultivating the Empty Field: The Silent Illumination of Zen Master Hongzhi,* rev. ed. (Boston: Tuttle, 2000), pp. 8–12.

Not Attaining, Not Knowing
22. Dharma Hall Discourse
Here is a story. [Tianhuang] Daowu asked Shitou, "What is the essential meaning of Buddha Dharma?"[53]

Shitou said, "Not attaining, not knowing."

Daowu said, "Beyond that, is there any other pivotal point or not?"

Shitou said, "The wide sky does not obstruct the white clouds drifting."

Not attaining, not knowing is Buddha's essential meaning. The wind blows into the depths, and further winds blow.[54] The wide sky does not obstruct the white clouds drifting. At this time, why do you take the trouble to ask Shitou?

Blue Mountains Walking; Giving Birth at Night
23. Dharma Hall Discourse
Deeply see the blue mountains constantly walking. By yourself know that the white stone [woman] gives birth to a child at night.[55]

Dōgen descended from his seat.

An Expression Never Before Expounded
24. Dharma Hall Discourse
In the entire universe in ten directions there is no Dharma at all that has not yet been expounded by all buddhas in the three times. Therefore all buddhas say, "In the same manner that all buddhas in the three times expound the Dharma, so now I also will expound the Dharma [reality]

---

53 This story is about Shitou's disciple Tianhuang Daowu, not Daowu Yuanchi, the disciple of Yaoshan, another successor of Shitou. See Yi Wu, *The Mind of Chinese Ch'an (Zen)* (San Francisco: Great Learning Publishing, 1989), pp. 77–78.

54 "Wind blows" (the literal translation) as a compound refers to freedom from attachments and societal conventions. "Winds" also refers to styles of practice. In this case the "further winds" refers to Buddha's going beyond Buddha, ever deepening.

55 "The blue mountains constantly walk and a stone [barren] woman gives birth to a child at night" is a saying by Furong Daokai, an important ancestor in the Chinese Sōtō lineage. Dōgen comments extensively on this saying in the Shōbōgenzō essay Sansuikyō (Mountains and Waters Sutra). See Kazuaki Tanahashi, ed., *Moon in a Dewdrop: Writings of Zen Master Dōgen* (San Francisco: North Point Press, 1985), pp. 97–107; or Cleary, *Shōbōgenzō: Zen Essays by Dōgen*, pp. 87–99.

without differentiations."[56] This great assembly present before me also is practicing the way in the manner of all buddhas. Each movement, each stillness is not other than the Dharma of all buddhas, so do not act carelessly or casually. Although this is the case, I have an expression that has not yet been expounded by any Buddha. Everyone, do you want to discern it?

After a pause Dōgen said: In the same manner that all buddhas in the three times expound the Dharma, so now I also will expound the Dharma without differentiations.

The Growth of Oneness

25. Dharma Hall Discourse for Winter Solstice on the First Day of the [Eleventh] Month [1240][57]

"Attaining oneness, heaven is clear; attaining oneness, earth is at rest."[58] Attaining oneness, a person is at peace; attaining oneness, the time becomes bright.[59] As this oneness grows, within the [days] growing longer, the buddha ancestors attain longevity. Everybody, within this growth you arouse awakening mind, practice, engage the way with effort, and attain

---

56 This quotation is from the Lotus Sutra, chap. 2, "Skillful Means." See Burton Watson, *The Lotus Sutra* (New York: Columbia University Press, 1993), p. 45; Hurvitz, *Scripture of the Lotus Blossom of the Fine Dharma*, p. 45; Bunnō Katō, Yoshirō Tamura, and Kōjirō Miyasaka, trans., *The Threefold Lotus Sutra: Innumerable Meanings, The Lotus Flower of the Wonderful Law, and Meditation on the Bodhisattva Universal Virtue* (New York: Weatherhill, 1975), p. 74.

57 The annual winter solstice occurs on the first day of the eleventh lunar month only every nineteen years. This Dharma hall discourse was given in 1240 C.E. The winter solstice occurs on different days of the eleventh lunar month in different years. The other winter solstice Dharma hall discourses are numbers 115, 135, 206, and 296. See the "Chronological Index of Dharma Hall Discourses with Dates" in the appendixes. The dates given therein are based on the comprehensive research into the dates in Eihei Kōroku in Shūken Itō, *Dōgen Zen Kenkyū* (Tokyo: Daizō Shuppan, 1998), now generally accepted in Sōtō scholarship.

58 This quotation is from Laozi's *Dao De Qing,* chap. 39. See Yi Wu, *The Book of Lao Tzu (Tao Te Ching)* (San Francisco, Great Learning Publishing, 1989), pp. 143. It is also quoted by Dōgen's teacher Tiantong Rujing and by Tiantong Hongzhi, whose writings are frequently quoted by Dōgen in Eihei Kōroku.

59 "The time becomes bright" literally means the time is yang, as opposed to yin. This refers to the time after the winter solstice when the days get longer, and brighter.

realization of a single phrase.[60] You have already attained the power and vitality that is within this growth.

Therefore, making a rosary with the bodies of buddha ancestors, you reach three hundred sixty days.[61] Every time this day [of winter solstice] arrives, [the length of days] proceeds just like this. This is exactly the body and mind of buddha ancestors, so [this growth] proceeds like this.

After a pause Dōgen said: The body and mind of each Buddha now can grow. The face and eyes of jade rings and round jewels are shaped in a heavenly palace.[62] Having counted each of them, how long and far do they reach? On this auspicious occasion, knowing the count is the single brightness.[63]

Complete Meeting of Host and Guest
26. Dharma Hall Discourse

Laying down the body here, shed the body there.[64] How is it there? Step by step, [the practice] is intimate and continuous. How is it here? The whole heart [beats], moment by moment. Put aside there and here for a while. How could [we discuss] such happenings?

The host devises a complete expression and the guest confirms it.[65] The guest devises a complete expression and the host confirms it. All people [in this assembly] devise a complete expression and this mountain monk

---

60 "A single phrase" refers to a statement or expression of clear understanding of Dharma.

61 "Rosary" is *juzu* in Japanese, a string of beads traditionally used by Buddhists to count chants or prostrations. Three hundred sixty days is one year in the lunar calendar, so Dōgen may be referring to multiplicity within oneness. Counting the days ends up with one year.

62 "Jade rings" are flat jade discs with a hole in the center used in China as jewelry. Both jade rings and round jewels might be used as beads strung on rosaries.

63 "Brightness" here is again literally "yang."

64 In "laying down the body here, shed the body there," "here" and "there" refer to this phenomenal world and the universal, or to saṃsāra (here) and nirvāṇa (there). "Shed" is *datsu* of *datsuraku,* or "dropping off," as in Dōgen's description of total awakening, "dropping off body and mind," as manifested in zazen.

65 "Host" is used for the teacher, and "guest" for the student, but host and guest also may refer to the universal and phenomenal. "Confirms" is *shōmei,* which refers to the verification of awakening.

[Dōgen] confirms it. This mountain monk devises a complete expression and all people [in the assembly] confirm it. When this mountain monk and all [you] people express it, the whisk and the staff confirm it.[66] When the whisk and the staff express it, this mountain monk and all [you] people confirm it. Shedding body [there] and laying down the body [here], what is there to say?

After a pause Dōgen said: Responding together in this enjoyable gathering is itself complete. The host is present from the beginning while the guest is in shashu.[67] A million times this has been said already. On this occasion, how can anybody not understand?

Our Own Work
27. Dharma Hall Discourse

Here is a story. In ancient days, when Venerable Mahākāśyapa was stamping on mud [to mix for making walls], a novice asked, "Why do you work like this yourself?"

The Venerable One said, "If I don't do this, who else would do it for me?"[68]

The teacher Dōgen said: The mind is like a fan in December, the body is like a cloud above the cold valley. If we can see that we act by ourselves, then we can see that someone is doing the work. If we can see that someone is doing the work, then we see that we ourselves are doing it.

Enter the Grass
28. Dharma Hall Discourse

Speaking a lot creates masses of complications, talking too little has no

---

66 Whisk and staff are insignia sometimes carried by Zen teachers. Dōgen carried at least his whisk with him during these talks, so he may have held up the whisk, and possibly the staff, as he said this.

67 *Shashu* is the formal gesture of holding one's hands together over the chest while standing.

68 This story is from one of the Chinese lamp transmission anthologies of stories, Shūmon Rentō Eyō (Collection of the Essence of the Continuous Dharma Lamp). This may be an apocryphal story, not in the sutras. The story is very similar to a story about a *tenzo,* chief cook in the monastery, who Dōgen saw during his experiences in China, told by Dōgen in his Tenzokyōkun (Instructions for the Chief Cook). See Leighton and Okumura, *Dōgen's Pure Standards for the Zen Community,* p. 40.

power. Not speaking a lot, and not talking too little, how will you say it? *After a pause Dōgen said:* Enter the grass and transmit the wind.[69]

Beyond the Marrow

29. Dharma Hall Discourse

It is rare to hear the Dharma, even in vast kalpas. For the sake of Dharma, previous wise leaders and worthies simply gave up their bodies. Truly, beings who have bodies, such as common people, animals, ants, mosquitoes, those with mistaken views, and those outside the way, all have bodies and lives. And yet, even of those who have not yet heard the Dharma, and need not be revered or treasured, how many of them have received bodies for innumerable lifetimes? Although they did not receive fortunate births, if they were able to hear the Dharma, then those were good lives.

Of those hearing the Dharma there are three kinds, highly capable, middling, and lowly. This is to say that highly capable people listen with spirit when hearing Dharma, the middling listen with the mind when hearing Dharma, and the lowly listen with their ears when hearing Dharma. We already have spirit, mind, and ears. How do you listen to the Dharma, and what Dharma do you listen to?

Don't you see that the old sage Śākyamuni said, "My Dharma enables separation from birth, old age, sickness, and death. This Dharma is not discriminative thinking."[70] Separating from birth, old age, sickness, and death, allow yourself to completely depart from these others. Not involved in discriminative thinking, allow yourself to completely be without these others.[71] We are already able to be like this.

Dōgen said: Break open this Dharma, and take the marrow from within

---

69 The wind blows and the grasses sway. "Entering the grass" can refer to manifesting in the ordinary world. "Wind" can refer to teaching styles or Dharma utterances. Dōgen is emphasizing the quality of expressions.

70 This quote is from the second chapter of the Lotus Sutra, "Skillful Means." See Watson, *Lotus Sutra,* pp. 23–46; Hurvitz, *Scripture of the Lotus Blossom of the Fine Dharma,* pp. 22–47; Katō, Tamura, and Miyasaka, *Threefold Lotus Sutra,* pp. 51–76.

71 These two sentences are difficult to understand. Literally, they could also be read as "Separating from birth, old age, sickness, and death, allow others to completely depart. Not involved in discriminative thinking, allow others to completely be without."

the Dharma; sift out the marrow, and take the essence from within the marrow. How would you say it?

After a pause Dōgen said: Even if awakened, the cold wind blows and chills me, and I don't yet know for whom the bright moon is white. This is a saying of practice together. How do you speak a statement that transcends Dharma and goes beyond marrow, that is without high, middling, and lowly, and that expresses the utmost heights? Still, do you thoroughly understand? A white heron stands in the snow, but they are not the same color. The bright moon [shines on the white] reed flowers, but one does not resemble the other.

Beyond Two or One
30. Dharma Hall Discourse

Here is a story. The great Guishan asked Yangshan, "Within the forty volumes of the Mahāparinirvāṇa Sūtra, how much is expounded by Buddha, and how much is expounded by demons?"[72]

Yangshan said, "It was entirely expounded by demons."

Guishan returned to the abbot's quarters.

Yangshan followed after him saying, "My mind and spirit were dull and dark just now when I answered you, like layers of rocks on a mountaintop."

Guishan said, "I know that your eye is correct."

The teacher Dōgen said: Guishan and Yangshan had such a conversation, but still they were careless and lazy. This mountain monk [Dōgen] will speak a word for them. On behalf of Yangshan I would have immediately gotten up from the assembly, made prostrations, and then returned to my place.

This single word was for Yangshan. I have another word to offer to the dragons and elephants here now before me.

After a pause Dōgen said: Mahāprajñāpāramitā (the great perfection of wisdom) is the same single profound conversation beyond any two or

---

72 The Mahāparinirvāṇa Sūtra is the Mahāyāna scripture supposedly spoken just before the Buddha's passing away into parinirvāṇa. One of its main teachings is that all beings have Buddha nature, which Dōgen questioned and clarified in his Shōbōgenzō essay "Buddha Nature" as "All beings totally are Buddha nature." See Waddell and Abe, *Heart of Dōgen's Shōbōgenzō*, pp. 59–98.

one.[73] Even if demons and buddhas speak through the same mouth, we should come forth and question whether or not it is necessarily true.

A Flat Path

31. Dharma Hall Discourse

Here is a story. Zen Master Deng Yinfeng was leaving Mazu [his teacher]. Mazu said, "Where are you going?"[74]

Deng Yinfeng said, "I'm going to Shitou."

Mazu said, "Shitou's path is slippery."

Deng Yinfeng said, "I'm bringing with me a tent-pole for traveling theaters. According to the situation I will improvise." He immediately departed.

As soon as he reached Shitou, Yinfeng immediately circumambulated the meditation hall one time, shook his monk's staff to make a sound, stood before Shitou, and asked, "What is the essential meaning?"[75]

Shitou said, "Blue sky, blue sky."[76]

Deng Yinfeng was speechless. He returned to Jiangxi [where Mazu taught] and told the story to Mazu.

Mazu said, "You should go again and when he says, 'Blue sky,' you should immediately make a sound of crying."

Deng Yinfeng went to Shitou again and asked the same question, "What is the essential meaning?"

Shitou immediately made a sound of crying.

Deng Yinfeng was again speechless and returned back [to Mazu].

Mazu said, "I told you that Shitou's path was slippery."

---

73 "Māhāprajñāpāramitā" means "the great perfection of wisdom," or prajñā, but also refers to a group of sutras including the Heart Sutra and the Diamond Sutra. This perfection of wisdom is the insight that sees reality beyond dichotomies or differentiations, "beyond any two or one." Demons and buddhas are not separate.

74 Deng Yinfeng was noted as an eccentric Dharma successor of Mazu's. For a slightly different version of this story, see Andy Ferguson, *Zen's Chinese Heritage: The Masters and Their Teachings* (Boston: Wisdom Publications, 2000), pp. 69–70.

75 The traditional monk's staff *shakujō* had metal rings on the top which clattered to warn off small animals or predators as the monk traveled. Yinfeng's actions here are discourteous according to the usual forms.

76 "Blue sky" is an expression of sorrow, usually accompanied by sighing and weeping.

The teacher Dōgen said: Some people who consider this single kōan believe that the person from Jiangxi [Mazu] spoke like this because he didn't dwell in any understanding. Also, people in the scholastic schools who count sand say, "[Mazu] didn't dwell in one-sided understanding and so he spoke thus." This mountain monk [Dōgen] is not like this. When Yinfeng said that he was going to Shitou, I would say to him: Shitou's path is flat.

Even if Shitou and Yinfeng at the same time made sounds, crying out, "Blue sky; blue sky," and also at the same time made the sound of crying together, when Yinfeng returned and spoke to this mountain monk, I would still tell him: Shitou's path is flat.

The Advantage of New Years

32. Dharma Hall Discourse

Today is the beginning of a new year [1241], and also a day with three mornings. I say three mornings because it is the beginning of the year, beginning of the month, and the beginning of the day.

Here is a story. A monk asked Jingqing Daofu, "Is there Buddha Dharma at the beginning of the new year or not?"

Jingqing said, "There is."

The monk asked, "What is the Buddha Dharma at the beginning of the new year?"

Jingqing said, "New Year's Day begins with a blessing, and the ten thousand things are completely new."

The monk said, "Thank you, teacher, for your answer."

Jingqing said, "This old monk today lost the advantage."[77]

A monk asked Mingjiao Zhimen Shikuan, "Is there Buddha Dharma at the beginning of the new year, or not?"

Mingjiao said, "There is not."

The monk said, "Every year is a good year, every day is a good day; why isn't there [Buddha Dharma in the beginning of the new year]?"

---

77 "Lost the advantage" here denotes that the speaker did not express the Dharma as fully as the monk in this dialogue, and was bettered by the monk.

Mingjiao said, "Old man Zhang drinks, and old man Li gets drunk."[78]

The monk said, "Great Elder, [you are like] a dragon's head and snake's tail."[79]

Mingjiao said, "This old monk today lost the advantage."

The teacher Dōgen said: [Both teachers] say the same, "This old monk today lost the advantage." Hearing such a story many people say, "These are good stories about [teachers] losing advantage [in a dialogue]." This mountain monk [Dōgen] does not at all agree. Although Jingqing and Mingjiao speak of one loss, they do not yet see one gain. Suppose somebody were to ask me, Kōshō, if there is Buddha Dharma at the beginning of the new year, or not.

I would say to them: There is.

Suppose the monk responded, "What is the Buddha Dharma at the beginning of the new year?"

This mountain monk would say to him: May each and every body, whether staying still or standing up, have ten thousand blessings.[80]

Suppose the monk said, "In that case, in accordance with this saying, I will practice."

This mountain monk would say to him: I, Kōshō, today have advantage after advantage.

Now please practice.

78 This is an expression from Yunmen's Extensive Record, in response to a monk's question about Yunmen's intention. See Urs App, trans. and ed., *Master Yunmen: From the Record of the Chan Teacher "Gate of the Clouds"* (New York: Kōdansha International, 1994), p. 184. This refers to the inconceivable interconnectedness of different beings and also expresses that the Dharma spreads wondrously, beyond our usual modes of perceiving. In this case the saying also refers to New Year's Day, a traditional time of drinking and celebrating in East Asian culture.

79 For "dragon's head and snake's tail" see explication in note 8 (Dharma hall discourse 4) above. This saying is originally from Mingjiao's teacher Yunmen.

80 This is a traditional, formal New Year's greeting in Zen monasteries from monks to teachers, still used by monks in New Year's cards. "Blessings" could also be translated as "happinesses."

A Place to Live

33. Dharma Hall Discourse

The ancient buddha ancestors understood Buddha Dharma and attained spiritual powers. Accomplishing buddhahood and becoming an ancestor cannot be done easily. Those who only attain spiritual power are called elders. Those who understand Buddha Dharma are called great ones. Understanding greatness and attaining respect as an elder simply depend on penetrating the principle and fully engaging the way.

Zhaozhou said, "Brothers, just sit and penetrate the principle. If you do so for twenty or thirty years and do not understand the way, then take this old monk's head and make it into a ladle for scooping up excrement and urine."

An ancient Buddha spoke like this, and present people do such practice. How could we be deceived? Simply because of being bound by sounds and colors and without realizing one's discriminative thinking, one is not yet able to be liberated. How pitiful. Such people are willing to vainly appear and disappear within the dusts of sounds and colors. Now we can encounter the current opportunity [to practice]. Abandon burning incense, prostrations, nenbutsu, practicing repentance, and reading sutras, and just sit.[81]

I remember Zhaozhou's visit to Yunju Daoying. Yunju said, "Great Elder, why don't you look for a place to reside?"[82]

Zhaozhou said, "What is a place where this person could live?"[83]

Yunju said, "In front of the mountain there is the foundation of an ancient temple."

Zhaozhou said, "High priest, it would be good for you to live there yourself."

---

81 "Just sit" is *shikan taza,* one of Dōgen's main expressions for sitting meditation (zazen). *Nenbutsu* is the practice of chanting a buddha's name, literally, "remembering Buddha." This sentence is from Dōgen's teacher Tiantong Rujing. Both Rujing and Dōgen in fact continued all these other practices in their monasteries, so we should not understand this admonition literally but see it as an emphasis on the centrality of just sitting. All these other practices, such as prostrations and reading sutras, are to be done in the spirit of just sitting.

82 At this time, Zhaozhou was already a Dharma successor of Nanquan and an accomplished adept. Yunju's birth date is unknown, but certainly Zhaozhou was much older than Yunju.

83 "What is a place where this person could live" could also be read as a declarative statement. This story is from Zhaozhou's Recorded Sayings; see James Green, *The Recorded Sayings of Zen Master Joshu* (Boston: Shambhala, 1998), pp. 146–147.

In such a manner, a person who understands Buddha Dharma manifests spiritual powers. This activity is not the same as that of those within the ten holy and three wise [stages].[84] I, Kōshō, on behalf of Yunju, will once more manifest spiritual power. Before, it was already said, "What is a place where this person could live." Later there was the saying, "High priest, live there yourself." Already having attained thus, you should be thus.[85] This is how to say, "Live; live."[86]

Penetrating Cold
34. Dharma Hall Discourse
If this greatest cold does not penetrate into our bones, how will the fragrance of the plum blossoms pervade the entire universe?

Dōgen descended from his seat.

Vision Beyond Buddhas and Demons
35. Dharma Hall Discourse
Is old sage Śākyamuni a buddha Tathāgata or the demon Pāpiyas?[87] If you call him a buddha Tathāgata, it will not be peaceful [anywhere] beneath

---

84 The "ten holy" refers to the ten stages, or bhūmis, of bodhisattva development, elaborated in the Daśabhūmika Sūtra. The "three wise" refers to the three groupings of ten ranks, or thirty steps, that precede the ten stages of the bhūmis, as elaborated in the Gaṇḍavyūha Sūtra. Both the Daśabhūmika and Gaṇḍavyūha Sūtra are also chapters within the Avataṃsaka Sūtra's vast depiction of the development of bodhisattvas becoming buddhas. Dōgen is saying that a person who understands Buddha Dharma transcends all such stages of development.

85 "Already having attained thus, you should be thus" is a statement by Yunju, quoted by Dōgen in the Shōbōgenzō essay "Suchness." See Cleary, *Shōbōgenzō: Zen Essays by Dōgen*, pp. 49–55.

86 Zhaozhou understood that in nirvāṇa, and in reality, there is no place to dwell. But Dōgen in this Dharma hall discourse is emphasizing the need beyond that to actually dwell, or manifest a life, in some place so as to express the living reality of just sitting for many years.

87 "Tathāgata" is a standard epithet for a buddha, literally, "the one who comes and goes in thusness." The demon Pāpiyas is another name for Māra, the spirit of temptation, who lives in the highest heaven in the realm of desire, and is derived from the Indian god Śiva. Māra appeared to Śākyamuni during the night of his awakening under the Bodhi tree to test him and try to unseat him, but Śākyamuni prevailed.

the heavens.[88] If you call him the demon Pāpiyas, you have not requited the benefaction of the ancestors. Saying it correctly for the first time, what will you call him?

After a pause Dōgen said: If you comprehend this mountain monk's words, I grant that you people have a single eye.[89]

Apparent in Every Color
36. Dharma Hall Discourse

> Having turned the ancient sutras in each inhale and exhale,[90]
> Now manifesting the ancient buddhas in each bowel
>   movement,
> In every place apparent, with every item precious,
> To express such a principle, how would you speak?

> *After a pause Dōgen said:*
> The high skies of Spring now darken,
> The green colors of the fields are clear,
> Amid the ten million peach blossoms,
> Where can we find the spirit clouds (Lingyun)?[91]

A Direct Question
37. Dharma Hall Discourse
Śākyamuni Buddha said, "When the bright star appeared, I together with all sentient beings attained the way."[92] How is this the principle of attaining the way? Originally there was no great way; however, today for the first

---

88 Sometimes Zen texts speak of the buddhas as breaking the peace and producing troubles for people who then mistakenly seek after some notion of enlightenment.

89 The "single eye" implies right view into the nonduality of the ultimate level of reality.

90 "Turning the ancient sutras in each inhale and exhale" refers to the saying by Prajñātāra; see Dharma hall discourse 20.

91 "Spirit Cloud" is the translation of the name of Lingyun Zhiqin, who is famous for awakening upon seeing peach blossoms. See Dharma hall discourse 457 and kōan case 72 in volume 9.

92 Śākyamuni is said to have awakened upon seeing the morning star.

time old sage Śākyamuni appears. What is it he calls sentient beings, and what is it he calls the way, and its attainment? Speak immediately, speak immediately!

The Difficulty of Such a Thing
38. Dharma Hall Discourse

Studying the way has been difficult to accomplish for a thousand ages. How difficult is this? Ordinary people cannot be compared to the seven wise and seven holy ones.[93] The seven wise and seven holy ones cannot be compared to the ten holy and three wise ones.[94] The ten holy and three wise ones cannot see the great way of all buddhas, even in a dream. Seeing in this way one immediately said, "If you want to attain such a thing, you should be such a person. Already being such a person, why worry about such a thing?"[95]

Can you say such a thing or not? If you can say this you attain the skin and marrow. If you cannot say this, still you attain the skin and marrow. Put aside for now whether you can say this or not, and whether you attain the skin and marrow or not. How is this suchness? Vipaśyin Buddha early on kept this in mind, and up until now has not grasped this mystery.[96]

The Remaining Raindrops
39. Dharma Hall Discourse

Here is a story. Jingqing Daofu asked a monk, "What is the sound outside the gate?"

The monk said, "The sound of raindrops."

Jingqing said, "Living beings are upside-down, deluded by self and chasing after things."

The monk said, "Teacher, how about you?"

Jingqing said, "I'm almost not confused by self."

---

93 The "seven wise and seven holy ones" refers to stages of the path in the pre-Mahāyāna practice.

94 The "ten holy and three wise ones" refers to stages on the bodhisattva path. See Dharma hall discourse 33 and note 84 above.

95 This quote is from Yunju Daoying.

96 Vipaśyin Buddha (Jap.: Bibashi) is the first of the seven primordial, mythical ancient buddhas, going back into previous cycles of ages, culminating in Śākyamuni as the seventh.

The monk said, "What does it mean, almost not confused by self?"

Jingqing responded, "It is most easy to be released from the self, but expressing this dropped off body is very difficult."[97]

The teacher Dōgen said: Since completely dropping the body, there is [still] the sound of the raindrops. Released from the self, what is the sound outside the gate? As for deluding the self or not deluding the self, which is difficult or which is easy I completely leave to you. As for chasing after things or chasing after self, are they upside-down or not upside-down?[98]

Clarifying Aspiration
40. Dharma Hall Discourse

Each of you without exception has the aspiration to penetrate the heavens. Just direct yourselves toward clarifying what the tathāgatas clarify.

Dōgen descended from his seat.

Loving Mountains in All Three Times
41. Dharma Hall Discourse

All buddhas and ancestors accomplish the way after passing through many kalpas, attaining the way sooner or later [than others]. However, the great way that they manifest is the same. All buddhas completely twirl a flower and attain the marrow.[99] All ancestors completely have transmitted buddhahood to each other. Yesterday's seeing the mountain, that was yesterday; today's seeing the mountain, that is today. [Their seeing the mountain is] completely thus and entirely the same. In ancient days, those who left the world sooner or later all aspired to enter the forest and see each other in order to expound the fundamental nature, and

---

97 For a variant rendition of this story, see Cleary and Cleary, *Blue Cliff Record*, case 46, p. 323.

98 In the Shōbōgenzō essay Ikka no Myōju (One Bright Pearl), Dōgen says that the whole universe "describes the ceaseless [process] of pursuing things to make them into self, and of pursuing things to make it into something." See Waddell and Abe, *Heart of Dōgen's Shōbōgenzō*, p. 33. Contrary to conventional understandings, Dōgen sometimes refers to "chasing after things" and "chasing after self" as positive.

99 Twirling a flower is a reference to the story of Śākyamuni's holding up a flower, twirling it, and then transmitting the "true Dharma eye storehouse, wondrous mind of nirvāṇa" to his disciple Mahākāśyapa, who had smiled. Attaining the marrow is a reference to the second Chinese ancestor, Dazu Huike, who Bodhidharma said had attained his marrow.

all the same are in the Lu family.[100] Each of them aspires to love mountains such as Nanyue, Wutai, Hengshan, and Songshan.[101] Once you enter a mountain, they are all the same single place. The Buddha Dharma is also like this.

After a pause Dōgen said: With the aspiration to love mountains established, although each mountain is different, thirty-one people [stay] on the same single mountain.[102]

Unobstructed Good Fortune

42. Bathing Buddha Dharma Hall Discourse [for Buddha's Birthday, 1241][103]

Today my original teacher Śākyamuni Tathāgata descended to be born at Lumbini Park.[104] Every year on this day we always have Lumbini Park. Tell me whether the great sage is born or not. If you say he has descended to be born, I grant you [have done] one portion of practice. If you say he has not descended to be born, I grant you [have done] one portion of practice. If you are already like this, you are not obstructed by mountains or oceans and will be born to a king's palace [like Śākyamuni Buddha]. If you are not obstructed by mountains or oceans, are you obstructed by birth or not? Even if previous buddhas and ancestors say that they are obstructed by birth, today this mountain monk [Dōgen] simply says that I am not obstructed by birth. If we are not obstructed by mountains or oceans, and are not obstructed by birth, all people in the entire earth and

---

100 A common family name, Lu was, for example, the family name of the author of the Spring and Autumn Chronicles, a Confucian classic.

101 These were all famous sacred mountains with many monasteries. Nanyue was the home of Nanyue Huairang and many other teachers. Wutai was the sacred mountain devoted to Mañjuśrī, the bodhisattva of wisdom. Hengshan was where Shitou Xiqian lived. Songshan was where Bodhidharma lived.

102 Genryū Kagamishima speculates that "thirty-one people" may refer to the total number of monks with Dōgen at Kōshōji at this time. This Dharma hall discourse does not appear in Manzan's version of the Eihei Kōroku.

103 Traditionally on the day of Śākyamuni Buddha's birthday (in Japanese Buddhism celebrated on April 8) Buddhists bathe a statue of the baby Buddha by ladling tea over it. This custom goes back at least to 462 C.E. in China.

104 It is said that Śākyamuni and other buddhas-to-be resided in the Tuṣita Heaven before descending to take birth in the human world and become incarnated buddhas.

the entire universe are born together with Śākyamuni Tathāgata and say, "Above the heavens and below the heavens, I alone am the World-Honored One."[105] After taking seven steps in the ten directions, this [statement] was the lion's roar, and a baby's crying. How do you express such a manifestation?

After a pause Dōgen said: In the entire universe and pervading the heavens, good fortune arrives. The grandmotherly intimate heart is [expressed by] the sage's descent to birth. How can we make offerings, serve, make prostrations, and bathe [to celebrate] the sage's descent to birth? Together with the pure great ocean assembly, let us enter the Buddha hall and perform the ceremony.

Sounds of the Ancestral Breeze
43. Dharma Hall Discourse

Do you people want to comprehend the ancestral teacher [Bodhidharma]? [He] leaped over oceans and mountains seeking [one who could] know himself.[106] Do you want to know the second ancestor [Dazu Huike]?[107] He moved heaven and earth and established great peace. Ultimately, how can one describe them? We do not know where those two buddhas have gone. The breeze of their truth has spread a joyful sound through ten thousand ages.[108]

---

105 "Above the heavens and below the heavens, I alone am the World-Honored One" is supposed to be the first statement the baby Buddha uttered. He said it after taking seven steps and pointing one hand up and the other down. Statues of the baby Buddha commemorate this posture and statement. This story goes back to the Pali suttas, in some of which it is described as the statement Śākyamuni made after his enlightenment, not at birth.

106 This sentence could be read in a variety of ways. It might be rendered as seeking one who knows his own self, as opposed to seeking someone who could understand him; or as seeking to know the "true self" as opposed to the self of either Bodhidharma or the other person. It also might be interpreted as Dōgen saying to his listeners that "you" should leap over mountains and oceans, in which case the sentence about moving heaven and earth would also be an instruction to the assembly.

107 In the Monkaku version of Eihei Kōroku, which we are generally using, the second ancestor is listed in the first sentence and Bodhidharma in the second reference. Manzan's version reverses this order, and we are following Genryū Kagamishima's lead in adopting the Manzan version in this instance.

108 "Breeze of their truth" is a literal translation of *shūfū,* which also means "the style of the school or lineage" of Bodhidharma and Huike.

Gathering Grasses

44. Summer Gathering Dharma Hall Discourse [1241][109]

Now the hundreds of grasses are actually gathering for the summer.[110] Plucked from the entire earth, there [would be] ten million stalks. One flower with five petals opens in the sky and the mud.[111] Without doubt it will naturally bear fruit.

The Ornaments of Perfect Wisdom

45. Dharma Hall Discourse

The years and months of one life are uncertain. When we look back at the ten thousand things, there is nothing to gain or lose. Who does not express the ornaments of the path of awakening?

[Everything is] Māhāprajñāpāramitā.[112]

The Dharma Pervades from Surface to Core

46. Dharma Hall Discourse

Here is a story. The first ancestor [Bodhidharma] requested to his disciples, "The time [of my passing] is finally coming. Why don't you each speak of what you have attained?"

Then his disciple Daofu replied, "My understanding is, without attaching to words and without separating from words, to perform the function of the way."

The ancestor said, "You have my skin."

---

109 "Summer Gathering Dharma Hall Discourse" refers to the first talk of the summer *ango,* or practice period. Going back to the time of Śākyamuni Buddha in India, the ninety-day summer practice period traditionally opened on the fifteenth day of the fourth lunar month, the rainy season.

110 The "hundred grasses" refers to the monks gathering for the practice period as well as to the grasses blooming in summer. This might also refer to the myriads of delusions that are plucked out in practice.

111 "One flower with five petals" refers to the Chinese Zen lineage that developed into five lineages or houses.

112 Māhāprajñāpāramitā (Great Perfection of Wisdom) here refers both to this wisdom itself and to a group of Mahāyāna sutras including the Heart Sutra and Diamond Sutra. In his essay in Shōbōgenzō called Māhāprajñāpāramitā, written in 1233, Dōgen says that the perfection of wisdom, both its form and emptiness, is "one hundred blades of grass, ten thousand things." See Cleary, *Shōbōgenzō: Zen Essays by Dōgen,* p. 25.

The nun Zongchi said, "My present understanding is that it is like Ānanda seeing the land of Akṣobhya Buddha once, and never seeing it again."[113]

The ancestor said, "You have my flesh."

Daoyu said, "The four great elements are fundamentally empty. The five skandhas do not exist; and my view is that there is not even one Dharma to attain."

The ancestor said, "You have my bones."

Lastly, [Dazu] Huike made a prostration, and then stood at his position. The ancestor said, "You have my marrow."

The teacher Dōgen said: Later people believe that these are shallow or deep [levels], but this is not the ancestor's meaning. "You have my skin" is like speaking of lanterns and standing pillars. "You have my flesh" is like saying, "This very mind is Buddha." "You have my bones" is like speaking of the mountains, rivers, and great earth. "You have my marrow" is like twirling a flower and blinking the eyes.[114] There is no shallow or deep, superior or inferior. If you can see like this, then you see the ancestral teacher [Bodhidharma], you see the second ancestor, and you can receive transmission of the robe and bowl.

This is one statement. Furthermore here is a verse that says:

The power of the buddha ancestors' Dharma wheel is great,
 turning the entire universe and turning each atom.
Even though the robe and bowl were transmitted into
 Huike's hands, the Dharma is heard by and universally
 pervades every man and woman.

---

113 Ānanda was Śākyamuni Buddha's cousin, attendant, and close disciple, who recited all of the sutras by memory after the Buddha's passing. Akṣobhya Buddha is the cosmic Buddha of the east. We do not know of a canonical reference to Ānanda's glimpse of this Buddha's pure land, or Buddha field, but it refers generally to glimpsing the ultimate reality of buddhas.

114 All of these phrases from "lanterns and standing pillars" to "twirling a flower and blinking" are expressions of ultimate truth. Dōgen also comments on this story in the Shōbōgenzō essay Kattō (Twining Vines); see Tanahashi, *Moon in a Dewdrop*, pp. 168–174.

The Primordial Thirty Blows

47. Dharma Hall Discourse

As soon as I happen to hear the two words "Buddha Dharma," my ears and eyes are stained. Even before you people stepped across the doorsill of the monks' hall or entered the Dharma hall, already I have given you thirty good blows.[115] Although it is thus, this mountain monk [Dōgen] today has fully exerted his powers for the sake of the assembly.

Dōgen gave one shout and descended from his seat.

Deceiving the Teacher

48. Dharma Hall Discourse

This mountain monk [Dōgen] has not passed through many monasteries. Somehow I just met my late teacher Tiantong [Rujing]. However, I was not deceived by Tiantong. But Tiantong was deceived by this mountain monk. Recently, I returned to my homeland with empty hands. And so this mountain monk has no Buddha Dharma. Trusting fate, I just spend my time. Morning after morning, the sun rises in the east. Evening after evening, the moon sets in the west. The clouds disperse and mountain valleys are still. After the rain, the mountains in the four directions are close. Every four years is a leap year. A rooster crows toward sunrise.[116]

The Ever-Present Dharma Discourse

49. Dharma Hall Discourse

This mountain monk has not lectured for the sake of the assembly for a long time. Why is this? Every moment the Buddha hall, the monks' hall, the valley streams, and the pine and bamboo endlessly speak on my behalf, fully for the sake of all people. Have you all heard it or not? If you say you

---

115 "Giving thirty blows" is a common Zen saying for expressing reality beyond speaking or not speaking. Although this may refer back to incidents of teachers hitting their students to awaken them, as a common expression it did not literally involve physical hitting.

116 This is one of the most famous of the Dharma hall discourses in Eihei Kōroku. Manzan moved it to become the first Dharma hall discourse in volume 1 of his edition, and it also begins the Eihei Dōgen Zenji Goroku, which was a very abridged selection from Eihei Kōroku edited by one of Tiantong's disciples in China, Wuwai Yiyuan. For the lines "However, I was not deceived by Tiantong. But Tiantong was deceived by this mountain monk" Wuwai substituted "I was not deceived by anybody, and returned to my homeland with empty hands." Wuwai's substitution was retained by Manzan in his edition.

heard it, what did you hear? If you say you have not heard it, you do not keep the five precepts.[117]

The Deafening Shout
50. Dharma Hall Discourse

Baizhang received a shout from Mazu, whereupon he became deaf for three days.[118] All people in the monasteries going back to ancient times call this [event] extraordinarily fine. This is not without meaning, and there is more to it that is extraordinary. This mountain monk [Dōgen] has not yet received a shout from Mazu, so how come I am completely deaf for one, two, three, even four lifetimes?[119] All buddhas in the three times have one deaf ear, and the six ancestral teachers [in China] were slightly deaf. How can we understand this principle [of deafness]?

After a pause Dōgen said: Where this favorable wind current spreads and pervades, do not let six ears [a third person] uselessly know about it.[120]

A Profusion of Weeds
51. Dharma Hall Discourse

[Fundamentally] all people are fully satisfied, each and every one with wholeness fulfilled. Why are the weeds seven feet deep throughout the Dharma hall? Do you want to understand this situation?

117 The five precepts are the first five of the ten major precepts: not to kill, not to steal, not to misuse sexuality, not to lie, and not to sell intoxicants.

118 The full story of Mazu's shout and his student Baizhang's resulting temporary deafness appears in the commentary to Hekiganroku, case 11. See Cleary and Cleary, *Blue Cliff Record,* pp. 73–74. This deafness expresses the intimacy of master and disciple. After this shout from his teacher, Baizhang did not need to hear anything else.

119 The "completely" in "completely deaf" is *shikan,* the same word translated as "just" in Dōgen's name for zazen, *shikan taza,* or "just sitting," so this could be read as "just deaf."

120 "Wind current" is the literal meaning of *fūryū,* which is also an expression for teaching styles; for going beyond convention; or for refined elegance. "Six ears" is from a statement by Mazu recorded in Keitoku Dentōroku, "Six ears [in other words three people] cannot make a plan." This refers to the teaching that only two people alone together can truly understand the way, as expressed, for example, in the Lotus Sutra: "Only a buddha together with a buddha can fathom the whole Dharma." Dōgen writes of this in his Shōbōgenzō essay Yuibutsu Yobutsu (A Buddha Together with a Buddha). See Tanahashi, *Moon in a Dewdrop,* pp. 161–167. Dōgen's statement about not letting a third person know in this instance may also be him joking about Baizhang bragging about the story of the shout to his student Huangbo.

After a pause Dōgen said: Flowers fall in our attachments, weeds grow following our aversions.[121]

Study of Sounds and Colors
52. Dharma Hall Discourse
It is recommended to win the entire bank, but definitely avoid creating head-on opposition. On the bright side [understanding distinctions] you deserve thirty blows; on the dark side [merging into unity] you deserve thirty blows.[122] You have already attained suchness. All people are not lacking, even a little. Why don't you realize it? Enlightenment does not begrudge enlightenment, but [you fail to realize it] simply because you are bound by sounds and colors. When sounds and colors bind up enlightenment, aren't sounds and colors bound by enlightenment? Although this is so, releasing your body into sounds and colors, opening your hands amid sounds and colors, remaining there using your effort, certainly you can realize standing pillar Zen and you can realize Nirgrantha Zen,[123] yet even in a dream you will not see Ancestor Zen or Tathāgata Zen. How very painful.

Once you mistakenly put on the robe of sounds and colors, and seek advantage through external forms, then you will have in your house paint-

---

121 This statement also appears near the beginning of Dōgen's famous essay Genjōkōan (Actualizing the Fundamental Point). See Tanahashi, *Moon in a Dewdrop*, p. 69

122 This sentence refers to a statement by Linji's friend Puhua, an eccentric trouble-maker, who said, "Come on the bright side and I'll hit you on the bright side. Come on the dark side and I'll hit you on the dark side." See Burton Watson, *The Zen Teachings of Master Lin-chi* (Boston: Shambhala, 1993), p. 87. One traditional interpretation of this kind of language is that brightness refers to the world of distinctions, the sounds and colors that Dōgen is about to discuss, while darkness refers to the ultimate, beyond sounds and colors.

123 Nirgrantha Jñatīputra, also known as Mahāvīra, is the name of the founder of Jainism, contemporary with Śākyamuni Buddha. The Jain tradition emphasizes asceticism and world-renunciation, so here "Nirgrantha Zen" might be Dōgen's expression for practice that attempts to reject the realm of sound and colors. "Standing pillar Zen" is an original expression here which might imply merely understanding, or meditation in stillness, without open expression and sharing of the teaching in the world outside the Dharma hall. Therefore this sentence might be interpreted as saying that rejection of the realm of sounds and colors is another form of attachment to the realm of sounds and colors. "Ancestor Zen" traditionally refers to practice as it functions in ordinary daily activity. "Tathāgata Zen" refers to practice based on teachings from the sutras.

ings of the goddess of good fortune, but you will also nourish the goddess of poverty.[124]

When without expectation, suddenly you break through the lacquered bucket of the ancestors' style, and lift your head and hit your chest [in unmediated expression], suddenly you attain realization of the way. When one person realizes the way, self and other together realize the way. In one morning of realizing the way, past body and future body together realize the way. For example, it is like [crossing a river] on a boat or a bridge, self and others go together, reaching and penetrating the way. Facing east or facing west, at the same time there is no standstill and no obstruction of each other. Someone facing east and someone facing west can use this single boat. The boat is the same, but the people are different. Going east or going west, each person reaches their destination. This is the characteristic of enlightenment. When we realize the way, we do not realize with something else, we realize only with sounds and colors. When we are deluded, we are not deluded with something else, we are deluded only with sounds and colors. A deluded person and an enlightened person at the same time use one boat, and each is not obstructed.

In ancient times, a monk once asked Fayan, "How can I transcend the two words, sound and color?"

Fayan said, "Great assembly, if you understand the point of this monk's question, it is not difficult to transcend sound and color."[125]

How can we investigate this one circumstance [of this story]? With your ears listen to the stringless lute, and with your eyes see the shadowless tree.[126] Great practitioners have known such a principle. However, there is a point you need to understand in detail. With your ears, [also]

---

124 "The goddess of poverty" is literally "the dark woman of misfortune," who, according to the Mahāparinirvāṇa Sūtra, is the twin sister who arrives together with the goddess of good fortune. Dōgen is speaking of the result of attachment to sounds and colors, or external forms.

125 This dialogue is case 39 of Hongzhi's collection of one hundred kōans with prose comments that were later expanded with commentary into the Record of Further Inquiries kōan anthology by Wansong Xingxiu, who had also written commentary to another of Hongzhi's kōan collections to form the Shōyōroku (Book of Serenity). This dialogue with Fayan appeared in the Jingde Transmission of the Lamp (Keitoku Dentōroku), vol. 24.

126 Lute is a translation of qin, a Chinese stringed instrument. "Listen to the stringless lute" is a saying from the Chinese poet Tao Yuanming (365–427).

listen to the lute that has strings; with your eyes, see the tree that has a shadow. Already you are like this. Now I ask the great assembly, what things do you call sounds and colors? Where are sounds and colors now?

Nothing Is Hidden
53. Dharma Hall Discourse
Directly it is said that not a single thing exists, and yet we see in the entire universe nothing has ever been hidden.[127]

Dōgen descended from the seat.

Who Saves All Beings?
54. Dharma Hall Discourse
Even if you manifest a body, and even if you expound the Dharma, say how you will save all beings.

After a pause Dōgen said: The nose is three feet long; the face weighs half a pound.

A Child with Red Heart
55. Dharma Hall Discourse
Who can know each piece of red heart? What a laugh, the child on the road to Huangmei.[128]

Taking Care of the Mustard Seed
56. Dharma Hall Discourse
Here is a story. A monk asked Master [Longji Shao]xiu, "A mustard seed contains Mount Sumeru. Mount Sumeru contains a mustard seed. What is this Mount Sumeru?"[129]

127 "Not a single thing exists" is from the famous verse by the sixth ancestor, Huineng, with which he is said to have earned the transmission.

128 "The child on the road to Huangmei" refers to the story of the fifth Chinese ancestor, Daman Hongren, who met the fourth ancestor as an old man in his previous life, and had to be reborn to become the person who would inherit the Dharma from the fourth ancestor, Dayi Daoxin. Huangmei was the name of the mountain where both the fourth and fifth ancestors taught. As a child he met the fourth ancestor again. Dōgen discusses their ensuing dialogue in the Shōbōgenzō essay Busshō (Buddha Nature); see Waddell and Abe, *Heart of Dōgen's Shōbōgenzō*, pp. 69–72.

129 According to Indian Buddhist cosmology, Mount Sumeru is the huge axial mountain at the center of the universe.

The master said, "It pierces your heart."
The monk said, "What is a mustard seed?"
The master said, "It covers your eyes."

Suppose somebody asks me, Kōshō, "What is Sumeru?" I would simply say to that person: Take care of your heart.
[As for] "What is a mustard seed?" I simply say: Take care of your eyes.

The Nightingale Tune and the Hollow Man
57. Dharma Hall Discourse
What is the mind of the ancient buddhas? I would say to someone: The song of the nightingale is the same everywhere.
What is the original person? I would say to someone: An emaciated man with withered skin.

Not Much to Sixty Blows
58. Dharma Hall Discourse
Don't say there's not much to the Buddha Dharma.[130] Grandmotherly Huangbo struck [Linji with] sixty blows.

What Is Intimacy?
59. Dharma Hall Discourse
Here is a story. Zen Master Fayan [Wenyi] once visited [his teacher] Zen Master [Luohan Gui]chen. The teacher asked, "Reverend, where are you going?"
Fayan said, "I will travel around on pilgrimage."
Guichen asked, "What is the meaning of pilgrimage?"
Fayan said, "I don't know."
Guichen said, "Not knowing is most intimate."
Fayan suddenly was greatly enlightened.[131]

130 When Linji awakened, after reporting to another teacher about beatings from his own teacher Huangbo, Linji said there was not much to Huangbo's Buddha Dharma. See Irmgard Schloegl, trans., *The Zen Teaching of Rinzai* (Berkeley: Shambhala, 1976), p. 78; and Cleary, *Book of Serenity,* case 86, pp. 367–368.

131 This story also appears in Shōyōroku, case 20. See Cleary, *Book of Serenity,* pp. 86–90. Dōgen also talks about this practice of pilgrimage, going around to visit different teachers, in the Shōbōgenzō essay Henzan (All-Inclusive Study). (*Henzan* is also a term for

The teacher Dōgen said: If this were Kōshō [Dōgen, in this situation] I would respond to Dizang [Guichen]: Is not knowing most intimate or is knowing most intimate?

I completely leave the greatest intimacy to intimacy, but now I ask Dizang [Guichen]: What is this intimacy?

This Genjōkōan
60. Dharma Hall Discourse

Everybody should just wholeheartedly engage in this genjōkōan "Full manifestation of ultimate reality."[132] What is this genjōkōan? It is just all buddhas in the ten directions and all ancestors, ancient and present, and it is fully manifesting right now. Do you all see it? It is just our present rolling up the curtain and letting down the curtain [at the entrance to the practice hall], and getting up and getting down from the sitting platform. Why don't you all join with and practice this excellent genjōkōan? Today this mountain monk [Dōgen], without begrudging my life or my eyebrows, for the sake of all of you expounds this again and repeatedly.[133]

Dōgen pounded the floor with his staff and immediately got down from his seat.

Maitreya Already Descended
61. Dharma Hall Discourse

Here is a story. Dongshan [Liangjie] said to Yunju, "Long ago Nanquan asked a monk who was lecturing on the Sutra of Maitreya's Descent,

---

such journeying by a student). There Dōgen says that without all-inclusive study, "studying the self is not complete." See Tanahashi, *Moon in a Dewdrop,* p. 200. In the Shōbōgenzō essay Jisshō Zammai (The Samādhi of Self-Verification), Dōgen says, "Widely visiting teachers *(henzan)* is widely visiting the self." See Nishijima and Cross, *Master Dogen's Shobogenzo,* book 4, pp. 31–42.

132 Genjōkōan is the name of one of Dōgen's most famous essays in Shōbōgenzō. It literally means "full manifestation" of the kōan. But by "kōan" Dōgen means not the traditional Zen dialogues or stories but the immediate crucial situation or problem of your life right now. For Dōgen, *genjōkōan* is thus a term implying the practice of facing immediate reality as it manifests in your life.

133 "Begrudging my eyebrows" refers to the common Chinese and Japanese notion that if you lie your eyebrows will fall out, similar to the Western expression that your nose will then grow.

'When will Maitreya descend?'[134]

"The monk replied, 'He is presently in the heavenly palace, and will be born in the future.'

"Nanquan said, 'There is no Maitreya up in heaven, and no Maitreya down on the earth.'"

Following this story, Yunju asked, "If it is simply that there is no Maitreya up in heaven and no Maitreya down on the ground, I wonder who granted his name [Maitreya]?"

Dongshan immediately shook his meditation chair and said, "Teacher [Yunju Dao]ying."[135]

The teacher Dōgen said: There is no Maitreya up in heaven, and no Maitreya down on the earth. Maitreya is not Maitreya; [and so] Maitreya is Maitreya. Even though this is so, doesn't everybody want to see Maitreya?

Dōgen raised his whisk and said: You have met with Maitreya. Already having met him, everyone, try to say whether Maitreya exists or does not exist.

Dōgen put down his whisk, got down from his seat, and circumambulated the hall.[136]

---

134 Maitreya is the archetypal bodhisattva who was predicted by Śākyamuni Buddha to be the next future incarnate Buddha. Presently he is said to be up in one of the meditative heaven realms waiting to descend to be reborn on earth in some unknown, perhaps very distant, future. For more information on Maitreya, see Taigen Dan Leighton, *Faces of Compassion: Classic Bodhisattva Archetypes and Their Modern Expression,* rev. ed. (Boston: Wisdom Publications, 2003), pp. 241–274; previously published as *Bodhisattva Archetypes: Classic Buddhist Guides to Awakening and Their Modern Expressions* (New York: Penguin Arkana, 1998).

135 Dongshan's response, "Teacher Ying," denotes that Yunju Daoying himself gave Maitreya his name. It also might be interpreted that Maitreya is right here, as the person Yunju Daoying. The "meditation chair" (literally, "Zen platform") of an abbot in traditional monasteries is separate from the sitting platform of the other monks.

136 "Circumambulate" is *jundō* in Japanese, and refers to the formal practice of walking around in front of all the monks, usually bowing. So in this instance, probably Dōgen was bowing to all the monks in the assembly as he passed them, thereby possibly implying that they were all Maitreya. "Put down his whisk" is literally "throw down" his whisk, a frequently described action throughout the Eihei Kōroku Dharma hall discourses. But even if Dōgen put it down abruptly, this action is generally understood as placing the object down, rather than actually flinging it.

Baizhang's Fox Is Clear
62. Dharma Hall Discourse
After relating the story of Baizhang and the wild fox, Dōgen said: I had mistakenly thought that the barbarian's beard was red, but surprisingly there is a red-bearded barbarian.[137] Not falling into [causality] or not ignoring [causality], cause and effect brings more cause and effect. Do all of you want to know causes and understand effects or not?

Dōgen raised his whisk and said: Look, look. Cause and effect are clear.
Dōgen put down his whisk and got down from his seat.

The Variety of Wind
63. Dharma Hall Discourse
Here is a story. An ancient raised a fan and said, "Even though this has a thousand kinds of usages, after all there are not two types of wind."[138]

The teacher Dōgen said: I, Kōshō, am not like this. Even though it has a thousand kinds of usages, I further see ten thousand types of wind.

After putting down his fan, Dōgen said: Great assembly, now what is it?

---

137 This first statement of Dōgen's is a quote from the famous, important Zen kōan of Baizhang and the Fox, which appears as case 77 in volume 9 of Eihei Kōroku. It is the second case in the Mumonkan (Gateless Barrier) kōan anthology. See Cleary, *Unlocking the Zen Kōan,* pp. 9–17; or Aitken, *Gateless Barrier,* pp. 19–27. It also is case 8 in Shōyōroku. See Cleary, *Book of Serenity,* pp. 32–36.

In the pivotal opening section of this complex and ironic story, an old man sitting in at the back of Baizhang's assembly reveals to Baizhang after a lecture that in a previous eon the old man had been the resident master there. A monk had asked him if a person of great cultivation was still subject to cause and effect. The old man had answered that such a person was not subject to causality, and because of this answer, the old man relates, he had been turned into a wild fox for five hundred lifetimes. He asks Baizhang for the assistance of a turning word, and Baizhang states that a greatly cultivated person does not ignore cause and effect. Thereupon the old man is released from his fox body.

"Here is a red-bearded barbarian" is Baizhang's praise for Huangbo, who challenges Baizhang in the discussion about the fox in the final section of the complete kōan. A red-bearded barbarian is a reference to Bodhidharma, a foreigner to China (and thus a "barbarian") sometimes said to have had a red beard and blue eyes.

For a full treatment of the meanings within this kōan and their intricate dynamics, and of the pivotal implications of Dōgen's own changing interpretations of this story, see Steven Heine, *Shifting Shape, Shaping Text: Philosophy and Folklore in the Fox Kōan* (Honolulu: University of Hawai'i Press, 1999).

138 This statement is attributed to Chengtian Huiyun, who appears in the Continued Lamp Record (Jap.: Seikoku Zoku Tōroku), no. 24. "Not two types of wind" implies that there is only one Buddha nature.

The Seven Wise Women and the Shout without Echoes

64. Dharma Hall Discourse

Here is a story. The Seven Wise Women were all daughters of kings of great countries.[139] During the season of praising flowers (i.e., spring), a hundred thousand people all wanted to go to a resort to enjoy themselves. Among the Seven Wise Women, one woman said, "Sisters, you and I should not go to scenic parks to partake of worldly entertainments like those people. Instead, let's go together to enjoy the charnel grounds."

The other women said, "That place is full of decaying corpses. What is such a place good for?"

The first woman said, "Sisters, just go. Very good things are there."

When they arrived in the forest, the woman pointed to a corpse and said to the other women, "The corpse is here; where has the person gone?"

The women witnessed the truth and realized the way. When they looked up at the sky, heavenly flowers fell around them and a voice praised them saying, "Excellent, excellent."

The woman said, "Who is praising us amid flowers raining from the sky?"

The voice from the sky said, "I am Indra.[140] Because I see the sacred women realizing the way, together with my attendants I came and scattered a rain of flowers."

He also said to the wise women, "I only request to the sacred women that if you need something, I might supply it until the ends of your lives."

The woman said, "At my house the four material offerings and seven jewels are all completely provided.[141] I only want three kinds of things.

---

139 "The Seven Wise Women" are from a story about Śākyamuni in the lamp transmission text called "Collection of the Essence of the Continuous Dharma Lamp" (Jap.: Shūmon Rentō Eyō), published in 1189. Dōgen quoted many stories from this text in his collection of three hundred kōans, Mana Shōbōgenzō. See Steven Heine, *Dōgen and the Kōan Tradition: A Tale of Two "Shōbōgenzō" Texts* (Albany: State University of New York Press, 1994).

140 Indra (Jap.: Taishaku Ten) is the Indian deity of the earth who acts as a guardian for the Dharma.

141 The four material offerings are food, clothing, bedding, and medicine. The seven jewels are gold, silver, lapis lazuli, crystal, agate, ruby, and carnelian.

First, I want one tree without roots. Second, I want one piece of land with no north and south.[142] Third, I want one valley where shouts do not echo."

Indra said, "I have all the things you could want, but those three things I truly do not have. I'd like to go together with you sacred women and discuss this with the Buddha."

Together they went to see the Buddha, and asked about this matter.

Buddha said, "Indra, all of the great arhats among my disciples cannot decipher the meaning of this. Only the great bodhisattvas understand this matter."

Then the teacher Dōgen said: The great śrāvakas do not know the meaning of the Tathāgata's unsurpassed bodhi (full awakening).[143] Only the bodhisattvas who are not involved in calculations gain advantage (i.e., understand the meaning) and let go of the advantage.

Although it is like this, I, Kōshō, say on behalf of Indra: Do you want a tree without roots? The cypress tree in the garden is it.[144] If you cannot use that, raise up this staff and say, "This is exactly it."

Do you want land without north and south? It is the charnel ground. If you cannot use that, the entire world in the ten directions is it.

Do you want a valley where shouts do not echo? Shout out, "Sisters!" to the seven wise women. If the women respond, immediately say to them, "I have given you a valley without echoes." If they do not respond tell them, "After all it doesn't echo."

Clouds Attracted to Mountains
65. Dharma Hall Discourse
Although the white clouds have no mind, wherever they go they seem to

---

142 "North and south" is literally "yin and yang," or "shadow and light," but is commonly used for north and south when applied to land.

143 "Śrāvakas" are disciples of a buddha who study the teachings but, from the Mahāyāna perspective, focus on personal rather than universal enlightenment.

144 "The cypress tree in the garden" was the response of the great master Zhaozhou to a monk's question about ultimate meaning: "What is the meaning of the ancestor Bodhidharma's coming from the west?" This dialogue is discussed by Dōgen in Dharma hall discourses 433 and 488, and in kōan case 45 in volume 9. It also appears in Shōyōroku, case 47, and in Mumonkan, case 37. See Cleary, *Book of Serenity*, pp. 197–200; Cleary, *Unlocking the Zen Kōan*, pp. 167–169; or Aitken, *Gateless Barrier*, pp. 226–230.

be attracted to the old mountains. What are these white clouds? What are these old mountains?

Dōgen struck the sitting platform with his whisk.

After a pause Dōgen said: No guests remain within the dragon gate. Turtles and cranes are inherently mountain sages.[145]

There Is a Mountain Path
66. Dharma Hall Discourse

Amid the spring colors of Ten Island in the east there is a mountain path.[146] In the heavens and in the human realm only I know it. Study this.

Suchness Beyond Struggle
67. Dharma Hall Discourse

Clearly show this to everybody. Directly reaching what has not been realized from the past to present, from beginningless time there is the actual suchness. Why should we struggle to become always intimate with it?[147]

Jumping and Stumbling in a Fragrant World
68. Dharma Hall Discourse

When we exhaust our strength to express it, the pillars help us from the sidelines with half a word. Training the mind and verifying enlightenment, a wooden ladle energetically adds another mouthful [of sustenance for practice]. For a person who can hear and who can practice, emotions are not yet born and forms have not yet appeared. Voices bab-

---

145 These two sentences are a quote from Dongan Changcha, an early Song dynasty master descended from Yaoshan.

Clouds are images for monks or practitioners; mountains are images of masters or of ultimate reality. The dragon gate is a legendary Chinese underwater gateway that fish swim through and become dragons. Fish do not stay there, but either become dragons or don't swim through. Similarly clouds visit but do not remain on any mountain. Turtles and cranes are symbols of longevity. "Mountain sages" are *sennin*, mountain hermits said to have very long lives.

146 This sentence is unclear. Ten Island is said to be the home of mountain sages, or *sennin* (see the preceding note). A story from the Qin dynasty (ca. 200 B.C.E.) tells that the emperor sent messengers to a legendary island to the east where *sennin* were said to live, in order to bring back a potion for longevity. Dōgen might be using this motif to refer to a pathway to a utopian realm of nirvāṇa.

147 Manzan omits this *jōdō* from his version of Eihei Kōroku.

bling on, every bit is naked. Without awakening, advancing each step we stumble over our feet, making seven mistakes and eight mistakes.[148] Without resting, taking a step backward we stumble over our exposed legs; arriving at two and arriving at three.[149] Jumping up and kicking over Mount Sumeru, pick it up and place it within everyone's eyeballs. Stumbling and overturning the great ocean, pick it up and place it within everyone's nostrils. Why doesn't everyone awaken and understand?

After a pause Dōgen said: Last night a flower blossomed and the world became fragrant. This morning a fruit ripened and bodhi (awakening) matured.

Presenting an Offering
69. Dharma Hall Discourse

Today this mountain monk [Dōgen] gives a Dharma hall discourse for the assembly. What I have just said I offer to all the three treasures in the ten directions, to the twenty-eight ancestors in India, to the six ancestors in China, to all the nostrils under heaven, to the eyeballs throughout the past and present, to dried shitsticks, to three pounds of sesame, to Zen boards, and to zafus.[150] Previously we offered incense for the limitless

---

148 "Making seven mistakes and eight mistakes" implies that we make mistake after mistake in our practice, which may be necessary for our practice to develop. In the Shōbōgenzō essay Sokushin Zebutsu (This Very Mind Is Buddha), Dōgen says, "Without making mistake after mistake one departs from the way." See Nishijima and Cross, *Master Dogen's Shobogenzo,* book 1, p. 49.

149 "Arriving at two and arriving at three" seems to imply something extraneous.

150 "Nostrils" refers to the original face, or true nature, as the nostrils are at the center of our face but we cannot see them. "Eyeballs" refers to understanding. When Dōgen returned from China he said that all he brought back was that his eyes were horizontal and nose vertical. "Dried shitsticks," referring to sticks that had been used as we now use toilet paper, was the response of the great master Yunmen to a monk's question, "What is Buddha?" For this dialogue see Cleary, *Unlocking the Zen Kōan,* case 21, pp. 102–105; and Aitken, *Gateless Barrier,* case 21, pp. 137–141. "Three pounds of sesame" (sometimes translated "three pounds of hemp") was Dongshan Shouchu's response to a monk's question, "What is the essential meaning of Buddha Dharma?" See Leighton and Okumura, *Dōgen's Pure Standards for the Zen Community,* p. 56 n. 46; Cleary and Cleary, *Blue Cliff Record,* case 12, pp. 81–87; Cleary, *Unlocking the Zen Kōan,* case 18, pp. 89–93; and Aitken, *Gateless Barrier,* case 18, pp. 120–125. "Zen boards" were support sticks placed under the chin to help maintain upright sitting during sleep. Zafus are round sitting cushions used in meditation.

excellent causal conditions, and we dedicate it so that toads may leap up to Brahma's heaven, earthworms may traverse the eastern ocean, and clouds and water monks may become horses and cows. All buddhas, ten directions, three times; all honored ones, bodhisattva mahāsattvas; Mahāprajñāpāramitā.[151]

Innumerable Simultaneous Dharma Hall Discourses
70. Dharma Hall Discourse
As this mountain monk [Dōgen] today gives a Dharma hall discourse, all buddhas in the three times also today give a Dharma hall discourse. The ancestral teachers in all generations also today give a Dharma hall discourse. The one who bears the sixteen-foot golden body gives a Dharma hall discourse.[152] The one endowed with the wondrous function of the hundred grasses (all things) gives a Dharma hall discourse. Already together having given a Dharma hall discourse, what Dharma has been expounded? No other Dharma is expressed; but this very Dharma is expressed. What is this Dharma? It is upheld within Shanglan temple; it is upheld within Guanyin temple; it is upheld within the monks' hall; it is upheld within the Buddha hall.[153]

Boundless Awareness Beyond Buddha Nature
71. Dharma Hall Discourse
Just see that karmic consciousness is totally boundless. All living beings are without Buddha nature.[154]

Dōgen descended from the seat.

---

151 "All buddhas…Mahāprajñāpāramitā" is the standard dedication at the end of a service or offering.

152 A sixteen-foot golden body is said to be an attribute of a buddha.

153 See Dharma hall discourse 5. Shanglan temple (Jap.: Jōran-in) was the temple where Shanglan Shun, a disciple of Huanglong Huinan, taught. Guanyin temple (Jap.: Kannon-in) was the temple where Zhaozhou taught.

154 "All living beings are without Buddha nature" is a reference to the saying in the Mahāparinirvāṇa Sūtra that "All living beings without exception have Buddha nature." In the Shōbōgenzō essay Busshō (Buddha Nature), which was written in 1241, the same year as this Dharma hall discourse and probably during this same time, Dōgen reinterprets that line to be "All living beings completely are Buddha nature." In that essay he further discusses "no Buddha nature" (or "without Buddha nature") as well as "with Buddha

Not Yet Attained

72. Dharma Hall Discourse

Right now, brother monks, is there someone who has attained it?

At that time a monk arose and made prostrations.

The teacher Dōgen said: This is what it is, only it's not yet [abiding] there.

The monk asked, "What is there to attain?"

The teacher Dōgen said: Truly I know that you have not attained it.

Then the teacher Dōgen said: How is the person who has attained?

After a pause Dōgen said: Body and mind are upright and direct, the voice is strong.

Memory of Spring

73. Dharma Hall Discourse

The voice is a sense object. Without being able to rely on what is external, can you bring forth one phrase for this mountain monk [Dōgen]?

After a pause Dōgen said: I always remember Jiangnan in the third month, when the partridges sing and a hundred blossoms open.[155]

Coming and Going within Life and Death

74. Dharma Hall Discourse

Here is a story. Zen Master Yuanwu said, "Coming and going within life and death is the genuine human body."

Nanquan said, "Coming and going within life and death is the genuine body."

Zhaozhou said, "Coming and going within life and death is exactly the genuine human body."

Changsha said, "Coming and going within life and death is exactly the genuine body of all buddhas."

The teacher [Dōgen] said: Those four venerable elders each unfolds their family style, and together they align our nostrils. They said what they could say, only it's not yet there. If this were Kōshō [Dōgen], I would not

nature" (or "is Buddha nature"). See the Shōbōgenzō essay "Buddha Nature," in Waddell and Abe, *Heart of Dōgen's Shōbōgenzō*, pp. 59–98, esp. pp. 60–65.

155 This is a quote from Fengxue Yanzhao, a prominent tenth-century Linji lineage teacher. It is also cited in Mumonkan, case 24; see Zenkei Shibayama, *The Gateless Barrier: Zen Comments on the Mumonkan* (Boston: Shambhala, 1974), pp. 175–181; Aitken, *Gateless Barrier*, pp. 155–159.

say it thus, but rather: Coming and going within life and death is just coming and going within life and death.

A Tired Infant

75. Buddha's Birthday Dharma Hall Discourse[156]

For a long time in the entire world the sky has been getting brighter. Today in heaven and earth the radiance is clear and beautiful.[157] Walking around for seven steps [the baby Buddha] exhausted all his energy.[158] Observers of this scene cannot avoid laughing.

Speechless in Autumn

76. Dharma Hall Discourse

In autumn, both the clouds and sun are calm and stately. They partly chase the time of year, and partly stand still. While facing [such autumn sky] I wonder how to speak, and can't find any transcendent response.

A Bright Full Moon

77. Mid-Autumn Dharma Hall Discourse [1241][159]

The laurel tree in the moon is completely broken.[160] This turning [of time]

---

156 This Dharma hall discourse may be out of chronological order. Dharma hall discourse 42 is Buddha's Birthday from 1241; Dharma hall discourse 98 is Buddha's Birthday from 1242. Genryū Kagamishima states that this Dharma hall discourse 75 is generally accepted as from 1243 but placed here out of sequence.

157 The characters for "heaven and earth" here are the names of the first two hexagrams in the I Qing, also called creative and receptive, and further imply yang and yin, or sun and moon. See Richard Wilhelm, trans., rendered into English by Cary Baynes, *The I Ching or Book of Changes* (Princeton, Princeton University Press, 1967), pp. 3–15; or Chih-hsu Ou-I, *The Buddhist I Ching*, trans. Thomas Cleary (Boston: Shambhala, 1987), pp. 1–30.

158 This refers to the story of the baby Śākyamuni's seven steps after birth. See note 105 above. According to Nāgārjuna's Commentary on the Mahāprajñāpāramitā Sūtra (Ch.: Dazhidulun; Jap.: Daichidoron), after the baby Buddha's seven steps and proclamation, he did not walk or talk until he was three years old. In this Dharma hall discourse, Dōgen is playfully teasing the baby Buddha.

159 Mid-Autumn is the fifteenth day (or the full moon) of the eighth lunar month. It is a traditional day for moon viewing, and on this occasion Dōgen always gathered with other monks to write poems.

160 In China a laurel tree was said to be in the moon, like the man in the moon in the

does not long for previous turnings. When a barbarian comes a barbarian appears, when a Chinese comes a Chinese appears.[161] Fifteen pieces of boundless pure light.[162]

The Sky in Each Object
78. Dharma Hall Discourse

Each and every thing is clear, and is present. Moment by moment, sit cutting off [all discriminations] in the ten directions, and thoroughly investigate each sense object. Completely investigating attains such power; completely enacting attains such form. Having counted ten emptinesses is like having nothing facing us; having verified half of emptiness resembles dropping away [of body and mind].[163] Do you want to comprehend this principle in detail?

After a pause Dōgen said: The black heaven and yellow earth do not stain my bright jewel.[164] In the pure mirror how can we dream of beautiful and ugly? [Even] without our knowing, the sun and moon [reflect] from the ocean onto the dusty lands.[165] Since last night, the highest heavens dwell in the coral.[166]

West. Breaking a laurel tree was also an expression for passing the traditional Chinese examinations for government positions. "Moon laurel" was an expression for moonlight.

161 "When a barbarian comes…" is a quotation from a talk by Zhaozhou in his section of Keitoku Dentōroku, vol. 10. Zhaozhou said, "It is like a bright jewel. When a barbarian comes a barbarian appears, when a Chinese comes a Chinese appears." This implies the functioning of Buddha nature, or perfect mirror wisdom, reflecting each thing just as it is. For another rendition, see Ogata, *Transmission of the Lamp,* p. 349.

162 "Fifteen pieces" refers to the fifteen nights, or phases of the moon, between new and full moon.

163 "Ten emptinesses" can refer to the empty worlds in ten directions.

164 The "bright jewel" is an image for the interconnectedness of the whole universe.

165 "Sun and moon" here is literally "the two wheels."

166 "Since last night, the highest heavens dwell in the coral" can imply that within the nondifferentiation of darkest night there remains the uniqueness of each form reflected on the bright coral beds of the ocean floor.

The Active Dharma Wheel
79. Dharma Hall Discourse

Buddha ancestors turn fifty thousand somersaults,[167]
The kōan is manifested in a hundred thousand pieces.[168]
One blade of grass erects temples in the ten directions.[169]
Without expectation, cloud and water monks manage to arrive.[170]

Ancestral Knowledge
80. Dharma Hall Discourse

There are many different kinds of knowledge. There is knowledge about a red-bearded barbarian, and there is knowledge about a barbarian's red beard.[171] There is knowledge about the heads of divine spirits, and there is knowledge about the faces of demons. All you people who want to study the way, do so by borrowing the body and mind of buddha ancestors. If buddha ancestors want knowledge, they borrow your knowledge and put it to use.[172] Therefore breaking into a smile and attaining the true eye is the profound

---

167 Somersaults can symbolize transforming the karmic body into a buddha body.

168 "The kōan is manifested" is *genjōkōan*, an important term for Dōgen and the name of one of his most famous essays in Shōbōgenzō. See Dharma hall discourse 60 and note 132 above.

169 "One blade of grass" refers to the story about the Indian deity Indra out on a walk with the Buddha, who pointed to the ground and said, "This is a good place for a temple." Indra stuck a blade of grass into the ground and said that the temple was built, and the Buddha smiled. See Cleary, *Book of Serenity,* case 4, pp. 17–19.

170 In the first three lines of this poem, Dōgen describes his practice at Kōshōji, done without expectation. Somehow monks have arrived anyway. "Clouds and water" is the literal translation of *unsui,* the term for monks in training, sometimes wandering freely like clouds and water.

171 The "red-bearded barbarian" is a reference to Bodhidharma from the kōan about Baizhang and the Fox. See Dharma hall discourse 62 and note 137 above.

172 "Put it to use" is *juyū,* as in the *jijuyū zammai* or "self-fulfilling samādhi," which Dōgen uses as a term for zazen. *Juyū* as a compound means fulfillment or enjoyment, so this samādhi, or meditative concentration, is the practice in which our self is fulfilled and thoroughly enjoyed. The Chinese characters *ju* and *yū* mean to accept or receive one's function or position. So this sentence is saying that buddha ancestors borrow people's knowledge and receive its usefulness, but also that the buddha ancestors are fulfilled by and enjoy the knowledge they see in practitioners.

style of Vulture Peak.[173] Cutting off the forearm and attaining the ancestor's marrow are the exceptional tracks from Mount Song.[174] If you are not like this, how can there be the suchness [of buddha ancestors' knowledge]? You already have attained suchness, but have you completely enacted it?

After a pause Dōgen said: Losing our bodies and lives repays our debt of gratitude for [receiving] the knowledge [of buddha ancestors]. Changing our face and turning our head, we thoroughly investigate our doubt. Even if we have thrown away both jewels and pebbles without concern, this is the time of [practicing with] the robe of the way, the Dharma of the way, and the mind of the way.

An Awakening Tree
81. Dharma Hall Discourse
Last night a clear wind blew down from the vast sky. This morning the cypress tree instantly attained buddhahood.[175]

Dōgen descended from his seat.

Plenty of Enlightenment
82. Dharma Hall Discourse
The spiritual root having no front or back, two or three scoops of great enlightenment have been cooked to make porridge with milk, and offered to monks in the ten directions.

After a pause Dōgen said: There is plenty, really plenty. Once we penetrate the ebb and flow of situations, the present resembles the ancient. Since we have a single storehouse world of sentient beings, [there is] a fist like a thunderclap, and grandmotherly mind.[176]

173 "Breaking into a smile and attaining the true eye" refers to the story of Śākyamuni Buddha's disciple Mahākāśyapa, who smiled when the Buddha held up a flower at Vulture Peak, whereupon the Buddha declared that Mahākāśyapa had attained the true eye. This true eye is referred to in the title of Dōgen's masterwork Shōbōgenzō (True Dharma Eye Treasury).

174 "Cutting off the forearm and attaining the ancestor's marrow" refers to the second ancestor, Dazu Huike, who is said to have gotten the attention of Bodhidharma by cutting off his arm. Bodhidharma's Shaolin temple was on Mount Song.

175 The cypress tree is a reference to Zhaozhou's response about the meaning of Bodhidharma's coming from the west. See Dharma hall discourse 64 and note 144 above.

176 "A fist like a thunderclap" and "grandmotherly mind" are two approaches, grasping and granting, to teaching and cultivating awakening in students.

An Ocean Deity Beyond Emptiness
83. Dharma Hall Discourse
Not mind, not Buddha, and not things either; not self and not other; [these understandings] do not allow you even a little effective knowledge.[177] Within the ocean of spring and autumn, there is an ocean deity.[178]

All-Pervading Melted Snow
84. Dharma Hall Discourse on a Snowy Morning
Bright whiteness manifests with boundless dignity. The radiance is clarifying and awesome.

The teacher Dōgen then brought up a story. Yunju asked Xuefeng, "Has the snow outside the gate melted or not?"[179]

Xuefeng said, "There is not a bit [of snow]. What is there to melt?"

Yunju said on behalf of Xuefeng [in answer to his own original question], "It's melted."

The teacher Dōgen comments: On Yunju's question, "Has the snow outside the gate melted or not?" I would say: I don't see any other person even a bit outside. The other person doesn't see me even a bit outside.

The teacher Dōgen comments: On Xuefeng's response, "There is not a bit. What is there to melt?" I would say: For every flake of falling snow, where could it fall and land?

The teacher Dōgen comments: On Yunju's statement on behalf of Xuefeng, "It's melted," I would say: What are the thousand great worlds?[180] Ten trillion people open the wondrous gate.[181]

177 "Not mind, not Buddha, and not things" is a saying of Nanquan.

178 Spring and autumn represent impermanence. Dōgen seems to be saying that within such fluctuations exists an ocean spirit or divinity (Jap.: *kami*). Ocean spirits often are depicted as dragons, a symbol of enlightenment. Ultimate reality exists right in impermanence.

179 Yunju and Xuefeng were roughly contemporaries. Xuefeng as a young monk had studied with Yunju's Dharma teacher Dongshan Liangjie, founder of the Caodong (Sōtō) lineage, but later received transmission from Deshan.

180 "The thousand great worlds" is a standard term for the universe of as many worlds as grains of sand in the Ganges River.

181 "Opening the wondrous gate" here implies opening the gates to liberation or to the teaching, and also opening any gates that separate inside and outside.

Maturing in the Way
85. Dharma Hall Discourse
Everybody, endeavor to practice the way and act accordingly. With this effort, everyone will naturally mature. Spending your days simply involved in human affairs, even in the monastery how will you find time to accomplish the way?

Everyday Serenity
86. Dharma Hall Discourse
Having enough gruel and rice is the wondrous function of spiritual power. Cloud and water monks arrive and manifest [Buddha's] body to express the Dharma. How is this?

    After a pause Dōgen said: Although it can't be explained in words, it's peaceful and serene.

The Function Enacted
87. Dharma Hall Discourse
The functional power of the twelve faces [of the bodhisattva of compassion] has ten million kinds of equanimity.[182] When we are deeply intimate with the great doubt, we cannot reach around and grasp this [power]. Why is it that we cannot fully comprehend? Where explanatory documents are of no use, [we should] enact in detail the ancient ones' intention.

Buddha Underfoot
88. Enlightenment Day Dharma Hall Discourse [1241][183]
The teacher Dōgen said: Two thousand years later, we are the descendants

---

182 One of the primary forms of the many diverse iconographical forms of the bodhisattva of compassion (Skt.: Avalokiteśvara; Jap.: Kannon or Kanzeon; Ch.: Guanyin; Tib.: Chenrezig) has eleven faces. Although it is not part of the formal iconography, among the many subsidiary forms of this bodhisattva one has twelve faces. This might derive from the eleven-faced form with the addition of the head of Amitābha Buddha, which regularly appears in the headdress of most forms of Avalokiteśvara. For more on Avalokiteśvara's iconography and practice see Leighton, *Faces of Compassion*, pp. 167–209. There is a story in the Records of Linji that refers to this twelve-faced version of the bodhisattva. See Watson, *Zen Teachings of Master Lin-chi*, p. 98.

183 In East Asia during Dōgen's time, Enlightenment Day, the commemoration of the day of Śākyamuni Buddha's awakening, was celebrated on the eighth day of the twelfth month (Jap.: Rōhatsu) by the lunar calendar. In modern times Rōhatsu (referring to both

[of Śākyamuni]. Two thousand years ago, he was our ancestral father. He is muddy and wet from following and chasing after the waves.[184] It can be described like this, but also there is the principle of the way [that we must] make one mistake after another. What is this like? Whether Buddha is present or not present, I trust he is right under our feet. Face after face is Buddha's face; fulfillment after fulfillment is Buddha's fulfillment.

Last night, this mountain monk [Dōgen] unintentionally stepped on a dried turd and it jumped up and covered heaven and earth.[185] This mountain monk unintentionally stepped on it again, and it introduced itself, saying, "My name is Śākyamuni." Then, this mountain monk unintentionally stepped on his chest, and immediately he went and sat on the vajra seat, saw the morning star, bit through the traps and snares of conditioned birth, and cast away his old nest from the past.[186] Without waiting for anyone to peck at his shell from outside,[187] he received the thirty-two characteristics common to all buddhas and, together with this mountain monk, composed the following four-line verse:

---

the eighth day and now Enlightenment Day) is celebrated on December 8. Senne, who collected the talks for this first volume of Eihei Kōroku, notes here that there was a question-and-answer session during this *jōdō*, which was not recorded. Scholars now speculate that this may have been the case in many other Dharma hall discourses, but this is the only place in the first volume where it is explicitly noted. See also Dharma hall discourses 136, 213, 297, 360, 406, 475, and 506.

184 "Following and chasing after the waves" can refer to the waves of suffering beings in the world whom buddhas seek to awaken.

185 "Dried turd" is the term used in a famous kōan for the great master Yunmen's (vulgar) response to a monk asking, "What is Buddha?" It might also be translated as "dried shitstick" (see note 150 above). See Cleary, *Unlocking the Zen Kōan,* case 21, pp. 102–105; or Aitken, *Gateless Barrier,* case 21, pp. 137–141. In the story in this Dharma hall discourse, Dōgen more likely stepped on a piece of dried excrement. This passage beginning with "Last night…" seems like a fantastic dream or vision that Dōgen might have had the previous night. In accord with Yunmen's memorable response, the "dried turd" in this vision of Dōgen's seems to have transformed into Buddha, who then proceeded to his great enlightenment.

186 This describes the great awakening of Śākyamuni under the Bodhi tree.

187 "Peck at his shell from outside" refers to the common Zen image of teacher and student being like the mother hen and chick embryo together both pecking at the eggshell, from outside and within, until the shell breaks and the chick emerges. This image originated with Jingqing Daofu, see Cleary and Cleary, *Blue Cliff Record,* case 16, pp. 104–109.

Stumbling I stepped on his chest and his backbone snapped,
Mountains and rivers swirling around, the dawn wind blew.
Penetrating seven and accomplishing eight, bones piercing
   the heavens,
His face attained a sheet of golden skin.

Mount Sumeru's Mistakes

89. Dharma Hall Discourse

Here is a story. Once a monk asked Yunmen, "Not arousing a single thought, is there any mistake or not?"

Yunmen said, "Mount Sumeru."[188]

After a pause, the teacher Dōgen said: Mount Sumeru speaks about Mount Sumeru. Upon seeing a flower twirl, naturally [one] breaks into a smile. One thought is one hundred years, or thirty thousand days. A woodcutter's shifting circumstances remain in the mountain.

New Year Blossoms

90. New Year's Dharma Hall Discourse [1242]

As the heavenly sky is vacant and clear, oneness attains oneness and is undefiled. The earth is covered with nourishing moisture, penetrating a thousand and soaking ten thousand.[189] How is it right at this time?

After a pause Dōgen said: News of spring spreads harmony and the entire world is fragrant. The deity of spring sits immovably in the cloud monks' hall. On each branch flowers bloom with coral color. The blossoms of the world open, and this is a heavenly realm.

An Everlasting Blossom

91. Dharma Hall Discourse

Since I attained buddhahood, I always remain here expounding

---

188 This dialogue with Yunmen also appears in case 19 of Shōyōroku. See Cleary, *Book of Serenity,* pp. 81–85. See also Dharma hall discourse 56 and note 129 above. Interpretations of this story might include that not arousing a single thought is as huge a mistake as Mount Sumeru.

189 The earth covered with humidity recalls the common Buddhist image of Dharma rain nurturing all beings, described, for example, in chapter 5 of the Lotus Sutra.

Dharma.[190] Don't say that in our school there are no words and phrases. Truly I am the third son of Xie.[191] All dharmas dwell in their Dharma positions; forms in the world are always present.[192] Wild geese return to the [north] woods, and orioles appear [in early spring]. Not having attained suchness, already suchness is attained. Already having attained suchness, how is it?

After a pause Dōgen said: In the third month of spring, fruits are full on the Bodhi tree. One night the blossom opens and the world is fragrant.

Meet the Teacher Not Knowing the Person
92. Dharma Hall Discourse

Great assembly, within this assembly there is a person of great enlightenment. Do you all know him or not? If now you know, you are facing each other without recognizing each other. If now you do not know, meet with the teacher and inquire about the way.

Meet the Teacher Knowing the Person
93. Dharma Hall Discourse

Within this assembly there is a person of great enlightenment. Great assembly, do you know the person or not? If you know, meet with the teacher and inquire about the way. If you do not know, you are facing each other without recognizing each other.

190 "Since I attained buddhahood, I always remain here expounding Dharma" is a quote from the Lotus Sutra, chap. 16, "Inconceivable Life-Span of the Buddha." See Hurvitz, *Scripture of the Lotus Blossom of the Fine Dharma*, p. 242. This indicates the ongoing activity of Buddha, dedicated to the one great cause of awakening sentient beings.

191 "The third son of Xie" is a reference to a saying by Xuansha that he and Śākyamuni Buddha studied together with the third son of Xie, which was Xuansha's family identity before he became a monk. This indicates Xuansha's intimate study of his own karmic self and conditioning, together with the ever-present guidance of Buddha. See the reference in Dōgen's Shōbōgenzō essay Henzan (All-Inclusive Study), in Tanahashi, *Moon in a Dewdrop*, p. 200. Henzan was written in 1243, the year after this Dharma hall discourse.

192 This sentence is a quote from the Lotus Sutra, chapter 2, "Skillful Means." See Hurvitz, *Scripture of the Lotus Blossom of the Fine Dharma*, p. 41. Hearing this Dharma hall discourse, one of Dōgen's major disciples, Tettsū Gikai, had a significant awakening experience; see the section in the introduction on "Dōgen's Great Disciples."

Baizhang's Fox and the Vanishing Flowers
94. Dharma Hall Discourse
After relating the story of Baizhang and the fox, the teacher Dōgen said:
Mountains, rivers, and the great earth are the cave of the wild fox.[193]
Receive and discard one piece of skin, flesh, and bone. Cause and effect
are very clear, and not a personal matter. Partridges sing incessantly [in late
spring], and a hundred flowers vanish.

The Wide Study of Ancient Buddhas
95. Dharma Hall Discourse
For twenty years I have been studying the ancestral schools, widely visiting teachers amid the autumn chrysanthemums and green pines.[194]
Beholding the wind and spreading apart the flowers [as I proceed through
them], I aspire to transmit the way. Ancient buddhas receive the merit and
leap beyond their boundaries.

The Unmastered Sounds and Colors of the Careful Heart
96. Dharma Hall Discourse
Study and practice of the Buddha Dharma is not achieved easily. In the
Eihei era in the Later Han dynasty, the name and form [of the teachings]
were heard a little bit; in the Putong era in the Liang dynasty the ancestral teacher [Bodhidharma] came from the west.[195] If the ancestral teacher
had not come from the west, nobody else would know where to find the
genuine Dharma. How could they know about going beyond Buddha?

---

193 For the story of Baizhang and the fox, see Dharma hall discourse 62 and note 137
above.

194 "Widely visiting teachers" is *henzan,* which refers to the practice of all-inclusive study
of monks traveling around to visit various teachers. See note 191 above and Tanahashi,
Moon in a Dewdrop, pp. 197–202. "Autumn chrysanthemums and green pines" can represent the passage of time, the variety of teachers Dōgen visited, and also the true nature
of all beings.

195 The Eihei (Ch.: Yongping) era in the Later Han dynasty lasted from 58 to 76 C.E. It
is said that in the tenth year of this era (67 C.E.), the first Buddhist sutras were introduced
to China. Later, in 1246, Dōgen would therefore rename the temple he founded in Echizen
after Eihei, and it is still called Eiheiji. The Putong era (Jap.: Futsū) lasted from 520 to 527
C.E., the period when it was supposed (in Dōgen's time) that the Chan founder Bodhidharma arrived in China from India. Modern scholars are still disputing many aspects of
the historicity of Bodhidharma's life.

Discussing the profound and expounding the mystery are not right. Expounding mind and nature are not right. If we release the profound mystery to the place of non-abiding, and if we send the mind nature to the place of nonattachment, this is still seeking after a livelihood within the realm of sounds and colors. When we remove the profound mystery mind nature, then sounds and colors are simply without masters.[196] Why is it like this?

After a pause Dōgen said: Coarse, grasping mind loses it; determined, careful heart attains it.

Radiance Responds
97. Dharma Hall Discourse
Everybody has their own radiant light. The Buddha hall and monks' hall can never be destroyed. Now I ask you, where do you all come from? The radiant light allows the radiant light to respond.

Bathing with the Baby Buddha
98. Bathing Buddha Dharma Hall Discourse [for Buddha's Birthday, 1242][197]
Our Buddha Tathāgata was born today, and at once took seven steps in all ten directions. Who knows that with each step he gave birth to many buddhas? These buddhas are simply transmitting today's voice, with the same life, same place, and same name in the past, future, and present. Homage to Śākyamuni Buddha.[198] We pour fragrant water over the head [of the statue of the baby Buddha] to bathe our elder brother. This is the principle of bathing the newborn one. How do we conduct this ceremony of bathing? For a long time our Buddha has bathed the assembly of monks; today the assembly of monks pours water on our Buddha.

After a pause Dōgen said: Great assembly, let's go together to the Buddha hall and bathe our Buddha.

Dōgen descended from his seat.

196 "Sounds and colors are simply without masters" (or without owners) refers to directly experiencing sense objects, not in the context of subject and object, but without any attachment, grasping, or seeking.

197 See Dharma hall discourse 42 and note 103 above, and also Dharma hall discourse 75.

198 "Homage to Śākyamuni Buddha" is literally "Namu (name of) Śākyamuni Buddha," representing paying homage to, and the ritual act of taking refuge in, Buddha.

No Sword Can Cut It
99. Dharma Hall Discourse

The great way has been simply transmitted by buddhas and ancestors, but our families don't yet know it, and our old friends have not yet expounded it. Why is this the case? [One must] speak of existence and speak of nonexistence, the four phrases and one hundred negations, thinking and not-thinking, Buddha's judgments and Buddha's non-judgments, and [speak of] transmitting the golden brocade robe, and besides the robe, transmitting the true Dharma eye treasury wondrous mind of nirvāṇa.[199] With all your strength express suchness and non-suchness; and [express] knowing being and not knowing being. Even if you exhaust your strength expressing this, and even if you cut off your arm or attain my marrow, when you show it to this mountain monk, I will say to you, there is no such sword in my royal storehouse.[200]

Using a Broken Key
100. Dharma Hall Discourse

Practice is not doing special practices; the way is not the familiar way. Therefore it is said, the buddhas do not know about devices for going beyond, and the ancestors don't understand how to accept what is right here. Only people who are going beyond [attainment of buddhahood] can use a broken key to open a lock with no keyhole.[201]

199 The four phrases and one hundred negations are classical formulations of Nāgārjuna's that explicate the nature and aspects of the teaching of emptiness. The four phrases are existence, nonexistence, both existence and nonexistence, and neither existence nor nonexistence. "The true Dharma eye treasury wondrous mind of nirvana" is what Śākyamuni Buddha is said to have transmitted to the first Zen ancestor, his disciple Mahākaśyāpa; and "the true Dharma eye treasury" in Japanese is *shōbōgenzō,* the name of one of Dōgen's masterworks.

200 "There is no such sword in my royal storehouse" is a saying by Changqing Da'an, a disciple of Baizhang. This indicates that whatever cutting edge, or insight, you use to express it or not express it, this still is not it. There is no expression (or nonexpression) that works.

201 "Going beyond" refers to transcending any attainment and not abiding in or attaching to buddhahood. See the Shōbōgenzō essay Bukkojoji (Going beyond Buddha), in Tanahashi, *Moon in a Dewdrop,* pp. 203–210. "Use a broken key to open a lock with no keyhole" is our interpretation of an unclear phrase about locks and keys that seems to refer to some type of ancient Chinese lock, but indicates a conventionally impossible situation.

Wrapped in Bamboo

101. Dharma Hall Discourse

Here is a story. Mountain Master [Qingqi Hong]jin asked Mountain Master [Longji Shao]xiu, "Clearly knowing the unborn nature of life, why are we caught up in life?"[202]

[Longji Shao]xiu said, "A bamboo shoot eventually becomes bamboo. Shall we use it now to make bamboo wrapping?"[203]

[Qingqi Hong]jin said, "Later you will realize it by yourself."

Longji Shaoxiu said, "I am just like this. What is your meaning?"

Qingqi Hongjin said, "This is the monastery director's quarters; this is the tenzo's [chief cook's] quarters."

Longji Shaoxiu thereupon did a prostration.

The teacher Dōgen after a pause said: The kōan manifests for three or four feet; newly bound in traps and snares for five thousand years.[204]

The More Mud the Bigger the Buddha

102. Dharma Hall Discourse upon Closing the Summer [Practice Period, 1242][205]

The ancient ones now manifest a body to save beings, manifesting Baizhang's body, or manifesting Linji's body, or manifesting the venerable Śākyamuni's body, or manifesting Great Teacher Bodhidharma's body, all for the sake of saving beings, manifesting in each of these ways

---

202 Qingqi Hongjin and Longji Shaoxiu were Dharma brothers, both disciples of Luohan Guichen and fellow Dharma brothers of the Fayan school founder Fayan Wenyi, but it seems that Qingqi Hongjin was the senior of Longji Shaoxiu. "Mountain master" is a name for an abbot of a temple. This story also appears as case 70 in Shōyōroku. See Cleary, *Book of Serenity*, pp. 295–298.

203 Bamboo wrapping is made from the skin of bamboo shoots; it is still used to wrap foods. Even though the bamboo is not fully mature, it can still be useful, just like a practitioner not yet thoroughly enlightened.

204 Dōgen's comment about being trapped for five thousand years seems like criticism, but he is echoing the theme of the story, of willingly "being caught up in life." Just to take one's "Dharma position," whether practicing as director, *tenzo*, or whatever, is the kōan manifesting, and is the meaning of bodhisattva practice to benefit beings.

205 The summer practice period ended on the fifteenth day of the seventh month.

in order to expound the Dharma.[206] For the sake of those who can be saved by a body remaining from ancient times, they immediately manifest a body remaining from ancient times to expound the Dharma.[207] For the sake of those who can be saved by a fresh body, they immediately manifest a fresh body to expound the Dharma. The current summer [practice period] manifests the total dynamic function, and ancient summers manifested the total dynamic function. It is already like this. The ninety-day practice period is great fortune and joy.[208] Already having completed this practice period, how much merit and virtue has arisen?

After a pause Dōgen said: For living beings on the great earth, the more mud the bigger the Buddha.[209]

Difficult to Hear

103. Dharma Hall Discourse

Buddha said, "There is no stopping the coming and going within the six realms."

It is difficult [to have the opportunity] to hear one phrase of true Dharma.

The Grain of Autumn

104. Dharma Hall Discourse

At the occasion of the mid-heaven festival on the first day of the eighth month, red mouths and white tongues vanish.[210] Clouds gather on the

206 "Manifesting in each of these ways in order to expound the Dharma" is a reference to the thirty-three forms of manifestation of Avalokiteśvara Bodhisattva (Jap.: Kanzeon). Each of these manifestations is produced for the benefit of saving the variety of diverse beings, as described in chapter 25 of the Lotus Sutra.

207 The "body remaining from ancient times" is a reference to Śākyamuni's inconceivably long life-span, proclaimed in chapter 16 of the Lotus Sutra, and also to the ancient buddha who appears in a stupa in chapter 7 of the Lotus Sutra.

208 "Practice period" is *ango*, literally "peaceful abiding."

209 "The more mud the bigger the Buddha" is a quote from Yuanwu's commentary to case 77 of Hekiganroku. See Cleary and Cleary, *Blue Cliff Record,* p. 507.

210 The autumn "mid-heaven" festival occurs when there is perfect balance between summer and autumn, according to traditional Daoist yin-yang theory. During this festival, the phrase "red mouths and white tongues vanish" was written on gateways to keep out demons, two of whom were named Red Mouth and White Tongue. Red Mouth was said to guard the east gate of hell, White Tongue the west gate.

peaks and the autumn waters are pure. The merit [having been] sowed, fields of grain are pleasing in the morning wind.

Tiantong Rujing Arrives from the West

105. Dharma Hall Discourse on the Occasion of the Arrival of the Recorded Sayings of High Priest Tiantong.[211]

The teacher Dōgen stood up, lifted up the Recorded Sayings above the incense, and said: Great Assembly, this is Tiantong [Rujing], who has leaped over the eastern ocean, causing great waves to astonish fish and dragons. But even though fish and dragons are astonished, they do not hide themselves. How shall we express this? Have these words previously arrived here? Has there been a previous arrival of these sayings? If you say they have not yet been spoken, it is essential that the pure great ocean assembly verify [Rujing's sayings].

After a pause Dōgen said: The ocean deity knows their nobility and value. [Rujing's Recorded Sayings] remain in the human and heavenly realms, and their radiance illuminates the night.

Dōgen descended from his seat, and together with the great assembly made three prostrations [to Tiantong's Recorded Sayings].

A Good Laugh

106. Mid-Autumn Dharma Hall Discourse [1242][212]

Previous buddhas and later buddhas are together equally verified in awakening. They all completely illuminate each other. Right here we directly receive the glorious radiance. Hitting the mark and bursting through delusions, there is killing and giving life. Endowed with such a standard, we attain such authority. Where is this not called venerable; where do we not express the Dharma? Although it is like this, having seen the cold ground, each scene is a good laugh. Is this clearly apparent?

---

211 On the sixth day of the eighth month of 1242, Dōgen first received a copy of the *goroku*, or "recorded sayings," of his Chinese teacher Tiantong Rujing, who had died in 1228. Senne, the compiler of this volume of the Eihei Kōroku, notes that "Many words were not recorded." Presumably, Dōgen spoke more, but he only wrote down what is included here.

212 Mid-autumn was the fifteenth (full moon) day of the eighth month.

After a pause Dōgen said: Before our eyes there is no Dharma that we can assess; outside of Dharma what is there for mind to examine?[213]

Holding the Universe in a Demon's Cave
107. Dharma Hall Discourse

Holding the entire universe in the ten directions, we take the first step; holding the entire universe in the ten directions, we engage in practice; holding the entire universe in the ten directions, we clarify Mind; holding the entire universe in the ten directions, we transform the activity of our bodies; holding the entire universe in the ten directions, we reverse our way of thinking.

Here is a story. A monk asked Xuansha, "The high priest [Xuansha] has said, 'The entire universe in the ten directions is one bright pearl.' How can this student understand?"

Xuansha said, "The entire universe in the ten directions is one bright pearl. What is the use of understanding?"

The next day Xuansha further asked the monk, "The entire universe in the ten directions is one bright pearl. How do you understand it?"

The monk replied, "The entire universe in the ten directions is one bright pearl. What is the use of understanding?"

Xuansha said, "Now I know that you are making a living in the black mountain demon's cave."

After relating the story Dōgen said: The entire universe in all directions is one bright pearl. The sun, moon, and stars resemble a rabbit and crows.[214] If you want to understand the complete roundness, but you don't understand, being in the black mountain demon's cave is good, strenuous practice.

213 In "no Dharma that we can assess" and "outside of Dharma" the word "Dharma" refers both to things, or dharmas, in the objective, phenomenal world and to the teachings of buddhas.

214 In East Asia it is said that there is a rabbit in the moon and three crows in the sun (which we call sunspots). The story in this Dharma hall discourse is the subject of Dōgen's Shōbōgenzō essay Ikka no Myōju (One Bright Pearl). See Waddell and Abe, *Heart of Dōgen's Shōbōgenzō*, pp. 31–37; and Cleary, *Shōbōgenzō: Zen Essays by Dōgen*, pp. 57–63.

Wind and Clouds Eating Sesame Cakes
108. Dharma Hall Discourse

> Go beyond all previous buddhas and ancestors,
> Not bound by south, north, east, or west.
> Wind and clouds meet together and eat sesame cakes.
> They strike sages and wise ones, hitting all equally.[215]

Iron Men with Red Heart
109. Opening the Fireplace Dharma Hall Discourse [1242][216]
Today the furnace opens its great mouth and widely expounds various sutras in sequence. It accomplishes the training of cold ashes and iron persons, and [like the burning embers,] every bit of heart before our eyes is red.[217]

Rolling Up One Piece of Skin
110. Dharma Hall Discourse on Behalf of the Deceased Monk Egi[218]
One flower opens with five petals, just dying, just being born. The fruits

---

215 This *jōdō* is in the form of a four-line poem, and the last two lines are especially difficult to understand and require speculative interpretation. Clouds are a common image for monks or practitioners, so wind and clouds might perhaps refer to monks traveling where the wind takes them. Manzan suggests that winds and clouds is an image for teachers and students. "Meet together" is our reading of *kan'e,* a compound that is unclear but whose two characters mean "to have some feeling" and "to meet."

In the context of Dōgen talking about going beyond buddhas and ancestors, "Eating sesame cakes" is a reference to a saying by Yunmen, which is case 77 in Hekiganroku. A monk asked Yunmen, "What is talk that goes beyond buddhas and ancestors?" Yunmen answered, "Sesame cake." See Cleary and Cleary, *Blue Cliff Record,* pp. 506–509.

"Sages and wise ones" refers to different levels of attainment of stages on the bodhisattva path. Hitting the sages echoes Linji's saying, "If you see the Buddha, kill the Buddha." This is an image of going beyond Buddha, or beyond attachment to any attainment of buddhahood.

216 "Opening the Fireplace" happened at the beginning of the tenth (lunar) month. This fireplace or furnace was a large metal container behind the altar used to burn charcoal and give heat. See Dharma hall discourse 14 and note 37 above.

217 "Iron person" is a traditional Zen image for a strong, determined practitioner who is settled in the way.

218 Nothing else is known about the monk Egi, but presumably he was one of the monks training with Dōgen at Kōshōji. His name means Wise Respectfulness.

naturally ripen, becoming buddhas, becoming ancestors.[219] Monk Egi, have you attained such a face and eyes or not? Do you clearly understand? Rolling up one piece of skin of this difficult World of Endurance, ten thousand years or one moment are just ashes.[220] Within this [world], buddhas and ancestors appear one after another; old Yama and karmic demons [from hell realms] become buddhas.[221]

The Sangha Ocean Dries Up

111. Dharma Hall Discourse on Behalf of the Deceased Head Monk Sōkai[222]
Dōgen recited Sōkai's Death verse:

> In twenty-seven years,
> My ancient debt is not repaid.
> Leaping over the empty sky,
> I shoot myself into hell like an arrow.

After reciting this the teacher Dōgen said: Last night Sōkai (Sangha Ocean) dried up. How profusely the cloud and water monks have been crying! Although I see you [Sōkai] down to the [ocean] bottom, tears fill my breast like an overflowing lake. Yesterday I held up and shook the

---

219 This passage quotes the verse traditionally attributed to the Chan founder Bodhidharma, which appears in the Jingde Transmission of the Lamp (Keitoku Dentōroku), vol. 3: "I first came to this land transmitting Dharma to save deluded beings. One flower will open with five petals, and the fruit naturally will ripen." See Ogata, *Transmission of the Lamp,* p. 71. This is presented as a prophecy, since it refers to the much later "five houses" of Chan, or Chinese Zen, and was probably written much later than Bodhidharma.

220 "World of Endurance" is a translation of the Sahā world, the name for this troublesome world system in which we live, and in which Śākyamuni was the incarnated Buddha. Living in this World of Endurance is considered a good opportunity to practice and develop patience.

221 Yama (Jap.: Emma) is the king of the afterlife and judge of the deceased.

222 Sōkai (1216–1242) had been *shuso,* or head monk of a practice period, sometime after Dōgen's senior disciple Koun Ejō in 1236. Sōkai's name means "Sangha Ocean." According to the Sanso Gōgyōki (Record of the First Three Ancestors) (Dōgen, Ejō, and Gikai), one of the oldest biographies of Dōgen, Sōkai had previously received Dharma transmission from Dōgen, after Ejō. The Sanso Gōgyōki says that Sōkai was one of three Dharma successors of Dōgen, along with Ejō and Senne, the compiler of this first volume of Eihei Kōroku. But some modern scholars question whether Senne received transmission.

whisk for your spirit. With this one word upon your departure, I don't wait for you to revive.

A Transformation in the Monastery

112. A Second Dharma Hall Discourse on Behalf of the Deceased Head Monk Sōkai

Here is a saying: Zhaozhou said, "Upon first seeing this old monk, thereafter you are not a different person."

Then the teacher Dōgen said: Upon seeing this old monk [Dōgen], [Sōkai] did not have the same old face. While he was alive he never left the monastery.[223] In the chill winds while the fruits were falling he transformed his thinking. A splash of water is his body; the clouds are his mind.

A Mouth Like a Bowl of Blood

113. Dharma Hall Discourse

The vital eye of total dynamic activity manifests before it functions. His fangs are like sword trees, his mouth is like a bowl of blood.[224]

The Ingredients for Making a Whisk

114. Dharma Hall Discourse

That which buddhas correctly transmit to buddhas definitely includes three things, a donkey's womb, a horse's belly, and an ox's skin. Herein are manifested whisks [for teaching the Dharma].[225]

---

223 "While he was alive he never left the monastery" is a reference to Zhaozhou's utterance "If you never leave the monastery for ten or fifteen years, even if you are wordless like a mute, even buddhas cannot budge you." For another version of this saying, with discussion by Dōgen, see the Shōbōgenzō essay Gyōji (Continuous Practice), in Tanahashi, *Enlightenment Unfolds*, pp. 121–122.

224 "His fangs are like sword trees, his mouth is like a bowl of blood" is a saying by Longtan Chongxin about his disciple Deshan Xuanjian, who became known for his wild, fierce teaching style, including shouts and striking his students. Sword trees and bowls of blood are depicted as among the implements of torture in the hell realms.

225 "A donkey's womb, a horse's belly, and an ox's skin" could represent our karmic life and condition in the realm of desire and attachment. Buddha transmission occurs right within karmic life, and exactly because we are caught in such karmic conditions we need to practice. Whisks are symbols of the teachings that help guide us to practice within saṃsāra.

Now We Can Enjoy Our Sleep
115. Winter Solstice Dharma Hall Discourse
Every year adds another to one of the three yangs.²²⁶ Not old and not new, its merit is very deep. This is an auspicious morning and an auspicious season with ten million changes. From now we can enjoy our sleep and eat our rice.

Buddhas Dance and Blossoms Open
116. New Year's Dharma Hall Discourse [1243]
The sky covering is clear, and moisture covers the earth. So it is said, Buddhas as numerous as the sands of the Ganges dance to exalted music, and throughout the entire world the blossoms on the branches facing south immediately open.²²⁷ I am delighted that the Spring Deity has unlocked the time, and spring clouds and water [monks] are coming.

Genuine Study in Spring
117. Dharma Hall Discourse
If our study of the way with genuine, focused aspiration is truly genuine, the way will be thoroughly penetrated.

After a pause Dōgen said: In spring, for each step of walking there is no hindrance. Each person advancing another year penetrates the situation.

Playing with the Buddha Ancestors
118. Dharma Hall Discourse Binding Together the Summer [Practice Period]
I tie up the bags of patch-robed monks, and play with them as a ball.²²⁸

---

226 The winter solstice was on the twenty-second day of the eleventh month in the lunar calendar in this year, 1242. The "three yangs" were three days commemorated each year, including New Year's Day (the first day of spring in the lunar calendar) and the winter solstice. After the winter solstice the days grow longer, and thus yang energy, or light, increases.

227 "Exalted music" is literally three *tai* (terraces or platforms), and here this is a reference to a particular piece of music. Three *tai,* among other things, refers to a type of multi-tiered tower, one of which was in the Chinese city of Ye. During the Wei dynasty (386–543 C.E.), a musical composition was written in honor of someone who held parties at that tower, and who named the music after it.

228 This Dharma hall discourse seems to be out of sequence, as the beginning of the summer practice period was on the fifteenth day of the fourth month, after the Dharma hall

Within this bouncing, numberless buddha ancestors appear. I keep them to give to the monastery so they can raise horses and oxen.

The Dharma Expounds the Buddha
119. Dharma Hall Discourse
Reward and Transformation are not buddhas; thinking is not sentient beings.[229] So it is said, before Buddha finishes expounding the Dharma, the Dharma has already expounded Buddha.[230]

The Single Vehicle
120. Dharma Hall Discourse
In the entire earth there is nobody outside the way; from ancient to present times, there are no two vehicles.[231]

---

discourse for closing the furnace (which is Dharma hall discourse 122). "Play with them as a ball" says literally that "Hōrin," i.e., Kōshō Hōrinji temple, or its abbot, Dōgen himself, plays with the monks' bags as balls. "Kōshō Hōrinji" literally means "Raising Sages Jeweled Forest temple." This summer practice period of 1243 was the last at Kōshōji before Dōgen moved to the north coast of Japan in Echizen (modern Fukui), where he eventually built Eiheiji. Dōgen and most of the Kōshōji monks moved north in July 1243, on the very next day after the end of this practice period. Historians don't know with any certainty about the reasons for moving and Dōgen's decision-making process. But perhaps he had already decided to move when this summer practice period began.

229 Reward and Transformation refer to the reward body of buddhas (Skt.: *saṁbhogakāya*) and the transformation body of buddhas (Skt.: *nirmāṇakāya*). The reward body is the blissful aspect or body of a buddha that results as a fruit of meditative practice. The transformation body is the historically incarnated human aspect or body of Buddha, e.g., Śākyamuni around 500 C.E. in northern India. These two are usually mentioned as part of the "three bodies" of a buddha, together with the *dharmakāya* or reality body, which is the totality of the whole universe. We may understand Dōgen as saying here that a buddha is not limited to any of the three bodies. The true Buddha is beyond such categories. In the Shōbōgenzō essay Gyōbutsu Igi (Awesome Presence of Active Buddhas), written in 1241 not long before this Dharma hall discourse, Dōgen says that *gyōbutsu*, i.e., practicing or active buddhas, are neither reward-body buddhas nor incarnate-body buddhas. The true Buddha is practicing actively in the world. Sentient beings are similarly not limited merely to their discriminative, cognitive, or deluded thinking. Sentient beings are not separate from buddhas.

230 At the end of Gyōbutsu Igi, Dōgen quotes a verse by Yuanwu that says, "In raging fires throughout the heavens, Buddha expounds the Dharma; throughout the heavens in raging fires, the Dharma expounds Buddha." From a translation of Gyōbutsu Igi by Taigen Leighton and Kazuaki Tanahashi, in Kazuaki Tanahashi, ed., *Beyond Thinking: Meditation Guide by Zen Master Dōgen* (Boston: Shambhala, 2004), pp. 79–96.

231 For the two vehicles, see note 47 above.

A Last Song at Midnight
121. Dharma Hall Discourse for the Gathering on Nirvāṇa [Day, 1243][232]
Amid a little rain and much wind the [full] moon resembles a drawn bow; with falling flowers and flowing stream, one complete roundness. At midnight Gautama manifested the divine transformation, and with square words and round sounds he sang nirvāṇa.[233]
Dōgen descended from his seat.

The Single Red Fire of a Life of Training
122. Dharma Hall Discourse upon Closing the Fireplace[234]
Look! Look at Kōshōji's single red fire. The entire universe in ten directions joins to form the pattern. Our life is training to become buddha ancestors. This morning I use my hands to offer tea gruel.[235]

Punching Out the Empty Sky to Sell Eyes of Compassion
123. Dharma Hall Discourse
One sheet of dull stubbornness is three inches thick. Three lengths of upside-downness is five feet long. Last night, this mountain monk [Dōgen] struck the empty sky with a single blow.[236] My fist didn't hurt, but the empty sky knew pain. A number of sesame cakes appeared and rushed to become the faces and eyes of the great earth.[237]

---

232 Nirvāṇa Day, the commemoration of Śākyamuni Buddha's passing away in parinirvāṇa, is commemorated on the fifteenth day of the second month. Other Nirvāṇa Day Dharma hall discourses are discourses 146, 225, 311, 367, 418, and 486.

233 Siddhārtha Gautama was Śākyamuni's name before he became the Buddha. "Square words and round sounds" is a literal translation, and as an expression shares the English connotations of straightforward words with soft, gentle sounds. This "singing" refers to his passing away into nirvāṇa and also to his expounding of the Mahāparinirvāṇa Sūtra shortly before he died.

234 "Closing the Fireplace" was observed on the first day of the third month. See also Dharma hall discourse 489. See Dharma hall discourses 14, 109, 199, 288, 353, 396, 462, and 528 for Opening the Fireplace celebrations.

235 "Tea gruel" is gruel (rice cooked as cereal with much water) with tea mixed in for flavor.

236 The entire story in this Dharma hall discourse is presented as if recounting a dream Dōgen had.

237 Sesame cakes probably refer in part to Yunmen's response in case 77 in Hekiganroku. See Dharma hall discourse 108 and note 215 above.

Suddenly a person came to this mountain monk and said, "I want to buy the sesame cakes."

This mountain monk said to him, "Who are you?"

The person replied to this mountain monk, " I am Avalokiteśvara Bodhisattva. My family name is Zhang, and my personal name is Li."[238]

This mountain monk said to him, "Did you bring any money?"

He said, "I came without any money."

I asked him, "If you didn't bring money, can you buy them or not?"

He didn't answer but just said, "I want to buy them, I really do."

Do you totally, thoroughly understand the meaning of this?

After a pause Dōgen said: When Avalokiteśvara Bodhisattva makes an appearance, mountains and rivers on the great earth are not dead ashes. You should always remember that in the third month the partridges sing and the flowers open.[239]

A Good Time for Zazen
124. Dharma Hall Discourse

These days are a good time for zazen. If you pass this time [vainly], how can you have full strength? If you have no strength, how can you fully engage and affirm the way? Borrowing energy from this time, we can easily cultivate the way.

Now the spring winds are a whirlwind, and the spring rains have continued [for many days]. Even this smelly skin-bag born from our father and mother cherishes this [time]. How could the bones, flesh, and mar-

---

238 In one of his major forms Avalokiteśvara Bodhisattva, the bodhisattva of compassion, has eleven faces and a thousand eyes, one eye on each hand of his thousand-handed form. See note 182 above. In case 82 of Shōyōroku, Yunmen says, "The Bodhisattva Avalokiteśvara brings money to buy a sesame cake: when he lowers his hand, it turns out to be a jelly-doughnut." See Cleary, *Book of Serenity,* p. 350. Perhaps in this dream of Dōgen's, Avalokiteśvara wants to buy the sesame cakes to acquire his hands and eyes. Zhang and Li are very common Chinese names, so this represents Avalokiteśvara as an ordinary person. For more on Avalokiteśvara's iconography and practice see also Leighton, *Faces of Compassion,* pp. 167–209.

239 Even without money, Avalokiteśvara managed to have many faces and eyes. Persistent intention and practice seem to be necessary. Do the spring partridges and flowers manifest stubbornness?

row correctly transmitted by buddha ancestors despise it? Those who despise it truly are beasts.

After a pause Dōgen said: In spring, beyond our own efforts, a withered tree returns to life and flowers. For nine years unknown by people, how many times did he cross the desert?[240]

Thirty Years of No Teachers
125. Dharma Hall Discourse

Without taking a step bow to the three governmental offices.[241] The entryway that has long been locked is now wide open. Sit and cut through the billions of tangled vines to penetrate all of the ten thousand functionings and arouse the wind and thunder.

Here is a story. Huangbo instructed his assembly saying, "All of you people have just been gorging on dregs. Traveling around like that to visit teachers, when will there ever be the matter of Today? Don't you know that there are no Zen teachers in all of Tang China?"[242]

Then a monk came forth and said, "What about all of those in various places who correct students and lead assemblies?"

Huangbo said, "I didn't say that there is no Zen; only that there are no teachers."

After a pause the teacher Dōgen said: Already for thirty years, I have not been saying that there is no Zen, but only that there are no teachers; self and self stand shoulder to shoulder.

---

240 "Nine years unknown by people" refers to the legendary Chinese Zen founder Bodhidharma, who is said to have sat alone in a cave in Northern China for nine years. "Crossing the desert" refers to the deserts of Western China between Bodhidharma and his Indian homeland.

241 "The three governmental offices" is three *tai;* see note 227 above. But here it refers not to music but to three government office buildings, going back to an ancient phrase for the three chief ministers in the Zhou dynasty (1122–255 B.C.E.). Here Dōgen is referring to authority generally, including Zen masters. In Hōkyōki, Dōgen's record of his studies in China, he quoted his teacher Tiantong Rujing as saying, "I am the general headquarters of Buddha Dharma." For Hōkyōki see Takashi James Kodera, *Dōgen's Formative Years in China: An Historical Study and Annotated Translation of the "Hōkyō-ki"* (Boulder: Prajñā Press, 1980), p. 123.

242 This story is case 11 in Hekiganroku, and case 53 in Shōyōroku. See Cleary and Cleary, *Blue Cliff Record,* pp. 72–80; and Cleary, *Book of Serenity,* pp. 223–228.

Drawing a Person at Midnight

126. Dharma Hall Discourse

Here is a story. Zen Master Daman Hongren [the fifth ancestor] in the middle of the night secretly visited the rice-pounding hut and questioned layman Huineng, saying, "Is the rice white or not?"[243]

Huineng said, "It's white but not yet sifted."

Daman tapped the stone mortar with his staff three times.

Huineng immediately took the rice on the bamboo winnowing basket and tossed it in the air three times to clean it; then entered the [master's] room.

After a pause the teacher Dōgen said: White but not yet sifted are two or three gallons.[244] Both of these threes [the taps by Daman and shakes by Huineng] joined as one and began to transmit the light. At midnight the flower opened five petals, and the brocade robe [was transmitted].[245] Drawing a layman so as to draw a [true] person is [how] to draw a monk.

243 In the story of Huineng's Dharma transmission from the fifth ancestor, it occurred at a meeting at midnight, beginning with this story. Huineng, a layman from the backwaters of southern China, had been assigned by the fifth ancestor to pound rice in the back of the kitchen after his arrival, and received the transmission while still a layman. See Philip B. Yampolsky, trans., *The Platform Sutra of the Sixth Patriarch* (New York: Columbia University Press, 1967); or Thomas Cleary, trans., *The Sutra of Hui-neng: With Hui-neng's Commentary on the Diamond Sutra* (Boston: Shambhala, 1998).

244 "Two or three gallons" is an approximate equivalent volume to the four or five *shō* measure in the original.

245 "Five petals" here may refer to the sixth ancestor, Huineng, as the fifth ancestor in the lineage after Bodhidharma.

DAIBUTSU GOROKU

RECORDED SAYINGS OF THE FOUNDER OF DAIBUTSUJI
TEMPLE ON KICHIJŌ MOUNTAIN IN ECHIZEN PROVINCE

COLLECTED BY EJŌ, ATTENDANT OF DŌGEN ZENJI

E K
I Ō
H R   THE EXTENSIVE RECORD OF EIHEI DŌGEN, VOLUME TWO
E O
I K
  U

The teacher Dōgen moved to this mountain on the eighteenth day of the seventh month of the second year of Kangen [1244]. In the next year [1245] many students from the four directions gathered like clouds to practice with him.[1]

1 Volume 1 of Eihei Kōroku was compiled by Dōgen's disciple Senne from Dharma hall discourses at Kōshōji outside Kyoto. Volume 2 begins with Dōgen's Dharma hall discourses after his community moved north to Echizen Province, and while they were at Daibutsuji (Great Buddha temple). Volume 2 was compiled by Koun Ejō, who was Dōgen's main Dharma successor.

Immediately after he moved to Echizen in the seventh month of 1243, Dōgen and his students stayed at Yoshiminedera, a Tendai temple. During this period Dōgen gave no formal *jōdō*, or Dharma hall discourses. In 1244 he moved to Daibutsuji, a temple newly constructed by Dōgen's patron in Echizen, Hatano Yoshishige, a local lord. In 1248 this temple was given the mountain name Mount Kichijō (Auspicious Mountain). The Dharma hall discourses of Eihei Kōroku did not resume until the fourth month of 1245, at the beginning of the first practice period Dōgen led in Echizen, at Daibutsuji. Thus there is a two-year gap between volumes 1 and 2 of Eihei Kōroku, during which time he wrote twenty-nine of the essays in Shōbōgenzō. Once Dōgen resumed these Dharma hall discourses, he added very little more to Shōbōgenzō, for example only writing six fascicles of the seventy-five-fascicle version.

Not Beginning, Not Going Beyond
127. Dharma Hall Discourse Binding Together the Summer [Practice Period]
Dōgen held up his whisk and drew a circle [in the air] and said: Practice period (peaceful abiding) goes beyond this.[2]

Again he made a circle and said: In the practice period we will thoroughly study this. So it is said, the Buddha Awesome Sound King of Emptiness was granted this life vein, and became a buddha and an ancestor.[3] The fist and staff gain the use of this [circle], and transmit the Dharma and the robe.

Bit by bit, from moment to moment, the summer practice period becomes the crown of the skull.[4] Even though this is so, don't take this as the beginning [of your practice]; don't take this as going beyond. Even if you see this as the beginning, kick over the beginning. Even if you see this as going beyond, stamp out going beyond. Already having attained such a thing, how do we not get caught up in the beginning, or in going beyond?

Then Dōgen picked up the whisk, drew a circle, and said: Within this nest, abide peacefully (this practice period).

The Evening Meetings and Full Expression of Great Monasteries
128. Evening Dharma Hall Discourse[5]
Dōgen said: Long ago in the assembly of Zen Master Ciming Quyuan, there was a discussion about [what makes] a great or small monastery.[6]

---

2 Practice Period is *ango*, literally "peaceful abiding," the ninety-day period of intensive practice, conducted once a year in Dōgen's time.

3 The Buddha Awesome Sound King of Emptiness is the Buddha described in chapter 20 of the Lotus Sutra, "The Bodhisattva Never Disparaging." See Hurvitz, *Scripture of the Lotus Blossom of the Fine Dharma*, pp. 279–281. This buddha's Sanskrit name is Bhīṣmagarjitasvarāja, and in the Lotus Sutra commentaries he is said to be the Buddha of the Empty Kalpa (the kalpa, or age, before the universe manifested). Thus Dōgen calls him Buddha Awesome Sound King of Emptiness.

4 "Crown of the skull" symbolizes something of ultimate value.

5 Evening refers to the evening meeting (Jap.: *bansan*), the formal Dharma meeting between the teacher and the assembly in the evening.

6 The assembly of Ciming Quyuan (986–1039) was known for having evening meetings.

Even though that was the discussion of former worthies, still it was missing the single eye. Just say, what do you call a great monastery, what do you call a small monastery? Do not consider as a great monastery one with many monks and large buildings. Do not consider as a small monastery one with few monks and small buildings. Even with many monks, if there are no people of the way truly this is a small monastery. Even with a small building, if there are people of the way, truly this is a great monastery. Do not take an assembly of many people as making a country; if there is one sage or one wise person, that is a [great] country.[7] People's families are also like this.

The great monasteries of buddhas and ancestors unfailingly have evening [Dharma] meetings. Therefore, in the assembly of Zen Master Fenyang Shanzhao, even though there were only seven or eight monks, they always conducted evening meetings, providing an excellent example. Although Zhaozhou had less than twenty monks, this was a great monastery. Yaoshan had less than ten monks, but that was the greatest monastery. In modern times, even though five hundred, seven hundred, or even a thousand monks gather together, how could we ever consider these to be great monasteries, compared to the assemblies of Yaoshan, Zhaozhou, or Fenyang? This is because there is not a single or even a half person of the way. Therefore the [modern] abbots also cannot compare with Yaoshan, Zhaozhou, or Fenyang. That is why in modern times [the practice of holding] evening meetings has died out.

My late teacher Tiantong [Rujing]'s emergence was [as rare as] one encounter in a thousand years. Without being caught up in the procedural regulations of this degenerate age, at midnight, or in the evening, or after lunch, generally without concern over the time, he [had someone] beat the drum for entering the room for general talks.[8] Sometimes he [had someone] beat the drum for small meetings and entering the room.[9]

7 That one sage or wise person constitutes a great country, rather than a large assemblage, is a common idea in Confucianism.

8 "Entering the room" refers to entering the abbot's quarters for group or individual discussion (although apparently in groups under Tiantong Rujing). "General talks" is *fusetsu* in Japanese, literally "universal preaching," which refers to a teacher giving an informal talk without offering incense or wearing robes.

9 "Small meetings" is *shōsan* in Japanese, referring to small group Dharma meetings in the abbot's quarters.

Sometimes he himself hit the wooden sounding block in the monks' hall three times, and gave a general talk in the illuminated hall.[10] After the general talk the monks entered the [abbot's] room. Sometimes he hit the hanging wooden block in front of the head monk's quarters, and gave a general talk in the head monk's room.[11] After the general talk the monks entered the [abbot's] room. These were very rare, excellent examples. Because I, Daibutsu, am a child of Tiantong [Rujing], now I also conduct evening meetings, which is happening for the very first time in our country.[12]

I remember that High Priest Danxia [Zichun] brought up a story and commented, "Deshan [Xuanjian] said to his assembly, 'There are no words or phrases in my school, and also not a single Dharma to give to people.' Deshan said such a thing, only he did not awaken to entering the grasses and searching for people with his whole body soaked in muddy water. Having observed him closely, he was endowed with only one single eye. Danxia [myself] would not have spoken like this. In my school there are words and phrases.[13] They cannot be cut open even with a golden sword. The mysterious, profound, wondrous meaning is that the jade woman becomes pregnant in the night."[14]

10 The monks' hall in formal monasteries was where monks sat in meditation, took meals, and also slept, each at their own assigned place, which was large enough to lie down at and had a cabinet for bedding. The "wooden sounding block" (Jap.: *tsui chin*) was a block a few feet high; it was hit on the top with a small mallet to signal announcements and also during the formal serving of meals with chanting in the monks' hall. The illuminated hall was a passageway with skylights, which led to the washrooms behind the monks' hall. For more on monastic procedures in the monks' hall see Leighton and Okumura, *Dōgen's Pure Standards for the Zen Community*.

11 The "hanging wooden block" (Jap.: *han*) is struck with a wooden hammer to signal regular daily events in the monastery. The head monk, *shuso*, is the guiding monk assigned for one practice period, who sometimes gives Dharma talks and otherwise helps the abbot.

12 Daibutsu, literally "Great Buddha," is the name of the new temple where these Dharma hall discourses were given, and thus refers to Dōgen himself.

13 Dōgen was himself in the Caodong (Jap.: Sōtō) lineage that descended from Danxia. Deshan was the ancestor from whom the Yunmen and Fayan lineages were descended.

14 "Jade woman" implies a barren woman who cannot get pregnant, but also a woman of precious value. This image also relates to the "stone woman" referred to by Danxia Zichun's teacher, Furong Daokai, who said, "A stone woman gives birth at night." The stone woman image was previously described in Song of the Precious Mirror Samādhi, by

The teacher Dōgen said: Danxia could say it like this. His eyes shined through the imposing coarseness of Deshan, as [Danxia] killed with laughter the lazy, worthless buddha ancestors of the past and present. Although it is like this, I, Daibutsu, would not have spoken like this. Great assembly, do you want to hear what I have to say?

After a pause Dōgen said: In my school there are only words and phrases. Eyes and mouths open one after another. Pick up and express it for the sake of other people, both [from] donkey wombs and horse wombs.[15]

The Host Lays Down the Law
129. Evening Dharma Hall Discourse
In ancient times during the [legendary] Chinese dynasties of Tang and Yu, when someone violated the law, [the punishment was] only that it was inscribed on their clothing.[16] However, nobody ever violated the law. Later, even though [the government] carried out the law severely with five punishments, often many people violated the law.[17] Even though in Tang and Yu they just wrote the crimes on clothing, nobody violated the law because people valued the way and the law. Now our community has encountered the Buddha Dharma, with which the law of Tang and Yu

---

Dongshan, the founder of the Chinese Sōtō lineage, which says, "The wooden man begins to sing; the stone woman gets up dancing." For Dongshan's Song of the Precious Mirror Samādhi, see Leighton and Wu, *Cultivating the Empty Field,* pp. 76–77; see also William F. Powell, trans., *The Record of Tung-Shan* (Honolulu: Kuroda Institute, University of Hawai'i Press, 1986), pp. 63–65.

15 "Donkey wombs and horse wombs" might be interpreted either as embryos of donkeys and horses or as those born from donkeys and horses. Donkeys may represent unenlightened sentient beings, and horses awakened persons. This passage has been considered by contemporary Sōtō Zen scholars in terms of Dōgen's view of Danxia and of Chinese Sōtō Zen generally. Dōgen says his school is "*only* words and phrases," as opposed to Danxia's merely acknowledging that "there are words and phrases," although Danxia's expression does counter Deshan's more extreme "no words or phrases." While Dōgen's statement certainly goes beyond Danxia's, it does not necessarily represent criticism of Danxia. Danxia's student Tiantong Hongzhi is frequently quoted by Dōgen in the ensuing volumes of Eihei Kōroku.

16 Tang and Yu, the dynasties ruled by the great mythical wise emperors Yao and Shun, are supposed to have lasted from about 2356 to 2205 B.C.E.

17 The five severe punishments included tattooing the nature of the person's crimes, cutting off the nose, cutting off the legs below the knees, cutting off male genitals, and capital punishment.

cannot compare.[18] Even if we don't inscribe [violations] on clothing, how could we ever violate Buddha Dharma? If someone violates it, then they don't value Buddha Dharma. How painful, Buddha.[19]

I remember that Nanquan asked Huangbo, "Where are you going?"

Huangbo said, "I'm going to gather some greens."

Nanquan said, "With what will you gather them?"

Huangbo held up a knife.

Nanquan said, "You only understand how to be the guest, you don't understand how to be the host."

Even though the meeting together of the experienced masters Nanquan and Huangbo is like this, if it had been I, Daibutsu, there would have been a difference in the deliberations. When Huangbo held up the knife, on behalf of Nanquan I would have said to Huangbo: In my royal storehouse there is no such knife.[20]

Stretching Out in the Circle

130. Dharma Hall Discourse upon Closing the Summer [Practice Period, 1245]

With his whisk Dōgen drew a circle and then said: Don't consider that this means that the practice period is fully completed, or smash your rice bowls because of this [complete roundness]. How is it at this very moment?

18 The character for "law" as described in the Tang and Yu eras is the same as that for "Dharma," as used for the Buddha's teaching after it was introduced to China.

19 We might imagine that this Dharma hall discourse was in response to some violation of monastic procedures in the community at Daibutsuji.

20 Dōgen makes a nearly identical statement, "There is no such sword in my royal storehouse," in Dharma hall discourse 99. Here it might imply that for Dōgen there is no distinction between guest and host. Knives or swords signify the incisive wisdom of Mañjuśrī, but also discriminating consciousness. Dōgen emphasizes nonduality, not production of or attachment to distinctions. If there had in fact been some minor violation by the monks, we might speculate that this may be Dōgen's way of saying there would be no other punishment, aside from its mention here, perhaps a clear reference to some incident for the assembly. For a different version of the dialogue between Nanquan and Huangbo, with a highly contrasting last line, see Ogata, *Transmission of the Lamp*, pp. 307–308.

After a pause Dōgen said: There is not an inch of grass for three thousand miles. Shitou stretched out his legs and lived on a high mountain.[21]

The Connecting Pivot Right Now

131. Evening Dharma Hall Discourse

Here is a story. Huangbo asked Baizhang, "What Dharma did the ancient ones long ago use to instruct people?" Baizhang sat without moving.

Huangbo asked, "What will our descendants in later generations transmit?"

Baizhang brushed out his sleeves, stood up, and said, "I had thought you were that person."

These two old men could only speak of a tiger's stripes, they could not speak of a person's stripes. Moreover, they could not speak of a tiger without stripes, a person without stripes, a phoenix without markings, or a dragon without markings. Why is this so? Great assembly, listen carefully. For the sake of people, the ancient ones just sat without moving. For the sake of people, later generations just return back to the abbot's quarters.[22] Although this is right, it is not yet fully complete. Where is it not complete?

Great assembly, you should know that if the question is not complete, the response is not complete. Why didn't Huangbo ask, "Ancient ones and those of later generations both receive the teacher [Baizhang]'s

---

21 "There is not an inch of grass for ten thousand miles" is a statement by the Chinese Sōtō founder Dongshan Liangjie at the end of a practice period. See Powell, *Record of Tung-Shan,* p. 44. Three thousand miles is literally ten thousand *li;* one *li* being about one-third of a mile.

Shitou, three generations before Dongshan, described the rhythm and simplicity of his practice life in his Song of the Grass-Roof Hermitage: "After eating, I relax and enjoy a nap." "Let go of hundreds of years and relax completely. Open your hands and walk, innocent." See Leighton and Wu, *Cultivating the Empty Field,* pp. 72–73.

22 After Baizhang said, "I had thought you were that person," in the above dialogue, he returned to his quarters. This dialogue is case 44 in the ninety kōans with Dōgen's verse comments in volume 9 of Eihei Kōroku, below. He also selected it as the second case in his Mana Shōbōgenzō (also known as Shinji Shōbōgenzō), the three hundred kōan cases he collected without comment. For a variant interpretation, see rendition in Gudo Nishijima, *Master Dogen's Shinji Shobogenzo,* book 1 (Woods Hole, Mass.: Windbell Publications, 2003), p. 5. The Mana (or "Chinese") Shōbōgenzō is a different work than the popular Shōbōgenzō with essays, often on kōans, written in Japanese. See the discussions of Dōgen's works and relation to kōans in the introduction.

instructions. What is the connecting pivot right now?" When it is asked like this, look, how will Baizhang instruct him?

If someone asked me, Daibutsu, "What Dharma did the ancient ones long ago use to instruct people?" then I would answer: Others put a rope through their own nostrils.

If also asked, "What will our descendants in later generations transmit?" then I would tell him: I pull myself by my own nostrils.[23]

If someone also asked, "What is the connecting pivot right now?" then I would say to him: One person transmits emptiness, and then ten thousand people transmit reality.[24]

One Cannot Avoid Losing Life

132. Dharma Hall Discourse

Raise your eyebrows completely without relying on others. Revolve your skull-top to pierce the heavens without dependence.[25] Therefore, the person who swallowed the buddhas of the three times has been reluctant to open his mouth.[26] Your mouth is my mouth. The person who shines through three thousand worlds is now reluctant to open his eyes. Others' eyes are exactly his own eyes. Although it is like this, if one neglects to respond to a phrase about going beyond, one cannot avoid losing body and life.[27]

---

23 Nostrils are the face's center, so they represent the original fundamental face. Pulling someone's nostrils implies leading them in a direction. Many Zen expressions refer to the nostrils. A rope through the nostrils is also used to lead oxen, another common Zen motif, as in the ten oxherding pictures. "Put a rope through the nostrils" is from the Hekigan-roku, case 4. See Cleary and Cleary, *Blue Cliff Record,* pp. 22–30.

24 On the surface level, "One person transmits emptiness, and then ten thousand people transmit reality" implies the positive continuity of the teaching tradition. But this saying also echoes an old ironic Chinese proverb, "One dog howls meaninglessly, and ten thousand dogs follow." This might imply that the teaching of emptiness is a provisional skillful means, although it does continue the manifestation of the true Dharma. Each person's practice can influence ten thousand.

25 "Raising your eyebrows completely" implies widely opening the eyes. "Revolve your skull-top to pierce the heavens" implies reversing discriminating thoughts to open one's unmediated awareness.

26 "Reluctance to open his mouth" recalls Śākyamuni Buddha's reluctance to teach immediately after his complete awakening. This could have come from the fear that nobody would understand, but also from the realization that there was no need to say anything.

27 "If one neglects to respond to a phrase about going beyond" indicates the necessity of

I remember Jingqing [Daofu] said to Xuansha [Shibei], "As a student first entering the monastery, I implore you for instruction about the path of entry."

Xuansha said, "Do you hear the sound of water flowing downstream over the weir?"

Jingqing said, "I hear it."

Xuansha said, "Enter through this."

From this Jingqing attained the entrance.

Wuzu Fayan said, "As a result of gaining entrance, one can freely move in all directions. If you have not yet done so, don't carelessly leave here."

If this were me, Daibutsu, as well, [the dialogue] would not have been like this. Truly you wish to gain this entryway, but unfortunately this is a hitching post [you are tied to]. If someone asks, "How is it at that very time?" I, Daibutsu, would say to him, after a pause: One scene of Māra.[28]

A Bow upon Meeting and the Single Phrase
133. Dharma Hall Discourse

Last winter I especially instructed all you brother monks: Whenever brother monks meet each other in the hall, on the walkway, by the stream, or under the trees, lower your head and bow in gassho to each other in accord with Dharma.[29] Then start to speak. Before bowing it is not permissible to speak to each other on great or minor matters. We should always make this a constant rule. This is the ordinary tea and rice custom for buddha ancestors meeting each other. How could buddha ancestors not conduct themselves with such decorum? Where buddha ancestors meet, there is offering incense, spreading fragrance; flowers raining, scat-

---

teaching. But this phrase might also be read as "if one responds with a mistake to a phrase that expresses going beyond," indicating the importance of responding correctly. Another interpretation of this reading is that mistakes are unavoidable, because going beyond cannot be fully expressed in words, yet teachers willingly "lose body and life" for the sake of sharing the Dharma with others.

28 The expression "one scene of Māra" connotes "What a shame!" Māra is the demon spirit of temptation who confronted Śākyamuni before his awakening.

29 *Gasshō* is a formal gesture expressing gratitude or respect, done with palms joined together in front of one's face, fingers straight up and fingertips about at nose level, hands one width away from the face. It may be performed while bowing or standing erect.

tering petals; consoling and asking after the harmony of the four elements [i.e., the other's health]; and inquiring as to whether those seeking instruction are difficult.[30] If this occurs, then the jewels of Buddha, Dharma, and Sangha will manifest.

I remember that a monk asked Muzhou [Daoming], "How is it when it is expressed completely in a single phrase?"

Muzhou said, "This old monk is inside your eating bowl bag."

Later a monk asked Yunmen, "How is it when it is expressed completely in a single phrase?"

Yunmen said, "Ripped apart from ancient times till now."

Someone may ask me, Daibutsu, "How is it when it is expressed completely in a single phrase?"

Dōgen threw his whisk down the stairs [from his seat up on the altar] and said: Great assembly, do you understand? If you don't yet understand, I am sorry for [throwing] this whisk.[31]

Subhūti's Silence Surpassing Vimalakīrti
134. Dharma Hall Discourse

When the government lacks wise people, it searches for the talented in the mountains and wilderness. As excellent examples, in this way they found Bairi Xi and entrusted him with the governance, and found Fushi Yan to serve the country.[32] Clearly understand that amid mountains and wilderness are certainly talented wise persons, and that such persons are abundant there. Therefore you cloud and water monks who lodge yourselves in the mountains and wilderness and study the Buddha way with body and mind should not be inferior to laypeople or government ministers. Now you do not yet match the determination of ministers; how can you reach the careful intention of wise sages? This is because you are lazy and do not study. You should be ashamed and saddened. You should know

30 "Flowers rain" refers to a phenomenon that occurs in some sutras when the Buddha expounds the Dharma.

31 "I am sorry for this whisk" might imply that Dōgen is sorry the monks did not understand his throwing the whisk down, or perhaps that he is sorry for the whisk itself, having gone through being thrown vainly.

32 Bairi Xi served as minister in the seventh century B.C.E. Fushi Yan was found in a cave but then served the government during the Yin dynasty (1766–1154 B.C.E.).

that time [flies] like an arrow, and human life is difficult to preserve. To study the way as if extinguishing the flames around your head is the face of the previous buddha ancestors, and the bones and marrow of the founding ancestor.[33]

I remember that Subhūti was holding up the bowl on begging rounds at the house of Vimalakīrti.[34] Vimalakīrti filled the bowl with fragrant rice and exclaimed to Subhūti, "If you can slander Buddha, crush the Dharma, and not enter within the Sangha, you can eat this." [According to the sutra,] Subhūti did not understand this, and put down his bowl and left.

For more than two thousand years, nobody has cooked this particular situation. Everybody simply says that Subhūti did not understand this meaning, and nobody has said that Subhūti did understand. Daibutsu [Dōgen] asks the previous worthies and ancient wise ones, have you seen through this case of Subhūti putting down his bowl and leaving, or not? Already Subhūti has put down the bowl and left. The voice of Subhūti is like the thunder that reaches until the present and has not yet rested.[35] Thus his voice sheds the voices of the śrāvaka vehicle, pratyekabuddha vehicle, and bodhisattva vehicle.[36] So it seems that Vimalakīrti was unable to hear.

Now I ask Vimalakīrti: Do you hear the voice of Subhūti that slanders Buddha, crushes the Dharma, and does not enter within the Sangha, or not? If you do not listen to his voice expounding it, I will make you

---

33 "Founding ancestor" refers to Bodhidharma.

34 This is an episode from the Vimalakīrti Sūtra. See Robert A. F. Thurman, trans., *The Holy Teachings of Vimalakīrti* (University Park: Pennsylvania State University Press, 1976), pp. 27–28; and Burton Watson, trans., *The Vimalakīrti Sutra* (New York: Columbia University Press, 1997), pp. 41–43.

35 Dōgen here is comparing Subhūti's action to the famous thunderous silence of Vimalakīrti, implying that Subhūti really did understand, but just departed silently. However, according to the Vimalakīrti Sutra itself, Subhūti later admitted that he had been "dumbfounded," not knowing what to say. We know of no canonical basis for Dōgen's creative re-creation of the event in support of Subhūti. See Watson, *Vimalakirti Sutra*, p. 43.

36 "Sheds" is *datsuraku*, which also means "drops away" or "casts off." Dōgen frequently uses this word to refer to the ultimate realization of shedding body and mind, letting go of self–other discrimination. Here Dōgen is saying that Subhūti let go of the categories of śrāvakas (those who heard the Buddha's teaching), pratyekabuddhas (those who awaken without teachers or students), and bodhisattvas, even though Subhūti himself was a śrāvaka.

remain holding up a bowl of rice and standing on the ground throughout one or two kalpas.

All the more, I, Daibutsu, say to Vimalakīrti on behalf of Subhūti: fill the bowl with fragrant rice even while you slander Buddha, crush the Dharma, and do not enter within the Sangha. Then I will eat it. Waiting for Vimalakīrti to respond, I [Subhūti] will quickly take the bowl of rice and proceed ahead.

Polishing a Jewel amid Snowfall
135. Winter Solstice Dharma Hall Discourse [1245]
When the ancient Buddha Hongzhi was residing at Mount Tiantong,[37] during a winter solstice Dharma hall discourse he said, "Yin reaches its fullness and yang arises, strength is exhausted and our state changes. A green dragon runs fleetly when his bones are exposed.[38] A black panther is transformed when he is clothed in mist. Take the skulls of the buddhas of the three times, and thread them onto a single rosary.[39] Do not speak of bright and dark heads, as truly they are sun face, moon face.[40] Even if your measuring cup is full and the balance scale is level, in transactions I sell at a high price and buy when cheap. Zen worthies, do you understand? In a bowl the bright pearl rolls on its own without prodding.[41]

---

37 Hongzhi Zhengjue (or Tiantong Hongzhi, as he was known after he became abbot at Tiantong) was the most important Caodong (Sōtō) figure in China in the century before Dōgen, and Hongzhi was abbot at the same Tiantong monastery where Dōgen later trained with his teacher Rujing. This is the first of many long quotes from Hongzhi by Dōgen in Eihei Kōroku, here from volume 4 of Hongzhi's Extensive Record.

38 Green Dragon was the name of a horse in a poem by the famous Chinese poet Dufu (712–770). The meaning of "bones are exposed" is not clear, and it also could be read as the bones recede, are in decline, or are removed.

39 "Rosary" is juzu in Japanese, a string of beads traditionally used by Buddhists to count chants or prostrations. See also Dharma hall discourse 25. In his verse comment to case 76 of the Shōyōroku Hongzhi says, "The skulls of the buddhas and ancestors are strung on a single line." See Cleary, Book of Serenity, p. 321.

40 "Sun face, moon face" refers to the response by Mazu to a question about his condition as his health was failing. Mazu, whose name means Horse Ancestor, replied, "Sun Face Buddha; Moon Face Buddha." See Cleary and Cleary, Blue Cliff Record, case 3, pp. 18–21; and Cleary, Book of Serenity, case 36, pp. 160–162. According to the Buddha Names Sutra, the Sun Face Buddha lives for many ages, the Moon Face Buddha lives for one night.

41 "In a bowl the bright pearl rolls on its own without prodding" is a slight expansion of

"Here is a story," [Hongzhi continued.]

"Xuefeng asked a monk, 'Where are you going?'

"The monk said, 'I'm going to do community work.'

"Xuefeng said, 'Go.'

"Yunmen said, 'Xuefeng understands people according to their words.'"

Hongzhi said [about this dialogue], "Don't move. If you move I'll give you thirty blows. Why is this so? For a luminous jewel without flaw, if you carve a pattern its virtue is lost."

The teacher Dōgen said: Although these three venerable ones spoke this way, I, old man Daibutsu, do not agree. Great assembly, listen carefully and consider this well. For a luminous jewel without flaw, if polished its glow increases.[42]

Today's first [arising of] yang [and the daylight's increase] is an auspicious occasion; a noble person reaches maturity. Although this is an auspicious occasion for laypeople, it is truly a delight and support for buddha ancestors. Yesterday, the short length [of day] departed, yin reached its fullness, and the sound of cold wind ceased. This morning the growing length [of day] arrived, and yang arises with a boisterous clamor. Now patch-robed monks feel happy and sustained, and the buddha ancestors dance with joy. How could directly transcending [going back before] the realm of Awesome Sound King of Emptiness have anything to do with the seasons of spring, autumn, winter, or summer?[43]

"The pearl in a bowl rolls of itself," the fourth line of Hongzhi's verse commentary on case 36 about Mazu's "Sun Face Buddha, Moon Face Buddha" in the Shōyōroku (Book of Serenity). Hongzhi picked the cases and wrote the main verse commentaries for the Shōyōroku.

42 Hongzhi's statement "For a luminous jewel without flaw, if you carve a pattern its virtue is lost" implies that the Buddha nature is perfect as it is; don't mess with it. Dōgen's version, "If polished its glow increases," implies that even though Buddha nature is perfect as it is, our practice can clarify and extend its manifestation. In both cases practice and enlightenment are one, but for Hongzhi the emphasis is on enlightenment, and practice is its natural function, like the pearl rolling on its own. For Dōgen, the emphasis is on practice, which expresses and actually deepens enlightenment.

43 Awesome Sound King of Emptiness is the name of the Buddha during the kalpa of emptiness. See Dharma hall discourse 127. So this expression means to go back before the empty kalpa, to the original self of the reality before any Buddha.

Although to see in this way [transcending the phenomenal world] is the life vein of wise people and sages, and the liver and kidneys [essential organs] of humans and heavenly beings, it is not yet the nostrils of Śākyamuni and the eyeballs of Mahākāśyapa. Do you people want to understand the occasion of this auspicious morning?

With his whisk Dōgen drew a circle and said: Look.

After a pause Dōgen said: Although the plum blossoms are bright amid the fallen snow, inquire further about the first arrival of yang [with the solstice].

This mountain [temple] is located in Etsu [Province] in the Hokuriku [northern] region, where from winter through spring the fallen snow does not disappear, at various times seven or eight feet, or even more than ten feet deep. Furthermore, Tiantong [Rujing, Dōgen's teacher] had the expression "Plum blossoms amid the fallen snow," which the teacher Dōgen always liked to use. Therefore, after staying on this mountain, Dōgen often spoke of snow.[44]

Meeting the World-Honored One

136. Enlightenment Day Ceremony Dharma Hall Discourse[45]

The old head of the house, after falling in the grass for six years, during the night entered the plum blossoms without realizing it.[46] The spring wind arising within [the plum blossoms] cannot stay put; the branches all red and white take pride in themselves.[47]

All of you venerable monks, do you want to know the causes and reasons for [the awakening of] Bhikṣu Gautama? The first cause for accomplishing the Buddha way is hearing Tiantong [Rujing] speak about

---

44 This paragraph seems to have been added later by Koun Ejō, the compiler of this volume.

45 For Enlightenment Day, see volume 1 (Dharma hall discourse 88), note 183. See also discourses 88, 213, 297, 360, 406, 475, and 506.

46 The "head of the house," referring here to Śākyamuni Buddha, is a common Zen expression for an experienced, skillful teacher. "Falling in the grass for six years," taken from a poem about Śākyamuni's enlightenment by Tiantong Rujing, refers not only to Śākyamuni's ascetic practices before his awakening but also to his manifestation in the world.

47 "Branches" here refers to the lineages descended from the Buddha.

dropping away.[48] The second is the power of Daibutsu's [Dōgen's] fist entering all of your eyeballs. Its spiritual power and wisdom transform and liberate living beings, who suddenly see the bright star, or [this fist's power and wisdom] take over your entire body so that you sit on the vajra seat [of Buddha's awakening]. Grasping and letting go are each brilliant. With one raised [fist], we meet thirty-three people.[49]

Although it is like this, how does the life root of the World-Honored One remain in all of your hands? Do you want to meet the World-Honored One?

Dōgen raised his fist and paused for a while, then opened his five fingers wide and paused, then said: You have already met the World-Honored One. How is it to have met him?

After a pause Dōgen said: Right now awaken the way and see the bright star. This is exactly the place where the Tathāgata eats porridge.[50]

Gratitude in the Assembly

137. Dharma Hall Discourse in Appreciation of the [Outgoing] Director[51] [This director] has overseen the temple for twenty-one months, almost two years, or more than six hundred days.[52] I bow with hands clasped in appreciation for his many labors. Furthermore, he did not neglect the effort of using his sitting cushion. This is the present great assembly

---

48 Dōgen himself is said to have awakened when his teacher Tiantong Rujing spoke of body and mind dropping away. So Dōgen here is speaking of himself—and then of all of his monks—as Buddha.

49 "Thirty-three people" refers to the traditional lineage of thirty-three ancestors from Śākyamuni to Huineng, the sixth Chinese ancestor.

50 Porridge, or gruel, refers here not only to the monks' breakfast at Dōgen's monastery but also to the nourishment Śākyamuni Buddha accepted before sitting down under the Bodhi tree and awakening.

51 "Director" is *kansu*, the administrative head of the monastery, one of the six main temple administrator positions. This discourse was given on the occasion of the director having finished his term in that position, and the following discourse is likewise for the *tenzo*.

52 "Overseen" is the interpretation of Manzan, which we have adopted. The earlier Monkaku version that we are primarily using says, "has pulled the noses," implying pulling the noses of the oxen to train them, a metaphor for leading the assembly.

expressing gratitude to each other. Tell me, how shall we speak of the buddha ancestors' gratitude to him?

After a pause, Dōgen hit the right side of his seat once with his whisk and said: Every buddha ancestor has already expressed gratitude to the former director.

A Wooden Ladle Striking in the Place We Cannot Avoid

138. Dharma Hall Discourse in Appreciation of the [Outgoing] Tenzo [Chief Cook]

I, Daibutsu, was the first to transmit the Dharma [procedures and attitude] for the tenzo to temples in Japan. Previously this did not exist here. Presently why do we have this? Truly this [Dharma of the tenzo] is the remains from ancient sages and former worthies such as Guishan, Jiashan, Wuzhuo, and Xuefeng, who practiced with outstretched hands. Their previous wholehearted engaging and affirming [of the practice of tenzo] is the greatest virtue. Who can assess their limits? They not only planted good roots at the places of one or two buddhas, or even three, four, or five buddhas, but we clearly realize that at the assemblies of immeasurable, countless buddhas they practiced many virtues, made diligent efforts, were accomplished, fulfilled [their practice], and actively and carefully managed their work. Therefore it is said, if you have nostrils, I will give you nostrils; if you do not have nostrils, I will take away your nostrils.[53]

Dōgen held his whisk upright and said: This is the principle of not taking away and not giving. Therefore the nostrils are not deceived by either me or you. If sometime suddenly your nose were replaced by a flute without holes, it could not be hung straight upon your beak as before. If you

---

53 Since nostrils are at the center of the face, in Zen rhetoric they sometimes represent the original face, or true self. In the Mumonkan (Gateless Barrier), case 44, Bajiao says, "If you have a staff, I will give you a staff. If you have no staff, I will take away your staff." See Aitken, *Gateless Barrier*, pp. 264–268; or Cleary, *Unlocking the Zen Kōan*, pp. 195–197.

Dōgen wrote extensively about the position of *tenzo*, most famously in Tenzokyōkun (Instructions for the Tenzo). A number of good translations exist, and it is included in Dōgen's Eihei Shingi, which also includes long sections on the responsibility of the *tenzo* in the Chiji Shingi essay "Pure Standards for the Temple Administrators." See Leighton and Okumura, *Dōgen's Pure Standards for the Zen Community*, pp. 33–57, 136–143, and 170–179. For a translation with commentary by a modern Japanese Sōtō master, see Thomas Wright, trans., *Refining Your Life: From Zen Kitchen to Enlightenment*, by Zen Master Dōgen and Kōshō Uchiyama (New York: Weatherhill, 1983).

desire to play the music of Shaolin, you will fall into playing "Enticing Plum Blossoms."[54] If you want to play the music of Jetavana Vihāra, you will fall into playing a Persian melody.[55] Like this, making mistakes we produce more mistakes, and hang our nostrils on the entryways of sun face and moon face, exhaling the energy that drills through our nostrils, and emitting light from our eyes to open our eyes. Then we have already attained faith. The buddhas of all times right now share the same hands and eyes with you, and practice and affirm this for the whole three hundred sixty days. The ancestors from all generations right now share one body and mind with you, and hold it carefully for twelve months. The sun is round and the moon is full; the merit returns to accomplish the way.

If suddenly the wooden ladle strikes the rice container or the serving pot, with the same voice different mouths chant, "Māhāprajñāpāramitā." Usually we chant without realizing that our single loud voice is chanting, "Māhāprajñāpāramitā." Surprisingly, whether we are hitting up against this or that, or striking fences or walls, wherever we go we cannot avoid arousing the Dharma body. How can we discuss this place we cannot avoid?

After a pause Dōgen said: Yunmen's every-atom samādhi can turn into both the wheel of food and the wheel of Dharma.[56] Bring a full container and fill the [monks'] bowls. The World-Honored One's confirmation [of the tenzo's practice] has been employed, and yet is fresh.

The Capabilities of Iron Persons
139. Dharma Hall Discourse Inviting the [Incoming] Director and Tenzo Temple administrators are protected and kept in mind by all buddhas of

---

54 "Enticing Plum Blossoms" is the name of a piece of Chinese secular music mentioned by Rujing. Shaolin is the temple of Bodhidharma.

55 Jetavana Vihāra was the temple donated to Śākyamuni where his monks practiced. Even though we desire to emulate the ancient buddhas, we fall into karmic patterns. We try to make our nostrils, or true self, into an instrument of Buddha Dharma, but we lack skill and end up with pop music.

56 In the Shōyōroku, case 99, a monk asked the great master Yunmen, "What is every-atom samādhi?" Yunmen said, "Rice in the bowl; water in the bucket." See Cleary, *Book of Serenity*, pp. 425–427. Here Dōgen is referring to the equivalence of food and teaching when meals are properly prepared according to the Dharma of the *tenzo*.

the three times.[57] Venerable Nanda was an excellent example, and Venerable Tōba practiced this diligently.[58] Now we are making efforts to establish this mountain [temple] from the ground up, and construction is not yet completed. The myriad things are desolate, and nobody can bear to be patient.[59] If you have no affinity to arouse the mind of awakening and become a seedling [of the Buddha way], how can you face your responsibilities?

Then Dōgen picked up his whisk and said: In the pure ocean [assembly] I fished for golden-scaled dragons, and without leaving the forest monastery selected these two shoots. Becoming oxen you need to pull the plow and the till; becoming horses you need to bite the reins and wear a saddle. Putting on fur, crowned with horns, swinging the tail, and shaking the head, kick over the barrier and enter straight through the dragon gate. Without seeking to become sages, be people who are capable of your duties. Without valuing personal spiritual development, be the host within the guest.[60] Leaping out from under the three beams [of the monks' hall and its meditation seats], still do not be concerned about the busy cross-streets. When meeting people, do not be mistaken in how you prac-

57 "Temple administrator" is *chiji,* literally "to know affairs," the main traditional positions for taking care of monasteries. Usually there are six main positions, the director, the *tenzo,* the assistant director, the monks' supervisor *(inō),* the work leader, and the treasurer. Dōgen discusses the responsibilities and practice of the temple administrators in detail in Pure Standards for the Temple Administrators, an essay in Eihei Shingi; see Leighton and Okumura, *Dōgen's Pure Standards for the Zen Community,* pp. 127–204.

58 Nanda was a half-brother of Śākyamuni Buddha and served as a temple administrator. See Leighton and Okumura, *Dōgen's Pure Standards for the Zen Community,* pp. 127–131. Tōba is the Japanese name (Ch.: Dapo) for an Indian monk referred to in volume 12 of the Shibun Ritsu (The Four-Part Vinaya), the main text for rules of discipline used in China.

59 At the time of this Dharma hall discourse in the twelfth month of 1245, amid the cold mountain winter, the Daibutsuji Dharma hall and monks' hall had just been completed, but other living quarters and necessary buildings were unfinished.

60 The "host within the guest" is a metaphor used in describing the relationship between the ultimate and the particular in the Sōtō five ranks systems, and also is used in a system of four relationships between guest and host described by Linji. Host and guest correspond to ultimate and particular, or to teacher and student. In this instance, "host within the guest" implies that the director and *tenzo* are students fulfilling the functions of the teacher, and being the hosts among the guests, or the other monks.

tice. Becoming buddhas, you must be iron persons. Do you want to hear about the phrase "iron person"?

After a pause Dōgen said: This is the director's office. This is the tenzo's office.

The Indestructible Nature in Deep Muddy Water

140. Dharma Hall Discourse

I remember that a monk asked Zhaozhou, "Before there was this world, already there was this nature. When this world is destroyed, this nature will not be destroyed. What is this indestructible nature?"

Zhaozhou said, "The four great elements and five skandhas."

The monk said, "These still can be destroyed. What is this indestructible nature?"

Zhaozhou said, "The four great elements and five skandhas."[61]

The teacher Dōgen said: Although Zhaozhou said it like this, I, Daibutsu have a further saying about this. When the water is deep, the boat rides high. When there is much mud, the Buddha is large.

Not Merely Glimpsing

141. Dharma Hall Discourse

Completely swallow all the buddha ancestors, then borrow their nostrils to exhale. Though Mahākāśyapa smiled in ancient years, even now this is not merely glimpsing the land.

Fishing for a Person

142. New Year's Dharma Hall Discourse [1246]

Here is a saying. The ancient Buddha Hongzhi, while residing at Tiantong, in a New Year's Dharma Hall Discourse said,

> In New Year's morning zazen, the myriad things are natural.
> Mind after mind is beyond dichotomies; Buddha after
>   Buddha manifests presently.

---

61 For a slightly different version, see Green, *Recorded Sayings of Zen Master Joshu,* pp. 141–142.

The snow on the river is completely pure and white.
The mind of the son of Xie is satisfied on his fishing boat.[62]
    Study this.

The teacher Dōgen said: This morning I, Daibutsu, respectfully continue this poem.
After a pause Dōgen said:

This great auspicious New Year's morning I enjoy zazen.
In accord with this occasion, offering congratulations is
    natural.
Mind after mind, the spring faces laugh with delight.
Buddha after Buddha pulls the oxen around before our eyes.
Presenting an auspicious sign, over a foot of snow covers the
    mountain,
Fishing for a person, fishing for a self, on the fishing boat.

Horns Hidden behind the Big Dipper
143. Dharma Hall Discourse
An old tree conveys the transformative function without moving even slightly. A large rock completely holds the mind seal but its markings are not apparent.[63] Reaching this ground, human and heavenly eyes cannot see. Deluded [worldly] wisdom and enlightened wisdom evaluate without understanding. Fundamentally, Gautama's eyeball rests in the hands of

---

62 The son of Xie is a reference to Xuansha Shibei. See Dharma hall discourse 91 and volume 1, note 191. Xuansha was a fisherman before he became a monk. This Dharma hall discourse poem is in Hongzhi's Extensive Record, vol. 4.

63 According to Genryū Kagamishima, the "old tree" represents Dharma nature, the "large rock" represents Buddha nature. Some interpreters say that an old tree refers to an ancient wooden statue of Buddha. "Large rock" is literally "rock head," which is also the name of the great eighth-century master and progenitor of the Sōtō lineage, Shitou Xiqian. If interpreted this way, then these two sentences might refer to Śākyamuni and Shitou. However, the point of this Dharma hall discourse as a whole seems to relate to the elements of nature and the way that they inherently express the Dharma. This interpretation is shared in the version of the Eihei Kōroku published by Manzan, in which the characters for "old tree" are instead given as "great potter" or "great potter's wheel." This could refer to the force of creation, as opposed to the elements of creation in the natural world, even rocks.

this mountain monk, like a soapberry [used in rosaries]; and this mountain monk's nostril rests in Gautama's hands, like a bamboo tube.[64] Therefore, when you see smoke from behind a mountain or river, you definitely know there is a fire; when you see horns behind a fence or wall, you definitely know there is an ox.[65]

Dōgen held up his whisk and said: All of you tell me, how do you intimately see this and definitely know what it is, without being separated from it? Do you want to completely understand this through your body? At dawn we are informed by the calls of mountain birds; at the beginning of spring we get the news from the fragrance of plum blossoms.

I remember that a monk asked Yunmen, "What is the phrase that goes beyond the Dharma body [dharmakāya]?"

Yunmen said, "The body is hidden in the Big Dipper."

The teacher Dōgen said: Old man Yunmen was only able to speak a phrase about the Dharma body, but was not able to speak a phrase going beyond the Dharma body. If someone were to ask Daibutsu, "What is the phrase that goes beyond the Dharma body?" I would say to him: The body is hidden within the Dharma body.[66]

Dōgen descended from his seat.

The Many Kinds of Great
144. Dharma Hall Discourse
Raising your fist or dangling your feet, expound the west and [also] speak

---

64 Soapberries are the fruit of a group of subtropical trees, sometimes used for soap but also as rosary beads. This sentence evokes the mutual relationship of Śākyamuni Buddha and Dōgen, as Buddha's representative in Dōgen's time, and this might apply to any of Buddha's true successors.

65 "When you see smoke...when you see horns..." is from the Mahāparinirvāṇa Sūtra, and is also the beginning of the pointer (introduction) to case 1 at the very beginning of the Hekiganroku; see Cleary and Cleary, *Blue Cliff Record*, p. 1. Given this story about Bodhidharma visiting the emperor, seeing smoke or horns in the pointer might refer to the possibility of seeing the traces of the Mind Seal held by Bodhidharma, even though the emperor failed to see.

66 Dōgen says the Dharma body (dharmakāya), or true ultimate body of Buddha, is hidden or stored within the Dharma body. The dharmakāya also refers to all phenomena, or the entire natural world. So Dōgen here points to awakening awareness as it is expressed in nature.

the east. Although allowed to overturn your bodies and turn your heads [to transform yourself], you cannot avoid losing your body and life.

I remember someone asked Zhaozhou, "What is the portrait of [the Dharmakāya Buddha] Vairocana like?"

Zhaozhou said, "This old monk has been a home-leaver since I was small, never with any [illusory] flowers in my eyes."

The teacher Dōgen said: Although the ancient Buddha Zhaozhou said it in that way, if someone asked this of Daibutsu, I would simply say to him: Among the great there are many kinds of great, and among the small there are many kinds of small.[67]

Dōgen put down his whisk and descended from his seat.

Dragons and Snakes, Horses and Cows
145. Dharma Hall Discourse

A three-inch tongue has no place to move; an empty hand cannot become a fist.[68]

I remember a monk asked Tongan [Daopi], "What is the master's family style?"[69]

Tongan said, "The golden fowl embraces its child and returns to the boundless sky. The jade rabbit holds its baby and goes to the heavenly palace of the Big Dipper."[70]

The monk said, "When you suddenly encounter a guest, how do you receive him?"

Tongan said, "In early morning a monkey takes the golden fruit and

---

67 "Great" refers to the universal Dharmakāya Buddha, personified as Vairocana. Statues of Vairocana are referred to as the Great Buddha, for example the large Vairocana Buddha statue at the Tōdaiji in Nara. Such a Great Buddha is *Daibutsu* in Japanese, also the name of Dōgen's temple at this time, and therefore of Dōgen himself. The "losing your life" Dōgen mentions above also can be an expression for transforming the small self into universal true being.

68 By referring to a three-inch tongue and an empty hand, Dōgen apparently is saying that reality cannot be fully expressed by any tongue or words, and that emptiness cannot be grasped.

69 "Family style," literally "house wind," is a common expression for the teaching style of a lineage.

70 "Golden fowl" refers to the sun. "Jade rabbit" refers to the moon, because of the image of a rabbit as seen on the moon.

leaves. In late evening a phoenix grabs the jade flower in its beak and goes home."

The teacher Dōgen said: The family style of the ancient ancestor Tongan was most unusual and excellent. The family style of this distant descendant, Daibutsu, is simply a diverse amalgamation.[71] If someone asks, "What is the master's family style?" I would say to him: If I were to say it clearly, horns grow on the head, dragons and snakes mix together, and there are many horses and cows. If suddenly encountering a guest, how would I receive him? "Before you arrive at this mountain gate, I already have forsaken giving you thirty blows."

Dōgen descended from his seat.

In Stagnant Water a Dragon Hides

146. Dharma Hall Discourse on the Fifteenth Day of the Second Month [Parinirvāṇa Day, 1246]

Now our original teacher, Great Master Śākyamuni, is passing away, entering nirvāṇa, under the sala trees by the Ajitavāti River in Kuśinagara. Why is this only about Śākyamuni Buddha? All buddhas in the ten directions in the past, future, and present enter nirvāṇa tonight at midnight. Not only all buddhas, but the twenty-eight ancestors in India and the six ancestors in China who have noses and headtops, all without exception enter nirvāṇa at midnight tonight. There is no before and after, no self and others. Those who do not enter nirvāṇa tonight at midnight are not buddha ancestors and are not capable of maintaining the teaching. Those who have already entered nirvāṇa tonight at midnight are capable of maintaining the teaching. Those who are already capable of maintaining the teaching are in this same family business.

Whether a tripod kettle has a broken leg or no legs, a ladle has a short or long handle, a nose is either broken and flat or long and straight, someone has one eye bulging and the other eye sunken, they all discern the

71 Tongan Daopi was an ancestor in the Caodong (Sōtō) lineage that Dōgen inherited from his teacher Tiantong Rujing. This Caodong lineage from Tongan Daopi through its great Song dynasty masters Touzi Yiqing, Furong Daokai, and Hongzhi Zhengjue may have seemed too elegant for Dōgen's teaching in Japan. This statement by Dōgen about the variety of his teaching belies the modern stereotype of the strict purity of Dōgen's teaching.

monk's staff and complete the matter of a lifetime. Stagnant water hides a dragon; in the entire earth there is no person.[72] Clods of mud or lumps of earth may break someone's front teeth or sever one's left arm.[73] Today we exist, tomorrow there's nothing. At midnight, holding this with empty hands is called practice for three immeasurable kalpas and another hundred kalpas.[74] With full exertion lift up this single stone, and call it the life-span of as many ages as the atoms in five hundred worlds.[75] The great assembly has already seen such a principle. However, there is a more essential point. Would you like to thoroughly experience it?

After a pause Dōgen said: On various people's faces hang Gautama's eyes, but still they beat their breasts with fists in empty grieving. I cannot bear the heavenly demon, or the demon of life and death, who roll around on the floor with laughter seven or eight times at seeing Buddha [dying].[76]

Dōgen put down his whisk and descended from his seat.

The Upright Staff of Daibutsu

147. Evening Dharma Hall Discourse

Dōgen held up his monk's staff, pounded it once on the floor, and said: This is the staff of Daibutsu. Buddhas and lands as numerous as the sands of

---

72 "Stagnant water" is literally "dead water." As well as still, stagnant water, this might also refer to the water placed in the mouth of a newly deceased person as a blessing. Either way, this refers to the dragon, or awakening, of parinirvāṇa upon the ceasing of the karmic self at death.

73 "Sever the left arm" refers to the second ancestor in China, Dazu Huike, said to have cut off his arm to prove his sincerity to his teacher, Bodhidharma. Mud and earth are images of the delusions of karmic conditioning.

74 This time span refers to Mahāyāna lore about the three *asaṃkhya*, or immeasurable kalpas (or ages), during which Śākyamuni is said to have practiced the ten bodhisattva stages in preparation for buddhahood, which he then followed with another hundred kalpas of practice to achieve the thirty-two marks of a buddha.

75 Dōgen here compares this moment of entering nirvāṇa (at death) to a single stone, referring to a "stone" placed as a move when playing the game Go. The life-span refers to the vast longevity described in the Lotus Sutra, chap. 16, about Śākyamuni's inconceivable life-span. Dōgen's "the atoms in five hundred worlds" is an abbreviation for the atoms in five hundred thousand myriads of millions and many more of worlds, an unimaginably vast number, as described in the sutra. See Hurvitz, *Scripture of the Lotus Blossom of the Fine Dharma*, pp. 237–238.

76 Whether enlightened, seeing with Buddha's eyes, or demons, those referred to here by Dōgen fail to recognize Buddha's vast life-span, and only see him as dying.

the Ganges River are all swallowed up in one gulp by this staff. All the living beings in these lands do not know and are not aware of it. All you people, where are your noses, eyes, spirits, and headtops? If you know where they are, within emptiness you can place the staff vertically or hold it horizontally. If you do not know, there is rice and gruel for you on the sitting platforms [in the meditation hall].

I remember that a monk asked Zen Master Baizhang Dazhi, "What is the special excellent matter?"[77]

Baizhang said, "Sitting alone on Great Hero Peak."[78]

Moreover, my late teacher Tiantong [Rujing] said, "If someone asks the venerable monk Rujing, 'What is the special excellent matter?' I would simply reply to him, 'What special excellence is there? Ultimately, what is it? I moved my bowls from Jingci Temple to Tiantong and ate rice.'"[79]

What these two venerable teachers said expresses it pretty well, and yet they cannot avoid the laughter of observers.

If someone asked me, Daibutsu, "What is the special excellent matter?" I would immediately reply to him: The staff of Daibutsu stands upright in Japan.

Dōgen pounded the staff and descended from his seat.

The Same Root and Body
148. Dharma Hall Discourse
An ancient [Sengzhao] said, "Heaven and earth and myself have the same root; the ten thousand things and myself have the same body."[80]

---

77 Dazhi, literally "Great Wisdom," was an honorific posthumous name given to Baizhang by the emperor.

78 "Great Hero" Peak (Daxiong) was the name of the summit above Baizhang's monastery.

79 Jingci Temple, where Rujing resided as abbot before Mount Tiantong, was the fourth-ranked of the five mountains, or major temples of the country. Tiantong was ranked third among the five mountains, so Rujing's move was an elevation in status.

80 This is a saying by Sengzhao, the great early Chinese Buddhist teacher and disciple of Kumārajīva, from his collected commentaries. See Richard Robinson, *Early Mādhyamika in India and China* (Madison: University of Wisconsin Press, 1967), pp. 212–232; and Walter Liebenthal, *Chao Lun: The Treatises of Seng-chao* (Hong Kong: Hong Kong University Press, 1968), pp. 45–80.

Dōgen held up his whisk and said: This is the whisk of Daibutsu. What is it that has the same body and the same root as this whisk? Now, without begrudging my life, I will expound this for the sake of everybody.

After a pause Dōgen said: The price of rice in Luling is high. The size of Chinese radishes in Zhenzhou is large.[81]

Dōgen put down his whisk and descended from his seat.

The Reality of Practice

149. Dharma Hall Discourse

Seeing Buddha, we make prostrations to Buddha; riding an ox, we search for the ox. Why is it like this? This is the reality of our practice. Where wisdom does not reach, totally avoid speaking. If you speak, horns grow on your head.

Dōgen held up his whisk and said: Horns have even now grown on our heads, and we have been speaking. Already there are horns. Is this an ox or a horse; Gautama or Bodhidharma? Wind whistles through the branches; rain breaks up the clumps of earth. Toads croak and earthworms cry out. Simply see that peach blossoms open by the mountain huts. A thousand gates and ten thousand doors face the valley streams in spring.

Dōgen put down his whisk and descended from his seat.

Immeasurable Kalpas on the End of a Staff

150. Evening Dharma Hall Discourse

Dōgen held up his staff and said: Buddha Dharma should be considered with the standards of Buddha's Dharma. Do not consider it based on the Dharma of heavenly demons, of those outside the way, of the triple realms of desire, form, and formlessness, or of the six destinies.[82]

---

81 "The price of rice in Luling" is from a saying by Qingyuan Xingsi, in response to a monk's question, "What is the essential meaning of Buddha Dharma." See Cleary, *Book of Serenity*, case 5, pp. 20–22. "The size of Chinese radishes in Zhenzhou is large" is a saying by Zhaozhou in response to a monk's asking whether or not Zhaozhou intimately met his teacher, Nanquan. See Cleary and Cleary, *Blue Cliff Record*, case 30, pp. 191–193.

82 The six destinies are the realms of heavenly beings, ambitious titans, humans, animals, hungry ghosts, and hell-dwellers, into which one can be reborn in various lives; they are also psychological states that one can assume in this life.

Śākyamuni Buddha completed three immeasurable kalpas of making offerings to buddhas, and thereafter himself became a buddha. Thus it is said that from the former Śākyamuni Buddha to Ratnaśikhin Buddha, he met seventy-five thousand buddhas and fulfilled the first immeasurable kalpa.[83] From Ratnaśikhin Buddha to Dīpaṅkara Buddha he met seventy-six thousand buddhas and fulfilled the second immeasurable kalpa. From Dīpaṅkara Buddha to Vipaśyin Buddha he met seventy-seven thousand buddhas and fulfilled the third immeasurable kalpa.[84] Finally, after that, he attained the way in the present day.

I, Daibutsu, will now expound about this for the sake of the great assembly. From the former Śākyamuni Buddha to our sitting cushions, we sit and cut off the seventy-five thousand hazy mists and fulfill the first immeasurable kalpa. From our sitting cushions to this monk's staff, we break up the seventy-six thousand clumps of earth and fulfill the second immeasurable kalpa. From the staff to the whisk, we bite through the seventy-seven thousand iron brows and fulfill the third immeasurable kalpa. Although it is like this, beyond this there are the fourth, fifth, sixth, seventh, eighth, ninth, and tenth immeasurable kalpas. Exhaustively study this in detail and you will attain this for the first time.

Great assembly, do you want to know the first immeasurable kalpa? *Dōgen held up his staff, pounded it once, and said:* Just this is it.

Do you want to see the second immeasurable kalpa? *Dōgen held up his staff, pounded it once, and said:* Just this is it.

Do you want to see the third immeasurable kalpa? *Dōgen held up his staff, pounded it once, and said:* Just this is it.

Simply practice in this way and you will attain it for the first time.

Do not face these images cast in a mirror and mistakenly understand

---

83 The "former Śākyamuni Buddha" is a very ancient Buddha who has the same name as the Śākyamuni Buddha of our era. These names of ancient buddhas are from volume 178 of the 200-volume Abhidharma Mahāvibhāṣāśāstra, a commentary translated into Chinese by the great translator Xuanzang (600–665). For "immeasurable kalpas," see note 74 above.

84 Dīpaṅkara Buddha first gave prediction of buddhahood to the present Śākyamuni after Śākyamuni (in a former life) put down his long hair for Dīpaṅkara to walk across over a mud puddle. Vipaśyin Buddha is the first of the seven buddhas so far in our kalpa, with the present Śākyamuni Buddha as the seventh.

that our present Śākyamuni is an image cast in a mirror by the former Śākyamuni.[85]

Abandon the Seven Ton Bow
151. Dharma Hall Discourse
Great teacher Śākyamuni Buddha said to Śāriputra, "You should not extensively expound the Dharma with great respect for the sake of people with sharp faculties, and then simplify your respectful expounding of the Dharma for the people with dull faculties."[86]

Śāriputra said, "I expound for people out of sympathy, not according to the capacity of the roots with which they have been endowed."

The World-Honored One said, "Whether to expound the Dharma extensively or in condensed form is not something that can be known by śrāvakas or pratyekabuddhas."[87]

This is a saying by the ancient Buddha at Vulture Peak. If someone asked who is a person with sharp faculties, I would say to him: The two ears on the head are like the wheels on a vehicle.[88]

If asked who is a person of dull faculties, I would respond to him: One whose skull and facial skin become a laughingstock. What is the meaning of Śāriputra saying, "I expound for people out of sympathy?" Because of this sympathy, I forsake giving him thirty blows.

Although this is so, what is the intention of the World-Honored One's statement "Whether to expound the Dharma extensively or in condensed form is not something that can be known by śrāvakas or pratyekabuddhas"?

---

85 One interpretation of this last sentence would be that the present, historically incarnated Śākyamuni Buddha, as a manifest nirmāṇakāya buddha, should not be understood merely as a reflection of some ancient Śākyamuni Buddha as a dharmakāya buddha, equal to the totality of the universe. Each manifest Buddha must actually practice and realize on their own, not simply as a reflection in a mirror.

86 Dōgen quotes this dialogue from the commentary by the sixth Tiantai patriarch, Jingqi Zhanran on the Great Treatise on Śamatha and Vipaśyanā Meditation (Ch.: Mohe Zhiguan) by the Tiantai founder Zhiyi.

87 For śrāvakas and pratyekabuddhas, see volume 1 (Dharma hall discourse 17), note 47.

88 "The two ears on the head are like wheels" implies that all people are not essentially different in their faculties.

After a pause Dōgen said: A seven-ton bow that can shoot a tiger must be abandoned if there is no person who can use it.[89]

Dōgen descended from his seat.

The Music of Snow and the Refreshing Flowers

152. Dharma Hall Discourse on the Third Month, Twentieth Day [1246]
The boundless sky is the nose of all people. The vast earth is the legs and feet of all people. Therefore, the ancestral teacher [Bodhidharma] came from the west and directly clarified how all buddhas appear in the world. The nose performs the Buddha work of the eyes; the eyes perform the Buddha work of the ears.[90] The six sense faculties function together, and all objects practice together. So it is said, "A stone person resembles you, and sings a popular song. You resemble a stone person, and are in harmony with the music of the snow."[91] Exactly thus, exactly now, all sense fields are perfect wisdom. Everybody, do you want to enact this reality in complete detail?

After a pause Dōgen said: Who would complain that spring radiance does not seek after anything? The bright green grasses and hundred flowers are refreshing.

Dōgen descended from his seat.

What Is This Laughter?

153. Dharma Hall Discourse
In the mountains, rivers, and great earth, in the entire world in ten directions, tiles shatter and ice melts. In what place in the mountains, rivers, and great earth, in the entire world in ten directions, could we establish a peaceful life? Is there anybody who can say something about this? If someone can express it, their eyes of practice are bright and clear. If they cannot speak of it for thirty years when they encounter someone, they cannot

89 This is a difficult sentence in the original, but the bow seems to represent skillful teaching, and shooting the tiger might represent saving beings.

90 This is a paraphrase from chapter 33 of the Avataṃsaka Sūtra, "The Inconceivable Qualities of Buddhas." See Thomas Cleary, *The Flower Ornament Sutra* (Boston: Shambhala, 1993), p. 916.

91 "A stone person..." is a quote from Luopu Yuanan. The music of the snow might refer to silence.

mistakenly bring this up. After thirty years, I, Daibutsu, will just laugh at them. What is this laughter? This laughing at them is encountering someone without being able to mistakenly bring this up.

Tuning the Strings on the Path without Mistakes
154. Dharma Hall Discourse
Here is a story. A monk asked Zhaozhou, "What is the path without mistakes?"

Zhaozhou said, "Clarifying mind, seeing the nature, is the path without mistakes."[92]

Later someone [Shexian Guisheng] said, "Zhaozhou only expressed eighty or ninety percent. I am not like this. If someone asks, 'What is the path without mistakes?' I would tell him, 'The inner gate of every house extends to Chang'an [the capital].'"[93]

The teacher Dōgen said: Although this was how it was said [by Shexian Guisheng], this is not worth considering. The ancient Buddha Zhaozhou's expression is correct. Do you want to know the clear mind of which Zhaozhou spoke?

Dōgen cleared his throat, then said: Just this is it.

Do you want to know about the seeing the nature that Zhaozhou mentioned?[94]

Dōgen laughed, then said: Just this is it.

Although this is so, the ancient Buddha Zhaozhou's eyes could behold east and west, and his mind abided south and north. If someone asked

---

92 For this statement from Zhaozhou, see Green, *Recorded Sayings of Zen Master Joshu,* p. 70.

93 This commentary is from the Recorded Sayings of Shexian Guisheng. Chang'an, the ancient capital of China, literally means "long peace," and that meaning is also implied here. Zhaozhou had said, "The great way leads to Chang'an." See Green, *Recorded Sayings of Zen Master Joshu,* p. 108.

94 "Seeing the nature" is *kenshō,* sometimes used as a name for opening or awakening experiences, although it is often used as a verb in traditional Zen, as in "to see the nature" of a particular experience or teaching. In modern Rinzai Zen, *kenshō* is frequently used for the experience of going beyond conceptual thinking. Dōgen criticized understandings of *kenshō* that negated the study of sutras and other Buddhist teachings. Rather than merely seeing the nature, Dōgen emphasized *genjō,* to actually manifest the nature.

Daibutsu, "What is the path without mistakes?" I would say to him: Do not leave this place abruptly.[95]

Suppose someone says to me, "Master, isn't this tuning the string by gluing down the fret?"[96] I would say to him: Do you fully understand tuning the string by gluing down the fret?

Seeing the Birth Right Now

155. Dharma Hall Discourse for Bathing Buddha on the Eighth Day of the Fourth Month [Buddha's birthday; 1246]

My root teacher, Great Master Śākyamuni Buddha, three thousand years ago this morning descended from the heavens and took birth in Lumbinī park, [as son] of King Śuddhodana. He took seven steps to the ten directions, pointed one hand to the heavens and one hand to the earth, looked to the four directions, and said, "Above the heavens and below the heavens, I alone am the venerable one."

The teacher Dōgen said: Great assembly, do you want to see the birth of the World-Honored One? *Dōgen held up his whisk, drew a circle, and said:* The World-Honored One has been born. In the entire world in ten directions, in mountains, rivers, and lands, all the human beings and all sentient or insentient beings, and all buddhas in the three times in the ten directions, all have been born simultaneously with Gautama, the World-Honored One. Not one thing is born before or after that. What is the reason for this? It is because the World-Honored One receives Daibutsu's taking birth and takes birth; receives Daibutsu's legs and takes seven steps; and receives Daibutsu's open mouth and then says, "Above the heavens and below the heavens, I alone am the venerable one."[97]

95 "This place" refers to the concrete phenomenal world, including our mistakes, including activities such as clearing the throat and laughing. So this might be interpreted that seeking the path without mistakes is a mistake; or that the unmistaken path is right in the middle of endless mistakes.

96 "Gluing down the fret" refers to the movable object that is placed underneath the strings up or down the length of a *koto* (a traditional Japanese zither) to tune them. The questioner is saying that you cannot change the tuning of a string when this is glued down, implying that one needs to be flexible to tune one's life. Dōgen's response might indicate the value of staying still, as in zazen, for true spiritual attunement.

97 This "Daibutsu," whose birth, legs, and mouth are received by Śākyamuni, refers throughout this volume to Dōgen himself, master of Daibutsu temple. But Daibutsu, literally "Great Buddha," here implies as well the dharmakāya, or ultimate body of Buddha,

Ultimately I should further state: Not receiving any receiving of sensation is what is called true receiving, or samādhi.[98] If this is so, drops of water do not fall in different places.[99] What is this principle of not falling in different places?

After a pause Dōgen said: If we do not transmit the Dharma and save living beings, our practice cannot be considered to repay the kindness of Buddha. What is this principle of transmitting Dharma and repaying kindness? I will descend from the seat and together with the great assembly go to the Buddha hall and respectfully bathe the pure Dharma body of the Tathāgata.

Seeing the Face of Maitreya

156. Dharma Hall Discourse

If I expound Buddha Dharma as an offering to my fellow practitioners, I cannot avoid my eyebrows falling out [from lying].[100] If I do not expound Buddha Dharma as an offering to my fellow practitioners, I will enter hell as fast as an arrow. Going beyond these two alternatives, what can I do today for you, my fellow practitioners?

After a pause Dōgen said: Above the heavens there is no Maitreya, below the earth there is no Maitreya, but seeing his face is superior to hearing his name.[101] If you meet him in person you cannot be deceived.

---

which is equal to all the beings of the world also born with Śākyamuni, as described in the previous sentence.

98 Literally "all receiving" or "any receiving" is also used as a term for the second skandha, sensation (Skt.: *vedanā*). "True receiving" is used as a term for samādhi, or settled meditative awareness.

99 The image of drops of water is like mindful attention that is concentrated in the same place, and can be as powerful as drops of water drilling holes in rocks.

100 In Asian custom, people who tell lies, or deviate from truth, are said to lose their eyebrows, similar to the Western notion of liars' noses growing long.

101 "Above the heavens there is no Maitreya, below the earth there is no Maitreya" is a reference to a story about a dialogue involving Nanquan. For this story and another comment on it by Dōgen, see Dharma hall discourse 61.

Greeting Monks Beyond Calculation

157. Dharma Hall Discourse Congratulating the New Guest Manager[102]
At this temple, today we appoint a guest manager for the first time. The
guest manager is the one who meets the cloud monks and water monks.
When the guest manager meets together with cloud and water monks, he
treats the monks as his own face and eyes. This is the practice of all buddhas, and nothing other than the single color of wholeheartedly engaging
the way. The person in this position upholds the mind of the way and
kindly looks after those arriving from all over, making the monastery
flourish with Buddha Dharma.

Then Dōgen said: If Buddha Dharma is not expounded by people, even
those with wisdom cannot fulfill it. Who is the person who reaches this
field where they can leap over barriers, and face south to see the North
Star? [The guest manager] allows visitors who are beyond calculation to
practice the incalculable matter. The person beyond calculation has
already seen and now also hears the incalculable Dharma. Although it is
like this, how can I utter a phrase that is not related to verbal expression?

After a pause Dōgen said: [When the guest manager] enters the realms
of both buddhas and demons, cloud monks and water monks are content.

In Disciplined Restraint a Sitting Cushion Bears Fruit

158. Dharma Hall Discourse Opening the Summer [Practice Period;
Fourth Month, Fifteenth Day, 1246]
Five or six cups of the buddha ancestors' mind and marrow is called ninety
days of peaceful abiding, or practice period. A hundred or a thousand
eyeballs of patch-robed monks are called three months of protecting life.
Clouds settle on the mountain, like children with their father. The water
is clear in the ocean assembly, like younger and older brothers together.
Bones and flesh practice together, dragons and snakes make a single
endeavor. Buddhas uphold and maintain this, eating their rice and wearing their robes. People protect this event, pacifying the mind and establishing their lives. Ancient buddhas from the ten directions settle down
like rocks with their entire bodies, committed to never departing
[throughout the practice period]. All the pillars with their entire substance

---

102 Guest manager (Jap.: *shika*) is one of the six heads of monastic departments in the traditional East Asian monastic establishment.

are wooden, in disciplined restraint.[103] Sitting cushions bear fruit, which ripen all the time. Flowers open on a monk's staff, fragrant every day. At this very time, the demon Pāpiyas sees buddhas and laughs joyfully; a rigid stone nods its head and is noisy with delight.[104] At what are they laughing joyfully, or making a delighted clamor? He laughs joyfully at a flower opening on a monk's staff, and it makes a delighted clamor at a sitting cushion bearing fruit.

The Body of Prajñā
159. Dharma Hall Discourse
Clouds appearing on the mountaintop are an auspicious omen. For Guishan's water buffalo, nine times nine equals eighty-one.[105] The moon settled on the surface of the deep river pool is bright and clear. For Xuefeng's turtle-nosed snake, nine times seven equals sixty-three.[106]

I remember that Zhaozhou asked Daci [Huanzhong], "What is the body of prajñā?"

---

103 "Disciplined restraint" is *kessei*, another term for the practice period along with *ango*, "peaceful abiding"; *kinsoku*, "committed to never departing" (or "forbidden to leave"); and *ketsuge*, "opening the summer." In modern Japan another common term for the practice period is *seichū*, "within restraint."

104 For Pāpiyas see Dharma hall discourse 35.

105 Guishan Lingyou said that after he died he would become a water buffalo down the hill from the mountain. "On the left side of the buffalo's chest five characters, *Gui, shan, monk, Ling,* and *you* will be inscribed. At that time you may call me the monk of Guishan, but at the same time I shall also be the water buffalo. When you call me water buffalo, I am also the monk Guishan. What is my correct name?" See Chang, *Original Teachings of Ch'an Buddhism,* p. 208.

106 These traditional references presented by Dōgen are complicated. The following comments in this note include the editor's merely speculative interpretations. Xuefeng said to his assembly, "On South Mountain there's a turtle-nosed snake. All of you people must take a good look." His disciple Yunmen threw down his staff (which represents the teaching) in front of Xuefeng and made a gesture of fright (as if it were a snake). For the comments by two of Xuefeng's other disciples, see Cleary and Cleary, *Blue Cliff Record,* case 22, pp. 144–153. Turtle-nosed snakes are poisonous. The teaching is medicine that sometimes seems dangerous.

Both of the multiplication citations are from the Extensive Record of Yunmen. "Nine times nine equals eighty-one" is Yunmen's answer to the question "What is the single path that goes beyond?" See App, *Master Yunmen,* pp. 90, 105. In his note to this dialogue, App says that Yunmen uses the phrase "nine times nine equals eighty-one" in five instances altogether in his Extensive Record. Because Tang dynasty multiplication tables begin with

Daci said, "What is the body of prajñā?"

Zhaozhou gave a hearty laugh, and departed.

The next day, Daci saw Zhaozhou sweeping the ground and asked, "What is the body of prajñā?"

Zhaozhou threw down his broom, clapped his hands, and roared with laughter. Daci immediately returned to his abbot's quarters.[107]

The teacher Dōgen said: Daci and Zhaozhou only were able to speak phrases that resembled [prajñā]. They were not able to speak phrases that were the body [of prajñā]. If someone asked me, Daibutsu, "What is the body of prajñā?" I would say to him: Come along and follow it.

The Power of Gruel and Rice
160. Dharma Hall Discourse

Here is a story. Guishan brought up the story of the causes and conditions of Linji's awakening to the way, and asked Yangshan, "At that time did Linji attain the power of [Gao'an] Dayu, or the power of Huangbo?"[108]

---

nine times nine, App speculates that this refers to the basic knowledge of anyone with minimal education, like "one plus one equals two" for us. Thus it may be equivalent to saying to the questioner, "Get the basics," or "First things first," before being concerned with going beyond.

Therefore, applied to Guishan's water buffalo, Dōgen's "nine times nine equals eighty-one" might refer to Guishan's becoming a water buffalo as the path of going beyond (into the next life, and into the realm of manifestation in the world). Conversely, this simple calculation may refer to Guishan returning to the basics of the animal realm. The clouds as an auspicious omen might refer to Guishan's self-prediction of becoming manifest in the world as a water buffalo in his next life, an irony as predictions of future buddhahood are traditionally considered auspicious omens.

"Nine times seven equals sixty-three" is Yunmen's response to the question "I came from a distance to study with you. What is the teacher's mind?" For a variation on this calculation, see App, *Master Yunmen*, p. 144. On the surface, in which the moon is clearly reflected, Yunmen's mind ("nine times seven is sixty-three") might seem as frightening as a snake.

107 This story about Zhaozhou and Daci appears in the Recorded Sayings of Zhaozhou. The two were contemporaries, but Zhaozhou did not have his own temple until late in his long life. So in this story he was practicing at the temple of Daci, a disciple of Baizhang. See Green, *Recorded Sayings of Zen Master Joshu*, p. 162.

108 The story about Linji is that when he studied with Huangbo, three times he asked, "How is the significance of Buddha Dharma manifested?" Each time he was immediately hit by Huangbo. Despite encouragement from Huangbo's head monk, Linji left in

Yangshan said, "[Linji] not only touched the tiger's whiskers but also rode on the tiger's head."

The teacher Dōgen said: Guishan and Yangshan spoke very well, but they managed to speak only eighty or ninety percent. If it was Daibutsu, I would not say it that way. Suppose someone asked, "At that time did Linji attain the power of [Gao'an] Dayu, or the power of Huangbo?" I would say to him: The power of gruel and the power of rice. Although it is like this, who knows that Huangbo attained the power of Linji's staff, and [Gao'an] Dayu attained the power of Linji's fist?

Not Saying Alive, Not Saying Dead

161. Dharma Hall Discourse Requested by Bhikṣuṇī Eshin for Her Late Father[109]

Penetrating one dharma is penetrating ten thousand dharmas. Knowing the three elements of heaven, humanity, and earth is knowing all buddhas. So it is said, knowing benefaction is repaying benefaction.

I remember that Jianyuan [Zhongxing], at a donor's house on a condolence visit with [his teacher] Daowu, rubbed the casket and asked, "Alive or dead?"

Daowu said, "I don't say alive; I don't say dead."

Jianyuan asked, "Why won't you speak?"

Daowu said, "I won't say; I won't say."[110]

---

frustration and visited Gao'an Dayu, who had been recommended by Huangbo. When Linji told Gao'an about Huangbo's treatment of him, Gao'an said that Huangbo was a kind old grandmother, spending so much effort on Linji. Linji thereupon awakened, and said, "After all there's not much to Huangbo's Buddha Dharma." When Gao'an challenged Linji, Linji hit Gao'an three times. Gao'an Dayu then said that Huangbo was Linji's true teacher. After Linji returned to Huangbo and told the story, Linji slapped Huangbo, who said, "You returned again to touch the tiger's whiskers." See Watson, *Zen Teachings of Master Lin-chi,* pp. 104–107.

Another version of the dialogue about this story between Guishan and Yangshan appears right in the Recorded Sayings of Linji immediately after the previous story.

109 Nothing is known about the Bhikṣuṇī (nun) Eshin, whose name means Blessing Faith. Dōgen had a number of women disciples.

110 For the full story of this encounter between Jianyuan and his teacher Daowu, which later included Jianyuan beating up his teacher for refusing to answer him, see Leighton and Okumura, *Dōgen's Pure Standards for the Zen Community,* pp. 138–139.

The teacher Dōgen said: Alive or Dead! All buddhas of the three times don't know it is. Dead or Alive! Cats and white oxen do know it is.[111] Not saying alive, not saying dead, as of old, an iron ox lies down in smoke and sand.

"Why don't you speak?" The tongue is too long and the mouth is too narrow.

"I won't say; I won't say." A tiger and a tiger become intimate for the first time.

Showing the Jewel in the Black Moon
162. Dharma Hall Discourse

I remember, Yangshan visited Dongsi [Ruhui], and Dongsi asked, "Where did you come from?"

Yangshan said, "I come from Guangnan."

Dongsi said, "I have heard that in Guangnan there is a bright jewel that pacifies the ocean. Is it so or not?"

Yangshan said, "Yes it is."

Dongsi said, "What is its shape and quality?"

Yangshan said, "In the white moon (the moon waxing in the first half of the month), it is hidden. In the black moon (the moon waning in the second half of the month), it appears."

Dongsi said, "Have you brought it or not?"

Yangshan said, "I brought it."

Dongsi said, "Why don't you show it to me?"

Yangshan said, "In the past I visited Guishan and was asked for this jewel, and I directly understood that there is no word to respond with and no truth that can be reported."

Dongsi said, "A true lion's child has a great lion's roar."

The teacher Dōgen said: In the monasteries this situation is called a story of showing the jewel. What is this jewel? *Dōgen drew a circle with his whisk and said:* Isn't this it? Leaving this aside for a while, where do we show this jewel?

---

111 "All buddhas of the three times don't know it is. Cats and white oxen know it is" is a saying by Nanquan. See Cleary, *Book of Serenity,* case 69, pp. 290–294.

Then Dōgen said: We have enough rice and bean gruel for our daily functioning. Even if you clarify the place where you have exerted your energy, I give you thirty blows of the staff.

Sky Flowers Fluttering

163. Dharma Hall Discourse

An ancient person said, "When the eyes are clouded over, flowers in the sky flutter down."[112]

Dōgen held up his whisk and said: Isn't this a cloud over the eyes? A hundred thousand buddhas all dwell at the tip of this whisk, manifest a sixteen foot, purple and golden body, ride around all the lands in the ten directions, and expound all dharmas, saving all beings. Isn't this flowers in the sky fluttering down? All ancestral teachers travel to Liang and visit Wei [like Bodhidharma], transmitting the robe and entrusting the Dharma.[113] Isn't this flowers in the sky fluttering down?

Now if there is someone who arrived before I held up this whisk and who can tumble freely, please come forward and meet with me. If you are not [such a person], you should never reach the place where the eyes are not clouded over, and where there are no flowers in the sky. *Then Dōgen threw down the whisk to the foot of his sitting platform and said:* Nevertheless, you cannot avoid the fact that this year salt is expensive and rice is cheap.[114]

---

112 This is a saying by Guizong Zhichang from Jingde Transmission of the Lamp (Keitoku Dentōroku), vol. 10. "Flowers in the sky" is usually used in Buddhism as an image for illusions or hallucinations, but Dōgen takes them as the flowering of Dharma. Dōgen also discusses this in his Shōbōgenzō essay Kūge (Flowers in the Sky), written in 1243, three years before this Dharma hall discourse. See Cleary, *Shōbōgenzō: Zen Essays by Dōgen*, pp. 64–75. This image originally appears in the Śūraṅgama Sūtra, where Śākyamuni refers to a person with clouded-over eyes as seeing flowers in the sky, perhaps what are called "floaters" by modern optometrists, as "clouded eyes" is also sometimes an expression for cataracts. But the character *kū* for sky, or space, also means emptiness, and Dōgen uses the image of flowers in the sky positively as the flowering of emptiness.

113 Liang is where Bodhidharma encountered Emperor Wu, as described in case 1 of the Hekiganroku; see Cleary and Cleary, *Blue Cliff Record*, pp. 1–9. After he told Emperor Wu there was nothing sacred, and departed from Liang, Bodhidharma went north to Wei, where he sat in a cave for nine years.

114 "Salt is expensive and rice is cheap" is a saying by Zhaozhou from his Recorded Sayings. See Green, *Recorded Sayings of Zen Master Joshu*, p. 84.

How to Speak with Lips Shut

164. Dharma Hall Discourse

I remember that when Guishan, Wufeng [Changguan], and Yunyan were attending to Baizhang, Baizhang asked Guishan, "Close your throat and lips; how will you speak?"

Guishan said, "Teacher, instead of me, you should speak."

Baizhang said, "I will not avoid speaking to you, but I fear that I would be bereft of my descendants."

Baizhang also asked this of Wufeng, and Wufeng replied, "Teacher, you should also close your mouth."

Baizhang said, "Even where there is no person, I'll shade my eyes with my hand and gaze out at you."

Baizhang also asked Yunyan, and Yunyan replied, "Teacher, are you there or not?"

Baizhang said, "I have lost my descendants."[115]

The teacher Dōgen said: [Guishan's] "Teacher, instead of me, you should speak" is breaking his bones and returning them to his father.

[Wufeng's] "Teacher, you should also close your mouth" is borrowing a grandmother's skirt and bowing to her many years.

[Yunyan's] "Teacher, are you there or not?" is inconveniencing him so that his eyebrows drop away.[116]

Where Flowers Rain From

165. Dharma Hall Discourse

Here is a story. When Subhūti expounded Dharma, Indra caused flowers to rain. The Venerable Subhūti asked, "Did these flowers come from heaven?"

Indra said, "No."

"Did they come from earth?"

Indra said, "No."

"Did they come from people?"

---

115 This story about Baizhang appears in the Hekiganroku as cases 70, 71, and 72. See Cleary and Cleary, *Blue Cliff Record,* pp. 473–482.

116 "Eyebrows dropping off" is usually a negative expression for lying, but here Dōgen uses it as a positive image of total dropping away of body and mind, as he praises all three responses.

Indra said, "No."

"Where are they from?"

Indra raised his hands.

The Venerable Subhūti said, "So it is; so it is."

Yunmen said, "What is the meaning of Indra raising his hands? Are your four elements and five skandhas the same or different from old man Śākyamuni's?"[117]

The teacher Dōgen then said: The venerable Subhūti inquired in this way, but his questioning is not yet complete. Indra replied like that, but his answer is not yet complete. If this were Daibutsu, I would ask Indra: Are these flowers in this old monk's eyes, or flowers in Indra's eyes?

If I were Indra, I would say to Subhūti: Eye flowers, eye flowers.

When Subhūti asked, "Are these flowers from heaven, from earth, or from people?" if I were Indra I would tell him: The sky is clear because of these flowers. Earth is peaceful because of these flowers. And people flourish because of these flowers.[118]

Waiting while Subhūti is trying to say, "So it is; so it is," it would be good for Indra to hold up the flowers and have them rain on top of the Venerable Subhūti's head. It is very good that Indra raised his hands, but I'm afraid that the flowers raining was an hour late.

Today I ascend the seat in the Dharma hall for the sake of the great assembly at Daibutsu, and the expounding of Dharma resounds like roaring thunder. Certainly we will see flowers raining down in profusion.

Dōgen put down his whisk and said: Now I ask the great assembly, which is first, expounding the Dharma or flowers raining?[119]

---

117 This story is from the Recorded Sayings of Yunmen.

118 Heaven, earth, and humanity are the three elements of the world in Chinese culture (see Dharma hall discourse 161). But the character for heaven also means sky, so the image in Dōgen's response for Indra is of the rain of flowers leaving a cleared sky, as well as purifying Heaven.

119 The flowers raining is the manifestation or expression of Dharma. Dōgen's question relates to whether the manifestation is before, during, or after the expounding of Dharma.

Shitou Disturbs the Water Buffaloes

166. Dharma Hall Discourse

If you speak the first phrase, you will be deceived by a monk's staff. If you don't speak the first phrase, you will be deceived by a bottle gourd.[120] When we cut off phrases about this and that, at Great Compassion Temple villagers make food offerings.[121]

Swallowing such phrases as these, Master Shitou arrived at [his master] Qingyuan. That eyes are set in, and noses protrude is [an example of] the seven vertical and eight horizontal [or numberless, freely used expressions and perspectives]. Asking this ancestral teacher about essential meaning, [Shitou] nodded and swayed and struck emptiness a little bit. He asked about this true Dharma eye, then clapped his hands, laughed loudly, and fell to the ground. [Trying to] depict a tiger, he [only] ended up with a cat, and completely fell into becoming a wild-fox spirit, disturbing water buffaloes.

Strong Legs Cannot Avoid Deceiving the Teacher

167. Dharma Hall Discourse

Here is a story. A monk asked Baofu [Congzhan], "What kind of saying did Xuefeng use in his ordinary life so that he could resemble an antelope when it hangs by the horns [not leaving any tracks]?"[122]

Baofu said, "If I had not become Xuefeng's disciple, I would not have realized that."

---

120 A bottle gourd, or calabash, is a kind of vine, sometimes cited in Zen expressions for its intertwining. "The first phrase" refers to an utterance of ultimate reality.

121 "At Great Compassion Temple villagers make food offerings" is from a saying in the Recorded Sayings of Linji by Linji's eccentric friend Puhua. Puhua went around town proclaiming, "If you come from the bright, I'll hit you in the brightness; if you come from the dark, I'll hit you in the darkness.... Come from the empty sky and I'll hit you with so many flails." When Linji asked, what if he did not come in any of those ways, Puhua announced the donor's feast at Great Compassion Temple, the name of a temple near Linji. See Watson, Zen Teachings of Master Lin-chi, p. 87.

122 The image used to inquire of Baofu about his famous teacher Xuefeng is based on the Chinese folklore or fable that antelopes hung from trees by their horns when they slept, to avoid leaving any traces or tracks on the ground for hunters. Therefore, this apparently fantastic expression is an image for the everyday, a master appearing as nothing special. This story is from the Recorded Sayings of Yuanwu.

[Commenting on this story,] Zen Master Yuanwu said [about the traceless expression of Zen masters], "The feathers of peacocks and kingfishers, and the horn of a Chinese unicorn, resplendent with brilliant colors, have been transmitted from one to another.[123] If you want to understand the workings of catching a tiger, you should offer such a saying [as Baofu's], which is like a sheer cliff. Nevertheless, he only knows how to come like this; he doesn't know how to go like this. Suppose someone asked this mountain monk [Yuanwu], 'What kind of saying did Wuzu [Fayan, Yuanwu's teacher] use in his ordinary life so that he could resemble an antelope when it hangs by the horns [not leaving any tracks]?' Then I would simply say to him, 'I dare not oppose my late teacher.' Do you thoroughly understand this? Although the mountain is high, it does not obstruct the white clouds drifting by."

The teacher Dōgen said: Monks in my lineage are not like this. Knowing about such sayings, just enjoy a rest. Nevertheless, [Baofu and Yuanwu] only know to grow a horn on their heads, and don't know about having strength in their legs. Someone with an iron tongue and spike beak can bite through the model kōans from ancient or modern times. Suppose such a person asked this mountain monk [Dōgen], "What kind of saying did Tiantong [Rujing, Dōgen's teacher] use in his ordinary life so that he could resemble an antelope when it hangs by the horns [not leaving any tracks]?" I would simply say to him: I cannot avoid deceiving my late teacher.

The Moon Brings Forth Two
168. Dharma Hall Discourse
The moon brings forth one, we pick up a brush and record it as good fortune. The moon brings forth two, the clear intention of the ancestral teachers. The moon brings forth three; a thousand ancient ones submit to Gautama.[124] Although this is the case, is there a dragon or elephant here who can come forth and meet with Daibutsu's staff?

123 A Chinese unicorn, known as *kirin* in Japanese, is a fabulous animal with the body of a deer, the tail of an ox, horse hooves, a fleshy horn, and multicolored fur with a yellow belly. This animal represents sages, with the horn representing their main teaching.

124 "The moon brings forth one,...two,...three" derives from the saying by Laozi in

After a pause Dōgen said: [Although the same fruit,] it is called an orange in Huaibei [north of the Huai River], and called a tangerine in Huainan [south of the Huai River].

The Grass That Doesn't Enter through the Gate

169. Dharma Hall Discourse on the Fifth Day of the Fifth Month [1246][125]
Dōgen pounded his staff once and said: The fifth day of the fifth month is the Festival of the Center of Heaven, when people throughout the world wear a medicine pouch.[126] I remember that Sudhana studied with Mañjuśrī.[127] Mañjuśrī said, "Go out and bring back one stalk of medicinal herb." Sudhana left and looked throughout the entire earth, but there was nothing that was not medicine. He came back to Mañjuśrī and said, "The entire great earth is medicine. Which one should I pick and bring you?"

Mañjuśrī said, "Bring back one stalk of medicinal herb." Sudhana plucked one blade of grass and gave it to Mañjuśrī. Mañjuśrī held up the single blade, showed it to the assembly, and said, "This one blade of grass both can kill a person and can give them life."

The teacher Dōgen said: Do you want to study this story? When Sudhana said, "The entire great earth is medicine. Which one should I pick and bring you?" he had already brought one blade of grass. And yet, Sudhana could only see with his eyes, he could not yet understand with his heart.

Mañjuśrī said, "Bring back one stalk." Mañjuśrī, do you know the truth that what enters through the gate is not the family treasure? If you don't know yet, Mañjuśrī, although you have brought [one stalk], you are not yet intimate with it. When Sudhana went out the gate, he was too hasty

---

chapter 42 of the frequently translated classic, Dao De Jing: "The Way brings forth One; One brings forth Two; Two brings forth Three; Three brings forth all things. All things carry the dark and embrace the light and make them harmonize with empty energy." See Wu, *Book of Lao Tzu,* pp. 154–156.

125 The fifth day of the fifth month is one of the traditional East Asian festival days, commemorated as Boys' Day.

126 The Period of the Center of Heaven is the name for one of the twenty-four "periods" in the traditional yearly calendar.

127 For another version of this story about Mañjuśrī Bodhisattva and the pilgrim Sudhana in the Gaṇḍavyūha Sūtra, see Dharma hall discourse 16 and volume 1, note 44.

and careless moving through the grass. Before he could grasp and bring [one stalk], he had already trampled it.

Sudhana plucked one blade of grass and gave it to Mañjuśrī, thereby having brought one or two kōans. At this very time, these two persons have strength in their arms. Mañjuśrī received the grass and said, "This one blade of grass both can kill a person and can give them life." But how does this kill people and how does it give life to people?

Dōgen pounded his staff once and said: This is exactly what kills people. *Again he pounded his staff and said:* This is exactly what gives life to people. Without being caught up by these two sides, there is one further principle. Does the great assembly want to know it? *Dōgen pounded his staff once and got down from his seat.*

A Clear-Eyed Layman
170. Dharma Hall Discourse

Here is a story. Lay practitioner Ganzhi from Chizhou visited Nanquan, offered breakfast gruel, and requested Nanquan to perform a chant honoring buddhas. Nanquan entered the hall, struck the upright wooden sounding block, and announced, "Great Assembly, let us recite the Māhāprajñāpāramitā on behalf of [this person, who is like] cats or white oxen."[128] The layperson immediately departed and went down the mountain. After eating breakfast gruel, Nanquan left the hall and asked the tenzo (chief cook) if the layperson was still there. The tenzo said, "He immediately brushed out his sleeves and left." Nanquan then hit the gruel pot.

---

128 In Shōyōroku, case 69, Nanquan said, "All buddhas in the past, present, and future do not know it is. Cats and white oxen know it is." See Cleary, *Book of Serenity*, pp. 290–294. This could imply that cats and white oxen have delusions based on how they see the world; whereas buddhas know that they cannot know the ultimate. But on the other hand, one might understand this saying as describing ordinary, humble creatures, without discriminating consciousness, as more fully aware even than buddhas. Therefore, cats and white oxen could be an image of the deluded, karmic self, or an image of awakened awareness. This story about Nanquan and the lay donor is from the Jingde Transmission of the Lamp (Keitoku Dentōroku), vol. 10. In Nanquan's original saying, and in Dōgen's comment on this story, cats and white oxen seem to be considered in the positive, awakened sense.

Dōgen said: [Nanquan] chanted the Māhāprajñāpāramitā searching for cats or white oxen. Even though Nanquan hit the gruel pot, how can he be as clear as the layman descending the mountain?

A Black Staff on Full-Moon Day
171. Dharma Hall Discourse
Before the fifteenth day (the full moon), if we do not sleep alike at our places in the monks' hall, how can we know that our quilt covering is worn through?[129] After the fifteenth day, when the pivotal wheel has not yet turned, if it turns it certainly will proceed including both sides.[130] Right on the fifteenth day, no matter how green or red the ancient wall, waiting for autumn the crickets sing. This being so, in the Daibutsu assembly, how can we raise this aloft?

Meeting with the ancient awl on Vulture Peak [Śākyamuni Buddha], we certainly open our hands and let go. Deceiving the old smelly barbarian at Caoxi [Bodhidharma], our hearts are worn soft and settle down.[131] Do you all want to thoroughly understand this truth?

After a pause Dōgen said: Every day I expound to people with my vital organs. How black the lacquer is on this single staff.[132]

A Buddha Ancestor at Your Feet
172. Dharma Hall Discourse
Buddha after Buddha extend their hands; ancestor after ancestor transmit

129 The fifteenth day of the month is the full moon, which represents enlightenment. So before the fifteenth day implies practice before awakening. This Dharma hall discourse was given on the fifteenth day of the fifth month in 1246. In the traditional monks' hall, monks slept at their sitting place, using for bedding a quilt that, during the day, was folded up in a cabinet at the head of their sitting place. "If we do not sleep alike at our places in the monks' hall..." is from the commentary to Hekiganroku, case 40. See Cleary and Cleary, *Blue Cliff Record,* p. 295.

130 "When the pivotal wheel has not yet turned..." is from the verse commentary to Hekiganroku, case 65. See Cleary and Cleary, *Blue Cliff Record,* p. 415. After awakening, first there is silence. When the wheel of teaching is expounded verbally, then both ultimate and conventional realities are included.

131 "Deceiving" a teacher has been used by Dōgen as an expression for becoming a successor to and surpassing one's teacher. See Dharma hall discourse 48 and the end of Dharma hall discourse 167. "Worn soft" is literally to tan and soften a hide.

132 Blackness connotes purity and nondiscrimination, with nothing mixed in.

to each other. What do they transmit to each other and what do they hand over? If the great assembly now knows its ultimate position, then the buddhas of past, present, and future, and the six generations of ancestral teachers [in China] wear through their sandals and break their wooden ladles, exhausting their strength in the effort, without being willing to stop. If you hesitate, I will remain at your feet.[133]

Thirty Incoherent Years of Fragrant Wind
173. Dharma Hall Discourse

Within ten thousand forms I appear alone; above the hundred grasses we meet each other. I do not see beyond my portion. The other does not see beyond his portion. For thirty years I have not been able to give a coherent explanation. Throughout the twenty-four hours, nothing hits the mark. So it is said, this is not divine power or wondrous function, and is not the Dharma as such. At this very moment, how is it?

After a pause Dōgen said: Today's eating bowl is like yesterday's. Tasting the arising of fragrant winds is itself the wind of spring.

Dye the Clouds White and Wash the Moon
174. Dharma Hall Discourse

What is higher than heaven is that which arises in heaven. What is thicker than earth is that which arises in earth. What is vaster than empty space is that which arises in empty space. What goes beyond buddhas and ancestors are those who arise from buddhas and ancestors.

Although this is so, for what reason does this abide on the eyebrows, for what reason does it abide in a grain of millet or rice? At this very time it is easy to clarify the essential within a phrase, but it is difficult to distinguish a phrase within the essential. The mind cannot relate to it; the mouth cannot discuss it. We should directly take a step back [in reflection], and then carry it carefully. Never go and stick your head into it. Everyone, do you want to thoroughly understand this?

After a pause Dōgen said: Carry the cleared sky and dye the clouds white; bring water from the valley stream to wash bright the moon.

---

133 "I will remain at your feet" implies Dōgen's pledge to continue to support the monks' practice.

The Moon in the Window

175. Dharma Hall Discourse

I remember that Zhaozhou asked Nanquan, "Where will the person go who knows it is?"

Nanquan said, "This person will go to a patron's house down the mountain and become a water buffalo."

Zhaozhou said, "I am grateful for the teacher's answer."

Nanquan said, "Last night at midnight the moon came in the window."

The teacher Dōgen said: Before the ox and after the person, there is an eye within the eye. The one who knows it is has a long nose. He is able to tie up last night's moon in the window. At midnight, as always, the mountain hall is illuminated.

Temporarily Wearing Dirty Clothes

176. Dharma Hall Discourse

When you directly take a step forward, you cannot avoid trespassing on the grasses and waters of the king. When you directly take a step back, you cannot avoid trampling the rice paddies of your grandfather. Without taking a step forward or backward, is there any path of emancipation?

After a pause Dōgen said: Temporarily wearing dirty clothes is what is called Buddha. When donning luxurious attire, who is it?

Renaming Eiheiji, Eternal Peace

177. Dharma Hall Discourse on the Occasion of Renaming Daibutsuji as Eiheiji (on the Fifteenth day of the Sixth Month in the Fourth Year of Kangen Period [1246])[134]

When heaven has the way, it is high and clear, when the earth has the way it is substantial and at rest, when people have the way, they are calm and peaceful. Therefore, when the World-Honored One descended and was

---

134 This Dharma hall discourse was given the day that Dōgen changed the name of Daibutsuji (Great Buddha Temple) to Eiheiji (Eternal Peace Temple), the name which it still has. A note in the text, presumably added by the compiler of volume 2, Koun Ejō, gives the date. Beginning with this Dharma hall discourse, Dōgen refers to himself as Eihei, rather than Daibutsu.

born, he pointed one hand to the heaven and one hand to the earth, took seven steps in each direction and said, "Above the heavens and below the heaven, I alone am the Honored One." Even though the World-Honored One had such a way, I, Eihei, have a way for the great assembly to verify.[135]

After a pause Dōgen said: Above the heavens and below the heaven, this very place is Eihei (Eternally Peaceful).

The Capacity of Students
178. Dharma Hall Discourse
Students must be endowed with the eyes of a patch-robed monk before they are capable. If you are already endowed with the eyes of a patch-robed monk, your eyes must be transformed into soapberry wood [for making a rosary] by your mentor, before you are capable.[136] If your eyes have been changed into soapberry wood, you will not be deceived by the great earth, by the entire heaven, by buddha ancestors, or by a monk's staff. Plunging into water or fire, you will not be drowned or burned. Whether seeing buddhas or seeing demons, wherever you are you are free.

After a pause Dōgen said: How do you understand what I have been saying? If you have it, come forth and demonstrate this for the assembly, and Eihei will affirm that the great matter of your study is complete. If it is not yet the case, this monk's staff will laugh at you. Although this may be so, if I call you such a person [who is not yet capable], then my eyebrows will fall out [from lying].

The Space of Returning to the Source
179. Dharma Hall Discourse
The World-Honored One said, "When one person opens up reality and returns to the source, all space in the ten directions disappears."[137]

---

135 This sentence might more commonly be read as "Even though the World-Honored One spoke thus, I [Dōgen] have a statement for the great assembly to verify." But since Dōgen—when speaking earlier of heaven, earth, and humanity—used the character that could be read as "statement" to mean "way," the phrase in this sentence probably also means "have a way."

136 For soapberry wood and rosaries, see Dharma hall discourse 143.

137 This statement of the Buddha's is from the Śūraṅgama Sūtra, chap. 9. These quotations are also cited and discussed by Dōgen in his Shōbōgenzō essay Tembōrin (Turning

Teacher Wuzu of Mount Fayan said, "When one person opens up reality and returns to the source, all space in the ten directions crashes together resounding everywhere."

Zen Master Yuanwu Keqin of Jiashan said, "When one person opens up reality and returns to the source, in all space in the ten directions flowers are added on brocade."

Teacher Fuxing Fatai said, "When one person opens up reality and returns to the source, all space in the ten directions is simply all space in the ten directions."

My late teacher Tiantong [Rujing] said, "Although the World-Honored One made the statement 'When one person opens up reality and returns to the source, all space in the ten directions disappears,' this utterance cannot avoid becoming an extraordinary assessment. Tiantong is not like this. When one person opens up reality and returns to the source, a mendicant breaks his rice bowl."

The teacher Dōgen said: The previous five venerable teachers said it like this, but I, Eihei, have a saying that is not like theirs. When one person opens up reality and returns to the source, all space in the ten directions opens up reality and returns to the source.

Maitreya Expounds Just This
180. Dharma Hall Discourse
I remember that Vasubandhu descended from Maitreya's inner palace. Asaṅga asked [his brother Vasubandhu], "Four hundred years in the human realm is one day and night in [Maitreya's] heaven. At one time, Maitreya led five hundred billion heavenly beings to realize completely the tolerance of the unconditioned nature of all things.[138] I do not understand, what Dharma did he expound to them?"

Vasubandhu said, "He only expounded the Dharma of just this [as it is]." Hearing this, Asaṅga immediately had attainment.

---

the Dharma Wheel). See Tanahashi, *Enlightenment Unfolds*, pp. 196–198.

138 "The tolerance of the unconditioned nature of all things" is *anutpattika dharma kṣānti* in Sanskrit. This refers to the ultimate insight of patience with the incomprehensibility, ungraspability, or emptiness of any entity or category.

Eihei Dōgen then asked: In the past, present, and future, how are fists and headtops, the pillars and the lanterns, the Dharma of just this? A monk's staff never reaches it; a whisk is no use. Isn't this a flower opening and closing? Isn't this sweeping the ground and sweeping the sitting platform in the monks' hall?

After a pause Dōgen said: The oceans in the three thousand lands completely become autumn. The bright moon illuminates and chills the coral.[139]

Simply the Yellow Scroll
181. Dharma Hall Discourse

I remember that a monk asked Shishuang [Qingzhu], "Is the intention of the ancestral teacher [Bodhidharma] within the sutras?"

Shishuang said, "It's there."

The monk said, "What is the intention of the ancestral teacher within the sutras?"

Shishuang said, "Do not seek it within those scrolls."

Yunmen said on behalf of Shishuang, "Do not be ungrateful to the old monk. What are you doing, sitting in a pile of shit?"[140]

The teacher Dōgen said: These two old masters said it right, but I'm afraid they only got eighty or ninety percent. Suppose someone asked Eihei, "Is the intention of the ancestral teacher within the sutras?" I would say to him: If it is not within the sutras, how could there be any intention of the ancestral teacher? If he then asked, "What is the intention of the ancestral teacher within the sutras?" I would say to him: Simply the yellow scroll, and the red spindle [that the sutra is rolled up on]. What is it ultimately?

Dōgen threw his whisk down in front of the steps below his sitting platform, and descended from his seat.

---

139 "The oceans in the three thousand lands...chills the coral" is a quotation from Tiantong Hongzhi's Extensive Record, vol. 4; except that Hongzhi originally says for the second part, "The bright moon and coral are cool and illuminate each other."

140 This dialogue of Shishuang with Yunmen's added comment is in the Recorded Sayings of Yunmen. Yunmen speaks of the sutras as the leftover excrement of buddhas. See App, *Master Yunmen,* p. 179.

Seeing the Buddha as a Tile Maker

182. Dharma Hall Discourse

My original teacher, Great Master Śākyamuni Buddha was a tile maker in a previous life.[141] His name was Great Radiance. At that time there was a buddha whose name was also Śākyamuni Buddha. The longevity, epithets, land, disciples, and the durations of the ages of true Dharma and of semblance Dharma of that world-honored Buddha were completely the same as for the present Buddha.[142] That Buddha, together with his disciples, visited the tile maker's house and stayed overnight. The tile maker offered grass seats, lamps, and rock candy water to the Buddha and his monks, and aroused a vow, "In the future, I will become a buddha in the world of five defilements in the final age of Dharma, and the lifespans of the Buddha and his disciples, and the epithets, the land, the height, the true Dharma, and the semblance Dharma of that Buddha will be completely the same as the present Śākyamuni Buddha, without any difference."

Just as in that ancient vow, today he has become the Buddha, and the land, disciples, true Dharma, semblance Dharma, longevity, and epithets all are the same as those of the ancient Śākyamuni Buddha.

In Echizen Province in Japan, I, monk Dōgen, the founder of Eihei Temple, also arouse a vow: In the future, I will become a buddha in the world of five defilements in the final age of Dharma, and the Buddha and

---

141 This story about one of Śākyamuni Buddha's past lives is from the Commentary on the Mahāprajñāpāramitā Sūtra (Ch.: Dazhidulun; Jap.: Daichidoron), translated by Kumārajīva, and attributed to Nāgārjuna. Many stories that Dōgen cites from the early teachings and from Śākyamuni's life appear in the Nikāyas of the Pali Suttas. But Dōgen usually quotes the versions of these stories that appear in this Mahāprajñāpāramitā Śāstra, or Commentary. So references in these footnotes will most often mention the section from this Commentary from which Dōgen cites them. Modern scholars believe that this text, translated by Kumārajīva, was not actually written by Nāgārjuna, though it is attributed to him traditionally. See Paul Williams, *Mahāyāna Buddhism: The Doctrinal Foundations* (London: Routledge, 1989), pp. 44, 56–57, 74–75, 174–175; and Sangharakshita, *The Eternal Legacy: An Introduction to the Canonical Literature of Buddhism* (London: Tharpa Publications, 1985), p. 147.

142 The ages of True Dharma and Semblance Dharma refer to a Buddhist theory of the degeneration of a buddha land. Supposedly the Buddha realm degenerates from the ages of True Dharma and Semblance Dharma to the final age of Dharma, and many of Dōgen's contemporaries believed the final degenerate age had arrived, although Dōgen generally refuted this theory and considered it a merely expedient teaching.

his disciples, the land, the epithets, the true Dharma, the semblance Dharma, the height, and the longevity of that Buddha will be the same as today's original teacher Śākyamuni Buddha, without any difference.[143]

I simply wish that the three treasures of Buddha, Dharma, and Sangha, the heavenly beings, the earthly beings, the cloud and water assemblies of monks, and this monk's staff and whisk would verify this vow. Nevertheless, the present Śākyamuni Buddha has himself resided in the country of the ancient Śākyamuni Buddha, and when the Buddha and his disciples stayed at his house, he offered them grass seats and rock candy and aroused his vow. Now he has accomplished that vow. Currently, does Dōgen also see the present Śākyamuni Buddha and the Buddha's disciples, and hear the Buddha expounding the Dharma?

Śākyamuni Buddha said (in the Lotus Sutra chapter on the Bodhisattvas' Emerging from the Ground), "If one sees my body and hears my teaching and then completely trusts and accepts it, then one enters the Tathāgata's wisdom."[144] Having heard the Buddha's teaching is like already seeing the Buddha's body. When one first sees the Buddha's body, one naturally is able to accept it and have faith, and enter the Tathāgata's wisdom. Furthermore, seeing Buddha's body with your ears, hearing Buddha's preaching with your eyes, and similarly for all six sense objects, is also like entering and residing in Buddha's house, and entering buddhahood and arousing the vow, exactly the same as in the ancient vow, without any difference.

A Repentance Ceremony after Ninety Days in Buddha's Hand
183. Dharma Hall Discourse at the Closing of Summer Practice Period [1246]
Uphold the essence of the true directive. Geese drinking water enjoy its genuine flavor, penetrating the way in a straight line. Bees taking nectar

---

143 The world of five defilements is in chapter 2 of the Lotus Sutra, "Skillful Means," which says that buddhas enter an evil world stained with these five: the defilement of the kalpa, the defilement of afflictions (kleśa), the defilement of beings, the defilement of views, and the defilement of life-span. See Hurvitz, *Scripture of the Lotus Blossom of the Fine Dharma*, p. 31.

144 The note about the citation from chapter 15 of the Lotus Sutra text is added, apparently by the compiler of this volume, Koun Ejō. See Leon Hurvitz, *Scripture of the Lotus Blossom of the Fine Dharma*, p. 227.

from flowers do not damage the remaining fragrance. At the end of the practice period we speak in the repentance ceremony, and the world in all ten directions at the same time speaks the repentance ceremony.[145] The sitting cushions have fully completed another year of their Dharma age, and the world in all ten directions at the same time has fully completed another year of Dharma age. Therefore, those with mind know, and what is without mind attains it. For the guest it functions, in the host it is venerated. According to their position, their effort is clear; according to their effort, their position is clear.[146] The spirits of father and children harmonize; the ways of lord and minister join together.

After a pause, Dōgen looked over all the monks and said: We have played for ninety days with Gautama's single hand. Extending a trusty hand, he passed along a wooden ladle by the handle. Consequently, clouds and water monks in the monastery who practice repentance are joyful together.

A Memorial to Tiantong Rujing, Deceived by Dōgen
184. Dharma Hall Discourse on the Memorial Day for Tiantong Rujing [1246]
When I entered China I studied walking to be like someone from Handan.[147] I worked very hard carrying water and hauling firewood. Don't say that my late teacher deceived his disciple. Rather, Tiantong was deceived by Dōgen.

---

145 The repentance ceremony (Skt: *uposatha;* Jap.: *fusatsu*) is done traditionally twice a month, on the full moon and new moon. In India, monks confessed their own violations of precepts to the other monks. Today the ceremony involves a ritual chanting of a general acknowledgment and repentance for unwholesome karma from many lifetimes. We do not know how the ceremony was done in Dōgen's time at Eiheiji, but within a few generations after Dōgen's time, in Keizan's monastic guidelines, the ceremony involved ritual chanting.

146 "According to their position, their effort is clear; according to their effort, their position is clear" is from Hongzhi's Extensive Record, vol. 8.

147 "Studying walking to be like someone from Handan" is a reference to a story by Zhuangzi in the chapter on "Autumn Water." In this story someone from the countryside went to the city of Handan and imitated the fashionable walking of the townspeople. But before he had succeeded in mastering their walking, he had forgotten his own country walking, and had to crawl home on his hands and knees. See Burton Watson, trans., *The Complete Works of Chuang Tzu* (New York: Columbia University Press, 1968), p. 187; or Sam Hamill and J. P. Seaton, trans., *The Essential Chuang Tzu* (Boston: Shambhala, 1999), p. 92. The memorial day for Tiantong Rujing was the seventeenth day of the seventh

In another version,[148] *Dōgen said:* When I entered China I studied walking to be like someone from Handan. I worked very hard carrying water and hauling firewood. Don't say that the King of Chin deceived Zhao to get their jewel.[149] Rather, Tiantong was deceived by Dōgen.

---

month. Other memorial Dharma hall discourses for him in Eihei Kōroku are discourses 249, 274, 276, 342, 384, and 515.

148 This is a different version of this same Dharma hall discourse included by the compiler Koun Ejō, presumably also written by Dōgen. This second version is not included by Manzan in his edition.

149 "The King of Chin deceived Zhao to get their jewel" is a reference to an ancient story about the king of Chin (ca. 250 B.C.E.), who promised fifteen cities in exchange for a famous large jewel that belonged to the king of Zhao. Handan was the capital city of Zhao. Upon receiving the jewel, Chin tried to renege on his promise, but the wise Minister Xiangru of Zhao was himself able to deceive the king of Chin and get the jewel back home safely. See Burton Watson, trans., *Han Fei Tzu: Basic Writings* (New York: Columbia University Press, 1969), p. 80.

EIHEI ZENJI GOROKU

RECORDED SAYINGS
AT EIHEIJI TEMPLE

COLLECTED BY EJŌ, ATTENDANT OF DŌGEN ZENJI

```
E  K
I  ō
H  R
E  O
I  K
   U
```

THE EXTENSIVE RECORD OF EIHEI DŌGEN, VOLUME THREE

The Teacher's Compassion and Disciple's Determination

185. Dharma Hall Discourse Given at the Request of Head Monk Ekan in Memorial for His Late Teacher, Wayfarer Kakuan[1]

After offering incense, Dōgen took his seat, held up his whisk, and said: Who can equal Ekan in their conduct of filial responsibility? Today's memorial dedication will be clearly examined by the [departed] sacred spirit. The deep determination of the disciple yearning for his late teacher is known only by the late teacher. The late teacher's compassion while sympathizing with his disciple is known only by the disciple. How can someone else know it? People without [such a relationship] cannot match it. So it is said, it cannot be known with mind, it cannot be attained without mind, it cannot be reached by practice-enlightenment, and it cannot be measured with spiritual power. Having reached this ground, how can it be calculated?

Dōgen pounded his staff and said: Only this staff always knows it distinctly. Why does the staff always know it distinctly? Because this is the

---

1 This first Dharma hall discourse of volume 3, given in summer of 1246, was requested by Dōgen's disciple Kakuzen Ekan (d. 1251). Ekan was a Dharma heir of Bucchi Kakuan (n.d.), who was himself a Dharma heir of Dainichi Nōnin (n.d.), founder of the Daruma sect. Koun Ejō had also been a disciple of Kakuan. Ekan became a disciple of Dōgen in 1241, bringing with him his disciples Tettsū Gikai (1219–1309), Kangan Giin (1217–1300), and Eihei Gien (d. 1314), who all became prominent disciples of Dōgen. Tettsū Gikai became the Dharma heir of Koun Ejō (1198–1280).

case, all buddhas in the past are thus, all buddhas in the present are thus, and all buddhas in the future are thus. Although this is so, this is exactly the affair of the buddha ancestors' realm. How is this the true principle of knowing and repaying our debt of kindness?

After a pause Dōgen said: Alas for the days of the past, [as the teacher becomes] a single piece of emptiness. Confused by flowers in the eyes, the great earth is red. Blood and tears filling my chest, to whom can I speak? I only wish that [the teaching of] this staff would spread widely. These are the very sayings that know and repay our debt of kindness.

What is this matter of going beyond buddhas and ancestors?

Dōgen threw his staff down before the platform, and descended from his seat.

The Moon Comes Naturally to the Pond
186. Dharma Hall Discourse

I remember that one day when Fayan was sitting, suddenly he pointed to the curtains in front of him [at the entry to the meditation hall]. At that time, two monks went and rolled up the curtains in the same manner.

Fayan said, "One attained; one lost."[2]

The teacher Dōgen said: I, Eihei do not speak like that.

After a pause Dōgen said: Creating a pond, do not wait for the moon. When you have built a pond, naturally the moon will come.[3]

Bodhidharma's Single Utterance
187. Dharma Hall Discourse

For nine years Bodhidharma bestowed a single utterance. Until now, people in various regions have mistakenly taken it up. Do you want to demonstrate it without mistakes? Eihei will again demonstrate it for the sake of all of you. The Iron Ring mountains surround Mount Sumeru at

---

2 This story appears in the Shōyōroku, case 27, and the Mumonkan, case 26. See Cleary, *Book of Serenity*, pp. 116–119; Cleary, *Unlocking the Zen Kōan*, pp. 125–128; and Aitken, *Gateless Barrier*, pp. 166–170.

3 "Creating a pond...the moon will come" is from Hongzhi's Extensive Record, vol. 4. A pond completely reflects the light of the full moon, but the pond can be prepared before the moon is full. If you build it, the moon will come. The evaluations and judgments are irrelevant.

the center.[4] This is just exactly right. Thus it is demonstrated completely. However, is it possible to demonstrate it unmistakably?

After a pause Dōgen said: The jade woman recalls her dream of the triple world. The wooden man sits, cutting off functioning of the six senses.[5]

Dōgen descended from his seat.

A Peaceful Lifetime of Wearing Through Straw Sandals

188. Dharma Hall Discourse

Under the heavens all is very peaceful. Wherever the monk's staff travels, you can eat rice. All the myriad common people have peace and bliss. Whenever [there is teaching] amid temple pillars, flowers blossom. Therefore, a smile broke out on Mahākāśyapa's face, and [Dazu] Huike made prostrations and attained the marrow. Having arrived at this field, then practice a full lifetime. What is the reason for this? Unless you climb a great mountain, you will not know the heights of heaven. Unless you cross the blue depths, you will not know the ocean's expanse. If one is a practitioner, heaven exists within one grain of millet, the ocean exists on the tip of a hair. The Flower Treasury World of Constant Tranquil Radiance is completely included in our eyebrows and eyelashes.[6] Please tell me, in what place does this [practice] person pacify the body and establish a life?[7] Do you thoroughly understand?

4 In Indian Buddhist cosmology, Mount Sumeru is the axial center of the world, surrounded by nine Iron Ring mountains. So Dōgen is just describing the reality of the world, as it is traditionally conceived in Buddhism.

5 This particular reference to the jade woman and wooden man is from Hongzhi's Extensive Record, vol. 1. The image of wooden man and stone (or jade) woman originally goes back to Dongshan's Song of the Precious Mirror Samādhi (Jap.: Hōkyō Zammai). See Leighton and Wu, *Cultivating the Empty Field*, p. 77. The triple world comprises the realms of desire, of form, and the formless realm. All three realms, including the lofty formless realm, are included in the rounds of transmigration, or samsāra.

6 The Flower Treasury World is the name used in the Avataṃsaka (Flower Ornament) Sūtra for the Buddha field of the dharmakāya, or total reality body, Vairocana Buddha. Constant Tranquil Radiance is a name used in the Lotus Sutra for the Buddha field of the dharmakāya buddha, who is sometimes identified in commentaries with the Śākyamuni Buddha of inconceivable life-span revealed in the Lotus Sutra. Here Dōgen combines the names for the ultimate reality realms from these two great sutras.

7 To "pacify the body and establish a life" recalls the common Buddhist expression for penetrating the Dharma and establishing faith. However, it is usually stated as "pacify the mind and establish a life."

After a pause Dōgen said: Crossing mountains and rivers, you polish and break straw sandals. Having accomplished this, just as before you are still deceived by your eyes.

The Moon Produces Joyful Vigor
189. Mid-Autumn Dharma Hall Discourse [1246]
In the heavens the moon is round and vast as the ancient mirror; in the middle of the month in the human realm, the full moon extends over the entire world. In the dark it rolls up two or three thousand, in the light it unfolds to pervade throughout seven or eight. [Seeing the moon as like] the eyeballs of the seven buddhas produces joyful laughter; [seeing it as like] Yunmen's sesame cake brings an uproarious clamor.[8] Having arrived at such a field, can you enjoy your practice like this or not?

After a pause Dōgen said: Illuminating hundreds of grasses in many lands, everywhere a toad is jumping around with vigor.[9]

Abiding in Mountains without Personal Preferences
190. Dharma Hall Discourse in Appreciation of the New and Previous Inō and Guest Managers[10]
Because these people have [third] eyes on their crowns, they can thoroughly illuminate the ten directions. Because they directly indicate how to conduct affairs without personal preference, they do not harbor a single predilection. They unlock the gateway to Magadha, and take up and reveal the profound function of Jetavana Vihāra.[11] Truly, each hit of the sounding block by the inō manifests many buddhas, and the guest manager's meeting with visitors turns the great Dharma wheel. This is not due to divine power or wondrous function, and also is not merely the

8 Yunmen, when asked what goes beyond speaking of buddhas and ancestors, answered, "Sesame cake." See Cleary and Cleary, *Blue Cliff Record,* case 77, pp. 506–509; and Cleary, *Book of Serenity,* case 78, pp. 332–334. The seven buddhas refer to a traditional Mahāyāna list of the prehistorical buddhas, with Śākyamuni as the seventh Buddha.

9 The moon is symbolized by a toad, like the rabbit seen in the moon, or the Western "man in the moon."

10 The *inō* is the manager of the meditation hall and supervisor of the monks' conduct. The guest manager, *shika* in Japanese, welcomes and takes care of visitors to the monastery.

11 Magadha is the kingdom containing Bodhgayā, where Śākyamuni realized awakening, and Jetavana Vihāra was the monastery where he taught.

natural manner of things. Already such manifestations have been accomplished. So tell me, who could achieve this?

After a pause Dōgen said: For the time being, abiding on top of the ten thousand peaks, I will wait above the mountains, grasping my monk's staff.

When Tired I Sleep

191. Dharma Hall Discourse

I remember that a monk asked Touzi [Datong], "What are the causes and conditions of this single great matter?"

Touzi said, "Minister Yin asked me to open the hall and give a Dharma hall discourse."[12]

The teacher Dōgen said: If it had been Eihei, I would not have spoken like this. Suppose someone asks me, "What are the causes and conditions of this single great matter?" I would just say to him: In the early morning I eat gruel and at noon I eat rice. Feeling strong, I practice zazen; when tired I sleep.

Small Fish Swallow Big Fish

192. Dharma Hall Discourse

I remember that a monk asked Yantou [Quanhuo], "How is the time before the ancient sail is unfurled?"

Yantou said, "Small fish swallow big fish."

If you want to understand this situation, listen to this verse by Eihei:

> Small fish swallow big fish;
> A Buddhist priest reads a Confucian text.
> Escaping from the net of buddhas and demons,
> Sweep away the dusts of the teachings.

12 This story is from the Jingde Transmission of the Lamp (Keitoku Dentōroku), vol. 15. Minister Yin is unknown, but presumably he was an important government official and lay devotee.

Thinking That Circles the Earth

193. Dharma Hall Discourse

This morning is the first day of the ninth month [of 1246].[13] Let us take out the cushions and practice zazen. The custom of not sitting before the ninth month is not observed precipitously at this monastery, and also zazen is not omitted before the fifth day meal.[14] Our thinking during immovable sitting circles the earth; our boundless karmic consciousness fills the heavens. Although this is so, do you want to understand the key to the gateway of going beyond?

After a pause Dōgen said: In the morning hitting three thousand, in the evening eight hundred, if you truly get the inner workings, never mistakenly circulate it.[15]

Rocks Nod and Sky Vanishes

194. Dharma Hall Discourse

As I remember, a monk asked an ancient worthy [Guizong Daoquan], "Is there Buddha Dharma or not on a steep cliff in the deep mountains?"

The worthy responded, "A large rock is large; a small one is small."

My late teacher Tiantong [Rujing] said, "The question about the steep cliff in the deep mountains was answered in terms of large and small rocks. The cliff collapsed, the rocks split, and the empty sky filled with a noisy clamor."

The teacher Dōgen said: Although these two venerable masters said it this way, I, Eihei, have another utterance to convey. If someone were to

---

13 In China, during the three months before the first day of the ninth month, because of the heat, meditation in the monastery was optional. However, in his early collection of talks, Shōbōgenzō Zuimonki, Dōgen says that when he was in China he himself kept up his zazen practice during the hot periods. See Shohaku Okumura, trans., *"Shōbōgenzō-Zuimonki," Sayings of Eihei Dōgen Zenji Recorded by Koun Ejō* (Kyoto: Kyoto Sōtō Zen Center, 1987), pp. 48–49.

14 Every fifth day, those ending with four or nine, is traditionally a day with a relaxed schedule in Zen monasteries, without meetings with the teacher. Our interpretation of this passage is that at Eiheiji, unlike Chinese monasteries, zazen was scheduled as usual on these fifth days.

15 "In the morning hitting three thousand, in the evening eight hundred" appears in the commentary to the last line of case 61 of the Hekiganroku, and refers to ceaseless practice from morning to night. See Cleary and Cleary, *Blue Cliff Record*, p. 396.

ask, "Is there Buddha Dharma or not on a steep cliff in the deep mountains?" I would simply say to him: The lifeless rocks nod their heads again and again.[16] The empty sky vanishes completely. This [kind of expression] is an affair existing within the realm of the buddha ancestors. What is [the reality of] such an affair within the steep cliff in the deep mountains?

Dōgen pounded his staff once, and descended from his seat.

A Demonstration of the Six Spiritual Powers
195. Dharma Hall Discourse

A capable master must be endowed with the six spiritual powers. The first is the power to go anywhere; second is the power to hear everywhere; third is the power to know others' minds; fourth is the power to know previous lives; fifth is the power to see everywhere; sixth is the power to extinguish outflows [attachments].

Everyone, do you want to see the power to go anywhere?
The teacher Dōgen raised his fist.

Do you want to see the power to know others' minds?
Dōgen let one of his legs hang down from his seat.

Do you want to see the power of hearing everywhere?
Dōgen snapped his fingers once.

Do you want to see the power of knowing previous lives?
Dōgen raised his whisk.

Do you want to see the power of seeing everywhere?
Dōgen drew a circle in the air with his whisk.

Do you want to see the power of extinguishing outflows?
Dōgen drew a single horizontal line [the character for "one"] with his whisk and said: Although this is so, ultimately, six times six is thirty-six.[17]

---

16 "The lifeless rocks nod their heads again and again" is a reference to Kumārajīva's great disciple and early Chinese Buddhist scholar, Daosheng. Daosheng saw in the Mahāparinirvāṇa Sūtra that all beings can become Buddha, so he went to the mountain and expounded the Dharma to the rocks. The rocks nodded in response.

17 "Six times six is thirty-six" is simple, like "one plus one equals two." So this could be understood as saying that spiritual powers are simple, everyday matters. But "six times six is thirty-six" also implies many powers beyond just six, indicating that there are not just thirty-six but innumerable spiritual powers.

Extending a Simple Wish for Health and Blessings

196. Dharma Hall Discourse

After relating the story of National Teacher Great Realization [Nanyang Huizhong] examining Tripitaka Master Da'er,[18] the teacher Dōgen said:
Numbers of people have taken up this story. There was a monk who asked Zhaozhou, "Tripitaka Master Da'er didn't see the national teacher the third time. Where was the national teacher?"

Zhaozhou said, "He was on the tripitaka master's nose."

A monk asked Xuansha, "Already on the [tripitaka master's] nose, why couldn't he be seen?"

Xuansha said, "Simply because he was so close."

A monk asked Yangshan, "Why didn't Tripitaka Master Da'er see the national teacher the third time?"

Yangshan said, "The first two times the [national teacher's] mind was interacting with objects, but later he entered the self-fulfilling samādhi, so he couldn't be seen."[19]

Haihui [Shou]duan said, "If the national teacher was on the nose of the tripitaka master, why was he difficult to see? [Zhaozhou] especially did not realize that the tripitaka master was in the national teacher's eyeball."

18 For the story of National Teacher Nanyang Huizhong examining Tripitaka Master Da'er, see Dharma hall discourse 17 and volume 1, note 45. "Great Realization" (Dazhang) was a posthumous honorific name given by the emperor to the national teacher.

To recount the basic story briefly, in the eighth century Tripitaka Master Da'er arrived from India to the Tang dynasty capital, claiming that he had the wisdom eye, which has the power to know others' minds. National Teacher Nanyang Huizhong tested him and asked Da'er where the national teacher was now (in his thoughts). Da'er responded that, though he was teacher of the nation, Huizhong was watching boat races. Nanyang Huizhong asked a second time, and the tripitaka master replied that the national teacher was on a famous bridge watching monkeys playing. But when Nanyang Huizhong asked a third time, the tripitaka master could say nothing, and Nanyang Huizhong called him a fox spirit, and said, "Where is his power to see others' minds now?"

The later commentaries that Dōgen discusses center on the supposed difference (which Dōgen challenges) between the first two times and the third time the national teacher inquired of Da'er.

19 "Self-fulfilling samādhi" is *jijuyū zammai,* a term Dōgen uses to describe zazen. It literally means self-fulfilling or self-enjoying meditation, or the samādhi of "accepting one's own function." Dōgen describes it as the criterion of zazen in his early writing Bendōwa (Talk on Wholehearted Practice of the Way). See Okumura and Leighton, *The Whole-Hearted Way,* pp. 14–19, 21–24, 94–123.

Xuansha questioned the tripitaka master by saying, "The first two times, did you really see him?"

Xuedou Chongxian said [of the tripitaka master], "Lost, lost."

These five respected people have not yet understood something about this story. If this were Eihei, it would not be so. Suppose the national teacher were present now, and wished to examine the tripitaka master by asking, "Tell me, where is this old monk now?" On behalf of the tripitaka master I would say: This autumn morning the frost is cold. I humbly wish that the teacher's venerable health and activities will be filled with blessings.

Two Monks and a Worm-Filled Puddle

197. Dharma Hall Discourse

I remember that when the World-Honored One was alive there were two bhikṣus who wanted to visit the Buddha. During their journey they became severely dehydrated, and then saw a puddle by the roadside with worms in it. One of them did not drink the water with its worms and died of thirst, after which he was born in heaven, saw the Buddha, and attained the way. The other drank the water, and later reached Buddha's place. After hearing what had happened, Buddha took off his monk's robe, revealing his golden body, and said, "You are a very foolish person. You think that this body made up of the four elements is who I am, but it is only a smelly phantom. To see the Dharma is to see my body."[20]

The teacher Dōgen said: The monk who was reborn in heaven saw the Buddha's Dharma body; the monk who remained in the human realm saw the Buddha's body of four elements. We don't know what it was that the monk who was Buddha saw.

After a pause Dōgen said: If you want to observe the teacher you should observe their disciples. After all, how are we?

The teacher Dōgen put his hands in gasshō (palms together) and chanted: I take refuge in Buddha; I take refuge in Buddha.

---

20 "Revealing his golden body" implies that Buddha displayed the dharmakāya body, or reality body, beyond the material, fleshy body. The second monk had violated the precepts by swallowing the worms.

Renewing Confirmation Beyond Ancient Predictions
198. Dharma Hall Discourse
The teacher [Songshan] Hui'an [spoke] about the time before the seven buddhas. Nanyue Huairang received confirmation from the Burning Lamp Buddha Dipankara. Ultimately, what is this about? If you say that their mind's eyes are certified at the same time, you are not yet free from the grogginess of being in a dream.[21]

A Seed Planted in the Sky and the Cold Ash Revived
199. Dharma Hall Discourse for Opening the Fireplace [1246][22]
Dig in the earth to search for heaven; meet with sun face and moon face buddhas.[23] Dig a hole in the sky to plant the seed of a lotus that will blossom neither red nor white [without any color]. Play with Linji's lump of red flesh, and penetrate the width of Xuefeng's ancient mirror.[24] Further-

---

21 This Dharma hall discourse has various possible interpretations. "The seven buddhas" refers to the ancient buddhas of this age, ending with Śākyamuni Buddha as the seventh. Dipankara, or Burning Lamp Buddha, was another ancient Buddha, not one of the seven, so apparently prior to those seven, or simply from a different teaching tradition. But Dipankara was the Buddha who is said to have given a prediction of buddhahood to Śākyamuni in a previous life. "Confirmation" in the text means a prediction of future buddhahood, such as Dipankara gave to Śākyamuni, and here to Nanyue, and as it is used in the Lotus Sutra where the Buddha gives predictions of future buddhahood to his disciples. But in his essay Juki in Shōbōgenzō, Dōgen interprets this as confirmation of what is already existing in potential in the person receiving it. We know of no other reference to Nanyue receiving a prediction from Dipankara Buddha.

Songshan Hui'an had been the teacher of Nanyue before Nanyue went to study with the sixth ancestor, Huineng. Dōgen frequently refers to the first dialogue between Nanyue and Huineng, which he recounts in the Shōbōgenzō essay Henzan (All Inclusive Study). See Tanahashi, *Moon in a Dewdrop*, p. 198. When Nanyue told Huineng he had come from studying with Songshan Hui'an, Huineng asked him, "What is this that thus comes?" After eight years of consideration, Nanyue was able to say that nothing could be said exactly about this. When Huineng asked if, in that case, there existed practice and realization, Nanyue said that it was just that practice-realization could not be defiled. Huineng thereupon approved him.

22 For Dōgen's previous Dharma hall discourses on the occasion of opening the fireplace, on the first day of the tenth month, see Dharma hall discourses 14 and 109.

23 "Sun Face Buddha, Moon Face Buddha" was Mazu's response about his health during his final illness. See Cleary and Cleary, *Blue Cliff Record*, case 3, pp. 18–21; and Cleary, *Book of Serenity*, case 36, pp. 160–162.

24 Linji's lump of Red Flesh refers to a famous saying by the great master Linji, "Here in

more, burn up Danxia's wooden Buddha, and smelt a hundred times the iron ox at Shanfu.[25] Don't laugh when the cold ash is revived. Return for a while to a warm place [the meditation hall] and deliberate about this.

Valley Streams and Mountains Speak Softly, and Readily Attend to Others

200. Dharma Hall Discourse

In studying the way, the mind of the way is primary. This temple in the remote mountains and deep valleys is not easy to reach, and people arrive only after sailing over oceans and climbing mountains. Without treading with the mind of the way, it's difficult to arrive at this field. To refine the rice, first the bran must be removed. This is a good place in which to engage the way. And yet, I'm sorry that the master [Dōgen] does not readily attend to others by disposition. However, by day or night, the voice of the valley stream happens to be conducive for carrying water. Also, in spring and fall, the colors of the mountain manage to be conducive for gathering firewood. I hope that cloud and water monks will keep the way in mind.

I remember, a monk asked Shoushan [Xingnian], "All the buddhas come from this sutra. What is this sutra?"

Shoushan responded, "Speak softly; speak softly."

The monk asked, "How should we receive and maintain it?"

Shoushan said, "It can never be defiled."[26]

---

this lump of red flesh is a True Man with no rank." See Watson, *Zen Teachings of Master Lin-chi*, p. 13.

"Xuefeng's ancient mirror" refers to a story in which Xuefeng says, "If the world is ten feet wide, the ancient mirror is ten feet wide. If the world is one foot wide, the ancient mirror is one foot wide." His disciple Xuansha asked, "Then how wide is the furnace?" and Xuefeng said, "As wide as the ancient mirror." This is recounted in Dōgen's Shōbōgenzō essay Kokyō (The Ancient Mirror). See Nishijima and Cross, *Master Dogen's Shobogenzo*, book 1, p. 254. All of the references in this Dharma hall discourse refer in some way to the fireplace, or its opening.

25 Danxia Tianran, a disciple of Shitou, is famous for having burned a wooden buddha statue to warm himself. At Shanfu was a huge iron statue of an ox, considered a guardian deity of the Yellow River. Its head and tail were in different provinces, Henan and Hebei, and it was said to have been built by the legendary Emperor Yu of the Xia dynasty (ca. 2200 B.C.E.).

26 "It can never be defiled" is a reference to the utterance of Nanyue. See note 21 (Dharma hall discourse 198) above.

Suppose someone asked me, Eihei, "What is this sutra?" I would say to him: If you call it "this sutra," your eyebrows will fall out [from lying].

As to "How should we receive and maintain it?" I would say: Reaching back for your pillow in the middle of the night.[27]

The Bottomless Bowl of a Monk
201. Dharma Hall Discourse
[When Bodhidharma] departed the western heaven [India] and entering the eastern earth [China], clouds followed the dragon and wind followed the tiger. Just leave it to the various people whether they nod their heads [in agreement] and transform themselves.[28]

Dōgen raised his whisk and said: How can you deliberate about this [teaching], as it just accepts three thousand times and rejects eight hundred times? If you can make this calculation, this is threading the nostrils of the seven buddhas and crushing the eyes of all people. If you cannot calculate it, you only have the bottomless bowl of a monk, filled with rice and soup.

Discriminations of the Unconditioned Dharma
202. Dharma Hall Discourse
It is said in the [Diamond] Sutra that all the wise sages know the unconditioned Dharma, and yet they make discriminations. If someone asks, "What is the Dharma that includes discrimination?" I would say to him, "It would not be right to make even a little discrimination." As to what is unconditioned Dharma, I would say, "It is difficult to clarify discriminating wisdom." After all, what is this principle? On the long sitting platform [in the monks' hall], there is gruel and rice.

Fields All in White, the Empty Sky Ages
203. Dharma Hall Discourse on a Snowy Day
When the ancient Buddha Hongzhi, abbot of Tiantong, was giving a

---

27 "Reaching back for your pillow in the middle of the night" is a saying by Daowu Yuanzhi to Yunyan Tansheng about the naturally responsive activity of Avalokiteśvara, the bodhisattva of compassion, with his one thousand hands and eyes. See Cleary and Cleary, *Blue Cliff Record*, case 89, pp. 571–577; and Cleary, *Book of Serenity*, case 54, pp. 229–232.

28 Although clearly referencing Bodhidharma's arrival in China from India, this attitude here also refers to Dōgen's own transmission of Dharma from China to Japan.

Dharma hall discourse, a monk asked, "How is it when snow covers a thousand peaks?"

Hongzhi said, "Each drop of water freezes as it drops."

The monk said, "The clear light is cold, illuminating the eye. With fields all in white, the house can't be found."

Hongzhi said, "The white ox [cart] outside the house, where does it go?"[29]

The monk said, "It remains."

Hongzhi said, "This is also horns growing on the head."

The monk said, "In the end, where does it go?"

Hongzhi said, "When the self is transformed from the bottom, the solitary peak is unquestionably not white."

The teacher Dōgen said: If someone were to ask Eihei, "How is it when snow covers a thousand peaks?" I would say to him: There is nothing other than this color.

To the question, "The white ox outside the house, where does it go?" I would say: Both nostrils are pierced.

To "In the end, where does it go?" I would say to him: Day and night in harmony, sun and moon equally bright, the empty sky ages and the eyebrows are white.

Rice Eats a Person
204. Dharma Hall Discourse
Old man Eihei suddenly gave you all a single sharp punch twenty years ago.[30] Do you all know about this? If you really know it, the temple pillars confirm that, and the wooden ladles study together with you. If you don't know it, my whisk will jump up and beat on Brahma's nose. Immediately, Brahma will clasp his hands in shashu and ask, "What is this?"[31] I, Eihei, will reply to him: A person eats rice and rice eats a person.

---

29 The white ox cart refers to the story in the Lotus Sutra about the comprehensive, all-inclusive One Vehicle, which is shown to the children by their father after they are lured from the burning house by stories about diverse splendorous carriages. See Hurvitz, *Scripture of the Lotus Blossom of the Fine Dharma*, pp. 58–60.

30 Twenty years before this, around 1226, is when Dōgen received Dharma transmission from his teacher Tiantong Rujing.

31 *Shashu* is the formal standing position in the monastery, with hands clasped at chest

The wooden ladles will do three informal prostrations and ask, "How do we go beyond this [in practice]?"[32] I, Eihei, will reply: There are no separate objects before my eyes. On the headtop is an open gate.

Stop Baizhang's Wild-Fox Monster
205. Dharma Hall Discourse

After relating the story of Baizhang and the wild-fox, Dōgen asked the great assembly: Because of the previous Baizhang's saying that he did not fall into cause and effect, why did he descend into a wild-fox body?[33] As to the later Baizhang's saying he was not blind to cause and effect, how did this cause the release from the wild-fox body?

The teacher Dōgen himself said: I can't stand this wild-fox monster shaking his head and wagging his tail. Stop, Stop!

The Blessings of Hongzhi and Dōgen on the Arising of Yang
206. Dharma Hall Discourse for Winter Solstice [1246]

When the ancient Buddha Hongzhi, abbot of Tiantong, was giving a Dharma hall discourse on the occasion of winter solstice, he said, "Yin reaches its fullness and yang arises, strength is exhausted and our state changes. A green dragon runs fleetly when his bones are exposed.[34] A black panther is transformed when he is clothed in mist. Take the skulls of the buddhas of the three times and thread them onto a single rosary. Do not speak of bright and dark heads, as truly they are sun face, moon

---

height. As to Dōgen hitting Brahma's nose, the meaning is unclear, but it was the god Brahma who persuaded Śākyamuni to teach after his great awakening.

32 "Informal prostrations" are *sokurei*, with a monk's bowing cloth folded up and placed before him, rather than spread on the ground where he bows. The wooden ladle represents ordinary daily activities, such as cooking or serving food, which are understood in Dōgen's monastic standards as full expressions of practice.

33 Dōgen has referred to the famous story of Baizhang and the wild-fox spirit in Dharma hall discourses 62 and 94. See also Mumonkan, case 2, Cleary, *Unlocking the Zen Kōan,* pp. 9–17; or Aitken, *Gateless Barrier,* pp. 19–27; and Cleary, *Book of Serenity,* case 8, pp. 32–36.

34 This entire long quote from Tiantong Hongzhi, including the dialogue by Xuefeng and comments by Yunmen and Hongzhi, is exactly the same as in the previous year's winter solstice Dharma hall discourse 135. For notes on Hongzhi, the Green Dragon, rosaries, "sun face, moon face," and the bright pearl rolling on its own, see the notes to that discourse. Dōgen's subsequent comments are different in the two Dharma hall discourses.

face. Even if your measuring cup is full and the balance scale is level, in transactions I sell at a high price and buy when cheap. Zen worthies, do you understand? In a bowl the bright pearl rolls on its own without prodding.

"Here is a story," [Hongzhi continued].

"Xuefeng asked a monk, 'Where are you going?'

"The monk said, 'I'm going to do community work.'

"Xuefeng said, 'Go.'

"Yunmen said, 'Xuefeng understands people according to their words.'"

Hongzhi said [about this dialogue], "Don't move. If you move I'll give you thirty blows. Why is this so? For a luminous jewel without flaw, if you carve a pattern its virtue is lost."

The teacher Dōgen said: I ask the great assembly, is this a saying of the ancient Buddha Hongzhi, or of old man Eihei? If you say this is a statement by the ancient Buddha Hongzhi, then when the first [arising of] yang [and the daylight's increase] reaches its culmination, we are delighted by this blessing. If you say that this is a statement by old man Eihei, then you cannot avoid practicing together with this old monk Eihei. Since this is already the case, does the assembly want to see the first yang reaching its culmination?

Dōgen put down his whisk and said: On the auspicious occasion of the first [arising of] yang, I respectfully wish the great assembly ten thousand blessings in both its sitting and standing.

The Zen School Never Has Existed
207. Dharma Hall Discourse

Practitioners should know wrong from right. It is said that after [the ancestor] Upagupta, there were five sects of Buddha Dharma during its decline in India. After Qingyuan and Nanyue, people took it upon themselves to establish the various styles of the five houses, which was the error in China. Moreover, in the time of the ancient Buddhas and founding ancestors, it was never possible to see or hear the Buddha Dharma designated as the Zen school, which has never actually existed. What is presently called the Zen school is not truly the Buddha Dharma. How could we call the Buddha Dharma a Zen school? If you call the Buddha Dharma the Zen school, your tongue will fall out. Beginners and experienced students should definitely know this. I know that students who call this the Zen school are not disciples of Śākyamuni.

I remember that a monk asked Yunmen, "I heard that an ancient said that although the Oxhead [founder Niutou] expounded horizontally and vertically, he did not know the key to the workings of going beyond. What is that key to the workings of going beyond?"

Yunmen said, "The eastern mountain and the western peak are green."

Suppose someone were to ask Eihei, "What is that key to the workings of going beyond?" I would simply reply to him: Indra's nose is three feet long.

The Nourishment of a Chunk of Clay

208. Dharma Hall Discourse

I can remember, there was a monk who visited venerable Qin [Muzhou Daoming], and the venerable teacher [Muzhou] said, "Aren't you a monk on pilgrimage?"[35]

The monk said, "Yes, that's so."

The venerable teacher [Muzhou] asked, "Have you bowed to Buddha?"

The monk replied, "What is the use of bowing to a chunk of clay?"

The venerable teacher [Muzhou] said, "You should go and make a confession."

The teacher Dōgen said: The venerable Qin [Muzhou Daoming] rejected students with great extravagance, and accepted them with great frugality. Although in meeting people he revealed his vital organs, he did not mix mud with water and provide people with their fundamental nourishment. Thus this monk tested his fortune and heard useless sounds.

Perfect Wisdom Drinks the Water and Carries Firewood

209. Dharma Hall Discourse

I can remember, Yunmen ascended the seat and said to the assembly, "Monks in training, you must clarify the nostrils of a patch-robed monk, and then you will finally get it. What are these nostrils of a patch-robed

---

35 Qin was the family name of Muzhou Daoming.

monk?" Then he said, "Mahāprajñāpāramitā. Today we have a great community work project." Then he descended from his seat.

The teacher Dōgen said: Clouds and water assembly, you must clarify the nostrils of a patch-robed monk, and then you will finally get it. What are these nostrils of a patch-robed monk? *Then Dōgen said:* Mahāprajñāpāramitā. What is this Mahāprajñāpāramitā?

Then Dōgen said: [It is] carrying water and gathering firewood. What is this carrying water? Those who drink it all die. What is this gathering firewood? Those who bear it have strength.[36]

The Virtue of Unwashable Bowls
210. Dharma Hall Discourse

Last night all the buddhas of the three times fell into the dwelling of Eihei, and they all brought rice and put it in the storehouse. The tenzo [chief cook] took the rice, made gruel, and brought it to the monks' hall. Brothers, have you eaten the gruel or not?

Then Dōgen said: We have eaten the gruel; we have eaten the gruel. Having eaten the gruel, have you washed your bowls? We haven't yet washed our bowls. Why haven't they been washed yet?

After a pause Dōgen said: Not having washed the bowls because they have no bottoms is better than receiving a prediction from Gautama.

Not Speaking about Juzhi's One Finger
211. Dharma Hall Discourse

In studying the way you should know about speaking and not being able to speak. Everyone, do you know how to speak or not? If you don't yet know, you should understand it. Why don't you say where it is that everyone speaks?

The teacher Dōgen related the story about [Jinhua] Juzhi's one-finger Zen.[37] *Then he said:* After [meeting Hangzhou Tianlong], Juzhi expounded the Dharma extensively for human and heavenly beings, explaining hor-

---

36 Mahāprajñāpāramitā, the perfection of great wisdom, is the teaching of emptiness, which is expressed right in everyday activity. Drinking or accepting this reality, the egoistic self is relinquished.

37 Jinhua Juzhi was famous for holding up one finger in response to all questions, a teaching device he took from his teacher Hangzhou Tianlong. Before he met Hangzhou

izontally and vertically without hesitation or obstruction throughout his life [simply by holding up one finger]. Thus if someone asked about Buddha, he spoke of Buddha; if someone asked about the way, he spoke of the way. For questions about yellow [Earth], he spoke of yellow; for questions about black [Heaven], he spoke of black.[38] Not only that, but Juzhi finished expounding the entire collection of the canon thirty-six times, and expounded the collection of eighty thousand teachings eighty-one times. The seven buddha tathāgatas expounded Dharma and saved beings through Juzhi's gesture, and the twenty-eight [Indian] ancestors expounded Dharma and saved beings through Juzhi's gesture.

Would you all like to meet old man Juzhi? *Dōgen raised his whisk and said:* Look!

Do you want to hear old man Juzhi expounding Dharma? *Dōgen hit his sitting platform with his whisk and said:* Listen!

Now you have met with Juzhi, and heard him expounding Dharma. However, do not open your mouth and talk with a long tongue [at length] about his finger.

It's Not Even in India
212. Dharma Hall Discourse
Not only does it not exist at Caoxi [where the sixth ancestor taught], it does not exist in India.[39] The person who understands Buddha Dharma

---

Tianlong, a nun once came to where Juzhi was teaching, and walked around him disrespectfully without taking off her rain hat. She said she would take off her hat if he could speak, but he was speechless, and she left. When he later met Hangzhou Tianlong, Juzhi related this story, and Tianlong held up one finger. Juzhi was awakened. Later when Juzhi was a noted teacher, someone asked one of his novice students about Juzhi's teaching, and the boy held up one finger. When the student related this to Juzhi, Juzhi cut off the student's finger. As he was running from the room in pain, Juzhi called the student, who turned, and Juzhi held up one finger. The novice was greatly awakened. Portions of this story were anthologized in all the major kōan collections. See Cleary and Cleary, *Blue Cliff Record*, case 19, pp. 123–128; see Cleary, *Book of Serenity*, case 84, pp. 356–360; see Aitken, *Gateless Barrier*, case 3, pp. 28–32; or Cleary, *Unlocking the Zen Kōan*, pp. 18–24.

38 Yellow and black are expression for earth and heaven in the I Qing. Again, all of Jinhua Juzhi's "speaking" was by silently holding up one finger.

39 "Not only does it not exist at Caoxi, it does not exist in India" is a response by Shitou when he arrived and spoke to his teacher Qingyuan. Shitou said that he had come from Caoxi, where he had studied with Huineng as a boy before the sixth ancestor's death.

attains it, but the teacher does not attain it.[40] The temple pillars are the ancient buddhas, and the lanterns are the new Tathāgatas.[41] This is what we study [sitting] on the long platforms. Going beyond this study, then what?

After a pause Dōgen said: I thought all barbarians' beards were red, but basically there is also a red-bearded barbarian.[42]

A Plum on Last Year's Branch

213. Enlightenment Day Dharma Hall Discourse [1246][43]

The old bandit Gautama entered the temptations of the demon Māra. When Gautama afflicted the human and heavenly realms with confusion, stirring up disturbance, people lost their eyes and so could not look for them. The plum blossom opens afresh on the same branch as last year.

Qingyuan held up his whisk and asked if anything like it existed in Caoxi, and Shitou responded, "Not only does it not exist at Caoxi, it does not exist in India." Qingyuan asked if Shitou had been to India, and Shitou said if he had been there, the whisk (signifying the teaching) would have been there also. When Qingyuan asked Shitou to speak from his own experience, Shitou asked Qingyuan to express that himself. Qingyuan said that if he did so, Shitou would never get it later. Dōgen cites this as case 18 of the ninety kōans with verse comments in volume 9 of this book, and also as the very first story in his early collection of three hundred kōans without commentary, the Mana Shōbōgenzō. See Nishijima, *Master Dogen's Shinji Shobogenzo,* p. 3.

40 "The person who understands…" refers to a story about the sixth ancestor, Huineng. A monk asked Huineng, "Who attained the mind of his teacher, the fifth ancestor Daman Hongren?" Huineng said, "A person who understands Buddha Dharma attains it." The monk asked if Huineng had attained it, and he replied he had not attained it. When the monk asked why, Huineng said that he did not himself understand Buddha Dharma. This story appears in the Platform Sutra of the sixth ancestor. See A. F. Price and Wong Mou-Lam, trans., *The Diamond Sutra and the Sutra of Hui Neng* (Berkeley: Shambhala, 1969), p. 80; or Cleary, *Sutra of Hui-neng,* p. 58.

41 This is a reference to a saying by Zhaozhou. When addressed by a young official as an ancient Buddha, Zhaozhou called him a young Tathāgata. See Green, *Recorded Sayings of Zen Master Joshu,* p. 168.

42 The saying about the barbarian's red beard was made by Baizhang Huaihai in praise of his student Huangbo at the end of the famous story about Baizhang and the wild fox. See Dharma hall discourses 62, 94, and 205.

43 For Enlightenment Day, or Rōhatsu, see Dharma hall discourse 88 and volume 1, note 183. For other Enlightenment Day Dharma hall discourses, see discourses 136, 297, 360, 406, 475, and 506.

Eyes Wide Open

214. Dharma Hall Discourse in Appreciation of the New and Former Tenzo and Director

[The directors and tenzos] buy yellow rice throughout the province for us, and [arrange] for firewood to be carried up to this nook in the mountains. With wind and clouds in cooperation, the dragons gain the water.[44] With this merit completed, their eyes are wide open.

The Place of Half a Person

215. Dharma Hall Discourse

Dōgen held up his whisk, pointed it at the assembly, and said: I ask the great assembly, where does this whisk come from?

I remember that Mingzhao [Deqian] visited Elder Tan in Quan Province.[45] Tan said, "Practitioners should visit even places where there is only a single person, and even visit places where there is a half person."

Mingzhao immediately asked, "I don't ask about the place where there is a single person, but what is a place where there is only half a person?"

Tan did not speak.

Later, Tan sent a junior disciple to ask Mingzhao, "Would you like to understand the place where there is only half a person? This is just a person playing with a clump of mud."

The teacher Dōgen said: I, Eihei, am not like that. If someone asked, "What is the place where there is only half a person?" I would simply tell him: The seven [ancient] buddhas could not avoid staying in the monks' hall, opening up their quilts at night, and folding them up in the morning. Moreover, they could not avoid searching for a phrase to express the way.

Delighted with Zazen

216. New Year's Dharma Hall Discourse [1247]

Dōgen quoted the words by Zen Master Hongzhi about New Year's morn-

---

44 "Dragons" refers to the assembly of monks, with wind and clouds representing their necessary provisions.

45 This Elder Tan is unknown aside from this story.

ing zazen the same as in the previous year. After a pause Dōgen said the fol-
lowing.[46]

On this great auspicious New Year's morning I am delighted with zazen. Patch-robed monks engaging the way are peaceful just as they are. Each person is joyful and at ease with a spring-like face.[47] Noses and eyes manifest presently. The snow on the river is completely pure and white. The mind of the son of Xie is satisfied on his fishing boat.[48]

Yunmen's Place of Great Intimacy
217. Dharma Hall Discourse
I can remember, Yunmen asked Caoshan, "Why don't we know that there is a place of great intimacy?"

Caoshan said, "Just because it is greatly intimate, we do not know it is there."

Suppose this were Eihei and someone asked me, "Why don't we know that there is a place of great intimacy?"

I would just hit his face with my whisk and ask him, "Is this knowing or not knowing?" If he tried to answer, I would hit him again with the whisk.

How to Encounter People for Their Sake
218. Dharma Hall Discourse
Seeing colors, clarifying mind, old man Śākyamuni turned a somersault. Hearing sounds, awakening to the way, the ancestral teacher Bodhidharma held out his bowl. Before the fifteenth day [on the full moon], there's talk of the moon on Vulture Peak; after the fifteenth day, flowers

---

46 This is a note added by the compiler, Koun Ejō. It refers to the poem by Hongzhi in the New Year's Dharma hall discourse 142: "In New Year's morning zazen, the myriad things are natural. / Mind after mind is beyond dichotomies; Buddha after Buddha manifests presently. / The snow on the river is completely pure and white. / The mind of the son of Xie is satisfied on his fishing boat. / Study this."

47 Again, New Year's Day in the traditional Japanese lunar calendar is in mid-February, and is considered the first day of spring.

48 The son of Xie refers to Xuansha Shibei. See Dharma hall discourse 91 and volume 1, note 191. Xuansha was a fisherman before he became a monk.

are added on brocade.[49] These are still not free from words and phrases. Beyond this, how can we encounter people for the sake of people?

After a pause, Dōgen said: If pure gold is not refined a hundred times, how will it reveal its radiance? If a precious jewel is not assessed, how can it be judged genuine or fake? What is it like, right at this time? Being early spring, it is still cold. I respectfully wish all you honored persons ten thousand blessings in your sitting and standing.

In Accord with Dignified Cushions and Ladles

219. Dharma Hall Discourse on the Fifteenth Day of the First Month [1247]

Abundant with ten thousand virtues, the sitting cushions and wooden ladles are dignified. Brushing away every bit of dust, the abbot's chair, and bamboo and wooden utensils, realize it physically. Picked up, they are transparent, and a thousand or ten thousand distinctions are clear. Released, they fall and scatter, and the ten directions and three times are clear. Tell me, how do you act so as to be in accord with such a thing? Do you really know?

After a pause Dōgen said: The family style is pure white, like plum blossoms, snow, and the moon. At the time of flowering, fortunately there is a way to protect the body. The clouds are bright, the water is delightful, and our effort is totally perfect. Without realizing it, our entire body enters the emperor's neighborhood.

No Wonderful Secret to the Single Function

220. Dharma Hall Discourse

Holding up one function completely pervades a thousand or ten thousand functions. Expounding one phrase circulates a thousand or ten thousand phrases. Without borrowing from the family style of the ancient buddhas, completely reveal your own nose. Already this is happening. We use a stick to kill the thousand wild foxes in Baizhang's cave, and give a

---

49 In the earlier Monkaku-bon version we are using for this translation, the second half of this sentence starts with "After the twelfth hour," i.e., after midnight. We are following Genryū Kagamishima's lead in adapting here the later Manzan version reading of "After the fifteenth day" to match the first half of the sentence.

loud yell to disperse the gang of thirty thousand monkeys at Xuefeng's.[50] This is not simply patience with the unconditioned nature of all things, but also allows the wondrous Dharma wheel to turn forever.[51] Even if you reach this field directly, you should know there is a path of going beyond. Do you want to know the path for going beyond?

After a pause Dōgen said: There is no wondrous secret [of Bodhidharma] at Shaolin to be transmitted from father to son. When hungry we eat; when thirsty we drink; when healthy we sit; when tired we sleep. When we understand this right here, this land is the Western Heaven [India].

Host and Guest Not Meeting; Then Sharing One House

221. Dharma Hall Discourse

In a Dharma hall discourse the ancient ancestor, great teacher Shitou said, "My Dharma gate has been transmitted by the former buddhas. Without discussing samādhi or effort, they simply reached the insight of buddhas."[52]

The teacher Dōgen said: I ask the great assembly, what is this insight of buddhas that Shitou mentioned?

Dōgen held his staff upright, pounded it once, and said: The previous, innumerable, excellent causes are dedicated to the insight of buddhas. [Shitou] manifested buddhas' insight while eating rice, putting on clothes, defecating, urinating, and engaging the way in the monks' hall while making effort on the sitting platforms. For Eiheiji students it is not like this. When I sit you should stand. When I stand you should sit. If we both stand or sit at the same time, we will both be blind people.[53] Therefore,

---

50 The foxes in Baizhang's cave relates to the kōan of Baizhang and the fox, often mentioned in Eihei Kōroku, for example in Dharma hall discourses 62, 94, and 205. Hongzhi relates a story about Xuefeng and Sansheng Huiran observing monkeys. Another time, Xuefeng was going to the local village with his disciples to do some work and met a band of monkeys on the road. Xuefeng said that each monkey "carries an ancient mirror, but they come to break off the tops of my rice plants." See Chang, *Original Teachings of Ch'an Buddhism,* pp. 281–282.

51 "Patience with the unconditioned nature of all things" is *anutpattika dharma kṣānti,* the patience with insight into emptiness, equivalent to unsurpassed wisdom. See volume 2 (Dharma hall discourse 180), note 138.

52 This is a quote from Shitou that appears in the Jingde Transmission of Lamp (Keitoku Dentōroku). For another version, see Ferguson, *Zen's Chinese Heritage,* p. 73.

53 One standing and the other sitting refers to the distinction between universal and

Dongshan arrayed the five ranks of lord and minister, and Linji enumerated the four kinds of guest and host.[54] A person within the gate sits solidly grounded, and even if he wants to leave, cannot. A person outside the gate shifts all over, like ocean waves, and even if he wants to enter, cannot. These different persons do not know each other and do not meet each other. You are you; I am I. We do not disturb each other, each protecting our own territory.

When suddenly those in the four directions change their positions and switch host and guest, the person on the path does not leave their house, and the person in the house does not depart from the path. Yours is mine, and mine is yours. We should say that he and I share one house; host and guest are equally strong. If we can see it like this, there is something that does not interact with the two paths [of host and guest] and cannot be included in the four phrases.[55] Where shall we meet together with that [reality beyond dichotomy]?

Dōgen held his staff upright, pounded it once, and said: Return back to the hall and consider this.

A Cock Crows at Dawn
222. Dharma Hall Discourse
A monk once asked Jiashan, "How is it when we remove the dust and see Buddha?"

Jiashan said, "You should simply swing the sword. If you don't swing the sword, the fisherman will stay in his nest."[56]

---

particular, or host and guest. Each side must abide in its own position.

54 The five ranks are a teaching presentation originated by the Caodong (Sōtō) founder, Dongshan Liangjie. Originally depicted in his teaching poem, the Song of the Precious Mirror Samādhi, these five positions elaborate the interrelationships of the particular and universal, which have sometimes been symbolized in the Sōtō tradition in terms of lord and minister, host and guest, upright and inclined, or teacher and student. The Linji (Rinzai) founder, Linji, presented a similar teaching of four relationships between guest and host.

55 The "four phrases" refers to the four categories of Nāgārjuna: existence, nonexistence, both existence and nonexistence, and neither existence nor nonexistence. So this is something beyond category or conceptualization.

56 Swinging the sword refers to cutting off delusion. When the fisherman remains at

The teacher Dōgen said: If this were Eihei, it would not proceed thus. Suppose someone asked, "How is it when we remove the dust and see Buddha?" I would say to him: Don't make trouble by hanging up a stone mirror. Naturally at dawn the cock crows.[57] Eating rice, drinking tea, we exit and enter at the same gate [as Buddha].

The Moon in the Ageless Cauldron

223. Dharma Hall Discourse
One nine and two nines (i.e., eighteen) face and encounter each other. Inquiry and response are like spring rain and spring wind. Zen Master Huangbo stuck out his tongue; the teacher Xuansha raised his eyebrows.[58] Even when such divine power transcends buddhas and goes beyond ancestors, it cannot avoid the limitations of west and east. If you remain in the temple of Eihei, it will become an especially fine place for patch-robed monks. Great assembly, do you want to thoroughly understand the fine place of patch-robed monks?

After a pause Dōgen said: Outside the window, plum blossoms open in secret, encompassing spring. [You] can catch the moon in the ageless cauldron of the sky.[59]

Nostrils Half Drilled

224. Dharma Hall Discourse
I remember, once a monk asked Dongshan [Liangjie], "What is the activity of a monk (srāmaṇera)?"

Dongshan said, "His head is three feet long, his neck two inches long."

---

home, he makes no catch. This dialogue of Jiashan is from Hongzhi's collection of kōans; see Cleary, *Book of Serenity,* case 68, pp. 286–289.

57 "Don't make trouble by hanging up a stone mirror. Naturally at dawn the cock crows" is a saying by Touzi Yiqing.

58 Huangbo stuck out his tongue when he heard his teacher Baizhang talk about having gone deaf for three days after Baizhang's teacher Mazu yelled at him. This story is in the Jingde Transmission of the Lamp (Keitoku Dentōroku), vol. 6, on Baizhang. See Ferguson, *Zen's Chinese Heritage,* pp. 78–79.

59 "Ageless cauldron" is based on a Taoist fable about an old man selling medicine who regularly returned back to his home of an eternal vessel that contained a marvelous palace with endless feasts. The cauldron of the sky could also be read as the cauldron of emptiness.

Another monk asked the teacher Guizong Danquan, "Actually, what was Dongshan's meaning?"

Guizong Danquan said, "This skin covering is two inches thick."⁶⁰

The teacher Dōgen said: Today if someone asked Eihei, "What was Dongshan's meaning?" I would say to him: The nostrils half drilled are still five feet long.

Seeing the Tathāgata's Life Vein in the Midnight Frost

225. Dharma Hall Discourse for the Ceremony for [Śākyamuni's] Nirvāṇa [1247]⁶¹

The twin sāla trees [under which Śākyamuni passed away] did not receive the power of the spirit of spring.⁶² After a snowfall, how can we know the midnight frost? [Buddha] held up and turned the empty sky, and laid himself down in the world. The Tathāgata emitted light twice from the curled hair on his forehead. Although it is the case [that he was lying down], who would say that when he lost his physical life, he would not also have liked dying while sitting or standing? The eating bowls of the

---

In Hongzhi's verse comment to case 98 of the Shōyōroku, he uses the three characters we translate here as "the ageless cauldron of the sky." In the context of that verse Thomas Cleary aptly translates them as "the emptiness of the pot of ages." See Cleary, *Book of Serenity*, pp. 422–424. See also Dharma hall discourse 481.

60 This dialogue with Dongshan is from the Jingde Transmission of the Lamp (Keitoku Dentōroku), vol. 15, on Dongshan. See Chang, *Original Teachings of Ch'an Buddhism*, pp. 67–68. One interpretation of this difficult Dharma hall discourse is that three-foot-long heads, two-inch-long necks, and two-inch-thick skins refer to the bodhisattvas manifesting bodies as various different kind of beings. "Skin covering" as a compound is commonly read as "envelope," by which reading Guizong Danquan's statement would indicate that the letter, or the meaning, is too thick, that is, too long, to ever be expressible. The activity of a monk is beyond discriminating mind.

61 The passing away into nirvāṇa, or *parinirvāṇa*, of Śākyamuni is celebrated in East Asia on the fifteenth day of the second month. Previous Parinirvāṇa Day commemorations in Eihei Kōroku are Dharma hall discourses 121 and 146.

62 The twin trees under which Śākyamuni entered parinirvāṇa are said to have withered after his death. Therefore they did not benefit from the spring season, which begins on the fifteenth day of the second lunar month. "Spirit of spring" is literally "Eastern Lord," the Chinese name for the deity of spring who is identified with the sunrise in the east. According to the Mahāparinirvāṇa Sūtra, sāla trees naturally split into two trunks from one root system, so there were two pairs of trees above Śākyamuni.

seven buddhas are bottomless, but for sentient beings, this disaster was awful. If you say [Śākyamuni] is extinguished, you are not his disciple. If you say he is not extinguished, your words do not hit the mark. Having reached this day, how do you respond?

Do you want to see the Tathāgata's life vein? Offer incense, make prostrations, and return to the [meditation] hall.

Zhaozhou's Dogs and Dōgen's Cats

226. Dharma Hall Discourse

A monk asked Zhaozhou, "Does a dog have Buddha nature or not?"
Zhaozhou said, "Yes."
Another monk asked, "Does a dog have Buddha nature or not?"
Zhaozhou said, "No."[63]

This single story has a truth to be studied. Do you want to thoroughly understand this truth?

After a pause Dōgen said: Buddha nature has a nose to grasp, but a dog does not have a horn [to hold]. [With Buddha nature] not avoiding entry into a skin-bag, cats give birth to cats.

Music Beyond the Three Phrases

227. Dharma Hall Discourse

A thousand blossoms open their five petals; ten thousand birds sing throughout the spring. This is the first phrase. Buddha is made from the self; the Dharma is not received from other people.[64] This is the second

---

63 Only half of this famous story is featured as the first case in the Mumonkan, which only includes Zhaozhou's answer "No," or *mu* in Japanese. But the full story with both of Zhaozhou's responses is cited by Hongzhi in case 18 of the Shōyōroku. When Zhaozhou answers, "No," the monk asks, "Why not?" And Zhaozhou says the dog has no Buddha nature because it has karmic consciousness. When he answers, "Yes," and the monk asks how the Buddha nature could enter such a skin bag, Zhaozhou responds that it knowingly and willingly transgresses. This represents the bodhisattva activity of the Buddha nature. See Cleary, *Book of Serenity,* pp. 76–80. For the abbreviated Mumonkan version, see Aitken, *Gateless Barrier,* pp. 7–18; and Cleary, *Unlocking the Zen Kōan,* pp. 1–8. Dōgen also cites the full version as case 73 of ninety kōans with his verse comments in volume 9 of Eihei Kōroku, below.

64 "Buddha is made from the self; the Dharma is not received from other people" is from Hongzhi's Extensive Record, vol. 4.

phrase. A mute child eats the most bitter squash; Mister Chang [a common person] drinks wine and gets drunk. This is the third phrase.

How is it not to be involved in the three phrases? Every handclap is fundamentally music. Li ming luo liao luo ming ling.[65]

An Upright Staff Turns the Wheel of Dharma
228. Dharma Hall Discourse
All buddhas in the three times dwell within flames and turn the great Dharma wheel.[66] A respected teacher known in the world remains as a free-standing pillar in the temple and turns the great Dharma wheel. Old man Eihei dwells within a monk's staff and turns the great Dharma wheel.

Do you understand? If you have not yet understood, the staff will repeatedly expound it, horizontally and vertically. *Dōgen held the staff upright and pounded it once.*

In the Realm of Broken Ladle Buddha
229. Dharma Hall Discourse
The millions of billions of transformation bodies [of buddhas] abide throughout a monk's staff, carry water and gather firewood to make offerings to buddhas as numerous as there are sitting cushions, and, on the tip of a whisk, simultaneously all attain unsurpassed complete perfect enlightenment.[67] They are all equally named Broken Wooden Ladle Tathāgata, Worthy of Offerings, Omniscient, Foot of Bright Practice, Well-Gone

65 "Li ming luo liao luo ming ling" are the Chinese characters for the tones made by a flute. This saying is also from Hongzhi's Extensive Record, vol. 4. It could be interpreted as meaning there is no need to explain. Just enjoy the music.

66 "All buddhas in the three times dwell within flames and turn the great Dharma wheel" is a saying by Xuefeng. All three of these sayings are given by Dōgen in his Shōbōgenzō essay Gyobutsu Igi (The Awesome Presence of Active Buddhas). See Tanahashi, *Beyond Thinking*, pp. 90–96.

67 Dōgen plays with three conventional sutra phrases: a buddha remaining throughout kalpas, making offerings to buddhas as numerous as grains of sand in the Ganges River, and attaining enlightenment while sitting under the bodhi tree. Dōgen substitutes a monk's staff for endless kalpas, sitting cushions for grains of sand, and the top of a whisk for underneath the bodhi tree.

One, World-Liberator, Supreme One, Tamer of Strong Persons, Teacher of Humans and Heavenly Beings, World-Honored Buddha.[68] The Country [of this buddha] is named Clump of Soil; the kalpa is named Fist. The duration of the True Dharma Age and Semblance Dharma Age are both twelve hours, and the Buddha's longevity is that of a dried turd from three thousand great thousands of worlds.[69] Do you all understand?

If you state your understanding you are making mistake after mistake. If you say you do not understand, even the five precepts are not maintained.

The Pines Are Chilling and Bodhidharma Is Long Gone
230. Dharma Hall Discourse
I can remember, Xuansha said to his assembly, "I will always take all of you to the ultimate [awakening], without ever making even a thread of a mistake."

The teacher Dōgen said: Xuansha is thus. He only knows that the moon and clouds mingled together are both white, and doesn't realize that the sound of [the wind in] the pines, wet with dew, is chilling. Tell me, what is Eihei's meaning?

It has been a long time since the one sandal went back home to India through Congling.[70] Stop asking what was the point of Bodhidharma's coming [to China].

---

68 Starting with "Tathāgata," these are the standard ten epithets for a buddha, in this case describing the new buddha invented here by Dōgen, named Broken Wooden Ladle, who might be a reference to all of the humble monks at Eiheiji.

69 "True Dharma Age and Semblance Dharma Age" refers to the first phases of a buddha age before its degeneration. "Dried turd" is a reference to a famous response by Yunmen as to what Buddha is. See, for example, Dharma hall discourse 229, and case 21 of the Mumonkan; Aitken, *Gateless Barrier,* pp. 137–141; and Cleary, *Unlocking the Zen Kōan,* pp. 102–105.

70 The one sandal returning to India refers to the legend of Bodhidharma being sighted on the Congling Plateau in Central Asia, barefoot but carrying a single sandal, as he returned to India after establishing Chan in China. The historicity of the many Bodhidharma legends remains uncertain, but other stories tell that he was poisoned by rivals and died in China. After he was buried at his temple, someone supposedly opened the tomb and found only one sandal.

Turning the Four Noble Truths

231. Dharma Hall Discourse

Dōgen held up his staff and said: This is the highest culmination of all dharmas. *Holding the staff horizontally he said:* This is the deepest source of Buddha Dharma.

Here I turn the Dharma wheel of the [four] noble truths, the truth of suffering, the truth of causation, the truth of cessation [of suffering], and the truth of the path. What is the truth of suffering? All of the ten thousand phenomena dwell in this single cup of tea. What is the truth of causation? The luster of the auspicious clouds glitters. What is the truth of cessation? When healthy, zazen; when tired, we sleep. What is the truth of the path? The great way pervades to eternal peace.[71]

All of this is within the boundary of the nirmāṇakāya [manifesting] Buddha. What goes beyond this? Do you want to see the truth of suffering going beyond? *Dōgen pounded his staff once.*

Do you want to see the truth of causation going beyond? *Dōgen pounded his staff once.*

Do you want to see the truth of cessation going beyond? *Dōgen pounded his staff once.*

Do you want to see the truth of the path going beyond? *Dōgen pounded his staff once.*

Although this is the matter of going beyond the buddha ancestors, what is Eihei's meaning? *Dōgen pounded his staff twice.*

Spring for the Single Family

232. Dharma Hall Discourse

Making the horse run around the lantern, you are not yet free from playing with shadows and light.[72] Even when you hide your body inside a temple pillar, you still are relying on grasses and trees. Even if you say you

---

71 "The great way pervades to eternal peace" (which is also the name of the Chinese capital Chang'an) is a saying by Zhaozhou. See Green, *Recorded Sayings of Zen Master Joshu,* p. 108; see also Dharma hall discourse 154.

72 The horse running around the lantern refers to a revolving lantern with the shadow picture of a horse on it. When rotated the horse seems to move. Shadow and light also refers to the passing of time.

are not the partner of the ten thousand things, you have not considered that you are surrounded by the ten thousand things. Even if you say that explaining a single thing is off the mark, you do not realize that a single thing still remains. Whether you turn to the left or turn to the right, from the east or from the west, practicing with sticks or shouts is still just following others. How do you speak a single phrase that is independent and free?

After a pause Dōgen said: Rain over a misty village in the third month; basically this is spring for a single family.

Realizing the Two Emptinesses
233. Dharma Hall Discourse

Here is a story. Master Huanglong [Huinan] said to the assembly, "Awakening is separate from language, and so far nobody has attained it. You should rely on the principle of the two emptinesses, and then you will confirm the body of the Dharma king. Tell me, what are the principles of the two emptinesses? These are the emptiness of persons and things, the emptiness of inside and outside, the emptiness of ordinary and saintly beings, and the emptiness of all dharmas. I have expounded the principle of two emptinesses for the sake of all of you. Tell me, what is the body of the Dharma king? The four great elements and five skandhas; walking, standing, sitting, and reclining; opening your lacquer place mat and setting out your eating bowls; the monks' hall and the Buddha hall; the kitchen and administrative offices building, and the temple gate; there is nothing that is not the body of the Dharma king. If you can cover this completely, then the heavens and the great earth, and the sun, moon, and stars, pierce the eyeballs of all of you, and the waters of the four great oceans flow into all of your nostrils. You should know that the prediction of Śākyamuni and of Maitreya [as the next future Buddha] are just vain names, and Linji's shout and Deshan's stick are just expedient, provisional means." Huanglong hit his chair with his whisk and descended from his seat.

The teacher Dōgen said: Although the ancestral teacher Huanglong said it like this, it not so for Eihei.

After a pause Dōgen said: If Gautama's prediction is not genuine, how can we realize the two emptinesses of the body of the Dharma king?

A Demonic Temptation
234. Dharma Hall Discourse

When you nod your head you haven't reached it; black and white are not distinguished. When you reach it you don't nod your head, mud and water are mixed together.[73] I don't care if a temple pillar leaps into a monk's staff. Why are all of your noses still on your faces? If you cover it completely, you will give a lash of the whip to Guishan's water buffalo.[74] If you haven't clarified this yet, what demonic temptation caused you to leave home and travel around to practice? Speak quickly.

The Stone Woman's Charms
235. Dharma Hall Discourse

Wash the darkness of the long night with the brightness of fundamental reality. At that very time, within earshot of each person, give one or two hits to the poison-smeared drum, and with the wisdom of the Dharma nature, break through the doubts of many kalpas.[75] At that very time, for each person's nose, burn a hundred or a thousand sticks of incense that bring back spirits [of the dead]. At that very time, how shall we practice?

After a pause Dōgen said: The iron ox has a white head and triangular hat; the stone woman in the prime of life is endowed with hundreds of charms.[76]

Not Receiving Sensation and the Vital Path Refreshed
236. Dharma Hall Discourse for Bathing [the Baby] Buddha [1247]

Here is a story. When Zen Master Hongzhi was abbot at Tiantong he

---

73 "When you nod your head you haven't reached it; when you reach it you don't nod your head" is a saying by Xinghua Cunjiang in response to a monk nodding his head.

74 Guishan said that after his death he would become a water buffalo at the foot of the mountain. See volume 2 (Dharma hall discourse 159), note 105.

75 The poison-smeared drum is an image from the Mahāparinirvāṇa Sūtra, chap. 9. This drum has poison such that anyone who hears it will die. The sutra itself is said to be like this drum, except that anyone who hears it will become free from greed, hate, and delusion.

76 A triangular hat was worn by elderly people. The prime of life here refers to the thirties and forties. This iron ox and stone woman echoes the image of the wooden man and stone woman used by Dongshan Liangjie in his teaching poem Song of the Precious Mirror Samādhi, in which he says, "The wooden man starts to sing, the stone woman gets up

said in a Dharma hall discourse on this day [of Buddha's birthday], "When the pure water of the emptiness of self-nature and the radiant body of the Dharma realm are only faintly distinguished, then this person is born. Without cleansing the dusts from the body, because of this water's wonderful touch he expresses clear realization. I ask you, for many years he has been departed, so how can he return to be near us today? On this day two thousand years ago, he pointed to heaven and to earth and gave the lion's roar. Yunmen remained at war while thinking about great peace by saying that he would kill the baby Buddha and assuredly feed him to the dogs. This is pointing east and calling it west, making nonexistence into existence. Although I pour foul water on you, don't get angry.[77] Now that I see you, how will you accept it? Buddha said, 'Not receiving any sensation is called right receiving.'[78] If you practice like this, each drop falls on exactly the same spot."

The teacher Dōgen said: Although the ancient Buddha Hongzhi said it like this, how should Eihei speak of the true meaning of this birthday? Dropping off the body within the ten thousand forms, naturally he had the conditions for this birth. In the single color after transforming the body, he saw the vital path afresh. What is the true meaning of our bathing the Buddha?

After a pause Dōgen said: Holding together our own broken wooden ladle, we pour water on his head to bathe the body of the Tathāgata.

Freeing the Circle and the Single Stroke
237. Dharma Hall Discourse
I can remember, once Mazu [Dao-I] sent somebody with a letter to Great

---

dancing." See Leighton and Wu, *Cultivating the Empty Field*, pp. 76–77. These images have been used by various Sōtō lineage teachers, and generally refer to the revival or awakening of spirit.

77 "Pouring foul water" is an added saying by Yuanwu in the Hekiganroku, case 55, referring to a teacher's strong rebuke of a student. See Cleary and Cleary, *Blue Cliff Record*, p. 366.

78 "Not receiving any sensation is called right receiving" is a quote from a commentary on the Sutra of Perfect Enlightenment by Guifeng Zongmi, the great Chan master who was also a patriarch of the Huayan school. "Right receiving" is also a term for samādhi that refers to receiving positive, negative, and neutral sensations equally, with equanimity.

Awakened Zen Master Jingshan Daoqin of Hangzhou in China. In the letter he had made one circle. Daoqin opened the envelope and made one horizontal stroke within the circle, then sealed the envelope again and sent it back. The national teacher Nanyang Huizhong heard this and said, "Teacher Daoqin is still misled by Master Mazu."

The teacher Dōgen said: Today Eihei sees that the national teacher, Mazu, and Daoqin, all three fall into the same pit. Now can Eihei allow them to get out of the hole or not? If they can get out of the hole, I'm afraid that they will lose their body and relinquish their lives. If they cannot get out of the hole, how can I call myself a good spiritual benefactor? Having reached this field, how can I finally practice?

After a pause, Dōgen threw down his staff and descended from his seat.

Pull Your Own Nose and Lift the Ancient Kōan

238. Dharma Hall Discourse Beginning the Summer Practice Period [1247]

Digging a hole in the sky, leveling the earth, and constructing a demon's cave, the monks' bad-smelling waters splatter, pouring over the heavens. Donkeys and cows mix together with buddhas and ancestors. Pull yourself by your own nose. Tell me, how shall we today lift up the ancient kōan from two thousand years ago?

After a pause Dōgen said: A copper head and iron brow keep practicing. A wooden ladle and a clump of soil clap their hands and laugh.

The Courage of Patch-Robed Monks

239. Dharma Hall Discourse

The courage of a fisherman is to enter the water without avoiding deep-sea dragons. The courage of a hunter is to travel the earth without avoiding tigers. The courage of a general is to face the drawn sword before him, and see death as just like life.[79] What is the courage of patch-robed monks?

After a pause Dōgen said: Spread out your bedding and sleep; set out your bowls and eat rice; exhale through your nostrils; radiate light from your eyes. Do you know there is something that goes beyond? With vital-

---

79 "The courage of a fisherman...see death just like life" is a paraphrase by Dōgen of a saying by the Daoist philosopher Zhuangzi. See Watson, trans., *The Complete Works of Chuang Tzu,* p. 185.

ity, eat lots of rice and then use the toilet. Transcend your personal prediction of future buddhahood from Gautama.

The Assembly's Statement Transcending Śākyamuni's Utterance
240. Dharma Hall Discourse
Great teacher Śākyamuni Buddha sat on the vajra seat under the bodhi
tree, saw the bright star, realized the way, and said, "When the bright star
appeared, I accomplished the way at the same time as the great earth and
all sentient beings."

The great earth and sentient beings say it this way; old man Śākyamuni
says it this way; what does the great assembly say? If the great assembly
cannot say it, then I, Eihei, will speak.

Dōgen held up his staff, pounded it once, and said: This is what I was
able to study on the long platform. Can you say something that goes
beyond it?

Again Dōgen raised his staff and pounded it once and said: Without being
involved with two sides, what more can you say?

After a pause Dōgen said: I have already met with you all in front of the
monks' hall.

An Eighty-Thousand Foot Cliff
241. Dharma Hall Discourse
Sun face and moon face are filled with gruel and rice.[80] When a Chinese
person comes, he appears as a Chinese person, with sufficient firewood
and water. The rice is from Luling; the wheat from the foot of the mountain.[81] The first ancestor [Bodhidharma] didn't come to the eastern land
[China]; the second ancestor [Dazu Huike] didn't go to the western
heaven [India].[82] Each of them stands like an eighty-thousand-foot cliff,
all of them right in front of your nose.

Dōgen pounded his staff once and descended from his seat.

---

80 During his final illness, Great Master Mazu was asked about his health and replied,
"Sun Face Buddha, Moon Face Buddha." See Cleary and Cleary, *Blue Cliff Record,* case
3, pp. 18–21; and Cleary, *Book of Serenity,* case 36, pp. 160–162.

81 When asked for the great meaning of Buddhism, Qingyuan Xingsi replied, "What is
the price of rice in Luling?" See Cleary, *Book of Serenity,* case 5, pp. 20–22.

82 "The first ancestor didn't come to the east; the second ancestor didn't go to the west"

No Two-Sided Speech and Rivers Flowing Upstream
242. Dharma Hall Discourse for the Fifth Day of the Fifth Month Celebration [1247][83]
When Zen Master Hongzhi was abbot at Tiantong he said in a Dharma hall discourse on the morning of this day, "The fifth day of the fifth month is the Festival of the Center of Heaven; we see killing and giving life on the hundred grass-tips. Licorice grass and mugwort are by nature sweet and bitter; ginseng and wolfsbane are dispensed according to cold and heat.[84] Grasses with pleasant and putrid fragrances are difficult to be ignored by our crookneck-squash nose. How can delicious tastes deceive our crescent moon tongue? Round and bright, with clear insight, consciousness is tranquil. Mahākāśyapa could differentiate, and for all Zen worthies, differentiation is a matter of discriminating mind.[85] For a long time, the venerable Mahākāśyapa extinguished the root of discriminating mind. Round and bright, clear insight does not rely on consciousness. So now, how can we go on in good shape? A settled person doesn't speak; placid water doesn't flow."

The teacher Dōgen said: The ancient Buddha Hongzhi said it like this, but what shall his descendant Eihei say about a settled person not speaking? No false speech, no deceiving speech, no dishonest speech; this does not mean no speaking, but no two-sided speech. What shall I say about placid water not flowing? If the great ocean thought it was full enough, the hundred rivers would flow backward.

---

is a saying by Xuansha. Dōgen also quotes this in the Shōbōgenzō essay Henzan (All-Inclusive Study). See Tanahashi, *Moon in a Dewdrop*, p. 197.

83 For the fifth day of the fifth month, see Dharma hall discourse 169.

84 As mentioned in Dharma hall discourse 169, also quoting Hongzhi, on this day people wore medicine pouches. Licorice grass, mugwort, ginseng, and wolfsbane are all herbs that were used as medicines.

85 The word we are translating as "consciousness" in this Dharma hall discourse is *shin'nen*, which means the mind and its functions, literally "mind" and "mindfulness." The word we are translating here as "discriminating mind" is *i*, which also means intention or thinking mind. In Cittamātra ("mind-only") or Yogācāra Buddhist teaching, *i* refers to *manas* in Sanskrit, the seventh level of consciousness, which discriminates self from others.

The Radiance of Each Place
243. Dharma Hall Discourse
Someone [in the assembly] asked, "What is Buddha?"[86]

The teacher Dōgen said: Finally, future births are prevented with the special attainment of cessation not arising through analysis.[87]

The monk said, "Master, don't teach people using Lesser Vehicle Dharma."[88]

Dōgen said: I am not teaching people using Lesser Vehicle Dharma.

The monk asked: "What is Buddha?"

The teacher Dōgen said: Finally, future births are prevented with the special attainment of cessation not arising through analysis.

Then Dōgen said: Heaven is not high; the earth is not dense. Mountains and rivers, and the sun and moon, are not separated. The radiant light of each place penetrates each place. A Persian riding on a white elephant enters the Buddha hall; Handan people with bare feet circumambulate the monks' hall.[89] What principle can we rely on to be like this?

After a pause Dōgen said: The bright moon follows someone as if there were a reason. Naturally white clouds provide rain with no mind.

86 This exchange, and Dharma hall discourse 72, are unique examples in Eihei Kōroku of actual dialogues recorded between Dōgen and one of his monks.

87 This is a quote from the Abhidharma Kośa by Vasubandhu, a commentary on the early Buddhist abhidharma psychology, which Dōgen first read when he was nine. This statement refers to a buddha's ending the chain of personal rebirth. "Cessation not arising through analysis" (Skt.: *apratisaṃkhyā nirodha*) is one of the three unconditioned dharmas (the unconditioned elements of reality according to this system of thought), the other two unconditioned dharmas being space and cessation arising as a result of analysis.

88 "Lesser Vehicle," sometimes given with the Sanskrit term "Hinayāna," was used in Dōgen's time to refer to pre-Mahāyāna teachings. Sometimes it was used by Mahāyāna people as a pejorative term for particular schools, but generally it refers to self-purification practice, not aimed at universal enlightenment. This is not an appropriate term for any modern Buddhist schools, all of which offer Dharma widely to all people. But "Lesser Vehicle" might be understood as the tendency we all sometimes have to practice for self-gain, not helping others.

89 "A Persian" may refer to Bodhidharma, sometimes described as having blue eyes and a red beard and being from Persia, but it may also just refer to any merchant or traveler from an exotic place. For people from Handan see Dharma hall discourse 184 and volume 2, note 147.

Expounding in Accord with Japan
244. Dharma Hall Discourse

Expounding Dharma should be in accord with time and season. If it is not in accord with the times, it is completely inappropriate, idle chatter. Is there anything here that is in accord with time and season, or not?

After a pause Dōgen said: Expounding Zen in the country of Japan is necessarily always previous to the Awesome Sound in the realm of the Empty King.[90] It cannot be the same as Huangmei [Daman Hongren], and cannot be [compared to] before or after Qingyuan.[91] Although it is like this, I cannot avoid being reviled by bystanders who would say, "Hey! This mountain barbarian only can expound wild-fox Zen."

Monks' Bowls Open Their Mouths
245. Dharma Hall Discourse

I can remember, once a monk asked Zhaozhou, "How can we use our mind throughout the twenty-four hours?"[92]

Zhaozhou said, "You are used by the twenty-four hours; this old monk [Zhaozhou himself] can use the twenty-four hours. Which time are you asking about?"

The teacher Dōgen said: Although Zhaozhou said it this way, how is it for me, Eihei, having arrived at this point?

You are used by the twenty-four hours, but I allow that you understand Ancestral Teacher Zen. This old monk [Zhaozhou] can use the

---

90 For the Buddha Awesome Sound King of Emptiness, see Dharma hall discourses 127 and 135. This Buddha is described in chapter 20 of the Lotus Sutra, "The Bodhisattva Never Disparaging." Here Dōgen is indicating that expressing Dharma must precede the emergence of the discriminations of the phenomenal world.

91 "It cannot be the same as Huangmei, and cannot be before or after Qingyuan" indicates that the true teaching is not a matter of imitation of, or comparison with, the ancient Chinese masters. In this case Dōgen, while citing Huangmei and Qingyuan, specifically also implies the changing seasons, since the names Huangmei and Qingyuan include the characters for yellow and blue, representing fall and summer. The changing seasons here also refers to Dōgen's changing situation of trying to teach Zen in a new country, Japan.

92 In Dōgen's Chinese, what we are translating as "twenty-four hours" is literally "twelve hours," the time division used traditionally in East Asia for one day. This story appears in Zhaozhou's Recorded Sayings; see Green, *Recorded Sayings of Zen Master Joshu,* p. 21.

twenty-four hours, so I allow that the old monk understands Tathāgata Zen.[93] This is the reality of going beyond buddhas and ancestors. What is the reality within the house of buddha ancestors?

After a pause Dōgen said: The monks' bowls open their mouths and eat rice.

Verses for the Original Mind
246. Dharma Hall Discourse

When Zen Master Hongzhi was abbot at Tiantong, in a Dharma hall discourse he gave this story. "A monk asked [Huguo Shoucheng] Jingguo, 'What is the original mind?' [Huguo] Jingguo said, 'Because a rhinoceros plays with the moon, a family crest appears on its horn. An elephant is startled by thunder, and a flower appears on its tusk.'"

Hongzhi said, "Not the same, not separated; not grasped, not discarded; from east to west, who is above and who below? Following the crooked ways of the world, you lose your merit; going straight in accord with the real, you will not be in debt. Tell me, how do you thoroughly express it? Do you understand? You should trust that within the jewel there is fire. Stop facing the sky and asking the sun."

The teacher Dōgen said: Although these two venerable ones said it like this, Eihei, also, will not keep silent. Suppose someone were to ask, "What is the original mind?" I would say to him: Indra constructs a splendid palace in the heavens.[94] A Persian from the southern ocean offers ivory.

---

93 See Dharma hall discourse 52 and volume 1, note 123. "Ancestor Zen" traditionally refers to practice as it functions in ordinary daily activity. "Tathāgata Zen" refers to practice based on teachings from the sutras.

94 Indra constructing a palace echoes the story cited by Hongzhi in the Shōyōroku, case 4. Indra was out walking with the Buddha, who pointed to the ground and said, "This is a good place for a temple." Indra stuck a blade of grass into the ground and said that the temple was built, and the Buddha smiled. See Cleary, *Book of Serenity,* case 4, pp. 17–19. See also Dharma hall discourse 79.

Wishes for the Emperor's Birthday

247. Dharma Hall Discourse on the Emperor's Birthday[95]

[The emperor is] the ancient Buddha from the heavens, most revered in the human world. Descending to be born in this continent of Jambudvipa, he reigns over ten thousand countries so that they revive and flourish. May the reign of this phoenix be thorough and long enduring, and sweep away the dusts of the whole world within the four oceans. May the body of this imperial dragon be ever in good health, so that we see him on the palace throne for a long time. Respectfully we pray that he have the longevity of South Mountain.[96]

Do you know the single phrase to completely express this wish? "On the occasion of the birthday of this emperor of the Hōji era, may his sacred life extend for ten billion years more."[97] This is the phrase for congratulations on the emperor's birthday. How shall his retainer monk, Eihei, express it? The waves on the four oceans are calm, and the dragon sleeps peacefully. The clouds are bright in the nine heavens, and the crane flies high.[98]

95 This was the fourth birthday, on the tenth day of the sixth month in 1247, of Emperor Gofukakusa, a relative of Dōgen. This emperor's paternal grandmother was either a cousin or a niece of Dōgen. There is still debate as to whether Dōgen's father was Minamoto Michichika, as believed in the traditional biographies, or Michichika's son, Minamoto Michitomo, the view of many modern scholars. Gofukakusa's father was the Emperor Gosaga, who reigned from 1242 to 1246. Gofukakusa was to reign from 1246 to 1259, and died in 1304. During most of Japanese history, including Dōgen's time, the emperors had no actual political power, although they were highly venerated. This is the only Dharma hall discourse in Eihei Kōroku for an emperor's birthday, and is therefore controversial among some modern Sōtō scholars. Dōgen calls himself a "retainer monk" herein, despite the issue in early Chinese Buddhism of whether monks should be subservient to the emperor. However, such Dharma hall discourses for the emperor's birthday were common in Song China, including those by Hongzhi and by Dōgen's teacher Tiantong Rujing.

96 "South Mountain" is short for Zhongnan Mountain, a sacred mountain south of the Chinese capital Xian.

97 This wish for ten billion years of life is a formulaic phrase used by all Japanese people to celebrate the emperor's birthday.

98 "The waves on the four oceans are calm…and the crane flies high," an expression of serene longevity, is a quote from the Recorded Sayings of Yuanwu, the commentator of the Hekiganroku.

Eyes and Nostrils Open

248. Dharma Hall Discourse for Closing the Summer Practice Period

On the fifteenth day of the fourth month we make a fist; on the fifteenth day of the seventh month we open our hand.[99] A single phrase in between transcends both sides. What is the phrase that transcends both sides? Eyelids are torn apart, nostrils are drilled open.

Tiantong Rujing's Troublemaking

249. Dharma Hall Discourse on the Memorial Day for [Dōgen's] teacher Tiantong Rujing[100]

Today my late teacher plays with spirit, fanning the family wind of the buddha ancestors to make clouds. Creating disorder and so much heartache in this Sahā world, his ignorant karmic consciousness extends to his descendants.

Meeting People of the Way

250. Dharma Hall Discourse on the First Day of the Eighth Month [1247]

I can remember, a monk asked Zhaozhou, "What do you do when you meet a wayfarer?"

Zhaozhou said, "I give him a lacquer bowl."

The teacher Dōgen said: The ancient Buddha Zhaozhou had superior power; however, he had a bearing together with which others could not study.[101] Suppose someone asked me, Eihei, "What do you do when you meet a wayfarer?" I would simply tell him: This mid-autumn morning it is getting cool. Respectfully I wish all the venerable ones in the great assembly ten thousand blessings in all your activities.

99 The fifteenth day (or full moon) of the fourth month is the beginning of the practice period; the fifteenth day of the seventh month is its end.

100 Tiantong Rujing's memorial day was the seventh month, the seventeenth day. He died in 1227, so this was the twentieth anniversary, considered the twenty-first by the traditional East Asian way of counting.

101 Zhaozhou is widely praised by all subsequent Zen people for the greatness of his practice and utterances. But it seems he was so lofty that none of his disciples could match him, and his lineage quickly died out.

A Mountain Homecoming from Kamakura

251. Dharma Hall Discourse on the Fourteenth Day of the Third Month of the Second Year of Hōji [1248][102]

On the third day of the eighth month of last year, this mountain monk departed from this mountain and went to the Kamakura District of Sagami Prefecture to expound the Dharma for patrons and lay students. On this month of this year, just last night, I came home to this temple, and this morning I have ascended this seat. Some people may have some questions about this affair. After traversing many mountains and rivers, I did expound the Dharma for the sake of lay students, which may sound like I value worldly people and take lightly monks. Moreover, some may ask whether I presented some Dharma that I never before expounded, and that they have not heard. However, there was no Dharma at all that I have never previously expounded, or that you have not heard. I merely explained to them that people who practice virtue improve; that those who produce unwholesomeness degenerate; that they should practice the cause and experience the results; and should throw away the tile and only take up the jewel. Because of these, this single matter is what this old man Eihei has been able to clarify, express, trust, and practice. Does the great assembly want to understand this truth?

After a pause, Dōgen said: I cannot stand that my tongue has no means to express the cause and the result. How many mistakes I have made in my effort to cultivate the way. Today how pitiful it is that I have become a water buffalo. This is the phrase for expounding Dharma. How shall I utter a phrase for returning home to the mountains? This mountain monk has been gone for more than half a year. I was like a solitary wheel placed in vast space. Today, I have returned to the mountains, and the clouds are feeling joyful. My great love for the mountains has magnified since before.

102 There is a seven-and-a-half-month gap between the previous Dharma hall discourse, given in the eighth month of 1247, and this one, in the third month of 1248. During this time, as he says, Dōgen traveled to the eastern capital of Kamakura, the headquarters of the new military rulers, or shōguns, only recently established in 1192. We do not know exactly what transpired there, or the full motivation for the trip. But apparently he was requested to teach there by patrons.

The Single Voice of Younger and Older Brothers

252. Dharma Hall Discourse

I can remember, Ānanda asked Mahākāśyapa, "Elder brother, besides transmitting his gold-embroidered monk's robe, what did Buddha transmit to you?"

Mahākāśyapa called, "Ānanda!"

Ānanda said, "Yes."

Mahākāśyapa said, "Take down the flagpole in front of the gate."[103]

Great Assembly, do you want to understand the principle of this?

After a pause Dōgen said: The calling and responding of younger and elder brothers have the same single voice. Before pulling out the nail, they have already removed the wedge.[104] Having pulled down the flagpole from in front of the gate, now, in which house will it become a dried shitstick?[105]

On the High Mountain, Spring Comes Late

253. Dharma Hall Discourse

Clapping hands and giving a hand have been transmitted and held by twenty-eight [Indian ancestors] and six [Chinese ancestors]. Knowing and repaying the debt of kindness, they constructed ten thousand trillion transformations [or methods of teaching]. The old plum tree is by the cliffside, and the peaches by the ocean.[106] The single dynamic activity is revealed in the samādhi that enters each and every thing. Although it is like this, because the mountain is high, the snow melts late, and because

---

103 This story of Ānanda and Mahākāśyapa appears in the Mumonkan, case 22. See Aitken, *Gateless Barrier,* pp. 142–146; and Cleary, *Unlocking the Zen Kōan,* pp. 106–109. The flagpole refers to the banner put out front of a monastery when ritual doctrinal debates were being conducted.

104 Genryū Kagamishima's interpretation is that the nail refers to doubt; the wedge is enlightenment.

105 For the reference to Yunmen's "dried shitstick," see, for example, Dharma hall discourse 229. This refers to the response by Yunmen as to what Buddha is. See case 21 of the Mumonkan; Aitken, *Gateless Barrier,* pp. 137–141; and Cleary, *Unlocking the Zen Kōan,* pp. 102–105.

106 The peaches by the ocean are legendary Daoist peaches that bestow immortality.

the tree is old, spring comes slowly. Why is this the case? Would you like to clearly understand?

The old crane, on the tree without shadows, dreams of the moon. The bees in the flowers of a budless branch find spring.

A Lion Knows a Lion's Roar
254. Dharma Hall Discourse

Here is a story. One day the World-Honored One, Śākyamuni, ascended the seat. Mañjuśrī pounded the sounding block and said, "Clearly observe the Dharma of the King of Dharma. The Dharma of the King of Dharma is thus." The World-Honored One stepped down from his seat.[107]

Teacher Zhimen Guangzuo said, "Pounding the block, Mañjuśrī announced and let the assembly know that the law of the Dharma King is like this. If there is a person of saindhava in the assembly, such a person does not wait for the light to shine from the hair-curl on the Buddha's brow."[108]

His disciple, the Zen elder Xuedou Chongxian, said, "Within the forests of successive sages, a capable person knows that the law of the Dharma King is not like this. If there were a person of saindhava in the assembly, why would it be necessary for Mañjuśrī to pound the block?"[109]

The teacher Dōgen said: Although both those venerable teachers practiced together with Mañjuśrī, they did not practice with the World-Honored One. Benevolent people, do you want to know the principle for

---

107 This story of Mañjuśrī pounding the sounding block is the first case in the Shōyōroku, and case 92 in the Hekiganroku. See Cleary, *Book of Serenity,* pp. 3–5; and Cleary and Cleary, *Blue Cliff Record,* pp. 588–591.

108 *Saindhava* is a Sanskrit word which, depending on context, can mean "salt," "horse," "bowl or basin," or "water," as described in chapter 9 of the Mahāparinirvāṇa Sūtra. It is used in Zen as a test for context, as the disciple must divine which item is intended by the master calling for *saindhava.* So a "person of *saindhava* "understands what is required without explanation." Dōgen wrote an essay in Shōbōgenzō called "A King Asks for Saindhava." See Heine, *Dōgen and the Kōan Tradition,* pp. 249–253; or Nishijima and Cross, *Master Dogen's Shobogenzo,* book 4, pp. 101–106.

109 "Within the forests of successive sages, a capable person,...why would it be necessary for Mañjuśrī to pound the block?" is a quote from the Hekiganroku. See Cleary and Cleary, *Blue Cliff Record,* case 92, pp. 590.

practicing together with the World-Honored One? The sound of a lion's roar is known by a lion. The Dharma of the Dharma King is the same. Everyone in the assembly is a person of saindhava, so Mañjuśrī must pound the block a second time.

Body and Mind Connected with the Ten Thousand Forms
255. Dharma Hall Discourse

All buddhas of the three times and the ancestral teachers of all generations carry and bring everything from under the heavens to store it under the heavens, then tear up society and reenter society. When we attain this key to the gateway, we can expound one foot and can practice one foot.[110] This body is not a lump of flesh; the mind is fences and walls. Our eyebrows arch like the low spring mountains; our eyes are blue as the autumn seas. Within a hundred thousand samādhis, many dusts appear; from immeasurable Dharma gates, the ten thousand forms emerge.

Washing an Unstainable Body
256. Dharma Hall Discourse for Bathing [the Baby] Buddha [Buddha's Birthday, 1248]

When Zen Master Hongzhi was abbot at Tiantong, in a Dharma hall discourse upon bathing Buddha he said, "This is the completely clear water of the emptiness of self-nature; the perfectly bright, pure wisdom body. Therefore, we do not need to wash the body; right here not a speck of dust exists. So he has become Buddha, overcome demons, [reached] that other shore, and [departed] this deluded riverbank. This "dada wawa" baby talk was at the beginning, then this random crawling around became the cause [for becoming Buddha].[111] On this occasion, Śākyamuni Buddha, do not get angry at our pouring foul water on your head. Why don't you invoke the power of Avalokiteśvara Bodhisattva, and then naturally [this injury]

---

110 "Can expound one foot and can practice one foot" here is in contrast to the common Zen expression that to practice one inch is better than expounding one foot.

111 "Baby talk" refers to Buddha's utterance that "I alone am the World-Honored One," and "crawling around" refers to his then taking seven steps, both occurring in legend shortly after the Buddha's birth. This Buddha's Birthday Dharma Hall Discourse by Hongzhi is similar in parts to the one Dōgen quotes in Dharma hall discourse 236.

will rebound to its originator.[112] Benevolent people, what is it like just when the ladle [for pouring water over the Buddha] is in your hand? Without the cause of [thoroughly studying] a single thing, we cannot develop any wisdom."

The teacher Dōgen said: This ancient Buddha, my Dharma uncle, was from the branch of Furong [Daokai], and a disciple of Danxia [Zichun].[113] Although Hongzhi said it like this, his descendant Eihei has a verse on this occasion:

> At the time of his birth, three thousand worlds trembled.
> At his awakening site, eighty thousand gates opened wide.
> Pouring water over the head of his unstained body
> Is an embarrassing scene of sincerity in play.

Practicing Together with the Tathāgatas

257. Dharma Hall Discourse for Beginning the Summer Practice Period
When Zen Master Hongzhi was abbot at Tiantong, in a Dharma hall discourse for beginning the summer practice period, he said, "Ordinary people and sages together share one house. We see our lives as in the Buddha field of tranquil radiance. Then we empty our minds in the hall for creating buddhas, where some naturally open their flower of awakening in this monastic garden in the hills.[114] Committed to never leaving for ninety days, we see the place where we were before we ever took a step.[115] For

---

112 "Invoke the power of Avalokiteśvara Bodhisattva, and this injury will rebound to its originator" is from chapter 25 of the Lotus Sutra, which is a separate sutra, "The Universal Gateway of the Bodhisattva Regarder of the World's Sounds." See Katō, Tamura, and Miyasaka, *Threefold Lotus Sutra*, p. 325; or Hurvitz, *Scripture of the Lotus Blossom of the Fine Dharma*, p. 317. This sutra to Avalokiteśvara (Jap.: Kannon; Chin.: Guanyin) was chanted regularly in Dōgen's time, and is still chanted in Japan today.

113 Hongzhi was the Dharma brother of Zhenxie Qingliao, another disciple of Danxia Zichun, from whom the lineage of Tiantong Rujing and Dōgen descends.

114 The "hall for creating buddhas," another name for the *zendō*, or meditation hall (Jap.: *senbutsujō*), literally means the hall for "selecting buddhas."

115 "Committed to never leaving" is one of the names for a practice period. See volume 2 (Dharma hall discourse 158), note 103.

three months of protecting life, enact the body and mind that does not attach to objects. Many bodies peacefully abide within one body, and one body engages the way within many bodies.[116] Therefore it is said that all buddhas' Dharma bodies enter my nature; my nature joins with and becomes the same as the tathāgatas.[117] Also it is said, 'Make great perfect awakening into your own sangha building.'[118] If we can proceed accordingly, how could there be a problem? So now, how can we thoroughly enact this to join the tathāgatas? Do you fully understand this? Do not manifest the bodily form of the karmic three realms of desire, form, and formlessness. Sit and cut off the ten directions and clarify the emptiness of self-nature."[119]

The teacher Dōgen said: Although the ancient Buddha Hongzhi joined with the tathāgatas, he has not yet peacefully abided together with the tathāgatas. Today Eihei joins in harmony with Hongzhi, and practices together with the tathāgatas. Do you understand this?

After a pause Dōgen said: Holding up a flower and smiling slightly is really making trouble. Truly Gautama created confusion in that scene. We [simply need to] hold each other's hands and visit the Buddha hall; with eyebrows knit together we just enter the monks' hall.[120]

116 "Peacefully abide" is the primary name for the three-month practice period.

117 "All buddhas' Dharma bodies enter my nature; my nature joins with and becomes the same as the tathāgatas" is a quote from the Song of Enlightenment by Yongjia Xuanjie. See Sheng-Yen, trans. and ed., *The Poetry of Enlightenment: Poems by Ancient Ch'an Masters* (Elmhurst, N.Y.: Dharma Drum Publications, 1987), p. 55.

118 "Make great perfect awakening into your own sangha building" is from the Perfect Enlightenment Sutra, the chapter on the "Perfect Enlightenment Bodhisattva." See Sheng-Yen, trans. and ed., *Complete Enlightenment: Translation and Commentary on the Sutra of Complete Enlightenment* (Boston: Shambhala, 1999), p. 59; and Charles Muller, trans., *The Sutra of Perfect Enlightenment* (Albany: State University of New York Press, 1999), p. 232.

119 "Cutting off the ten directions" implies cutting through our sense of separation from the objective, external world in all directions.

120 Dōgen seems to be emphasizing the everyday simplicity of practice as its purpose. He seems basically in accord with what Hongzhi stated, but perhaps Dōgen somewhat disagrees with Hongzhi's last two sentences in this quote, which seem to somewhat advocate transcending this phenomenal, karmic world and physical body.

Eihei Zenji Goroku

RECORDED SAYINGS
AT EIHEIJI TEMPLE

COLLECTED BY EJŌ, ATTENDANT OF DŌGEN ZENJI

E K
I Ō
H R   THE EXTENSIVE RECORD OF EIHEI DŌGEN, VOLUME FOUR
E O
I K
U

Playing the Iron Flute

258. Dharma Hall Discourse

At midnight put on your shoes and depart after stealing Bodhidharma's eyeballs. At dawn put on your hat and come after grabbing Xitang [Zhizang]'s nostrils.[1] One departs and one arrives, just like autumn sounds and spring sounds; half open, half closed, something like sun face and moon face.[2] Reaching back for his pillow, the hands and eyes throughout [Daowu Yuanzhi's] body are clear.[3] Cutting off his arm to offer it to the

---

1 This refers to a story that Dōgen discusses in the Shōbōgenzō essay Kokū (Space). Xitang's older Dharma brother Shigong asked Xitang if he could demonstrate space. After Xitang pawed the air, Shigong said he didn't understand, stuck his finger in Xitang's nostril and yanked his nose. When Xitang screamed, Shigong said, "Now you understand space." Dōgen cites this story as case 53 in his kōans with verse comments in volume 9, below. For Kokū (Space) see Tanahashi, *Enlightenment Unfolds*, pp. 202–203.

2 "Sun face and moon face" refers to Mazu's response to a question about his failing health, and refers to buddhas said to live a very long time, or for merely one night. Dōgen mentions this phrase regularly in Eihei Kōroku, and includes it as case 80 in his kōans with verse comments in volume 9. See also Cleary and Cleary, *Blue Cliff Record*, case 3, pp. 18–21; and Cleary, *Book of Serenity*, case 36, pp. 160–162.

3 "Reaching back for his pillow, the hands and eyes throughout the body are clear" is a reference to the dialogue between Yunyan Tansheng and his brother Daowu Yuanzhi concerning the function of the many arms of the bodhisattva of compassion, Avalokiteśvara (Jap.: Kannon). When Yunyan asked how Avalokiteśvara uses so many hands and eyes, Daowu said it's like reaching back for a pillow in the middle of the night. When Yunyan said this is like hands and eyes all over the body, Daowu responded that the hands and

first ancestor, only [Dazu Huike] transmitted the Dharma and attained the marrow. Although this is so, you should directly open the lock to nonduality and finally attain it. What is this lock to nonduality?

After a pause Dōgen said: Throw away the sutras, vinaya, and commentaries, and freely blow on the iron flute to play the melody "Enticing Plum Blossoms."[4]

A Day of Just Sitting and Just Sleeping

259. Dharma Hall Discourse on the Twenty-Fifth Day of the Fourth Month [1248]

While Zen Master Yuanwu lived as abbot at Yunju (Cloud Dwelling) Mountain, he gave a Dharma hall discourse on this day and said, "An ancient one said, 'On this eleventh day of the summer practice period, how is Hanshan?' Another person said, 'On this eleventh day of the summer practice period, how is the water buffalo?' This mountain monk [Yuanwu] is not like that. On this eleventh day of the summer practice period, how are the lanterns and temple pillars? If you penetrate the lanterns and temple pillars, you will immediately recognize the water buffalo. If you recognize the water buffalo, you will immediately see Hanshan. If you hesitate, this old monk is beneath your feet."

Old man Yuanwu said it this way, but today Eihei will try to give you comments on each statement. The lanterns are a piece of orange peel. The temple pillars are originally dried shitsticks.[5] Water buffaloes are animals. How many of the temple's seedlings do they eat? Speaking to Hanshan, you are a worldly person.[6] If you do not understand, Eihei is

eyes are throughout the body. Dōgen discusses this dialogue in the Shōbōgenzō essay Kannon. See Francis Cook, *Sounds of Valley Streams: Enlightenment in Dōgen's Zen; Translations of Nine Essays from Shōbōgenzō* (Albany: State University of New York Press, 1989), pp. 89–95. See also Cleary, *Book of Serenity,* case 54, pp. 229–232; and Cleary and Cleary, *Blue Cliff Record,* case 89, pp. 571–577.

4 "Enticing Plum Blossoms" is a song mentioned by Tiantong Rujing. See Dharma hall discourse 138. Here Dōgen is encouraging the freedom of practice, rather than theoretical understandings.

5 "Dried shitsticks" is a reference to Yunmen's statement about Buddha, often referred to by Dōgen. See, for example, Dharma hall discourse 69 and volume 1, note 150.

6 Hanshan is thought to have been a layperson, even though he lived in the mountains near a monastery.

treading on top of Yuanwu's head. Do you all clearly understand this point? If you hesitate, how will all of you benevolent people remain within Eihei's fist and continue your efforts?

Although this is so, I, Eihei also say: On this eleventh day of the summer practice period, what are you doing inside the monks' hall? Everyone, I ask what you will say. If you do not speak, Eihei will speak for all of you.

After a pause Dōgen said: In the early morning we eat gruel, at midday rice. When the wooden sounding block is struck, we just sit zazen; when we open our quilts, we just sleep.

The Fifth Ancestor's Three Hits

260. Dharma Hall Discourse

I can remember, the sixth ancestor entered the assembly of Huangmei, and stayed at the rice pounding hut. Once the fifth ancestor [Daman Hongren] secretly came by himself to the rice pounding hut and asked, "Is the rice refined or not?"

Huineng said, "It is refined, but it is not sifted yet."

The fifth ancestor hit the mortar three times with his staff. Huineng immediately sifted the rice three times, and entered the fifth ancestor's room.[7]

The teacher Dōgen said: Tell me everyone, do you want to meet with these two ancient buddhas? *Dōgen pounded his staff three times.*

Suppose someone says that this is what is studied in the realm of buddha ancestors, so what is the reality of total liberation? *Dōgen pounded his staff three times.*

Suppose someone further says that this is what is studied on the long platform in the monks' hall, so what is the reality that does not cross into twos or threes? *Dōgen pounded his staff three times.*

The Spread of Healing Wisdom

261. Dharma Hall Discourse for the Fifth Day of the Fifth Month Celebration [1248]

---

7 This story precedes Huineng's receiving Dharma transmission in the Platform Sutra of the sixth ancestor. See Price and Wong, *Diamond Sutra and Sutra of Hui Neng*, pp. 18–19; and Cleary, *Sutra of Hui-neng*, pp. 10–11.

Dōgen quoted the Dharma Hall Discourse for the Fifth Day of the Fifth Month by Zen Master Hongzhi, previously discussed [in Dharma hall discourse 242] and then, after a pause, Dōgen said the following.[8]

The fifth day of the fifth month is the Festival of the Center of Heaven. Above the hundred grass-tips we see the mountain of medicine. Large and small rocks discuss prajñā.[9] These sounds flow out and spread to reach the human world.

Scooping Up the Dharmakāya
262. Dharma Hall Discourse

I can remember, a monk asked Yunmen, "What is the phrase that pervades the Dharma body?"[10]

Yunmen said, "Hide the body within the Big Dipper."

The teacher Dōgen said: Yunmen gave a very good answer, but he was only able to say eighty or ninety percent. Suppose someone asked Eihei, "What is the phrase that pervades the Dharma body?" I would say to him: The dipper scoops up Śākyamuni; a measuring cup assesses Bodhidharma.

Meeting It without Recognition
263. Dharma Hall Discourse

I can remember, a monk asked Shishuang [Qingzhu], "How is Buddha nature like empty space?"

Shishuang responded, "When we lie down it's there; when we sit it's not there."

---

8 For other Dharma hall discourses on this Fifth Month Festival day, see Dharma hall discourses 169 and 242. The first sentence in the text, "Dōgen quoted...said the following" is a note added here by the compiler of this volume, Koun Ejō. The excerpt by Hongzhi referred to here is given in full in Dharma hall discourse 242, ending with "A settled person doesn't speak; placid water doesn't flow."

9 "Mountain of medicine" refers to a mountain covered with medicinal herbs (see Dharma hall discourses 169 and 242) but also to the Zen teacher Yaoshan Weiyan, as "Yaoshan" means Medicine Mountain. "Rocks" (in "large and small rocks") is *shitou* and therefore refers to Yaoshan's teacher, Shitou Xiqian, progenitor of Dōgen's Caodong, or Sōtō lineage. So this passage also refers to the teaching of this lineage spreading into the world.

10 "Dharma body" (Skt.: *dharmakāya*) is the True Reality body of Buddha, equivalent to the whole phenomenal world.

Today I, Eihei, will give you all a comment to break through this statement. What is the meaning of Shishuang's saying that it is there when we lie down? When the jewel wheel functions and turns, we laugh loudly. What is the meaning of Shishuang's saying that it is not there when we sit? Right here we meet without knowing each other. Study this.

The Function of Emptiness and the Protection of the Mind Seal
264. Dharma Hall Discourse
The function before the empty kalpa is used without having traces, and the mind seal tucked under the arm is empty, but exists within conditions.[11] How shall we describe such a situation? Raising the banner of ignorance and karmic consciousness, upside down, we pick up and come with the dried shitstick.[12]

Just Come and Go
265. Dharma Hall Discourse
Life has no place where it comes from, just bear it and come, again and again. Similarly, death has no place to go, just bear it and go, again and again.

Demonstrations of Practice Clarified in the Dawn Wind
266. Dharma Hall Discourse
Sometimes I, Eihei, enter the ultimate state and offer profound discussion, simply wishing for you all to be steadily intimate in your mind field.[13]

---

11 "The mind seal tucked under the arm," literally "seal below the elbow," refers to the Buddha Mind Seal, said to be what is transmitted in Zen. "Below the elbow" is an old Chinese phrase for talismanic papers tied to a string around the neck and tucked under the arm for protection. This whole first sentence about the function and the mind seal is from Hongzhi's Extensive Record, vol. 4.

12 "The dried shitstick" is an expression of Yunmen's discussed previously in Eihei Kōroku. Here Dōgen seems to be using it as a positive expression for Buddha, indicating the mind seal and its functioning as existing right in the world of delusion.

13 This "sometimes," repeated four times in this Dharma hall discourse, is the same phrase, uji, used by Dōgen as the title of his celebrated essay "Being-Time" in Shōbōgenzō. In that essay, Dōgen presents a teaching and philosophy about the multidimensionality of time as our very existence. See Tanahashi, Moon in a Dewdrop, pp. 76–83; Cleary, Shōbōgenzō: Zen Essays by Dogen, pp. 102–110; or Waddell and Abe, Heart of Dōgen's Shōbōgenzō, pp. 48–58.

Sometimes, within the gates and gardens of the monastery, I offer my own style of practical instruction, simply wishing you all to disport and play freely with spiritual penetration. Sometimes I spring quickly leaving no trace, simply wishing you all to drop off body and mind.[14] Sometimes I enter the samādhi of self-fulfillment, simply wishing you all to trust what your hands can hold.[15]

Suppose someone suddenly came forth and asked this mountain monk, "What would go beyond these [kinds of teaching]?"

I would simply say to him: Scrubbed clean by the dawn wind, the night mist clears. Dimly seen, the blue mountains form a single line.

Nanquan Not Involved with the Demon Spirits
267. Dharma Hall Discourse
I can remember, once Officer Lu requested Nanquan, "I ask the teacher to expound the Dharma for the sake of the assembly."

Nanquan said, "What do you want this old man to expound?"

The officer said, "Master, don't you have some skillful means for teaching?"

Nanquan said, "What are those in the assembly lacking?"

The officer said, "What will you do about those in the four births and six realms?"[16]

---

14 "Spring quickly leaving no trace" is from Zhuangzi. "Spring" is literally "to race or gallop," but here it implies Dōgen's instant leap into reality. "Drop off body and mind" is *shinjin datsuraku,* an important phrase for Dōgen, referring to zazen as well as complete awakening.

15 "The samādhi of self-fulfillment" is *jijuyū zammai,* a phrase often used by Dōgen to refer to zazen. *Juyū* as a compound means fulfillment or enjoyment, so this samādhi is the practice in which our self is fulfilled and thoroughly enjoyed. The individual Chinese characters *ju* and *yū* mean to accept or receive one's function or position. Dōgen describes this as the criterion of zazen in his early writing Bendōwa (Talk on Wholehearted Practice of the Way). See Okumura and Leighton, *The Wholehearted Way,* pp. 14–19, 21–24, 94–123.

16 In traditional Buddhist cosmology, the four births are beings who are womb-born, egg-born, moisture-born, and born through metamorphosis, but this refers generally to all living beings; as do the six realms of karmic existence: heavenly beings, titans, humans, animals, hungry ghosts, and hell-dwellers.

Nanquan said, "This old monk does not teach them."

The officer had no response.[17]

The teacher Dōgen said: That mountain barbarian did not leave Mount Nanquan for more than thirty years. The demon spirits finally had an opportunity to observe Nanquan.[18] Although this was the story, if it were Eihei, and someone were to request me to expound the Dharma for the sake of the assembly, this is what I would say to him: I have been expounding it for a long time.

Suppose he were to ask, "What will you do about those in the four births and six realms?" I would say to him: Fortunately, right here I am able to have a bowel movement. Why would I be involved with those in the four births and the six realms?[19]

Sparrows and Crows in the Vast Universe

268. Dharma Hall Discourse

When you climb a mountain you should reach the peak. When you enter the ocean you should reach the bottom. If you climb a mountain and don't reach the peak, you will not know the unlimited vastness of the universe. If you enter the ocean and don't reach the bottom, you will not know the shallows or depths of the blue-green sea. If you already know the unlimited vastness and the shallows and depths, you can overturn the four oceans with one kick, and topple Mount Sumeru with one push. As for a person who opens their hands like this and reaches home, how could he not be aware of the sparrows singing and crows cawing among the cypress trees? Do you all want to understand this clearly?

---

17 Officer Lu (b. 764), a high government minister, was a prominent lay disciple of Nanquan. Their dialogues appear in a number of kōans. This dialogue appears in the Jingde Transmission of the Lamp. See Chang, *Original Teachings of Ch'an Buddhism*, pp. 158–159. For another story of Officer Lu, see Cleary, *Book of Serenity*, case 91, pp. 390–393.

18 "Demon spirits" refers to a story about a villager making preparations for Nanquan's unannounced visit, thanks to being forewarned by spirits, much to Nanquan's chagrin. See Chang, *Original Teachings of Ch'an Buddhism*, pp. 154–155. Dōgen cites this story as case 63 of his 90 kōans with commentary in volume 9 below, as well as in his collection of three hundred kōans. See Nishijima, *Master Dogen's Shinji Shobogenzo*, case 18, p. 27.

19 "Why would I be involved with those in the four births and the six realms?" also could be read as "How would I control those in the four births and the six realms?"

After a pause Dōgen said: After twenty-one days of facing the tree, and doing walking meditation, the morning star appeared and illuminated the Milky Way. Unexpectedly he sat and broke through the vajra seat. Who could fathom the wall-gazing of our house?[20]

The Land Is the Entire Body of Buddha
269. Dharma Hall Discourse

Here is a story. A monk asked National Teacher [Nanyang Hui]zhong, "In the teachings we only see that sentient beings become buddhas, but we do not see that nonsentient beings receive confirmation of attaining buddhahood. Among the thousand buddhas in the present kalpa, who is a nonsentient buddha?"

The national teacher said, "When a prince has not yet received his dominion, he is only an individual person. After receiving his dominion, the land of the whole nation belongs to the king. How will the national land receive its own dominion? Now, when only sentient beings are receiving confirmation of becoming buddhas, the nation's land in the ten directions is the Buddha body of Vairocana. How will nonsentient beings receive confirmation?"

The ancient Buddha Hongzhi said, "The Buddha within the land manifests a body everywhere. The lands within the Buddha are also all like this in every particle. Can you thoroughly experience this?"

After a pause [Hongzhi] said, "The six kingdoms [of China] naturally were purified [and unified] after a period of chaos. A solitary person dared on his own to build a foundation for great peacefulness."[21]

---

20 This passage refers to Śākyamuni's sitting under the Bodhi tree before his great awakening. "Facing the tree" refers to his practice of facing a tree, like Dōgen's facing the wall in zazen. Walking meditation is *kinhin,* the walking done between longer periods of sitting. "Wall-gazing" is a phrase for sitting meditation, implying facing the wall, a practice going back to Bodhidharma sitting in the cave in Northern China. It also implies observing the world as a wall does, beyond self-projection or discriminative judgments.

21 This "solitary person," on one level, historically, refers to the founder of the Qin dynasty, who ruled from 255 to 250 B.C.E. He had succeeded in unifying the country of China from six smaller feudal states, besides the seventh, former small Qin kingdom. Historically this emperor was known both for initiating the Great Wall of China to protect the nation and for burning many books in an attempt to destroy the lore of Chinese

The teacher Dōgen said: The ancient Buddha has spoken like this, but why should I not say more? The Buddha of the land pervades the body and is the entire body. The lands of the Buddha are the suchness of reality, and their non-suchness. Can you thoroughly experience this?

After a pause Dōgen said: The host within the host, and the host within the host, go beyond objects and transcend people to establish the foundation for an empire.[22]

Speak of Not Speaking
270. Dharma Hall Discourse

Polishing a tile to make a mirror is diligent effort. How could the way of thinking within steadfast, immovable sitting be careless?[23] If you want to visit that realm of glimpsing the ground [of buddhahood], you should further come here and close your mouth in silence.

Tell me great assembly, are Eihei and the ancient ones the same or different? Try to say something and I'll see how you do. If you do not speak, I will speak for all of you.

---

culture, much of which was indeed lost. However, this passage by Hongzhi could also be read as a statement about the relationship between a buddha and the land, or the objective world. The six kingdoms might refer to the six sense gates, which must be purified to produce the foundations for the great peacefulness of a buddha, which Dōgen then refers to as the host within the host.

22 The repetition in "The host within the host, and the host within the host" expresses that both the personal Buddha and the lands of the phenomenal world are ultimately the host within the host. This is an expression for the epitome of suchness, or the ultimate integration and identification of the universal and the phenomenal. "The host within the host" is an expression used by Dongshan Liangjie at the end of the Song of the Precious Mirror Samādhi, his important teaching poem, in which the Caodong (Sōtō) teaching of the five ranks is first suggested. Therefore Dōgen's statement echoes the original language of the national teacher in the first dialogue in this Dharma hall discourse, when the national teacher discusses the dominion of the prince and the land, since "dominion" is our translation in that context for "rank."

23 Polishing a tile to make a mirror refers to a story about Mazu and his teacher Nanyue Huairang. Nanyue asked why Mazu was sitting, and Mazu said he was trying to become a buddha. Nanyue started polishing a tile and Mazu asked what he was doing. Nanyue said he was making the tile into a mirror. See Ogata, *Transmission of the Lamp,* pp. 162–163. Conventionally, this story is understood as a warning against sitting meditation, but Dōgen encourages polishing mirrors and zazen, though without seeking to become a buddha. "Steadfast, immovable sitting" refers to a story about Yaoshan Weiyan. A monk asked what he was thinking, as he sat so firmly, and Yaoshan replied that he was thinking

After a pause, Dōgen struck his abbot's chair with the handle of his whisk, and got down from his seat.[24]

Freely Using a Black Staff
271. Dharma Hall Discourse
Dōgen held up his staff and said: Holding this horizontally or using it upside-down, I strike and open the eyes of all buddhas. Going to brightness and coming from darkness, I knock off the noses of the ancestral teachers. At that very time, Maudgalyāyana and Śāriputra are stunned, and swallow their vital spirits and voices. Linji and Deshan laugh loudly. Tell me, what are they laughing at? They are laughing at this thoroughly black staff.

What Should Be Cherished
272. Dharma Hall Discourse
Cherish the dropping away of body and mind. Eyes like lightning illuminate the Milky Way. Value sitting that breaks through the vajra seat. Who knows the wall-gazing of our house?

What Kind of Place Is This?
273. Dharma Hall Discourse
What kind of place is this where we cannot explain, we cannot practice, we cannot enter the room, we cannot give Dharma hall discourses, we cannot make a comment, we cannot enter the gate, and we cannot be liberated? How should we classify this?

It is not that there is no practice-realization. "A high place is high level" is like Mount Sumeru and the nine mountains surrounding it. "A low

---

of not thinking. When the monk asked how to do that, Yaoshan replied, "Beyond-thinking." See Dharma hall discourse 373. For both polishing a mirror and "steadfast, immovable sitting," see "Zazenshin" in Carl Bielefeldt, *Dōgen's Manuals of Zen Meditation* (Berkeley: University of California Press, 1988), pp. 188–205. Both stories are also referred to in Dōgen's writing Fukanzazengi (Universally Recommended Instructions for Zazen). See the end of volume 8, below; also Shohaku Okumura, trans. and ed., *Shikantaza: An Introduction to Zazen* (Kyoto: Kyoto Sōtō Zen Center, 1985), pp. 39–50; and Tanahashi, *Enlightenment Unfolds*, pp. 32–34.

24 "Abbot's chair," literally "Zen floor," refers to the chair, separated from the monks' long sitting platform, on which abbots sat.

place is low level" is like the eight seas and the great ocean around them.[25] Going beyond, he's not called [Yunju] Daoying.[26] Right here there is no second person.

Tiantong Rujing's Last Pilgrimage
274. Dharma Hall Discourse at the Memorial for Master Tiantong [Rujing]
On this day Tiantong [Rujing] mistakenly made a pilgrimage. He did not travel to Mount Tiantai or Mount Wutai.[27] How sad that for ten thousand miles there is not an inch of grass.[28] The old master Guishan became a water buffalo and came here.[29]

25 "A high place is high level; a low place is low level" is a quote from Yangshan. While out working in the fields he told his teacher Guishan that the ground was uneven. Guishan suggested that Yangshan use water to level the ground, and Yangshan responded that "It is unnecessary. A high place is high level; a low place is low level." See Chang, *Original Teachings of Ch'an Buddhism*, p. 210. Dōgen quotes this saying in various writings—for example, in the "Instructions for the Tenzo"—to exemplify each dharma having its appropriate position. See Leighton and Okumura, *Dōgen's Pure Standards for the Zen Community*, p. 36. In traditional Buddhist cosmology, Mount Sumeru is the great axial mountain at the center of the world, with nine mountains around it, interspersed with eight oceans, all surrounded by a great ocean.

26 Dongshan Liangjie asked his student Yunju Daoying what his name was. When Yunju Daoying said, "Daoying," Dongshan asked him to say something going beyond that, and Daoying said that when going beyond he was not named Daoying. See Powell, *Record of Tung-Shan*, pp. 38–39.

27 This Dharma hall discourse was on the seventeenth day of the seventh month (1248), commemorating the day of Tiantong Rujing's passing away. Death is commonly referred to as a "pilgrimage" in Mahāyāna Buddhism. Mount Tiantai and Mount Wutai are sacred mountains in China, with many monasteries and pilgrims. Tiantai was home to Zhiyi, the founder of the Tiantai school (Jap.: Tendai). Dōgen was initially ordained in the Tendai school. Mount Wutai is said to be the home of the bodhisattva of wisdom, Mañjuśrī.

28 "For ten thousand miles there is not an inch of grass" is a saying by Dongshan Liangjie in a Dharma hall discourse at the end of a summer practice period. He told the monks that when they departed the monastery they should go only where there is not an inch of grass for ten thousand miles. See Cleary, *Book of Serenity*, case 89, pp. 382–384; and Powell, *Record of Tung-Shan*, p. 48 and also p. 44, for a related use of this expression by Dongshan.

29 Guishan Lingyou told his assembly, "After I have passed away I will become a water buffalo at the foot of the mountain." See Chang, *Original Teachings of Ch'an Buddhism*, p. 208. Here Dōgen seems to be equating Tiantong Rujing with the great ancient master Guishan.

The Fruit of Past Lives

275. Dharma Hall Discourse

Śākyamuni Buddha spoke to human and heavenly beings and said, "Because of superior causal conditions [from previous lives], some are born on this southern continent. Because of the worst causal conditions [from previous lives], some are born on the northern continent."[30]

Now I ask the great assembly, what are the worst causal conditions? Just pissing and shitting. What are superior causal conditions? In the early morning we eat gruel; at midday, rice. In the early evening, just zazen, in the middle of the night we sleep.

Tiantong Rujing's Last Somersault

276. Dharma Hall Discourse at the Morning Memorial for Master Tiantong [Rujing][31]

Today Tiantong [Rujing] turned a somersault, and kicked over a donkey's womb and horse's womb.[32] Within this scene of violence, the bottom of the bucket fell out. The school of Dongshan entrusted this ancestral teacher, and now it has come to us.

Polishing the Second Moon

277. Mid-Autumn Dharma Hall Discourse

Drawing a circle [in the air] with his whisk, Dōgen said: What is this? Which number moon is this? Truly this is the second moon, transcending not only sun face and moon face but also brightness and darkness.[33]

---

30 This is a quote from the Mahāparinirvāṇa Sūtra, chap. 37. The southern continent, Jambudvipa in Sanskrit, is the human realm, that is, this world. The northern continent is a realm of great pleasure where the life-span is a thousand years; but because of that, those who dwell there find it difficult to arouse the mind of practice and awakening.

31 This memorial discourse for Tiantong Rujing appears right after another similar memorial in discourse 274. Genryū Kagamishima speculates that since there is no memorial discourse for 1251, either Dharma hall discourse 274 or this one, 276, is actually from 1251 and was mistakenly included here with the Dharma hall discourses from 1248.

32 "A donkey's womb" is an expression referring to karmic self, and a "horse's womb" is an expression referring to Buddha nature. See also Dharma hall discourse 4.

33 "The second moon" refers to a story about Yunyan Tansheng and his brother Daowu Yuanzhi. Yunyan was sweeping and Daowu said, "Too busy." Yunyan said, "You should know that there is one who is not busy." Daowu said, "Do you mean there is a second

Can we call it a patch-robed monk's eye? Can we call it all buddhas' eyes? Can we call this the round moon in the sky? Can we call this the full moon in the human world? Since we say that ancient people saw this moon, and modern people see this moon, why is it difficult for modern people to explain the hearts of the ancient people?

For some time, I, Eihei have been striking this [circle], making it into two pieces. One piece fell into the autumn waters. Master Chuanzi [Decheng, the boatman,] took it to make a fishing hook and fished throughout the rivers and oceans. Fishing for a golden-scaled fish, the hook was three inches short, but he finally made his disciple speak.[34]

The other piece flew up to the edge of the twilight clouds, and Master Shigong [Huizang] bent it into a bow, which could shoot a deer, shoot the self, shoot a herd of deer, and shoot half a sage.[35] Although this was so, he did not know that by shooting once or shooting a half, there is giving life and there is killing.

---

moon?" Yunyan held out the broom and said, "Which moon is this?" Dōgen cites another version of this story as case 12 of the 90 kōans in volume 9 of Eihei Kōroku, below. See also Cleary, *Book of Serenity,* case 21, pp. 91–94. This story uses the image of two moons to discuss nonduality, and also the transcendence of ideas about nonduality. Later Keizan Jōkin, Dōgen's most prominent third-generation descendant, would tell one of his disciples that descendants in the Sōtō lineage must know that there are two moons. See Thomas Cleary, trans., *Timeless Spring: A Sōtō Zen Anthology* (Tokyo: Weatherhill, 1980), pp. 138–139. "Sun face and moon face" is a reference to Mazu's response about his failing health, already mentioned in previous Dharma hall discourses.

34 Chuanzi is known as the boatman because during a persecution of Buddhism he became a ferryman, although he was still looking for a disciple. Chuanzi's Dharma brother Daowu Yuanzhi sent the monk Jiashan to Chuanzi. After an exchange, the boatman told Jiashan that Jiashan was fishing with a hook three inches short. Chuanzi asked Jiashan to say something, but when he started, Chuanzi knocked him into the water two times. Jiashan awakened, and nodded three times. The entire story is detailed by Dōgen in Dharma word *hōgo* 8 below in volume 8. Portions of it are further cited as kōan cases 10, 22, and 28 in volume 9. See also Ferguson, *Zen's Chinese Heritage,* pp. 147–148.

35 Shigong Huizang was a hunter chasing a deer who accidentally wandered into Mazu's monastery. The story relates that Shigong disliked monks. Mazu stopped him and asked what he was doing. Shigong said he was following a deer that he wanted to shoot. Mazu said that he, unlike Shigong, could shoot a whole herd with one arrow; then he suggested that Shigong shoot his self instead. Shigong became a disciple of Mazu. See Cheng Chien, *Sun Face Buddha,* pp. 71–72. "Half a sage" refers to Shigong's meeting with Sanping Yizhong. When Shigong later became a teacher, he would meet students by aiming an arrow at them. When Sanping arrived and faced Shigong's arrow, Sanping opened his robe, bared his breast, and said, "This arrow is for killing. What arrow gives life?" Shigong

Somewhere [the circle] makes a jeweled rabbit; somewhere it makes a tile or a pebble. Although Eihei says it this way, it is only what I studied sitting on the long platform.

Dōgen drew a circle and said: When I speak facing this [actuality], how is it? Great assembly, would you like to clearly understand?

After a pause, Dōgen said: I polished a tile to make a mirror and hung it in the sky, but people say the moon in the mid-autumn sky is the full circle. Who would not laugh at our useless efforts? Isn't the karmic consciousness of ignorance the condition of our birth?

Not Knowing Samādhi
278. Dharma Hall Discourse

An ancient person [Langye Huijue] said, "Mahākāśyapa did not know the World-Honored One's samādhi. Ānanda did not know Mahākāśyapa's samādhi. Śānavāsin did not know Ānanda's samādhi. Up to now, although I have samādhi, you do not know it."

At that time a monk asked [Langye], "I wonder, who can know the teacher's samādhi?"

Another ancient person said, "True gold does not need to be examined in a smelting furnace. The trophy for first place in the examination for officials is the most beautiful of flowers, completely splendid."

The teacher Dōgen said: Although the ancients said it that way, I won't speak like that. The World-Honored One did not know the World-Honored One's samādhi. Mahākāśyapa did not know Mahākāśyapa's samādhi. Ānanda did not know Ānanda's samādhi. Śānavāsin did not know Śānavāsin's samādhi. I have samādhi, but I don't know it. You have samādhi, but you don't know it.[36]

---

plucked the bowstring three times; Sanping made three prostrations. Shigong said that after thirty years, he had finally met half a sage, and then he broke his bow. This story appears in the Jingde Transmission of the Lamp, in the section on Sanping.

36 This not knowing one's own samādhi is discussed by Dōgen in his writing about self-fulfillment samādhi in Bendōwa. They "do not mix into the perceptions of this person sitting, because they take place within stillness without any fabrication, and they are enlightenment itself. If practice and enlightenment were separate as people commonly believe, it would be possible for them to perceive each other." Okumura and Leighton, *The Wholehearted Way*, p. 23.

Suppose someone came forth and asked why I don't know. I would say to him: Tomorrow there will be a meal offered at Great Compassion Temple.[37]

Just Sitting in the Timeless Spring

279. Dharma Hall Discourse on the First Day of the Ninth Month [1248][38]

Sit on your cushions and think beyond thinking; play vividly and energetically, and don't be fooled by any demonic spirits. The old monk abiding on this mountain swallows buddhas and living beings with one gulp. The crouching lion catches rabbits and enraged elephants with one swipe of his paw. Smashing the polished tile of trying to become a buddha by sitting as a buddha, laugh and destroy the net of doubts of the three vehicles and five vehicles.[39] Completely avoid following others in order to realize the way and clarify the mind. Why should we fear the upside down illusions related to "It [is exactly me,] I [am not it]"?[40]

For a long time, [those with such illusions] have put aside directly pointing and simply transmitting, and they only receive falsehoods derived from [mere] echoes. Do you want to completely understand the principle I am discussing?

---

37 "Tomorrow there will be a meal offered at Great Compassion Temple" is a saying by Linji's friend Puhua. Puhua went around town proclaiming, "If you come from the bright, I'll hit you in the brightness; if you come from the dark, I'll hit you in the darkness.... Come from the empty sky and I'll hit you with so many flails." When Linji asked what would happen if he did not come in any of those ways, Puhua announced a donor's feast at Great Compassion Temple, the name of a temple near Linji. See Watson, *Zen Teachings of Master Lin-chi,* p. 87. When he got to the feast itself, Puhua overturned the table filled with food.

38 See Dharma hall discourse 193. Traditionally this date was when sitting cushions were brought out and the relaxed summer meditation schedule ended.

39 The five vehicles are śrāvakas, pratyekabuddhas, bodhisattvas, humans, and heavenly beings. The three vehicles are the first three of these five.

40 "Completely avoid following others" is from Dongshan Liangjie's verse upon his awakening, when he looked at his reflection in a stream that he was crossing, after leaving his teacher Yunyan Tansheng. Dongshan wrote, "Completely avoid seeking from others. Now I travel alone; everywhere I can meet it. It is now truly me, but I am not it. Understanding like this, we finally harmonize with suchness." Dōgen's second sentence in this passage might be read literally as "Why should we fear the upside-down illusions

After a pause Dōgen said: The five-petaled flower opens in the timeless spring. The single circle of the moon is white in the dawn sky.

The Staff and Fist of Grandmother Mind
280. Dharma Hall Discourse
This staff is "direct pointing at the human mind." This fist is "this mind is itself Buddha." This grandmotherly mind is only for the sake of all of you. Unsurpassed awakening is the great rest.

The Daily Activity of Clouds and Water
281. Dharma Hall Discourse
Going to the seashore to count grains of sand vainly wastes one's strength. Polishing a tile to make a mirror is a meaningless use of effort. Don't you see that the clouds above the tall mountains naturally wind and unwind around each other, so how could they be intimate or estranged? The water of a deep river channel follows along the straight stretches and curves without preferring this way or that. The daily activity of living beings is like clouds and water. Clouds and waters are like this, but people are not. If they could be like this, how could they ever transmigrate in the triple world?[41]

The Jewel Illuminating All Things
282. Dharma Hall Discourse
Everyone without exception holds on to the jewel that glows in the night. All houses naturally embrace the jewel of Mount Jing.[42] Unless we turn the

---

of others or myself?" But the characters for "it" (or "others") and "me" probably refer directly to the third line of Dongshan's verse. Dōgen is warning about upside-down illusions concerning self and other and their relationship. For the context of Dongshan's verse see Powell, *Record of Tung-Shan,* pp. 27–28, 63–65; and Cleary, *Book of Serenity,* case 49, pp. 206–209.

41 "The triple world" refers to the realms of desire, form, and formlessness, all of which are included in the karmic, conditioned world of samsāra, or suffering. "Clouds and water" is a traditional term for monks, so ideally they should live like clouds and water, without preference or attachments.

42 The jewel of Mount Jing refers to a story in the Spring and Autumn Chronicles (and other Chinese classics) about a person named Bianhuo who found a rock containing a great jewel (supposedly in the period 400–200 B.C.E.). He offered it to a king who did

light within to illuminate the self, how can we hold close the jewel when we are lost in the outlying countryside?[43] Don't you know the words, "When the ear is in accord it is like the [receptive] spirit of the empty valley, and loud and soft sounds are never lacking. When the eye is in accord it is like the illumination of a thousand suns, and the ten thousand forms cannot escape their images"?[44] If we seek outside of sounds and colors, Bodhidharma's coming from the west is a great fault.

The Sounds of Emptiness
283. Dharma Hall Discourse
The sounding of the mind must be simply the sounding of emptiness. What we call the sounding of mind is actually the sounding of a bell. If the windbell does not sound, the mind does not sound. How can we call this the mind's sounds?[45]

The Eyeballs of Mindfulness
284. Dharma Hall Discourse
Although people in the past who left the world to become teachers said that the body and mind of ancient buddhas become attached to grasses

---

not recognize its value, and ordered Bianhuo's left foot cut off. Bianhuo then offered it to another king, who repeated the mistake and cut off Bianhuo's right foot. Finally he offered it to a third king, who accepted the offering, recognizing its value. See Watson, *Han Fei Tzu,* p. 80.

43 "Turn the light within to illuminate the self," *ekō henshō* in Japanese, is a phrase used by Dōgen for the principle of zazen. Dōgen uses it, for example, in Fukanzazengi (Universally Recommended Instructions for Zazen). See the end of volume 8 below.

44 This quotation is from the Chinese Chan monk and poet Gaocheng Fazang, but we can find no other reference to him.

45 This Dharma hall discourse is a response to a story about Sanghānandi and Gayaśāta, the seventeenth and eighteenth ancestors in the Indian ancestral lineage as recognized in Zen. After hearing a temple windbell, Sanghānandi asked Gayaśāta if the wind or the bell made the sound. Gayaśāta said it was neither wind nor bell, but the mind. When Sanghānandi asked what mind is, Gayaśāta said that both are tranquil. Sanghānandi then approved of him as his sole disciple. This story is from the Jingde Transmission of the Lamp (Keitoku Dentōroku), in the section on Sanghānandi. See Ogata, *Transmission of the Lamp,* p. 35. In this Dharma hall discourse Dōgen disagrees with Gayaśāta's description of mind as sounding. Dōgen also cites this story in the Shōbōgenzō essay Immo (Suchness). See Cleary, *Shōbōgenzō: Zen Essays by Dōgen,* pp. 49–55.

and trees, they never said that [mindfulness of] body, sensations, mind, and phenomena are the eyeballs of the ancestral teachers.[46]

Spring and Autumn on the Ancient Road

285. Dharma Hall Discourse

The arrival of geese and the flight of nightingales are both the Buddha work [of Śākyamuni] at Jetavana Vihāra.[47] The opening flowers and reddening leaves are nothing other than the family style [of Bodhidharma] at Shaolin temple. People who have fully attained like this directly mount the sounds and straddle the colors, transcend seeing and go beyond hearing, and freshly join with others.[48]

Tell me, what were the practice activities of Vipaśyin Buddha?[49]

After a pause Dōgen said: Movement and appearances uphold the ancient road, no [longer] sinking into debilitating activities.[50]

---

46 "Becoming attached to grasses and trees" is an expression for manifesting in the world for the sake of beings. Awareness of body, sensations, mind, and phenomena are the four foundations of mindfulness, recommended as objects of awareness in traditional Buddhist meditation practice.

47 Jetavana Vihāra was a monastery of Śākyamuni. In East Asia, geese arrive in the fall, and nightingales in the spring.

48 "Directly mount the sounds and straddle the colors, transcend seeing and go beyond hearing" is a phrase used by Hongzhi in various of his writings. See, for example, Leighton and Wu, *Cultivating the Empty Field,* p. 55. There is also a Dharma hall discourse in Hongzhi's Extensive Record, vol. 1, which is almost identical with this entire Dharma hall discourse by Dōgen. It differs only in a few details. Hongzhi's Dharma hall discourse refers in the first sentence to Avalokiteśvara Bodhisattva, who Dōgen changes to Śākyamuni. Hongzhi then refers to Mañjuśrī Bodhisattva, who Dōgen changed to Bodhidharma. Hongzhi further refers to Samantabhadra Bodhisattva, who Dōgen changes to Vipaśyin Buddha. In addition to changing these archetypal bodhisattvas to the legendary Zen founders, Dōgen's discourse here differs only in changing Hongzhi's "wild flowers" and "fragrant grasses" to "flowers" and "leaves." For more on the iconographical, doctrinal, and practice contexts on the archetypal, cosmic bodhisattvas Avalokiteśvara, Mañjuśrī, and Samantabhadra, see Leighton, *Faces of Compassion,* pp. 109–209.

49 Vipaśyin Buddha (Jap.: Bibashi) is the first of the seven primordial, mythical ancient buddhas, culminating in Śākyamuni as the seventh. See also Dharma hall discourse 38.

50 Dōgen's statement after the pause is from the verse by Xiangyan Zhixian after he was awakened by the sound of a pebble hitting bamboo. See Chang, *Original Teachings of Ch'an Buddhism,* pp. 219–220. This quote is also cited exactly by Hongzhi in his earlier version of this Dharma hall discourse.

The Genuine Body and Mind
286. Dharma Hall Discourse

This very body and mind are not merely the five skandhas.[51] Our wondrous existence is most excellent, and should not be an object of desire. Without coming or going, we simply respond to sounds and colors. Further, we turn around from our center, and move out in the eight directions. Negating all dualities, our feet are on the ground. How could there be arising and perishing, as our magnanimous energy pierces the heavens? Although it is like this, do not say that killing Buddha after all has no results.[52] The genuine cause of attaining buddhahood is zazen.

Mind-Nature in Young and Old
287. Dharma Hall Discourse

Here is a story. The venerable Śāṇavāsin asked Upagupta, "How old are you?"

Upagupta replied, "I am seventeen years old."

The teacher Śāṇavāsin asked, "Is your body or your nature seventeen years old?"

Upagupta replied, "Teacher, your hair is already white. Is it your hair or your mind that is white?"

The teacher Śāṇavāsin said, "It is only my hair that is white, not my mind."

Upagupta said, "My body is seventeen, not my nature."[53]

The teacher Dōgen said: I am considering these two venerable people, and what they said. What are they calling body; what are they calling nature? What are they calling mind; and what are they calling hair? One

---

51 The five skandhas, literally "aggregates," are the accumulations of the aspects of which a person is composed: forms, perceptions, sensations, predilections, and consciousness. See also Dharma hall discourse 20.

52 In this context, "killing Buddha" refers to going beyond our delusions about enlightenment, and is a description of the heart of zazen. In the Shōbōgenzō essay Zazenshin (The Acupuncture Needle of Zazen), Dōgen says, "When you are sitting Buddha, you are killing Buddha." See Bielefeldt, *Dōgen's Manuals of Zen Meditation*, p. 196.

53 This story is from the Jingde Transmission of the Lamp (Keitoku Dentōroku), in the section on Śāṇavāsin. See Ogata, *Transmission of the Lamp*, p. 11.

person expressed nature as body; the other person expressed mind as hair. How laughable to say that one gained and one lost.[54]

Although this is so, suppose someone asked Eihei, "What is the truth of the preceding story?" I would simply say to him: Enthusiastically observing spring mountains and autumn mountains, we still cannot avoid calling them two sides of one coin.[55]

The Warmth of Practice

288. Dharma Hall Discourse for Opening the Furnace [1248][56]

Before spring, peach and plum blossoms open. Patch-robed monks pick them and come to make fire in the furnace. From making considerations in a warm place one becomes sleepy. What a pity that Baizhang wasted his efforts.[57]

54 "One gained and one lost" was a comment by Fayan Wenyi when two monks made the exact identical action of rolling up the blinds in the door of the meditation hall. See Cleary, *Book of Serenity*, case 27, pp. 116–119; Aitken, *Gateless Barrier*, case 26, pp. 166–170; and Cleary, *Unlocking the Zen Kōan*, case 26, pp. 125–128.

55 "Two sides of one coin" refers to the non-separate relationship of Śāṇavāsin and his disciple Upagupta, and also to the relationship of their age and youth. But in contrast to Śāṇavāsin and Upagupta stating the primacy of mind-nature over the body and its hair, Dōgen seems to be also indicating that mind-nature is only expressed and can only manifest in the particular phenomenal situation of a body with hair, whether it is aged or youthful. Mind and body are also two sides of one coin, and for Dōgen, Buddha nature is expressed in impermanence.

56 The Opening the Furnace ceremony happened on the first day of the tenth month. See Dharma hall discourses 14, 109, and 199.

57 "Making considerations" seems to refer to hazy thinking during meditation. "What a pity that Baizhang wasted his effort" is Dōgen's ironic way of actually saying, "We should be appreciative of Baizhang's kindly effort." But perhaps the monks are not appreciative if they are too sleepy. This reference is to the story of Baizhang asking his student Guishan to look in the fireplace for a burning coal. When Guishan said the fire was completely extinguished, Baizhang reached in with tongs and pulled out a live ember. This story appears in the Jingde Transmission of the Lamp and is referred to by Dōgen in various writings, for example, in Eihei Shingi. See Chang, *Original Teachings of Ch'an Buddhism*, pp. 200–201; and Leighton and Okumura, *Dōgen's Pure Standards for the Zen Community*, pp. 136–137. Here Dōgen seems to be warning his monks not to get too warm and comfortable once the fireplace is going in the monks' hall. However, this is an example of Dōgen's humor, as Eiheiji in the winter is extremely cold, even with a fireplace.

Down in Śākyamuni's Cave

289. Dharma Hall Discourse

Here is a story. Xuansha said, "Now all [Zen] successors say they receive the teaching from Śākyamuni. I say that I practiced together with Śākyamuni. You tell me, in what assembly did we practice together?"[58]

Although Master Xuansha spoke like this, he was only imitating the one who abandoned his father and departed to wander in other lands.[59] He had not yet attained through practice the field of a peaceful body and settled life. He also does not know that today Eihei has appeared in the world, and has something to say. Now I say to Xuansha, although you say that you practiced together with Śākyamuni, in fact you practiced under Śākyamuni, and were a successor to him. Do you want to know why this is the case?

After a pause Dōgen said: Not only Xuansha but all buddha ancestors from the beginning fall down into Śākyamuni's cave and spring around [sharing the teaching].

The Colors of Eiheiji

290. Dharma Hall Discourse

Together buddhas extend their hands; ancestors transmit to each other. Tell me, what do they transmit, and what do they give? Everyone, if you know the place to settle down, you will see all buddhas of the three times and all generations of ancestral teachers, holding hands and pulling, without affirming advancement. If you hesitate in deliberation, this mountain monk will be in your nostrils. At that very time, how is it?

After a pause Dōgen said: Although the colors of Eihei mountain are marvelous, in front of us is the highest peak.[60]

---

58 Dōgen refers to this claim by Xuansha in various places. See, for example, Dharma hall discourses 91, 142, and 216, and Tanahashi, *Moon in a Dewdrop,* "All-Inclusive Practice," pp. 200–201.

59 "The one who abandoned his father and departed to wander in other lands" refers to the prodigal son in the Lotus Sutra. See Hurvitz, *Scripture of the Lotus Blossom of the Fine Dharma,* pp. 85–95.

60 "In front of us is the highest peak" could refer to the endless path of going beyond Buddha, wherever one is. On the literal level, the nearby mountain one sees looming above Eiheiji, Hakusan, came to be revered as a protective spirit of the Sōtō school.

The Way Is Not Easy

291. Dharma Hall Discourse

You should know that studying the way is not at all easy. For example, Linji remained at Huangbo's mountain for twenty years, planting pines and cedars, and yet he had not exhausted Huangbo's mind and intention.[61] Deshan remained for thirty years as attendant for Longtan [Chongxin], attending to towels and carrying water for washing, and yet he did not understand Longtan's mind. Deeply we should sympathize; deeply we should sympathize. Although this was the case, these days if we search from east to west and south to north for smelly fists like Linji or Deshan, we cannot find any.

Don't you see that someone said, "Atop Mount Wutai, the clouds are making steamed rice; below the steps to the Buddha hall, a dog urinates up toward the heavens. At the top of a flagpole, dumplings are cooking; three monkeys are sorting coins in the night."[62]

Brothers, if you can comprehend this saying, you will know the mind of the three vehicles and twelve divisions of the teaching. Do you want to clearly understand the meaning of the ancestor [Bodhidharma] coming from the west?

After a pause Dōgen said: Pierce your nostrils for yourself. Search for the fiery lotus in the water of mind.[63] Study this.

61 Dōgen also refers to the story of Linji planting trees in the remote mountains at Huangbo's in Eihei Shingi. See Leighton and Okumura, *Dōgen's Pure Standards for the Zen Community,* pp. 148–150. Linji responded to Huangbo's inquiry by saying that he planted trees to provide scenery for the mountain gate and a guidepost for later generations.

62 The saying "Atop of Mount Wutai..." is by Dongshan Shouchu from the Jingde Transmission of the Lamp, vol. 7, and is quoted in the commentary to Hekiganroku, case 96. See Cleary and Cleary, *Blue Cliff Record,* p. 609. Mount Wutai is a sacred mountain in northern China, dedicated to Mañjuśrī Bodhisattva. "Clouds making steamed rice" could refer to the clouds above the mountain resembling steam rising from rice, but it also might refer to monks (known as "clouds and water") preparing steamed rice at the temples on the mountain. Dongshan Shouchu is praised by Dōgen as an exemplary *tenzo,* or chief cook, in Eihei Shingi. See Leighton and Okumura, *Dōgen's Pure Standards for the Zen Community,* p. 49.

63 The "fiery lotus," or lotus in the middle of flames, is an image that recalls the Buddha sitting in the middle of fire, used, for example, by Dōgen in the Shōbōgenzō essay Gyōbutsu

Repaying for Your Food in the Solitary Reality

292. Dharma Hall Discourse

I remember, Nanquan said to his assembly, "Master Kiangsi [Mazu Dao-i] said, 'This very mind is Buddha,' but he also said, 'No mind, no Buddha.' I do not speak like this. This is not mind; this is not Buddha; this is not a thing. I also say that mind is not Buddha; wisdom is not the way. I also say that ordinary mind is the way."[64]

The teacher Dōgen said: These two elders have spoken like this, but elder Eihei does not speak that way either. Now I ask you, Kiangsi [Mazu] and Nanquan: What kind of place is this where you expound mind, expound the way, expound things, expound Buddha, and expound not Buddha, not mind?

You should know that the single entirety is not at all two things. In the ten directions, the solitary [reality] appears, perceived as mountains and rivers. We cannot say whether this is Buddha nature or causes and conditions. Why is it like this? To repay the money for the rice you have eaten. Ultimately, what is it?

After a pause Dōgen said: Bottle gourds entwine with bottle gourds.[65]

Danger in Practice

293. Dharma Hall Discourse

Making a livelihood in a demon's cave in the mountains, a wild-fox spirit demonstrates supernatural powers. He plays with a monk's bowl that has a handle, not in conformity with the herd among the ten thousand forms. Examine and inquire, then say quickly, whose family style is this?

Igi (The Awesome Presence of Active Buddhas). See Kazuaki Tanahashi, ed., *Beyond Thinking*. This image refers to practice in the middle of the karmic world of desire.

64 The first part of this statement by Nanquan, up to "This is not a thing," is from Jingde Transmission of the Lamp, vol. 8. See Ogata, *Transmission of the Lamp*, p. 258; or Chang, *Original Teachings of Ch'an Buddhism*, p. 155. The stories about Mazu's saying "This very mind is Buddha" and "No mind; no Buddha," as well as Nanquan's saying "Ordinary mind is the way," are featured in cases 30, 33, and 19 in the Mumonkan; see Aitken, *Gateless Barrier*, pp. 126–131, 189–194, 204–207; and Cleary *Unlocking the Zen Kōan*, pp. 94–98, 144–145, 155–157.

65 For bottle gourds, or calabashes, see Dharma hall discourse 166 and volume 2, note 120. This twining is the same idea as the twining vines in Dōgen's Shōbōgenzō essay Kattō (Twining Vines); see Tanahashi, *Moon in a Dewdrop*, pp. 168–174.

After a pause Dōgen said: Zihu has a single dog. On South Mountain there is a turtle-nose snake.[66]

Not Denigrating Buddha
294. Dharma Hall Discourse
Dropping off body and mind does not prevent us from recognizing the original source. The Dharma is not apart from arising and extinction, and yet we still mistakenly have discussions about its falseness or truth. Therefore it is said, seeing Buddha in every bit of dust does not denigrate Buddha; hearing the sutras in every bit of earth we are not apart from the sutras. Do you want to attain intimate prediction on Vulture Peak?[67] Large and small stones nod their heads and come.

After a pause Dōgen said: After thirty years, you will not be able to make mistakes when bringing this forth.

Practicing with No Mind
295. Dharma Hall Discourse
With a monk's bowl with a handle and a monk's robe with horns, a monk's staff blooms and bears fruit, a sitting cushion spreads out roots that grow sprouts.[68] Śākyamuni blocked the barrier gate, and Dipankara

66 The story of Zihu's dog is related in the commentaries to Hekiganroku cases 22 and 96. Below the gate at Zihu's temple was a sign that read, "At Zihu there is a dog. On top he takes people's heads; in the middle he takes their torso; below he takes their legs. Hesitate and you will lose your life." When greeting newcomers, Zihu would shout and say, "Look at the dog." If the guest turned his head, Zihu would return to his room. "On South Mountain there is a turtle-nose snake" is the statement by Xuefeng that begins Hekiganroku case 22. A turtle-nose snake is poisonous, and the case gives warning against danger. The case ends with Xuefeng's great disciple, Yunmen, throwing down his staff and mocking a gesture of fright. See Cleary and Cleary, *Blue Cliff Record,* pp. 144–153, 610–611. Dōgen's view of the practice in this discourse might be read as positive or negative. If you practice in such a dangerous way you may lose your life. But might this loss be dropping off body and mind?

67 The "prediction on Vulture Peak" refers to Śākyamuni's predictions throughout the Lotus Sutra of future buddhahood for bodhisattvas and his disciples.

68 "A monk's bowl with a handle and a monk's robe *(okesa)* with horns" are impossible, nonexistent items, but from such inconceivability practice bears fruit, as symbolized by a staff blossoming or a sitting cushion sending out shoots.

had to walk around him.[69] Inside or outside there is no body or mind; from ancient times to the present there are no buddha ancestors. Master Zhaozhou in the north and Zen teacher Xuefeng in the south meet and do not recognize each other, but although not recognizing each other, they still meet together.[70] Do you want to enact this truth?

After a pause Dōgen said: A person of the way with no-mind is able to be like this; not yet having realized no-mind, you will have great difficulty.[71]

In Lengthening Daylight, a Horse Gallops

296. Winter Solstice Dharma Hall Discourse [1248]

As before, after relating Hongzhi's Winter Solstice Dharma Hall Discourse that begins, "Yin reaches its fullness and yang arises," Dōgen then said the following.[72]

Zen Master Hongzhi has previously spoken like this, but I, Eihei, have something further to say. Today I accomplish the primary subtle, wondrous, true Dharma, which consists of precepts, samādhi, wisdom,

---

69 Dipaṅkara is the ancient Buddha from a previous age who predicted the future buddha-hood of Śākyamuni during a former life of Śākyamuni.

70 Yunmen responded to an inquiry about the primary meaning of the Zen tradition by saying, "In the south there's Master Xuefeng; in the north there's Master Zhaozhou." See App, *Master Yunmen,* p. 128. Zhaozhou and Xuefeng may have never met in person, but there are a number of stories of monks traveling between them and exchanging teachings. Once Zhaozhou told a monk who was going to visit Xuefeng that if Xuefeng asked about the ultimate, the monk should tell Xuefeng that the monk himself had come from Zhaozhou, and was not a verbal messenger. Upon hearing this, Xuefeng said that such a statement could only come from Zhaozhou. See Chang, *Original Teachings of Ch'an Buddhism,* pp. 171–172. Once when Zhaozhou asked a monk coming from Xuefeng about the latter's teachings, the monk reported that Xuefeng was saying, "The whole world is the eye of a monk. Where will you take a shit?" Zhaozhou responded that if the monk went back to Xuefeng he should take a trowel (used for digging a hole and covering excrement while traveling). On one occasion after hearing Zhaozhou's response to one of his own sayings, Xuefeng called Zhaozhou an old Buddha. See Green, *Recorded Sayings of Zen Master Joshu,* pp. 5, 140, 141.

71 "No-mind" is a common phrase in Zen teachings. Guishan said that no-mind is the way. Huangbo said that no-mind is all minds. From *mushin* entry in Zengaku Daijiten Hensansho, *Zengaku Daijiten* (Zen Studies Dictionary) (Tokyo: Daishūkan Shoten, 1978), p. 1208. For Dōgen, no-mind refers to awareness without discriminative thinking or grasping.

72 This introduction is a note added to the text by the compiler of this volume, Koun Ejō. Hongzhi's Winter Solstice Dharma hall discourse referred to here was previously cited in full by Dōgen in his own Winter Solstice Dharma hall discourses 135 and 206.

liberation, and awareness of liberation.[73] I give rise to anuttara samyak-sambodhi (complete perfect enlightenment), without regressing or being diverted. Yunmen's wooden horse neighs and gallops; Guishan guides elephants with spiritual transformation.[74]

The noses of the buddhas of past, present, and future are pierced in one long line together with large and small rocks, long and short boards, the clear face of heaven, and the peaceful face of earth, and all receive support.[75] My "measuring cup is full and the balance scale is level," but in the marketplace I buy what is precious and sell it cheaply.[76] How is it that the bright pearl in a bowl starts to roll on its own?[77] The original master within the ten thousand forms is magnificent, imposing![78] With the ancestral teachers on top of the hundred grass tips, all is unmistakably clear.[79]

73 Precepts, samādhi, wisdom, liberation, and awareness of liberation are the five aspects of the dharmakāya, or reality body of Buddha, in traditional Buddhist teaching.

74 A monk asked, "What is the neighing of the wooden horse of Yunmen?" Yunmen said, "Mountains and rivers are running." See Chang, *Original Teachings of Ch'an Buddhism*, p. 293. A conflicting version of this dialogue (somewhat longer) appears in Yunmen's Recorded Sayings; see App, *Master Yunmen*, p. 102. But the former version, from the Jingde Transmission of the Lamp, is more appropriate to Dōgen's context in this Dharma hall discourse.

75 "The noses of the buddhas of past, present, and future are pierced in one long line" refers back to a line from the Dharma hall discourse by Hongzhi that Dōgen cited in the beginning. Hongzhi said, "Take the skulls of the buddhas of the three times, and thread them onto a single rosary." Dōgen here implies that all phenomena in the universe are connected in the same line with all the buddhas, interconnected through the dependent co-arising of all things.

76 Dōgen here is reversing the statement in Hongzhi's Winter Solstice Dharma hall discourse, "Even if your measuring cup is full and the balance scale is level, in transactions I sell at a high price and buy when cheap." (See Dharma hall discourses 135 and 206.) Dōgen may be demonstrating bodhisattva generosity by instead buying the precious teaching and selling it cheaply. Buddha's head and karmic phenomena may be more or less precious, but all still balance evenly on the scale.

77 With the exception of one character, Dōgen's statement "The bright pearl in a bowl starts to roll on its own" is the same, and it has the same meaning, as a line in Hongzhi's Winter Solstice Dharma hall discourse: "In a bowl the bright pearl rolls on its own without prodding."

78 "Magnificent! Imposing!" was Baizhang's remark upon first meeting his future successor Huangbo, who is described as seven feet tall with a lump like a round pearl on his forehead. See Cleary and Cleary, *Blue Cliff Record*, case 11, p. 73.

79 This sentence is a paraphrase from a saying of the layman Pangyun. See Dharma hall discourse 9.

Blossoming in the Snow
297. Enlightenment Day Dharma Hall Discourse (1248)[80]
The snowball hits! The snowball hits![81] It hits the cold plum so that it blossoms in the snow. On this eighth day of the twelfth month, the bright star in heaven and a wooden ladle on the earth arrive before spring.

Thunderbolts That Help Lotuses Open
298. Dharma Hall Discourse in Appreciation of the Previous Inō[82]
An iron hammerhead without a hole is always like a thunderbolt, immediately dispersing wild-fox Zen.[83] This morning, would you like to know the ultimate summit? On top of Dayu Peak there is a lotus flower on the twelfth month.[84]

A Fire Boy's Dedicated Play
299. Dharma Hall Discourse in Appreciation of the Previous Director
After relating the story about the director [Bao'en] Xuanze and the fire boy, the teacher Dōgen said: Before, when [Bao'en Xuanze] heard, "The fire boy comes seeking fire," he did not understand, but later when he heard

---

80 Enlightenment Day, the commemoration of the day of Śākyamuni Buddha's awakening, is celebrated in East Asia on the eighth day of the twelfth month (Jap.: Rōhatsu). See also Dharma hall discourses 88, 136, 213, 360, 406, 475, and 506.

81 "The snowball hits! The snowball hits!" is from the verse comment to a story about Layman Pang playing in the snow in the Hekiganroku, case 42. See Cleary and Cleary, *Blue Cliff Record*, p. 304.

82 The *inō* is the person who manages the meditation hall and supervises the monks' conduct. See Dharma hall discourse 190 in honor of the prior *inō* at Eiheiji.

83 "An iron hammerhead without a hole" is a reference to the wooden block pounded loudly on a wooden pedestal (Jap.: *tsui chin*) in the monks' hall by the *inō* to precede all announcements. This block is shaped like the head of a sledge hammer. See volume 2 (Dharma hall discourse 128), note 10.

84 Dayu Peak is where the sixth ancestor, Huineng, went after first receiving transmission; there he was challenged by the monk Huiming, whom Huineng then awakened. See Yampolsky, *Platform Sutra of the Sixth Patriarch*, p. 134; or Cleary, *Sutra of Hui-neng*, pp. 12–13; and Aitken, *Gateless Barrier*, case 23, pp. 147–154; or Cleary, *Unlocking the Zen Kōan*, pp. 110–115. Here Dōgen seems to be comparing the impact of the previous *inō* to that of the sixth ancestor.

this he was completely awakened.[85] Tell me, great assembly, where is the key to this change?

Now I will exert myself completely to compose a verse in order to express appreciation to Director Tai.[86]

After a pause Dōgen said: The fire boy comes seeking fire. With complete dedication, do not stop when you have only seen the smoke. Play with the golden star (Venus), manifesting so brightly. A December plum blooms colorfully on the tip of an old branch.

The Livelihood in the Innermost Hall

300. Dharma Hall Discourse for Appointing the New Director

The predictions at Vulture Peak pull patch-robed monks by the noses. [Dazu Huike's] attaining the marrow at Shaolin was the root of many descendants.

Going beyond the old and the new, respond to this and that: the tenzo priest and the director priest, food in the bowl and water in the bucket. If you love each moment for ten thousand years, this is like the three virtues and six tastes.[87] We should not only encounter each other on the narrow path, but please assist the World-Honored One within the innermost hall.[88] At this very time, what is the livelihood that is manifesting? Does the great assembly want to activate this completely?

85 The story about [Bao'en] Xuanze and the fire boy, or fire spirit's apprentice, is given in full in Dharma hall discourse 15.

86 Nothing else is known about this monk Tai, who had been director of Eiheiji.

87 In his Instructions for the Tenzo, Dōgen says that the chief cook is only serving the community when meals are endowed with the three virtues and six tastes. The three virtues are food that is soft, clean, and prepared appropriately. The six tastes are sweet, spicy, salty, bitter, sour, and simple. See Leighton and Okumura, *Dōgen's Pure Standards for the Zen Community,* pp. 35, 50.

88 "Encountering each other on the narrow path" refers to the encounters outside the monastery of the director Yangqi (later an important teacher) with his teacher Ciming. Yangqi kept insisting on an explanation of the Dharma, and Ciming told him simply to take care of his work. See Leighton and Okumura, *Dōgen's Pure Standards for the Zen Community,* pp. 133–135. Assisting within the innermost hall implies both understanding the essential matter and taking care of temple affairs.

After a pause Dōgen said: For the three months of spring, the results are fulfilled and bodhi (awakening) is complete. One night, a flower opens and the world arises.[89]

The Ultimate Function within Stages

301. Dharma Hall Discourse

The beginning and advanced ordinary practitioners are like bamboo on the mountain and the cypress tree in the garden. The incomplete and ultimate sages are like spring flowers and the autumn moon.[90] Practice so that there is no Zen in the world of Zen, and to be clear that you have no desires within the world of desire. Throughout the entire world, there is nobody who understands Buddha Dharma. In all the great country of Tang China, there are just gobblers of dregs.[91] Expounding one thing does not hit the mark. Not accompanied by the ten thousand things, what stages could there be?[92] What do you use this for?

89 "The results are fulfilled and bodhi is complete; a flower opens and the world arises" is a saying by the Indian ancestor Prajñātāra, teacher of Bodhidharma. See Ogata, *Transmission of the Lamp,* p. 55.

90 "Beginning and advanced ordinary practitioners" refers to people in the first ten, and then the next thirty, of the fifty-two stages of bodhisattva development. "Beginning and advanced" are literally outer and inner, the former still subject to backsliding and leaving the path. These fifty-two stages are depicted in the Gaṇḍavyūha Sūtra, the final chapter of the Avataṃsaka Sūtra (Flower Ornament Sutra). "The incomplete and ultimate sages" refers to the final twelve stages for the incomplete sages, and the stage of buddhahood, beyond the fifty-two, for the ultimate sage. See Cleary, *Entry into the Realm of Reality.*

91 "In all the great country of Tang China, there are just gobblers of dregs" is a paraphrase of a saying by Huangbo to his assembly. Huangbo called his monks dreg slurpers and said there were no teachers of Chan in all of China. See Cleary and Cleary, *Blue Cliff Record,* case 11, pp. 72–80; or Cleary, *Book of Serenity,* case 53, pp. 223–228.

92 "Expounding one thing does not hit the mark" is the response of Nanyue Huairang, after eight years of consideration in practice, to the question addressed to him by the sixth ancestor, Huineng. When Nanyue first arrived Huineng had asked him, "What is this that thus comes?" See Ogata, *Transmission of the Lamp,* p. 162. "Not accompanied by the ten thousand things" is from Layman Pangyun's question to Mazu, "Who is the person not accompanied by the ten thousand things?" Mazu responded, "When you can swallow the whole West River in one gulp, I'll tell you." Layman Pang then remained with Mazu for two years, studying with him. See Ogata, *Transmission of the Lamp,* pp. 293–294. "What stages could there be?" is a saying by Huineng. When Qingyuan Xingsi asked him how to practice so as not to fall into stages, Huineng asked what practice he had been doing. Qingyuan said he did not even practice the sacred truth, and Huineng said, in that case,

The One Self at Year's End

302. Dharma Hall Discourse on the Twenty-Fifth day of the Twelfth Month

The sun is setting on this year, and we meet the spring.[93] The causes and conditions of birth and death, how they disturb people! Take up the thousand differences and ten thousand distinctions, and make them one, letting go of subject and object. Although this is so, do not recognize the self as the pure dharmakāya.[94]

The Smiling Face at New Year's

303. New Year's Dharma Hall Discourse [1249]

After relating Zen Master Hongzhi's New Year's Dharma Hall Discourse, as before, Dōgen said the following.[95]

On this great auspicious New Year's morning, patch-robed monks in zazen engage the way peacefully. Everyone has a smiling face with the color of spring. Buddhas' eating bowls appear, and the plum song is heard amid the thousand snowy peaks.[96] The mind of the son of Xie is satisfied on his fishing boat.

"What stages could there be?" See the commentary to case 5 about Qingyuan in the Shōyōroku; Cleary, *Book of Serenity*, p. 20.

93 In the Chinese lunar calendar, the first day of the first month is considered the first day of spring. There was not the same special significance for Dōgen of the twenty-fifth day of the twelfth month as there is in the West. However, according to another Chinese lunar calendar system, in some years there are two beginnings of spring, one before New Year's. This date in 1248 was one of those years, so this was a day designated as one of the beginnings of spring. See also verse 97 in volume 10, and its note 148.

94 "Do not recognize the self as the pure dharmakāya" is a response to the emperor by the national teacher Nanyang Huizhong. See Ogata, *Transmission of the Lamp*, p. 182.

95 This introduction is a note added to the text by the compiler of this volume, Koun Ejō. Hongzhi's Dharma hall discourse referred to here was previously cited in full by Dōgen in his own New Year Dharma hall discourse 142, and then again referred to in New Year Dharma hall discourse 216. The first two sentences here are slight variations from the beginning of Dharma hall discourse 216. And the final sentence in this Dharma hall discourse, referring to Xuansha, is identical to the final sentence in Dharma hall discourse 216.

96 The plum song is a reference to a piece of music, "Enticing Plum Blossoms," referred to in Dharma hall discourse 138 and volume 2, note 54.

Bodhidharma's Not Knowing

304. Dharma Hall Discourse

Great assembly, the study of the way is not very easy. Therefore, ancient sages and former worthies studied in the assemblies of good teachers, where they practiced penetratingly for nearly twenty or thirty years. Yunyan and Daowu engaged the way for forty years. Teacher Chuanzi (the boatman) stayed with Yaoshan for thirty years, clearly attaining this matter. Nanyue [Huairang] Dahui studied at Caoxi [with Huineng] for fifteen years. Linji stayed at Huangbo Mountain for thirty years, planting pines and cedars, engaging in this matter.

Therefore, brothers on this mountain should cherish their days and nights, engaging the way in zazen. Do not be swayed by conditions. If you are swayed by conditions, you will remain within the dusts of the mundane world, and will waste every bit of your time. Raising your head and snapping your fingers, or sighing, you should regret every bit of the time you have wasted, because we cherish the Dharma body and zazen.

The first ancestor, Bodhidharma, came from the west, and did not engage in various activities or give lectures on sutras or commentaries, but simply faced the wall in zazen for nine years at Shaolin. Sitting is exactly the true Dharma eye treasury of the wondrous mind of nirvāṇa. Generation after generation give face-to-face transmission, intimately receiving the secret seal, actually transmitting the bones and marrow between teachers and disciples. Just this is the single genuine matter; other things are not like this.

Therefore, Emperor Wu of Liang asked the first ancestor, "What is the highest meaning of the sacred truth?"[97]

The first ancestor said, "Vast emptiness, nothing sacred."

The emperor said, "Who is the person facing me?"

The ancestor said, "I don't know."

This very "not knowing" has not been understood by anybody for the past several generations. Now, among the mountains in Great Song [China], those abbots sitting in lion's seats, calling themselves teachers of humans and heavenly beings, have never understood this. How miser-

---

97 This story is case 1 in the Hekiganroku, and case 2 in the Shōyōroku. See Cleary and Cleary, *Blue Cliff Record*, pp. 1–9; and Cleary, *Book of Serenity*, pp. 6–10.

able, how miserable! It's goes without saying that among people within our country of Japan, nobody has understood. All of you people, do you want to understand the first ancestor's "not knowing"?

In the house of buddha ancestors, originally there is no principle of mind nature, Buddha nature, or consciousness nature. Simply depending on the combinations of causes and conditions of wind and fire, there are movements and activities. And yet, stupid people consider movements and activities as eternal souls.[98] Great assembly, do you want to understand this point?

After a pause Dōgen said: With the vast emptiness of nothing sacred, and not knowing, you attain skin, flesh, bones, and marrow.[99] If someone asks further about this, make him do three prostrations and return to his place.

Nurturing Spring under Two Moons

305. Dharma Hall Discourse on the Tenth Day of the First Month

Here is a story. A monk asked Touzi [Datong], "What is the first moon?"[100]

Touzi said, "In the early spring it is still cold."

The monk asked, "What is the second moon?"

Touzi said, "In mid-spring it gradually warms."

Although Touzi responded in this way, a discussion of the first moon and second moon appeared in the Complete Enlightenment Sutra.[101] This

---

98 "Eternal souls," literally "conscious spirits," refers to the idea of a fixed permanent self that persists through life and death.

99 For Bodhidharma's transmission of skin, flesh, bones, and marrow, see Dharma hall discourse 46.

100 In asking about the first and second moon, the monk is referring to these moons as symbols of the ultimate reality and the relative, conventional reality of sentient beings. Touzi appears to respond as if the monk was asking about the first and second month (the same character in Chinese as moon).

101 In the chapter on Mañjuśrī in the Complete Enlightenment Sutra, a second moon is introduced as an image for illusory visions, and the relationship between ultimate and illusory realms is then discussed throughout the sutra. See Charles Muller, *Sutra of Perfect Enlightenment*, p. 79; and Sheng-Yen, *Complete Enlightenment*, p. 17. The theme of two moons is also central to a dialogue between Yunyan and Daowu; see Dharma hall discourse 277 and note 33 above, which Dōgen also uses as case 12 of the ninety kōans with verse comments in volume 9 of Eihei Kōroku.

evening I, Eihei, have something to say to the clouds and water monks. If someone asked me, "What is the first moon?" I would say to him: I have enough gruel and rice.

If someone also asked me, "What is the second moon?" I would say to him: I have enough grass and water.

Suppose someone asked, "What is the point of this?" I would say to him: Bring me the hundreds of grasses from all around, and I will nurture spring on every branch and leaf.

A Breakfast for Dropping Off Body and Mind
306. Dharma Hall Discourse

Dropping off body and mind is good practice.[102] Make a vigorous effort to pierce your nostrils. Karmic consciousness is endless, with nothing fundamental to rely on, including not others, not self, not sentient beings, and not causes or conditions.[103] Although this is so, eating breakfast comes first.

The Sameness and Difference of the Four Elements
307. Dharma Hall Discourse

An ancient Buddha said, "Each of the four great elements has its own nature, and has its own form."

Today, for the sake of you monks, I, Eihei, will discuss the nature and form of the four elements. So it is said, the nature of earth is wall-gazing; the nature of water is washing your bowls; the nature of fire is the tenzo's activity; the nature of wind is a fan in December. As for the forms of the four elements, the form of earth is steady immovability; the form of water is eyes; the form of fire is the expounding of Dharma by all buddhas in the three times; the form of wind is nostrils.[104]

Tell me, is what I am saying the same or different from what the ancient Buddha said? Do you want to clearly understand?

102 "Practice" here is *sanzen,* which Dōgen uses sometimes for zazen, or sitting meditation, but also more generally for practice. "Dropping off body and mind" is a phrase Dōgen uses often for practice-realization.

103 The same phrase, "Karmic consciousness is endless, with nothing fundamental to rely on," appears in a question by Guishan in the Shōyōroku, case 37. See Cleary, *Book of Serenity,* p. 163.

104 "Steady immovability" is *gotsu-gotsu* in Japanese, a phrase Dōgen uses to refer to unshakable upright zazen posture.

After a pause Dōgen said: A white heron perches in a snowy nest; in sameness there is difference. A crow alights on a black horse; within difference there is sameness.[105]

Amid Changing Scenery, Mountains Are Mountains
308. Dharma Hall Discourse
Arising and perishing has no place to come from or go to, but Lingyun [Zhiqin] smiled at the flowering trees that had grown from hundreds of years of peach pits.[106] Delusion and enlightenment retain their places; the spring wind is delighted to belong amid the cold plum blossoms during the first month.

Although this is so, the blue mountains, as of old, are blue-green with majestic peaks.

Resting and Going Ahead within Unceasing Samādhi
309. Dharma Hall Discourse
Just resting is like the great ocean accepting hundreds of streams; arriving here, there is no forward or backward. Freely going ahead is like the great surging tides riding on strong winds; coming here, there is inner and outer.[107] Buddhas don't know it is; cats and cows know it is.[108] Those with heads above their legs do not see the Tathāgata's parinirvāṇa. Within our house, the unceasing samādhi of removing [all obstructions] is transmitted.[109]

---

105 This Dharma hall discourse about sameness and difference refers to the poem "Harmony of Difference and Sameness" (Jap.: Sandōkai) by Shitou Xiqian, which says, "The four elements return to their natures... Fire heats, wind moves, water wets, earth is solid." See Leighton and Wu, *Cultivating the Empty Field,* pp. 74–75; and Shunryu Suzuki, *Branching Streams Flow in the Dark: Zen Talks on Sandokai* (Berkeley: University of California Press, 1999).

106 Lingyun is famous for awakening upon seeing peach blossoms in a mountain valley. See Dharma hall discourse 457 and kōan case 72 in volume 9.

107 "Just resting...riding on the strong winds" is from Hongzhi's Extensive Record. See Leighton and Wu, *Cultivating the Empty Field,* p. 46. In this context, just resting might refer to zazen, while going ahead implies activity in the world. Dōgen's use of inner and outer here implies the discrimination of familiar and alien.

108 "Buddhas don't know it is; cats and cows know it is" is a saying by Nanquan, selected by Hongzhi as case 96 in the Shōyōroku. See Cleary, *Book of Serenity,* pp. 290–294.

109 We are speculating that "samādhi of removing" is an abbreviation for the "samādhi of removing all obstructions," which is referred to in the Mahāvairocana Sūtra.

Dōgen's Four Foundations of Mindfulness
310. Dharma Hall Discourse
Our Buddha [Śākyamuni] said to his disciples, "There are four foundations
of mindfulness on which people should depend. These four foundations
of mindfulness refer to contemplating the body as impure; contemplating
sensation as suffering; contemplating mind as impermanent; and contemplating phenomena as non-substantial."

I, Eihei, also have four foundations of mindfulness: contemplating the
body as a skin-bag; contemplating sensation as eating bowls; contemplating mind as fences, walls, tiles, and pebbles; and contemplating phenomena as old man Zhang drinking wine, old man Li getting drunk.[110]

Great assembly, are my four foundations of mindfulness the same or
different from the ancient Buddha's four foundations of mindfulness? If
you say they are the same, your eyebrows will fall out [from lying]. If you
say they are different, you will lose your body and life.

Freedom in Life and Death
311. Parinirvāṇa Day Dharma Hall Discourse [1249][111]
The Māra of Death saw Buddha [passing away], and both the Buddha and
Māra laughed.[112] Human and heavenly beings were disturbed and could
not stop crying. Do not have doubts about this mountain monk [Dōgen]
neither laughing nor crying. All buddhas in the ten directions also nod
their heads. This [crying] is true for common people, but how is it for
patch-robed monks?

---

110 "Old man Zhang drinks, and old man Li gets drunk" is an expression from Yunmen's
Recorded Sayings, referring to the inconceivable interconnectedness of different beings,
and also expressing that the Dharma spreads beyond our usual modes of perceiving. See
Dharma hall discourse 32 and volume 1, note 78.

111 Parinirvāṇa Day, commemorating Śākyamuni's passing away into nirvāṇa, is commemorated on the fifteenth day of the second month. Other Parinirvāṇa Day Dharma hall
discourses in Eihei Kōroku are discourses 121, 146, 225, 367, 418, and 486.

112 The Māra of Death is one of the four aspects of Māra, or demonic spirits that obstruct
practice. The four are the Māra of Delusion, the Māra of the Five Skandhas, the Māra of
Death, and the Māra of Heaven, who controls human fate. These four aspects of Māra
appear in Nāgārjuna's Commentary on the Mahāprajñāpāramitā Sūtra (Ch.: Dazhidulun; Jap.: Daichidoron), chap. 5.

After a pause Dōgen said: Thoroughly investigate life in order to study death. Letting go and taking hold of life and death depend on your refinement.

Clarifying the Harmony of Light and Dark

312. Dharma Hall Discourse

People who study Buddha Dharma should first know the sayings of buddhas and ancestors, without being confused by those outside the way. Brothers, you should know that the beliefs that there is no brightness or darkness; that darkness vanishes and returns to brightness; that brightness and darkness are the same form; or that good and bad are the same mind, are all views that are outside the way. If you consider the outsiders' views as the same as the sayings of buddhas and ancestors, you are as foolish as those who grasp a rock as if it were a jewel.

Brothers, don't you see that Shitou [Xiqian] said, "Right in light there is darkness, but don't meet it as darkness. Right in darkness there is light, but don't see it as light."[113] Do you want to know the saying of our past ancestor Shitou that right in light there is darkness? *Dōgen pounded his staff once.*

Do you want to know Shitou's saying that right in darkness there is light? *Dōgen pounded his staff once.*

Why did the ancestor say to not meet it as darkness? Do you want to illuminate this point? *Dōgen pounded his staff once.*

Why did the ancestor say not to see it as light? Do you want to illuminate this point? *Dōgen pounded his staff once.*

The ancestor also said, "Light and darkness face each other like the front and back foot in walking." Great assembly, do you want to know the front and back foot in walking? *Dōgen pounded his staff twice and said:* We cannot call our front foot the back one, and we cannot call our back foot the front one. What is the meaning of such a principle? *Dōgen pounded his staff twice.*

---

113 This saying by Shitou, and the one that follows, are from his important teaching poem "Harmony of Difference and Sameness," which expresses the interactions of the phenomenal and the universal. See Dharma hall discourse 307 and note 105, above.

Practice That Continues Beyond Magical Offerings
313. Dharma Hall Discourse
I can remember that before Niutou had met the fourth ancestor [Dayi Daoxin], hundreds of birds brought Niutou flowers in their beaks as offerings. After their meeting, the birds brought no more flowers.

I, Eihei, have a verse about this:

> Carrying flowers, hundreds of birds made offerings
> to Niutou.
> Touzi [Datong] appeared to be selling oil.[114]
> Talented and untalented are thirty-five miles apart.[115]
> People in the past and present have expressed
> progress and practice.

Roaring Lions Do Not Fear Disappointment
314. Dharma Hall Discourse
Here is a story. One day National Teacher Dazheng [Nanyang Huizhong] called his attendant. The attendant responded. The national teacher called like this three times, and each time the attendant responded. The national teacher said, "I thought I had disappointed you, but it is you who has disappointed me."[116]

The teacher Dōgen said: The national teacher called three times, and the attendant responded three times. A buddha and a demon discern the sequence of events, and both the dog and Zhaozhou have no Buddha nature. My disappointing you means that I do not become one of the ten thousand things. Your disappointing me means that I had thought the barbarian's beard was red, but there is also a red-bearded barbarian.

---

114 Zhaozhou visited Touzi Datong's hermitage, but Touzi was away. Touzi returned carrying a bottle of oil for lamps. Zhaozhou said that although he had heard of Touzi's fame, he could only see an old man selling oil. Touzi said that Zhaozhou only saw an old oil seller, and did not see Touzi. Zhaozhou asked, "What is Touzi like?" Touzi said, "Oil, oil." From the Jingde Transmission of the Lamp (Keitoku Dentōroku), vol. 15.

115 In an old Chinese story, one person understood the writing in a puzzle immediately, but another only understood after he had walked thirty-five miles farther. For Dōgen, both ways are complete practice.

116 This story about the national teacher is case 17 in the Mumonkan. See Cleary, *Unlocking the Zen Kōan*, pp. 85–88; or Aitken, *Gateless Barrier*, pp. 113–119.

Although this is so, do you wish to thoroughly understand the essential point of National Teacher Nanyang?

After a pause Dōgen said: Why would hundreds of thousands of roaring lions fear the old wild foxes in the human and heavenly realms?

The Ordinary Tea and Rice of Turning the Great Dharma Wheel
315. Dharma Hall Discourse

All dharmas are born from causes and conditions. This Dharma expounds causes and conditions, and it exhausts all conditions. The Great Teacher [Śākyamuni] expressed it like this. How is it to practice this reality? When Aśvajit heard the teaching, he cut off the root of life [and death], and when Śāriputra heard the teaching his face broke open.[117] This is the ordinary tea and rice in the house of buddha ancestors. If we are descendants of buddha ancestors, we can begin to build a sanctuary for the jewel king on Vairocana Buddha's headtop, and turn the great Dharma wheel that goes beyond Dongshan [Liangjie]. Tell me, what is this turning of the great Dharma wheel?

Then Dōgen held up his whisk and said: Even if you can turn it, you cannot avoid my whisk.

Eminent and Vigorous in Tattered Robes
316. Dharma Hall Discourse

Remain solitary without dependency and drop off all of reality. Mixed together within the ten thousand forms, be clear and apparent. Eminent and vigorous on each bit of ground, be like the moon stamped on the water, flowing but not flowing. Like the wind in the sky, move but do not move. Having become thoroughly like this, when you proceed, in mean alleys do not ride on a golden horse; when turning back, wear tattered robes.

---

117 Aśvajit (Assaji in the Indian Pali language) was one of the five companions of the Buddha during his ascetic practices on the path to awakening, and later became an arhat and follower of the Buddha. Śāriputra was one of the Buddha's ten great disciples, who awakened with the help of Aśvajit; see Dharma hall discourse 381.

The Certainty before the Peaches Blossomed
317. Dharma Hall Discourse

The eyes are not sense faculties, but actually soapberry beads.[118] Peach blossoms are not objects, but rather Linji's slab of red meat.[119] Consciousness is not perception, but the ancient eyes blinking at Vulture Peak. Mind is not the ability to think, but attaining and entrusting the marrow at Shaolin.[120] Do you want to understand in detail why it is like this?

After a pause Dōgen said: Amid spring rain, spring wind, and spring grasses and trees are yellow nightingales, earthworms, and toads. It is impossible to doubt this saying by Eihei: Why was it necessary for Lingyun to see the peach blossoms?

Truly Dropping Off Body and Mind
318. Dharma Hall Discourse

My late teacher [Tiantong Rujing] instructed the assembly, "Sanzen (Zen study and practice) is dropping off body and mind."

Great assembly, do you want to understand thoroughly the meaning of this?

After a pause Dōgen said: Sitting upright and dropping off body and mind, the ancestral teachers' nostrils are flowers of emptiness. As for the true transmission of the samādhi of wall-gazing, the later generations of disciples are expounding mistakes.[121]

---

118 For more on soapberry beads used in rosaries, see Dharma hall discourse 143 and volume 2, note 64.

119 Linji said, "In this slab of red meat is a true person of no rank, always going out and in through the portals of your face." See Watson, *Zen Teachings of Master Lin-chi,* p. 13; and Cleary, *Book of Serenity,* case 38, p. 167. Peach blossoms refer to the incident of Lingyun Zhiqin's awakening.

120 The "eyes blinking at Vulture Peak" refers to Śākyamuni blinking and holding up a flower at the first transmission; and "entrusting the marrow at Shaolin" refers to Bodhidharma's transmitting the mind seal.

121 "Later generations of disciples are expounding mistakes" implies that they are clinging to the forms of upright sitting, or the study of Zen *(sanzen),* rather than enacting the crucial activity of dropping off body and mind.

Mind Is Walls; Buddha Is Mud

319. Dharma Hall Discourse

The true Dharma correctly transmitted by buddhas and ancestors is simply just sitting. My late teacher Tiantong [Rujing] instructed the assembly saying, "You know the circumstances of Zen Master Damei Fachang when he studied with great teacher Kiangsi Mazu, don't you? He asked Mazu, 'What is Buddha?' and Mazu said, 'Mind itself is Buddha.' Immediately Damei made prostrations and departed, and entered the peaks of Plum Mountain (Meishan) where he ate pine nuts and wore lotus leaves, spending his whole life practicing zazen day and night. For thirty years he was unknown by rulers or ministers, and did not receive any support of patrons. This is an excellent example of the Buddha way."[122]

We should know that zazen is the decorous activity of practice after realization. Realization is simply just sitting zazen. At this monastery we have the first monks' hall, so in this country of Japan this is the first we have heard of this, the first time we have seen it, the first time we have entered it, and the first time of sitting in a monks' hall. This is fortunate for people studying the Buddha way.

Later a monk asked Damei, "What principle did you attain when you saw great teacher Mazu and came to reside on this mountain?"

Damei said, "Mazu told me that this mind itself is Buddha."

The monk said, "These days Mazu's Buddha Dharma is different."

Damei asked, "How is it different?"

The monk said, "These days he says 'Neither mind nor Buddha.'"

Damei said, "This old man confuses people endlessly. I will let him have neither mind nor Buddha; for me it's just this mind itself is Buddha."

The monk returned and reported to Mazu, and Mazu said, "The plum has ripened."

So we see that the person who clearly understood that this mind itself is Buddha abandoned human society and entered the deep mountains

---

122 This story about Damei and Mazu also appears in Dharma hall discourse 8, and Dharma words 9 in volume 8. It is referred to in the Mumonkan, cases 30 and 33. See Cleary, *Unlocking the Zen Kōan*, pp. 144–145, 155–157; or Aitken, *Gateless Barrier*, pp. 189–194, 204–207. The story also appears in the Jingde Transmission of the Lamp; see Ogata, *Transmission of the Lamp*, p. 240.

and valleys, only practicing zazen day and night. Brothers on this mountain, you should straightforwardly, single-mindedly focus on zazen. Do not pass your days and nights in vain.[123] Human life is impermanent; how could we wait for some other time? I prayerfully beseech your practice. Great assembly, do you want to understand the truth of this mind itself is Buddha?

After a pause Dōgen said: This mind itself is Buddha is very difficult to understand. Mind is fences, walls, tiles, and pebbles, and Buddha is a glob of mud or a clump of soil. Kiangsi [Mazu] expressed trailing mud and dripping water; Damei realized lurking in the grasses and sticking to trees.[124] Where can we find this mind itself is Buddha?

The Ladle Is in Your Hands
320. Dharma Hall Discourse for Bathing Buddha [on Buddha's Birthday, 1249]
As before, Dōgen quoted all of Hongzhi's Dharma Hall Discourse for Bathing Buddha that begins, "This is the completely clear water of the emptiness of self-nature," and then Dōgen said the following.[125]

Urging two dragons to carry water for her, Queen Māyā bathed her newborn son's body. Thus Buddha abandoned the bliss of Tuṣita Heaven and seemed to be stained by the six sense objects of the human realm. He grasped a glob of mud to make it into a buddha, and scooped the moon from the water, considering it the spirit. The oceanic vow of great compassion has no shore or limit, and saves living beings with release from the

---

123 "Do not pass your days and nights in vain" is the conclusion of Shitou's poem "Harmony of Difference and Sameness." See Leighton and Wu, *Cultivating the Empty Field,* pp. 74–75.

124 "Trailing mud and dripping water" appears in the introduction to Hekiganroku, case 2: "To say the word 'Buddha' is trailing mud and dripping water." See Cleary and Cleary, *Blue Cliff Record,* p. 10. "Lurking in the grasses and sticking to trees" appears at the very beginning of the introduction to Shōyōroku, case 73: "Lurking in the grasses and sticking to trees one turns into a spirit." See Cleary, *Book of Serenity,* p. 307. This is a traditional expression for the lingering attachment of ghosts or spirits to this realm. In this Dharma hall discourse, Dōgen is using both of these expressions to indicate the vow to remain in the phenomenal world of sentient beings to pursue bodhisattva activity.

125 This introduction is a note added to the text by Koun Ejō, compiler of this volume, and refers to the Dharma hall discourse by Hongzhi, quoted in its entirety in Dōgen's Dharma hall discourse 256.

harbor of suffering. The very last body is the true beginning, and his birth, saying, "I alone am the World-Honored One," is the genuine cause [for saving beings]. On this fine occasion, both old and young cut off ignorance, greed, and anger. When you nurture the power of the wooden ladle at Vulture Peak, you become eminent people within the cave of patch-robed monks.

All of you benevolent people, what is it like just when the handle of the ladle is in your hands? The lowest person has the highest wisdom.[126]

Asking about the Unknowable
321. Dharma Hall Discourse
Difficult delusions and delusions of wrong view; this mind and this Buddha; throughout the body and the entire body; unknowable things and nonexistent things: If someone asks what these mean, I'll hit him once in the face with my whisk.[127]

Offering Rice to Demons
322. Dharma Hall Discourse for Opening the Summer Practice Period
As before, Dōgen quoted all of Hongzhi's Dharma Hall Discourse for Open-

---

126 "The lowest person has the highest wisdom" is from the Platform Sutra of the sixth ancestor, Huineng, when he is questioned about having his own poem written on the wall. See Cleary, *Sutra of Hui-neng,* p. 10; or Price and Wong, *Diamond Sutra and Sutra of Hui Neng,* p. 17.

127 "Difficult delusions and delusions of wrong view" refers to the ten basic delusions. The first five delusions, greed, hatred, ignorance, arrogance, and doubt, are considered difficult to extinguish. The second five delusions of wrong view are the view that the self exists, the view of extinction or permanence of the self, the view that negates causality, attachment to views, and clinging to misguided rules. In the Abhidharma Kośa, by Vasubandhu, there are six delusions, the first five and wrong view, which includes the second five of the ten mentioned by Dōgen. See Leo Pruden, English trans., *Abhidharma Kośa Bhāṣyam,* translated into French by Louis de La Vallée Poussin, vol. III (Berkeley: Asian Humanities Press, 1990), pp. 767–770. "Throughout the body" and "the entire body" are the responses of Daowu and Yunyan, respectively, about how to understand the presence of the thousand hands and eyes of the bodhisattva of compassion, Avalokiteśvara. See Dōgen's Shōbōgenzō essay Kannon, in Cook, *Sounds of Valley Streams,* pp. 89–95; and Cleary, *Book of Serenity,* case 54, pp. 229–232. "Unknowable things and nonexistent things" is literally "What things and no things."

ing the Summer Practice Period that begins, "Ordinary people and sages together," and then Dōgen said the following.[128]

Whereas the ancient Buddha Hongzhi joined with the tathāgatas, his descendant Eihei also joins with the ancient Buddha Hongzhi. Do you want to understand this point in detail?

After a pause Dōgen said: Monks sharing the practice period become capable practitioners. Picking out the ordinary from the sage, how can we settle in this lifetime? Patch-robed monks pierce their nostrils, so that in the summer the five-petaled flower becomes more fragrant. Offering one portion of rice to the demon Pāpiyas, allow him to drop off even the place of a peaceful body and settled life.[129] Time after time, scoop up the toads and jellyfish in your net and have them put their minds to the work of jumping clear of the net to reach the shore.

All the buddhas in ten directions gather on top of Eihei's staff and do practice period. Eihei's staff engages the way on the headtops of all the buddhas in the ten directions. "Therefore it is said that all buddhas' Dharma bodies enter my nature; my nature joins with and becomes the same as the tathāgatas. Also it is said, 'Make great perfect awakening into your own sangha building.'"[130] Practice period with body and mind is the wisdom of the nature of equality. If this can be so, what is it that joins with the tathāgatas? Solitary and silent, for ninety days of summer practice period, go beyond appearances. Immovable sitting is boundless in the twenty emptinesses.

128 This introduction is a note added to the text by Koun Ejō, compiler of this volume, and refers to the Dharma hall discourse by Hongzhi, quoted in its entirety in Dōgen's Dharma hall discourse 257. In this Dharma hall discourse Dōgen further refers to this Dharma hall discourse for Opening the Summer Practice Period from Hongzhi, concerning joining with the tathāgatas.

129 For the demon Pāpiyas, see Dharma hall discourse 35 and volume 1, note 87.

130 These quotes are from Hongzhi's Dharma hall discourse for Opening the Summer Practice Period, cited by Dōgen here. "All buddhas' Dharma bodies enter my nature; my nature joins with and becomes the same as the tathāgatas" is from the Song of Enlightenment by Yongjia Xuanjie. "Make great perfect awakening into your own sangha building" is from the Complete Enlightenment Sutra. See Dharma hall discourse 257 and volume 3, notes 116 and 117.

This Very Mind Cutting Notches in the Boat
323. Dharma Hall Discourse
An ancient said, "This very mind, this very Buddha."[131] Now there are
only a few who can understand this. Although he said, "This very mind,"
this is not the first five consciousnesses; or the sixth, eighth, or ninth consciousness; or the various elements of the mind.[132] Also it is not citta, the
mind of grasses and trees, or the mind as the heart essence.[133] Excluding
all of these, what mind is there that we can call "this very mind"? It is not
thinking, knowing, memory, or sensation, not views or understanding,
not spiritual knowledge or clarified knowledge. Arriving at such a ground
[where we understand it is not any of these kinds of mind], who can
fathom "this very mind, this very Buddha"?

There were more than eighty good teachers who were disciples of Mazu,
but only Zen Master Ruhui of Dongsi temple in Hunan understood the
meaning of "this very mind, this very Buddha." Why do I say this?

131 "This very mind, this very Buddha" refers to the saying of Mazu that "This very mind
itself is Buddha." See the Mumonkan, case 30, in Cleary, *Unlocking the Zen Kōan*, pp.
144–145; and Aitken, *Gateless Barrier*, pp. 189–194. When a monk asked about "this very
mind, this very Buddha," Mazu responded, "No mind, no Buddha." See Cheng Chien,
Sun Face Buddha, p. 78; and Ogata, *Transmission of the Lamp*, p. 188.

132 These various consciousnesses refer to the Yogācāra theory that includes the five senses
as the first five consciousnesses, and the mind faculty observing mind objects (i.e.,
thoughts) as the sixth sense, and the sixth consciousness. The eighth consciousness, or
ālaya vijñāna in Sanskrit, is the repository of all experiences and resulting dispositions, both
wholesome and unwholesome, which can be strengthened or weakened depending on our
conduct. The seventh consciousness, *manas* in Sanskrit, not mentioned here by Dōgen,
is the egoistic faculty of human consciousness that distinguishes self from other and objec-
tifies the world. This seventh consciousness is not likely to be mistaken for Buddha, as it
may be considered the source of delusion. A basic text for the eight consciousnesses is the
Thirty Verses (Trimśikā) by Vasubandhu. See translations and commentary in David
Kalupahana, *The Principles of Buddhist Psychology* (Albany: State University of New York
Press, 1987); or Stefan Anacker, *Seven Works of Vasubandhu: The Buddhist Psychological
Doctor* (Delhi: Motilal Banarsidass, 1984). The ninth consciousness, expounded especially
in Shingon, or Vajrayāna Buddhism, and described in the Vajra Samādhi Sūtra, is the
transformed and purified eighth consciousness. "The various elements of the mind," literally the various "dharmas" of mind, refers to the abhidharma psychological teachings of
the variety of component elements of reality, most of them mental qualities.

133 *Citta* is the Sanskrit term that refers generally to the human mind and all its aspects.
"The mind of grasses and trees" and "the mind as the heart essence" are given by Dōgen
as the Sanskrit terms *hṛdaya* or *karida* and *vṛddha* or *irida*. These are aspects of mind
delineated very near the beginning of the chapter "Awakening the Mind" in the Tiantai

After [Mazu Daoyi] Daji left the world, this teacher [Dongsi Ruhui] always grieved that Mazu's students continued to ceaselessly recite and memorize the saying "This very mind, this very Buddha." He would say, "Where does Buddha dwell that could be called 'This very mind?' The mind is like the painter [of the world], but you call it 'This very Buddha.'"

Finally the teacher [Ruhui] said to the assembly, "Mind is not Buddha; wisdom is not the way. The sword is long gone, yet you are cutting notches in the boat."[134] After that time people called Dongsi temple the cave of Zen.[135]

The meaning of "this very mind, this very Buddha" is like this. I sincerely implore you not to be demented and confused.

Clarifying Morning and Evening
324. Dharma Hall Discourse on the Twenty-Fifth Day of the Fourth Month [1249]
As before, Dōgen related Yuanwu's saying that begins, "On this eleventh day of the summer practice period," and then said the following.[136]

---

text Mohe Zhiguan by the Tiantai founder Zhiyi. See Neal Donner and Daniel Stevenson, *The Great Calming and Contemplation: A Study and Annotated Translation of the First Chapter of Chih-I's Mo-Ho Chih-Kuan* (Honolulu: Kuroda Institute, University of Hawai'i Press, 1993), p. 140. Most of Dōgen's leading disciples, to whom he was speaking these Dharma hall discourses, had also been Tendai monks like Dōgen and would have known these technical terms. Dōgen also refers to these same three aspects of mind at the beginning of his Shōbōgenzō essay Hotsu Bodaishin (Arousing the Bodhi Mind). See Nishijima and Cross, *Zen Master Dogen's Shobogenzo*, book 3, pp. 265–266; or Yūhō Yokoi with Daizen Victoria, trans., *Zen Master Dōgen: An Introduction with Selected Writings* (Tokyo: Weatherhill, 1976), p. 107. In that passage Dōgen says that *bodhicitta*, the mind directed toward awakening, arises through using the mind of thinking and knowing, or *citta*. The "mind of grasses and trees," *hṛdaya*, refers to life force as seen via ideas of Buddha nature, or of tathāgata-garbha, the world as the womb of buddhas. The "mind as the heart essence," or *vṛddha*, refers to the heart or core.

134 "The sword is long gone, yet you are cutting notches in the boat" refers to a story about a foolish person whose sword fell overboard and who then cut a notch in the side of the boat to mark where it was lost. The story is from the classic Lu Spring and Autumn Annals, a third-century-B.C.E. encyclopedic collection of Chinese philosophical writings.

135 This whole paragraph is from the Jingde Transmission of the Lamp. See Ogata, *Transmission of the Lamp*, p. 245.

136 This introductory note is by the compiler, Koun Ejō, and refers to Dharma hall discourse 259, given on this same date in the previous year, in which Yuanwu's saying is quoted in full.

It is the eleventh day since beginning the summer practice period, and each day has morning and evening. If you clarify that each day has morning and evening, you will penetrate the lanterns and temple pillars. If you penetrate the lanterns and temple pillars, you will immediately recognize the water buffalo. If you recognize the water buffalo, you will immediately see Hanshan.[137]

If you hesitate, I, Eihei, will be present wherever you walk, stand, sit, or lie down, and wherever you put on your robe or eat your rice.

Harvesting Practice amid the Rainy Season
325. Dharma Hall Discourse on the First Day of the Fifth Month
When oxhide covers the temple pillars, the temple pillars cry, "Boo hoo."[138] Someone crosses over the bridge; the bridge flows but the water does not.[139]

Although ancient worthies spoke like this, do people today understand or not? Patch-robed ones drop off body and mind within the fist of ignorant karmic consciousness. Here at this mountain hut, amid the fifth-month plums, the rain falls.[140] Under the heavens, right now is harvest season for the new wheat.

Feeding Sixteen-Foot Grasses to the Water Buffalo
326. Dharma Hall Discourse for the Fifth Day of the Fifth Month Celebration [1249]

---

137 "If you penetrate the lanterns and temple pillars...you will immediately see Hanshan" is quoted exactly from Yuanwu's Dharma hall discourse in Dōgen's Dharma hall discourse 259.

138 A monk asked Guizong Zhichang, "This matter is never-ending, how can we take care of it?" Guizong Zhichang said, "When oxhide covers the temple pillars, the temple pillars cry, 'Boo hoo.'" He continued, "Ordinary people listen and do not hear, but all sages laugh joyfully." See Ogata, *Transmission of the Lamp*, p. 249.

139 "Someone crosses over the bridge; the bridge flows but the water does not" is from a poem by the great layman Fu. The preceding lines say, "Grasping a hoe with empty hands; walking while riding on a water buffalo." This appears in Jingde Transmission of the Lamp, vol. 27.

140 The fifth month in Japan is part of the rainy season, and it is unpleasantly humid.

As before, the teacher Dōgen quoted the Dharma Hall Discourse for the Fifth Day of the Fifth Month by Hongzhi, and then after a pause Dōgen said the following.[141]

The fifth day of the fifth month is the Festival of the Center of Heaven, when Samantabhadra and Mañjuśrī appear as worldly people, and pick a sixteen-foot stalk of grass to nurture the water buffalo of Guishan.[142]

The Ancient Crane Flying throughout the World

327. Dharma Hall Discourse

Although the true Dharma eye treasury, wondrous mind of nirvāṇa, is what buddhas protect and keep in mind, it cannot be defiled by the Buddha Dharma.[143] Although it was correctly transmitted by arhats, the true Dharma eye treasury did not descend into the dharma of śrāvakas. Although it was correctly transmitted by common people, it did not descend into the dharma of sentient beings. If this were not true, how could it have ever reached us now? Great assembly, do you want to clearly know the key to why this is so?

After a pause Dōgen said: After midnight the moon sets and the nest is chilled with night. The thousand-year-old crane does not remain in the jewel forest.

141 For other Dharma hall discourses on this Fifth Month Festival day, also known as Boys' Day, see Dharma hall discourses 169, 242, and 261. This introduction is a note added by the compiler of this volume, Koun Ejō. The excerpt by Hongzhi referred to here is given in full in Dharma hall discourse 242, ending with "A settled person doesn't speak; placid water doesn't flow."

142 In the first Dharma hall discourse for the fifth month festival, discourse 169, Mañjuśrī asked the pilgrim Sudhana to bring him a single stalk of medicinal herb. Here Samantabhadra and Mañjuśrī pluck a sixteen-foot stalk, which refers to the image of a sixteen-foot-tall body of a buddha. Dōgen often refers to Guishan Lingyou's water buffalo. Guishan said that after he died he would become a water buffalo down the hill from the mountain. See Dharma hall discourse 159 and volume 2, note 105. The water buffalo became a common image for referring to monk trainees developing their practice.

143 The true Dharma eye treasury not being defiled by the Buddha Dharma can refer to defilement from attachments to the Dharma, or from provisional teachings included in the Dharma.

Don't Have Deluded Thoughts

328. Dharma Hall Discourse

Here is a story. Government Minister Zhu asked Changsha [Jingcen], "When an earthworm is cut into two, I wonder which piece has the Buddha nature?"

Changsha said, "Don't have deluded thoughts."

The officer said, "What about when both pieces are moving?"

Changsha said, "That is only because the wind and fire has not yet dispersed."

After further discussion, Changsha said, "Ignorant people call this [consciousness that is the root source of life and death] the original person."[144]

Then the teacher Dōgen said: The root of life and death from beginningless ages is what ignorant people call the original person. Even though they turn upside down and disseminate their views in the process, the great earth, mountains, and rivers are still the pure body.

Neither Right nor Wrong

329. Dharma Hall Discourse

The bright clarity of the ancestral teacher's mind is the bright clarity of the hundred grass-tips.[145] With others it is never one; with the self it is never different. If you are only right, you are offending someone to their face. If you are only not right, where can you escape or hide? Therefore it is said, be neither right nor wrong; neither attached nor separate. All the tathāgatas in the three times alike proclaim this truth; all the ancestral teachers together transmit this wonder.

---

144 The title of "Government Minister" of this questioner Zhu was for one of the three main officials of the government, in charge of distributing decrees. This dialogue is also discussed by Dōgen near the end of the Buddha Nature essay in Shōbōgenzō. See Waddell and Abe, *Heart of Dōgen's Shōbōgenzō,* pp. 94–96. Dōgen includes the full version of this dialogue as case 65 in the ninety kōans with his verse comments in volume 9 of Eihei Kōroku, below; and also as case 20 in his collection of three hundred kōans, Mana Shōbōgenzō. See Nishijima, *Master Dogen's Shinji Shobogenzo,* p. 30.

145 This is a saying cited by the famed eighth-century Chan adept Layman Pang to his daughter Lingzhao. See Dharma hall discourse 9 and volume 1, note 17.

I dare to question the great assembly, tell me, what does this mean?

After a pause Dōgen said: Freely play the single iron flute; unless you know its sound, we cannot listen together.[146]

Slander!

330. Dharma Hall Discourse

I can remember, a monk asked Zhaozhou, "Does a dog have Buddha nature or not?"[147]

Zhaozhou said, "No."

The monk asked, "All living beings have Buddha nature, why doesn't the dog?"

Zhaozhou said, "Because it has karmic consciousness."

The teacher Dōgen said: Zhaozhou said it like this for the sake of this person, and was most kind. However, if someone asked me, "Does a dog have Buddha nature or not?" I would say to him: Whether you say yes or no, either one is slander.

If the person were to ask "What?" at the very moment of his speaking he would be hit with my stick.

The Indestructible Tiles and Pebbles

331. Dharma Hall Discourse

A monk asked Zhaozhou, "Before this world existed, this nature existed. When this world is destroyed, this nature will not be destroyed. What is this indestructible nature?"

Zhaozhou said, "The four great elements and five skandhas."

The monk said, "These still can be destroyed. What is this indestructible nature?"

Zhaozhou said, "The four great elements and five skandhas."[148]

---

146 An iron flute has no finger holes or hollow to blow through.

147 For references for the famous story of Zhaozhou's responses to this question about a dog's Buddha nature, see Dharma hall discourse 226 and volume 3, note 63.

148 This story also appeared in Dharma hall discourse 140. See a slightly different version in Green, *Recorded Sayings of Zen Master Joshu,* pp. 141–142.

The teacher Dōgen said: Although the ancient Buddha Zhaozhou said it like this, old monk Eihei also has something to say. Suppose someone asked, "Before this world existed, this nature existed. When this world is destroyed, this nature will not be destroyed. What is this indestructible nature?" I would say to him: Fences, walls, tiles, and pebbles.

If he were to say, "This is still something fabricated and perishable, what is the indestructible nature?" I would simply say to him: Fences, walls, tiles, and pebbles.

The Fallen Flower Still Blooms Here
332. Dharma Hall Discourse

The true Dharma eye treasury transcends brightness and darkness. Patch-robed monks' nostrils disregard both enlightenment and delusion. So it is said, "A broken mirror does not illuminate or reflect. A fallen flower does not jump back onto the branch."[149] Why is this so? Great assembly, do you want to understand this clearly?

After a pause Dōgen said: Buddha's children abide in this land, and this is Buddha's fulfillment.[150] Always remaining among them, [Buddha] does walking meditation, sits, and lies down.[151]

---

149 "A broken mirror does not illuminate or reflect. A fallen flower does not return to the branch" is a saying by Baoji [Huayan] Xiujing in response to a monk's question, "How is it when a person of great enlightenment becomes deluded again?" Dōgen discusses it also in the Shōbōgenzō essay Daigo (Great Enlightenment); see Thomas Cleary, trans. and ed., *Rational Zen: The Mind of Dōgen Zenji* (Boston: Shambhala, 1993), pp. 110–115.

150 "Fulfillment" is *juyū*, which, read as separate characters, could be interpreted as (the Buddha) "accepts their functioning" or "accepts and utilizes them." This could also refer to the practice of self-fulfillment samādhi, *jijuyū zammai*, which Dōgen discusses in Bendōwa; see Okumura and Leighton, *The Wholehearted Way*, pp. 19–24. Here Dōgen says that Buddha's fulfillment exists in the practice of his followers right now.

151 This entire last statement, "Buddha's children abide in this land...does walking meditation, sits, and lies down" is from the very end of chapter 17 of the Lotus Sutra, on "Discrimination of Merits." See Hurvitz, *Scripture of the Lotus Blossom of the Fine Dharma*, p. 257; Watson, *Lotus Sutra*, p. 244; or Katō, Tamura, and Miyasaka, *Threefold Lotus Sutra*, p. 268.

The Fist Like a Thunderbolt

333. Dharma Hall Discourse

Not letting in any [view of] outside, not letting out any [view of] inside, a single fist like a thunderbolt completes the ten thousand affairs. Although this is so; no two, no duality, no discriminations, Māhāprajñā-pāramitā.[152]

The Unceasing Smile without Any Separation

334. Dharma Hall Discourse

Directly pointing to the human mind is like the separation between heaven and earth. Seeing the nature and becoming Buddha is like this slightest deviation.[153] Huangbo sticking out his tongue does not yet cover the three thousand worlds. Qingyuan [Xingsi] lowers his leg and kicks over great empty space.[154] Why is this so? Great assembly, do you want to clearly understand the meaning of this?

152 The first sentence is a quote from Tiantong Rujing's Recorded Sayings. "No two, no duality, no discriminations" is from the Māhāprajñāpāramitā Sūtra and is also quoted by Tiantong Rujing.

153 "Directly pointing to the human mind; seeing the nature and becoming Buddha" is from Huangbo's Transmitting the Essence of the Mind and Dharma, as a quote from Bodhidharma. See John Blofeld, *The Zen Teaching of Huang Po: On the Transmission of Mind* (New York: Grove Press, 1958), p. 66. "The slightest deviation is like the separation between heaven and earth" is from the Inscription on Faith in Mind, traditionally attributed to the third ancestor, Jianzhi Sengcan. See Sheng-Yen, *Poetry of Enlightenment*, p. 25.

154 Sticking out his tongue was Huangbo's response to hearing the story about his teacher Baizhang going deaf for three days after a shout by Baizhang's teacher Mazu. Dōgen discusses this story in Dharma hall discourse 50, and also as case 82 in his ninety kōans with verse comments in volume 9. The full story of Mazu's shout and his student Baizhang's resulting temporary deafness appears in the commentary to the Hekiganroku, case 11. See Cleary and Cleary, *Blue Cliff Record*, pp. 73–74. The reference to Huangbo's tongue as "not yet covering the three thousand worlds" is a comparison to Śākyamuni Buddha, whose tongue can cover them (according to the chapter on the "Form of Buddha's Tongue" in the six-hundred-volume version of the Māhāprajñāpāramitā Sūtra). Qingyuan lowering his leg refers to the gesture he used in giving his final approval to his disciple Shitou Xiqian, before Shitou departed to live in his own hermitage. In this Dharma hall discourse, Dōgen is criticizing the idea of "directly pointing to the human mind; seeing the nature and becoming Buddha," as an expression for avoiding textual study and also for seeing nature (Jap.: *kenshō*) as the attainment of some awakening experience. Dōgen rejected the priority sometimes given to such attainment. Praising Qingyuan, antecedent of the Sōtō lineage, perhaps implies some comparative criticism by Dōgen of the lineage of Huangbo and his disciple Linji (Rinzai).

After a pause Dōgen said: Mahākāśyapa's face breaking into a smile has not yet ceased.[155]

A Pitiful Condition
335. Dharma Hall Discourse
Tathāgata Zen and Ancestral Zen were not transmitted by the ancients, but only transmitted falsely in the Eastern Land (China).[156] For several hundred years some have been clinging with delusion to these vain names. How pitiful is the inferior condition of this degenerating world.

Transcribing Dharma
336. Dharma Hall Discourse for Appointing the New Scribe[157]
Buddhas bestow [the Dharma] by hand to buddhas; ancestors fully pour out their water [Dharma] for other ancestors. Tie together your affinities with the cloud and water monks, plant seeds in the forest of the monastery. At this very moment, make Mount Sumeru your brush and take the water of the great ocean as your ink. Using these, what do you copy and what do you write?

Great assembly, do you want to clearly understand this? Practice this in accord with Dharma, do not practice without accord with Dharma. Whether now or later, if you practice the Dharma you will be at peace. Having made copies in this way, how do you penetrate these circumstances?

After a pause Dōgen said: Make three prostrations and stand at your place.

---

155 "Mahākāśyapa's face breaking into a smile" refers to his response to Śākyamuni Buddha's silently holding up a flower at Vulture Peak. This is said to be the first Zen transmission of the true Dharma eye treasury. See Aitken, *Gateless Barrier*, case 6, pp. 46–53; or Cleary, *Unlocking the Zen Kōan*, pp. 33–38.

156 "Tathāgata Zen" refers to practice based on the teachings from the sutras. "Ancestral Zen" refers to practice outside of words and letters. See also Dharma hall discourse 52. Here Dōgen criticizes the distinction between the two.

157 The person in the position of monastery scribe, or secretary (Jap.: *shoki*), is the head of one of the six monastic departments. He sits next to the head monk in the monks' hall and otherwise assists the head monk, and also handles correspondence for the monastery. The *shoki* may have also taken the notes for these Dharma hall discourses. See Leighton and Okumura, *Dōgen's Pure Standards for the Zen Community*, pp. 52, 90, 105, 228.

The Reality of Just Sitting

337. Dharma Hall Discourse

Great assembly, do you want to hear the reality of just sitting, which is the Zen practice that is dropping off body and mind?

After a pause Dōgen said: Mind cannot objectify it; thinking cannot describe it. Just step back and carry on, and avoid offending anyone you face. At the ancient dock, the wind and moon are cold and clear. At night the boat floats peacefully in the land of lapis lazuli.[158]

Not Designing Buddha

338. Dharma Hall Discourse

In seeking for buddhahood through Zen practice, have no designs on becoming a buddha. If you practice Zen by designing a buddha, Buddha becomes increasingly estranged. When the tile is shattered and the mirror vanishes, where is your face?[159] Thereupon we understand that reaching here requires some effort.

Not Escaping Buddha; Not Escaping Delusion

339. Dharma Hall Discourse

As I remember, the ancient Buddha Zhaozhou, when he was residing at Guanyin temple, gave a Dharma hall discourse in which he said to the assembly, "It is like a bright jewel held in your palm, when a barbarian comes, a Chinese person is reflected. This old monk holds one stalk of grass to use it as a sixteen-foot golden body, and holds a sixteen-foot golden body to use as one stalk of grass. Buddha is delusion; delusions are Buddha."[160]

Then a monk asked, "I wonder, whose delusion is Buddha?"

Zhaozhou said, "It's the delusion of everybody."

---

158 "At the ancient dock...the land of lapis lazuli" is from volume 1 of Hongzhi's Extensive Record. The land of lapis lazuli is the abode of the Medicine Buddha, Bhaisajyaguru. See Raoul Birnbaum, *The Healing Buddha*, rev. ed. (Boston, Shambhala, 1989).

159 "Tiles shattered and mirror vanished" is an image for ending views of self or of objectified Buddha.

160 This quote from Zhaozhou is from Jingde Transmission of Lamp, vol. 10. See Chang, *Original Teachings of Ch'an Buddhism*, p. 166; Ogata, *Transmission of the Lamp*, p. 349. The original of Zhaozhou's first response to the monk might be read as "It's delusion for

The monk said, "How can we escape it?"

Zhaozhou said, "What's the use of escaping it?'

The teacher Dōgen said: Although old Buddha Zhaozhou said it like this, I, Eihei, also have a little bit to say. Great assembly, do you want to hear it? Suppose someone asks me, "I wonder, whose delusion is Buddha?" I would say to him: One stalk of grass is the delusion of one stalk of grass. The sixteen-foot golden body is the delusion of the sixteen-foot golden body.

If he asks, "How can we escape it?" I would say to him: If you want to escape it, just escape it.

The Richness of Cultivation
340. Dharma Hall Discourse

Holding up and using the bright, clear hundred grasses, nurture the water buffalo and its horns will grow. When the horns mature, forthwith the water buffalo matures. In spring, Nanquan and Guishan plow the field.[161] Tell me, great assembly, when plowing the field in spring, what circumstances arise?

After a pause Dōgen said: Cultivating the fields, then preparing food, are everyday household affairs. The bright moon cleared by the wind is the richness of a lifetime.[162]

---

the sake of everybody." The version in the Recorded Sayings of Zhaozhou, perhaps compiled around the same time as the Jingde Transmission of the Lamp, uses slightly different characters for the dialogue, which emphasize the "for the sake of" interpretation. See Green, *Recorded Sayings of Zen Master Joshu,* p. 34. "When a barbarian comes, a Chinese person is reflected" as quoted by Dōgen is an abbreviation of Zhaozhou's original statement, "When a barbarian comes, a barbarian is reflected; when a Chinese person comes, a Chinese person is reflected." "Delusion" here is *bonno,* which refers to emotional and mental attachments and afflictions.

161 Nanquan and Guishan both said that they would return in the next life as water buffaloes.

162 "Cultivating the fields, then preparing food, are everyday household affairs" is from Hongzhi's Extensive Record, vol. 2, which became the verse comments for the Shōyōroku. See Cleary, *Book of Serenity,* case 12, p. 52. "The bright moon cleared by the wind is the richness of a lifetime" is from Hongzhi's verse comment to the Shōyōroku, case 60. See Cleary, *Book of Serenity,* p. 254.

Further Effort Beyond Counting

341. Dharma Hall Discourse for Ending the Summer Practice Period [1249]

When he was residing at Tiantong monastery, Zen Master Hongzhi gave a Dharma hall discourse for ending the summer practice period and said the following. "Before the fifteenth day, I don't put the seven-jeweled crown on my head. After the fifteenth day, I pull out the five-colored thread from underfoot.[163] Putting the seven-jeweled crown on my head is upright sitting without a view of sitting. Pulling out the five-colored thread from underfoot is directly leaving without a view of leaving.

"Right on the fifteenth day [on the full moon], seeing and breaking through both ends, directly attain the way of lord and minister in cooperation, and the spirit energy of parent and child in harmony. Up in the lapis lazuli palace, the jade woman rolls her head; in front of the bright moon hall, the stone man rubs his hands.[164]

"Taking a backward step, open your hands in front of the ten-thousand-foot cliff. Taking a step forward, turn your body on the top of the hundred-foot pole. Arising and perishing, coming and going, in motion and calm, emerging and sinking; right at this time gather up the functional essence of all these many activities. Letting go and grasping are entirely up to myself. Tell me, how is it at just such a time? Do you understand? Those walking in front have not arrived, still lost in the self; those in the rear have already passed it, and require further effort."

The teacher Dōgen said: This is the ancient Buddha Hongzhi's utterance about ending the summer practice period. I also have a small corresponding statement in the same tone. Great assembly, do you want to hear it?

After a pause Dōgen said: Although nobody has yet recognized our sweating like horses, we simply need to remind ourselves again and again about all the generations of effort.

---

163 "The five-colored thread" refers to the cravings or delusions arising from the five senses.

164 The jade woman and stone man is an example of Hongzhi's echoing of the image of the stone woman and wooden man in the Song of the Precious Mirror Samādhi by Dongshan Liangjie. See Leighton and Wu, *Cultivating the Empty Field*, pp. 62, 64, and p. 77, for other related references by Hongzhi.

This is a statement expressing the same tone as the ancient Buddha Hongzhi. What is a statement for having completed another year of Dharma practice?

After a pause Dōgen said: Who will expound this matter twenty years from now? Even for immeasurable kalpas, there will be no end of counting.

Remembering Tiantong Rujing

342. Dharma Hall Discourse for the Memorial Offering for Tiantong [Rujing][165]

Today I offer incense for my late teacher, an ancient Buddha. I do not know where his nostrils presently exist. Five thousand miles of ocean are filled with my sorrowful tears; for twenty years now, so much heartbreak!

Zazen Beyond Categories

343. Dharma Hall Discourse

Buddhas' and ancestors' zazen is not movement or stillness, not practice and realization, not limited to body or mind, not the opposition of delusion and enlightenment, not emptying the various conditions, not bound by various realms. How could it be connected to form, sensation, perception, mental formations, or consciousness? Studying the way does not use sensation, perception, mental formations, or consciousness. If you practice sensation, perception, mental formations, or consciousness, that is only sensation, perception, mental formations, or consciousness, and is not the study of the way.

Sitting on the Autumn Moon

344. Mid-Autumn Dharma Hall Discourse

I remember that when he was residing at Tiantong monastery, Zen Master Hongzhi gave a mid-autumn Dharma hall discourse and said the following. "In the pure, cool world, the vessel of fresh air soaks the autumn. The clear body and mind disperses appearances and embraces the moon at midnight. It is spiritually self-illuminated, vast and always empty. Cut-

---

165 Dōgen's teacher Tiantong Rujing died in 1228. This is the Dharma hall discourse for his memorial service in 1249.

ting off the causal conditions of arising and cessation, it leaves discriminating assessments about existence and nonexistence. People, having
arrived at such a field, can you play this out in your activity or not?"

After a pause [Hongzhi] said, "Completely break the laurel tree in the
moon and the clear light will increase."[166]

The teacher Dōgen said: People, would you like to make prostrations to
the ancient Buddha Hongzhi?

Dōgen raised up his whisk, and said: The ancient Buddha Hongzhi has
already appeared in this world and received prostrations from everybody.
Do you furthermore hear the Dharma that the ancient Buddha Hongzhi
is expounding?

After a pause Dōgen said: Why has our ancestor Yunyan's "Which moon
is this?" suddenly appeared as a round sitting cushion?[167]

Not Misled by Duality, a Clay Ox Melts into the Ocean
345. Dharma Hall Discourse

When polishing a tile to make a mirror, our body is not the four great elements, but is suchness, imposing and magnificent.[168] When polishing a
hammer to make a needle, our mind is not the five skandhas but is the

---

166 This Dharma hall discourse by Hongzhi is echoed in Dōgen's previous mid-autumn
Dharma hall discourse eight years before in 1241; see Dharma hall discourse 77. In China
a laurel tree was said to be in the moon, like the Western man in the moon, so removing
the tree would seem to increase the moon's brightness. "Moon laurel" was also an expression for moonlight.

167 "Yunyan's 'Which moon is this?'" refers to the story in the Shōyōroku, case 21, also
cited by Dōgen as kōan case 12 in volume 9, below. As Yunyan was sweeping the ground
his brother Daowu commented, "Too busy." Yunyan responded, "You should know there
is one who is not busy." But Daowu challenged, "Then there is a second moon." Yunyan
then held up the broom and said, "Which moon is this?" See note 33 above, and Cleary,
Book of Serenity, pp. 91–94. In Japan the mid-autumn full moon is a pleasant occasion for
celebration with a moon-viewing festival. Here Dōgen celebrates this full moon with Yunyan's utterance.

168 Polishing a tile to make a mirror refers to the story of Nanyue doing so in front of his
student Mazu when Mazu said he was sitting zazen to make a buddha. See Dharma hall
discourse 270 and note 23 above. "Imposing and magnificent" (although in reverse order)
is the description of Huangbo by his teacher Baizhang when they first met. See Dharma
hall discourse 296 and note 78 above. Both Baizhang's teacher Mazu and his disciple
Huangbo were celebrated as very tall, striking persons.

absolute, completely clear and bright. Therefore, no colors obstruct our eyes, no sounds plug our ears, no interactions bind our body, no affairs mislead our mind. Taking away objects is like a donkey looking at a donkey; taking away the person is like the well seeing the well.[169] Ultimately, what is it? A wooden horse neighing in the wind freely settles in the mountains; a clay ox bellowing at the moon is able to enter the ocean.[170]

169 "Taking away the object" and "taking away the person" are from the beginning of the section on "Teachings to the Assembly" in the Recorded Sayings of Linji. Linji says that sometimes he takes away the person (or subject), sometimes he takes away the object, and sometimes he takes away both or neither. See Kazumitsu Kato, *Lin-chi and the Record of His Sayings* (Nagoya: Nagoya University of Foreign Studies, 1994), p. 86; and Watson, *Zen Teachings of Master Lin-Chi*, pp. 21. "A donkey looking at a donkey" and "the well seeing the well" refer to the story about Caoshan in the Shōyōroku, case 52. A student answered Caoshan that the response of the reality body was like an ass looking at a well, and Caoshan said that, beyond that, it is like the well looking at the ass. See Cleary, *Book of Serenity*, pp. 219–222.

170 In Dharma hall discourse 296 Dōgen says that "Yunmen's wooden horse neighs and gallops." This refers to a dialogue in which a monk asked, "What is the neighing of the wooden horse of Yunmen?" Yunmen said, "Mountains and rivers are running." See note 74 above. In the Recorded Sayings of Dongshan, when Dongshan asked the hermit Longshan why he dwelled deep in the mountains, Longshan replied, "I saw two clay oxen fighting until they entered the ocean. Since then there has been no news of them." This relates to the dissolution of dualism, as clay or mud statues would dissolve in water. See Powell, *Record of Tung-Shan*, pp. 32–33; and Ogata, *Transmission of the Lamp*, pp. 292–293.

EIHEI ZENJI GOROKU

RECORDED SAYINGS
AT EIHEIJI TEMPLE

COLLECTED BY GIEN, ATTENDANT OF DŌGEN ZENJI

Encouragement for the Autumn Rocks

346. Dharma Hall Discourse

The bright years of a single lifetime exist within an evening thunderbolt. Who can bind up the ten thousand conditions, which are empty from beginning to end? Even if you sympathize with your nostrils hanging in front of your face, still you should cherish the merit of engaging the way, even for a short time.

Are these words encouragement for other patch-robed monks, or are they words for the sake of this old mountain man [Dōgen himself]; what do you think?

After a pause Dōgen said: The ten thousand peaks are stained with autumn colors by the light rain. Why would this immovable rock set in the mountains ever chase after the wind?

The Fist with No Hands

347. Dharma Hall Discourse on the First Day of the Ninth Month [1249][1]

This morning is the first day of the ninth month. With three hits on the han [the wooden sounding block], we sit zazen. Dropped off body and mind are unshakable, like making a fist with no hands.

---

1 See Dharma hall discourses 193 and 279. Traditionally this date was when sitting cushions were brought out and the relaxed summer meditation schedule ended.

Like a Lotus in Flames
348. Dharma Hall Discourse

The sitting cushions of the seven buddhas are now about to be worn through; the sleeping stick of my former teacher [Tiantong Rujing] has been transmitted.[2] Eyes and nose should be upright and straight, headtop reaching up to the blue sky, and ears aligned above the shoulders. At this very time, how is it?

After a pause Dōgen said: Do not control the monkey mind or horse will. Make an effort like a lotus in fire.

The Conditions of Awakening
349. Dharma Hall Discourse

An ancient worthy said, "As things arise due to the many conditions, don't things also perish due to many conditions?" He answered, "Because there are many conditions things arise, and after arising, naturally they perish."[3]

If this were Eihei, I would not say it like that. Suppose someone asked, "As things arise due to the many conditions, don't things also perish due to many conditions?" I would say to him: Because there are many conditions things arise; because there are many conditions things perish. Because arising has already arisen due to many conditions, there is the perishing that perishes due to many conditions. Ultimately, what is this [arising and perishing]? Great assembly, do you want to understand this clearly?

After a pause Dōgen said: At Shaolin [Dazu Huike] did three prostrations and returned to his place; at Vulture Peak [Śākyamuni] held up a flower and [Mahākāśyapa] broke into a smile.

---

2 "Sleeping sticks" *(zenpan),* literally "Zen boards," were flat sticks placed between the seat and one's chin to prevent monks from falling over when they slept sitting up all night. Apparently this was the practice at Eiheiji in Dōgen's time.

3 The speaker of this question and response is not known, but Dōgen criticizes his idea of "naturally" perishing.

Deepen Intimacy with Self and Others
350. Dharma Hall Discourse

Please cherish your skin, flesh, bones, and marrow.
Knowing each other, intimate friends grow
   even more intimate.[4]
When someone asks the meaning of coming from the west,
[Bodhidharma] faces the wall for nine years,
   abiding at Shaolin.

The Lineage of Study of No-Mind
351. Dharma Hall Discourse
I can remember, the ancient Buddha, High Ancestor Dongshan [Liangjie] said,

With no-mind, the way joins with people;
With no-mind, people join with the way.
Do you want to know the meaning of this?
One is old and one is not old.[5]

Dongshan's distant descendant Eihei respectfully makes another verse using his closing rhyme, to investigate the meaning of the founding ancestor.[6]

---

4 Intimate friend is *chi'in,* literally "knowing the sounds." This expression comes from an old classic Chinese story. A great musician had a friend who deeply appreciated his music. When the friend died he broke the strings of his instrument and did not play any more.

5 This verse is from the Recorded Sayings of Dongshan. "One is old and one is not old" refers to chapter 15 of the Lotus Sutra, in which Śākyamuni, upon being questioned, states that the myriad venerable bodhisattvas that spring forth from the ground have studied with him for many ages, even though they seem much older than Śākyamuni himself. See Hurvitz, *Scripture of the Lotus Blossom of the Fine Dharma,* pp. 228–236.

6 "Distant descendant" is literally "cloud descendant," a term usually used in Chinese genealogy for ninth-generation descendants. However, Dōgen was actually thirteen generations after Dongshan, the founder of the Caodong (Jap.: Sōtō) lineage. "Closing rhyme" refers to the sounds of the ends of the second and fourth lines ("way" and "old"), which are *dao* and *lao* in Chinese in Dongshan's poem. In Dōgen's ensuing verse, "way" and the ending character of "shrimp" are also *dao* and *lao.* Writing such a verse using a former verse's rhyme ending was a standard means for poets to express respect for a previous poet.

After a pause Dōgen said:

> With no-mind, the great way joins with people;
> With no-mind, people join with the way.
> How can we know the meaning of this?
> Toads never study with shrimp.[7]

Just Raising the Whisk

352. Dharma Hall Discourse

I can remember, Xiangyan asked a monk, "Where did you come from?"

The monk said, "I came from Guishan (Xiangyan's teacher)."

Xiangyan said, "What does the teacher have to say these days?"

The monk said, "When someone asked about the meaning of [Bodhidharma] coming from the west, the teacher [Guishan] raised his whisk."

Xiangyan after hearing this asked, "How did the brothers there understand the teacher's meaning?"

The monk said, "The monks there deliberated and thought this was 'Right within forms, clarifying the mind; adhering to things, demonstrating the principle.'"

Xiangyan said, "Those who understand just understand. Why should those who do not understand die from hurrying?"

The monk asked further, "What was the teacher's [Guishan's] meaning?"

Xiangyan also raised his whisk.

The teacher Dōgen said: Old man Xiangyan is exactly right. And yet I do not yearn to practice together with Xiangyan, and would not be glad to walk together with Guishan. Suppose someone asked, "What was the teacher's [Guishan's] meaning?"

After a pause Dōgen also raised his whisk, then descended from his seat.

---

7 The characters for "shrimp" in Sino-Japanese literally mean "ocean elder," or old man of the sea. In East Asia shrimp are associated with old age because of their bent back and whiskers. While Dongshan may have been negating the distinction of old and young, Dōgen seems to be emphasizing here that aside from their age, buddha ancestors or people of no-mind study only with other buddha ancestors or people of no-mind.

Everyday Practice of the Ancient Mirror
353. Dharma Hall Discourse for Opening the Fireplace [1249][8]
Today I, Eihei, open the fireplace, bringing forth the ancient mirror to make a design. As usual, I expound the Dharma and everybody listens, wearing their monk's robes and using their eating bowls.

Monkey Mind Is Not Buddha
354. Dharma Hall Discourse
The ancestors in India said that no-mind is Buddha. Kiangsi Mazu said, "This mind itself is Buddha."[9] Mazu said that this mind itself is Buddha; however, he was not saying that the monkey mind and horse will themselves are Buddha. Many students in modern times understand this mistakenly. Someone said that once you return to "This mind itself is Buddha," you will not have another birth. Understanding like this is the same as the view of extinction of those outside the way.

After a pause Dōgen said: What is the essential meaning of "This mind itself is Buddha"? Wanting to stop an infant from crying, it is a single punch that kills the baby.

Seeing the Smoke and the Primary Destination
355. Dharma Hall Discourse
Master Longya said in a verse,

> Study the way like boring wood to make fire.
> When smoke arises do not stop.
> Just wait until the golden star appears.
> Returning home is arriving at your destination.

Master Longya is a founding ancestor of our family lineage. Can his ocean of virtue ever be measured? It is inevitable that his descendant Eihei would respectfully make another verse using his closing rhyme.

8 For Opening the Fireplace, the first day of the tenth month, see Dharma hall discourses 14, 109, 199, and 288.

9 For other discussions by Dōgen of Mazu's "This mind itself is Buddha," see Dharma hall discourses 8, 292, 319, and 323. The phrase "samādhi of no-mind" occurs in chapter 47 of the Commentary on the Mahāprajñāpāramitā Sūtra (Ch.: Dazhidulun; Jap.: Daichidoron) attributed to Nāgārjuna.

After a pause Dōgen said:

> Study the way as if boring wood to make fire.
> Seeing the smoke you should not stop.
> Immediately the golden star appears.
> Within the world this is the primary destination.

The Understanding of Temple Pillars

356. Dharma Hall Discourse

Here is a story. A monk asked Shitou, "What is the meaning of the ancestral teacher [Bodhidharma] coming from the west?"

Shitou said, "Ask the temple pillars."

The monk said, "I don't understand."

Shitou said, "I understand even less than you."[10]

The teacher Dōgen said: The student asked Shitou about the meaning of the ancestral teacher. His saying "Ask the temple pillars" is a great dawn. If you say that trees and rocks do not understand, then this mountain monk will explain further.

After a pause Dōgen said: When poor one resents this single body as too much [to feed]. When wealthy one dislikes having only a thousand mouths as too few [for consuming].

Overseeing Fragrance

357. Dharma Hall Discourse Inviting the New Tenzo

I have invited a wooden ladle for this mountain, and would like to transmit the family style of clouds and water monks. The nostrils pervading the heavens oversee the fragrant realm; virtue is completely accomplished within the kitchen and temple administration offices.[11]

10 See Ferguson, *Zen's Chinese Heritage,* p. 74.

11 "Fragrant realm" is a name for the kitchen in Buddhism. It is derived from the name of the Buddha who appears in the Vimalakīrti Sūtra from the distant Buddha realm "Many Fragrances." See Thurman, *Holy Teachings of Vimalakīrti,* pp. 78–83; and Watson, *Vimalakirti Sutra,* pp. 112–120. "Kitchen and temple administration offices" is the *kuin,* the temple building which also houses the food storehouse. See Leighton and Okumura, *Dōgen's Pure Standards for the Zen Community,* pp. 50, 192, 221.

Did the Saga Empress Hear a Partridge Sing?

358. Dharma Hall Discourse

People in Japan heard the word "jōdō" for the first time when I, Eihei, transmitted it.[12] At the time of the reign of Emperor Saga, during the Kōnin era (810–823), the Saga empress was from the Tachibana family, and she was a former wife of the previous emperor and mother of the future emperor Nimei. She invited Huiyuan, a disciple of National Teacher Yanguan Qi'an from distant Great Tang China, and had him stay at the Sai'in temple of Tōji, and asked him about the way, mornings and evenings.[13] She greatly respected and venerated him, and supported him with unusually lavish offerings. However, Huiyuan never gave Dharma hall discourses and never followed the practice of students entering the room for discussion with the teacher.

Much more discussion [by Dōgen] followed, which is not recorded.[14]

12 *Jōdō,* literally "ascending the hall," which we have translated throughout Eihei Kōroku as "Dharma hall discourse," was the standard form of teaching in Song China. It occurred regularly in the Dharma hall, and the monks were standing while the teacher sat on the high seat on the altar. In Chanyuan Qingui, the Chinese monastic regulations Dōgen borrowed heavily from for his own Eihei Shingi, or Pure Standards, the *jōdō* were supposed to be given on special occasions, as well as six times a month, on the 1st, 5th, 10th, 15th, 20th, and 25th. Many of the recorded sayings *(goroku)* of the classical masters include these *jōdō.* Although there might sometimes have been questions and discussions from the monks, in Eihei Kōroku usually only Dōgen's words were recorded.

13 The Saga empress, Tachibana Kachiko (786–850), sent a Japanese monk to China to bring back a Chan (Zen) teacher, as she had heard about Chan from the great Japanese Shingon founder Kukai (known as Kōbō Daishi, 774–835), who had visited China. The monk she sent found the national teacher Yanguan Qian, who sent to Japan his disciple Yikung (n.d.; Jap.: Giku), who is mistakenly called Huiyuan (Jap.: Egen) in this Dharma hall discourse in Eihei Kōroku. Yikung first taught at a subtemple of Tōji, the great Shingon temple in southern Kyoto founded by Kukai, as described here by Dōgen. Later, the Saga empress founded a temple, Danrinji, in the Arashiyama section of Saga in the west of Kyoto, where Yikung was the first abbot. Danrinji could be said to have been the first Zen temple in Japan, although Yikung later returned to China without having established any enduring Zen lineage in Japan. The empress Tachibana Kachiko herself became a nun. So the first Zen practitioner in Japan was a woman. Danrinji was destroyed by fire in 928. It was reconstructed in 1345 as Tenryuji, which was one of the main headquarters temples of Rinzai Zen and still remains in western Kyoto.

14 This is a note by Gien, the compiler of this volume of Eihei Kōroku. Presumably he thought that Dōgen's extended discussion of aspects of Japanese Buddhist history was not important enough to record.

Body and mind dropped off is neither form nor consciousness. Do not speak about delusion or enlightenment, or what are beings and what is Buddha.[15] Ultimately, how is this?

After a pause Dōgen said: If you want to know a person from Jiangnan, go toward where the partridges sing.[16]

Reality Blossoms on Top of a Staff
359. Dharma Hall Discourse

> This patch-robed monk's staff is as black as lacquer.
> It is not in the class of ordinary worldly wood,
> but breaks apart traps and snares, and actualizes reality.[17]
> In the snow, a plum blossom suddenly opens on a branch tip.

The Wondrous Fragrance of Wisdom and Virtue Amid Snow
360. Enlightenment Day Dharma Hall Discourse [1249][18]
Under the bodhi tree, where the two wheels of practice and Dharma are intimately turning, the flower of awakening is bright. In immeasurable, innumerable great thousands of worlds, at this time, for himself and the entire surroundings, ease and bliss arose. My original teacher, the World-Honored One, Great Master Śākyamuni Buddha, on this morning

---

15 Not speaking about "what are beings and what is Buddha" here implies not discussing what the distinction is between (unenlightened) sentient beings and buddhas.

16 This comment relates to a saying by Fengxue Yanzhao, "I always remember Jiangnan in the third month, when the partridges sing and a hundred blossoms open." See Dharma hall discourse 73. Jiangnan is the area south of the Yangzi River. Here Dōgen is encouraging personal experience of body and mind dropped off.

17 "It breaks apart traps and snares, and actualizes reality" repeats, in inverted order, a line from Dōgen's early writing Fukanzazengi (Universally Recommended Instructions for Zazen), which says, "When reality is actualized, traps and snares cannot reach it." See the end of volume 8 below. "Actualizes reality" could also be read literally as "manifests the kōan." It is the same *genjōkōan* as the name of Dōgen's famous essay. See Tanahashi, *Moon in a Dewdrop*, pp. 69–73.

18 Enlightenment Day, the commemoration of Śākyamuni Buddha's awakening, is celebrated on Rōhatsu (the word used to name these Dharma hall discourses), i.e., the eighth day of the twelfth month. See also Dharma hall discourses 88, 136, 213, 297, 406, 475, and 506.

remained under the bodhi tree sitting zazen on the vajra seat, accomplishing unsurpassed true awakening.

When first expressing it, he said, "Three quarters of this night has passed; in the remaining quarter the brightness will dawn. The various kinds of conditioned and unconditioned beings all remain unmoving. At this time, the unsurpassed venerable great sage extinguishes the various afflictions, attains bodhi, and becomes known as the one with wisdom about everything in the world."[19] What is the meaning of the World-Honored One speaking like this? Great assembly, do you want to clearly understand this?

After a pause Dōgen said: In the snow is a single branch of jeweled plum blossoms. Wondrous fragrance strikes the nose, arriving before spring.

At that time the World-Honored One also said, "Because of the virtue and benefit I created in ancient times, everything wished for in my heart has been accomplished, my mind of samādhi has been instantly verified, and I have reached the shore of nirvāṇa. All my various enemies or foes and even the demon Pāpiyas (Māra) in the Iśvara level of the realm of desire cannot trouble me, and so they all take refuge in Buddha.[20] This is because of the power of my virtue and wisdom. If you can courageously make diligent efforts to seek sacred wisdom, this will be attained without difficulty. Once it is attained all afflictions will be exhausted, and all your accumulated offenses and faults will be extinguished."

This is the first expounding of Dharma for the sake of human and heavenly beings at the time when the World-Honored One attained awakening. His Dharma children and Dharma descendants should not fail to know this. Already having known this, how do you express it? This morning for the sake of clouds and water monks, Eihei will tell it. Do you want to hear this?

19 The passage "Three quarters of this night has passed" through "known as the one with wisdom about everything in the world" is from the Buddhacarita Saṃgrāha Sūtra (Sutra of the Collection of Buddha's Original Practices), translated from the Sanskrit into Chinese by Jñānagupta between 587 and 591. This sutra is again quoted in the following paragraph.

20 Pāpiyas is another name for Māra, the spirit of temptation who opposed Śākyamuni before his awakening. Iśvara is the name of the highest of the heavenly realms in the world of desire.

After a pause Dōgen said:

> When the morning star finally appeared,
>   Buddha accomplished the way.
> In the snow is a single branch of plum blossoms.[21]
> On the great earth,
>   sentient beings together with grasses and trees
> Attained joy as never before at this time.

The Benefits of Performance of the Tripitaka

361. Dharma Hall Discourse upon the Arrival of a Letter from the Great Lord of Izumo Province [Hatano Yoshishige] about His Having the Tripitaka Copied to Be Donated to This Temple[22]

Here is a story. A monk asked Touzi [Datong], "Is there anything marvelous or special in the teachings expounded in the Tripitaka?"

Touzi said, "The performance of the teachings expounded in the Tripitaka."

The ancient Buddha, Touzi [Datong], has spoken like this, and this [donation] brings much joy to this mountain gate [of Eiheiji]. On this occasion, I have an utterance to offer on behalf of the cloud and water monks. The performance of the teachings expounded in the Tripitaka is the protective talisman, which you should know is fortunately obtained by tamers of strong persons, heavenly beings, and wise sages.[23] At this very time, what does this mean?

---

21 "In the snow is a single branch of plum blossoms" is a quote from a verse by Tiantong Rujing, which Dōgen also quotes in the Shōbōgenzō essay Baika (Plum Blossoms). See verses on plum blossoms by Tiantong Rujing in Tanahashi, *Moon in a Dewdrop*, pp. 119–122.

22 "Great Lord of Izumo Province" (Jap.: Unshū Daishu) was a title referring to Hatano Yoshishige, Dōgen's major patron. Yoshishige resided in Kamakura and Kyoto but also owned land in Echizen Province, some of which he donated as the site for Eiheiji. The Tripitaka, the collection of the sutras, vinaya, and abhidharma, the entire Buddhist canon, is literally the great collection of sutras (Jap.: Daizōkyō). There have been several such collections made in East Asian history. This donation of the Tripitaka became important to Dōgen's later teachings, in which he quoted it extensively.

23 "Protective talisman" here refers to a piece of paper with names of buddhas, bodhi-

After a pause Dōgen said: There are certainly arhats in the world. With good and bad, how could there not be the process of cause and effect?

The Ten Thousand Peaks Shine with the Golden Tripitaka

362. Dharma Hall Discourse about a Joyful Letter from the Great Lord [Hatano Yoshishige] That Has Arrived in Response to [Our Accepting the Donation of] the Tripitaka Being Copied for This Temple

The Ocean Storehouse of Vairocana has been transmitted from ancient times to the present.[24] This is the threefold revolution of the Dharma wheel in the great thousands [of worlds].[25] The thousand summits and ten thousand peaks are the color of golden leaves. Sentient beings attain the way completely at this time.

In Gratitude to my Father

363. Dharma Hall Discourse for the Memorial for My Nurturing Father, Counselor of State Minamoto[26]

---

sattvas, or sutras written on it, kept as a protective charm. "Tamers of strong persons" is one of the ten epithets for a buddha; see Dharma hall discourse 229.

24 "The Ocean Storehouse of Vairocana" is a term for the ocean of Buddha nature and of Dharma nature, also referred to as the Buddha womb (Skt.: Tathāgata garbha). This is the world as the matrix for awakening, a teaching that was highly influential in East Asian Buddhism.

25 "The threefold revolution of the Dharma wheel" refers either to the paths of insight *(darśana mārga),* meditation *(bhāvanā mārga),* and mastery *(aśaikṣa mārga)* or to the three phases of teaching of the Theravāda four noble truths, the Mādhyamika perfection of wisdom, and the Vijñānavāda teachings about the two truths. See Thurman, *Holy Teaching of Vimalakīrti,* p. 110, n. 37.

26 This was the memorial service for Minamoto Michitomo (1170–1227) who has traditionally been considered Dōgen's guardian and brother. Michitomo was a son of Minamoto Michichika (1149–1202), who has been considered Dōgen's biological father, dating back to the Teiho Kenzeiki biography of Dōgen by Menzan Zuihō written in 1754. Previous sources were unclear as to who Dōgen's father was. Many modern Sōtō scholars now believe that Minamoto Michitomo, eulogized in this Dharma hall discourse, was Dōgen's actual biological father. Minamoto Michichika and Minamoto Michitomo (and therefore Dōgen himself) were directly descended from the Murakami emperor (926–67), who reigned from 946 to 967. Minamoto Michitomo had been counselor of state (Jap.: *dainagon),* an important court position. This is one of the very few places in Dōgen's writings where he refers directly to his family background. This memorial day was held on the second day of the ninth month, so it is out of sequence, and should probably be right after

Eihei's staff is a branch of plum blossoms. It is from a seed planted in the Tenryaku era [947–957; the beginning of the reign of the Murakami Emperor], but the fragrance of its five petals endures without fading up to the present. Its roots, stems, and fruit are truly far-reaching.

Spring Arises Beyond All Control
364. Dharma Hall Discourse
[Today,] where the clouds are smiling and when the snow's will is bright, over the mountains and forests are spring wind and rain. At this very time, how is it?

After a pause Dōgen said: Do not say that someone holds the handle of creation. The causes and conditions for proceeding on the way give rise to good karmic roots.

The Fruits of No-Mind and This Mind
365. Dharma Hall Discourse
The voicing of "No-mind is exactly Buddha" arose in India. The utterance of "This mind is exactly Buddha" originated in China.[27] If you understand in these ways, you are as distant as the separation between heaven and earth. If you do not understand in these ways, you are a mere mediocre person. Ultimately, how is it?

Throughout the three months of spring, fruit is abundant on the bodhi tree. One night the flower blossoms and the world is fragrant.

The Tripitaka Is Embroidered on the Eiheiji Brocade
366. Dharma Hall Discourse
Here is a quotation. Many heavenly beings uttered verses of praise, saying, "At first, the Buddha sat under the tree and with his power overcame demons. He attained the sweet dew of nirvāṇa and accomplished the way of awakening. Three times in the great thousands of worlds he turned the Dharma wheel that is originally and continuously pure and clear. This is

---

discourse 347, assuming this was in 1249. There is one more later Memorial Dharma Hall Discourse for Minamoto Michitomo: Dharma hall discourse 524, in 1252.

27 See also Dharma hall discourse 354.

verified whenever humans or heavenly beings attain the way. At this time the three jewels appear in the world."[28]

Now I, Eihei, am delighted that the three jewels have manifested in the world and that the Dharma wheel has actually arrived at this mountain.[29] I have a simple mountain verse.

After a pause Dōgen said:

> He realized the sweet dew and accomplished buddhahood.
> Three times he turned the Dharma wheel in the great
>   thousands of worlds.
> All human and heavenly beings together attained the way.
> Thus the three jewels appeared in the world.

When the three jewels manifest in the world, how is it? In this mountain home, spring flowers are added on brocade.

Filled with Sadness Despite Trusting His Words

367. Dharma Hall Discourse for the Parinirvāṇa Ceremony [1250][30]
Again and again I declare that I am entering into nirvāṇa [as a skillful means]. All beings are sad with longing, and their tears overflow. Although we trust his words that he always resides on Vulture Peak, how can we not be sorry about the coldness of the twin sāla trees?[31]

28 This quotation is from the Vimalakīrti Sūtra, chap. 1. See Watson, *Vimalakirti Sutra,* p. 22; and Thurman, *Holy Teaching of Vimalakīrti,* pp. 13–14. Watson's translation is from the Chinese version translated by Kumārajīva, which Dōgen also used, whereas Thurman's translation is from the Tibetan version, which varies slightly in this and other cases.

29 Presumably the copy of the Tripitaka commissioned by Hatano Yoshishige had arrived at Eiheiji soon before this Dharma hall discourse.

30 Other Parinirvāṇa Day Dharma hall discourses are discourses 121, 146, 225, 311, 418, and 486.

31 "Again and again I declare that I am entering into nirvāṇa [as a skillful means]" and "All beings harbor longing" are from the sixteenth chapter of the Lotus Sutra, "The Inconceivable [Long] Lifespan of the Buddha." Śākyamuni reveals that he has been present for an unimaginably long time, and will remain so. But as a skillful means for the sake of beings, over and over again he pretends to pass away into nirvāṇa, because they might otherwise become lax in their practice. After he appears to be gone, they yearn for the Buddha, and practice diligently. See Hurvitz, *Scripture of the Lotus Blossom of the Fine Dharma,*

At this very time, what more can be said? At midnight he turned head over heels. We do not realize it when the dawn arises [as if the night never ended].

Exposing Wild Foxes
368. Dharma Hall Discourse
This very mind, this very Buddha, is madness. Directly pointing to the human mind is also as distant as heaven from earth, like desiring to exhaust the water of the gigantic ocean with three scoops.[32] At this instant, these are exposed as wild-fox Zen.

Responding to the Fifth Ancestor as One
369. Dharma Hall Discourse
Here is a story. The fifth ancestor [Daman Hongren] visited lay worker Lu [Dajian Huineng] at the rice pounding hut and said, "Has the rice been refined or not?"

The lay worker said, "It is refined, but not yet sifted."

The fifth ancestor hit the stone mill with his staff three times. The lay worker shook the rice winnow three times and entered the room [of the fifth ancestor, later at midnight].

The teacher Dōgen said: If this were Eihei, I would not act like that. If the fifth ancestor asked me whether the rice had been refined or not, I would simply tell him, "Stars are aligned with the North Star; the sun rises in the east." If I saw that the fifth ancestor wanted to strike with his staff, I would grab his staff and say to him, "Morning or evening, while engaged in Dharma meetings, we join together as one."[33]

---

pp. 238, 241; Katō, Tamura, and Miyasaka, *Threefold Lotus Sutra*, pp. 251, 253; and Watson, *Lotus Sutra*, pp. 226, 229. Historically, Śākyamuni passed away under twin sāla trees in Kuśinagara.

32 Here Dōgen again criticizes the misunderstanding of "This very mind is Buddha" as equated with grasping monkey mind. See Dharma hall discourse 354. He also again criticizes "Direct pointing to the human mind." See Dharma hall discourse 334.

33 "Dharma meetings" here is *shinsan*, literally "inviting the teacher for study," which refers to various types of formal lectures and discussions, including *jōdō*, or Dharma hall discourses.

Not Mind, Not Things, Not Buddha

370. Dharma Hall Discourse

Here is a story. Once Nanquan said to the assembly, "Kiangsi Mazu said, 'This very mind itself is Buddha.' Old teacher Wang [Nanquan] doesn't talk like this. It is not mind, not a thing, not Buddha. Is saying it like this a mistake or not?"

Zhaozhou made prostrations and left.

Then a monk followed him and asked Zhaozhou, "Elder monk, after making prostrations you departed. What was your meaning?"

Zhaozhou said, "You should go ask the teacher."

The monk went up to Nanquan and asked, "Just now, what was elder monk [Zhaozhou] Congshen's meaning?"

Nanquan said, "He fully received this old monk's meaning."[34]

The teacher Dōgen said: Although Nanquan and Zhaozhou, father and son in the life vein, said it like this, now Eihei will disrupt them a little and speak. Great assembly do you want to clearly embody this?

After a pause Dōgen said: He fully received this old monk's meaning, and also fully received Nanquan's meaning.

Garuḍas Choose to Eat Dragons

371. Dharma Hall Discourse

Here is a saying. The third ancestor, Great Teacher [Jianzhi Sengcan], in "Inscription on Faith in Mind" said, "The supreme way is not difficult; only disdain picking and choosing."[35]

Great assembly, have you ever studied the third ancestor's meaning? Tell me, what is the third ancestor's meaning?

Passing through three kalpas, without fail we arrive; passing through numberless kalpas, without fail we arrive; without arising from our seat,

---

34 This story appears in the section on Nanquan in the Jingde Transmission of the Lamp. See Ogata, *Transmission of the Lamp*, p. 258; and Chang, *Original Teachings of Ch'an Buddhism*, p. 155.

35 "Inscription on Faith in Mind" (Shinjinmei) is a celebrated teaching poem, traditionally attributed to the third Chan ancestor, Jianzhi Sengcan, although it is now clear to scholars that it was written later. See D. T. Suzuki, *Manual of Zen Buddhism* (New York: Grove Press, 1960), pp. 76–82; and Sheng-yen, *Poetry of Enlightenment*, pp. 25–29.

without fail we arrive; without arising in a single moment, without fail we arrive. Therefore, [the third ancestor] said, "The supreme way is not difficult." Simply to disdain picking and choosing is like a garuḍa not eating anything but dragons.[36]

Undisturbed by Thunderclaps
372. Dharma Hall Discourse
Here is a story. The World-Honored One was staying under a tree in the forests of the region of Atama, and while sitting he entered dhyāna samādhi.[37] At that time a rainstorm came suddenly, lightning and thunder crashing. There were two people plowing with four oxen, and hearing the sound they died of terror. After a little while it cleared up. The Buddha stood and did walking meditation.

A layperson was there and did prostrations at Buddha's feet, then followed behind him, and said to Buddha, "World-Honored One, in the recent crashing of lightning and thunder, there were two people plowing with four oxen, who, hearing the sound, died of fright. World-Honored One, did you hear it or not?"

Buddha said, "I did not hear it."

The layperson said, "Buddha, were you sleeping then?"

Buddha said, "I was not asleep."

The layperson said, "Had you entered the samādhi beyond mental perception?"

Buddha said, "I had mental perceptions, but I had entered samādhi."

The layperson said, "I have never heard of such a thing. The buddhas'

---

36 A garuḍa is a mythological Indian bird that is a guardian of the Dharma, often present in the Buddha's assembly in sutras. Garuḍas are famed for eating dragons. Here Dōgen uses the characters for "golden-winged kingly bird," a standard epithet of garuḍas. In this Dharma hall discourse, Dōgen is pointing out a paradox in the Inscription on Faith in Mind. Disdaining or avoiding is a kind of preference, a kind of picking and choosing. But for garuḍas it is simply natural to eat dragons; for Buddhist practitioners it is simply natural to follow the way.

37 "Dhyāna samādhi" is *zenjō,* or Zen samādhi, but in this case *zen* refers to the *dhyāna* meditative states, practiced by Śākyamuni Buddha. Sometimes referred to as trance states, they are states of elevated awareness, derived from refined nonattachment, in the form and formless realms of karmic consciousness beyond the conventional desire realm. Atama (Azuma or Anpi in Sino-Japanese) is a village in an area near Kuśinagara.

dhyāna samādhi is great and very profound. There is mental perception, but in this dhyāna samādhi, even though awake, you did not hear such a loud sound."[38]

The teacher Dōgen said: I, Eihei, respectfully speak a verse of praise:

There is a mind of perception entering dhyāna samādhi.
The thirty-four minds can deliberate.[39]
Buddha functions with four in the morning and three at
    evening.
In this state, the skin-bag is exhausted.[40]

The Vitality of Beyond-Thinking
373. Dharma Hall Discourse
Here is a story. Once a monk asked Yaoshan, "What are you thinking while in steadfast, immovable sitting?"
    Yaoshan said, "I think of not thinking."
    The monk said, "How do you think of not thinking?"
    Yaoshan said, "Beyond-thinking."[41]

38 This story is from Nāgārjuna's Commentary on the Māhāprajñāpāramitā Sūtra (Ch.: Dazhidulun), translated by Kumārajīva, chap. 21.

39 The thirty-four minds refers to eight patiences, eight wisdoms, nine nonobstructions, and nine liberations. These are from the Abhidharma Kośa by Vasubandhu. The eight patiences and wisdoms are in the *darśana mārga,* or path of insight. See Pruden, *Abhidharma Kośa Bhāṣyam,* vol. III, p. 946.

40 "Four in the morning and three at evening" refers to a story in Zhuangzi's chapter on the equality of all things. Some monkeys were irate at only receiving three nuts in the morning and four in the evening, but when they instead were given four in the morning and three at evening, they were content. See Hamill and Seaton, *Essential Chuang Tzu,* p. 12; and Watson, *Complete Works of Chuang Tzu,* p. 41. The "skin-bag" here refers to the self of karmic consciousness.

41 Dōgen also quotes this story about Yaoshan and meditation in Fukanzazengi (Universally Recommended Instructions for Zazen), in Dharma hall discourse 524, and in Zazenshin (The Acupuncture Needle of Zazen). "Not thinking" is *fushiryō* in Japanese; "beyond-thinking" is *hishiryō.* "I think of not thinking," might be interpreted as, "I think of the activity, or realm, of not thinking." "Beyond-thinking" implies an aware mind that may include either thinking or not thinking, but is not attached to either. In Dōgen's view of zazen, one does not follow thoughts, nor stop them, but thoughts come and go

The teacher Dōgen said: The existing mind has already withered. Non-mind has not yet appeared. In the vitality of this lifetime purity is supreme.[42]

Protection of Nondefilement

374. Dharma Hall Discourse

Here is a story. When Nanyue [Huairang] first visited the sixth ancestor [Dajian Huineng], the ancestor asked him, "Where are you from?"

Nanyue said, "I came from the place of National Teacher Songshan [Hui]an.

The ancestor said, "What is this that thus comes?"

Nanyue never put this question aside. After eight years he told the sixth ancestor, "[I,] Huairang can now understand the question 'What is this that thus comes?' that you received me with upon my first arriving to see you."

The sixth ancestor said, "How do you understand it?"

Nanyue said, "To explain or demonstrate anything would miss the mark."

The sixth ancestor said, "Then do you suppose there is practice-realization or not?"

Nanyue said, "It is not that there is no practice-realization, but only that it cannot be defiled."

The sixth ancestor said, "This nondefilement is exactly what the buddhas protect and care for. I am thus, you are thus, and the ancestors in India also are thus."[43]

---

freely. It cannot be called thinking, because thoughts are not grasped. It cannot be called not thinking because thoughts continue to come and go. In samādhi the brain continues to function, as Dōgen described in the previous Dharma hall discourse. For Fukanzazengi, see the end of volume 8 below. For Zazenshin, see Carl Bielefeldt, *Dōgen's Manuals of Zen Meditation,* pp. 188–205.

42 "Existing mind" and "non-mind" are *u-shin* and *mu-shin,* linguistic opposites. Existing mind implies mental functioning or thinking. Non-mind here might imply mind without thinking. In Gakudō Yōjinshū (Points to Watch in Study of the Way), Dōgen says that Buddha Dharma cannot be attained with either *u-shin* or *mu-shin.* See Shohaku Okumura, trans. and ed., *Dōgen Zen* (Kyoto: Kyoto Sōtō Zen Center, 1988), p. 12. "Purity is supreme" implies its importance, and also purity as an ideal direction or objective.

43 Dōgen cites this story as case 59 of the ninety kōans with verse comments in volume 9. Dōgen also quotes it in the Shōbōgenzō essay Henzan (All-Inclusive Study). See Tanahashi, *Moon in a Dewdrop,* p. 198. An earlier version of the story, without Dōgen's under-

The teacher Dōgen said: Caoxi [Huineng] and Nanyue have spoken like this. Today, how can I not say something? Tell me, great assembly, do you want to understand this clearly? The highest fruit of arhat practice is the new attainment of extinction through discernment.[44] [Ājñāta]kauṇḍinya was verified in his attainment of [patience with] non-arising.[45] At just such a time, again, how is it?

After a pause Dōgen said: We must smile at the beginning of this story about that fellow [Nanyue Huai]rang. Upon exerting his power, he could express eighty or ninety percent.

The Importance of Zazen
375. Dharma Hall Discourse
The essence of patch-robed monks' study of the way is meditation.[46]

The Dharma of dropping off body and mind has been transmitted to the present.

All right and wrongs are never executed.

[Bodhidharma's arrival in China in] the years of Universal Penetration is not the same as a petty matter.[47]

What Is Behind the Back of Just This
376. Dharma Hall Discourse
Here is a story. Nanquan arrived to study with National Teacher [Nanyang Hui]zhong. The national teacher asked, "Where are you from?"

---

standing of the oneness of practice-realization, appears in Jingde Transmission of the Lamp; see Ogata, *Transmission of the Lamp,* p. 162.

44 "Extinction through discernment" is one of the three unconditioned dharmas in the abhidharma psychological study. It refers to attainment of nirvāṇa, or extinction of all future lives, by thorough comprehension of the chain of causation. This is the goal of arhat practice.

45 Ājñātakauṇḍinya was one of the five attendants of Śākyamuni during his ascetic practice, who became the first arhat after Buddha's awakening. Patience with the non-arising of all things, *anutpattika dharma kṣānti,* is an expression for supreme realization. See Dharma hall discourse 220 and volume 3, note 51.

46 "Meditation" here is *sanzen,* referring to the practice of zazen, or seated meditation.

47 "Years of Universal Penetration" *(futsu)* was the name of the era when Bodhidharma was supposed to have arrived in China, in 520–26 C.E.

Nanquan said, "I came from Kiangsi [the place of Mazu Daoyi].

The national teacher said, "Have you come after attaining the truth of Master Ma or not?"[48]

Nanquan said, "Just this [i.e., myself] is it."

The national teacher said, "Is there something behind your back?"

Nanquan stopped [talking] and left.

The teacher Dōgen said: The national teacher and Nanquan are both right, exactly right, and have spoken, but not yet fully spoken. Why do I say this? The characters for "crow" and "how" are difficult to differentiate; the characters for "fish" and "foolish" are clearly distinguished.[49] Although it is like this, I want to ask a question to those two old guys. Can all buddhas and all disciples of buddhas be like this or not?

The Offering Beyond Seeking
377. Dharma Hall Discourse

Unsurpassed bodhi is not for the sake of self, not for the sake of others, not for the sake of fame, and not for the sake of profit. And yet, single-mindedly seeking unsurpassed bodhi, diligently proceeding without

---

48 The "truth" (Jap.: *shin*) of Master Ma here might be short for "true portrait" (Jap.: *shinzō*), according to some Sōtō scholars. This *shinzō* would refer to an actual portrait of Mazu, since teachers sometimes bestowed portraits of themselves to disciples as an emblem of Dharma transmission. It is not clear if these "true portraits" were given in Mazu's time, in the Tang dynasty, but this was the common practice in Song China when Dōgen visited there. So here the national teacher might be asking if Nanquan had received formal transmission, i.e., the true Dharma, from Mazu, but also perhaps verification of this with Mazu's portrait. Historically, we do not know if most of these dialogues actually go back to their Tang dynasty protagonists, or were instead created in the Song, which is when many were first recorded in writing. It is certainly possible that Dōgen would have interpreted this "truth" as the "portrait" of Mazu verifying Nanquan's transmission, and the whole story might be read in that way, although the underlying truth indicated by the portrait would still be signified. This story appears in the Jingde Transmission of the Lamp; see Ogata, *Transmission of the Lamp,* p. 179.

49 The Chinese characters that Dōgen gives here for "crow" and "how," which are *u* and *en* in Japanese, look very similar. The characters used for "fish" and "foolish" (*gyo* and *ro* in Japanese) are easily distinguishable, even though *gyo* is the top part of the character for *ro*. Dōgen is using the appearance of these characters as examples of sameness and difference. Applied to this story, the issue is the sameness and difference of Nanquan's "Just this," referring to his own concrete being, with the national teacher's "Something behind your back," which refers to the entire universe that is expressed in concrete phenomena.

retreat, is called arousing bodhi mind. After this mind has already manifested, not seeking after bodhi, even for the sake of bodhi, is the genuine bodhi mind. If you do not have this mind, how could it be the study of the way? Brothers at this temple, single-mindedly seek bodhi mind, and never quit out of laziness. If you have not yet attained bodhi mind, you should pray to the previous generations of buddhas and ancestors. Further, you should dedicate the good karma from your practice to bodhi mind and sincerely seek it.

I can remember, a monk asked Zhaozhou, "The ten thousand things return to the one. Where does the one return?"

Zhaozhou said, "When I lived in Qingzhou I made a cotton shirt weighing seven pounds."[50]

The ancient Buddha Zhaozhou has spoken this way. Suppose a monk asked Eihei, "The ten thousand things return to the one. Where does the one return?" I would say: It returns going beyond.

If the monk says, "Why do you say so?" I would say: I stay right here and make offerings to a thousand billion buddhas.

Rare and Wonderful
378. Dharma Hall Discourse
Here is a story. A monk asked Baizhang, "What is the rare and wonderful affair?"

Baizhang said, "Sitting alone on Daxiong Peak."[51]

Suppose someone asked this old monk, "What is the rare and wonderful affair?" I would say to him: Today, I, Eihei, go up to the hall [to give a Dharma hall discourse].

The universal is completely expressed in phenomena, the particulars completely express the universal, or ultimate, but both aspects need to be integrated in practice. Buddha's universal truth is expressed concretely in the practice of a buddha's disciples.

50 This dialogue of Zhaozhou is case 45 in the Hekiganroku; see Cleary and Cleary, Blue Cliff Record, pp. 318–322.

51 This dialogue of Baizhang is case 26 in the Hekiganroku; see Cleary and Cleary, Blue Cliff Record, pp. 172–175.

A Timeless Appeal to Buddhas and Bodhisattvas for Clear Skies
379. Dharma Hall Discourse in Supplication for Clear Skies on the Tenth Day of the Sixth Month [1250]

Last year and this year, through spring, summer, autumn, and winter, below the heavens the rains have fallen without cease. The whole populace laments as the five grains do not ripen. Now elder Eihei, for the sake of saving our land from lamentation, will again make supplications by lifting up the Dharma hall discourse praying for clear skies that was given by my late teacher Tiantong [Rujing] when he resided at Qingliang Temple. What is the reason? What can we do if the Buddha Dharma does not relieve the suffering of human and heavenly beings? Great assembly, do you clearly understand Eihei's intention?

When my late teacher had not yet given a Dharma hall discourse, all buddhas and ancestors had not yet given a Dharma hall discourse. When my late teacher gave a Dharma hall discourse, all buddhas of the three times, the ancestral teachers of the six generations, and all nostrils and the ten thousand eyeballs [of all teachers], at the same time all gave a Dharma hall discourse. They could not have been an hour earlier, or half an hour later. Today's Dharma hall discourse by Eihei is also like this.

After a pause Dōgen said: Without ceasing, one, two, and three raindrops, drop after drop fall continuously morning to night, transformed into torrents, so that we can do nothing.[52] The winds and waves overflow throughout the mountains, rivers, and the great earth.

[Tiantong Rujing] sneezed once and said, "Before one sneeze of this patch-robed monk is finished, the clouds part and the sun appears."

[Tiantong Rujing] raised his whisk and said, "Great assembly, look here. The bright clear sky swallows the eight directions. If the waters continue to fall as before, all the houses will float away to the country of demons.[53] Make prostrations to Śākyamuni; take refuge in Maitreya. Capable of saving the world from its sufferings, wondrous wisdom power of Avalokiteśvara, I call on you."

52 This entire section after the pause, from "Without ceasing, one, two, three raindrops..." until the end of this Dharma hall discourse, is quoted exactly from the Recorded Sayings of Tiantong Rujing, vol. 1.

53 The country of demons is the place of dangerous demons that is mentioned in chapter 25 of the Lotus Sutra, "The Universal Gateway of Regarder of the Cries of the

Just Practice Buddha's Way
380. Dharma Hall Discourse
Descendants of buddha ancestors, do not study the Āgama teachings, the teachings of Brahmans, the methods of making sacrifices, teachings about the pursuit of pleasure, or the teachings of the [extremist] opponents of pursuing pleasure.[54] Save your head from fire, and just study the fists, eyeballs, staffs, whisks, sitting cushions, Zen sleeping boards, ancestral minds, and ancestral sayings of the buddhas and ancestors. If it is not the activity of buddha ancestors, do not practice it; if it is not the talk of buddha ancestors, do not say it. Great assembly, do you want to clearly understand the key to this?

After a pause Dōgen said: [Practice with] sitting cushions, Zen boards, and Zhaozhou's tea, not expressing evil throughout the whole day.[55] The ancient buddhas have studied the true meaning. Śāṇavāsin received transmission and wore Buddha's monk's robe.[56]

Wisdom Is Not the Way
381. Dharma Hall Discourse
Buddha Dharma is not something that can be understood depending on

---

World." The sutra says that when in peril in such a place, if you call on the power of the compassionate bodhisattva Avalokiteśvara, "Regarder of the Cries of the World," the bodhisattva will appear and save you. See Katō, Tamura, and Miyasaka, *Threefold Lotus Sutra,* p. 320.

54 The Āgama teachings are the early Pali suttas. In this instance they refer to pre-Mahāyāna scriptures, traditionally considered lesser teachings by most Mahāyānists. Brahman is the ancient Indian religion. "Sacrifices" here probably refers to the Indian Vedic sacrificial rituals. Teachings "about the pursuit of pleasure" is literally given by Dōgen as a transliteration of the Indian materialist "Lokāyata" school. "Opponents of the Lokāyata" refers to those who taught extreme ascetic practices.

55 "Zhaozhou's tea" refers to the story about Zhaozhou receiving monks and, whether they answered that they had been there before or not, telling them to go have some tea. When the head monk inquired about this, Zhaozhou told him as well to go have some tea. See Green, *Recorded Sayings of Zen Master Joshu,* p. 146.

56 Śāṇavāsin was the successor to Ānanda, and the first ancestor not to study directly under Śākyamuni. Śāṇavāsin means "Natural Robe," as he was said to have been born wearing a robe, which was spontaneously transformed to monk's robe when he aroused the thought of leaving home. For his story see Ogata, *Transmission of the Lamp,* pp. 10–12; and Francis Cook, *The Record of Transmitting the Light: Zen Master Keizan's*

brilliance and keen wisdom. Moreover, it cannot be patiently sustained by those who are without brilliance or keen wisdom. If those with keen wisdom were vessels of the way, Śāriputra could not have attained the first fruit, stream-entry, by attending to the expounding by Aśvajit.[57] Furthermore, even after Śāriputra attained arhatship, he was not able to give monk ordination to Śrivati.[58] When Śāriputra was only eight years old, he had already overcome all the teachers of philosophical debate.

Therefore as a verse says, "All living beings, excepting only the World-Honored Buddha, when compared to Śāriputra can only reach one sixteenth of his wisdom and erudition."[59]

Once, seeing Aśvajit's dignified presence and refined elegance, Śāriputra asked him, "Who is your teacher? Whose disciple are you?"

Aśvajit replied, "Prince Siddhartha abandoned birth, old age, sickness, and death; left home to practice the way; and attained supreme perfect awakening. He is my teacher."

Śāriputra asked again, "What Dharma does your teacher expound?"

He answered, "I am like a young child, having only studied the precepts for a short time. How could I express the ultimate truth of the supreme meaning of what he widely expounds?"

Śāriputra said, "Then explain the essential points in simplified form."

Denkōroku (Boston: Wisdom Publications, 2003), pp. 42–45; or Cleary, *Transmission of Light: Zen in the Art of Enlightenment by Zen Master Keizan* (San Francisco: North Point Press, 1990), pp. 16–17.

57 Śāriputra, one of the ten great disciples of the Buddha, especially known for his wisdom, first became a disciple of Śākyamuni Buddha thanks to seeing the Elder Aśvajit (Assaji in Pali) going on his alms round. Aśvajit was one of the five companions of Gautama during his ascetic practices who later became the Buddha's first disciples. Although Aśvajit was not particularly noted for wisdom, Śāriputra was deeply impressed with his dignified bearing during his alms round and inquired who his teacher was. Stream-entry is the first fruit, or result of practice, in the path to arhatship. For this story, see Nyanaponika Thera and Helmuth Hecker, *Great Disciples of the Buddha: Their Lives, Their Works, Their Legacy* (Boston: Wisdom Publications, 1997), pp. 6–8.

58 Śrivati was a wealthy man who sought to become a monk. But because he was already more than a hundred years old, Śāriputra refused him. The character *do* in the text, referring to *tokudo*, or monk ordination, literally means "to save."

59 This saying about Śāriputra's wisdom and knowledge, and the ensuing story about Śāriputra and Aśvajit, and about Maudgalyāyana hearing about it from Śāriputra, are from Nāgārjuna's Commentary on the Māhāprajñāpāramitā Sūtra (Ch.: Dazhidulun), chap. 11.

Aśvajit said, "All phenomena arise according to conditions. His teaching expounds the causes and conditions [of phenomena]. These phenomena and conditions can be exhausted. My teacher expounds it like this." Having heard this, Śāriputra attained the first fruit of stream-entry.

When Aśvajit had gone out that morning, the Buddha had told him, "The one you will meet today will be a bright person. You should expound the Dharma in simplified form." So Aśvajit expounded in condensed form three of the four noble truths. That all dharmas arise from conditions is the truth of suffering. His Dharma expounding causes and conditions is the truth of the combination [of conditions leading to suffering]. That dharmas together with conditions are exhausted is the truth of the cessation [of suffering].

After hearing this, Śāriputra returned to where he was staying. Maudgalyāyana first arose to meet him, and then said, "You have attained sweet dew. I want to taste it as well."⁶⁰ Śāriputra then explained what he had heard. Maudgalyāyana heard this and also attained the first fruit.

You should all know that Aśvajit saved Śāriputra, which is testimony to the Buddha Dharma. The point is clear that within the Buddha Dharma, wisdom and wide learning are not of primary importance.

When the World-Honored One was staying at the Bamboo Garden in Venuvana Vihāra (monastery) in Rājagṛha, there was a wealthy person in Rājagṛha city whose name was Śrivati.⁶¹ He was one hundred years old. Hearing that the merit and virtue of leaving home was immeasurable, he thought to himself, "Why shouldn't I leave home and practice the way of the Buddha Dharma?" Immediately he said farewell to his wife and children, his servants, and all the old and young relatives in his household, saying he wanted to leave home. He was old and senile, and there were none of the old and young in his home who were not disgusted and tired with him. They had disregarded and ridiculed what he said, and never followed it. Hearing that he wanted to leave home, everyone was delighted

60 "Sweet dew" is a phrase for nirvāṇa, or the teaching that leads to nirvāṇa.

61 This story about Śrivati is from one of the Jātaka sutras, or from the Sutra on the Causes and Conditions of the Wise and Foolish, translated into Chinese by Huijue. Dōgen is perhaps quoting these stories at such length to share some of the materials from the new copy of the Tripitaka at Eiheiji; see Dharma hall discourse 361 and 362.

and said, "You should leave soon. Why are you delaying? Now is the right time."

Śrivati left his home and went to the bamboo grove, wishing to meet the World-Honored One, to find out how to become a home-leaver monk. After arriving at the bamboo grove he asked many bhikṣus, "The Buddha, World-Honored One, great sage, great compassionate one who widely benefits humans and heavenly beings, where is he now?"

A bhikṣu replied, "The Tathāgata, World-Honored One, went somewhere to teach and benefit others, so he is not here."

Śrivati asked again, "Next after the Buddha, great teacher, who else here would be the senior wise person?"

The bhikṣu pointed out the venerable Śāriputra. Then Śrivati went to Śāriputra, threw down his cane, made prostrations, and said, "Venerable One, permit me to leave home." Then Śāriputra looked at this person and thought that he was aged and lacking in three aspects: he could not study, could not do seated meditation, and could not help out with many matters. So Śāriputra told him, "You should leave. You are old, with too many years to be able to become a home-leaver."

Next Śrivati went to Mahākāśyapa, Upāli, Aniruddha, and, in order of seniority, visited five hundred great arhats, all of whom asked him, "Previously have you asked someone else or not?"

He would reply, "I previously went to the World-Honored One, but he was not there. Next I went to the Venerable Śāriputra."

They asked, "What did he say?"

He replied, "He told me, 'You are old, with too many years to be able to become a home-leaver.'"

The bhikṣus said, "Śāriputra is preeminent in wisdom, and he did not give you permission. We as well do not give you permission. This is like when a skilled physician clearly diagnoses an [incurable] liver disease, and gives up treating it. Other junior physicians also would throw up their hands, clearly recognizing that the patient had unquestionable signs of a fatal disease."

Because Śāriputra in his great wisdom did not allow it, so also the other bhikṣus would not allow it. Śrivati sought out many bhikṣus, but could not become a home-leaver monk. Then he left the bamboo grove and sat on the threshold of the temple gate, weeping with sadness and vexation. He screamed and wailed, "Since I was born I have never committed any great misdeeds. Why do they especially forbid me to become a home-leaver? Upāli had been a humble barber; Sunita had cleaned out excrement from latrines; Aṅgulimālya had murdered innumerable people; Dāsaka had been a despicable, lowly person [a former slave]. All these people could become home-leavers. Because of what crime am I prevented from becoming a home-leaver?"

When Śrivati said this, the World-Honored One appeared before him, emitting brilliant radiance. The magnificent adornments of his marks of buddhahood could be likened to the lofty, seven-jeweled carriage of Indra, the king of the Trayastriṃśāḥ Heaven. The Buddha asked Śrivati, "What have you come for?"

At that time, this wealthy person heard the Brahma-like voice, and his heart was comforted and danced with joy, like a child meeting his father. With five parts of the body touching the ground, he made prostrations to the Buddha.[62] Then Śrivati cried and said to Buddha, "All sentient beings, including murderers, thieves, liars, those who slander, and those of the lowest class, all are able to leave home. For what crime am I alone forbidden from becoming a home-leaver in Buddha Dharma? Because I am old and senile, both old and young in my home do not respect me. If I cannot become a home-leaver in Buddha Dharma, when I return to my own home they certainly will not accept me. Where can I go? I must now definitely end my life right here."

Then the Buddha said to Śrivati, "Who was it who raised their hand into the sky and decided that while some people could become home-leavers, this person could not because of old age?"

The wealthy Śrivati said, "World-Honored One, you are the supreme wise person among Dharma-wheel-turning rulers, but second to the Buddha among the leading teachers in the world is the venerable Śāriputra, and he will not permit me to leave home in the Buddha Dharma."

Then the World-Honored One, with great compassion, comforted and instructed Śrivati, just like a compassionate father comforting and instructing a filial child. Buddha said to him, "Do not be distressed or despair. Now I allow you to become a home-leaver monk. Śāriputra is not

62 The five parts of the body touching the ground in such prostrations are the knees, elbows, and forehead.

someone who diligently engaged in ascetic practices for three asaṃkhya kalpas, or practiced merit for hundreds of kalpas. Śāriputra did not follow difficult practices lifetime after lifetime, such as cutting off his head or removing his eyes, or making offerings of his marrow, brain, blood, flesh, skin, bones, arms, legs, ears, or nose. Śāriputra did not throw his body down to a hungry tiger, enter a pit of fire, have a thousand nails pounded into his body, or engrave his body with a thousand lamps.[63] Śāriputra did not offer countries and cities, his wife and children, servants and slaves, horses and elephants, or seven jewels. Śāriputra did not make offerings to eighty-eight thousand buddhas in the former asaṃkhya kalpas, did not make offerings to ninety thousand buddhas in the middle asaṃkhya kalpas, and did not make offerings to one hundred thousand world-honored buddhas in the later asaṃkhya kalpas. He did not then leave home, maintain the precepts, and fulfill the perfection of ethical conduct. Śāriputra is not free to oversee the Dharma. How could he judge and declare that some person should leave home, and another person cannot leave home because of old age? I am the only person free to oversee the Dharma. I alone ride the jeweled vehicle of the six perfections, don the armor of patience, sit at the vajra seat under the bodhi tree, overcome the demon king's enmity, and alone attain the Buddha way. Nobody is equal to me. You came to follow me. I will make you a home-leaver monk."

Like this, the World-Honored One in various ways comforted and instructed Śrivati. His distress and despair were removed, and his heart was greatly delighted. Then he followed behind Buddha and entered Buddha's monastery, and Buddha had Maudgalyāyana give him the ceremony to become a home-leaver monk.

What is the reason that sentient beings accord with the affinity to receive monk ordination? If someone has affinity with Buddha, nobody else is able to ordain them. If they have affinity with someone else, Buddha cannot ordain them. If someone has affinity with Śāriputra, then Maud-

---

63 These actions all represent self-sacrifices by Śākyamuni in his previous lives. For example, one of the Jātaka tales of his past lives describes a prince who threw his body down a cliff to feed a hungry tigress and her cubs. See Peter Khoroche, trans., *Once the Buddha Was a Monkey: Ārya Śūra's Jātakamala* (Chicago: University of Chicago Press, 1989), pp. 5–9. This entire section on the past deeds that Śāriputra had not practiced, ending with "I alone ride the jeweled vehicle of the six perfections," is removed in Manzan's version of Eihei Kōroku.

galyāyana, Mahākāśyapa, Aniruddha, Śābira, or other disciples are not the ones to give that person monk ordination. Extending this in accord with the person's affinity, other people do not give them monk ordination.

At that time, Maudgalyāyana also thought, "This person is extremely old and senile. The three matters of reciting sutras, sitting in meditation, and helping out with affairs are completely impossible for him. And yet, Buddha, the ruler of Dharma, has ordered that Śrivati be given home-leaver ordination, so this could not be improper. Therefore, I will allow him to leave home, and receive the complete precepts. In previous lives, this person has already planted seeds of affinity for this ordination, and already has swallowed the Dharma hook like a fish who swallows a hook and will definitely leave home."

Śrivati must have already practiced and accumulated many good virtues. Day and night he diligently practiced, reading and reciting the sutras, the vinaya, and abhidharma, deeply penetrating the sutra treasury.

You should all know that Śāriputra's great wisdom could not match the virtues of the buddhas.[64] We clearly realize that ultimately we cannot compare Śāriputra's great wisdom with the World-Honored Buddha. Moreover, foolish people these days search out a few words and phrases from the ancient writings or sayings and try to make them into seeds of wisdom, but ultimately they cannot meet the singular transmission and direct pointing of the buddhas and ancestors. Even using Śāriputra's wisdom this cannot be attained, so how much more so for other people's wisdom. If even those searching with wisdom cannot meet this, how could those searching with the seeds of upside-down views ever attain the great way of buddha ancestors?

Brothers on this mountain, do not make a mistake, do not make a mistake. Don't you see that an ancient person said, "Mind is not Buddha, wisdom is not the way."[65] Great assembly, do you want to clearly understand this point?

---

64 Here begins Dōgen's commentary on the preceding story from a sutra.

65 "Mind is not Buddha, wisdom is not the way" is a saying by Nanquan used as case 34 in the Mumonkan. See Cleary, *Unlocking the Zen Kōan,* pp. 158–160; or Aitken, *Gateless Barrier,* pp. 208–212.

After a pause Dōgen said: The Dharma for monks is not to go to bed before your teacher.

Demon Zen
382. Dharma Hall Discourse

> Those with demons attached to them distinctly explain Zen.
> When the demons have left they are as if deranged.
> Without knowing and carrying out the transmitted truth,
> Who would know they do not realize their harmful
> inclinations?

Keep the Faculties Sharp and Clear
383. Dharma Hall Discourse
As a reward for seeds of prajñā planted in previous lives, we are born in the southern continent, and encounter Buddha Dharma. Clearly know that we are without hindrance, and have affinity with Dharma. Our only regret would be not practicing, and not yet having attained verified realization. Not practicing means not yet having discarded fame and profit, and having attachments to ourselves and our positions. In India and China, buddhas and ancestors swiftly cast away fame and profit, forever abandoned themselves and their positions, and single-mindedly engaged the way. They committed no violations or misdeeds. Therefore they accomplished Buddha Dharma.

You should know that between the practitioners in the True Dharma Age and the Semblance Dharma Age there was already a difference in the accomplishment of the Dharma by those practitioners.[66] Five hundred

---

66 "True Dharma Age" and "Semblance Dharma Age" refer to the historical theory of the three-stage degeneration of the Buddha Dharma, a popular theory in Dōgen's time. Many of Dōgen's contemporaries believed that they were in the "Final Dharma Age" *(mappō)*, in which practice and enlightenment were impossible. Dōgen refers to this theory, for example, in Dharma hall discourse 182. In an early writing, Bendōwa, in response to one of the questions (number 15), Dōgen says clearly that "In the true teaching of Mahāyāna there is no distinction of true, semblance, and final Dharma, and it is said that all who practice will attain the Way." Okumura and Leighton, *The Wholehearted Way*, p. 37. In this Dharma hall discourse, Dōgen is referring to the *mappō* theory to encourage his monks, but he still does not say that it is impossible to accomplish the way in such an age.

years after [Śākyamuni], there was already the difference between the strength of liberation [of the True Dharma Age] and the strength of samādhi [remaining in the Semblance Age]. Moreover, now we are encountering the Final Dharma Age and its degenerate conditions, so even if we act diligently and courageously, trying to save our heads from fire, I am afraid that we cannot equal the people from the True Dharma and Semblance Dharma Ages. In India, right within the True Dharma and Semblance Dharma Ages, there were already those who accomplished the Dharma and those who did not, depending on their diligence or lack of it. Considering this remote country in the present Final Dharma Age, between the True and Semblance Ages and our age, the faculties of humans are as distant as heaven from earth.

Considering our own situation resulting from the past, people from India, the center [of the teaching], and those from our country are as difficult to compare as gold and sand. However, we have no serious obstructions, and have received superior connections [with the teaching]. With humility, we should not slacken and regress. Such not slackening nor regressing involves making diligent effort. To be diligent means not seeking fame and profit, and not having attachments to sounds and colors.

Therefore we should not look at the words and phrases of Confucius or Laozi, and should not look at the Śūraṅgama or Complete Enlightenment scriptures.[67] *Many contemporary people consider the Śūraṅgama and Complete Enlightenment Sutras as among those that the Zen tradition relies on. But the teacher Dōgen always disliked them.*[68] We should exclusively study the expressions coming from the activities of buddhas and ancestors

---

67 Although Dōgen himself sometimes quotes Confucius or Laozi, here Dōgen is emphasizing the difference between Buddhism and either Confucianism or Daoism. Dōgen also occasionally quotes the Śūraṅgama, or Complete Enlightenment Sutra. However, he distinguishes between scholarly teachers, who depend on sutras, and teachings based on experience of practice-awakening.

68 These two sentences are a note added to the text by Gien, the compiler of volume 5. Although he occasionally did quote these two sutras, in some of his earlier writings Dōgen directly criticizes them as unreliable and apocryphal. In Hōkyōki, Dōgen's writing about his study in China with Tiantong Rujing, Dōgen questions the authenticity of these two sutras, and Rujing agrees, saying they were written in China. Based on modern historical knowledge, scholars now concur. See Kodera, *Dōgen's Formative Years in China*, sec. 6, pp. 121, 175–176. However, in the Shōbōgenzō essay Tembōrin (Turning the Dharma Wheel) Dōgen says that even if these sutras are spurious, because they have been

from the time of the seven world-honored buddhas to the present. If we are not concerned with the activities of the buddha ancestors, and vainly make our efforts in the evil path of fame and profit, how could this be study of the way? Among the World-Honored Tathāgata, the ancestral teacher Mahākāśyapa, the twenty-eight ancestors in India, the six generations [of ancestors] in China, Qingyuan, and Nanyue [Huairang], which of these ancestral teachers ever used the Śūraṅgama or Complete Enlightenment Sutra and considered them as the true Dharma eye treasury, wondrous mind of nirvāṇa? Further, what ancestral teachers would have tasted the saliva of Confucius or Laozi, and made it into the sweet dew of the buddha ancestors? Now it is most faulty that many monks in Great Song China often discuss the expression "The three teachings are as one."[69] How painful it is that in Great Song, the Buddha Dharma has weakened and been swept onto the ground. All the ancient worthies disliked the comparison of Laozi with the World-Honored One. These days, all the monks discuss how the Tathāgata and Laozi are one and the same. We should know that in the present time, because there are no honorable people, such a calamity has arisen.

Brothers, if you want to read sutras, you should follow the scriptural teachings recommended by Caoxi [the sixth ancestor, Dajian Huineng], such as the Lotus, the Mahāparinirvāṇa, and the Prajñā [Pāramitā] Sutras. What is the use of sutras not recommended by Caoxi? Why are they useless? Ancient people opened the sutras and commentaries simply for the sake of awakening. Modern people open the sutras and commentaries merely for the sake of fame and profit. Buddhas expound the sutras in order to enable all living beings to attain awakening. When modern people open the buddhas' sutras only for the sake of fame and profit, how greatly it opposes the intention of the buddhas.

---

commented on by genuine buddha ancestors, they become useful material for Dharma discourse, even as have tiles and pebbles. See Tanahashi, *Enlightenment Unfolds*, p. 197.

69 In Song China, because Buddhism was supported by the mainstream establishment, many Buddhists emphasized the cooperation of the three religious traditions. This attitude was conveyed to Japan by other teachers in Dōgen's time, but Dōgen emphasized the uniqueness of Buddhism. In our modern age of globalization and religious pluralism, one might well question the attitude Dōgen expresses here, which was perhaps appropriate while encouraging the practice focus of his monk disciples at Eiheiji.

Needless to say, likening short sighted thinking to extensive study and wide knowledge is truly extreme foolishness. Fortunately, we have escaped from becoming government officials or following worldly vocations, and have left home to become monks. Therefore do not seek or desire sounds and colors or fame and profit. If we chase after sounds and colors, this is shameful for home-leavers. Sound and color objects are the basis of the five sense desires. Never allow the five sense faculties to indulge and enter into the five desires.

Don't you see that the World-Honored One said, "You bhikṣus already abide in the precepts. Restrain the five faculties and do not allow yourselves to indulge and enter into the five desires. For example, this is like a person who tends an ox, holding a staff and keeping watch so that it never violates the seedlings in others' fields. If we indulge the five senses, then the five desires will simply grow beyond all bounds, and go beyond all control."[70]

Therefore, the descendants of buddha ancestors should not direct themselves on the evil paths of sounds and colors or fame and profit. Not directing oneself toward sounds and colors means that you should immediately discard fame and profit, and make the five faculties sharp and clear. To be sharp and clear means that once we hear that we should discard fame and profit and should discard self-centeredness, we immediately discard them. Such practitioners can be said to enact great functioning and have superior qualities. People who cannot yet be like this are called inferior vessels. This being the case, how can we tend an ox? How is the staff? How are the seedlings? How is our watching? And how is the master of the seedlings? Worldly people certainly do not know this; it is only correctly transmitted by buddha ancestors.

This staff is now in Eihei's hands; sometimes vertical, sometimes horizontal, I hold it up and keep watch. Furthermore I ask you, are you able to tend the ox?

After a pause Dōgen said: I have this monk's staff, and it follows me when I eat rice and when I enter the hall to give Dharma hall discourses.

---

70 This quote is from the Sutra of the Last Discourse of Buddha. See Phillip Karl Eidmann, trans., *The Sutra of the Teaching Left by the Buddha* (Osaka: Koyata Yamamoto, 1952), section 2, pp. 3–4.

Once I strike the faces of self and others, in the heavenly and human realms all separation is transcended.

Tiantong Rujing's Single Gaze

384. Dharma Hall Discourse at the Memorial for Master Tiantong [Rujing][71]

Today, Tiantong [Rujing] turns a somersault and lifts up his hands in the great three thousand worlds. Although he saw the eastern land of Akṣobhya Buddha, his eyes never reached the place of other persons.[72]

The Echoes of Emptiness

385. Dharma Hall Discourse in Appreciation of the Previous Inō[73]

The iron mallet singularly transmitted by buddha ancestors has no hole.[74] [This inō] upheld and used it to receive [the sounds of] emptiness and continue its echoes, with a single hit slaying wild-fox Zen.

Genuine Faith and the Teaching of Causality

386. Dharma Hall Discourse

An ancient Buddha said, "Some eight hundred years after [the Buddha's] entering nirvāṇa at the twin [sāla] trees, the world has become a decayed burial mound and the trees are all withered. People have no sincere faith,

---

71 This memorial discourse for Tiantong Rujing was in 1250, the seventeenth day of the seventh month. For previous memorial discourses for Rujing, see discourses 274, 276, and 342.

72 Akṣobhya Buddha is the Buddha of the five directions who lives in the east. He is especially discussed in the Vimalakīrti Sūtra, among others. In Dharma hall discourse 46, Bodhidharma's disciple Zongchi refers to Ānanda as seeing but not entering Akṣobhya's Buddha land. "His eyes never reached the place of other persons" could be interpreted as saying either that Rujing never saw other people as separate from himself, or that Rujing was paying attention only to his disciple Dōgen, or that Rujing never saw Akṣobhya Buddha as other than himself.

73 See Dharma hall discourses 190 and 298 for other discourses of appreciation for a departing inō (director of the monks and monks' hall).

74 The iron mallet with no hole refers to the tsui chin, a block used by the inō to signal events in the monks' hall. Except in this poetic expression, the mallet is made of wood, and sits on a larger wooden block, on which it is pounded.

and true mindfulness has dimmed, so that they do not trust genuine reality but merely love spiritual power."[75]

Moreover, now two thousand two hundred years have passed since the parinirvāṇa under the twin [sāla] trees, and we clearly see that people have no sincere faith, and true mindfulness has dimmed.[76] If people who study Buddha Dharma have no genuine faith or true mindfulness, they will certainly dispense with and ignore [the law of] causality.

An ancient said, "When causes are complete and the results fulfilled, true awakening is accomplished."[77]

Tell me great assembly, among the disciples of Eihei, how should we assess causality within Buddha Dharma? Do you wish to clearly understand this?

After a pause Dōgen said: Holding up the flower at Vulture Peak is compassion descending to the grasses. Shigong [Huizang teaching by] pulling back his bow still shows the remains of bad habits.[78]

The Cause for Buddhas' Appearance
387. Dharma Hall Discourse
I can remember, when instructing the monk Fata, whose practice was to recite the Lotus Sutra, the ancient Buddha Caoxi [the sixth ancestor, Dajian Huineng] said, "The essential point of this sutra concerns the causes and conditions for [buddhas] appearing in the world."[79] The

---

75 This is a saying by the seventeenth Indian ancestor, Sanghānandi. It is in the Jingde Transmission of the Lamp (Keitoku Dentōroku), vol. 2; see Ogata, *Transmission of the Lamp*, p. 33.

76 According to the understanding of Sanghānandi and Dōgen, Śākyamuni had died around the eighth century B.C.E., whereas most contemporary historians now believe he died in the fifth century B.C.E.

77 The saying "When causes are complete and the results fulfilled, true awakening is accomplished" is from Yongming Yanshou.

78 Shigong Huizang was a hunter who became a monk. Later, as a teacher, he would draw back his bow to challenge arriving students. See Dharma hall discourse 277 and volume 4, note 35.

79 The story of this interaction between Huineng and the monk Fata (Jap.: Hōtatsu; unknown aside from this story) is discussed at length by Dōgen in the Shōbōgenzō essay Hokke Ten Hokke (The Lotus Turns the Lotus). See Nishijima and Cross, *Master Dogen's Shobogenzo*, book 1, pp. 203–220. The Lotus Sutra, chap. 2, says that the single great cause

ancient Buddha Caoxi spoke like this. His descendant Eihei cannot avoid saying something. How shall I say it?

I would say that the essential point of this sutra concerns all buddhas appearing in the world. Tell me great assembly, are Caoxi's saying and Eihei's saying the same or different? I ask you to judge and discern this.

Do not say they are the same; do not say they are different. This is because all buddhas' appearance in the world could not be involved with sameness or difference. Don't you see that it is said that myself and the buddhas in ten directions are the ones who can know this matter?[80]

Practice without Scattering Flowers
388. Dharma Hall Discourse
In ancient times, someone was up in a high tower and saw two monks walking by.[81] Two heavenly beings were sweeping the road and scattered flowers behind the monks. When the two monks returned, two demons shouted and spit at the monks, and swept away their footsteps. The person observing this finally descended from the tower and asked the two monks what had happened. The two monks said, "When we were going, we were discussing the principles of buddhas. When we were returning, we were engaged in random talk. That is the reason." Realizing this deeply, the two monks were repentant and continued on their way.

Listen, although this story concerns [the two monks'] coarse realms of consciousness, if we examine it minutely, this is the most important aspect of people's study of the way. Why is that so? It is because when even a bit of sentimental thinking arises, external conditions appear before us. If such thoughts do not arise, there can be no particular condition.[82]

---

for buddhas appearing in the world is to help all suffering beings enter the path toward awakening. See Katō, Tamura, and Miyasaka, *Threefold Lotus Sutra*, pp. 59–60.

80 "Myself and the buddhas in ten directions are the ones who can know this matter" is a paraphrase from the Lotus Sutra, chap. 2, "Only a buddha together with a buddha can fathom the Reality of All Existence." See Katō, Tamura, and Miyasaka, *Threefold Lotus Sutra*, p. 52.

81 This story is recorded in Engo Zenji Shinnyō (The Mind Essence of Zen Master Yuanwu), a collection of Yuanwu Keqin's writings.

82 "Particular condition" is *kyō*, whose meanings include "realm," "boundary," or "sense objects." This is related to *kyōgai*, translated earlier in the paragraph as "realms of

An ancient [Yuanwu Keqin] said, "Although it was like this, it was exactly because those heavenly beings scattered flowers on the road that the demonic spirits could see [the two monks]."

If there had been no road upon which the heavenly beings could scatter flowers, and there were no means for the demonic spirits to observe them, then what would have happened? Great assembly, do you want to clearly understand this? Nobody in previous generations has discussed this, but I will now speak about it.

After a pause Dōgen said: Buddhas do not appear in the world by [depending on] the sixteen especially excellent meditation methods, which generate the spiritual powers.[83] Even when ordinary people with sharp capacity practice these kinds of meditation, the cessation of outflows does not occur. When tathāgatas expound the teaching, the cessation of outflows does occur.

The Senses as Tuned by Zazen

389. Dharma Hall Discourse

This morning is the first day of the ninth month [1250].[84] As in the past, now we strike the han, and do zazen. Also I ask, what is required in the zazen of buddhas and ancestors? What is most essential is simply the following.

In the zazen of patch-robed monks, although the two eyes are like grapes, it is necessary to further transform them into soapberries [used as

---

consciousness," but which also connotes "place" or "behavior." See the excellent article by Victor Hori, "Kōan and Kensho in the Rinzai Zen Curriculum," in Steven Heine and Dale Wright, eds., *The Kōan: Texts and Contexts in Zen Buddhism* (Oxford: Oxford University Press, 2000), pp. 292–295.

83 "The sixteen especially excellent meditation methods" refers to sixteen techniques of awareness in early Buddhism. These include awareness of breath as inhalation or exhalation or as long or short, receiving delight or bliss, contemplating impermanence, contemplating the cessation of desires, and contemplating cessation (nirvāṇa). These are from the Anapanasati Sutta. See Thich Nhat Hanh, *Breathe! You are Alive: Sutra on the Full Awareness of Breathing* (Berkeley: Parallax Press, 1996), pp. 5–7. Dōgen here is emphasizing the practice of buddhas, which is not directed toward gaining some exalted state, unlike special meditation techniques.

84 For the first day of the ninth month, when the regular meditation schedule resumes after the summer, see Dharma hall discourses 193, 279, and 347.

beads in rosaries].⁸⁵ Although the two ears are like the whirling of wheels, it is also necessary that right and left each be a single fan extended [to listen]. Although the nostrils are pierced, it is necessary that they also be two crookneck squashes on the face.⁸⁶ Although the tongue speaks for the entire three-thousand-fold world, it is also necessary that it be a bright crescent moon. Although the body is like a long drum [narrow in the middle], we should further study it as a collection of droplets of water. Although the mind is [fleeting] like the wind, it is also necessary that we think of not thinking.⁸⁷

How to Breathe in Zazen
390. Dharma Hall Discourse
In the zazen of patch-robed monks, first you should sit correctly with upright posture. Then regulate your breath and settle your mind. In the lesser vehicle originally there were two gateways, which were counting breaths and contemplating impurity. In the lesser vehicle, people used counting to regulate their breath. However, the buddha ancestors' engaging of the way always differed from the lesser vehicle.

A buddha ancestor said, "Even if you arouse the mind of a leprous wild fox, never practice the self-regulation of the two vehicles."⁸⁸ The two vehicles refer to such as the school of the four-part vinaya, and the [Abhidharma] Kośa school, which have spread in the world these days.⁸⁹ In the Mahāyāna there is also a method for regulating breath, which is knowing

85 For soapberries and rosary beads, see Dharma hall discourse 143. See also discourse 25 and volume 1, note 61.

86 For the nose as a crookneck squash, see Dharma hall discourse 242.

87 "Think of not-thinking" refers to a story about Yaoshan often cited by Dōgen. See Dharma hall discourse 373 and note 41 above; see also volume 4 (Dharma hall discourse 270), note 23.

88 This quote is from Nāgārjuna's Commentary on the Mahāprajñāpāramitā Sūtra (Ch.: Dazhidulun), later also quoted by Zhiyi in the Mohe Zhiguan (Great Treatise on Śamatha and Vipaśyanā Meditation).

89 The four-part vinaya is Shibun Ritsu, the version of the vinaya from the Dharmaguptaka school in India, which became the most popular vinaya text in China. The Abhidharma Kośa is a pre-Mahāyāna commentary on the early Buddhist abhidharma psychological teachings, written by Vasubandhu. The Japanese Ritsu or Vinaya school and the Japanese Kusha school of Buddhism were established in the early Japanese Nara

that one breath is long, another breath is short. The breath reaches the tanden and comes up from the tanden.[90] Although exhale and inhale differ, both of them occur depending on the tanden. Impermanence is easy to clarify, and regulating the mind is easy to accomplish.

My late teacher Tiantong [Rujing] said, "Breath enters and reaches the tanden, and yet there is no place from which it comes. Therefore it is neither long nor short. Breath emerges from the tanden, and yet there is nowhere it goes. Therefore it is neither short nor long."

My late teacher said it like that. Suppose someone were to ask Eihei, "Master, how do you regulate your breath?"

I would simply say to him: Although it is not the great vehicle, it differs from the lesser vehicle. Although it is not the lesser vehicle, it differs from the great vehicle.

Suppose that person inquired again, "Ultimately, what is it?"

I would say to him: Exhale and inhale are neither long nor short.

Someone asked Baizhang, "The Yogācārabhūmi Śāstra and the Jewel Necklace Sutra contain the Mahāyāna precepts.[91] Why don't you practice according to them?"

Baizhang said, "What I take as essential is not limited to the greater or lesser vehicles, and does not differ from the greater or lesser vehicles. I condense and combine the extensive scope [of regulations] to establish standards for appropriate conduct."[92]

---

period (eighth century). The Ritsu school was still quite active in Dōgen's time, and the Kusha teachings had been absorbed into the Hossō (Yogācāra) school, also active in Dōgen's Kamakura period.

90 *Tanden* is originally a Daoist alchemical and yogic term, referring to the center of energy and vitality in the lower abdomen, about two and a half inches below the navel.

91 The Yogācārabhūmi Śāstra, or Commentary on the Stages (or Grounds) of the Yogācāra Teaching, is by Asaṅga, although formally attributed to the bodhisattva Maitreya. The Jewel Necklace Sutra (more formally called the Bodhisattva Jewel Necklace Original Conduct Sutra) was written in China and discusses the three pure precepts: sustaining all precepts (to refrain from evil), sustaining all good conduct, and including and sustaining all beings. This text is the source for these three of Dōgen's sixteen bodhisattva precepts.

92 This quote is from Baizhang's legendary Qingguei (Jap.: Shingi; Pure Standards), which was the inspiration for Dōgen's Eihei Shingi. See Leighton and Okumura, *Dōgen's Pure Standards for the Zen Community*. Although scholars now doubt that there was ever

Baizhang said it this way, but Eihei is certainly not like this. It is not the case that it is not limited to the great or small vehicles, or not different from the great or small vehicles. What is this small vehicle? The affairs of the donkey are not complete. What is this great vehicle? The affairs of the horse have already arrived.[93] Not the extensive scope means the extremely great is the same as the small. Not condensed means the extremely small is the same as the great. I do not combine, but gallop over and drop away great and small. Already having accomplished this, how shall we go beyond?

After a pause Dōgen said: When healthy and energetic we do zazen without falling asleep. When hungry we eat rice, and know we are fully satisfied.

Life and Death without Abode
391. Dharma Hall Discourse Requested by Bhikṣuṇī Egi for Her Late Mother[94]
Life has no place whence it comes. It is like putting on one's pants. However, our face is solemn. Therefore it is said, the ten thousand things return to the one. Death has no place to go. It is like taking off one's pants. However, our traces are dropped away. Therefore it is said, to where does the one return?[95] At this very time, how is it?

After a pause Dōgen said: From the beginning, life and death do not involve each other. Offense and happiness are both empty with no place to abide.

---

actually such a text by Baizhang, a supposed excerpt of the legendary text appears in the Jingde Transmission of the Lamp, including this quote cited here by Dōgen. See Ogata, *Transmission of the Lamp,* p. 218.

93 This use of donkey and horse echoes Dōgen's phrase in Dharma hall discourse 4, "a donkey in front with a horse behind." See volume 1, note 8.

94 Bhikṣuṇī (Nun) Egi, whose name means "Cherish the Meaning," was a Dharma sister of Koun Ejō and disciple of Bucchi Kakuan. See Dharma hall discourse 185 and volume 3, note 1.

95 A monk asked Zhaozhou, "The ten thousand things return to the one; where does the one return?" Zhaozhou said, "When I was at Qingzhou, I made a robe of seven pounds." See Dharma hall discourse 377. This story is in the Recorded Sayings of Zhaozhou, and also appears in the Hekiganroku, case 45. See Green, Recorded Sayings of Zen Master Joshu, p. 82; and Cleary and Cleary, Blue Cliff Record, pp. 318–322.

A Warm Tear in the Freezing Mountain
392. Dharma Hall Discourse on the Tenth Day of the Twelfth Month
[1250][96]
After relating the story of the second ancestor [Dazu Huike] standing in the snow and cutting off his arm, Dōgen said: Whenever it comes to the evening of the ninth and this morning of the tenth and I see the winter snow, I recall that time on Shaoxi Peak at Mount Song, so that deep emotion fills my chest and tears of sadness wet my robe. I now speak for the sake of Buddha Dharma and the sake of respected teachers. Standing in the snow and cutting off your arm actually is not difficult. I only regret that we do not have such a teacher. Shouldn't you all elicit the aspiration to yearn for the ancients?

In verse Dōgen said:

Snowfall covers for many thousands of miles,
Every flake neither the same nor different.
After this song and dance, heaven and earth are refreshed.
It buries the moon and clouds, and smothers flames from gas wells.
The five petals and six flowers respond to time and season.[97]
He did not fear freezing night or icy times.
Valley pines and mountain bamboo preach with empty mind.

Caring for the Family Style
393. Dharma Hall Discourse
We surely have the opportunity to encounter the family style of the buddha ancestors. Black lacquer emits light unlimited by inside or out.[98] Further observing, the mountains in four directions turn blue or yellow. The reeds on the grass-roof hut grow old, and I cover it with firewood. Although the moon descends and colors the window, we should take care that refined beauty not turn into shiny trinkets.

96 The tenth day of the twelfth month is traditionally commemorated as the day the second Chinese ancestor, Dazu Huike, cut off his arm to prove his sincerity to Bodhidharma.

97 "Five petals" refers to the five houses of classical Chan. "Six flowers" refers to the six Chinese ancestors.

98 Black lacquer is an image for the undifferentiated universal, in which all distinctions merge in sameness.

The Final Power

394. Dharma Hall Discourse

I can remember, the World-Honored One was once asked by a mountain sage with five divine powers, "The World-Honored One has six divine powers, but I only have five. What is the other remaining power?"

The World-Honored One asked him to come closer and then said, "O five-powered sage."

The sage responded, "Yes."

The World-Honored One said, "That is the one power you asked me about."[99]

The World-Honored One of the three realms called with a single voice. The mountain sage with five powers responded with a single voice. [They demonstrated] five powers, six powers, and that single power. [Penetrating] the realm of being, the realm of nonbeing, and the realm of both nonbeing and being, bring a basin of water or make tea for the master.[100]

How is this among the disciples of Eihei?

The five-powered mountain sage originally desired to steal the eye of the small Śākyamuni, and to see the small Śākyamuni. But suddenly he saw the great Śākyamuni. How was it then?

After a pause Dōgen said: The mountain sage did not achieve his previous wish. A mendicant smashes his rice bowl.[101]

The Natureless Nature

395. Dharma Hall Discourse

All sentient beings have Buddha nature, therefore milk has cheese nature. All sentient beings have no Buddha nature, therefore milk has no cheese

---

99 This story is from the Recorded Sayings of Xuedou. Traditionally, the first five powers are the all-seeing heavenly eye, the heavenly ear, the power to see previous lives, knowing other's minds, and divine legs to travel everywhere rapidly. The sixth power traditionally is the power to eliminate all outflows and purify all defilements.

100 "Bring a basin of water or make tea" refers to the story of the spiritual powers of Guishan's disciples Yangshan and Xiangyan, who could intuit their master's needs. See Dharma hall discourse 17 and volume 1, note 48.

101 "A mendicant smashes his rice bowl" is a saying by Tiantong Rujing. See Dharma hall discourse 179.

nature.[102] Sentient beings do not have sentient being nature, therefore milk does not have milk nature. Buddha nature does not have Buddha nature as a nature, therefore cheese has no cheese nature.

Although this is the case, suppose someone asked Eihei, "What about holding up a flower at Vulture Peak or the three prostrations at Shaolin?"

After a pause Dōgen said: Cheese has no milk nature.

The Warmth of Bodhidharma's Spirit

396. Dharma Hall Discourse for Opening the Furnace [1250][103]

This morning at Kichijō Mountain, we bring forth the eyes of Bodhidharma to open the crimson fireplace. Even though this year is cold, how could we wish for another fire rather than the single plum blossom with five petals in the snow?

Sitting on the Ground of Prajñā

397. Dharma Hall Discourse

There is no place the great way of the buddha ancestors does not pervade, and not a thing that is not endowed with it. However, only people who have the seeds of prajñā planted in past lives can patiently sustain it. Therefore it is said, "Do not see in terms of shapes; do not seek in terms of sounds."[104]

---

102 "All sentient beings have Buddha nature" is a paraphrase from the Mahāparinirvāṇa Sūtra. Dōgen discusses this teaching extensively in his Shōbōgenzō essay Busshō (Buddha Nature). He retranslates the sentence from the sutra "All sentient beings completely have Buddha nature" into "All sentient beings' entire being is Buddha nature." He also discusses the ideas of existence of Buddha nature and nonexistence of Buddha nature, which are variant ways of reading "have Buddha nature" and "have no Buddha nature." See Waddell and Abe, *Heart of Dōgen's Shōbōgenzō*, pp. 60–65.

103 For other Dharma hall discourses on the occasion of beginning to use the fireplace hibachi behind the altar in the monks' hall, see discourses 14, 109, 199, 288, 353, 462, and 528. Because this occurred on the first day of the tenth month, this discourse must have actually been given before discourse 392, which was on the tenth day of the twelfth month, but after discourse 389, given on the first day of the ninth month.

104 This quote is from the Diamond Sutra, which includes similar teachings in various passages. See, for example, Price and Wong, *The Diamond Sutra and the Sutra of Hui Neng*, pp. 28, 37, 43–45.

The wind is still in the great thousands of worlds.
Birds sing and mountain peaks are profoundly quiet.
The roads in all four directions brighten with dawn.
The six doorways are chill with autumn.
Sharing the seat on the ground beyond doubt,
A reflection of a bow floats in the wine cup.[105]

The True Dragon Sharing the Seat

398. Dharma Hall Discourse for Appointing the New Head Monk
The true dragon is coiled up, having grasped the essence, able to drill
through the skulls of patch-robed monks. The heaven rains jeweled flowers in joyful celebration, and the earth willingly offers auspicious signs of
harmony and gentleness. Between the [teacher sitting with his] whole
being and the one sharing his seat there can be no discriminations. This
is the head monk of Eiheiji.

Before and After Come Together

399. Dharma Hall Discourse
Our Buddha once said, "First I expound the three vehicles to encourage
the progress of living beings, then later, with only the Mahāyāna, I liberate them."[106]

I have a question for the great assembly. If the Tathāgata used early and
later explanations, this would have been no different from [the teachings
of] human and heavenly beings, and also would have been the same as the
stages of the ten kinds of sages and the three levels of wise ones.[107] But if

---

105 "Sharing the seat," literally "half sitting," refers to Buddha sharing his teaching seat
with Mahākāśyapa, or to anyone sharing the Dharma seat with a buddha. "A reflection of
a bow floats in the wine cup" refers to an old Chinese story about someone seeing the form
of a snake in his wine cup as he drank. Looking up, he realized it was only the reflection
of a drawn bow that was nearby. So this refers to not becoming confused by the distor-
tions from the senses, but seeing things clearly as they are.

106 This quote is from the Lotus Sutra, chap. 3, on parables. See Hurvitz, *Scripture of the
Lotus Blossom of the Fine Dharma*, p. 64; Katō, Tamura, and Miyasaka, *The Threefold
Lotus Sutra*, p. 91.

107 "The ten kinds of sages and the three levels of wise ones" refers to levels of progres-
son the bodhisattva path. See Dharma hall discourse 301 and volume 4, note 90.

he did not use previous and later teachings, why did he say this? Great assembly, do you want to clearly understand this?

After a pause Dōgen said: Before the affairs of the donkey are finished, the affairs of the horse arrive.[108]

Expressing the Seamless Transmission
400. Dharma Hall Discourse

Perfectly matching, as seamless as silk, completely clear with nothing covered up or hidden, even though it was transmitted to Mahākāśyapa on Vulture Peak, how was it entrusted to Shenguang [Dazu Huike] at Shaolin? Manifesting everywhere with words that really meet, everyone is fully endowed with the fragrance of insight. The empty sky widely expresses it, and the whole web of creation hears. Without flapping your lips, bring it forth to flourish widely.[109]

All of you people in the clouds and water assembly, throughout the hours of the day it fills your eyes and ears, transcending ancient and present. Who is self? Who is other? What is delusion? What is realization? Are you able to fully enact this?

After a pause Dōgen said: Raise up the Chinese radishes of Zhenzhou. Determine the price of rice in Luling.[110]

The Merit of the Tenzo's Activity
401. Dharma Hall Discourse for Appointing the New Tenzo

Heaven and earth are one finger; the ten thousand things are one horse.[111]

---

108 See Dōgen's similar use of this phrase in Dharma hall discourse 390.

109 This paragraph uses some expressions from a Dharma hall discourse by Hongzhi Zhengjue in his Extensive Record, vol. 1.

110 "The Chinese radishes of Zhenzhou" refers to Zhaozhou's response about whether or not he had personally seen his teacher Nanquan. Zhaozhou replied that Zhenzhou produces big radishes. See Cleary and Cleary, *Blue Cliff Record*, case 30, pp. 191–193. "The price of rice in Luling" refers to Qingyuan Xingsi's response about the essential meaning of Buddha Dharma. Qingyuan replied, "What is the price of rice in Luling?" See Cleary, *Book of Serenity*, case 5, pp. 20–22. These two sayings are also cited together by Dōgen in Dharma hall discourse 148.

111 This is a quotation from Zhuangzi, the chapter on the equality of all things. See Watson, *Complete Works of Chuang Tzu*, p. 40.

The two exist depending on the one, but the one also should be cast aside.[112] Rice in the bowl and water in the bucket, for the sake of others equally speak prajñā.[113] Dig in the ashes and pull out some fire; and wash the sand from the rice.[114] The merit [from all these works] returns and enters this community.

Although it is like this, such "entering" does not involve the distinctions between ordinary people and sages, self and others, delusion and realization, ultimate and particular, inside and outside, or beginning and end. So how is it? Can you clearly understand and express this?

After a pause Dōgen said: Near the pot, the tenzo is not concerned about Mañjuśrī.[115] Taking a piece of firewood and blowing on it three times is not standing mute.[116]

---

112 "The two exist depending on the one" is an idea from Laozi, for example, in chapter 42 of the Dao De Jing: "The Way brings forth one; One brings forth two; Two brings forth three; Three brings forth all things." See Wu, *Book of Lao Tzu*, pp. 154–156.

113 "Rice in the bowl and water in the bucket" is Yunmen's response to the question "What is every-atom samādhi?" See Cleary, *Book of Serenity*, case 99, pp. 425–427. "For the sake of others equally speak prajñā" is from Tiantong Rujing's poem about the functioning of a windbell hanging in emptiness. See Okumura and Leighton, *The Wholehearted Way*, pp. 46–47.

114 "Dig in the ashes and pull out some fire" is Baizhang's request of Guishan when Guishan was *tenzo*. When Guishan couldn't find any fire, Baizhang used some tongs to pull an ember from the ashes of the fireplace. See Ogata, *Transmission of the Lamp*, p. 297. Dōgen also cites this story in Eihei Shingi. See Leighton and Okumura, *Dōgen's Pure Standards for the Zen Community*, pp. 136–137. "Wash the sand from the rice" refers to the story of Dongshan Liangjie inquiring of Xuefeng, who was *tenzo*. When he asked Xuefeng whether Xuefeng washed the sand from the rice or the rice from the sand, Xuefeng said both, and overturned the whole container of rice, whereupon Dongshan said that Xuefeng would need to find another teacher. Dōgen tells this story in his Instructions for the Tenzo. See Leighton and Okumura, *Dōgen's Pure Standards for the Zen Community*, p. 35.

115 "Near the pot not concerned about Mañjuśrī" refers to the story about Wuzhuo when he was *tenzo* on Mañjuśrī's sacred mountain Wutai and Mañjuśrī appeared above the cooking pot. Wuzhuo finally hit Mañjuśrī and drove him away. Dōgen cites this story in the section on the *tenzo* in his Pure Standards for the Temple Administrators. See Leighton and Okumura, *Dōgen's Pure Standards for the Zen Community*, p. 139.

116 "Taking a piece of firewood and blowing on it three times" refers to a later story about Baizhang questioning Guishan as *tenzo*. While working together in the mountains, Baizhang asked Guishan for fire. Guishan picked up a stick and blew on it three times. Baizhang agreed. Dōgen also cites this story in his Instructions for the Tenzo. See Leighton and Okumura, *Dōgen's Pure Standards for the Zen Community*, pp. 49, 57.

An Unbeneficial Philosophy about Self and Spirit

402. Dharma Hall Discourse

Students of Buddha Dharma should know the difference between false and true paths, and between the Buddha way and other ways. If your view is that of other ways, ultimately you will not benefit from Buddha Dharma. Although there are many other ways, they all have three main ancient progenitors. Among them a primary person is named Kapila.[117]

This name [Kapila] is translated as "Yellow Head." His head was a golden color. It is also said that his head and face were both golden, and so he was named thus. He was frightened of dying, so he visited the heavenly being Iśvāra and inquired about it. The heavenly being took him to Binda Mountain and let him eat some of the olives there to gain longevity. After eating them, he was transformed into a rock in the forest as big as a bed. Those who could not catch him before wrote verses of inquiry to the rock. Later Dignāga Bodhisattva wrote a verse scolding him, and the rock split apart. Then [Kapila] gained five powers and had knowledge of eighty thousand kalpas from the past and future, and searched throughout the entire world for someone who could be saved [by receiving his teaching].

He saw one Brahman, whose name was Śri, wandering around in the human realm and asked him, "Are you only playing?" The Brahman answered, "Yes." After two thousand years had passed, Kapila asked again, "Are you able to practice the way?" He answered, "Yes, I can."[118] Then

---

117 The following lengthy section of this Dharma hall discourse, beginning "This name [Kapila] is translated" all the way down to "with the objects that were just discussed, make up twenty-five principles," is a quotation from the most prominent commentary to Zhiyi's Mohe Zhiguan (Great Treatise on Samatha and Vipaśyanā). This commentary is called Makashikan Bugyōden Guketsu in Japanese, or Extensive Clarification and Transmission of the Guide to Practice of the Great Treatise on Samatha and Vipaśyanā. It was written by Jingqi Zhanran, the sixth ancestor of the Chinese Tiantai school. This long passage quoted by Dōgen here consists of an elaborate description of a complex Indian philosophical teaching, Sānkhya, which attempts to correlate human faculties with natural elements. The Sānkhya teachings, which seem to slightly antedate Śākyamuni Buddha, are attributed to a legendary founder, Kapila. However, its main text, discussed directly in the passage quoted by Dōgen, is the Sānkhya Kārikās (Sānkhya Verses), written by the Indian philosopher Iśvārakrishna (ca. 350–425). This text was translated into Chinese around the sixth century. See Ian McGreal, ed., *Great Thinkers of the Eastern World* (New York: HarperCollins, 1995), pp. 194–197.

118 This "Śri" probably refers to the Sānkhya philosopher Iśvārakrishna (see the preceding note). The following paragraph refers to Iśvārakrishna's one hundred thousand verses.

Kapila expounded on three kinds of pain. The first is inner pain, referring to such things as hunger and thirst. The second is outer pain, referring to the threat from tigers and wolves. The third is heavenly pain, referring to winds and rain.

He expounded a scripture of one hundred thousand verses called Sānkhya. Here this [Sānkhya school] is called the Enumerated Method. It uses twenty-five principles to clarify that the results are already within the [primordial] cause. It considers that there is a single source.[119] These twenty-five principles begin with the single [source], and from this primordial origin arises intellect [the second principle]. Before the eighty thousand kalpas passed, all was dark and unknown. [This intellect] can be simply seen as the first arising from the original indeterminate state.[120] With the power to see past ages, it constantly contemplates this [original state]. This is called the principle of darkness. This is also called the nature of the world. Living beings in the world exist depending on that primordial origin, and so it is called the original nature of the world. Also they call it natural, because it does not rely on anything. From this, intellect appears. Also this is called greatness, which is the consciousness of this indeterminate state. Then from this intellect arises personal-self mind, which is the self of arrogance, not the self of spirit self, and which is the third principle.[121]

From this personal-self mind is produced colors, sounds, fragrance, and tastes, and from these five dusts appear the five elements, which are the four great elements [earth, water, fire, wind], along with space. The dusts are minute and the great elements are coarse, but the dusts when collected produce the great elements. So it is said that from the dusts arise the great elements, and in how the great elements are produced there are some

119 This single source or primordial matter is called *prakṛti* in Sanskrit.

120 "Indeterminate state," often translated as "intermediate state," refers to the realm between lifetimes, as described, for example, in the Tibetan Book of the Dead, as well as in East Asian views of the period of transmigration between manifestations. In this case, it refers to such an intermediate state, but before any life has ever appeared. See Robert Thurman, trans., *The Tibetan Book of the Dead* (New York: Bantam Books, 1994).

121 This "personal-self mind" is our ordinary ego consciousness. "Spirit self" (Skt.: *puruṣa*) refers to the idea of an ultimate goal of evolution, which exists as a multiplicity, independent from the primordial source or from any unity.

variations. From sounds are produced the great space; from sounds and touch are produced the great wind; from colors, sounds, and touch are produced the great fire; from colors, sounds, touch, and tastes are produced the great water; and from all five dusts the great earth is produced. The earth element depends on many dusts, so its power is weakest. And finally the space element depends on the fewest dusts, so its power is the strongest. Therefore the four wheels [the first four elements] make up the world, and the space wheel is its foundation, followed by wind, fire, water, and earth.

From these five great elements are produced the eleven faculties. These include what are called the faculties of eyes and so on, which are able to perceive, and so are called the five cognizing faculties. The hands, legs, and eyes and the large and small excretory organs have the ability to function, and so are called the five active faculties. Together with mind, which is the faculty uniting all of them, there are eleven faculties. The mind is able to make everything its object, and so is called the faculty uniting all.

Each of the five cognizing faculties uses one of the great elements. So the color dusts make up the fire element, the fire element makes the eye faculty, and the eye faculty also sees the colors. Space dusts make the ear faculty, and the ear faculty hears sounds. The earth making the nose, the water making the tongue, and the wind making the body are also like this.

These twenty-four principles are possessions of the self, and all depend on this spirit self, which is thus called the principal master. This subject, along with the objects that were just discussed, make up twenty-five principles.[122]

These twenty-five principles are not the teaching of the buddhas and ancestors. If we discuss the mind of buddha ancestors, it is fences, walls, tiles, and pebbles. Their eyes are just soapberry beads. Their noses are just sections of bamboo. Their tongues are like the new crescent moon. When we study like this, how is it?

After a pause Dōgen said: I thought the barbarian's beard was red, but there is a red-bearded barbarian.

---

122 What follows this long quotation, ending "make up twenty-five principles," is Dōgen's brief comment. Perhaps Dōgen mentions at such length this abstract Indian Sānkhya philosophy as a corrective to the misguided interest of some Eiheiji monks.

A Donkey with a Vital Eye

403. Dharma Hall Discourse

Here is a story. Caoshan asked elder monk De, "A buddha's true Dharma body is like empty space, manifesting forms in response to beings like the moon in water. How do you express the truth of this response?"

De said, "It is like a donkey looking in a well."

Caoshan said, "What you have said is very good, but it is only eighty or ninety percent."

De asked, "How would you say it master?"

Caoshan said, "It is like the well looking at the donkey."[123]

The teacher Dōgen said: The donkey looks in the well; the well looks at the donkey. The well looks in the well; the donkey looks at the donkey. The appearance of the body and presence of the mind are boundless. The forms manifested in response to beings are abundant. The vigorous eye within the circle illuminates vast emptiness and wondrously penetrates the origin, even until the castle is filled with mustard seeds and the rock of ages is worn away.[124] While carrying a traveling bag by your side, why don't you write a letter home?

The Bright Grasses Meet Spring Anew

404. Dharma Hall Discourse

Here is a story. When the World-Honored One was out walking with his assembly, he pointed to the ground and said, "This is a good place to build a sanctuary."

---

123 This story appears in the Shōyōroku, case 52. See Cleary, *Book of Serenity*, pp. 219–222. Caoshan's first statement, "A buddha's true Dharma body is like empty space, responding to things and manifesting shapes like the moon in water," is from the Suvarṇaprabhāsa Sūtra (Golden Light Sutra).

124 "The vigorous eye within the circle...the rock of ages is worn away" is a quote from Hongzhi's verse commentary to case 63 of the Shōyōroku. See Cleary, *Book of Serenity*, p. 266. A castle gradually filling up with mustard seeds refers to the time it takes for a kalpa, or long age. The rock of ages similarly refers to an image for the duration of a kalpa, which lasts as long as it takes to wear away a rock measuring one cubic mile if a heavenly being flies over it once every hundred years, brushing it with its sleeves. A variation on this image involves a bird flying over Mount Everest every hundred years, brushing it with a piece of silk in its claws.

Indra took a blade of grass, stuck it in the ground, and said, "I have finished building the sanctuary."

The World-Honored One smiled.[125]

The teacher Dōgen said: The bright hundreds of grasses encounter spring again. He takes one blade and lets it function intimately. The sixteen-foot golden body erects a sanctuary. The lotus shrine has never been tainted by the mud in the water. In this hall he is the original host, and there he receives guests. Peacefully following the Buddha in walking meditation in this place, people of the Buddha way are not like those of the conditioned triple world.

A Cold Lotus
405. Dharma Hall Discourse
"Atop Mount Wutai, the clouds are making steamed rice; below the steps to the Buddha hall, a dog urinates up toward the heavens. At the top of a flagpole, dumplings are cooking; three monkeys are sorting coins in the night."[126]

The teacher Dōgen said: If you face this saying and can clearly comprehend, you are like the black dragon with the pearl who can create clouds and rain wherever it goes. Otherwise, if it is not like this, you are still delighted by the lotus in the cold of December. Study this.

Uphold the Plum Blossom Ceremony
406. Enlightenment Day Dharma Hall Discourse [1250][127]
Previous generations in Japan have transmitted Buddha's Birthday and Parinirvāṇa Day ceremonies. However, the ceremony for Buddha's attaining the way had not yet been transmitted or practiced. I first introduced it twenty years ago. From now on and through the future, transmit and practice it.

---

125 This story is in Shōyōroku, case 4. See Cleary, *Book of Serenity,* pp. 17–19.

126 "Atop Mount Wutai…" is a saying by Dongshan Shouchu, also cited by Dōgen in Dharma hall discourse 291. See volume 4, note 62.

127 For other Enlightenment Day Dharma hall discourses, see discourses 88, 136, 213, 297, 360, 475, and 506.

The teacher Dōgen repeated what he had quoted before from the Tathāgata upon his accomplishing the way, from "Three quarters..." to "...wisdom about everything in the world." Then Dōgen said the following.[128]

At this very time, students of Eihei, what do you have to say?

A branch of plum blossoms opens in the snow. It does not avail itself of the spring winds that will gradually blow.

From "Because of the virtue and benefit I created in ancient times" to "will be extinguished" the teacher again related the previous quote and then said the following.[129]

Great assembly, do you want to clearly understand the meaning of this?

After a pause Dōgen said: The world in ten directions is blessed with radiant light, and all living beings hear the Buddha preaching. The staff and okesa (monks' robes) together laugh with joy, and the monks' hall, Buddha hall, and eating bowls are delighted.

Endless Practice Amid Flames

407. Dharma Hall Discourse

The ancestral teachers have this skillful means. In the seventh tumble the eighth downfall is still not finished. Zen sleeping sticks, sitting cushions, and monks' staffs at this time become lotuses in the fire.[130]

---

128 This paragraph is a note by Gien, the compiler of this volume. Dōgen restated the following quote from Śākyamuni from Dharma hall discourse 360: "Three quarters of this night has passed; in the remaining quarter the brightness will dawn. The various kinds of conditioned and unconditioned beings all remain unmoving. At this time, the unsurpassed venerable great sage extinguishes the various afflictions, attains bodhi, and becomes known as the one with wisdom about everything in the world."

129 This paragraph is also a note by Gien. Dōgen had again repeated a quote given in Dharma hall discourse 360. The entire quote reads, "Because of the virtue and benefit I created in ancient times, everything wished for in my heart has been accomplished, my mind of samādhi has been instantly verified, and I have reached the shore of nirvāṇa. All my various enemies or foes and even the demon Pāpiyas (Māra) in the Iśvara level of the realm of desire cannot trouble me, and so they all take refuge in Buddha. This is because of the power of my virtue and wisdom. If you can courageously make diligent efforts to seek sacred wisdom, this will be attained without difficulty. Once it is attained all afflictions will be exhausted, and all your accumulated offenses and faults will be extinguished."

130 For "sleeping sticks" see note 2 above. "The eighth downfall" refers to the unending inevitability of problems in the world. Because of this, the endless practice of ancestral teachers needs to be maintained.

The Right View of Deep Snow
408. Dharma Hall Discourse
At this time snow was falling, piling high on the mountain peaks.[131]

For people studying the way, it is difficult to attain the right view, and difficult to be free of mistaken views. Even if you can cut off [views of] causal conditioning or the natural arising [of events], and views of extinction or permanence, if you fall into views such as that the world of form is great and the self is small, or that the self is great and form is small, this is still among the sixty-two false views.[132] It has been stated that space arising within great enlightenment is like a bubble emerging from the ocean. It has also been stated that empty space arises within your mind like a cloud marking the great purity. Although this is described as our Buddha's teaching, this is actually the view of self as great and form as small. If you see it like this, you are not disciples of the buddhas of the three times, and you are not the descendants of the ancestral teachers in each generation.

Since ancient times, true worthies with the mind of the way unfailingly and sincerely have totally clarified the difference between the Buddha way and divergent ways, and thereafter studied the teachings of buddhas. Because of this, the [right] view is accomplished.

I remember that Yunju asked Xuefeng, "Has the snow outside the gate melted or not?"

Xuefeng said, "Not a single flake exists, how can it melt?"

Yunju said, "It's melted."[133]

---

131 This is a note inserted by Gien, compiler of this volume.

132 The sixty-two false views are mentioned in the Lotus Sutra, chap. 2, on "Skillful Means," in which they are described as the obstacles of those hard to save, for whose sake the Buddha employs tactful means. The number sixty-two is derived from four possibilities (existence, nonexistence, both existence and nonexistence, or neither) in each of the five skandhas and in the three times (past, present, or future). To these sixty views are added the two views that matter and spirit are either the same or different. The sixty-two are listed in chapter 48 of Kumārajīva's translation of the Prajñāpāramitā Sūtra in 25,000 lines. See Hurvitz, *Scripture of the Lotus Blossom of the Fine Dharma*, p. 36.

133 This dialogue between Yunju and Xuefeng is also discussed by Dōgen in Dharma hall discourse 84, while he was still at Kōshōji in Kyoto, and where there was much less snow than at Eiheiji.

Today I, Eihei, will make comments on each statement. As to Yunju asking, "Has the snow outside the gate melted or not?" if we comment even a little in terms of past and future, we fall into the distinctions of this and that. Ultimately [beyond duality], what is it? Like this [with the snow around us], it is such.

Xuefeng said, "Not a single flake exists, how can it melt?" How did the first ancestor become Bodhidharma? This is an embarrassing scene.[134]

Yunju's saying "It's melted" provides laughter, as it fills in the ditches and blocks up the valley, with eyes and skulls covering the fields.

Remembering My Mother
409. Dharma Hall Discourse on the Memorial Morning for My Late Mother[135]

> In an abandoned village, a plum blossoms on an old bare branch.
> A snowflake falls on a fiery furnace.[136]
> The black dragon's jewel is behind the straw sandals.
> Who would regret the moon in the vast sky?

Further extending what I just said, students of Eihei, how is this?

Today this mountain monk offers some words for repaying my debt of gratitude. My monk's staff expresses it intimately for her.

Arousing the Mind amid Shifting Sands
410. Dharma Hall Discourse
I can remember, a monk asked Zhaozhou, "Without polishing, is the ancient mirror illuminating or not?"

---

134 "This is an embarrassing scene" is from Yuanwu's comment in Hekiganroku, case 1, about Bodhidharma's leaving Emperor Wu and crossing the river to north China. See Cleary and Cleary, *Blue Cliff Record*, p. 2, where it is rendered as "He can't avoid embarrassment."

135 Dōgen's mother died when he was seven, according to traditional accounts, which state that he awakened to impermanence seeing the incense arise at her funeral. Historically, not much is known with certainty about Dōgen's parents. See Dharma hall discourse 363 and note 26 above.

136 "A snowflake falling on a fiery furnace" is a simile for a patch-robed monk who has passed through a forest of thorns, from the introduction to Hekiganroku case 69. See Cleary and Cleary, *Blue Cliff Record*, p. 434.

Zhaozhou said, "The previous lives are the cause; the present life is the result."[137]

Who knows that the ancient mirror, of itself, is in the house of the buddha ancestors? The condition of the ancient mirror cannot be compared to the great perfect mirror, and cannot be compared to a crystal mirror.

Even though this is so, suppose someone asked Eihei, "Without polishing, is the ancient mirror illuminating or not?" I would simply say to him: In the birth before buddhahood, the bodhisattva will be born in Tuṣita Heaven. The Heaven of the Thirty-Three [deities] is ruled by Indra.[138] Why is this so? Great assembly, do you want to clearly understand the meaning of this?

After a pause Dōgen said: The bodhisattva arouses the mind of awakening within karmic consciousness. How could we hate or love the autumn moon or the spring wind? Do you know the land of this Sahā [Endurance] Realm or not? It is east of the world of all the grains of sand in the Ganges River.

The Undeceiving Mirror
411. Dharma Hall Discourse

I can remember, a monk asked Nanyue, "If the mirror is cast into an image, to where does the brightness return?"

Nanyue said, "Great worthy, your face before you left home, to where has it returned?"

The monk said, "After the image is completed, why does it not reflect and illuminate?"

Nanyue said, "Although it does not reflect and illuminate, it does not deceive at all."[139]

---

137 This saying by Zhaozhou is in his Recorded Sayings. See Green, *The Recorded Sayings of Zen Master Joshu,* p. 35.

138 Tuṣita Heaven is where the Bodhisattva Maitreya waits to be born as the next Buddha after Śākyamuni. The Heaven of the Thirty-Three (Skt.: Trayastrimśāḥ) is another of the six heavens of the desire realm. In Buddhist cosmology it is atop Mount Sumeru, with Indra at its center. Here this is given as simply the nature of reality, and of the reality of buddhas' manifesting.

139 Dōgen also discusses this dialogue of Nanyue in the Shōbōgenzō essay Kokyō (Ancient Mirror), written in 1241. See Nishijima and Cross, *Master Dogen's Shobogenzo,*

Twenty years ago, the situation of this story first pierced my ears. Since I realized its power, I have grasped it in my fist and never let it go. This mountain monk has a modest mountain verse.

After a pause Dōgen said:

How can the mirror of suchness be cast
    into ten thousand images?
The pure brightness has never been shattered.
Refined for ten thousand years,
    melted down a hundred thousand times,
How could it create even a bit of deception?

Eighty-Four Thousand Teachings in One Fist

412. Dharma Hall Discourse on the Fifteenth [Full Moon] Day of the First Month [1251]

Recently in the Song dynasty, people call this day's Dharma hall discourse the Original Evening Dharma Hall Discourse.[140] It seems to be an event of the mundane world, and truly not the way of the buddha ancestors. The so-called high origin, middle origin, and low origin are names from worldly texts.[141] In the Tang dynasty, Zheng Zhuhui wrote the Miscellaneous Records of the Bright Emperor, and said, "The emperor stayed in the Eastern capital, and on the full moon evening of the first month, he visited the Shangyang Palace. Candles and torches were set up and kept burning, and a tower was built sixty yards wide and fifteen feet high, decorated with colorful silks. Many jewels were hung on it, so the breezes created delightful chiming. The torches were set up in the shapes of dragon, phoenix, tiger, and leopard."

---

book 1, p. 244. A slightly different version of this story appears in the Jingde Transmission of the Lamp; see Ogata, *The Transmission of the Lamp*, p. 164.

140 The Dharma hall discourses were delivered at different times of day. Perhaps this was the first during the year given in the evening. In China, in celebration of a Daoist holiday, on the fifteenth day of the first month people sang and danced all night.

141 These names, high origin, middle origin, and low origin, refer to traditional celebrations on the evenings of the fifteenth (full moon) days of the first month, seventh month, and tenth month, respectively.

The Shiji, or Historical Annals, say, "In the Han dynasty, they lit torches for the Festival of the North Star on the full moon day of the first month."[142]

Deliberating on these things, it is very clear that these are all worldly celebrations. Monks in Great Song China say that Confucianism, Daoism, and Buddhism are one, but this is very wrong. Eighty-four thousand medicines have been offered [by Buddha], but the worldly dusts are what are treated, and the Dharma medicine is what treats them. Do you want to hear about the eighty-four thousand Dharma gates? From ancient times it is said that the collections of Śākyamuni's expounding the Dharma number up to eighty thousand. You should know that the tathāgatas in the three times without fail opened the eighty-four thousand Dharma gates.

It has been said that the eighty-four thousand Dharma gates are not outside the one mind. It has been said that the eighty-four thousand Dharma gates are not outside the four noble truths of suffering, the collection of its causes, its cessation, and the path.[143] It has been said that the eighty-four thousand Dharma gates are all contained in a square inch. It has been said that Buddha expounded the Dharma from beginning to end for the sake of living beings and placed them in a storehouse, and in this way they became eighty-four thousand.[144] It has been said that one seating of expounding the Dharma makes a storehouse, and this extends to eighty-four thousand. It has been said that Buddha on his own expounded sixty-six thousand verses making a storehouse, and this extended to eighty-four thousand. It has been said that beings are weary from eighty-four thousand sufferings due to sense desires, and therefore

---

142 The Shiji (Jap.: Shiki; Historical Annals) was written by Shima Qian (145–86 B.C.E.) and includes 130 volumes.

143 The idea of eighty-four thousand faults of sentient beings, and eighty-four thousand appropriate remedies, appears in chapter 11 of the Lotus Sutra; see Katō, Tamura, and Miyasaka, Threefold Lotus Sutra, p. 204. The first two statements about the eighty-four thousand Dharma gates are from Zhiyi's Mohe Zhiguan.

144 A "storehouse" could also be read as a basket, or *pitaka* in Sanskrit, possibly referring to the classical three baskets or Tripitaka of the Buddhist canon: the sutras, the vinaya, and the abhidharma. The passage from "It has been said that Buddha expounded the Dharma from beginning to end" to "this extends to eighty-four thousand" is from the Sutra of Great Skillful Means Repaying the Debt of Gratitude of Buddha (Jap.: Dai Hōben Butsu Hō-on Kyō), vol. 6, a text written in China.

eighty-four thousand Dharma medicines have been expounded. It has been said that expounding the precepts every half month makes a storehouse, and this extends to eighty-four thousand. It has been said that eighty-four thousand Dharma gates are included in the two skandhas [of form and mental formations]. If the substance [of the eighty-four thousand Dharma gates] is spoken, they are included in the skandha of form; if their substance is given in [abstract] names, they are included in the skandha of formations.¹⁴⁵ It has been said that from the time Buddha first aroused awakening mind until his relics were divided [to be distributed for veneration], there were eighty-four thousand Dharma teachings.

Although these previous ten presentations are as stated, I, Eihei, have not yet been released from the dens of these ten statements, and I have something further to say. The so-called eighty-four thousand Dharma gates are dropped off completely by this [immediate] Dharma. Great assembly, would you like to understand clearly why this is so?

The blinking eyes at the Deer Park [at Varanasi where Buddha first preached] vigorously drove away [delusions]. His loquacious mouth at Vulture Peak [preaching the Lotus Sutra] organized all the commotion. In grasping, he directly cut through even the tiniest hairsbreadth [of delusion]. In letting go, why would he prevent the destruction of attachment to sense objects?

Today, I, Eihei, borrow his skillful means to open the gates and universally display this for the sake of humans, heavenly beings, and the eight kinds of [mythic] beings.¹⁴⁶

Dōgen raised up his whisk and said: Look; look. The halfway and the fulfilled of provisional and genuine [teachings], the partial and complete of gradual and sudden, the three thousand great parables and eight hundred small parables, the boundless ocean of meaning, and the inexhaustible Dharma gates—they all exist on the tip of Eihei's whisk. I trust my hand

---

145 The sentence "It has been said that eighty-four thousand Dharma gates are included in the two skandhas…included in the skandha of formations" is from Vasubandhu's Abhidharma Kośa, vol. 1.

146 The eight kinds of beings, described in the Lotus Sutra assembly as well as in other sutras, are heavenly beings (Skt.: *deva*), dragons *(nāga)*, demonic wood-spirits *(yakṣa)*, fragrance spirits *(gandharva)*, fighting spirits *(asura)*, huge dragon-eating birds *(garuḍa)*, musical bird spirits *(kiṃnara)*, and huge snake spirits *(mahoraga)*.

to hold this up and take the opportunity to use it. Not blind to the eye of self, I do not doubt the tongues of all beings beneath the heavens. Thus I have heard, at one time the Buddha abided, and [the assembly] attained great liberation, faithfully receiving and humbly practicing it.[147] In each sentence I see the truth, in each phrase I go beyond the essence. There is no Dharma that is not complete, no aspiring student who is not covered within it. At just such a time, how is it?

After a pause Dōgen said: A fist lets fly a thunderbolt that covers the heavens; a grandmother bleeds drop by drop for your sake.[148]

The Perfect Moon of Practice

413. Mid-Autumn Dharma Hall Discourse [1250][149]

> Who would say that a mirror[-shaped moon] wanes
>   like a fan [closing]?
> Going here and there, this evening everyone sees
>   a complete circle.
> In the lands and seas of three thousand worlds,
>   no timepieces.
> The mouth of an eating bowl has risen to the sky.

147 "Thus I have heard, at one time the Buddha abided" is the standard beginning of sutras, spoken by Ānanda to verify Buddha's words. "Attained great liberation, faithfully receiving and humbly practicing it" is the standard ending for sutras, describing the assembly's joy at having received and being awakened by the sutra.

148 This sentence is from a poem that Dōgen's teacher, Tiantong Rujing, wrote to be calligraphed on a portrait of himself, included in Rujing's Recorded Sayings. See Dōgen's similar Verses of Praise on Portraits of Himself in volume 10 below. Rujing's saying here refers to hitting students to awaken them in the meditation hall.

149 Mid-autumn is the full moon day of the eighth month. This Dharma hall discourse is recorded out of order, as the previous discourse is from the first month of 1251.

EIHEI ZENJI GOROKU

RECORDED SAYINGS
AT EIHEIJI TEMPLE

COLLECTED BY GIEN, ATTENDANT OF DŌGEN ZENJI

E K
I ō
H R
E O
I K
  U

The One Vehicle in Daily Activity

414. Dharma Hall Discourse

Here is a story. In Hongzhou Province in China on Mount Huanglong, Huanglong Huinan, Zen Master Pujue, once said in a Dharma hall discourse, "Within the Buddha lands in the ten directions, there is only the Dharma of the one vehicle.[1] With heaven above our heads and the ground beneath our feet, how shall we expound the Dharma of the one vehicle?"

After a pause [Huanglong Huinan] said, "Opening your lacquered place mat and setting out your bowls, is this not the Dharma of the one vehicle? Holding your spoon or your chopsticks, is this not the Dharma of the one vehicle?" Then, he held up his monk's staff and said, "What is this? If you call it the Dharma of the one vehicle, your eyebrows will fall out [from lying]." [Huanglong Huinan] pounded his staff on the sitting platform and got down from his seat.

The teacher Dōgen said: Although Huanglong spoke like this, how should Eihei speak?

Then Dōgen held up his staff, pounded it once and said: What place is

---

1 "Within the Buddha lands in the ten directions, there is only the Dharma of the one vehicle" is a quote from the Lotus Sutra, chap. 2, which discusses all teachings as included through skillful means in the great One Vehicle. See Hurvitz, *Scripture of the Lotus Blossom of the Fine Dharma*, p. 34; or Katō, Tamura, and Miyasaka, *Threefold Lotus Sutra*, p. 64.

this? At the time they are thoroughly penetrated, pits, mounds, sentient beings, buddhas, and empty space, all are always without self-nature, and arise propelled by conditions. [Buddha] uses his tongue to spread out over the entire universe, and trusts his hands to display it. When our Buddha appeared, although it was not yet the evil age, because of his original vow he expounded the Dharma of the three vehicles. Because of his original vow, he also expounded the Dharma of the one vehicle. How shall we expound this Dharma of the one vehicle?

After a pause Dōgen said: When tired we sleep; when lively we practice zazen. After filled with rice, we use our chopsticks for soup and then vegetables. Isn't this the Dharma of the one vehicle? In the evening eight hundred, in the morning three thousand, life after life, age after age, eyelids are open. Kalpa after kalpa, year after year, nostrils pierced, isn't all of this the Dharma of the one vehicle?

Then Dōgen held up his staff, pounded it once, and said: What is this? If we call this the Dharma of the one vehicle, there are no horns on the ox's head. If you do not call this the Dharma of the one vehicle, there is a horn on the horse's head.

Not Understanding Mind Only
415. Dharma Hall Discourse

Here is a story. Xuansha asked Luohan [Guichen, his student], "The triple world is mind only; how do you understand this?"

Luohan [Guichen] pointed to a chair and asked Xuansha, "Teacher, what do you call this?"

Xuansha said, "Chair."

Luohan said, "Teacher, you do not understand the triple world is mind only."

Xuansha pointed to the chair and asked Luohan, "I call this bamboo and wood. What do you call it?"

Luohan said, "Guichen also calls this bamboo and wood."

Xuansha said, "If you search the entire great earth for one person who understands the Buddha Dharma, nobody can be found."[2]

---

2 This story appears in the Jingde Transmission of the Lamp, volume 21. Dōgen also discusses it in Shōbōgenzō Sangai Yuishin (The Triple World Is Mind Only), written in

These ancient worthies spoke like this, but today what shall I say?

A chair and bamboo, bamboo and a chair, are not the same and not different. [Whichever you call it,] within this there is no triple world; within the triple world there is no such thing as this. Having reached this situation, again, how is it?

After a pause Dōgen said: Even though the boundless triple world is mind only, searching for someone who understands Buddha Dharma, finally we cannot find even one. Even though the bright, clear mind-only is the triple world, searching for someone who does not understand Buddha Dharma, we cannot find even half a person.

The Samādhi of Fresh Rice
416. Dharma Hall Discourse for Inviting the [New] Tenzo
A fresh bowl full of rice has pleasant color and fragrance. Yunmen's samādhi is in every atom.[3] You should never waste a single grain. Turn both the Dharma wheel and the wheel of food with excellence. At this very time, how do you speak?

After a pause Dōgen said: Exalted music should be performed by adepts; our tradition is supported by mature elders.[4]

Plum Blossoms Do Not Know Spring
417. Dharma Hall Discourse
I can remember, a monk asked Zhaozhou, "The ten thousand things return to the one, to where does the one return?"

Zhaozhou said, "When I lived in Qingzhou I made a cotton shirt weighing seven pounds."[5]

1243. See Nishijima and Cross, *Master Dogen's Shobogenzo*, book 3, pp. 47–49. "The triple world" refers to the three realms of samsara: the desire, form, and formless realm.

3 "Yunmen's samādhi is in every atom" refers to his answer to a monk's question, "What is samādhi in every atom?" Yunmen's response, "Rice in the bowl, water in the bucket," is the subject of Hekiganroku case 50 and Shōyōroku case 99. See Cleary and Cleary, *Blue Cliff Record*, pp. 342–344; and Cleary, *Book of Serenity*, pp. 425–427.

4 The phrase we have translated as "exalted music" literally means "three *tai*," which refers to a particular musical piece. See Dharma hall discourse 116, and volume 1, note 227.

5 This dialogue, which appears in Dharma hall discourses 377 and 391, is also case forty-five of the Hekiganroku. See Cleary and Cleary, *Blue Cliff Record*, pp. 318–321.

Also a monk asked an ancient worthy, "The ten thousand things return to the one, to where does the one return?"

The ancient worthy said, "The Yellow River turns nine times."[6]

The teacher Dōgen said: These two elders spoke like this for the sake of people. But if this were me, Eihei, it would not have gone like this. Suppose someone asked, "The ten thousand things return to the one, to where does the one return?" I would simply say to him: A single staff is seven feet long.

Great assembly, do you want to understand this clearly?

After a pause Dōgen said: I want to ask the meaning of spring's coming, but even the plum blossoms do not know.

Impermanence within the Timeless

418. Dharma Hall Discourse for the Ceremony for Parinirvāṇa Day [1251]

Today the prime teacher of this Sahā world, the Great Master, the Tathāgata Śākyamuni, entered nirvāṇa between the twin sāla trees in the town of Kuśinagara. Since then, two thousand two hundred years have passed. Although this is so, our Buddha once said, "If you say I perish, you are not disciples belonging to my clan. If you say I do not perish, you are also not disciples in my clan. If you say I both perish and do not perish, you are all not disciples in my clan."

Already we are not disciples of his clan, so finally what are we called? Aren't we all practicing together alongside Śākyamuni Buddha? If we are practicing alongside him, then whom are we practicing under? Tell me, great assembly; I inquire and will see what you say. If you cannot speak, for your sake I will talk.

After a pause Dōgen said: We meet and practice under Śākyamuni Buddha. If we meet and practice under Śākyamuni, we are Śākyamuni Buddha's disciples and among his kinfolk. Those who have already become his disciples and kin include commoners and sages, icchantikas, those who have committed the five deadly crimes, and heavenly beings and humans, in immeasurable, boundless, uncountable, and unthinkable

6 The "ancient worthy" in this dialogue is Yunfeng Wenyue. This dialogue is recorded in the Continuing Record of the Lamp (Jap.: Kenchū Seikoku Zokutōroku), published in 1101.

numbers.[7] Already having reached all of them, how was the teaching established? All sentient beings having Buddha nature; the World-Honored
One opens and shows this to transform both commoner and sage. What
a pity that after the parinirvāṇa [of Buddha] this evening, all sentient beings
have no Buddha nature. This is all in the realm of commoner and sage.
What goes beyond this? Great assembly, do you want to hear about it?

After a pause Dōgen said: An old turtle always nests on a lotus.[8] An old
person frequently doubts the mirror. This is the matter of going beyond.
What is the portion of this patch-robed monk?

After a pause Dōgen said: How regrettable, the broken wooden ladle at
Vulture Peak. Though we search the great thousand worlds, there is no
handle.

The Clumsiness of Body and Mind Dropped Off
419. Dharma Hall Discourse
Dōgen drew a circle with his whisk and said: Dropping body and mind,
function without effort.

Dōgen drew another circle with his whisk and said: Body and mind
dropped off is serene but not departed.

Those of the two vehicles are distressed and fall into empty voidness;
ordinary people are attached and tangled up in discriminations.[9] Bodhisattvas arrive here and practice diligently through various modes. Buddhas
arrive here and lavishly make speeches. Their excellence surmounts the
three vehicles and their merit extends beyond ten thousand kalpas. The
moon on the water is vast and boundless, the boat oars quiet. The snow
clouds gradually gather, and the crossroads vanish. Having arrived at such
a field, again, how does it feel?

---

7 An *icchantika* is someone who is said not to possess Buddha nature, according to early
Mahāyāna teachings, particularly some branches of Yogācāra, although not subscribed to
by Dōgen. The five grave misdeeds (or five deadly crimes), leading to immediate rebirth
in hell, are killing one's father, killing one's mother, killing a saint, causing dissension in
the Sangha, and wounding a buddha.

8 "An old turtle always nests on a lotus" is from Hongzhi's verse comment to case 81 of
the Shōyōroku. See Cleary, *Book of Serenity*, p. 347.

9 "Those of the two vehicles" refers to śrāvakas and pratyekabuddhas, who through attachment to emptiness or oneness fall into nihilistic views.

After a pause Dōgen said: Great eloquence seems like stammering; great skill seems clumsy.[10]

The Three Barriers within a Single Mudrā
420. Dharma Hall Discourse
Master Huanglong [Huinan] had three barriers.[11] These are known as: How do my hands resemble Buddha's hands? How do my legs resemble a donkey's legs? Each person has their own life conditions.

I, Eihei, want to add some footnotes. "How do my hands resemble Buddha's hands?" is to say, "How do my hands resemble my hands?" and "How do Buddha's hands resemble Buddha's hands?"

"How do my legs resemble a donkey's legs?" is to say, "How do my legs resemble my legs?" and "How do a donkey's legs resemble a donkey's legs?"

"Each person has their life conditions" is to say, "Each person has each person" and "Life conditions have their life conditions."

Why do I speak like this? Great assembly, do you want to clearly understand this principle?

After a pause Dōgen said: The three thousand worlds are within this single mudrā; the meaning of each word is apparent.[12] The eighty thousand Dharma gates exist within an atom, and are endowed with all categories.

Realization in between Clouds and Waters
421. Dharma Hall Discourse
The shifting clouds drift above the mountains; the murmuring waters flow down the mountains. I question, for people in between the clouds and the waters, where do we find our self? When the mind is dropped away, the Dharma (reality) transcends seeing and hearing. When this wisdom is thoroughly investigated, the way transcends emotional thinking.

10 "Great eloquence seems like stammering; great skill seems clumsy" is from Laozi's Dao De Qing, number 45. See Wu, *Book of Lao Tzu,* pp. 163–165.

11 "Barrier" is *kan,* as in the Mumonkan kōan collection, and also has the meanings of an entryway or checkpoint at a boundary place.

12 "This single mudrā" might refer to the hand position, and thereby the posture, of zazen, which includes everything, beyond all duality, when the two hands become as one.

At this very time, how are the bodies of all of you people? From birth, both ears are aligned with the shoulders. The spiritual cloud, Lingyun [Zhiqin], was enlightened at the site of peach blossoms.[13]

The Great Profit Beyond the Marketplace
422. Dharma Hall Discourse
How do great and small benefits avoid the market place? For now, let's put aside old teacher Wang [Nanquan Puyuan] selling himself.[14] Will someone pay the price of rice from Luling?[15] If nobody will pay it, Eihei will sell by myself and buy by myself.

After a pause Dōgen said: Wish-fulfilling jewels fill the great thousands of worlds, so there is nothing more to do than sit alone beneath the bright window. If you do not know this, how many days and nights you will spend in vain? If you know, why don't you practice it?

The Flower Transmitted
423. Dharma Hall Discourse
I can remember, Huangbo asked Baizhang, "What Dharma did the previous sages present to people?"

Baizhang remained silent.

Huangbo asked, "What will descendants of later generations transmit?"

Baizhang said, "I had thought you were such a person." Then he immediately returned to the abbot's quarters.[16]

---

13 Here Dōgen is punning with the name of Lingyun, or Spirit Cloud, who is famous for awakening upon seeing peach blossoms.

14 This refers to a story in which Nanquan offered before the assembly to sell himself. When a monk responded, Nanquan said, "If I charge neither a high or low price, how will you purchase me?" See Ogata, *Transmission of the Lamp,* p. 260.

15 A monk asked Qingyuan Xingsi, "What is the meaning of the Buddha Dharma?" and Qingyuan responded, "What is the price of rice in Luling?" See Ogata, *Transmission of the Lamp,* p. 161; and Cleary, *Book of Serenity,* case 5, pp. 20–22.

16 This dialogue of Baizhang and Huangbo is in Shūmon Tōyūshū (Collection of the Essence of the Tradition of the Essential Gate), volume 4, published in 1133. This collection, though less important to his later work, was one of the main sources for Dōgen's Mana Shōbōgenzō, his early collection of three hundred cases. See Heine, *Dōgen and the Kōan*

Suppose someone asked Eihei, "What Dharma did the previous sages present to people?" I would simply say to him: I show people my sitting cushion. So it is said, "I came to this land fundamentally in order to transmit the Dharma and save deluded beings."

As to "What will descendants of later generations transmit?" I would simply tell him: I transmit it with my fist. Therefore it is said, "One blossom opens with five petals and naturally bears fruit."[17]

Awakening in a Cold Nest
424. Dharma Hall Discourse

An ancient worthy said, "The skin is completely dropped off."[18]

My late teacher [Tiantong Rujing] said, "Body and mind are dropped off."

Already having arrived here, how is it?

After a pause Dōgen said: Who says this very mind is this very Buddha? No mind, no Buddha is not the way.[19] If someone wants to know the ancestral teachers' meaning, [in the moonlight of] the old rabbit, a crane in its cold nest awakens from a dream.[20]

Work in the Triple World
425. Dharma Hall Discourse

I can remember, Dizang [Luohan Guichen] asked Mountain Master [Longji Shao]xiu, "Where are you from?"

Longji Shaoxiu said, "From the south."

Tradition, p. 11. Dōgen also cites this story as case 44 in his collection of ninety kōans with verse comments in volume 9. It is also case 2 in Mana Shōbōgenzō; see Nishijima, *Master Dogen's Shinji Shobogenzo,* p. 5.

17 "I came to this land fundamentally in order to transmit the Dharma and save deluded beings. One blossom opens with five petals and naturally bears fruit," is the verse attributed to Bodhidharma. The five petals refer to the five houses of Chan, or possibly the next five ancestors up to the sixth ancestor.

18 The statement "The skin is completely dropped off" is attributed to Yaoshan Weiyan in Shūmon Rentō Eyō (Collection of the Essence of the Continuous Dharma Lamp), published in 1189.

19 "This very mind is Buddha" and "No mind, no Buddha" are both statements by Mazu, discussed frequently by Dōgen—for example, in Dharma hall discourse 8.

20 The old rabbit is an image for the moon.

Dizang asked, "In the south these days, how is the Buddha Dharma?"
Shaoxiu said, "There is extensive deliberation."

Dizang said, "It is better for me to stay here and sow the fields, make rice balls, and eat."

Shaoxiu asked, "What will you do about the triple world?"

Dizang said, "What is it you call the triple world?"[21]

Teacher Dizang and Mountain Master Shaoxiu spoke like this, but old man Eihei also has something to say. Seeing the triple world but not in the manner of the triple world, how can entering or leaving disturb the nonexistence of [the dichotomy of] inside and outside?[22] Be that as it may, "There is extensive deliberation," but what worldly people love, how can I love?[23] Having reached here, ultimately how is it?

After a pause Dōgen said: In the spring, Teacher Dizang must work the farm quickly in order to "Stay here and sow the fields, make rice balls, and eat."

Patch-Robed Monks Arrive in Daylight
426. Dharma Hall Discourse

The ten thousand functions fully rest; the thousand sages do not take the lead.[24] My father and mother are not my intimates; the buddhas are not on my path.[25] Putting aside for now intimacy and the path, what is it that you call "mine"? Patch-robed monks in their fundamental form can arrive

---

21 This dialogue is in the Shōyōroku, case 12. See Cleary, *Book of Serenity*, pp. 51–55.

22 "Seeing the triple world but not in the manner of the triple world" is from the Lotus Sutra, chap. 16. See Hurvitz, *Scripture of the Lotus Blossom of the Fine Dharma*, p. 239. In Dōgen's Shōbōgenzō Sangai Yuishin (The Triple World Is Mind Only), he turns this statement in characteristic fashion to say that "It is best for the triple world to see the triple world." See Nishijima and Cross, *Master Dogen's Shobogenzo*, book 3, p. 44.

23 "What worldly people love, I do not love" is from Shitou Xiqian's Song of the Grass Hut. See Leighton, *Cultivating the Empty Field*, pp. 72–73.

24 "The ten thousand functions fully rest; the thousand sages do not take the lead" is a statement by Xiangyan Zhixian, from the Jingde Transmission of the Lamp. See Chang, *Original Teachings of Ch'an Buddhism*, p. 221.

25 "My father and mother are not my intimates; the buddhas are not on my path" is also from the Jingde Transmission of the Lamp, in a statement by Buddhamitra. The response of his teacher, Buddhānandi, included that it was not appropriate to seek an external

on the single vital path and stroll along. So it is said, although there is arising and perishing, there is no coming and going. Although there are classifications of stages, [such practitioners] are free of these discriminations. It is not that there is no practice-realization, only that it cannot be defiled.[26] They turn their back on the dusts and join with awakening, opening the flower and bearing fruit. After thorough investigation, all buddhas and living beings are nothing other than the genuine appearance [of reality]. Already being this genuine appearance, why are all buddhas immeasurable and boundless, and living beings limitless and inexhaustible? Great assembly, do you want to clearly understand the point of this?

After a pause Dōgen said: It is not permitted to go in the nighttime; you must arrive in daylight.[27]

A Blossoming Monk's Staff
427. Dharma Hall Discourse for Bathing Buddha [on Buddha's Birthday, 1251]
[On this day] living beings find their father and manage the family business. Sages see their teacher and become cheerful. Hibernating insects must be glad for the present auspicious happiness. As the spring proceeds we increasingly love the thundering voice. Who says that he descends from Tuṣita Heaven? Why does only Māyā [Śākyamuni Buddha's mother] have a sacred womb? With virtue and wisdom as abundant as the sands of the Ganges River, in the great thousands of worlds the udumbara blossoms.[28] Although this principle is as such, how is the house of patch-robed monks?

Buddha, and that the original mind is neither in you nor apart from you. See Ogata, *Transmission of the Lamp,* p. 19.

26 "It is not that there is no practice-realization, only that it cannot be defiled" is a quote from Nanyue Huairang, frequently cited by Dōgen. See, for example, Dharma hall discourse 3 and kōan case 59 in volume 9.

27 "It is not permitted to go in the nighttime, you must arrive with the brightness" is a response by Touzi Datong. Zhaozhou asked him, "How is it when attaining vitality after the great death?" Touzi gave this response. See Cleary and Cleary, *Blue Cliff Record,* case 41, pp. 297–300. Dōgen is pointing out that buddhas and awakening manifest right in the world of form or phenomena.

28 An udumbara is a flower that blooms once every three thousand years from a mythi-

After a pause Dōgen said: Destroying emptiness and tearing apart existence brings inexhaustible benefit. Through playing with a monk's staff, another branch sprouts.

Zhaozhou's Tea at Vulture Peak
428. Dharma Hall Discourse
Here is a story. The World-Honored One, staying with the assembly at Vulture Peak, held up and twirled an udumbara flower in front of a million beings, and announced, "I have the true Dharma eye treasury, wondrous mind of nirvāṇa, which I entrust to Mahākāśyapa." At that time, Mahākāśyapa had broken into a smile.

In ancient days, the World-Honored One wished to transmit the Dharma. In front of a million beings, he held up and twirled a flower, blinked his eyes, and announced, "I have the Dharma." [Mahākāśyapa] broke into a smile, and alone met his father.[29]

This is what I attained through study on the sitting platform, but what goes beyond that? Great assembly, do you want to understand this clearly?

After a pause Dōgen said: Do not ask what kind of livelihood is here. Zhaozhou's tea exists in India.[30]

A Hairy Turtle on Zhaozhou's Single Staff
429. Dharma Hall Discourse
After relating the story about Zhaozhou's dog having no Buddha nature, and

---

cal kind of fig tree; it is used as a symbol for the rarity of the appearance of a buddha or the Dharma.

29 This passage is unclear. The reading of the modern Japanese translators is that, after saying, "I have the Dharma," Śākyamuni continued saying that he himself "broke into a smile, and alone met his father." In that reading, Śākyamuni would be saying, in effect, that when Mahākāśyapa smiled, Śākyamuni himself also broke into a smile and met his own Buddha nature. In the previous Dharma hall discourse, 427, when Śākyamuni Buddha was born all living beings found their true father. So "father" in both these Dharma hall discourses might indicate Buddha nature or true nature. In the text it is not clear whether Dōgen is referring to Śākyamuni, Mahākāśyapa, or Dōgen himself "alone meeting his father."

30 "Zhaozhou's tea" refers to the story about his greeting newly arrived monks, asking if they had been "here" before, and offering tea whether they said they had or not. When his attendant inquired about this, Zhaozhou also suggested he have some tea. See Green, *Recorded Sayings of Zen Master Joshu,* p. 146.

then his dog having Buddha nature,[31] *the teacher Dōgen said:* Today I, Eihei, have a mountain verse:

> A turtle with hair and a rabbit with a horn
>   are not of the same kind.
> On a spring day a flower's brightness
>   is like the moon opening.
> The nature of karmic consciousness
>   together with all Buddha natures,
> Zhaozhou's single staff arrives.

The Nonduality of Buddha Nature
430. Dharma Hall Discourse

Although there are twenty-five realms of transmigration, there are situations that are most difficult to attain.[32] First is to be born so as to encounter the Buddha Dharma. Even if you have already been introduced to the Buddha Dharma, it is still most difficult to arouse bodhi mind. Already having gained entry into Buddha Dharma, furthermore abandoning parents and leaving home is most difficult to do. Even if you have left your parents and gone from your home, it is moreover most difficult to lead your six relatives to enter the Buddha way.[33] After accomplishing the way, all buddhas practice five things, one of which is to expound the Dharma for the sake of one's father and mother to help them enter the Buddha way. If the father, mother, or six relatives cause these children who are srāmaṇera, whether bhikṣus or bhikṣuṇīs, to return home to lay

---

31 This refers to the previously cited story about Zhaozhou on one occasion saying a dog has no Buddha nature because it has karmic consciousness, and at another time saying a dog does have Buddha nature because it knowingly and deliberately transgresses. See Dharma hall discourses 226 and 429; kōan case 73 in volume 9; and Cleary, *Book of Serenity,* case 18, pp. 76–80.

32 The twenty-five realms of transmigration include fourteen in the realm of desire *(kāmadhātu).* These are the six realms of heavenly beings, angry titans, humans, animals, hungry ghosts, and hell beings, as well as various other heavenly realms. In the realm of form *(rūpadhātu)* there are seven heavenly realms. There are four realms also in the formless realm *(ārūpyadhātu).* These twenty-five are described in the Mahāparinirvāṇa Sūtra.

33 The six relatives are one's father, mother, spouse, children, elder siblings, and younger siblings.

life, or lead them into causes and conditions for obstructing the Buddha way, you should know that they are bad parents, and should not be followed. If they support causes and conditions for leaving home and practicing the way, you should know that they are bodhisattva parents.

High Ancestor Caoxi [the sixth ancestor, Dajian Huineng] when he was lay practitioner Lu and left his impoverished mother, desiring to visit and study with Huangmei [Daman Hongren], provided only forty silver coins to his mother to provide for her food and clothing. Truly this is one of the most difficult things to carry out. It seems that none before or since match his stature. Finally he visited Huangmei, and for eight months spent day and night pounding rice to offer to the assembly, without sleeping or resting. How magnificent! He became a good teacher until he was eighty, and graciously was willing to be the thirty-third ancestral teacher [after Śākyamuni]. So as a result, although he was the crowning peak of all laypersons, he was able to transmit the Tathāgata's robe and Dharma. In India and China few have compared with him. We have never heard of anyone like him.

In the eighth day of the first month of the Yifeng era (676 C.E.), [Dajian Huineng] arrived at the Faxing (Dharma Nature) temple in Nanhai. In the evening he was resting on a temple walkway, and two monks were arguing about the wind and a banner. The ancestor resolved their questionings.[34]

There was a Dharma teacher named Yinzong, who regularly lectured on the Mahāparinirvāṇa Sūtra and was highly esteemed by the assembly. He appreciated the uniqueness of [Huineng's] words and invited him for further discussion. The ancestor clarified [Yinzong's questions] with his understanding of truth. Yinzong, astonished, stood up and asked, "How have you verified this?"

The ancestor immediately described the story of his attainment of the Dharma from beginning to end, and brought out the robe that had been entrusted to him, and allowed [Yinzong's assembly] to examine it and

---

34 In this famous story, one monk said the banner moved, the other said that it was the wind that moved. Huineng told them it was actually their mind that was moving. See the Platform Sutra in Price and Wong, *Diamond Sutra and The Sutra of Hui Neng*, pp. 22–23; and Cleary, *Sutra of Hui-neng*, p. 14. This story also appears in the Mumonkan, case 29; see Aitken, *Gateless Barrier*, pp. 184–188; or Cleary, *Unlocking the Zen Kōan*, pp. 141–143.

make prostrations. After Yinzong and the others had done prostrations, he asked again, "In great teacher [Daman Hong]ren's entrustment of you, what instruction did he give?"

[Huineng] said, "He only discussed Buddha nature, unfabricated without outflows, and did not comment on meditation or liberation."[35]

[Yinzong] further inquired, "Why did he not comment on meditation or liberation?"

[Huineng] said, "Dharma that is dualistic is not the Buddha Dharma. Buddha Dharma is the teaching of nonduality."

Again [Yinzong] asked, "What is it you call the Dharma of nonduality?"

[Huineng] said, "Dharma teacher, you lecture on the Mahāparinirvāṇa Sūtra and clarify Buddha nature, which is the Dharma of nonduality. As Lofty Precious King of Virtue Bodhisattva said to the Buddha, 'World-Honored One, those who violate the four prohibitory precepts, or commit the five grave misdeeds, or are icchantikas, have they severed the good roots of Buddha nature or not?'[36]

"Buddha replied, 'Lofty Precious King of Virtue Bodhisattva, there are two kinds of good roots, one permanent and the other impermanent. Buddha nature is neither permanent nor impermanent, and therefore it is never cut off. This is called nonduality. One side is good; the second side is not good. Buddha nature is neither good nor not good. Therefore it is never cut off. This is called nonduality. The [five] skandhas and the [eighteen] realms [of sense objects, faculties, and consciousnesses] ordinary people see

35 Dōgen is quoting this story from the section on Huineng in the Jiatai Record of the Universal Lamp (Ch.: Jiatai Pudenglu; Jap.: Katai Futōroku), published in 1201, one of the five main lamp transmission texts in Zen. According to Genryū Kagamishima, Dōgen does not ever cite the Platform Sutra, which he considered an unreliable text. Modern scholars have come to agree with Dōgen, based on the political agenda of the distorted account of Huineng's transmission given in the Platform Sutra. In this dialogue, Dōgen uses "Buddha nature" in exchange for the Katai Futōroku's original version, which uses the term, "seeing the nature," or kenshō. This term has been understood at times to refer to an experience of attainment of realization, which Dōgen believes is a dualistic misunderstanding and should not be emphasized. For Dōgen, Buddha nature is not something that can be seen as an object to acquire, but that must be lived and manifested.

36 Lofty Precious King of Virtue Bodhisattva appears in this dialogue from the Mahāparinirvāṇa Sūtra, chap. 23. The four prohibitory precepts are the first four of the ten grave bodhisattva precepts: not killing, not stealing, not committing sexual misconduct, and not lying. For the five grave misdeeds (five deadly crimes) and the icchantika, see (Dharma hall discourse 418) note 7 above.

dualistically, but those with wisdom clearly realize that their nature is non-dualistic. This nondualistic nature is exactly their true nature.'"

[Huineng added,] "Therefore we know that Buddha nature is exactly the Dharma of nonduality."

After hearing this, Yinzong stood up with hands joined in gasshō, and asked humbly if Huineng would become his teacher. Then Yinzong also announced to his assembly, "This layperson is a bodhisattva in the flesh. What I expound is like tiles and pebbles; what he discusses is like refined gold. Do you all believe this?"

The whole assembly made prostrations and took refuge [with Huineng]. On the day of the fifteenth, Yinzong gathered many renowned worthies, and shaved Huineng's head. On the eighth day of the second month, Huineng received the full precepts from Vinaya Master Zhiguang.

The teacher Dōgen said: Caoxi and Yinzong conversed together as teacher and student in such a manner. What the World-Honored Tathāgata and Lofty Precious King of Virtue expounded and heard was also in such a manner. This morning, I, Eihei, would like to repeat and expound this for the sake of the cloud and water assembly.

After a pause Dōgen said: To open the lock of going beyond, how is Buddha nature concerned with nonduality? All dharmas basically have no self-nature. People of today mistakenly call them oranges [north of the Huai River], or tangerines [south of the Huai River, even though they are the same fruit].[37]

Southern Buddha Nature
431. Dharma Hall Discourse
I can remember, lay practitioner Lu [later the sixth ancestor, Dajian Huineng] visited the fifth ancestor [Daman Hongren].

The [fifth] ancestor asked, "Where are you from?"

Lu replied, "I am from Lingnan in the south."[38]

---

37 For a previous use of this expression about names of oranges, see Dharma hall discourse 168.

38 Lingnan is a large section of Canton, in south China. People from Lingnan were considered provincial and ignorant. Dōgen discusses this story in his Shōbōgenzō essay on Buddha nature; see Waddell and Abe, *Heart of Dōgen's Shōbōgenzō*, pp. 72–75.

The ancestor asked, "What is it you are seeking?"

Lu said, "I seek to become a buddha."

The ancestor said, "People from the south have no Buddha nature."

Lu said, "People have south or north; the Buddha nature does not have south or north."

The ancestor realized that this person was a vessel [of Dharma], and allowed him to enter the hall for lay postulants.

Although the fifth ancestor and sixth ancestor spoke like this, I, their descendant Eihei, have a bit more to say. Great assembly, would you like to understand this clearly? Although [Lu] picked up a single blade of grass, he had not yet offered five flowers.[39]

Removing Poison Arrows in Vigorous Sitting

432. Dharma Hall Discourse

The family style of all buddhas and ancestors is to engage the way in zazen. My late teacher Tiantong [Rujing] said, "Cross-legged sitting is the Dharma of ancient buddhas. Practicing meditation (sanzen) is dropping off body and mind. Offering incense, doing prostrations, chanting nembutsu, repentance, and reading sutras are not essential; in just sitting it is finally accomplished. In zazen, first of all do not fall asleep. Even for a single moment, fearless vigor must be primary.

Our ancestral teacher said, "A young forest hermit practiced zazen alone in a forest, and became inattentive and lazy.[40] Within the forest there was a divine spirit who was Buddha's disciple. He entered into the bones of a corpse, and appeared singing and dancing. Then he chanted a verse, saying, 'Young forest bhikṣu, why did you become inattentive and lazy? If you are not afraid of my appearing in the daytime, in the night I shall come again.'

"The monk was startled and scared, and arose from sitting. He reflected and considered this, but during the night, yet again fell asleep. This spirit

---

39 The "five flowers" may refer to the five houses of Ch'an that derived from Huineng. But Dōgen's statement implies the need to see multiplicity as well as the oneness of Buddha nature.

40 This ancestral teacher is Nāgārjuna, and this story is from his Commentary on the Mahāprajñāpāramitā Sūtra (Ch.: Dazhidulun), chap. 15.

again appeared, and from the mouths of his ten heads flames burst forth. His fangs and claws were like swords, his eyes red like flames. He glared and said as he grabbed the monk, 'You lazy, inattentive bhikṣu, at this place you must not be idle and careless. Why are you like this?'

"At this time the bhikṣu had great terror and arose to consider this, and single-mindedly contemplated the teaching and attained the path of arhats. This is called the diligence from one's own strength. With the power of non-indulgence he could attain the fruit of the path."

This is so true! When there is encouragement, we can be diligent and engage the way in zazen, and the causes and conditions of the great way are ripened and fulfilled.

Furthermore, when the World-Honored One was in the world, there was a bhikṣu who considered and contemplated the fourteen difficult [questions Buddha refused to entertain], but he could not penetrate them.[41] His mind could not endure this, so, holding his robe and bowl, he went before the Buddha and asked him, "Buddha, if you can resolve for me these fourteen difficult questions, and allow my mind to understand, I will become your disciple. If you cannot resolve them, I shall seek further from other paths."

Buddha said, "Foolish person, did you originally tell me that you vowed to become my disciple only if I would answer these fourteen difficult questions?"

The monk said, "No."

The Buddha said, "You are a foolish person. Now why is it that you say that if I do not answer you will not become my disciple? I expound the Dharma for the sake of saving people from old age, sickness, and death, but these fourteen difficult questions are merely issues for contentious argument. They are of no benefit to the Dharma, but idle chatter. What

41 This story is also from Nāgārjuna's Dazhidulun, chap. 15, before the previous story. It also appears in the Pali sutta in the Majjhima Nikāya about the monk Māluṅkyāputta, the "foolish person" in this story. See Bhikkhu Ñāṇamoli and Bhikkhu Bodhi, trans., *The Middle Length Discourses of the Buddha: A Translation of the Majjhima Nikāya*, rev. ed. (Boston: Wisdom Publications, 2001), pp. 533–537; and "On What It Is Important to Know," in Henry C. Warren, trans., *Buddhism in Translation* (Cambridge: Harvard University Press, 1922, originally published 1896), pp. 117–122. The fourteen questions Buddha refused to answer are theoretical and not directed at ending suffering.

is the use of your question? Even if I answer you, your mind will not understand. Until your death these will not be resolved, and you will be unable to be liberated from birth, old age, sickness, and death.

"For example, it is like a person shot by a poisoned arrow. His family and relatives called for a doctor in order to remove the arrow and apply medicine. But the person said [to the doctor], 'Do not yet remove the arrow. First I must know your family name, hometown, parents, and age. Next I want to know where this arrow is from, who made the arrowhead, and with what kinds of wood, feathers, and iron it was made. I also want to know about what mountain's wood or animal horn the bow was made from. I also want to know where this medicine is from, and what its name is. After I have completely understood all these things, then I will allow you to remove the arrow and apply the medicine.'"

The Buddha asked this bhikṣu, "Is it possible for this person to know all of these things, and then still remove the arrow or not?"

The bhikṣu said, "It is not possible to know. If he waits until knowing all of these things he will die."

The Buddha said, "You are also like this, because the arrows of evil view, poisoned with attachment, have already entered your mind. Because you wanted to remove this arrow, you became my disciple. And yet, you do not want to remove the arrow, but only want to seek after such things as whether the world is permanent or impermanent, or whether it is limited or boundless. Before you can attain what you seek, you will lose your wisdom life, you will die like an animal, and will throw yourself into black darkness."

The bhikṣu was ashamed, deeply appreciated Buddha's words, and immediately attained the path of arhats.

These days we are very remote from the time of sages, and we should lament in sadness. This is because some two thousand years after the Tathāgata's parinirvāṇa, people's arrows have not been removed, and none of Buddha's disciples have become forest spirits to encourage my friends. What shall we do about this? Although this is so, we should not spend our days and nights in vain. We should engage the way in zazen as if extinguishing flames from our heads. Buddhas and ancestors, generation after generation, face-to-face transmit the primacy of zazen. Because of this, the World-Honored One engaged the way in upright sitting for six years.

First he did zazen, day after day, night after night, and after that he expounded the Dharma. The founding ancestor at Mount Song [Bodhidharma] faced the wall for nine years, and now his descendants have spread throughout the world. Thus the great way of the buddha ancestors has been transmitted to this mountain as the fortune and the joy for people of our time. Shouldn't we practice it?

Zazen is dropping off body and mind. It is not the four formless absorptions, nor the four dhyāna.[42] Even the ancient sages did not comprehend it, so how could it be assessed by ordinary people? Suppose someone asked me, "What is Eihei's meaning in saying this?" I would simply say to him: During the summer, the lotus blossom opens toward the sun.[43] Suppose he says, "This is what we can attain through study on the sitting platforms. What is it that goes beyond the buddhas and ancestors?"

After a pause Dōgen said: The nose is aligned with the navel, the ears aligned with the shoulders.

The Meaning of the Cypress Tree
433. Dharma Hall Discourse
I can remember, a monk asked Zhaozhou, "What is the meaning of the ancestral teacher [Bodhidharma] coming from the west?"

Zhaozhou said, "The cypress tree here in the garden."

The monk said, "Master, do not instruct people using objects."

Zhaozhou said, "I am not instructing anyone by using objects."

The monk said, "What is the meaning of the ancestral teacher coming from the west?"

Zhaozhou said, "The cypress tree here in the garden."[44]

42 The four *dhyāna* are meditation or trance states that were practiced before Buddha's time and also by Śākyamuni. In these practices one achieves lofty states of nonattachment, but they are still part of the conditioned realm, and not liberation in the Buddhist sense. The character for *dhyāna* is the same that was adopted for "Chan," or "Zen" in Japanese, but here refers to the original dhyānic states rather than meditation generally.

43 "During the summer" might imply during the summer practice period. This Dharma hall discourse was given sometime near the beginning of the summer *ango* practice period in 1251.

44 This story of Zhaozhou and the cypress tree is widely quoted. Dōgen cites it in Dharma hall discourse 488 in volume 7; as kōan case 45 with his verse comment in volume 9; in

The teacher Dōgen said: Homage to the ancient Buddha Zhaozhou, who settled the essential meaning of the coming from the west.[45] The meaning of the ancestral teacher's coming from the west is the cypress tree in the garden. Not using objects to instruct people, how did he demonstrate it with the cypress? At this very time, how do you distinguish between this and that? You Zen worthies, do you wish to clearly understand this point?

After a pause Dōgen said: The ancient cypress stands in Zhaozhou's garden. From south to north, who would doubt orange and tangerine [as two names for the same thing]?[46]

The Moon Shining on All Beings and Oneself
434. Dharma Hall Discourse
The family style of all buddhas and ancestors is to first arouse the vow to save all living beings by removing suffering and providing joy. Only this family style is inexhaustibly bright and clear. In the lofty mountains we see the moon for a long time. As clouds clear we first recognize the sky. Cast loose down the precipice, [the moonlight] shares itself within the ten thousand forms. Even when climbing up the bird's path, taking good care of yourself is spiritual power.

The Purity of the Present Dream
435. Memorial Dharma Hall Discourse for Master Butsuju [Myōzen][47]
When wishing to open and display the true Dharma eye treasury, there

---

informal meeting 9 in volume 8; and as number 119 in Mana Shōbōgenzō, his collection of three-hundred kōans without comment (see Nishijima, *Master Dogen's Shinji Shobogenzo*, p. 166). The monk's statement might also be understood as "Master, do not indicate the subject using objects." This dialogue also appears in the Recorded Sayings of Zhaozhou (see Green, *Recorded Sayings of Zen Master Joshu*, p. 16); in the Shōyōroku, case 47 (see Cleary, *Book of Serenity*, pp. 196–200); and in Mumonkan, case 37 (see Aitken, *Gateless Barrier*, pp. 226–230; and Cleary, *Unlocking the Zen Kōan*, pp. 167–169).

45 "Homage" is *namu*, which also means to take refuge.

46 For Dōgen's use of orange and tangerine (our translations of two Chinese words for the same Chinese citrus fruit) for different names of the same thing, see Dharma hall discourses 168 and 430.

47 Butsuju Myōzen, a disciple of the Japanese Rinzai founder Eisai, was Dōgen's teacher in Japan before he went to China. Myōzen accompanied Dōgen to China but died at Tiantong monastery in 1225.

is the gate of the first meaning and the gate of the second meaning: holding up a whisk, raising a fist, headtops, eyeballs, nostrils, and legs. *After throwing his staff down the steps from the high seat Dōgen said:* These are all the helpful implements of the gate of the second meaning. Now tell me, what is the gate of the first meaning?[48] This mountain monk today will open and demonstrate the gate of the first meaning of the buddha ancestors, and I dedicate the merit produced by this to my late teacher, the great master [Butsuju Myōzen].

Thereupon Dōgen said: Venerable Mahākāśyapa asked Venerable Ānanda, "Which single verse gave rise to the thirty-seven elements and all the teachings of Buddha?"[49]

Ānanda said, "Not performing any evil, respectfully practicing all good, purifying one's own mind, this is the teaching of all buddhas."

Mahākāśyapa agreed.

Great assembly, do you want to clearly understand this principle?

After a pause Dōgen said: The most profound and wondrous message of the buddha ancestors is exactly like the present dream, never having awakened. Younger and elder brothers are both children born from Buddha's mouth, and his single verse is solely transmitted as the fundamental, grateful filial conduct.[50]

48 Traditionally in Buddhism, dating back to Nāgārjuna's first truth and second truth, the gate of the first meaning refers to ultimate truth, and the gate of the second meaning refers to conventional truth. Teaching implements used by Zen masters are usually considered gateways to the ultimate truth.

49 This refers to the thirty-seven elements or wings of bodhi. These are discussed by Dōgen in his Shōbōgenzō essay, Sanjushichi Hon Bodai Bunpo (Thirty-Seven Elements of Awakening). See Nishijima and Cross, *Zen Master Dogen's Shobogenzo*, book 4, pp. 1–27. These thirty-seven supports for enlightenment are mentioned in the Lotus Sutra, chap. 27; see Hurvitz, *Scripture of the Lotus Blossom of the Fine Dharma*, p. 325. This story of Mahākāśyapa and Ānanda is from the Ekottara Āgama, or Aṅguttara Nikāya, volume 1 (Jap.: Zōitsu Agon Kyō).

50 "Younger and elder brothers" refers here to Ānanda and Mahākāśyapa as fellow disciples of Śākyamuni, even though Ānanda later was considered Mahākāśyapa's disciple. "Solely transmitted" is *tanden,* implying that this verse is the single thing transmitted, with single-mindedness, from one person to another.

Washing a Painting of Breakfast
436. Dharma Hall Discourse
I can remember, a monk asked Zhaozhou, "This student has just entered
the monastery. Please, master, give me some instruction."
    Zhaozhou asked, "Have you eaten breakfast?"
    The monk said, "I have eaten."
    Zhaozhou said, "Wash your bowls."[51]

    The ancient Buddha Zhaozhou has spoken like this. Now I, Eihei, have
a mountain verse.
    After a pause he said:
    Green bamboo and plum blossoms are a painting.
    Bottle gourd vines are entwined with gourds.
    The barbarian's beard is red,
        and there is also a red-bearded barbarian.[52]
    Having eaten breakfast, wash your bowls.

The Results of Wrong Views
437. Dharma Hall Discourse
For people who study the Buddha Dharma, how to use the mind and
deport oneself physically is very difficult. Commoners and outsiders both
may engage in zazen. However, the zazen of commoners and outsiders is
not the same as the zazen of buddha ancestors. This is because the zazen
of outsiders includes mistaken views, attachments, and arrogance. If your
understanding is the same as that of outsiders, then even if your body and
mind suffer and toil, in the end it will not be beneficial. Furthermore, if
[your view] is the same as those who have committed the five grave mis-

---

51 This story appears in The Jingde Transmission of the Lamp (see Ogata, *Transmission
of the Lamp*, p. 353); in Shōyōroku, case 39 (see Cleary, *Book of Serenity*, pp. 171–172); and
in Mumonkan, case 7 (see Aitken, *Gateless Barrier*, pp. 54–59, and Cleary, *Unlocking the
Zen Kōan*, pp. 39–41). Dōgen cites this also as number 67 in his Mana Shōbōgenzō; see
Nishijima, *Master Dogen's Shinji Shobogenzo*, p. 94.

52 For bottle gourds, see Dharma hall discourse 166. For the red-bearded barbarian, see
Dharma hall discourse 62 and voume 1, note 137.

deeds, or the same as icchantikas, how can this be the body and mind of Buddha Dharma?[53]

Once the World-Honored One was staying at Vulture Peak in Rājagṛha together with five hundred bhikṣus. At that time, Devadatta caused disruption in the Sangha, injured the Tathāgata's foot, made Ajātaśatru capture and kill his father the king, and also himself killed arhats and bhikṣuṇīs. Then within the great assembly he put forth explanations for his conduct, saying, "Where there is evil, from what does evil arise? Who makes this evil and receives its consequence? I myself do not receive the results from this evil."[54]

At that time there were many bhikṣus who entered the city of Rājagṛha to beg for food, and they heard people saying, "The foolish person Devadatta was in the great assembly and asked, 'Where there is evil, from what does evil arise? Who makes this evil and receives its consequence?'" At that time, those many bhikṣus, after eating, gathered up their robes and bowls, put their bowing cloths over their right shoulders, went to where the World-Honored One was, made prostrations at his feet, and sat facing him. Then those many bhikṣus said to the World-Honored One, "The foolish Devadatta was in the great assembly and spoke this way, 'Doing evil is without blame. Blessed actions have no reward. There is no result received from doing good or evil.' What do you think?"

At that time the World-Honored One declared to those bhikṣus, "If there is evil conduct, there is retribution. All good and bad actions have their recompense. If the foolish Devadatta knew that there were consequences to good and evil, he would be withered with thirst, and grieve and lament his unhappiness. Boiling blood would spurt from the orifices of his face. Because Devadatta does not know about the retribution from good and bad deeds, therefore in front of the great assembly, he spoke saying, 'There is no retribution for good and evil; misconduct is without blame; virtuous actions bring no fortune.'" At that time the World-Honored One expounded this verse, "Foolish people clarify their own view that

---

53 For the five grave misdeeds and for icchantikas, see Dharma hall discourse 430, and note 7 above.

54 This story about Devadatta is from Ekottara Āgama, or Aṅguttara Nikāya, volume 5 (Jap.: Zōitsu Agon Kyō). Devadatta is here misapplying the teaching of no-self to rationalize that there is nobody who commits or suffers from misdeeds.

there is no results to evil conduct. I now clearly know the retribution for good and bad. Therefore, all you bhikṣus, depart far from evil. Do not become tired of good actions. All bhikṣus should study this."

At this time, all the bhikṣus, hearing the Buddha's preaching, were joyful and practiced respectfully. The World-Honored One again spoke to the bhikṣus, declaring, "When Devadatta had committed the five grave misdeeds, his body was destroyed and life finished, and he was born within the terrible Avīci Hell."[55]

Because of this we should know that, to get rid of wrong views, we do not think or say, "There is no retribution for good and bad deeds. Where there is evil, from what does evil arise? Who makes this evil and receives its consequences?" Speech like this is an evil view, and certainly the Buddha Dharma will be eliminated from your body and mind. If the Buddha Dharma is extinguished in body and mind, you cannot engage the way of zazen of the buddha ancestors.

My late teacher Tiantong [Rujing] said, "Sanzen (practicing Zen, or zazen) is dropping off body and mind." Already having dropped body and mind, definitely you will not have mistaken views, attachments, or arrogance. I sincerely pray on behalf of all of you.

The Importance of Practicing with Good Friends
438. Dharma Hall Discourse
From ancient times, people who study Buddha Dharma either reside alone in grass huts or else practice with others in monasteries. People who reside alone are often haunted by various demons and spirits, whereas those who practice together rarely are disturbed by demons such as Pāpiyas.[56] Before having clarified the passageways and blockages within the Buddha way, it is vain and extreme folly to maintain a solitary dwelling.

---

55 Buddhist legend is that Devadatta fell into a pit immediately after injuring the Buddha, although historically it is known that he actually outlived Śākyamuni, and Devadatta's teaching lineage survived in India until the seventh century c.e. Avīci Hell is the worst, most dreadful of the hell realms in Buddhist cosmology, where those who have committed any of the five grave misdeeds sojourn for a very long time.

56 The Chinese characters we translate as "various demons and spirits" include general and specific kinds of spirits, including one with four legs and a human face emanating from

How could this not be a mistake? Now, always practicing the way by staying day and night on the long platform in the monastery, demons cannot disturb us, and evil spirits cannot haunt us. Truly we are good spiritual friends and excellent companions.

Then Dōgen said: Here is a story. Once a monk asked Zhaozhou, "Master, I've heard that you intimately knew Nanquan. Is that so?"

Zhaozhou said, "In Zhen Province they raise large radishes."[57]

The ancient Buddha Zhaozhou has spoken like this, but fully understanding what Zhaozhou said is impossible. Today, suppose a monk asked me, Eihei, "Master, did you intimately know Tiantong [Rujing] or not?" I would say to him: Eihei's staff is from an old plum tree.[58]

Buddha Nature beyond Conditions
439. Dharma Hall Discourse
All tathāgatas are without Buddha nature, but at the same time, previously they have fully accomplished true awakening. Bodhisattvas studying the way should know how Buddha nature produces the conditions for Buddha nature.[59]

Awakening Shines through All Things
440. Dharma Hall Discourse
Already being an iron man with copper head, why not be the main beam

---

mountains or forests, and another spirit that eats the brains of corpses. "Pāpiyas" is another name for Māra, the demonic spirit who tempted Buddha.

57 This story appears in the Recorded Sayings of Zhaozhou (see Green, *Recorded Sayings of Zen Master Joshu*, pp. 17); and in the Hekiganroku, case 30 (see Cleary and Cleary, *Blue Cliff Record*, pp. 191–193).

58 Tiantong Rujing spoke often about plum blossoms.

59 The second sentence might also be read as follows: "Bodhisattvas studying the way should understand. How could Buddha nature produce the conditions for Buddha nature?" This Dharma hall discourse might be interpreted in a variety of ways. In his Shōbōgenzō essay "Buddha Nature," Dōgen discusses Buddha nature as existing or not existing, in terms of "being Buddha nature" and "non-being Buddha nature." In the first sentence in this Dharma hall discourse, Dōgen refers to "non-being Buddha nature." The second sentence, "Buddha nature produces the conditions for Buddha nature," might imply that there is no such thing as Buddha nature, since a thing cannot be its own cause. It also implies Buddha nature being made into an object, separate from itself as a subject. In terms of "being Buddha nature," this sentence might also be interpreted as indicating

for a magnificent structure?[60] A wish-fulfilling jewel and either fireflies, fireworks, or the sun [facing it] do not obstruct each other.[61] At this very time, how is it? Great assembly, do you want to clearly understand the meaning of this?

After a pause Dōgen said: Loving emptiness and hating existence is not the way. Why would buddha ancestors want such delusion again? Do not wish to become Brahma or Indra, but simply seek for unsurpassed awakening.

The Day Spring Arrived

441. Dharma Hall Discourse on the Memorial Day for Zen Master, Great Teacher Myōan [Eisai] Senkō, Former Sōjō Hōin of the Second Rank[62]
The teacher [Dōgen] first studied with master Butsuju [Myōzen], who was a student of Myōan [Eisai].[63]

Here is a story. My teacher's teacher [Eisai] asked his teacher Xuan [Huaichang], "When this student does not think in terms of good or bad, how is it?"

Xuan said, "The first dawning of your original life."[64]

Eisai said, "If this is so, I will never depart from this day."

Xuan said, "If so, nothing prevents you from departing today."

Eisai made a prostration.

Xuan said, "Facing south, see the North Star."

---

that Buddha nature is unconditioned, not arising from any objective condition beyond itself. See Waddell and Abe, *Heart of Dōgen's Shōbōgenzō*, pp. 59–98; and also Dharma hall discourse 429 and note 31 above.

60 "Iron man" and "Copper head" are expressions for settled practitioners with great determination.

61 Wish-fulfilling jewels, or *maṇi* jewels, are transparent so they absorb all kinds of light and allow it to pass through them.

62 Myōan Eisai was the founder of Japanese Rinzai Zen. Dōgen may have met Eisai as a young monk. *Sōjō* was the highest office and *hōin* also an important position in the government's Office of Monastic Affairs overseeing all monastic appointments. Eisai's memorial day was the fifth day of the seventh month, in this case, in 1251.

63 "The teacher [Dōgen] first studied with Master Butsuju [Myōzen], who was a student of Myōan" is a note by Gien, the compiler of this volume. Myōzen, Dōgen's early teacher, accompanied Dōgen to China, and died there.

After a pause Dōgen said: The ancestral teacher's first dawning of his original life is the complete renewal of breaking into a smile.[65] Without relying on peach blossoms or green bamboo, on this day, the mulberry of Japan encountered spring.[66]

Completion of a Dharma Year

442. Dharma Hall Discourse Closing the Summer Practice Period
[Seventh Month, Fifteenth Day, 1251]
After three months of protecting our lives without departing the monastery, the completion of another Dharma year has come. Now, striking the wooden sounding block on the bare ground, patch-robed monks at this time open their traveling bags to go back out into the world.[67]

The Excellence of Rice Baskets and Water Buckets

443. Dharma Hall Discourse
Even if you have an iron eye or a copper eye, still you are a person sighing.[68] When you thoroughly study rice baskets and water buckets, finally you will be able to express a little bit.

I can remember, once a monk asked Baizhang, "What is the most excellent matter?"

Baizhang said, "Sitting alone on Daxiong Peak."[69]

---

64 "Original life" is *honmyō,* which also is used for the Chinese astrological animal for one's year of birth. "First dawn," or *genshin,* also is an astrological term used in Chinese divination. In this dialogue these terms are apparently used to refer to true self or original face.

65 "Breaking into a smile" refers to Mahākāśyapa's smile that occasioned his transmission of Śākyamuni's true Dharma eye treasury. See note 29 above.

66 In Chinese legend, a giant mulberry tree was said to grow in the eastern island of Japan. Here Dōgen is referring poetically to Eisai as the first who transmitted Zen in Japan.

67 The wooden sounding block here is the *tsui chin,* a thin wooden block a few feet high, with a small wooden block above it, set next to the altar in the monks' hall, and sounded to make announcements. The "traveling bag," or literally "cloth bag" (Jap.: *hotei*), was used as the name of the legendary tenth-century Chan monk who became the model for the fat laughing Buddha in Chinese temples, and who is considered an incarnation of Maitreya, the future Buddha.

68 "Even if you have an iron eye or a copper eye" is from the commentary to the Hekiganroku, case 1. See Cleary and Cleary, *Blue Cliff Record,* p. 7.

69 Daxiong, or Great Bravery, is another name of Mount Baizhang, where this master lived and taught.

Suppose someone were to ask me, Eihei, "What is the most excellent matter?" I would simply tell him: Giving a Dharma hall discourse on Mount Kichijō.[70]

The Excellent Continuity of Inhale and Exhale
444. Dharma Hall Discourse

I can remember, Ānanda said, "Today when we left the town, I saw a most unusual thing."

The World-Honored One asked, "What unusual thing did you see?"

Ānanda said, "When we entered the town I saw a bunch of musicians dancing. Upon leaving the town, I saw they had all vanished."[71]

The World-Honored One said, "Yesterday I also saw an unusual thing."

Ānanda said, "I wonder what unusual thing the World-Honored One saw."

The World-Honored One said, "When I entered the town I saw musicians dancing. Leaving the town, I again saw musicians dancing."

The World-Honored One and Ānanda both saw the unusual. Although the musicians were the same, their existence and disappearance were different. This morning, suppose someone were to ask me, Eihei, "Teacher, do you also see an unusual thing or not?" I would say to him: I do not leave or enter the town, and I do not see musicians dancing, but I also see that there is an unusual thing.

Suppose someone were to ask, "Teacher, what unusual thing do you see?" I would tell him: Yesterday there was the leaving and entering of inhaling and exhaling. This morning as well, there is this leaving and entering.

---

70 Mount Kichijō, or Auspicious Mountain, was the mountain name given by Dōgen to Eiheiji.

71 "They had all vanished" is literally "they were not permanent." This story is from Shūmon Rentō Eyō lamp anthology, volume 1.

Returning from the Cage of Dharma
445. Dharma Hall Discourse
Holding up a flower and breaking into a smile, a fish plays in a net; making three prostrations and transmitting the robe, a bird enters a cage.[72] Penetrating the causes and conditions of all phenomena, return to make your livelihood within the black mountain.[73]

The Difference between Buddhas and Ancestors
446. Dharma Hall Discourse
Buddhas and ancestors should not be confused with each other. Those called buddhas are the seven buddhas. The seven buddhas include the three buddhas within the kalpa of Adornment: Vipaśyin Buddha, Śikhin Buddha, and Viśvabhū Buddha. In the Wisdom kalpa there are four buddhas: Krakucchanda Buddha, Kanakamuni Buddha, Kaśyāpa Buddha, and Śākyamuni Buddha.[74] Outside of these, nobody can be called a buddha. It is the case that, although there were many disciples remaining who received transmission of the Dharma treasury from Vipaśyin Buddha, we call them ancestral teachers or bodhisattvas. We never mistakenly call them buddhas or world-honored ones. When Śikhin Buddha appeared in the world, he unfailingly was called a buddha. This is because he completed his practice throughout many kalpas. Up through and after Śikhin and Viśvabhū Buddhas, during their True Dharma and Semblance Dharma ages, it was also like this.

During the Wisdom kalpa, although Krakucchanda Buddha also had many disciples who received transmission of the Dharma treasury and

---

72 "Holding up a flower and breaking into a smile" refers to the transmission from Śākyamuni to Mahākāśyapa. "Making three prostrations and transmitting the robe" refers to the second ancestor, Dazu Huike, becoming successor to Bodhidharma.

73 "The black mountain" refers to the demon cave in the black mountain, often as a trap for practitioners attached to emptiness. But here it indicates bodhisattvic reentry into the karmic world of samsāra. At the end of Shōbōgenzō Ikka no Myōju (One Bright Pearl) Dōgen says, "Forward steps and backward steps in a demon's black-mountain cave are just the one bright pearl itself." See Waddell and Abe, *Heart of Dōgen's Shōbōgenzō*, p. 37; and Cleary, *Shōbōgenzō Zen Essays by Dōgen*, p. 62.

74 These seven are said to be the buddhas of the past ages, ending with Śākyamuni Buddha, the seventh. In Japanese these buddhas' names are Bibashi, Shiki, Bishafu, Kuruson, Kunagonmuni, Kashō, and Shakamuni.

succeeded to and maintained the Buddha Dharma, none of them were ever called buddhas. With Kanakamuni Buddha's appearance in the world, he unfailingly was referred to as a buddha, a world-honored one. Up through Kaśyāpa Tathāgata this was also the case, and now with the teaching of Śākyamuni Buddha, this is also true.

Venerable Mahākāśyapa was the first ancestor in India. Bodhidharma was the twenty-eighth ancestor. Venerable Mahākāśyapa was endowed with thirty marks, lacking only the white curling hair [on the forehead, emitting light], and the protuberance on the headtop.

Buddha was abiding in Kāraṇḍa Venuvana monastery together with five hundred monks. When Mahākāśyapa was begging for food, he arrived where Buddha was and sat facing him. The Buddha said, "You are very aged, your intensity decreased and faculties weakened. You should abandon begging rounds and the twelve dhūta austere practices, including henceforth accepting invitations to receive food [in laypeople's homes] and accepting offerings of additional robes."[75]

Mahākāśyapa said, "I will not follow Buddha's instruction. If the Tathāgata had not fulfilled buddhahood, I would have become a pratyekabuddha. The teaching of pratyekabuddhas is to practice throughout one's whole life by doing the austere practice of remaining in a remote, quiet place."[76]

The Buddha said, "Very good; very good; this has abundant benefits. If Mahākāśyapa does these austere practices while in this world, my Dharma will remain for a long time and will increasingly benefit humans and heavenly beings. The three evil destinies will perish, and the ways of the three vehicles [śrāvakas, pratyekabuddhas, and bodhisattvas] will be fulfilled."

---

75 The twelve austere practices, *dhūta* in Sanskrit, also include only wearing material discarded at gravesides, living under a tree, eating only one meal a day, and never lying down, even to sleep at night. The full list is itemized by Dōgen in Shōbōgenzō Gyoji (Continuous Practice). See Francis Cook, *How to Raise an Ox: Zen Practice as Taught in Zen Master Dōgen's Shōbōgenzō* (Boston: Wisdom Publications, 2002), pp. 131–132; or Tanahashi, *Enlightenment Unfolds*, p. 132. This and the following stories about Mahākāśyapa are quoted by Dōgen from Zhiyi's commentary on the Lotus Sutra, although they all appear in the Agamas, the early pre-Mahāyāna sutras. See Zenno Ishigami, ed., *Disciples of the Buddha*, trans. Richard Gage and Paul McCarthy (Tokyo: Kōsei, 1989), pp. 35–36.

76 "The austere practice of remaining in a remote, quiet place," alone or with only a few monks rather than in a large monastery, is the first of the twelve *dhūtas*.

Another time, Mahākāśyapa heard heavenly beings refer to him as Buddha's teacher. He arose and made a prostration at [Śākyamuni] Buddha's feet and said, "Buddha, you are my teacher; I am your disciple." When Mahākāśyapa uttered these words, the doubts of human and heavenly beings were dispersed. Even though he was endowed with such virtues, we do not call Mahākāśyapa a buddha.

Later, when Mahākāśyapa had been following austere practices for a long time so that his hair and beard had grown long and his robes were tattered, he went to visit Buddha. All the monks regarded him with contempt. Buddha requested that Mahākāśyapa share his seat and that they sit side by side. Mahākāśyapa refused. Buddha said, "I stay in the fourth dhyāna in my meditation, putting my mind at rest from beginning to end but without losing awareness, and Mahākāśyapa is also like this.[77] I have great compassion and benevolence, including all beings, and you are also like this, with compassionate body and nature. My great compassion saves all sentient beings, and you are also like this. I have four divine samādhis: the first, beyond appearance; the second, immeasurable mind; the third, accumulation of purity; and the fourth, without backsliding, and you are also like this. I have six spiritual powers, and you are also like this. I have four settled minds: the first is settled meditation; the second, settled knowledge; the third, settled wisdom; and the fourth, settled in precepts, and you are also like this."

Then a brahman asked Buddha, "Yesterday a brahman came to my house. Who was that?"

The Buddha pointed to Mahākāśyapa. Again he inquired, "But he is a monk, not a brahman."

Buddha said, "I know the regulations of both monks and brahmans and Mahākāśyapa does as well. Mahākāśyapa's virtue is no different from mine. Why should he not sit with me?"

Hearing all of Buddha's praises, the monks were astonished, their hair standing on end.

---

77 The *dhyāna* were the pre-Buddhist Indian meditations, with four stages of increasingly refined nonattachment. The fourth is the highest mental state in the conditioned world. In China this word *dhyāna* was also used more generally for meditation, and the name Chan in China, pronounced Zen in Japan, came from this word.

The World-Honored One then related their previous causes and conditions [in past lives] in ancient times when there was a sage king named Murdhajāta, who was highly talented, beyond common people. The deity Indra, valuing his virtue, sent a thousand chariots and then went to the gate of his heavenly palace and received the king. When Indra went out to greet him, he shared the same seat with the king. After greatly enjoying being together, Indra sent the king back to his palace. In those ancient times, Mahākāśyapa [as Indra] asked me [as the king] to sit together with him on a seat of birth and death. I now have attained buddhahood, and with the seat of true Dharma, I repay his former meritorious deed."[78]

When he was sitting facing Buddha, heavenly beings referred to Mahākāśyapa as Buddha's teacher. Although he was endowed with such virtue, he could not yet be called a buddha. Furthermore, in this degenerate age, people without even a single virtue inappropriately proclaim themselves to be buddhas, and thereby undeniably slander Buddha, Dharma, and Sangha. How could these ignorant fools avoid falling down into the three evil realms?

For twenty-seven generations from Mahākāśyapa until Bodhidharma, there were either arhats or bodhisattvas who transmitted the true Dharma eye treasury of the Buddha, the World-Honored One, and yet they were not referred to as buddhas. This is because only after fulfilling the practice of buddhas does one become a buddha. The ancestors' understanding is complete and they succeed to the Dharma. But the awakening that is the fruit of buddhahood is not fulfilled readily. Those who clearly understand this point can truly be successors to the buddha ancestors. To become a buddha, one must definitely pass through three asaṃkhya (immeasurable) great kalpas; or must definitely pass through incalculable, countless, unthinkable kalpas; or else must definitely pass through one moment of thought.[79] Although these three [time periods] are not the

---

78 Murdhajāta (Jap.: Bundakatsu) was said to be a previous incarnation of Śākyamuni and to have been born from his mother's head. In a very different version of the story cited here by Dōgen, Murdhajāta is said to have been expelled from Indra's heavenly palace after having aroused the ambitious desire to succeed Indra as ruler of heaven.

79 This "one moment of thought" echoes Zhiyi's teaching that there are three thousand thoughts in one moment. For Dōgen, one moment can include immeasurable kalpas.

same, [fulfilling buddhahood] is neither difficult nor easy, and is neither a far distant time nor a sudden instant of time. Some fulfill buddhahood within a fist; some fulfill buddhahood at the top of a monk's staff; some fulfill buddhahood on the headtop of a patch-robed monk; and some fulfill buddhahood within the eyeball of a patch-robed monk. Although this is so, one who becomes a buddha invariably has received a former Buddha's prediction in regards to the [new Buddha's] kalpa, name, land, disciples to be taught, longevity, True Dharma age, and Semblance Dharma age. Ancestral teachers also are given predictions by these buddhas, but this should not cause confusion. Clearly understanding this point is exactly the entrustment of the true Dharma eye treasury wondrous mind of nirvāna of buddhas and ancestors. Great assembly, do you want to clearly understand the meaning of this?

After a pause Dōgen said:

> Unfailingly sweeping away all of great empty space,
> Ten thousand distinctions and a thousand gaps
>   are fully exposed.
> A lion teaches her cubs the secrets of lions.
> All equally remain within a painting.

Beyond Knowing and Not Knowing

447. Dharma Hall Discourse

I can remember, Guifeng Zongmi said, "The quality of knowing is the gateway of all excellence."

Zen Master Huanglong Sixin [Wuxin] said, "The quality of knowing is the gateway of all evil."

Later students have recited what these two previous worthies said without stopping up to today. Because of this, ignorant people have wanted to discuss which is correct, and for hundreds of years have either used or discarded one or the other saying. Nevertheless, Zongmi's saying that knowing is the gateway of all excellence has not yet emerged from the pit of those outside the way. What is called knowledge is certainly neither excellent nor coarse. As for Huanglong [Sixin]'s saying that knowing is the gateway of all evil, what is called knowledge is certainly neither evil nor good.

Today, I, Eihei, would like to examine those two people's sayings. Great assembly, would you like to clearly understand the point of this?

After a pause Dōgen said: If the great ocean knew it was full, the hundreds of rivers would all flow upstream.

A Pure Autumn Moon
448. Mid-Autumn Dharma Hall Discourse [Full Moon of the Eighth Month, 1251]
Yunmen's sesame cake hangs up in the sky, called the circle of the full moon of autumn.[80] The heavenly lord in blue robes now sits upright. The purity of the clear light will never surpass this splendid occasion.

The Endless Shoots of Zazen
449. Dharma Hall Discourse
What is called zazen is to sit, cutting through the smoke and clouds without seeking merit. Just become unified, never reaching the end. In dropping off body and mind, what are the body and limbs? How can it be transmitted from within the bones and marrow? Already such, how can we penetrate it?

Snatching Gautama's hands and legs, one punch knocks over empty space. Karmic consciousness is boundless, without roots. The grasses shoot up and bring forth the wind [of the Buddha way].

Making Fire with Ice
450. Dharma Hall Discourse
Whose strength can we depend on to rub pieces of ice together and make a fire? We risk our lives in the effort to enter the gates of death. Dropping our bodies while crossing over, we can return to life. Within a scene of shame, play with spirit. This is what we attain from our study on the long sitting platform. How is it when going beyond this cave?

After a pause Dōgen said: Proceed slowly and cut off the sound of flowing water. Freely observe and follow the traces of the birds' flight.

---

80 When asked about words that surpass the buddhas and ancestors, Yunmen responded, "Sesame cake." See Cleary and Cleary, *Blue Cliff Record,* case 77, pp. 506–509; and Thomas Cleary, *Book of Serenity,* case 78, pp. 332–334. Dōgen also refers to this story in his mid-autumn Dharma hall discourse 189.

Zazen Beyond Birth and Death

451. Dharma Hall Discourse on the First Day of the Ninth Month [1251]
Making ferocious efforts to combat birth and death, who would love the
four [attachments] or five [desires] of the world?[81] Even if we yearn for the
ancient who made three prostrations at Shaolin, how could we forget the
six long years of upright sitting?[82] Disciples of Eihei, if you can see like this,
how will you express it?

After a pause Dōgen said: This morning is the first day of the ninth
month.[83] We hit the han and sit zazen according to the olden manner, and
you are urged to avoid sleep and to seek the elimination of all doubts. Do
not let yourself blink your eyes or raise your eyebrows.[84]

The Dharma Expounded by Nonsentient Beings

452. Dharma Hall Discourse
I can remember, when Dongshan [Liangjie] first visited Yunyan he asked,
"Who can hear the Dharma expounded by nonsentient beings?"

Yunyan said, "Nonsentient beings can hear the Dharma expounded by
nonsentient beings."

Dongshan asked, "Master, do you also hear it?"

---

81 The four attachments of the world are youth, peace, longevity, and wealth. The five
desires are for sex, material wealth, fame, food, and sleep.

82 "The ancient who made three prostrations at Shaolin" refers to the second Chinese
ancestor, Dazu Huike, who made three prostrations before Bodhidharma and received
Dharma transmission. The "six long years" refers to Śākyamuni Buddha's austere practice
before his awakening.

83 The first day of the ninth month was traditionally when the relaxed period with
decreased meditation came to an end and the regular schedule resumed. Other Dharma
hall discourses by Dōgen on this date are discourses 193 (in 1246), 279 (1248), 347 (1249),
389 (1250), and 523 (1252).

84 "Not letting yourself blink your eyes or raise your eyebrows" is from a statement by
Mazu Daoyi to Yaoshan Weiyan, which Dōgen discusses in Shōbōgenzō Uji (Being-
Time). Mazu said, "Sometimes I let him raise his eyebrows and blink his eyes. Sometimes
I do not let him raise his eyebrows and blink his eyes. Sometimes letting him raise his eye-
brows and blink his eyes is right. Sometimes letting him raise his eyebrows and blink his
eyes is not right." Hearing this, Yaoshan had a great realization. See Tanahashi, *Moon in
a Dewdrop*, pp. 80–83; and Cleary, *Shōbōgenzō: Zen Essays by Dōgen*, pp. 108–109. In this
Dharma hall discourse, this utterance refers to the degree of intensity in zazen.

Yunyan said, "If I could hear it, you would not hear the Dharma that I expound."

Dongshan said, "If so, then I do not hear the Dharma expounded by the master."

Yunyan said, "If you do not even hear the Dharma I expound, how can you hear the Dharma expounded by nonsentient beings?"

Finally, [Dongshan] offered a verse saying:

> "How marvelous! How marvelous!
> The Dharma expounded by nonsentient beings
>   is inconceivable.
> If you listen with your ears,
>   it will be difficult to ever understand.
> Hearing the sounds with your eyes, surely you can know it."[85]

Once a monk asked National Teacher Nanyang [Huizhong], "Do nonsentient beings expound the Dharma?"

The national teacher said, "They vigorously expound the Dharma."

The monk asked, "Who can hear the Dharma expounded by nonsentient beings?"

The national teacher said, "All the sages can hear it."

The monk asked, "Master, do you also hear it or not?"

The national teacher said, "If I heard it, I would be the same as the sages."

The teacher Dōgen said: The national teacher said that all the sages can hear it, and Yunyan said that nonsentient beings can hear it. Although

---

85 This seminal story in the awakening of Dongshan, founder of the Caodong (Jap.: Sōtō) school, is given as Dōgen's kōan case 52 with verse comment in volume 9, below, and in Dōgen's Mana Shōbōgenzō, case 148; see Nishijima, *Master Dogen's Shinji Shobogenzo,* p. 197. Dōgen also discusses this story at length in Shōbōgenzō Mujō Seppō (Nonsentient Beings Expound the Dharma); see Tanahashi, *Enlightenment Unfolds,* pp. 185–195. The amplified version of this story, including Dongshan's recounting of the dialogue that follows with the national teacher, is given in the Recorded Sayings of Dongshan; see Powell, *Record of Tung-shan,* pp. 23–26. The story as Dōgen gives it here is recounted in the Jingde Transmission of the Lamp; see Chang, *Original Teachings of Ch'an Buddhism,* p. 59.

they said it like that, why did they not say that ordinary beings can hear it? Please tell me, what is the Dharma that nonsentient beings expound?

If someone were to ask me, Eihei, I would tell him that they expound, "This very Dharma."

After a pause Dōgen said: The Dharma expounded by nonsentient beings is inconceivable. The tathāgatas in the three times faithfully accept this. Who else can also understand it? This simple monk's staff effortlessly knows it.

Polishing a Mirror
453. Dharma Hall Discourse
Polishing a tile to make a mirror is our reward for accumulating merit and virtue.[86] Polishing a mirror to make a tile certainly depends on the nourishment from wisdom. Polishing a mirror to make a mirror brings a laugh; how are my hands and a buddha's hands similar? Practicing zazen to make a buddha is making a grass seat at the site of awakening.[87] Why is it like this?

After a pause Dōgen said: When one cart is hit, many carts go quickly.[88] One night a flower blooms and the world is fragrant.

86 "Polishing a tile to make a mirror" refers to a story about Mazu sitting zazen. When his teacher Nanyue Huairang asked what he was doing, Mazu said that he was sitting to become a buddha. Nanyue started polishing a tile, and when Mazu inquired, Nanyue said that he was polishing the tile to make a mirror. Usually this has been interpreted as that one cannot produce buddhahood from zazen. Dōgen gave his unique interpretation of this story, saying that polishing a tile does make a mirror, in Shōbōgenzō Zazenshin (The Acupuncture Needle of Zazen). See Bielefeldt, *Dōgen's Manuals of Zen Meditation,* pp. 188–205.

87 "How are my hands and a buddha's hands similar?" is one of Huanglong Huinan's three barriers. See Dharma hall discourse 420. "Practicing zazen to make a buddha is making a grass seat at the site of awakening" might also be read as "Practicing zazen to make a buddha is taking our weeds and sitting at the site of awakening." The former reading implies the preparation for awakening; the latter implies that we awaken in the context of our karmic consciousness.

88 Hitting a cart also comes from the story about polishing a tile. In the original story, Nanyue Huairang asked how Mazu could become a buddha by sitting, any more than Huairang could polish a tile to make a mirror. When Mazu asked how then to practice, Huairang said, "When an ox cart stops, do you hit the ox or the cart?" In Zazenshin, unlike Huairang, Dōgen suggests hitting the cart. For the original story, see Cheng Chien, *Sun Face Buddha,* pp. 59–60; and Ogata, *Transmission of the Lamp,* pp. 162–163.

Meeting with Teachers, Meeting with Self
454. Dharma Hall Discourse
I can remember, Xuefeng pointed to the assembly and said, "At Wang-zhou Pavilion I have met with all of you. On Wushi Peak I have met with all of you. In front of the monks' hall I have met with all of you."

Later Baofu [Congzhan] brought this up and asked Ehu [Zhifu], "Put aside for a while the front of the monks' hall. How was your meeting with Xuefeng at Wangzhou Pavilion and Wushi Peak?"⁸⁹

Ehu quickly walked back to the abbot's quarters, and Baofu immediately returned to the monks' hall.

I, Eihei, offer a modest mountain verse. I have met with all of you. Do you want to see it clearly?

After a pause Dōgen said: At Wangzhou Pavilion, Wushi Peak, and in front of the monks' hall, I have met with all of you not due to minor affinities, [but from such causes as] exchanging eyeballs, breaking into a smile, or cutting off your arm. Dropping off body and mind is practicing Zen. You have no Buddha nature; I am just like this. Zen boards and sitting cushions are also thus. Having seen it like this, what can you say? We pierce our own nostrils.⁹⁰

Accepting the Emptiness of Attainment
455. Dharma Hall Discourse
I can remember, Yaoshan asked novice Gao, "Is your attainment from reading sutras or from hearing lectures?"

The novice said, "I did not attain either from reading sutras or from hearing lectures."

89 Wangzhou (View of the Province) Pavilion and Wushi (Crow Rock) Peak were both noted places on Mount Xuefeng, part of or near to Xufeng's temple. Baofu Congzhan and Ehu Zhifu were both disciples of Xuefeng.

90 "You have no Buddha nature" refers to the statement of the fifth ancestor, Daman Hongren, to the sixth ancestor, Dajian Huineng. See Dharma hall discourse 431. "I am just like this" refers to Huineng's statement to Nanyue. See Dharma hall discourse 374. "Zen boards" refer to the implement placed under the chin to prevent nodding off to sleep during late-night sitting. "Piercing the nostrils" refers to Zen training in terms of the ox-herding pictures and, specifically, taming the ox by putting a ring in his nose to lead him.

Yaoshan said, "There are a great many people who do not read sutras and do not hear lectures. How come they have no attainment?"

Novice [Gao] said, "I do not say they do not have it, but only that they are not willing to accept it."

Today I, Eihei, will comment on each statement. Yaoshan said, "Is your attainment from reading sutras or from hearing lectures?" *The teacher Dōgen appended a comment saying:* Attainment and nonattainment come only from this fist.[91]

The novice said, "I did not attain either from reading sutras or from hearing lectures." *The teacher Dōgen commented:* Even before arriving at Zhaozhou's place, having drank Zhaozhou's tea.[92]

Yaoshan said, "There are a great many people who do not read sutras and do not hear lectures. How come they have no attainment?" *The teacher Dōgen commented:* All living beings have no Buddha nature.

The novice said, "I do not say they do not have it, but only that they are not willing to accept it." *The teacher Dōgen commented:* All living beings have Buddha nature.

The teacher Dōgen further said: Suppose someone suddenly asked me, Eihei, why I spoke like this. I would say to him: Originally we need all of emptiness to break through existence. Already having no existence, what emptiness is needed?[93]

Faith in Fresh Blossoms
456. Dharma Hall Discourse
I, Eihei, have this phrase that was correctly transmitted to me: In the midst of snow, plum blossoms only on a single branch.

Among the middling and lowly, many hear this, but not many believe. Mahāyāna bodhisattvas trust without doubt.[94]

---

91 "Appended a comment" is *jakugo,* a word in the kōan literature for a brief added comment to a single line of a kōan story.

92 For Zhaozhou's tea, see note 30 above.

93 "All of emptiness" might be read as "all the emptinesses." Nāgārjuna spoke about eighteen kinds of emptiness, including the emptiness of emptiness itself.

94 "Mahāyāna bodhisattvas trust without doubt" is from Shitou Xiqian's Song of the Grass-Roof Hermitage. See Leighton, *Cultivating the Empty Field,* p. 72.

Fallen Flowers throughout the Seasons

457. Dharma Hall Discourse

Among those who study and practice the great way of the buddha ancestors, those from the human realm are most prominent. In the three continents [the Buddha way] actively functions, and there are even some
[practitioners] in the animal realm.⁹⁵ As for the occasions for clarifying the
great matter, the four seasons are all equal. Among them, in the spring
Lingyun clarified the great matter upon seeing peach blossoms, and in
the autumn, Xiangyan [Zhixian] clarified the great matter upon hearing
green bamboo.

Once, Master Lingyun suddenly became clear about the great matter
at the cave of peach blossoms. He composed a verse to present to the great
Guishan [Lingyou, his teacher], saying,

> "Over thirty years I have been seeking a swordsman;
> How many years have the leaves fallen and branches grown anew?
> Since having once seen the peach blossoms,
> Without wavering, up to the present I have never doubted."⁹⁶

We understand that [Lingyun] engaged the way for thirty years, and
people today should emulate his example.

Furthermore, when Master Xiangyan had passed a number of years in
the circle of Guishan [Lingyou], Guishan said, "Other than what you
remember from commentaries or have heard from the sermons of this old
monk, bring me a single utterance."

---

95 The three continents refer to all but the northern one of the four continents surrounding the axial Mount Sumeru in traditional Indian Buddhist cosmology. In the northern continent, Uttarakuru, which is said to be a paradise, nobody is moved to awaken to
suffering, and therefore nobody practices. The southern continent, Jambudvīpa, considered the abode of humans and identified with India, is encouraging of practice because of
the suffering there.

96 This story about Lingyun is from the Jingde Transmission of the Lamp, volume 11, the
section on Lingyun. Dōgen discusses it in Shōbōgenzō Keisei Sanshoku (The Sounds of
Valley Streams, the Colors of the Mountain). See Cook, *How to Raise an Ox*, pp. 72–73;
and Cleary, *Rational Zen*, pp. 119–120.

Xiangyan looked within the commentaries, but could not find even a single utterance. He said to Guishan, "I am unable to speak, but I ask you to say it, master."

Guishan said, "I do not refuse to speak for you, except that later you would scold me."

Xiangyan said, "In this present lifetime, I no longer expect to understand Zen. For its duration, I will become a monk who just serves food." Then he held up his written commentaries and said, "A painting of a rice cake does not satisfy hunger." Then he burnt them all.[97]

Later he traveled to the site of the former hermitage of National Teacher Nanyang Huizhong and built a hut where he stayed. One day while taking a break to sweep the path, at the moment a pebble shot up and knocked against a bamboo, the great matter suddenly became clear. Then he composed a verse saying,

With one blow, subject and object vanish.
I no longer practice to solve things on my own.
In all my activities I celebrate the ancient path,
And do not fall into passivity.

Then he bathed and dressed in formal manner, faced toward Guishan [Lingyou] in the distance, offered incense, made prostrations, and said, "Great Master Guishan is my excellent teacher. My gratitude to him surpasses that to my father and mother. If he had spoken for me at that time, how could I have had today's experience?"[98]

---

97 Dōgen comments extensively and creatively on this utterance by Xiangyan, "A painting of a rice cake does not satisfy hunger," in Shōbōgenzō Gabyo (A Painted Rice Cake). See Tanahashi, *Moon in a Dewdrop*, pp. 134–139.

98 This story about Xiangyan is from the Jingde Transmission of the Lamp; see Chang, *Original Teachings of Ch'an Buddhism*, pp. 219–220. Dōgen discusses this story, along with the former story of his Dharma brother, Lingyun, in Shōbōgenzō Keisei Sanshoku (The Sounds of Valley Streams, the Colors on the Mountain). See Cook, *How to Raise an Ox*, pp. 71–73; and Thomas Cleary, trans., *Rational Zen: The Mind of Dōgen Zenji*, pp. 118–119.

Master Xiangyan as well [as Lingyun] is like a steep precipice in the ocean of our study. People of today should deeply appreciate the fragrant traces of these two teachers.

I, Eihei, humbly continue the verse of Zen Master Lingyun:

> From north to south,
>   searching for the sword with a notch on the boat,[99]
> Through the languid spring days,
>   how many branches did he examine?
> Unexpectedly, he viewed the peach blossoms.
> His eyes split open and his mind was pierced,
>   with nothing more to doubt.

Here is another verse as an expression of Master Xiangyan:

> He inadvertently swept up a pebble on an ancient path.
> What was it like, first hearing the sound of bamboo?
> At this very time, what will you say?
> Although the four oceans are boundless,
>   we add in the dew from the grass.
> Before eight years are over, an utterance is born.[100]

Great assembly, please tell me, how can you discern the virtue of these two venerable ones?

After a pause Dōgen said: A hundred thousand shards of a mirror no longer shine. Flowers fallen and scattered never return up to the branch.[101]

---

99 "Searching for a sword with a notch on the boat" refers to an old Chinese story about a foolish person who cut a notch on his boat to help find the sword that had just fallen overboard. "From north to south" is literally "from Hu [a barbarian region north of China] to Yue [a southern province of China]."

100 "Before eight years are over" refers to the time it took Nanyue to respond to Huineng's first question to him, "What is this that thus comes?" This story is discussed by Dōgen in Dharma hall discourse 374 and kōan case 59 in volume 9; and he refers to it in a number of places in Eihei Kōroku; for example, see Dharma hall discourse 3 and volume 1, note 6.

101 "A broken mirror no longer reflects. Fallen flowers never return up to the branch" is a saying by Baoji [Huayan] Xiujing, a disciple of Dongshan Liangjie. Dōgen refers to it in Shōbōgenzō Daigo (Great Enlightenment). See Cleary, *Rational Zen*, pp. 110–111.

The Whole Reality in the Perfume of Practice

458. Dharma Hall Discourse

When one bit of dust is raised, it includes the great earth; when one flower opens, the whole world is aroused.[102] When a single moment of thinking is dropped away, the eighty-four thousand afflicting delusions are removed. When one phrase hits our true function, eighty-four thousand Dharma gates are fulfilled. For example, it is like when one pulls the main line and immediately the whole net follows, or when one lifts the collar and the whole cloth quickly comes as well. The one is uncountable, and the uncountable is one. The large manifests within the small, and the small manifests within the large. On one hairtip, the sanctuary of the jewel king appears; within an atom, the great Dharma wheel turns. Great assembly, please tell me, how does the sanctuary of the jewel king appear; how does the great Dharma wheel turn?

Then Dōgen raised his whisk and said: Look, look! This is the jewel king's sanctuary. This is turning the Dharma wheel. This is the perfuming practice of immeasurable precepts, samādhi, wisdom, liberation, and the awareness of liberation; this is the fulfillment of immeasurable samādhi, dhāranīs, and the radiance of the hundred jewels.[103] Great assembly, do you wish to clearly understand this principle?

After a pause Dōgen said: The ancestral teachers expound and demonstrate the study of Zen; swallows profoundly discuss the true form [of all things].[104] Among living beings and buddhas there are the unlimited and limited. How could we slander twirling a flower and blinking the eyes?

102 "When one flower opens, the whole world is aroused" is from a verse attributed to Prajñātāra, Bodhidharma's teacher in India. See Ogata, *Transmission of the Lamp,* pp. 54–55.

103 "Immeasurable precepts, samādhi, wisdom, liberation, and the awareness of liberation" are the five aspects of the Dharma body of a buddha.

104 Upon hearing the chirping of baby swallows, Xuansha Shibei said, "This is profound expounding of the real form." Dōgen quotes this in Shōbōgenzō Shōhō-Jissō (The True Form of All Things). See Nishijima and Cross, *Zen Master Dogen's Shobogenzo,* book 3, p. 91.

The Continuous Practice of Cranes and Ducks
459. Dharma Hall Discourse

Ten million did not see the twirling of the flower at Vulture Peak. The entrustment of the marrow [by Bodhidharma] at Mount Song is the single arm of the entire body. There are a thousand divisions and ten thousand continuities between the cranes and ducks.[105] They flatten a hundred thousand peaks and fill up a hundred gullies. Already they have diligently engaged the way like this. Transcending the mundane and going beyond the sacred, things dwell in their Dharma positions and the forms of the world constantly abide.[106]

At this very time, what do you have to say? Great assembly, do you want to clearly understand this?

After a pause Dōgen said: Nobody knows how many straw sandals I have worn through. Returning to my home mountain, I just rest.

The Brush Mightier than Rocks
460. Dharma Hall Discourse for Appointing the [New] Scribe[107]

Great Penetrating [Surpassing Knowledge Buddha] counts the numerous ink drops ground from three thousand worlds.[108] Although these are imagined as three thousand, they are [unreal] as a lotus in the twelfth month.

---

105 Cranes and ducks can represent teachers and students. The original Monkaku version reads, "A thousand continuities and ten thousand continuities." Manzan changed it to "a thousand divisions (or cuts)," a reading that Genryū Kagamishima also follows, and which echoes the reference to Dazu Huike cutting off his arm in the previous sentence.

106 "Dharmas [or things] dwell in their Dharma positions and the forms of the world constantly abide" is from the Lotus Sutra, chap. 2, "Skillful Means." See Hurvitz, *Scripture of the Lotus Blossom of the Fine Dharma*, p. 41; and Katō, Tamura, and Miyasaka, *Threefold Lotus Sutra*, p. 70.

107 The scribe or secretary (Jap.: *shoki*) is one of the six department heads *(chōshū)* in the monastic system of positions.

108 This Buddha, Great Penetrating Surpassing Knowledge (Skt.: Mahābhijñājñānā-bhibū) is discussed in the beginning of chapter 7 of the Lotus Sutra. He is famed for having sat under the Bodhi tree, just previous to realizing perfect buddhahood, for ten minor kalpas. The image of ink drops is used in the sutra to denote the time since his extinction, an exceptionally vast number of kalpas, being the number of atoms in all the lands passed through if one were to drop one drop of ink after passing a thousand worlds. See Katō, Tamura, and Miyasaka, *Threefold Lotus Sutra*, pp. 145–169; or Hurvitz, *Scripture of the Lotus Blossom of the Fine Dharma*, pp. 130–155.

Elevate the three-foot brush made of tortoise hair to inscribe the destruction of the tough rock body of the outsider.[109]

Serene Illumination beyond Distinctions
461. Dharma Hall Discourse

Sitting on our cushions we can give birth to immeasurable buddhas, a birth which is exactly no-birth. Holding up Zen boards we can turn the pure Dharma wheel, a turning in which nothing is turned. Directly, bit by bit, we ceaselessly see the Buddha with no special marks, who is exactly true. Moment by moment, without falling into sounds and colors, we ceaselessly hear the sutra that is truly wondrous. Although it is like this, the person who can understand the gateways of light and shadow can attain it, just like at the time when guest and host have not yet been differentiated and shadow and form have not yet been distinguished. How can this be carried out?

After a pause Dōgen said: The nose smiling with mouth open, the eyes gaze at the North Star and Altair.[110] Wind and clouds do not mar the dawn, and sky and water join together in autumn.

Proper Respect for Fire
462. Dharma Hall Discourse for Opening the Furnace [1251][111]

Dōgen drew a circle with his whisk and said: This is Eihei's vast furnace. If you meet it, your eyebrows and beard will fall out; if you destroy it, every drop of water will turn to ice. At this very time, how is it?

The fire boys race forward, and I laugh heartily at Danxia [Tianran], greedy for the fire.[112]

---

109 "The tough rock body of the outsider" refers to Kapila, who is discussed in Dharma hall discourse 402. The rock body represents the idea of substantial existence.

110 Altair is a star celebrated every year on the seventh day of the seventh month for the Tanabata festival. According to legend, this star is a cowherd in love with another star, who is a weaver maiden. These two stars come together in the sky only on this night every year.

111 For other Dharma hall discourses for the opening of the furnace, or fireplace, on the first day of the tenth month, see Dharma hall discourses 14, 109, 199, 288, 353, 396, and 528.

112 "Fire boy" *(heiteidōji)* refers to the story of Bao'en Xuanze and his misunderstanding on the saying about "the fire boy seeking fire." See Dharma hall discourse 15. Danxia Tianran is famous for burning a wooden buddha statue to stay warm.

The Innocence of Dropping Off Body and Mind
463. Dharma Hall Discourse
Dropping off body and mind; and skin, flesh, bones, and marrow; how could these be involved with self or other? Upon breaking into a smile, earth, water, fire, and air have never been separated. At exactly such a time, do you want to clearly understand this point?

After a pause Dōgen said: In previous years we have determined the positions of dragons and snakes, but today we are again the same as children singing.

Hear the One Vehicle
464. Dharma Hall Discourse
I can remember, a monk once asked Baizhang, "The Yogācārabhūmi Commentary and the Jewel Necklace Sutra contain the Mahāyāna precepts. Why don't we follow them?"[113]

Baizhang said, "What I take as essential is not limited to the greater or lesser vehicles, and does not differ from the greater or lesser vehicles."

I, Eihei, have a humble mountain verse. *After a pause Dōgen said:*

Where ten vehicles race, one vehicle appears.
Sharing together with a guest, he scoops his own tea.
Although many listen, few know him.
The great king expounds saindhava.[114]

The Vital Eye of Kirins and Lions
465. Dharma Hall Discourse
To sit cutting off right and wrong, and to transcend nonattachment to worldly details, is the molding of buddha ancestors and the sphere of

---

113 A longer version of this story appears in Dharma hall discourse 390. The Yogācārabhūmi Śāstra, or Commentary on the Stages of the Yogācāra Teaching, is by Asaṅga. The Jewel Necklace Sutra, or the Bodhisattva Jewel Necklace Original Conduct Sutra, was written in China, and discusses the three pure precepts.

114 *Saindhava* refers to a request that is understood and responded to immediately thanks to familiarity with the person asking. See Dharma hall discourse 354 and volume 3 (Dharma hall discourse 254), note 108.

practice-realization.[115] This is the vital eye within the brow of a skull, and the mysterious working of phrases about the empty kalpa. The reddish-brown kirin of Qingyuan [Xingsi] walks calmly.[116] The golden-haired lion of Yaoshan is completely dignified.[117] When meeting each other they unfailingly hold hands, and together return as one to the great way.

Practice Beyond Letting Go and Holding Tight
466. Dharma Hall Discourse
What buddhas' sermons do not reach and what the ancestral teachers' displays do not arouse still entirely abides inside the seams between my fingers. Do you really see? Do you know this? Letting go is exactly like three heads and eight arms [acting freely and effectively]; holding tight is exactly like water not leaking through. Tell me, how is it when we neither let go nor hold tight?

After a pause Dōgen said: After proceeding to cut off the path of ten thousand distinctions, just practice on Vairocana's headtop.

The Thundering Canon
467. Dharma Hall Discourse for Appointing the [New] Librarian
The traces of the teachings are here from the Buddha's transformation of the great thousandfold world. A raised fist produces clouds and thunder. In this place converges the ocean of boundless meanings. He is able to open the eighty thousand Dharma gates.

---

115 This entire Dharma hall discourse is almost identical to one by Hongzhi Zhengjue in his Extensive Record, volume 9. The minor differences in Dōgen's version are his use of "cutting off" to replace "forgetting" in Hongzhi's version, and "transcend" to replace Hongzhi's "thoroughly see." Dōgen also added several words that do not significantly alter the meaning: "mysterious," "calmly," "completely," "unfailingly," and "one."

116 A *kirin* (Ch.: *qilin*) is a fabulous, auspicious animal with the body of a deer, tail of an ox, hooves of a horse, one fleshy horn, a yellow belly, and multicolored back. It is used in Zen lore to describe an eminent person. In this instance, it refers to Qingyuan's disciple Shitou Qixian, whom Qingyuan called a qilin/kirin in the section on Qingyuan in the Jingde Transmission of the Lamp.

117 Yaoshan's golden-haired lion refers to his disciple Yunyan Tansheng.

The Stark Peace of Mountains

468. Dharma Hall Discourse

For a pine by the blue mountain torrent, and for a crane in its cold nest, the nature of sadness is calm and peaceful, and its entire body is eminent.[118] The deep valley stream embraces the bright moonlight; the broad mountains cherish the colorfully glowing clouds. Each single spot is distinct; the ten directions are clear and open.[119] At this very time, do you understand this point or not?

After a pause Dōgen said: Huangbo did not mind [Linji] stroking the tiger's whiskers. Qingyuan was delighted with the horn of the kirin [Shitou].[120]

A Traceless Life

469. Dharma Hall Discourse

I can remember, a monk asked Baofu [Congzhan], "What kind of saying did Xuefeng use in his ordinary life so that he could resemble an antelope when it hangs by the horns [not leaving any tracks]?"[121]

Baofu said, "If I had not become Xuefeng's disciple, I would not have realized that."

118 The character for "sadness" here is very similar to one meaning "constancy," which may have been Dōgen's original meaning here.

119 This Dharma hall discourse, up to "ten directions are clear and open," is based on a Dharma hall discourse by Hongzhi in his Extensive Record, volume 9. Hongzhi's original version reads: "For a pine by the blue mountain torrent, and for a crane in its misty nest, its wild nature is calm and peaceful, and its thin body is eminent. The wide river embraces the bright moonlight and continues its training; the waters and sky merge in the boundless autumn. Each single spot is distinct; the ten directions are empty and open."

120 After Linji awakened and said there was not much to Huangbo's Zen after all, he returned to Huangbo and slapped him. Thereupon Huangbo said that Linji was stroking the tiger's whiskers. See Watson, *Zen Teachings of Master Lin-chi,* pp. 106–107. At the end of their first dialogue after Shitou arrived to study with Qingyuan, Qingyuan said about Shitou that "although there are many horns, one kirin is enough."

121 Up until Dōgen's comment, this Dharma hall discourse repeats the same dialogue and ensuing commentary by Yuanwu that is in Dharma hall discourse 167. See notes to that discourse for more material on Chinese folklore. This question is based on the Chinese fable that antelopes hung from trees by their horns when they slept, to avoid leaving any traces or tracks on the ground for hunters. Therefore, this apparently unusual expression is an image for anonymity of appearing ordinary.

Zen Master Yuanwu commented, beginning with a verse, "The feathers of peacocks and kingfishers, and the horn of a kirin, resplendent with brilliant colors, have been transmitted from one to another. If you want to understand the workings of catching a tiger, you should offer such a saying [as Baofu's], which is like a sheer cliff. Nevertheless, he only knows how to come like this; he doesn't know how to go like this. Suppose someone asked this mountain monk [Yuanwu], 'What kind of saying did Wuzu [Fayan, Yuanwu's teacher] use in his ordinary life so that he could resemble an antelope when it hangs by the horns?' Then I would simply say to him, 'I dare not oppose my late teacher.' Do you thoroughly understand this? Although the mountain is high, it does not obstruct the white clouds drifting by."

The teacher Dōgen said: Suppose someone asked me, Eihei, "What kind of saying did Tiantong [Rujing] use in his ordinary life so that he could resemble an antelope when it hangs by the horns?"

I would reply to him: In previous days, Tiantong used his fist to destroy the longtime cave of a wild fox.

Suppose I was further asked, "This is a phrase from Tiantong's ordinary life. What about your own response, master?"

I would say to him: Throughout my life, I, Eihei, never fall asleep before Tiantong.

The Way Beyond Grasping and Discarding
470. Dharma Hall Discourse

In a Dharma hall discourse, Zen Master Huanglong [Huinan] Pujue said, "The third ancestor [Jianzhi Sengcan] said, 'The perfection [of the supreme way] is the same as primordial emptiness, with nothing lacking, nothing extra. Indeed because of grasping and discarding, suchness is lost.'[122] For buddhas it does not increase, with ordinary beings it does not decrease. If it is without increase or decrease, how do some verify unsurpassed bodhi, while others fall into birth and death? How is it that simply due to grasping and discarding, suchness is lost? Because all buddhas

---

122 This quote is from the Inscription on Faith in Mind, traditionally attributed to the third ancestor. See, for example, Suzuki, *Manual of Zen Buddhism*, p. 77; and Sheng-yen, *Poetry of Enlightenment*, p. 25.

have no [discriminating] mind, they verify the unsurpassed way, and because ordinary beings have [discriminating] mind, they fall into birth and death. Therefore in a sutra it says, 'Dream phantoms and imagined flowers in the sky are like the moonlight in water, and birth and death, and nirvāṇa, are the same as those flowers in the sky.' If you can see this, stop the conference in front of the Pippāli Cave and consider well the path of Caoxi [Dajian Huineng]."[123] Then [Huanglong] hit his Zen seat with his whisk, and descended from the platform.

Today, I, Eihei, remove the horn from Huanglong's head, and respectfully raise up the jewel in the topknot of Huanglong's crown.[124] Great assembly, do you want to clearly understand this point?

"Its perfection is the same as primordial emptiness, with nothing lacking, nothing extra." Therefore, all buddhas verify the supreme way. "Its perfection is the same as primordial emptiness, with nothing lacking, nothing extra." Therefore, ordinary people fall into birth and death. How is it possible to avoid grasping and discarding, and drop off lack of suchness? Do you want to know this principle? In their last moments [before becoming buddhas], bodhisattvas unfailingly sit on the vajra seat; in their first arousal of the mind [of aspiration], bodhisattvas unfailingly arouse awakening mind. If you can see this, "Its perfection is the same as primordial emptiness, with nothing lacking, nothing extra."

123 Pippāli Cave, near Rājagṛha, was where a meeting convened soon after Śākyamuni Buddha's death to formulate the Buddhist scriptures. So Huanglong here is recommending study of Zen, as represented by the sixth ancestor, Dajian Huineng, rather than the study of the sutras.

124 "The jewel in the topknot of Huanglong's crown" refers to a parable in the Lotus Sutra, chap. 14, about a king with a crown jewel in his topknot, his most precious possession, which he bestows only with utmost care. See Katō, Tamura, and Miyasaka, *Threefold Lotus Sutra*, pp. 231–232. Here Dōgen is set to both criticize and praise aspects of Huanglong's statement, and to emphasize the importance of actual bodhisattva practice (which is described in the sutras).

EIHEI ZENJI GOROKU

RECORDED SAYINGS
AT EIHEIJI TEMPLE

COLLECTED BY GIEN, ATTENDANT OF DŌGEN ZENJI

The Snow at Midnight

471. Dharma Hall Discourse

Having questions and answers, we smear everything with shit and piss. Not having questions and answers, thunder and lightning crash. The great earth in ten directions is leveled, and all of space is torn open.[1] Not allowed to enter from outside; not allowed to leave from inside, a gavel strikes the sounding block and the ten thousand affairs are completed.[2] At such a time, how is it?

After a pause Dōgen said: Time and again, everything exists within a painting. Even allowing for what is split apart, snow falls at midnight.[3]

---

1 "Having questions and answers...thunder and lightning crash" and "The great earth...torn open" are quotes from part of a Dharma hall discourse in Tiantong Rujing's Recorded Sayings, volume 2. In between these two quotes, Rujing had said, "Eyebrows are blessed and cheerful, and nostrils are in high spirits."

2 "Not allowed to enter from outside . . . ten thousand affairs are completed" is from another Dharma hall discourse by Tiantong Rujing, in the same section as the previous one. "A gavel strikes the sounding block," refers to the story in Shōyōroku, case 1, in which Mañjuśrī Bodhisattva strikes the sounding block to end the talk immediately upon Śākyamuni's taking the lecture seat. See Cleary, *Book of Serenity*, pp. 3–5.

3 "Snow falls at midnight" is an image of nondiscrimination, all the myriad things equally covered.

The Pickiness of Garuḍas

472. Dharma Hall Discourse

Here is a statement. The third ancestor, Great Teacher [Jianzhi Sengcan] said, "The supreme way is not difficult, simply dislike picking and choosing."⁴ Upon hearing this, people who do not understand might say, "All dharmas are without good and bad; every [action] is neither evil or upright. Simply trust your nature and stroll along. Following conditions, let go of everything. Therefore with all good and bad or evil and upright, do not pick or choose, but just go on your way."

Another may say, "In order to not do this so-called picking or choosing, do not speak using words. This can be done by simply making a circle, holding up a whisk, pounding a monk's staff, throwing down the staff, clapping hands, giving a yell, holding up a sitting cushion, or raising a fist."

Views like this do not depart from the cave of common beings. Suppose someone were to ask me, Eihei, "What is the point of 'simply dislike picking and choosing'?"

I would say to him: A garuḍa does not eat anything but raw dragons. The Bodhisattva Next in Line [for buddhahood, i.e., Maitreya] is not born except in Tuṣita Heaven.⁵

Frost Added on Snow

473. Dharma Hall Discourse

The high ancestor on Mount Song [Bodhidharma] said, "For eight thousand years after my death, my Dharma will not shift by even a hairsbreadth, remaining as it was while I have been in this world."

Our Buddha, the Tathāgata said, "After my death, in order to protect my disciples to whom I have bestowed the Dharma, I bequeath the merit and virtue from the mark of my white hair curl."⁶ He also said, "In order

---

4 This quotation is the beginning of Inscription on Faith in Mind, traditionally attributed to the third ancestor. See Suzuki, *Manual of Zen Buddhism,* p. 76; and Sheng-yen, *Poetry of Enlightenment,* p. 25. Dōgen comments similarly on this same saying from Inscription on Faith in Mind in Dharma hall discourse 371.

5 For garuḍas see Dharma hall discourse 371 and volume 5, note 36. Bodhisattvas predicted to become the next future Buddha, such as Maitreya after Śākyamuni, are said to reside in Tuṣita Heaven, a meditative bliss realm within the realm of desire.

6 The merit of the white hair curl on a buddha's forehead, one of the thirty-two marks,

to benefit disciples to whom I have bestowed the Dharma, I bequeath twenty years of a buddha's allotted life-span to protect and safeguard these disciples."

Today, I, Eihei, happen to have a verse.

After a pause Dōgen said:

A cold plum blossom in the twelfth month is bright
  in the moonlight.
Frost is added to the snow on the snowy mountains.
The mark of the Tathāgata's hair still present now,
Benefits his remote descendants; how inconceivable.

The Buddha Nature of Milk and Cheese
474. Dharma Hall Discourse

The Buddha nature of time and season, causes and conditions,
Is perfectly complete in past and future, and in each moment.
Despite differences between merits gathered, or layers of virtue,
Milk and cheese completely earn their names in their own times.

Joining the Fulfillment of Completion
475. Enlightenment Day Dharma Hall Discourse [1251]⁷
*What the World-Honored One had said in his first sermon upon fulfilling the way, from "Three quarters of the night has passed" to "the one with wisdom about everything in the world," was related as before by the teacher Dōgen, who then gave this added comment.*⁸

---

was bequeathed by the Buddha to take care of the worldly needs of his later disciples, as with the merit of the twenty years mentioned in the next sentence.

7 Śākyamuni's Enlightenment Day is celebrated on the eighth day of the twelfth month in East Asia. Other Enlightenment Day Dharma hall discourses in Eihei Kōroku are discourses 88, 136, 213, 297, 360, 406, and 506.

8 This paragraph is a note by Gien, the compiler of this volume. This quote was given before by Dōgen in Dharma hall discourse 360 (see notes to that discourse for sources). The entire quote: "Three quarters of this night has passed; in the remaining quarter the brightness will dawn. The various kinds of conditioned and unconditioned beings all remain unmoving. At this time, the unsurpassed venerable great sage extinguishes the

Boundless merit and virtue has already manifested on this day. In December a fan leaps about in my hand.[9]

From "Because of the virtue and benefit I created in ancient times" to "will be extinguished" was quoted as before by the teacher Dōgen, who then said the following.[10]

I, Eihei, respectfully join and continue the completion of the fulfillment of the way. It is not that there is no practice-realization, but the way of awakening is complete. What kind of classifications exist? The dawn sky is bright. At this time we are delighted that our great compassionate father added a stalk to his eyebrows.[11]

Grateful Practice
476. Dharma Hall Discourse

Practice-realization manifests completely, not exhausted throughout the ages of time. The cause and its fruit are completely fulfilled, unlimited by their beginning or end. In the realm of Dharma, there is no center or edge. For the body of wisdom, there is no front or back. Tell me, how is it when we practice in such a way?

After a pause Dōgen said: The three thousand worlds gratefully receive [Buddha's] beneficent blessing, and all living beings follow his guidance.

---

various afflictions, attains bodhi, and becomes known as the one with wisdom about everything in the world."

9 A fan in December is an expression for something useless, here implying that Buddha's enlightenment was good for nothing.

10 Another note by Gien. This quote was also given before by Dōgen in Dharma hall discourse 360. The entire quote from the Buddha: "Because of the virtue and benefit I created in ancient times, everything wished for in my heart has been accomplished, my mind of samādhi has been instantly verified, and I have reached the shore of nirvāṇa. All my various enemies or foes and even the demon Pāpiyas (Māra) in the Iśvara level of the realm of desire cannot trouble me, and so they all take refuge in Buddha. This is because of the power of my virtue and wisdom. If you can courageously make diligent efforts to seek sacred wisdom, this will be attained without difficulty. Once it is attained all afflictions will be exhausted, and all your accumulated offenses and faults will be extinguished."

11 Adding a stalk to thicken the eyebrows might imply making something complete that is already complete.

Buddha and the Many Forms

477. Dharma Hall Discourse

I can remember, Zhaozhou said, "A wooden buddha does not pass through fire; a golden buddha does not pass through a furnace; a clay buddha does not pass through water. The true Buddha sits inside."[12]

Great assembly, do you understand?

What is a wooden buddha? It is Krakucchanda Buddha.

What is a golden buddha? It is Kanakamuni Buddha.

What is a clay buddha? It is Kaśyāpa Buddha.[13]

What is a true buddha? It is Śākyamuni Buddha.

Why do I say it like this?

After a pause Dōgen said: There's nothing in the world that matches the Tathāgata's wondrous form body.[14]

Karmic Consciousness Opened in Radiance

478. Dharma Hall Discourse on the Memorial Morning for my Late Mother[15]

When a mendicant breaks his begging bowl, even if peaches and plums must pass through frost and snow, our Buddha emits illumination from the hair on his forehead out to the ten directions.[16] Each bit of radiance is subtle and wondrous, displaying and expounding the Dharma. This is

---

12 For the context of this saying by Zhaozhou, see Green, *Recorded Sayings of Zen Master Joshu*, p. 77.

13 Krakucchanda, Kanakamuni, and Kaśyāpa (Jap.: Kuruson, Kunagonmuni, and Kashō) are the buddhas previous to Śākyamuni, who is said to be the seventh in this series of primordial buddhas. See also Dharma hall discourse 446.

14 "There's nothing in the world that matches the Tathāgata's wondrous form body" is a quote from the Sutra of Queen Śrīmālā. See Alex Wayman and Hideko Wayman, *The Lion's Roar of Queen Śrīmālā* (New York: Columbia University Press, 1974), p. 61. Although the wondrous body of Buddha is incomparable, from Dōgen's perspective on Buddha nature, he might be implying here that all buddhas, and all forms (including wood, gold, and clay) are ancient buddhas, and are wondrous.

15 See the previous memorial for Dōgen's mother, Dharma hall discourse 409, as well as notes for the memorial for his father, Dharma hall discourse 363.

16 "When a mendicant breaks his begging bowl" recalls Tiantong Rujing's statement cited by Dōgen in Dharma hall discourse 179, "When one person opens up reality and returns to the source, a mendicant breaks his rice bowl."

the activity of buddha ancestors; can you further tell me what is the conduct of patch-robed monks?

Dōgen threw down his staff, looked around at the great assembly, pointed with a finger of his right hand, and said: Look! Look! This patch-robed monk's staff turns a somersault, and wherever it touches, at once karmic consciousness is cracked open.

The Root of Ignorance
479. Dharma Hall Discourse
There is one Dharma that buddhas in the three times and all generations of ancestral teachers offer as a means for the sake of all assemblies of human and heavenly beings.

[Buddha] said, "Life and death is long; life and death is short.[17] If we rely on greed, anger, and foolishness, then [the cycle of suffering of] life and death is long. If we rely on precepts, samādhi, and wisdom, then this life and death is short."

At that time, a virtuous woman was before the Buddha, and asked him, "World-Honored One, on what do greed, anger, and foolishness depend?"

Buddha replied to the good woman, "Their existence depends on ignorance."

The good woman said, "If greed, anger, and foolishness depend on ignorance, then all things have existence."

Buddha replied to the good woman, "Does the ignorance you speak of exist within you?"

The woman said, "It does not."

Buddha asked, "Does it exist outside you?"

The woman said, "It does not."

Buddha asked, "Does it exist neither inside nor outside?"

The woman said, "It does not."

Buddha said, "This is how it exists."

---

17 Dōgen quotes the story that follows, from the beginning of Buddha's statement, up until the end of the dialogue with Buddha's statement "This is how it exists," from Zhiyi's Mohe Zhiguan, chap. 5. It is taken therein from Nāgārjuna's Commentary on the Mahāprajñāpāramitā Sūtra (Ch.: Dazhidulun), chap. 6.

The World-Honored Tathāgata has already spoken like this, but I, Eihei, his remote descendant, cannot avoid speaking further. Suppose today a virtuous woman were to ask me, Eihei, "Where does ignorance abide?" I would simply say to her: Even if you can recognize what ignorance depends on, you cannot escape Eihei's whisk.

A Teacher of Not Understanding
480. Dharma Hall Discourse
For all living beings passing through the life and death of samsāra, it is most difficult and rare to receive a body in the southern continent.[18]

One day the Tathāgata picked up a piece of dirt, put it on his fingertip, showed it to the assembly, and said, "Is there more soil in the three-thousand thousand-fold worlds, or on my fingertip?"

At that time Ānanda replied to Buddha, "There is more soil in the three-thousand thousand-fold worlds; it cannot be compared to the soil on your fingertip."

The World-Honored One said, "Those who receive human bodies in the southern continent are like the soil on my fingertip. Those who do not receive human bodies in the southern continent are like the soil in the three-thousand thousand-fold worlds. To be born and encounter the Buddha Dharma is even more rare than this."

Great assembly, we have already received a human body difficult to receive, and we have already encountered the Buddha Dharma difficult to encounter. We should engage the way as if extinguishing flames on our head.

I can remember, Venerable Aśvaghoṣa asked Venerable Punyayaśas, "I want to understand What is Buddha?"[19]

Punyayaśas said, "If you want to understand Buddha, it is that which does not understand."

18 For the southern continent of Jambudvīpa, the most auspicious birthplace for humans, see Dharma hall discourse 457 and volume 6, note 95.

19 This story of the dialogue between Punyayaśas and his disciple Aśvaghoṣa is from the Jingde Transmission of the Lamp. See Ogata, *Transmission of the Lamp*, pp. 22–23.

Aśvaghoṣa said, "If Buddha is not understanding, how can we know what it is?"

Punyayaśas said, "If Buddha is not understanding, how can we know what it is not?"

Aśvaghoṣa said, "This is the principle of a saw."

Punyayaśas said, "That is the principle of wood." Then Punyayaśas asked, "What is the principle of a saw?"

Aśvaghoṣa said, "I will the share the cost with the teacher." Then Aśvaghoṣa asked, "What is the principle of wood?"

Punyayaśas said, "You can understand through me."

Aśvaghoṣa suddenly had some experience of enlightenment.

Suppose someone asked me, Eihei, "What is the principle of a saw?" I would say to him: It is as distant as heaven from earth.

"What is the principle of wood?" I would say to him: There is a hairsbreadth's deviation.

The Spring within a Cold Flower
481. Dharma Hall Discourse on the Fifteenth [Full Moon] Day of the First Month [1252][20]

> How can white reed flowers covered in snow be defiled by dust?
> Who knows that there are many people on the pure earth?
> A single plum flower in the cold,
>   with fragrant heart blossoming,
> Calls for the arising of spring in the emptiness of the pot of ages.[21]

The Single Black Staff of Zazen
482. Dharma Hall Discourse
The Buddha Dharma entered China twice. The first time was when Buddhabhadra Bodhisattva came and transmitted it, staying at Waguan Temple and

---

20 For the fifteenth day of the first month see Dharma hall discourses 219 and especially 412 with its notes.

21 "The emptiness of the pot (or cauldron) of ages" is from Hongzhi's verse comment to case 98 of the Shōyōroku. See Cleary, *Book of Serenity*, p. 423. See also Dharma hall discourse 223, and volume 3, note 59.

transmitting to Ancestral Teacher [Seng]zhao.[22] The other was when the venerable High Ancestor Bodhidharma of Mount Song stayed at Shaolin Temple and transmitted to [Dazu] Huike from the land of Qi. The lineage of transmission to Dharma Teacher Sengzhao has already been cut off, but what was imparted to Great Teacher Huike has spread throughout the nine provinces [of China]. As a reward for seeds of prajñā planted in previous lives, my fellow lineage members have been able to encounter the most excellent, supreme, single transmission, and have studied and practiced it. We should practice diligently to save our head from flames.

The Buddha said, "There are two blameworthy wrongdoers. The first killed all the living beings in the three thousand great thousands of worlds. The other attained great wisdom, but slandered zazen practitioners. Between the two crimes, which is graver?" The Buddha continued, "The person who criticized zazen is still superior to the one who killed all beings in the three thousand great thousands of worlds."

We should consider and realize that the merit and virtue of zazen is most excellent and very profound. *Dōgen also said:* Wayfarers who study Zen, remaining on the sitting platform for many kalpas, also watch the single black staff. At this very time, is there the principle of dropping away or not?

After a pause Dōgen said: I thought the barbarian's beard was red, but there is furthermore a barbarian with a red beard.

True Home-Leavers Relieve the Needy
483. Dharma Hall Discourse
In discussing this affair, all buddhas in the ten directions are not without practice-realization, and all ancestral teachers cannot defile it. Therefore, among the hundred million people at Vulture Peak, only Mahākāśyapa was able to abide and maintain it. Among the seven hundred eminent monks at Mount Huangmei, [the fifth ancestor, Daman Hongren] selected only one lay worker to receive transmission of the Dharma.

How can this be attained by the mediocre or common? Those who are not common or mediocre are called true home-leavers. Those who are

---

22 This story about Buddhabhadra and Sengzhao is related in the commentary to Hekiganroku, case 62. See Cleary and Cleary, *Blue Cliff Record*, p. 401.

true home-leavers must maintain the commitment to strength and intense determination, and should erect the banner of diligence and fierce courage. Finally, they must hold forth the key of buddha ancestors, open the barrier of going beyond, and carry out their own family property to benefit and relieve all the abandoned and destitute. At this very time, we first requite our gratitude for the blessings and virtues of the buddhas. *Dōgen then struck the sitting platform with his whisk and descended from his seat.*

The Unfathomable Jewel of Awakening
484. Dharma Hall Discourse
The Honorable Sengzhao said, "The way of awakening cannot be measured. It is lofty and unsurpassable, vast and inexhaustible. It is a bottomless abyss, unfathomably deep."[23]

Today I, Eihei, cannot avoid making a comment on each phrase for the sake of the clouds and water assembly:

About "the way of awakening," the teacher Dōgen said: Practice the way riding the ox.

About "cannot be measured," I say: Return home and assess its measure.

About "lofty and unsurpassable," I say: A yellow nightingale sings in a willow.

About "vast and inexhaustible," I say: Its form reaches to the smallest atom.

About "the bottomless abyss," I say: The diamond wheel remains above the wind wheel.[24]

About "unfathomably deep," I say: Boundless flames pervade the sky, an unfathomable jewel.

The Three Kinds of Karma
485. Dharma Hall Discourse
The descendants of the buddhas and ancestors without fail simply transmit the great way of the buddha ancestors. Our Buddha Tathāgata said,

23 This quote is from Sengzhao's Treatises, the section called "Nirvāṇa Has No Name." See Liebenthal, *Chao Lun,* pp. 111–112.

24 In Indian Buddhist cosmology, the world is supported at the base by a wheel of wind, above which rests a diamond wheel.

"Even after a hundred kalpas have passed, the karma of our actions does not disappear, and when we encounter these causal conditions we receive their results ourselves."[25]

The nineteenth ancestor, Venerable Kumārata, instructed Venerable Jayata, saying, "Retribution for good and bad actions occurs in three times (past, present, and future). Common people only see that the benevolent die young and the violent live long, the unjust are fortunate and the just unfortunate, and so they think that there is no cause and effect, and that evil and virtuous actions are in vain. They do not realize that the shadow and echo of conduct follows without a hairsbreadth of discrepancy, and even after a hundred thousand kalpas have passed, [unless you have received its fruit] it has not been erased."[26]

The way of the buddha ancestors is like this. Descendants of buddha ancestors should carve this in their bones and etch it in their skins.

The first of the six non-Buddhist teachers, Pūraṇa Kaśyāpa, preached to his disciples as follows, "There is no black [evil] karma, and no retribution for black karma. There is no white karma, and no fruit of white karma. There is no gray [neutral] karma, and no result of gray karma. There is no ascending or descending karma."[27]

The sixth of those teachers, Nirgrantha Jñatīputra, preached to his disciples as follows, "There is no good and bad, no father and mother, no present and future lives, and no arhats or practice of the way. All living beings after eighty thousand kalpas will naturally be released from the cycle of birth and death. Both those who have and have not committed evil will equally share this."[28]

Clearly know that the teaching of buddha ancestors and the wrong views of those outside the way are ultimately not the same. It is said that there are three kinds of karmic retribution: the first is karmic results received

25 This quote is from volume 6 of the Sarvāstivādin Vinaya.

26 This statement by Kumārata is from the Jingde Transmission of the Lamp. See Ogata, *Transmission of the Lamp*, pp. 37–38.

27 Pūraṇa Kaśyāpa (Jap.: Furanakashō) was one of the six well-known non-Buddhist teachers during Śākyamuni's time.

28 For Nirgrantha Jñatīputra, the historical founder of Jainism, see Dharma hall discourse 52 and volume 1, note 123.

in the present life; the second, karmic results received in the next life; and the third, karmic results received in the future. These three kinds of karma are as shadows and echoes following us, like an image reflected in a mirror.

When Will We Meet the Compassionate Buddha?

486. Dharma Hall Discourse for the Ceremony for Buddha's Parinirvāṇa [1252][29]

Two thousand years ago today, our original teacher, the Tathāgata Śākyamuni, entered nirvāṇa under the bodhi tree in India in the Sahā world. Every year when we encounter this day, the branches lower and the leaves become withered, saddened by the Tathāgata's [passing away into] nirvāṇa. The meaning of this nirvāṇa is that we are not seeing the place where the first ancestor [Mahākāśyapa] broke into a smile.[30] We are not able to recognize the time of the second ancestor [Dazu Huike] doing prostrations. How could we assess a patch-robed monk drawing a circle? How could we deliberate about a capable person striking the sitting platform?

The sixth ancestor, the ancestral teacher of Caoxi, Dajian [Huineng], instructed Zen teacher [Guangzhou] Zhidao saying, "Unsurpassed great nirvāṇa is perfectly bright and always serenely illuminated. Common people think it is death, and those outside the way cling to it as annihilation. The people who seek after the two vehicles [of śrāvakas and pratyekabuddhas] take this as their own non-doing. These are examples of sentimental calculations, and are roots of the sixty-two [mistaken] views [of self]."[31]

Therefore [nirvāṇa] is neither departing nor entering [the world], nor hiding in despair. Nor is it birth or extinction, nor going or coming. And yet, simply when the opportunity and conditions join together, parinirvāṇa is manifested. This night [Buddha] entered nirvāṇa under the

29 For Dōgen's earlier Parinirvāṇa Day Dharma hall discourses, see discourses 121, 146, 225, 311, 367, and 418.

30 "This nirvāṇa" might be interpreted as the sadness at this idea of nirvāṇa as Buddha's extinction, as opposed to his continuing through the buddha ancestors.

31 This exchange between the sixth ancestor and Guangzhou Zhidao is from the Jingde Transmission of the Lamp. See Ogata, *Transmission of the Lamp*, pp. 156–158.

twin sāla trees, and yet it is said that he always abides on Vulture Peak.[32] When can we meet our compassionate father? Alone and poor, we vainly remain in this world. Although it is like this, his remote descendants in this thousandfold Sahā world, at this very time, what can you say?

After a pause Dōgen said:

> In Crane Forest with the moon fallen, how could dawn appear?[33]
> In Kuśi[nagara] flowers wither, and spring is not spring.
> Amid love and yearning, what can this confused son do?
> I wish to stop these red tears, and join in wholesome action.[34]

Spring Crimson Penetrating All Minds
487. Dharma Hall Discourse

> In both arousing the mind and the ultimate stage,
>   how do we practice fully?
> Engaging these two minds like this
>   is the style of buddha ancestors.
> Forgetting self and freeing others
>   with the strength of merit and virtue,
> My homeland's spring color, peach blossom crimson.

A Song for the Cypress Tree
488. Dharma Hall Discourse
I can remember, a monk once asked Zhaozhou, "What is the meaning of the ancestral teacher [Bodhidharma] coming from the west?"

Zhaozhou said, "The cypress tree here in the garden."

The monk said, "Master, do not use objects to guide people."

Zhaozhou said, "I am not using objects to guide people."

---

32 "It is said that he always abides on Vulture Peak" refers to the inconceivably long life-span described in chapter 16 of the Lotus Sutra.

33 Crane Forest was a name for Kuśinagara, where Śākyamuni passed away, because upon his passing it is said that many flowers immediately bloomed and turned as white as cranes, or that many cranes arrived as well.

34 "Red tears" is an expression similar to bitter tears. "Wholesome action" is, literally, "good karmic causes" of future effects.

The monk [again] asked, "What is the meaning of the ancestral teacher coming from the west?"

Zhaozhou said, "The cypress tree here in the garden."[35]

Students in recent times do not understand Zhaozhou's meaning and do not study Zhaozhou's words, so we should deeply pity them. Someone claimed that Zhaozhou said "The cypress tree in the garden" before, and again said "The cypress tree in the garden" later, only in order to not allow the student to create any understanding. Another claimed that all words without exception expound Zen, so before and after he used the same phrase, "cypress tree." Such kinds of people are as numerous as rice, sesame, bamboo, and reeds. And yet they try to affix their spring dreams to Zhaozhou's words, but they cannot.

Now suppose someone asked me, Eihei, "What is the meaning of the ancestral teacher coming from the west?" I would say to him: Crossing over the remote blue waves for three years.

Suppose he said, "Master, do not use objects to guide people." I should say to him: I am not using objects to guide people. Suppose he again asked, "What is the master's expression that does not use objects to guide people?"

I would say to him:

How could blinking the eyes at Vulture Peak
   be a special occasion?
Breaking into a smile has never ceased.
Four or five thousand willows and flowering trees
   along the street,
Twenty or thirty thousand musicians
   play strings and winds in the balconies.

35 The story of Zhaozhou's cypress tree is case 45 in Dōgen's kōan collection with verse comments in volume 9, and is also discussed by Dōgen in Dharma hall discourse 433. It appears in Green, *Recorded Sayings of Zen Master Joshu,* pp. 15–16; Cleary, *Book of Serenity,* case 47, pp. 197–200; and the Mumonkan, case 37 (see Aitken, *Gateless Barrier,* pp. 226–230; and Cleary, *Unlocking the Zen Kōan,* pp. 167–169). The monk's statement might also be read as "Master, do not use objects to instruct the subject."

The Fire of Life's Passing
489. Dharma Hall Discourse for Closing the Fireplace [1252][36]

> The whole circle arrives in spring.
> Opened or closed according to the times,
>   it resembles a painting.
> Feeding coals and gazing at the ashes we add a flake of snow.
> Patch-robed monks call this a red furnace.

A Green Hut in the Sunlight
490. Dharma Hall Discourse
I can remember, when Zen Master Nanyue Huairang first visited Caoxi, the sixth ancestor [Dajian Huineng] asked him, "Where are you from?"[37]

Nanyue Huairang said, "I came from National Teacher Songshan [Hui]an's place."

The ancestor said, "What is this that thus comes?"

Nanyue Huairang never put this question aside. After eight years he told the sixth ancestor, "[I,] Huairang can now understand the question 'What is this that thus comes?' that you received me with upon my first arriving to see you."

The sixth ancestor said, "How do you understand it?"

Nanyue said, "To explain or demonstrate anything would miss the mark."

The sixth ancestor said, "Then do you suppose there is practice-realization or not?"

Nanyue said, "It is not that there is no practice-realization, but only that it cannot be defiled."

The sixth ancestor said, "Only this nondefilement is exactly what the buddhas protect and care for. You are thus, I am thus, and the ancestors in India also are thus."

---

36 Shutting down the fireplace in the monks' hall occurred on the first day of the third month. The only other Dharma hall discourse in Eihei Kōroku on this occasion is discourse 122 in the year 1243.

37 Dōgen also recounts this story as case 59 in the kōan collection with verse comments in volume 9, and in Dharma hall discourse 374, given two years before in 1250. See note 43 to that discourse for other citations.

The teacher Dōgen said: Do you want to clearly understand the meaning of this? If the sixth ancestor were to ask, "Where are you from?" I would say on behalf of Nanyue: For a long while I have yearned for the atmosphere of the master's virtue. Arriving here to humbly make prostrations, I cannot bear how deeply moved I feel.

Suppose the sixth ancestor also asked, "What is this that thus comes?" On behalf of Nanyue, facing the sixth ancestor, I would bow and lower my head with hands clasped in shashu position and say: This morning in late spring it is fairly warm, and I humbly wish the venerable master ten thousand joys in your activities.

Suppose someone asked what was the meaning of Nanyue's statement, "To explain anything would miss the mark." I would simply say to him: Even though the reeds are young and green, these spring days the sunlight remains later, and I would like to build a grass hut.[38]

Suppose I was asked, "What did the sixth ancestor mean when he said, 'Just this nondefilement is exactly what the buddhas protect and care for. You are thus, I am thus, and the ancestors in India also are thus'?" Then I would like to say: A blue lotus blossom opens toward the sun.[39]

There Is No Zen School
491. Dharma Hall Discourse

Within the transmigrations of birth and death, encountering a tathāgata in this world is the most excellent reward. Even if we do not meet a tathāgata in this world, encountering the true Dharma is the next best thing. Even if we do not encounter the true Dharma, meeting the semblance Dharma is next.[40] Even if we do not meet either the true Dharma or the semblance Dharma, still, if we are born during the age of final

---

38 The word translated here as "reeds" refers to a kind of grass used for building thatched roofs. A grass hut is a metaphor for the space of practice.

39 A blue lotus is *utpala* in Sanskrit, one of the four kinds of lotus flowers in India. The Mahāparinirvāṇa Sūtra, chap. 24, says that it represents diligence.

40 According to the theory of the decline of Dharma, popular during Dōgen's time, the age of Semblance Dharma, when the practice and teaching remain, follows the age of True Dharma, when the Buddha's enlightenment is present as well as the practice and teaching. The Semblance Dharma is followed by the Final Dharma age, in which only the teaching remains. Dōgen usually disputes the ultimate truth of this theory, believing in the current possibility of practice and awakening. But he does use this theory, as here, as an

Dharma but before the Buddha Dharma has completely vanished, this is still [as rare as] the udumbara flower in the world, and a white lotus for people. A wheel-turning king or being born in the northern continent cannot compare with this.[41] Having already been able to encounter this, it is the time when we must most genuinely practice and engage the way. What our predecessors have been seeking is simply this right view. They wished to attain unmistaken views.

Now it is a mistake to arbitrarily call the Tathāgata's unsurpassed awakening of the true Dharma eye treasury wondrous mind of nirvāṇa by the name, Zen school. How could this not be a poisonous view?

In India for twenty-eight generations it has been passed along, heir to heir. The twenty-eighth ancestor, Venerable Bodhidharma, undeterred by ten thousand miles as he sailed the ocean for three years, finally arrived in China and reached Nanhai in Guangzhou. That was the eighth year of the Putong era of Emperor Wu of the Liang dynasty [527]. After his encounter with Emperor Wu of Liang, the emperor did not value him.[42] Then Bodhidharma left that country and entered Mount Song of the Wei dynasty.

Dwelling at Shaolin temple on Shaoshi Peak, he sat facing the wall for nine years. He had a Dharma heir, Shenguang [Dazu Huike], and transmitted the Dharma and robe. After being transmitted five times, it reached Caoxi [Dajian Huineng], who had two eminent disciples. They were Great Master Qingyuan [Xingsi] Hongji and Zen Master Nanyue [Huairang] Dahui. Qingyuan had only one successor, Shitou. Nanyue had only one successor, Kiangsi [Mazu Daoyi]. Those in later generations should know that even in ancient times there were not many [verified] people. In those times, how could there not have been evil demons and spirits, as in these days? Kiangsi [Mazu] was succeeded by Baizhang, and

---

expedient means to encourage students, going on to say that this is especially the time to practice diligently.

41 A wheel-turning king (Skt: *chakravartin*) is a benevolent world ruler with the physical signs of a buddha. The northern continent in Buddhist cosmology is without suffering. See volume 6 (Dharma hall discourse 457), note 95.

42 The legend of Bodhidharma's encounter with Emperor Wu is a famous story in Zen lore; see Cleary and Cleary, *Blue Cliff Record,* case 1, pp. 1–9; and Cleary, *Book of Serenity,* case 2, pp. 6–10. See also Dharma hall discourse 304.

Shitou was succeeded by Yaoshan. Today we do not have ancestral teachers like Kiangsi [Mazu], Shitou, Yaoshan, and Baizhang. When ancestral teachers like these were in the world, it was never heard that they called the Buddha Dharma the Zen School; but for the last two or three hundred years, mistakenly it is designated as Zen School. It is not yet clear where this title originated, but it is an extremely foolish name.

It is said in the Record of the Rock Gate in the Woods, "Bodhidharma first went from Liang to Wei.[43] He did walking meditation at the foot of Mount Song, rested his staff at Shaolin temple, and simply sat calmly facing the wall, not doing any practice of 'Zen.'[44] Later, worldly people could not fathom why he did this, and called his practice Zen. This dhyāna 'Zen' is only one of many practices; how could it suffice to describe the exhaustive practices of the sage? And yet people at that time and those who compiled historical accounts listed him among the biographies of dhyāna masters, and included him within the group of withered trees and dead ash.[45] However, the sage was not simply practicing dhyāna, and yet was not apart from dhyāna."

So we see, in past generations there were teachers who clarified the way, but now there is nobody who listens to the way. How sad; how sad! Evil demons and spirits, wild beasts, and domesticated animals now call themselves the Zen School, and furthermore falsely discuss its superiority and inferiority with schools such as the Lotus and Huayan.[46] This is because there are no [true] people in this degenerate age. What is simply trans-

---

43 The Record of the Rock Gate in the Woods (Ch.: Shimen Rinjian Lu; Jap.: Sekimon Rinkan Roku) is by Juefan Huihong, who lived at Shimen (Rock Gate) temple. This work was recommended to Dōgen by his teacher Tiantong Rujing.

44 The word "Zen" is the Japanese pronunciation of *chan*, the Chinese transliteration used sometimes for the technical Indian practice of *dhyāna*. *Chan* was also used generally in early Chinese Buddhism for all meditation. Here, Juefan Huihong is saying that Bodhidharma did not do any technical meditation practice. Dōgen critiqued the name "Zen School" in much the same way twenty years earlier in his response to question 5 in Bendōwa. See Okumura and Leighton, *The Wholehearted Way*, pp. 28–29.

45 "Withered trees and dead ash" refers to pre-Mahāyāna practitioners who seek to eliminate all desires and delusions in order to escape from the world.

46 The Lotus School was a name for the Tiantai (Jap.: Tendai) school, which most esteemed the Lotus Sutra; and the Huayan (Jap.: Kegon) school was based on the Avataṃsaka (Flower Ornament) Sūtra.

mitted by buddha ancestors is only the true Dharma of our Śākyamuni Buddha, which is anuttara samyaksambodhi. Therefore, we should know that within Buddha Dharma there are the Lotus and Huayan and other [teachings]; and it is not that within each of the Lotus and Huayan and so on there are various different buddha dharmas. Therefore, the eighty-four thousand Dharma treasures within the Lotus, Huayan, and so on are all without exception what is simply transmitted by buddha ancestors. It is not that outside of the Lotus and Huayan there is the way of ancestral teachers. So we should not compare various schools, as it is simply like a country having its king [who includes all].

People seeking the way for the sake of unsurpassed awakening do not designate the simply transmitted, directly indicated, unsurpassed true Dharma of buddha ancestors as the Zen School. If you use the name Zen School, you are not descendants of buddha ancestors and also have poisonous views.

After a pause Dōgen said: The Buddha Dharma fundamentally has no outer name or form. Later people falsely established many random names. Although facing the wall at Shaolin resembled [dhyāna], do not call it Zen School and misguide sentient beings.

The Good Karma of Thundering Silence
492. Dharma Hall Discourse
People who study the Buddha Dharma are called those who create good karma.[47] Those who seek fame and profit in worldly paths, or as government officials, are called people who create bad karma. It is bad karma because one falls into the three evil realms, and good karma because it allows us to attain the way of buddhas. Therefore, good teachers and home-leavers in the previous generations did not engage in worldly paths or as government officials. Why would they become attached to fame or profit? Such home-leavers should study the way as if extinguishing flames from their heads, without being caught up in writing Chinese poems or [Japanese] waka verses. Moreover, human life is impermanent, like dew on the grass or a splash of water. Although fragile as dew on the grass or

---

47 Good and bad karma here are, literally, "white" and "black" karma. See Dharma hall discourse 485.

a splash of water, if we support the way of buddha ancestors, we are joyful and fortunate within the ocean of birth and death.

I can remember, Yaoshan had not gone up to the hall [to give a talk] for some time. The director said, "For a while the great assembly has been missing the master's kind instruction."[48]

Yaoshan said, "Strike the bell." The bell was sounded and the assembly gathered. Yaoshan ascended the seat. After a while he simply descended from the seat, and returned to the abbot's quarters.

The director followed after him and said, "Master, you agreed before to expound the Dharma for the assembly. Why didn't you offer us a single word?"

Yaoshan said, "There are sutra teachers for sutras, and commentary teachers for commentaries. Why do you blame this old monk?"

The teacher Dōgen said: Do you want to understand "There are sutra teachers for sutras, and commentary teachers for commentaries. Why do you blame this old monk?"

Why are you criticizing? This old monk is the teacher, and you are the disciple.

Do you want to understand "Master, you agreed before to expound the Dharma for the assembly. Why didn't you offer us a single word?"

The sound of thunder shakes in the distance. Therefore [the director] said that [Yaoshan] did not offer a single word.

A Grandmother's Sixty Blows
493. Dharma Hall Discourse
Here is a story. After Linji was hit sixty times with Huangbo's staff, he visited Gao'an. After understanding Huangbo's mind, he returned to Huangbo. Huangbo said, "Such a crazy person, go practice in the monks' hall."[49]

Great assembly, do you want to understand this circumstance?

48 This story appears in Shōyōroku, case 7. See Cleary, *Book of Serenity*, pp. 28–31.

49 For the full story, see case 51 of the kōans with verse comments in volume 9, and volume 2 (Dharma hall discourse 160), note 108. See also Watson, *Zen Teachings of Master Lin-chi*, pp. 104–107.

After a pause Dōgen said:

The eye on the tip of the staff is like a hundred thousand suns,
Shining through old dreams to bring awakening.
The painful place of neither punishment nor reward is
    intimate.
How could the kindness of a grandmother's mind be small?[50]

Portraying Just This

494. Dharma Hall Discourse

I can remember, Great Teacher Dongshan [Liangjie] Wupen, when making offerings to the portrait of [his teacher] Yunyan, then related the story about portraying [Yunyan's] reality.[51] There was a monk who asked, "What was the meaning of Yunyan's saying, 'Just this is it'?"

Dongshan said, "At that time I nearly misunderstood my late teacher's meaning."

The monk said, "It's not yet clear. Did Yunyan know 'It is' or not"?

Dongshan said, "If he did not know 'It is,' how could he have understood to speak thus? If he did know 'It is,' how would he be willing to speak thus?"

The teacher Dōgen after a pause said: "How could he have understood to speak thus?" A bright star appears and the great thousand worlds brighten.

---

50 When Linji returned to Huangbo after awakening, he said, "It's all because of your grandmotherly kindness." See ibid., p. 106.

51 This story and dialogue is related in the Shōyōroku, case 49. See Cleary, *Book of Serenity*, pp. 206–209. The story refers back to a dialogue that had occurred previously when Dongshan left his teacher and asked Yunyan how, in the future, he could truly portray Yunyan. This could be interpreted as how to draw his portrait, as portraits were then passed from teacher to student to verify Dharma transmission. See volume 5 (Dharma hall discourse 376), note 48, for the use of the word "reality" to indicate "portrait," and more on this use of portraits in Zen transmission ceremonies. After Dongshan's question about this, Yunyan paused, and then replied, "Just this is it." Dongshan did not understand until later. See Powell, *The Record of Tung-shan*, pp. 27–28.

"How would he be willing to speak thus?" Chicken Foot Mountain opens and Mahākāśyapa is aged.[52] The ancient mirror is round and bright, illuminating upright and inclined.[53] The mysterious mechanism revolves on high, both naturally arriving within together.[54] For many kalpas their family style continues. The voice of father and son is boundlessly radiant.

A Joyful Culmination of Practice

495. Dharma Hall Discourse for Bathing [Baby] Buddha [on Buddha's Birthday, 1252][55]

The eight forms of accomplishing the way are the manners of transformation of buddhas.[56] Therefore, Māyā (Śākyamuni Buddha's mother) arrived at Lumbinī Park, and the bodhisattva was born and entered the world. Indra held up the bodhisattva on his [swaddling] cloth, and human and heavenly beings for the first time made prostrations upon seeing the face of the single most venerable one. At that very time, jeweled lotuses blossomed to support the bodhisattva's feet. Heavenly beings rained down

---

52 Chicken Foot Mountain (Skt.: Kukkutupāda) is the mountain in India where Mahā-kāśyapa practiced and passed away. He is said to be still waiting inside the mountain for Maitreya to appear as the next Buddha, at which time Mahākāśyapa will present Śākyamuni's robe to Maitreya. So here Dōgen is referring to the arrival of Maitreya at Mahākāśyapa's mountain.

53 Upright and inclined, also known as ultimate and phenomenal, or universal and particular, are the two polarities of the dialectic presented by Dongshan in his teaching of five ranks, and in his teaching poem "Song of the Precious Mirror Samādhi." See Leighton, *Cultivating the Empty Field,* pp. 7–12, 76–77; and Powell, *Record of Tung-Shan,* pp. 61–65. Beginning with "The ancient mirror is round and bright...," Dōgen's commentary is patterned very closely after Hongzhi's verse commentary to this story. See Cleary, *Book of Serenity,* p. 207.

54 "Both Arrive Within Together" is the fifth rank, in which the ultimate and phenomenal interact freely and are not seen as at all separate. The first four ranks are named, first, the "Phenomenal Within the Ultimate"; second, the "Ultimate Within the Phenomenal"; third, "Emerging from Within the Ultimate"; and fourth, "Going Within Together." Dōgen generally de-emphasizes the five ranks as this system can be misused as overly formulaic, and thereby misleading to actual practice.

55 The previous Buddha's Birthday Dharma hall discourses are numbers 42, 75, 98, 155, 236, 256, 320, and 427.

56 "The eight forms of accomplishing the way" are descending from Tuṣita Heaven to earth, entering a mother's womb, leaving the mother's womb, leaving home, overcoming demons, attaining the way, turning the Dharma wheel, and entering parinirvāṇa.

flowers upon the bodhisattva. Then he took seven steps in each of the four directions, and gazed to the four directions without blinking. The words naturally emerged from his mouth, "Within the world, I am the most excellent. Within the world, I am the most venerable. From today on my share of births have been exhausted; this is my final body, and I will become a buddha."

From the earth two ponds emerged as offerings to the sacred mother, and from the sky two showers fell and bathed the bodhisattva. [The park was] filled with precious necklaces and jeweled robes, and fully equipped with a golden bed and jeweled parasol, presumably offered by heavenly beings in accord with the genuinely matured function of his [past] conditions. Twenty thousand heavenly maidens surrounded Māyā and assisted her. Five hundred heavenly beings attended the bodhisattva with praises. The grasses and trees in the three thousand great thousand worlds suddenly produced beautiful flowers. All living beings without exception were illuminated with radiance. Those who were suffering were all relieved of their misery, and those in comfort all increased their joy. Who could fully express the auspicious appearance of this great good fortune? The benefit of this joyful happiness is still fresh today. Why is this so? Great assembly, do you want to clearly understand the meaning of this?

After a pause Dōgen said: [He] sat cutting through the dried turds of patch-robed monks, and wore through straw sandals while diligently engaging the way.[57] How could this be the same as the shell of ignorance? From this moment, he became the king of the great thousand worlds.

Responding to the Mystery
496. Dharma Hall Discourse

Brothers, this is a good time; just make effort. Time does not wait for people. Extinguish the flames from your head. Entrusting what is in front of your face, how could this depend on expression in words? One who actively responds to what meets their eyes is called a superior person who studies the mystery. If you can be like this, the style of our tradition will not fall. At this very time, how is it?

---

57 "Dried turds" here is a translation of Yunmen's response to "What is Buddha?" See Dharma hall discourses 69 and 88, and volume 1, notes 150 and 185. In this context it may refer simply to the karmic body.

After a pause Dōgen said: Drawing legs for the four snakes is not my intention, but rather to diligently practice the buddha ancestors' heart for this lifetime.[58]

Diligent Efforts of an Intimate Tradition
497. Dharma Hall Discourse

The first ancestor [Bodhidharma] came from the west, and China grew warm. Although [others who came] before and after were wonderful, Mount Song [where Bodhidharma stayed] alone was intimate. He sailed across the ocean over great distances for three years, then sat immovably facing the wall for nine years, and his descendants spread throughout the world until authentic successors came to our country. We can say that this country for the first time gratefully received the original lord of precepts, samādhi, and wisdom, like people gaining a king. People then could determine the good roots of body, speech, and mind, like receiving a lamp in the darkness. Truly the udumbara flower blooms and everyone loves and respects it; a lion roars and phantoms vanish.

Therefore, Qingyuan determined the price of rice in Luling, and Nanyue expressed that nothing hits the mark.[59] Sun face, moon face, eyes are wide open.[60] Bright head, dark head, the nose is high and straight. Huangmei [Daman Hongren] and Huangbo snapped apart their staffs; Yunyan and Yunju came holding their sitting cushions.[61] Already having

58 Drawing legs on a snake refers to something unnecessary or superfluous. The four snakes here implies the four elements: earth water, fire, and wind.

59 Qingyuan, when asked about why Bodhidharma came from the west, responded, "What is the price of rice in Luling?" See Cleary, *Book of Serenity,* case 5, pp. 20–22. For Nanyue not hitting the mark, see Dharma hall discourse 490.

60 "Sun face, moon face," frequently referred to by Dōgen, was Mazu's utterance when asked about his failing health, and refers to buddhas said to live a very long time, or for merely one night. See Cleary and Cleary, *Blue Cliff Record,* case 3, pp. 18–21; and Cleary, *Book of Serenity,* case 36, pp. 160–162. "Polishing a tile to make a mirror" in Dōgen's closing verse that follows this is also a reference to a story about Mazu. See volume 4 (Dharma hall discourse 270), note 23, or volume 6 (Dharma hall discourse 453), note 85.

61 Dōgen is playfully referring to various great masters in the lineage after Bodhidharma. The fifth ancestor, Huangmei, used his staff to signal Huineng in the rice pounding hut. Huangbo used his staff sixty times on Linji. See Dharma hall discourses 126 and 493, respectively.

attained such a thing, do not spend time vainly, but immediately you should energetically extinguish the flames on your head, and courageously make undaunted effort. At just such a time, how do you practice? Do you want to clearly understand this?

After a pause Dōgen said:

Who would laugh at polishing a tile to make a mirror?
Green bamboo and yellow flowers enter into a painting.
Not engaging in extensive deliberation,
When sowing the fields you must work diligently.

Practicing and Expounding in the Deep Mountains
498. Dharma Hall Discourse

Those who are truly endowed with both practice and discernment are called ancestral teachers. What is called practice is the intimate practice of the ancestral school. What is called discernment is the discerning understanding of the ancestral school. The practice and discernment of buddha ancestors is simply to discern what should be discerned and to practice what should be practiced. The first thing to practice is to cut away all attachments and have no family ties, to abandon social obligations and enter the unfabricated.[62] Without sojourning in towns, and without being familiar with rulers, enter the mountains and seek the way. From ancient times, noble people who yearn for the way all enter the deep mountains and calmly abide in quiet serenity.[63]

The ancestral teacher Nāgārjuna said, "All zazen people reside in the deep mountains." You should know that for departing the troubling bustle and attaining quiet serenity, there is nothing like the deep mountains. Even if you are foolish, you should abide in the deep mountains, because

62 The unfabricated, or unconditioned, in Buddhism refers to the state where no karma is created. It is also literally "non-action," the same term used in Daoism for harmoniously being in the world.

63 "Without sojourning...in quiet serenity" echoes the admonitions by Dōgen's teacher Tiantong Rujing—for example, "You must immediately make your dwelling in steep mountains and dark valleys, and nurture the sacred embryo of the buddhas and patriarchs for a long time. You will surely reach the experience of the ancient virtuous ones." See Kodera, *Dōgen's Formative Years in China,* p. 122.

the foolish abiding in towns will increase their mistakes. Even if you are wise, you should abide in the deep mountains, because the wise abiding in towns will damage their virtue.

I, Eihei, in my vigorous years searched for the way west of the western ocean [in China], and now in my older years I abide north of the northern mountains. Although I am unworthy, I yearn for the ancient traces. Without discussing our wisdom or unworthiness, and without discriminating between sharp or dull functioning, we should all abide in the deep mountains and dark valleys.

Daci [Huanzhong] instructed the assembly saying, "Being able to expound ten feet does not match practicing one foot; being able to expound one foot does not match practicing one inch."

Dongshan [Liangjie] said, "Expound what you are not able to practice, and practice what you are not able to expound."

Yunju [Daoying] said, "When practicing there is no way to expound. When expounding there is no way to practice. Neither practicing nor expounding, which path should we tread?"[64]

Luopu [Yuanan] said, "When both practice and expounding do not arrive, the original matter exists. When both practice and expounding arrive, the original matter does not exist."

Hongzhi [Zhengjue] said, "Transcend right and wrong, and erase all traces. Although encountering each other, we do not recognize our faces; if we recognize our faces we do not recognize each other [as others]. These [four] venerable masters all have good points. On the tip of the tongue at the present moment, there is no barrier at the crossroads; right beneath our feet, there are no links [attached] to the five sense objects. If you want to practice, just practice; if you want to expound, just expound. Suppose someone asked Changlu [Hongzhi], 'What is this: wanting to practice, just practice?'[65] I, Hongzhi, would say, 'Walk on.' To 'What is this: wanting to expound, just expound?' I, Hongzhi, would say, 'Ah!'"

---

64 In Shōbōgenzō Gyōji (Continuous Practice), Dōgen quotes in the same order these same three sayings by Daci, Dongshan, and Yunju and gives some commentary to each, validating the role of both practice and expounding. See Tanahashi, *Enlightenment Unfolds*, pp. 128–129. See also Dharma hall discourse 10.

65 Changlu is the name of a temple where Hongzhi Zhengjue resided before moving to Tiantong Temple in 1130, where he remained until his death in 1157, and thus he is

The teacher Dōgen said: Each of those five venerable masters spoke in such a way. Today, how can I, Eihei, not speak? Expounding horizontally and vertically is one and the same as wondrous, intimate practice. Wondrous, intimate practice is one and the same as expounding horizontally and vertically.

Prepare Tea and Hit the Cart
499. Dharma Hall Discourse
The flower in my hand opens toward the sun, but at times we prepare Zhaozhou's tea.[66] A patch-robed monk's [calligraphed] circle is the moon in mid-autumn, but still we ask, "What are the three pounds of sesame?"[67] Right at such a time, how can we speak further?

After a pause Dōgen said: What is the intention when the robe is transmitted? Instead of hitting the ox you should hit the cart.[68]

The Universal Expounding Right Now
500. Dharma Hall Discourse
When one comments on Zen, expounds the way, discusses the mystery, demonstrates the wonder, or raises up the style of the school, this is simply the appropriate portion from each person. Within the tip of a single hair there are innumerable buddhas and ancestors who arouse bodhi mind, diligently carry out the great practice, accomplish unsurpassed true awakening, turn the great Dharma wheel, and widely do Buddha's work. Do you understand, and do you also see this or not? Furthermore, within a single atom, manifest the sanctuary of the jeweled king and erect the Dharma banner. Buddha, the Dharma, monks, the lands, atoms, living beings, and the mountains, rivers, and great earth, from ancient to present,

---

sometimes referred to as Tiantong Hongzhi. Presumably this quote is from before Hongzhi moved to Tiantong.

66 For Zhaozhou's tea, see volume 6 (Dharma hall discourse 428), note 30.

67 Three pounds of sesame, often translated as three pounds of flax, is the response of Dongshan Shouchu to "What is the essential meaning of Buddha Dharma?" For references, see volume 1 (Dharma hall discourse 69), note 150.

68 For Nanyue Huairang's question about hitting the cart or the ox, see Dharma hall discourse 453 and volume 6, note 88.

all expound it at the same time without ceasing. Already it can be like this. Do not neglect or take lightly the manifestation of the study of the way that has been singularly transmitted by buddha ancestors. At this very time, whether our position is that of buddha ancestor, ordinary person, or sage; experienced student or newcomer, how do we speak?

After a pause Dōgen said: Simply realizing that a flower opens and the world becomes fragrant, who knows that our nostrils are pierced at the same time? *Dōgen threw down his whisk and descended from his seat.*

Moonlight over the Pregnant Temple Pillars
501. Dharma Hall Discourse

Body and mind dropped off is the beginning of our effort, but when a temple pillar becomes pregnant, how do we discern their absence? The thick cloud matting spread over the mountain peaks is still, and above the heights the round moon shines in all directions. It stands alone, eminent, not relying on anything. The lofty Buddha body does not fall into various kinds. Therefore, an ancient worthy said, "The sage empties out his heart. The ten thousand things are nothing other than my own production. Only a sage can understand the ten thousand things and make them into oneself."[69] At this very moment how is it? Do you want to understand this clearly?

After a pause Dōgen said: The moon moves following the boat, with the ocean vast. Spring turns following the sun, with the sunflowers red.

The Sound of the Mountains
502. Dharma Hall Discourse

In a Dharma hall discourse my late teacher Tiantong [Rujing] instructed the assembly, saying, "I can remember, a monk asked an ancient worthy [Guizong Daoquan], 'Is there Buddha Dharma or not on a steep cliff in the deep mountains?'[70]

---

69 This is a quote from Sengzhao's Treatises, chap. 4, "Nirvāṇa Has No Name." See Liebenthal, *Chao Lun,* pp. 101–129. See also Dharma hall discourses 482 and 484. This passage by Sengzhao had a profound impact on Shitou Xiqian. See Cook, *The Record of Transmitting the Light,* p. 181–182; or Cleary, *Transmission of Light,* p. 153.

70 This story is recounted almost exactly from Dharma hall discourse 194, although here the recounting of the story is also given as a quote from Tiantong Rujing.

"The worthy responded, 'There is.'

"The monk said, 'What is this Buddha Dharma on a steep cliff in the deep mountains?'

"The worthy said, 'A large rock is large; a small one is small.'"

My late teacher Tiantong [Rujing] said, "The question about the steep cliff in the deep mountains was answered in terms of large and small rocks. The cliff collapsed, the rocks split, and the empty sky filled with a noisy clamor."

The teacher Dōgen said: Do you want to clearly understand the meaning of this? The steep cliff asked about Buddha Dharma in the deep mountains, and large and small rocks gave ten million responses about existence and nonexistence, the kalpa of arising and the kalpa of destruction. At this very time, students of Eihei, how is this?

After a pause Dōgen said: The deep mountains are not necessarily peaks and steep cliffs, but when you strike through the supreme barrier there is [still] a noisy clamor.

Healing with Words That Needle
503. Dharma Hall Discourse

I can remember, a monk asked Yunmen, "What is Buddha?"

Yunmen said, "A dried piece of shit."[71]

My late teacher [Tiantong Rujing] composed a verse, saying:

> Yunmen took a shit from the opposite end,
> Upsetting Gautama, like an acupuncture needle in a painful spot.[72]
> We need to see the ocean dried up clear to the bottom,
> To know the person dead, without remaining mind.

Today, I, Eihei, would like to continue this rhyme:

71 For Yunmen's "a dried piece of shit," sometimes translated as "a dried shitstick," see volume 1, notes 150 and 185 (Dharma hall discourse 69 and 88).

72 "Took a shit from the opposite end," literally "upside down," implies that the words from Yunmen's mouth were like excrement.

How could myriad activities lead to this careless nature?
When Buddha was sick, Jīvaka offered a needle.[73]
Even if we see the ocean dried up without any bottom,
Who can clarify the person dead, without a mind remaining?

Clarifying Cause and Effect in the Formless

504. Dharma Hall Discourse for the Memorial Morning for My Late Teacher Butsuju [Myōzen][74]

Here is a story. An ancient Buddha said, "Our body received birth from the formless, just like conjured shapes and images. The body and consciousness of phantoms originally do not exist. Actions leading to punishment and fortune are both empty, not abiding anywhere."[75]

The teacher Dōgen said: Put aside for now receiving birth. What is the meaning of this formlessness? Do you want to hear it? This Dharma abides in its dharma position, and the form of the world constantly abides. This is the principle that only a buddha together with a buddha can thoroughly fathom.[76] Today, with what saying can I know and repay my gratitude [to my teacher Myōzen]?

After a pause Dōgen said: Tathāgatas never go beyond clarifying cause and effect; a bodhisattva [in the last life before buddhahood] unfailingly is born in Tuṣita Heaven.[77]

---

73 Jīvaka was Śākyamuni's physician, and a son of King Bimbisāra.

74 For the memorial service for Butsuju Myōzen in the previous year, 1251, see Dharma hall discourse 435. Myōzen had been Dōgen's Rinzai lineage teacher in Japan. They journeyed to China together, where Myōzen died.

75 This statement is attributed to Vipaśyin Buddha, the first of the legendary seven buddhas leading to Śākyamuni. See Dharma hall discourses 38 and 446. This verse is from the story in the Jingde Transmission of the Lamp. See Ogata, *Transmission of the Lamp*, p. 1; the Eihei Kōroku version here is "body and consciousness," however, while in the Transmission of the Lamp it is "mind consciousness."

76 "This Dharma abides in its dharma position, and the form of the world constantly abides" and "Only a buddha together with a buddha can thoroughly fathom it" are quoted from the Lotus Sutra, chap. 2, "Skillful Means." See Katō, Tamura, and Miyasaka, *Threefold Lotus Sutra*, pp. 70, 52; and Hurvitz, *Scripture of the Lotus Blossom of the Fine Dharma*, pp. 41, 22, respectively.

77 In Shōbōgenzō Sanji gō (Karmic Retribution in the Three Times), Dōgen refers to a similar idea as in the quote attributed to Vipaśyin Buddha, as stated by Changsa Jingcen,

Sitting through Midsummer
505. Dharma Hall Discourse
From this morning, the first day of the sixth month, we let go of striking the wooden sounding block *(han)* to signal zazen. But at the height of summer, we never discard our old Zen boards.[78] Don't forget that we are transmitting the Dharma and saving deluded beings.

The Black Glow of Enlightenment
506. Dharma Hall Discourse for Enlightenment Day on the Eighth Day of the Twelfth Month [1252][79]
On this night the Tathāgata [Śākyamuni] completed true awakening. With effort and dropping away [body and mind], his eyes became clear. Together with him, all the various living beings in the three thousand worlds smiled. Although this is so, what is the situation of patch-robed monk students of Eihei?

After a pause Dōgen said: The spring color of plum blossoms in the snow is wonderful. The black glow of a single monk's staff is pure.

---

that the essential nature of karmic retribution is empty. Dōgen in that essay criticizes Changsha, upholding the central importance of cause and effect. See Yokoi and Victoria, *Zen Master Dōgen,* pp. 148–149; and Nishijima and Cross, *Master Dogen's Shobogenzo,* book 4, pp. 123–124. In this Dharma hall discourse, Dōgen again upholds that buddhas never go beyond cause and effect. But in citing the Lotus Sutra, here he also seems to be trying to integrate the primacy of cause and effect with the statement "Actions leading to punishment and fortune are both empty." That cause and effect each abide in their dharma position is the principle, or meaning, of formlessness.

78 Traditionally in monasteries zazen was optional or reduced in schedule from the sixth month to the ninth. This is the first Dharma hall discourse noting the day when that period traditionally began. See Dōgen's comments on the day for resuming regular zazen schedule, Dharma hall discourses 193 (in 1246), 279 (1248), 347 (1249), 389 (1250), 451 (1251), and 523 (1252). Dōgen makes a point of not reducing zazen during these periods.

79 This Dharma hall discourse is obviously out of chronological order in the text. It is the final dated Dharma hall discourse given by Dōgen, as there were none dated from 1253, and it may indeed be Dōgen's final formal teaching. Other Enlightenment Day Dharma hall discourses in Eihei Kōroku are discourses 88, 136, 213, 297, 360, 406, and 475.

A Fragrant Period of Zazen

507. Dharma Hall Discourse Requested by Scribe Gijun as a Memorial for the Sake of Venerable [Kakuzen] Ekan[80]

> The old crane nests in the clouds, not yet awakened from sleep.
> Frost piles up on snow in the icy cauldron.
> For adorning his reward in the Buddha land, nothing is needed
> Besides the slight fragrance of practice during one stick of incense.

Just say, what is the situation today of you patch-robed monks?

After a pause Dōgen said: Stop saying that the other shore is not before your eyes. This single staff is the bridge.

The Cause and Fruits within the Complete Circle

508. Dharma Hall Discourse

> A circle is one complete wheel.
> Transmitting the robe is well-known from olden times.
> The auspicious flower has ten million petals.
> Bearing fruit is accomplished depending on causes.

Does a Wriggling Earthworm Have Buddha Nature?

509. Dharma Hall Discourse

In studying the Buddha way, the view and understanding should be true. If our view and understanding is false, we waste our time. In modern times everyone says, "Where people respond immediately is their fundamental life nature.[81] Where people immediately know cold and heat by themselves is their own lord and master. This is exactly Buddha nature, and there should not be another secondary person." This kind of understanding is what ancient worthies condemned.

---

80 Previously, in 1246, Dōgen had given a Dharma hall discourse requested by Kakuzen Ekan for his late teacher, Bucchi Kakuan. See Dharma hall discourse 185. Ekan had died in 1251, although the date is somewhat uncertain.

81 "Fundamental life nature," literally "original life," is the phrase used in East Asia to refer to one's life quality based on the astrological implications of the day and year of one's birth. But here it is used as a name for Buddha nature.

Don't you see that Government Minister Zhu asked Teacher Chang-sha Jingcen, "When an earthworm is cut into two pieces, and both parts are moving, I wonder which piece has the Buddha nature?"[82]

Changsha said, "Don't have deluded thoughts."

The official said, "What about their moving?"

Changsha said, "That is only because the wind and fire has not yet dispersed."

The official did not respond.

Changsha called out, "Government Minister!"

The official responded.

Changsha said, "This [response] is not your fundamental life nature."

The official said, "Apart from this present response, there should not be a secondary lord and master."

Changsha said, "You should not call or consider a government minister as like our present emperor."

The official said, "If so, when I do not respond to the teacher at all, then wouldn't that be this disciple's lord and master?"

Changsha said, "It is not about responding or not responding to this old monk, but from beginningless kalpas, this [response or non-response] is the fundamental root of life and death [the transmigration in samsāra, as opposed to the fundamental Buddha nature]."

Then Changsha gave instruction with a verse that said:

> "People who study the way do not understand truth
> Simply because they have acquiesced to discriminating
>   consciousness.
> The root of life and death from beginningless kalpas
> Ignorant people consider as the fundamental true person."

---

82 This story appears as case 65 of the ninety kōans with Dōgen's verse comment in volume 9. Abbreviated versions of this story are discussed by Dōgen in Dharma hall discourse 328, and in Shōbōgenzō Busshō (Buddha Nature). See Waddell and Abe, *Heart of Dōgen's Shōbōgenzō*, pp. 94–96. Dōgen gets this story from Shūmon Rentō Eyō (Collection of the Essence of the Continuous Dharma Lamp). There are different versions of this story in the Jingde Transmission of the Lamp, which seem to have been combined and adapted for the full Shūmon Rentō Eyō story, given by Dōgen here. See Ogata, *Transmission of the Lamp*, pp. 333, 336, 340–341.

This verse is a bright mirror for students of later generations. It illuminates the ancient and present, and illuminates false and true. If you take up this ancient mirror, you can abandon the mistake of considering a government minister as like the present emperor, and also abandon the mistake of having deluded thoughts about Buddha nature.

Last night Changsha came to stay on the tip of my whisk, and fell asleep. Then he made sounds, talking in his sleep, repeatedly chanting this verse. Therefore I, Eihei will humbly continue his rhyme.

After a pause Dōgen said:

Students of the way must actually penetrate the truth.
Ancestral teachers never play around with discriminating
    spirit.
Even if a government minister called himself the present
    emperor,
For ten million years there has never been a person.[83]

Causes for a Black Staff's Transformation
510. Dharma Hall Discourse
Students of the way cannot dismiss cause and effect. If you discard cause and effect, you will ultimately deviate from practice-realization.

---

83 As mentioned in note 77 above, in Shōbōgenzō Sanji gō, speculated to have been written around the same time as this Dharma hall discourse, Dōgen criticizes Changsha and strongly upholds the primacy of cause and effect. Furthermore, in Hōkyōki, Dōgen's journals from his studies with Tiantong Rujing in China in 1227, he asks Rujing about whether "people immediately knowing cold and heat by themselves" is itself enlightenment, which Rujing strongly denies. So this issue was apparently a longtime concern of Dōgen's. Shortly after that in Hōkyōki, Rujing strongly criticizes Changsha for equating karma and emptiness. See Kodera, *Dōgen's Formative Years in China*, pp. 119, 125; and Tanahashi, *Enlightenment Unfolds*, pp. 5, 11. To further complicate matters, some modern scholars believe that Dōgen's journals from China were not actually written until his last years, around the time of this Dharma hall discourse, as these supposed student journals were only discovered by Koun Ejō after Dōgen's death in 1253.

At any rate, in this Dharma hall discourse 509 Dōgen seems to be wrestling with the question of the relationships of emptiness to causality and of Buddha nature to karmic consciousness. He seems to be reasserting the emptiness of cause and effect and their implications for Buddha nature, as well as definitely praising Changsha. The issue of how Dōgen in his final years understood the significance of causality, also discussed in the next Dharma hall discourse, has been a major topic for recent Dōgen studies. See Heine, *Shifting Shape, Shaping Text.*

After relating the story of Baizhang's wild fox,[84] *Dōgen said:* Someone doubted this, saying, "A wild fox is an animal. How could it remember five hundred lifetimes?" This doubt is most foolish. You should know that various living beings, either animal or human, are inherently endowed with the power to know past lives.

Someone said, "Not falling into [cause and effect], and not ignoring are one and the same, and yet either falling or being released simply happens spontaneously." Such views are completely outside the way. Today, I, Eihei, will add a comment. If you say [people of great cultivation] do not fall into cause and effect, you are certainly dismissing cause and effect. If you say they do not ignore cause and effect, you have not yet avoided counting the neighbor's treasure.

After a pause Dōgen said: After many years of residing on this mountain, a black staff becomes a dragon, and this morning arouses wind and thunder.[85]

Zazen within Desire and Stumbling
511. Dharma Hall Discourse

I can remember, Dharma Teacher Dayi of the Tang dynasty asked Master Ehu, "There is no dhyāna in the realm of desire, how can we cultivate the samādhi of dhyāna?"

Ehu said, "You only know that there is no dhyāna in the realm of desire. You do not yet know that there is no desire in the realm of dhyāna."

Dayi had no response.[86]

---

84 For the story of Baizhang and the fox, frequently referred to by Dōgen, see volume 1 (Dharma hall discourse 62), note 137, and kōan case 77 in volume 9 with Dōgen's verse comments.

85 "Black staff" is literally "crow staff," and probably implies that it is black with age. "This morning" might also be read as "all at once."

86 The text has an error. As recorded in the Jingde Transmission of the Lamp, the dialogue takes place between an unnamed monk and Ehu Dayi, a disciple of Mazu, whereas in Dōgen's text Ehu and Dayi are two people. This is a small part of that dialogue, held at a debate sponsored by and presented before the emperor in 805. See Ogata, *Transmission of the Lamp*, pp. 229–230. This *dhyāna* is also "Zen" (or "Chan" in Chinese). So in the original dialogue it seems that the question and response may likely have related to the establishment of a Chan school in China by disciples of Mazu. But as Dōgen is using this story here, this term seems to refer more to meditation generally, and at times perhaps to the four *dhyāna*.

After a pause Dōgen said: Within seven tumbles and eight falls we still take up and use [meditation]. Both "no desire" and "no dhyāna" are not true. In steadfast immovable effort there is nothing to seek. How can this be equated with the three realms [of desire, form, and the formless]?

Lovebirds for Eisai

512. Dharma Hall Discourse on the Memorial Day for Great Teacher Zen Master Senkō [Myōan Eisai], Former Sōjō Hōin of the Second Rank[87]

The eye on his headtop opened with vitality, seeing through to the deep source of the buddha ancestors. The spirit talisman tucked under his arm broke through the lock of the barrier of life and death.[88] He could use his total functioning to illuminate everything with nothing left out. He let go his hold from the steep cliff, casting his body into the empty kalpa.[89] Going beyond he passed up through the headtops of buddhas; getting down he passed through the sense roots and dusts. His eyes did not make seeing a merit; his ears did not make hearing a virtue. The six sense faculties revolved together, and the ten thousand objects were vacant at ease. Entering [the realms of] buddhas and demons, he thereby transcended the forms of sameness and difference. Completely living and completely dying, he thereby dropped off the dynamic function of coming and going. [He is] already like this, but please say, where does my teacher's teacher, Senkō [Myōan Eisai], abide right now?

After a pause Dōgen said: I have vainly employed couples of lovebirds to somehow embroider these expressions.[90] Nevertheless, people struggle to search for golden needles.

---

87 See the prior memorial Dharma hall discourse for Eisai, discourse 441 in the previous year, 1251, and volume 6, note 62, for Eisai's titles, also given here.

88 For the talisman tucked under his arm, see volume 4 (Dharma hall discourse 264), note 11.

89 "Let go his hold from the steep cliff" is also used at the end of the closing verse from case 32 in Mumonkan. See Shibayama, *Gateless Barrier,* pp. 229; and Aitken, *Gateless Barrier,* p. 199.

90 "Couples of lovebirds" refers to the parallel structure of the pairs of lines in Dōgen's previous flowery statement about Eisai, recalling the parallelism that is the basis of Chinese poetry.

An Attractive Demon and Sickness
513. Dharma Hall Discourse
Studying the Buddha Dharma is most difficult to accomplish. Why is that? Even when people have genuinely aroused the mind of awakening, without knowing it they might fall in with demons, or unaware they might become sick, and their way-seeking mind will be broken, their practice-realization regressing and collapsing. Truly we must sympathize. Students these days are fascinated by the demon of brilliance and imagine it as the enlightenment of the way. Encountering the onset of the disease of fame and fortune, they imagine it as verification of the merit of their practice. These not only damage and destroy a single life or person, but they also can damage and destroy the merits and virtue of good roots from many lives through vast kalpas. This is the saddest thing for students. So-called satori (enlightenment) is very difficult to realize. It cannot be understood by thinking or discrimination, and it cannot be clarified by brilliance or keen wisdom. Considering fascination with this demon as great enlightenment, and clinging to the sickness and its ailments as merits and virtue, how could this not be a mistake?

Brother disciples, you should study in detail how to subdue demons and cure disease. The demons I speak of may appear as parents, teachers or seniors, brother disciples, relatives, close friends, or servants, repeatedly and strongly persuading us toward causes and conditions for regressing on the way. They also may manifest bodies such as buddhas, bodhisattvas, heavenly beings, or arhats, and may then instruct students saying, "The Buddha way is long and remote, and you must diligently bear suffering for a long time. So rather than this, follow your own inclinations. Nourish this body and life, and enjoy peace and comfort, always dwelling in the world with abundant clothing and food, satisfying the five desires, and you will naturally attain the way. How could the great way be related to this or that [lifestyle]? Just fall over amid the bustle, and return to your nature." Or they may say that causal conditioning is difficult to abandon, and cause students to backslide and turn from the way. Students should understand this and not follow them.

I can remember, a monk asked Zen Master [Baoji] Huayan Xiujing of Jingchao, "How is it when a person of great enlightenment returns to delusion?"

[Baoji Huayan] Xiujing said, "A broken mirror does not reflect anymore. A fallen flower has difficulty returning to the branch."[91]

The teacher Dōgen said: Although today I, Eihei, have entered the realm of [Baoji] Huayan, I have not yet exhausted his limits. Because I cannot avoid it, I will flap my lips. Suppose someone asks me, "How is it when a person of great enlightenment returns to delusion?" I would simply say to him: If the great ocean knew it was full, the hundred rivers would flow backward.[92]

Sudden Autumn Colors

514. Dharma Hall Discourse for Ending the Summer Practice Period [1252]

Considering the wisdom of playing with the spirits as your self, before you finish expounding the other, express yourself. Considering the Dharma of beyond-thinking as your realm, it is both existent and non-existent.[93] When we discuss this responsive function, the pure wind is pervasive. When we discuss this practice-realization, the ancient crane sleeps. Already like this, above the precious glazed hall are suddenly autumn colors, before the bright moon hall appears the abundant dawn sky. At just this very time, do you understand how it is?

After a pause Dōgen said: In the garden are eight hundred donkeys and three thousand horses. Although the next [buddha] to be born [Maitreya] is in the fourth heaven, inclined and upright have never departed from their original positions. How can the unborn speak about causes and conditions?[94]

---

91 Dōgen also discusses this dialogue of Baoji Huayan in Shōbōgenzō Daigo (Great Enlightenment). See Cleary, *Rational Zen,* pp. 110–115; and Nishijima and Cross, *Master Dogen's Shobogenzo,* book 2, pp. 85–90.

92 Dōgen also uses this expression, "If the great ocean knew it was full, the hundred rivers would flow backward," at the end of Dharma hall discourses 242 and 447.

93 This beyond-thinking is *hishiryō,* as discussed by Dōgen from the dialogue of Yaoshan about the mind of zazen. See Dharma hall discourse 373.

94 Donkeys and horses refer to monks in the monastery. The fourth heaven refers to Tuṣita Heaven, where Maitreya awaits his birth as the next Buddha in this world. The last two lines, "Inclined and upright have never departed from their original positions. How can the unborn speak about causes and conditions?" is from Hongzhi Zhengjue's Extensive Record, volume 5. Inclined and upright, also referred to as apparent and real, or

Grieving for my Late Teacher
515. Dharma Hall Discourse in Memorial for Tiantong [Rujing, 1252][95]
On this day my late teacher suddenly went on pilgrimage, kicking over the
barrier of his previous births and deaths. The clouds grieve, the wind
moans, and the valley streams are turbulent, as his young child (Dōgen)
yearns and looks for his beloved face. This is a statement about his passing away in complete tranquillity. Students of Eihei, what can you say as
a statement about realizing and repaying our debt of gratitude?

After a pause Dōgen said: After months and years of devotion to my
kind benefactor, how can the clouds dissipate? My tears have stained more
than a spot on my patched robe.

Sitting with Eyes Open in the Flames of the World
516. Dharma Hall Discourse
The ancestral teacher Nāgārjuna said, "Zazen is exactly the Dharma of all
buddhas, and yet, those outside the way also have zazen. However, those
outside the way make the error of attaching to its taste and to the thorns
of false views. Therefore it is not the same as the zazen of buddhas and
bodhisattvas. The two vehicles of śrāvakas [and pratyekabuddhas] also
have zazen. However, those two vehicles [seek to] control their own
minds, and have the tendency of seeking after nirvāṇa. Therefore, this is
different from the zazen of buddhas and bodhisattvas."[96]

The teacher Dōgen said: The ancestral teacher Nāgārjuna spoke like this.
We should know that although the name of zazen (sitting meditation) is
used by those of the two vehicles and those outside the way, it is not the
same as the sitting transmitted by buddha ancestors. These days in the
mountains and temples of Song dynasty China, many careless, lazy elders do not understand this point. This is undoubtedly the degeneration of

---

particular and universal, are the dialectical poles of the five ranks teaching, although here
it is said that they abide in their original positions. The "unborn" in the last sentence is
probably an abbreviation for the "patience with the unconditioned (unborn) nature of all
things" (Skt.: *anutpattika dharma kṣānti*) a synonym for perfect enlightenment.

95 The memorial day for Tiantong Rujing was the seventeenth day of the seventh month.
Previous Dharma hall discourses for Rujing were numbers 184, 249, 274, 276, 342, and 384.

96 This quote is from Nāgārjuna's Commentary on the Mahāprajñāpāramitā Sūtra (Ch.:
Dazhidulun), volume 17.

the Buddha Dharma. Brothers, you should know that only the ancestral teacher [Bodhidharma] transmitted the true vein of Buddha Dharma, doing zazen facing the wall. Since the Eihei era of the Later Han dynasty, although there was sitting based on interpretations of writings, this was completely outside the correct manner, which was only transmitted by the ancestral teacher.[97] Was this not truly the intimate transmission of the Buddha Dharma? The buddha ancestors transmit zazen facing the wall, which is not the same as the meditation of the two vehicles or those outside the way. The eye that sees before anything happens can open before anything happens, just like the lotus blossom in flames in the twelfth month.[98]

The Three Periods of Karma

517. Dharma Hall Discourse

I can remember, the twentieth ancestor in India, Jayata, asked Venerable Kumārata, "My father and mother always had faith in the three treasures. However, they frequently were sick, and whatever they did turned against their will. On the other hand, the neighbor family engaged in impure activities (such as butchering) for a long time, but their health was always strong and their business went well. Why were they happy, and what crime had we committed?"

The Venerable [Kumārata] said, "Why do you bother questioning this? The retribution for good and bad actions occurs in three times. Generally, people only see that the good die young, the violent live long, the wicked are fortunate, and the just have misfortune, and thereby they believe that there is no cause and effect, and actions worthy of punishment or fortune are in vain. Especially they do not know that shadows and echoes follow along without the slightest gap, and that even after a billion kalpas have passed, [the unmanifested consequences of actions] are not ground away."

---

97 The Eihei Era of the Later Han dynasty, 58–76 C.E., when the first Buddhist text was brought from India to China. Dōgen named his temple Eiheiji (which also gave Dōgen his own temple name, Eihei) after this era.

98 A lotus in flames implies practice in the midst of worldly desires, unlike those in the two vehicles seeking the cessation of nirvāṇa. Its blossoming in the twelfth month is yet another image of something rare and precious, like the transmission of the true practice.

At that time, after hearing these words, Jayata was immediately released from his doubts.[99]

Suppose someone asked me, Eihei, what was retribution in the present lifetime. I would simply tell him that retribution in the present lifetime is just like buckwheat [planted in the spring and harvested that same autumn].

Suppose someone asked about retribution in the next lifetime. I would simply tell him that retribution in the next lifetime is just like barley [planted in the fall and harvested in the following summer].

Suppose someone asked about retribution in future lifetimes. I would simply tell him that retribution in future lifetimes is like an old-growth tree.[100]

The Dharma Body in Everyday Activity
518. Dharma Hall Discourse

Dōgen drew a circle in the air with his whisk, held up the whisk, and said: If I hold this up, you call it buddhas appearing in the world. If I put it down, you call it the ancestral teacher [Bodhidharma] coming from the west. If I draw a circle, you call it what is protected and cared for by the buddhas and ancestral teachers. When I do not hold it up, put it down, or draw a circle, how do you assess this? Even if you can assess it, you should laugh at both the view of the unconditioned and at the livelihood in the demon's cave. Although it is like this, students of Eihei, there is another excellent place. Great assembly, do you want to see that excellent place?

Again Dōgen held up his whisk, and after a pause said: Great assembly, do you understand? If you understand, the Dharma body of all buddhas enters my nature. If you do not understand, my nature in the same way joins together with the Tathāgata.[101] Great assembly, what is the meaning

---

99 This story is from the Jingde Transmission of the Lamp, the section on Kumārata. See Ogata, *Transmission of the Lamp,* pp. 37–38.

100 "An old-growth tree" is our translation for *haojan* tree (Jap.: *kōken*), literally, "good, hard" tree. Supposedly, this tree grows after the seed has been in the ground for a century.

101 "The Dharma body of all buddhas enters my nature. My nature in the same way joins together with the Tathāgata" is from the Song of Enlightenment by Yongjia Xuanjie. See Sheng-yen, *Poetry of Enlightenment,* p. 55.

of "the Dharma body of all buddhas enters my nature" and of "my nature in the same way joins together with the Tathāgata"?

After a pause Dōgen said: In the early morning eat gruel, at lunchtime rice. In the early evening do zazen, and at night sleep.

The Upright Lotus

519. Dharma Hall Discourse

Following the sages in dwelling upright is like yearning for the wise ones. The lotus mind loves to be dry, not damp from the [muddy] water. You should know that here is the auspicious and dignified matter, passed on face to face for twenty-two hundred years.

The Flowing of This Moment in the Wind

520. Dharma Hall Discourse

When held up it is the essence, when let go it is transmitted by the wind. When neither held up nor let go, seven or eight are pervaded. The valley stream, with its nighttime flowing and daytime waters, washes the moon and washes the sun. The mountain, with clouds in the south and rain in the north, is dyed green and dyed red.[102] Zhaozhou's cypress tree could never be an object; [Hangzhou] Duofu's bamboo became a grove.[103] The three times seem to never move forward or backward; the great thousand worlds seem to hang in the empty sky. Each moment is neither me nor you; practice-realization is from the west and from the east.

Radiance of the Enduring Moon

521. Mid-Autumn Dharma Hall Discourse [1252][104]

The moon is neither round nor lacking, how could it wax or wane? Even

---

102 The north side of the mountain dyed red implies an earlier start to the colored leaves of autumn.

103 For Zhaozhou's cypress tree, see Dharma hall discourse 488 and kōan case 45 in volume 9. The bamboo of Hangzhou Duofu, a disciple of Zhaozhou, refers to the following dialogue, recorded in the Gotō Egen collection Five Lamps Merged into the Source (Ch.: Wudeng Huiyuan). A monk asked, "How is Duofu's bamboo grove?" Duofu said, "One or two stalks are leaning." When the monk said he didn't understand, Duofu said, "Three or four stalks are bent over."

104 Mid-autumn is the fifteenth day (the full moon) in the eighth month. Other Dharma

if it is good for offering, when we pause our restrictions it is good for practice.[105] The second moon of Xuansha is about to set. Yunyan's "which is this?" moon does not flourish.[106] Although this is so, for descendants of the buddha ancestors there is also the matter of going beyond.

When the World-Honored One was in the world, the Asura king Rāhula wanted to swallow the moon.[107] The heavenly moon was frightened and appeared before Buddha and recited to Buddha this verse, "World-Honored Buddha of great wisdom and pure effort, now I take refuge and make prostrations. This Rāhula is upsetting me. I entreat the Buddha to look upon me with pity, and help and protect me."

The Buddha recited a verse to the Asura king Rāhula saying, "The moon can illuminate the darkness, pure and cool. This is the great bright lamp in the empty sky. Its color is white and pure with a thousand rays. Do not swallow the moon, but immediately release it." At this time the Asura king Rāhula sweat with fear and shame, immediately letting go of the moon.

---

hall discourses on this date in Eihei Kōroku are discourses 13, 77, 106, 189, 277, 344, 413, and 448. This was Dōgen's last mid-autumn moon at Eiheiji. He died just a little more than a year later after a long sickness in Kyoto. He wrote the following waka poem about the 1253 autumn full moon. "Just when wondering / If I would again see it / In this fall— / Under tonight's full moon / How can I sleep?" Another version is in Steven Heine, *The Zen Poetry of Dōgen: Verses from the Mountain of Eternal Peace* (Boston: Tuttle Publishing, 1997), pp. 94–95.

105 This refers to a story about Mazu enjoying the full moon with his disciples Xitang Zhizhang, Baizhang, and Nanquan. Mazu asked, "How is it right now?" Xitang Zhizang said it was a good time for offering. Baizhang said it was a good time for practice, and Nanquan shook out his sleeves and left. See Dharma hall discourse 13 and other versions in Ogata, *Transmission of the Lamp*, p. 210; Cheng, *Sun Face Buddha*, p. 69; and the commentary to case 6 in Cleary, *Book of Serenity*, p. 25.

106 The reference to Xuansha and Yunyan refers to the story recorded in Shōyōroku, case 21. When Yunyan was sweeping the ground, his brother Daowu commented, "Too busy." Yunyan said, "You should know there is one who is not busy." Daowu then said, "So is there a second moon?" Yunyan held out the broom and said, "Which moon is this?" Xuansha had later commented, "Indeed this is the second moon." See Cleary, *Book of Serenity*, pp. 91–94. Dōgen saying Yunyan's moon does not flourish implies the moon waning.

107 This story is from volume 10 of Nāgārjuna's Commentary on the Māhāprajñāpāramitā Sūtra (Ch.: Dazhidulun). This occurred while the Asuras, or angry spirits, were at war with the heavenly beings. This incident might perhaps be based on an eclipse of the moon.

Seeing that the Asura king Rāhula was scared into releasing the moon, the Asura king Vādiṣa gave a verse asking, "Why did you, Rāhula, shiver with fear and immediately release the moon, with your whole body sweating as if you were sick and your mind agitated with fear?"

Then the Asura king Rāhula gave this verse in answer, "The World-Honored One gave a verse ordering that if I did not release the moon, my head would split into seven pieces. Even if I kept my life, there would be no peace. Therefore, I now have released this moon."

The Asura king Vādiṣa in a verse said, "Buddha is difficult to encounter; he appears in the world [only after] a very long time. When he expounded this pure verse, Rāhula promptly released the moon."

Therefore now the moon in the sky has maintained its life-span throughout five hundred heavenly years, simply to requite the World-Honored One's help and protection. The life-span of that heaven is such that fifty years of human life is like one day and night in that heavenly time span. Multiply that [fifty-year span] by thirty days in a month, and twelve months in a year, and then by those [heavenly] five hundred years. Cloud and water monks, you should know that today the autumn moon is radiant, pure, and cool, illuminating the darkness in the world, just as does the World-Honored One's eyes in their conditioned capacity.

On this very occasion of the autumn full moon, I, Eihei, wish to raise up the word brightness expounded by the World-Honored One in his verse, to increase the radiance of the moon palace and illuminate the darkness of delusion in the great thousands of worlds. This must be the transmission of the lamp and the command of Buddha.

Then Dōgen expounded a verse saying:

Because of Buddha's majestic power, the palace is bright.
A thousand glorious rays appear at once.
Even if humans love the moon in mid-autumn,
The brightness of the half moon is boundless in the heavens.

The Offering of Zazen

522. Dharma Hall Discourse

I can remember: When my late teacher, Tiantong [Rujing], was dwelling at Tiantong [monastery], he instructed the assembly with a Dharma hall discourse saying, "Right at the very time of sitting, patch-robed monks can make offerings to all the buddhas and ancestors in the whole world in ten directions. All without exception pay homage and make offerings ceaselessly with various materials such as fragrant flowers, lamps, precious jewels, or excellent robes. Do you know and see this? If you know this, do not say you are wasting time. If you do not yet know it, do not avoid what you are facing."

The teacher Dōgen said: I, Eihei, graciously became the Dharma child of Tiantong, but I do not walk the same as Tiantong. And yet, I have been sitting the same as Tiantong. How can I not penetrate the expressions of the innermost hall of Tiantong [Rujing]? Please say, what is the meaning of such a statement?

After a pause Dōgen said: At the very time of patch-robed monks sitting, do not say that polishing a tile or hitting the cart is making offerings to the buddha ancestors in the ten directions with excellent robes, precious jewels, or fragrant flowers. At just such a time, are there any further instructions for the cloud and water monks?

Dōgen scanned the great assembly and said: How can the hearing and seeing of ordinary beings compare to taking a drink of Zhaozhou's tea for oneself?[108]

New Impressions on Old Cushions

523. Dharma Hall Discourse

This morning is the first day of the ninth month.[109] With the striking of the wooden sounding block, the members of the great household do zazen. Never lower your head and sleep. Thinking of equality is seeing the coming of wisdom. Stop discussions based on grasping at trees and relying on

108 For Zhaozhou's tea, see volume 6 (Dharma hall discourse 428), note 30.

109 For other Dharma hall discourses on the first day of the ninth month, when the relaxed period with decreased meditation time was finished, see discourses 193, 279, 347, 389, and 451.

grasses.[110] Do not seek externally for the lotus that blooms in the last month of the year. Body and mind that is dropped off is steadfast and immovable. Although the sitting cushions are old, they show new impressions. At this very time, how is it?

After a pause Dōgen said: It is not that there is no practice-realization, but who could defile it? How could this be the same as the ten holy and three wise [stages]?[111]

The Reward Land of Beyond-Thinking

524. Dharma Hall Discourse for the Memorial for Counselor of State Minamoto[112]

Repaying our debts of gratitude to our fathers is exactly the traces of excellent footprints left by the World-Honored One. How shall I state a phrase about knowing and repaying this debt of gratitude? Abandon our benefactors and quickly enter the unconditioned. How do frost and dew dissolve in the brightness of the sun's wisdom? For the nine generations born in heaven we are very delighted.[113] How could our parents' [rebirth in] the land of reward be an idle boast?

Here is a story. When Yaoshan was sitting, a monk asked, "What are you thinking while so steadfast and immovable?"

Yaoshan said, "I think of not thinking."

The monk said, "How do you think of not thinking?"

Yaoshan said, "Beyond-thinking."[114]

---

110 For "grasping at trees and relying on grasses," here an expression for attachment to intellectual understandings, see volume 1 (Dharma hall discourse 1), note 2.

111 For the "ten holy and three wise stages," see volume 1 (Dharma hall discourse 33), note 84.

112 This is the memorial for Minamoto Michitomo, either Dōgen's brother or more likely his father (at the least his adopted father). See the one previous memorial discourse for him, Dharma hall discourse 363 and volume 5, note 26, for details. This memorial was on the second day of the ninth month.

113 It is said that when one is ordained as a home-leaver monk, nine generations of one's relatives will be reborn in heavenly realms, going backward and forward four generations as well as in the present generation, although there are many variations about how this is understood.

114 Dōgen quotes this story about Yaoshan frequently, for example in Dharma hall discourse 373. See volume 5, note 41, for other references.

Today I especially adorn the reward land [of my father] with this virtue [of beyond-thinking].

After a pause Dōgen said: While thinking during steadfast sitting, Li and Chang almost finish arguing about the black and also speaking of the yellow.[115] Who knows that above the sitting cushions and Zen boards, the hot water in the cauldrons and charcoal in the fires [in hell] are naturally pure and cool?[116]

The Single Practice Beyond Perception

525. Dharma Hall Discourse

An old man in ancient times [Sikung Benjing] said, "In studying the way, we do not use the perceptions of seeing and hearing. If we practice with the perception of seeing and hearing, that is simply the perception of seeing and hearing, not the awakening of the way."

Therefore I, Eihei, say that in the Buddha way we do not expect enlightenment from using the spirit.[117] Few have ever received transmission through writing and discussion. Even if you study with booming roars of thunderclaps, how can you let go of the bounds of senses and objects and the naming of forms? Wall-gazing and polishing a tile are meeting face to face, with effort and diligence continuous. Finally affirming the empty kalpa with body and mind, we truly see that the mouths of our eating bowls are round. This is what we can study on the long platforms [in the monks' hall], and this is also how one goes beyond the buddha ancestors.

After a pause Dōgen said: Mazu and Aśvaghoṣa are true from head to tail; [Daman] Huangmei and Huangbo play in the wind.[118] Turning a

---

115 Li and Chang are common family names, representing common people. In Chinese traditional symbolism, going back to the I Qing, or Book of Changes, black is the color of heaven (as in the night sky) and yellow the color of earth. So this sentence implies thinking about all the multitude of phenomena.

116 "Water in the cauldrons and charcoal in the fires" is a common expression for the tortures of hell.

117 "Spirit" is *kami,* which can mean spirits or deities, but here refers to psyche, intellection, and spiritual capacities.

118 Dōgen here is playing with the names of these great ancestral teachers. Mazu and Aśvaghoṣa (Ch.: Ma-ming; Jap.: Memyo) both have the character for horse starting their

somersault in one-practice samādhi, the kesa (monk's robe) of the seven buddhas is covering their shoulders.[119]

Green Leaves Turn Red
526. Dharma Hall Discourse
You should know that becoming a buddha is not something new or ancient. How could practice-realization be within any boundary? Do not say that from the beginning not a single thing exists.[120] The causes are complete and the results are fulfilled through time. Great assembly, please tell me, why is it like this?

After a pause Dōgen said: Opening flowers will unfailingly bear the genuine fruit; green leaves meeting autumn immediately turn red.

Waters Rise and Fall
527. Dharma Hall Discourse
A drop of water into a drop of ice; how does it transform, how does it freeze? Cultivating causes and experiencing fruits, we join horizontally and ascend vertically. If I were to comment, predictions [of buddhahood] are like determining the price of rice in Luling.[121] If I were to comment,

name, thus he calls them "true from head to tail". Huangmei (the fifth ancestor) and Huangbo both have the character for yellow starting their name. Huangmei means "Yellow Plum," and Huangbo means "Yellow Chinese cork tree." "Playing in the wind" in this sentence probably implies their enjoying the blossoms of those plants in the wind.

119 "One-practice samādhi" is the exclusive focus on a single practice. The sixth ancestor, Dajian Huineng, said, "In every place, whether walking, standing, sitting, or lying down, always practice with one straightforward mind." See Price and Wong, *Diamond Sutra and Sutra of Hui Neng,* p. 43; and Cleary, *Sutra of Hui-neng,* pp. 31–32.

120 "From the beginning not a single thing exists" is a famous statement attributed to the sixth ancestor, Dajian Huineng. See Cleary, *Sutra of Hui-neng,* p. 10; and Price and Wong, *Diamond Sutra and Sutra of Hui Neng,* p. 18.

121 What is the price of rice in Luling?" is the response of Qingyuan Xingsi to being questioned about the essential meaning of Buddha Dharma. See Cleary, *Book of Serenity,* case 5, pp. 20–22. "Prediction," or *juki,* refers to the predictions of future buddhahood given by Śākyamuni in the Lotus Sutra. But in Dōgen's interpretation this *juki* implies the "confirmation" of buddhahood implicit right now. See Nishijima and Cross, *Master Dogen's Shobogenzo,* book 2, pp. 197–209.

becoming a buddha brings rain in repayment of the clouds' ascending. What I have just said are simply phrases about the way in accord with the way, but furthermore there is discussion about descending to the grasses with compassion.[122] How is that?

After a pause Dōgen said: The first lamp lit immediately breaks the previous ancient darkness. Even if we add on so that the brightness increases, do not hold it up again as it will make no difference. A billion lamps are within the room.

Just Sitting in the Ancient Mirror
528. Dharma Hall Discourse for Opening the Fireplace [1252][123]
If we measure the boundaries of the world, the ancient mirror is not simply its painting.[124] Baizhang did not know one *zhang* measure. Xuefeng created the mold for the first time.[125] At just such a time, what is the portion of patch-robed monks?

After a pause Dōgen said: Today patch-robed monks quarrel about opening the fireplace. A great person did not dig in the cold ashes.[126] Let go of discussing the mystery and expounding the wonder; return here and shut your mouth.

122 The image of rainfall recalls the image of Dharma rain in the Lotus Sutra, chap. 5, falling to equally nourish all the varied beings. "Descending to the grasses" implies a buddha's descent to the world of suffering beings for their sake.

123 For previous Dharma hall discourses for Opening the Fireplace, held on the first day of the tenth month, see discourses 14, 109, 199, 288, 353, 396, and 462.

124 "The ancient mirror is not simply a painting" implies that the ancient mirror does not merely show a reflection. The ancient mirror is an image for the fundamental reality, or Dharma, of all things.

125 Xuefeng said that if the entire world were the width of one *zhang* (Jap.: *jō,* a measure equal to about ten feet), then the ancient mirror would also be one *zhang*. Xuansha then pointed to the fireplace and asked, "Then how wide is the fireplace?" Xuefeng responded, "As wide as the ancient mirror." See Shōbōgenzō Kokyō (The Ancient Mirror) in Nishijima and Cross, *Master Dogen's Shobogenzo,* book 1, pp. 254–257. This measure *zhang* is also the second character of Baizhang's name.

126 Not digging in the cold ashes refers to the story of Baizhang asking his disciple Guishan if there was fire amid the ashes in the fireplace. Guishan did not search in the ashes, but said there was no remaining fire. Baizhang reached in with tongs and pulled out an ember. See Leighton and Okumura, *Dōgen's Pure Standards for the Zen Community,* pp. 136–137; and Chang, *Original Teachings of Ch'an Buddhism,* pp. 200–202.

A Teacher Sells His Body

529. Dharma Hall Discourse

I can remember, Nanquan pointed to the assembly and said, "Old Master Wang [Nanquan himself] wants to sell his body.[127] Is there someone who will buy it?"

Then a monk came forward and said, "I will buy it."

Nanquan said, "Not making it too expensive, or too cheap, how much will you pay?" The monk could not respond.

Zhaozhou answered, "Next year I will make a cotton robe for the master [Nanquan]."[128]

Great assembly, can you grasp this situation? I, Eihei, would like to dispense this to the cloud and water monks, and see if you clearly understand.

After a pause Dōgen said:

> Before the sale of [Nanquan's] body was settled,
> [Zhaozhou already] bought it cheaply.
> We pity the person plundered in the marketplace.
> How much is asked for mugwort or chinaberry?[129]
> An excellent warhorse or eight [ordinary] workhorses
> all enjoy spring's arrival.[130]

A Cold Crane Looks to Spring

530. Dharma Hall Discourse

Here is a story. King Prasenajit asked Venerable Piṇḍola, "I have heard that the venerable one [Piṇḍola] personally saw the Buddha. Is that true?"

The Venerable Piṇḍola raised his eyebrows to reveal his eyes.[131]

---

127 "Selling his body" implies transmitting his Dharma.

128 Another version of this story appears in the Jingde Transmission of the Lamp, see Chang, *Original Teachings of Ch'an Buddhism*, p. 157; or Ogata, *Transmission of the Lamp*, p. 260.

129 Mugwort is a weed, available cheaply, eaten cooked or used as moxa for healing. Chinaberry (Jap.: *sendan*) is an expensive plant used in incense.

130 An "excellent warhorse" is the expression written literally as a "dragon horse."

131 This story, and the following verse by Tiantong Rujing, are in Dōgen's Shōbōgenzō essays Baika (Plum Blossoms) and Kenbutsu (Seeing Buddha). In Rujing's version, the

My late teacher Tiantong [Rujing] said in a verse:

Raising his eyebrows he answered the question.
He personally saw Buddha and was not deceived.
Even now he receives offerings from all under heaven.
Spring is present on a plum branch tip, covered in cold snow.

Today, I, Eihei, speak, respectfully continuing this lofty rhyme for the sake of the clouds and water assembly. Great assembly, do you want to hear it?

After a pause Dōgen said:

He personally saw Buddha and spoke directly.
Raising his eyebrows he wished not to deceive.
Springtime in the field of merit, flowers have not yet fallen.
In the jewel forest, the old crane's wings are still cold.

Nothing Lacking in the Triple World
531. Dharma Hall Discourse

In Qingyuan's White House tavern, three cups of wine,[132]

---

king in the story is Prasenajit, a patron contemporary with Buddha. This version is discussed by Dōgen in Shōbōgenzō (Plum Blossoms); see Tanahashi, *Moon in a Dewdrop*, pp. 120–121. In Kenbutsu, Dōgen cites another version of the story that seems more likely, in which the aged Piṇḍola is meeting King Aśoka, who lived more than a century after Śākyamuni. See Nishijima and Cross, *Master Dogen's Shobogenzo*, book 3, pp. 201–204.

132 "In Qingyuan's White House tavern three cups of wine" is a saying of Caoshan Benji (successor of Caodong/Sōtō school founder Dongshan), quoted by Dōgen from the Shūmon Rentō Eyō (Collection of the Essence of the Continuous Dharma Lamp). Caoshan tells a student he has had three cups of wine at this White House but claims that his lips are not wet, perhaps as if the wine had no effect, or dissolved like a snowflake. Another version of the story appears in the section on Caoshan in Jingde Transmission of the Lamp. See Chang, *Original Teachings of Ch'an Buddhism*, p. 73. This version also appears in case 10 of the Mumonkan; see Aitken, *Gateless Barrier*, pp. 70–75; and Shibayama, *Gateless Barrier*, pp. 82–85. However, in those stories there is no reference to Qingyuan.

On Shitou's red fireplace, one flake of snow,[133]
A flower blooming on a monk's staff has merit.
Smiling on our sitting cushions, there's nothing lacking.[134]

At this very time, students of Eihei, what do you say?
After a pause Dōgen said:

What we call karma creates the triple world.
Realizing these stories makes the one mind.[135]
Nāgārjuna received a person with a bowl of water.
Kānadeva approached the way holding a needle.[136]

133 "One flake of snow on the red fireplace" is a saying by Changzi Kuang, a disciple of Qingyuan's successor Shitou. During the conversation when they met, Shitou asked if Changzi wanted an eye-opening. When Changzi said yes, Shitou lifted his foot. Changzi made a prostration. When Shitou asked why, Changzi said, "One flake of snow on the red fireplace."

134 The "nothing lacking" might also refer to the round sitting cushions being completely round, like the full moon.

135 The triple world refers to the desire, form, and formless realms. "The triple world is one mind only" is a saying from the Avataṃsaka (Flower Ornament) Sūtra, discussed by Dōgen in Shōbōgenzō Sangai Yuishin. See Nishijima and Cross, *Master Dogen's Shobogenzo,* book 3, pp. 43–49.

136 Nāgārjuna received Kānadeva by presenting a bowl of water. Kānadeva dropped a needle in, and Nāgārjuna approved him as his disciple. The needle in a bowl of water could represent the particular phenomena (product of causes and conditions) right within the universal Dharma or Mind. See Ogata, *Transmission of the Lamp,* p. 29; and Cleary and Cleary, *Blue Cliff Record,* case 13, pp. 88–93.

ESHU EIHEI ZENJI DŌGEN OSHŌ SHŌSAN

MASTER DŌGEN'S INFORMAL TALKS
AT EIHEIJI TEMPLE IN ECHIZEN PROVINCE

COLLECTED BY EJŌ, ATTENDANT OF DŌGEN ZENJI, AND OTHERS

E K
I Ō
H R
E O
I K
  U

THE EXTENSIVE RECORD OF EIHEI DŌGEN, VOLUME EIGHT

Shōsan

The Suchness of Grasping and Letting Go

1. Informal Meeting at the End of the Summer Practice Period[1]

Both ancients and moderns clarify and engage that and this as they manifest.[2] If you do not know it is, how could you accomplish such a thing?

---

1 *Shōsan*, which we are translating as "informal meeting," is only informal in comparison to the *jōdō*, or Dharma hall discourses, of volumes 1–7 of Dōgen's Extensive Record. The *jōdō*, literally "ascending in the hall," were given from the Dharma seat platform in the Dharma hall while the monks were standing. This was the traditional form used in most of the Recorded Sayings of individual masters compiled in Song dynasty China. It was the form favored by Dōgen once he settled at Eiheiji. The written form of *jishu*, used by Dōgen in Shōbōgenzō, was used much less, or scarcely at all, once he started giving the *jōdō* at Eiheiji. Volume 8 starts with informal meetings (*shōsan*), literally "small meetings," which were given somewhat more informally than the *jōdō*, usually in the abbot's quarters. The informal meetings included discussion, although only Dōgen's talks are recorded in the Eihei Kōroku *shōsan*. Traditionally these informal meetings were given only on calendar days ending in 3 or 8 (i.e., 3, 8, 13, 18, 23, 28). The following days, ending with 4 or 9, traditionally had a more relaxed monastic schedule. However, the *shōsan* in volume 8 were given upon other, annual ceremonial occasions. Following the *shōsan* in this volume are a collection of *hōgo*, literally "Dharma words," which were written to individual students. While we know the dates of many of the Dharma hall discourses in volumes 1–7, the dates of these *shōsan* are uncertain, although they all were given after Dōgen settled at Eiheiji.

2 "Both ancients and moderns clarify and engage that and this as they manifest" could be read in a variety of other ways. The first part might be read as meaning "from ancient to modern times." The next as "clarify distinctions (between that and this)." The last part, "as

If you do know it is, how could you accomplish such a thing?[3] Although it is like this, if you only see by grasping and do not see by letting go, your eyebrows will mislead you, and your true eye will be caught in attachments. Essentially, if we practice in accord with the order [of the Buddha way], all people on the great earth will drink tea.

Dwelling Thoroughly in the Mountains
2. Informal Meeting on New Year's Eve
Great assembly, with more than three hundred pieces of empty sky I can buy one branch of plum blossoms at the end of the twelfth month, which, with auspicious clouds at the top of the cliff and the moon above the cold valley, contains spring and warmth promising sounds of laughter. Study of the way should directly follow the Dharma manner of ancient buddhas and previous ancestors. A deceased elder [Dongan Changcha] said, "We should direct ourselves toward how the Tathāgata practiced," which is the same meaning. Clouds and water brothers, you have departed far from your home villages, and have forever put aside family and kin. Completely forget trying to control fame and fortune or right and wrong. Although we should diligently study the details of our practice activity, and each and every dignified manner, first we must study the single affair of the ancient buddha ancestors. That is abiding in the mountains.

In ancient times a monk asked Great Teacher Yunju [Daoying] Hongjue, "Ultimately, how is a monk?"

Great Teacher [Yunju] said, "Abiding well in the mountains."

The monk did a prostration and arose.

Great Teacher [Yunju] said, "How about you?"

The monk, said, "Within the realms of good and bad, life and death,

---

they manifest," might be read as "and see completely" or "and become set as views." The reading given in the text is the one we deem most likely.

3 "If you do not know it is, how could you accomplish such a thing? If you do know it is, how could you accomplish such a thing?" is a slight paraphrase of a comment that Dongshan Liangjie made about his teacher Yunyan Tansheng. Before leaving Yunyan, Dongshan asked him how to express his teaching. After a pause, Yunyan said, "Just this is it." Later, a monk asked Dongshan whether Yunyan truly knew "it is" or not. Dongshan replied, "If he did not know it is, how could he be able to say such a thing? If he did know it is, how could he be willing to say such a thing?" See Dharma hall discourse 494; and Cleary, *Book of Serenity,* case 49, p. 206; or Powell, *Record of Tung-shan,* p. 28.

or favor and adversity, a monk's mind ultimately is immovable like a mountain."

Great Teacher [Yunju] immediately hit [the monk] once with his staff and said, "You have betrayed the former sages and destroyed my descendants."

Great Teacher [Yunju] then asked the monk standing next to the first monk, "How do you understand this?"

That monk made prostration, stood up, and said, "A monk ultimately abides in the mountains, his eyes not seeing the colors black and yellow [of sky and earth], his ears not hearing the music of bamboo and strings."

Great Teacher [Yunju] said, "You have betrayed the former sages and destroyed my descendants."

Therefore, all of you, what the former sages and ancient buddhas wish for is simply "abiding well in the mountains." Already abiding in the mountains, all of you should meet together with the ancient buddhas and previous ancestors. Even if you have not yet met together with the ancient buddhas and previous ancestors, you should be delighted that you are abiding well in the mountains. Keeping and maintaining this matter without regressing or being turned around is itself single-minded engaging of the way.

The World-Honored One said, "Sleeping in the mountain forests is what delights buddhas. Diligent effort in the towns does not please buddhas."

Therefore great ancestral teachers on Vulture Peak [Śākyamuni], Chicken Foot Mountain [Mahākāśyapa], Mount Song [Bodhidharma], Huangmei [Daman Hongren], Caoxi [Dajian Huineng], Nanyue, Qingyuan, Shitou, Yaoshan, Yunyan, Dongshan [Liangjie], Yunju, Xuedou, Furong [Daokai], and Dabai [either Hongzhi Zhengjue or Tiantong Rujing], all simply abided in the mountains. Furthermore, even laypeople who were noble wayfarers all hid themselves in the deep mountains and left excellent examples, such as at Mount Ji, Mount Nan, Shouyang, and Kongtong.[4]

---

4 The teachers in the previous sentence are all in the glossary. Mount Ji is where Xuyou hid when the legendary Emperor Yao tried to make him ruler. Mount Nan, or Zhongnan

Right now, if you are someone who has the mind of the way, at first you should seclude yourself and dwell in mountain valleys. Ignorant people who are truly without the mind of the way, who crave fame and love possessions, cannot abide in the mountains. All of you people already are dwelling in the mountains, so how could you not practice? Everyone, you should never betray the former sages, or destroy my descendants. Truly you must never dismiss abiding well in the mountains. Dwelling in the assembly throughout death and lifetimes is more excellent than [dwelling with] one's own flesh and blood. As this is superior to one's own flesh and blood, we should practice and train, joining in harmony in accord with Dharma. If you do not practice today, you will have spent three hundred sixty days in vain. If you do not spend a single day in vain, you will not waste three hundred sixty days. The former ancestor Shitou said, "Do not pass your time in vain," which is exactly the meaning of this.[5] A person practicing and one not practicing are a person reflecting on oneself and not reflecting, respectively, which is the saying of an ancient sage that is clear and obvious, and contains an admonition.

Long ago Master Foyan [Qingyuan] became fundraiser monk at Wuweijun, and once hit his heel in the street and had some realization. After returning [to his temple], he brought this up to [his teacher] Wuzu [Fayan]. Later, when he was staying at the guest house, one night during sitting he stirred the fire, and suddenly had a forceful realization. Although this was the case, whenever he entered the [teacher's] room he was never able to enter deeply to the inner sanctum. Calmly he asked Wuzu for instruction. Wuzu said, "I will express it for you with a parable. It is just like a person pulling an ox, and the ox passes by the window. Both horns and four hooves pass by, but only the tail cannot pass by."[6]

Mountain, was where government minister Zhuge Kongming (181–234) hid. After being dismissed by the emperor for giving highly moral advice, Boyi and Shuqi hid on Mount Shouyang, where they died of starvation. According to Zhuangzi, Kongtong Mountain is where the sage Guang Chengzi lived and where the Yellow Emperor went for advice that led him to give up his kingdom. See Hamill and Seaton, *Essential Chuang Tzu,* pp. 75–76.

5 Shitou's "Do not pass your time in vain" is the last line of his Harmony of Difference and Sameness (Jap.: Sandōkai). See Leighton, *Cultivating the Empty Field,* pp. 74–75; and Shunryu Suzuki, *Branching Streams Flow in the Dark.*

6 The story of the ox's tail not passing by the window appears in Mumonkan, case 38. It has

Wuzu instructed Foyan like this. Both horns and four hooves have passed by. Why is it that only the tail cannot pass by? People, look at this in detail in your Zen practice.[7]

The World-Honored One said, "For example, it is like a great elephant passing by a window. The entire body has gone by, but only the tail cannot get by. Worldly people are also like this. Home-leavers entering the way who altogether abandon associations, but only are not yet able to abandon name and gain, are like the elephant's tail not able to pass by."

Because of this [remaining attachment], we transmigrate through the six destinies in the three realms [desire, form, and formless], and are tossed around through birth and death. Therefore, although the elephant spoken of by the World-Honored One and the ox spoken of by Wuzu are different, yet they are the same. Thus we should know that if the tail has not yet been studied in practice, the horns also have not yet been studied. If the horns have already passed by, the tail has already passed by. Great assembly, do you wish to understand the meaning of horns and tail?

After a pause Dōgen said: Leading the ox along, do not seek for a perfect balance point. The three realms are alike duckweed floating on the water. Studying the way, the tail has not yet passed by; on what day will the entire body pass by the window?

Great assembly, you have been standing for a long while. I respectfully hope you will take good care.

The Dynamic Relationship of Ancient and Present
3. Informal Meeting for the End of the Summer Practice Period
In ancient times there were those who heard one and attained ten; nowadays there are none who hear ten and attain one. What is the principle of this? What face did ancient people cherish? They cherished this iron-beaked face, and opened these vajra eyes. As to what face current people cherish, they cherish this iron-beaked face, and open these vajra eyes.

---

sometimes been translated as the ox passing *through* the window; a vivid, fantastic image. But this is more conventionally understood as passing by, or in view of, the window. See Shibayama, *Gateless Barrier*, pp. 265–272; and Aitken, *Gateless Barrier*, pp. 231–234.

7 "Zen practice" here is *sanzen*, which Dōgen sometimes uses interchangeably for zazen. If so, this is an unusual instance of Dōgen directly recommending reflection on a kōan in meditation.

An ancient buddha [Baoming Renyong] said, "[The examples left by] ancient people are what current people use; current people are what ancient people have brought about. Ancient and present ones neither turn their back nor face each other, but how many present or ancient people know this?"[8]

Therefore, current people [practicing the way] are the ongoing outcome of ancient people; and what ancient people have brought about is exactly the ancient ones' ability to give rise to current people. Ancient people's [example] is the intimate functioning of current people; and current people's functioning is exactly so that current people can use [the example of] ancient people. Because of this, the ancient ones cannot avoid being used by current people, and current people cannot avoid being an outgrowth of the ancient ones.

It is impossible to diminish a single thread or to add on a single hair. Therefore we have peacefully abided [in practice period] for ninety days, not departing the monastery for three months. Having reached such a field, it is all right to call ourselves ancient people; it is all right to call ourselves modern people; it is all right to call ourselves neither ancient nor modern people. We can call ourselves as such for the first time.

After a pause Dōgen said: Just this seeing and hearing goes beyond seeing and hearing, and there are no more sounds or colors to offer to you.[9] Having completely settled within this, you are genuinely beyond concerns. Whether or not you make distinctions between ancient and modern, what is the problem? I respectfully hope you will take good care.

Nine Times Nine in the Deep Snow
4. Informal Meeting on Winter Solstice
An ancient worthy said, "Nine times nine makes eighty-one, but nobody can understand this calculation. Two times five hundred coins are originally one string of cash."[10]

---

8 This is a quote from Shūmon Rentō Eyō, volume 15, the section on Baoming Renyong.

9 "Just this seeing and hearing goes beyond seeing and hearing, and there are no more sounds or colors to offer to you" is a quote by Sanping Yizhong, cited by Hongzhi Zhengjue in case 85 of his kōan collection, The Record of Further Inquiries. Yunmen also cites this saying; see App, *Master Yunmen,* p. 160.

10 "Nine times nine makes eighty-one" is a frequent saying of Yunmen, used, for example,

An ancient worthy spoke like this. Everybody, do you want to understand this clearly? "Nine times nine makes eighty-one, but nobody can understand this calculation," horizontally a thousand, vertically ten thousand, horizontally ten, vertically one; this is responding to the occasion and receiving support. "Two times five hundred coins are originally one string of cash," copper, iron, silver, and gold coins; this is the first [arising of] yang and [the daylight's increase] reaching its culmination. Already being like this, everybody, how do you speak a phrase to congratulate each other for encountering the buddha ancestors?

After a pause Dōgen said: Although around our mountain home each night the snow is deep, with the plums blossoming in the snow, the great earth is fragrant. I respectfully hope you will take good care.

A Great Dōjō
5. Informal Meeting on New Year's Eve

After expressing appreciation for the temple administrators, monastic department heads,[11] *and the great assembly, Dōgen said:* Bodhisattvas arouse the mind [of awakening] and enter the kitchen. The nostrils are well pierced, and the rice is fragrant.[12] With [the monks] again and again carrying water and gathering firewood, I become aware that Eiheiji is a great practice place.[13]

I can remember, a monk once asked Zhaozhou, "Two mirrors face each other, which is brighter?"

---

to answer the question, "What is the way beyond?" It is suggested by Iriya Yoshitaka that Tang dynasty multiplication tables began with nine times nine, so this indicates the most common, basic knowledge. See App, *Master Yunmen,* pp. 90, 105. "Two times five hundred coins are originally one string of cash" refers to two ancient units of currency, but basically is like saying one hundred pennies is originally one dollar. The source of this quote is unknown.

11 Temple administrators are the *chiji,* including the *tenzo,* or chief cook, and monastic department managers are the *chōshū.* All these are the various officials responsible for maintaining the monastery. See Leighton and Okumura, *Dōgen's Pure Standards for the Zen Community,* pp. 50, 52, 208–209.

12 "Nostrils are well pierced" is literally "loftily pierced." Since piercing nostrils is an ox-training image used for training disciples, this is here an image of developed practitioners.

13 "Practice place" here is *dōjō,* literally "place of the way," used for the Bodhi seat where

Zhaozhou said, "Elder monk, your eyelids cover Mount Sumeru."[14]

Suppose this were Eihei, and someone asked me, "Two mirrors face each other, which is brighter?" I would simply face him and, holding up my staff, say: This is a monk's staff.

Suppose he said to this old man, "This is what you were able to study on the long monks' platform. What is the way of going beyond buddha ancestors?"

Dōgen threw down his staff, descended from his seat, and said: I respectfully hope you will take good care.

Our Temple Is Great Awakening

6. Informal Meeting for Beginning the Summer Practice Period
Gathering together at the place to select buddhas, we engage and affirm the matter of our journey of practice.[15] Not leaving the monastery, how do my legs resemble a donkey's? Protecting life, all people have their own life conditions.[16] As for Yunmen's ninety days of money for rice, how could this rice not be the self?[17] As for Dongshan [Liangjie]'s "Not an inch of grass for ten thousand miles," there are gates to both east and west.[18] The old teachers in the various directions all dwell on the tip of Huangbo's staff.[19] Hundreds of thousands of samādhis are not separate

---

Buddha awakened, but also commonly used for various training centers, including for martial arts.

14 See Green, *Recorded Sayings of Zen Master Joshu,* p. 118.

15 "Place to select buddhas" is *senbutsujō,* another name for the monks' hall. "Journey of practice" is *angya,* or "pilgrimage," here referring to ceasing travels for the practice period.

16 "How do my legs resemble a donkey's?" and "Each person has their own life conditions" are two of the "three barriers" of Huanglong Huinan. See Dharma hall discourse 420.

17 Once at the end of a summer practice period, Yunmen demanded the monks give him back the money for ninety days' worth of food. See App, *Master Yunmen,* p. 130.

18 At the end of a summer practice period, Dongshan suggested that the departing monks should go where there is not an inch of grass for ten thousand miles. See Cleary, *Book of Serenity,* case 89, pp. 382–384.

19 For Huangbo's staff, see Dharma hall discourse 493.

from [Hongzhou] Shuiliao's chest.[20] Therefore it is said, "Make great perfect awakening into our own temple building." Now our temple building is great perfect awakening. "Body and mind dwell peacefully in the wisdom of the nature of equality."[21] Many selves are peacefully dwelling within one self; the one body within the many bodies engages the way.

Everyone, do you want to understand this truth? We must eat rice with the mouth of the assembly; our vitality must be the strength of the assembly. I respectfully hope you will take good care.

A Complete Dharma Year
7. Informal Meeting for the End of Summer Practice Period
Do you want to see the completion of the Dharma year?[22]

Dōgen made a circle [in the air with his whisk] and said: It comes from this.

Again Dōgen made a circle and said: Being here it is complete. Being able to practice big radish Zen, we fulfill the wombs of donkeys and bellies of horses.[23] Being able to practice glass water jar Zen, we smash it and seven flowers are torn into eight pieces.[24] Being able to practice Tathāgata Zen,

---

20 When Hongzhou Shuiliao asked his teacher Mazu about Bodhidharma's coming from the west, Mazu kicked him in the chest; Shuiliao, knocked down, was greatly enlightened. He arose laughing and, rubbing his hands, said, "How excellent. The source of the hundreds of thousands of samādhis and immeasurable meanings can be understood on the tip of a hair." Later he said to his students, "Since I was kicked by my teacher Mazu until now, I cannot stop laughing." See Ogata, *Transmission of the Lamp,* pp. 289–290; and Cheng Chien, *Sun-Face Buddha,* p. 77.

21 This is quoted from the Complete Enlightenment Sutra, the chapter on "Complete Enlightenment Bodhisattva." See Muller, *Sutra of Perfect Enlightenment,* p. 232; and Sheng-yen, *Complete Enlightenment,* p 59. Dōgen also cites this quote in the Shōbōgenzō essay Ango (Practice Period); see Tanahashi, *Beyond Thinking;* and Nishijima and Cross, *Master Dogen's Shobogenzo,* book 4, p. 85.

22 At the end of the summer practice period, monks were considered to have completed another "Dharma year" of seniority since their ordination, which affected their position in the monastery, including the order of their places in the monks' hall.

23 "Big radish Zen" refers to a story about Zhaozhou, and so could be interpreted as "Zhaozhou's Zen." See Dharma hall discourse 438. When asked whether he had closely studied with his teacher Nanquan, Zhaozhou said, "In Zhen Province they raise large radishes." For donkeys' wombs and horses' bellies, see Dharma hall discourses 114, 128, 276, and 390.

24 "Glass water jar" refers to a phrase by Dahui in his kōan commentaries, Zen Master

our eyes have no strength and this life is impoverished. Being able to practice Ancestral Zen, this disaster reaches our descendants.[25]

Practicing in such ways, please tell me, what is the intention of Eihei? Just see the sun rising in the east. Who can then drink Zhaozhou's tea?[26]

Ninety Days of Great Peace
8. Informal Meeting for Opening the Summer Practice Period

Master Cihang [Fapo] was a venerable teacher in the Huanglong lineage. When he resided at Four Clarities temple at Mount Tiantong, at an informal meeting for opening the summer practice period he said, "Zen practitioners should first have their noses upright, then must have clear, bright eyes. Next they must value penetrating both the essence and its expression. After that they arrive equally into energetic capacity and its function, and then enter buddhas and demons, self and other arriving together. Why is this? When the nose is upright, everything is upright. This is like a person dwelling in a household; if the master is upright, all below him are naturally transformed. So how can we make our nose upright? An ancient sage [Huangbo] said, 'Be determined not to flow into a second thought, and you will enter our essential gate.' Doesn't this make a standard for you that approaches [your true self] before your parents were born?" Then he said, "The long period of ninety days starts tomorrow. Your practice should not go outside the guidelines."

The teacher Dōgen said: Although an ancient sage said, "Be determined not to flow into a second thought," I, Eihei, also say: Be determined not to flow into a first thought; be determined not to flow into no thought. Everyone, if you practice and study like this, you will finally attain it.

This evening, I, Eihei, do not begrudge the karma of words, and say to all of you: The long period of ninety days starts tomorrow. Your practice should not go outside the guidelines. Sit on your cushions unconcerned

---

Dahui Pujue's Arsenal of the Essential Gate, compiled in 1186. Dahui was the leading Linji school master in Song China in the period before Dōgen, and Dōgen sometimes strongly criticized him. This is probably also implied here in the smashing of this Zen.

25 For "Tathāgata Zen" and "Ancestral Zen" see Dharma hall discourse 52 and volume 1, note 123. Generally, Tathāgata Zen refers to practice based on sutra study, and Ancestral Zen refers to practice applied to everyday activity.

26 For Zhaozhou's tea see volume 6 (Dharma hall discourse 428), note 30.

by other affairs; all through the day, silently, serenely appreciate the great peace.

The Meaning of the Green Pine
9. Informal Meeting for Winter Solstice
Here is a story: A monk asked Zhaozhou, "What is the meaning of the ancestral teacher [Bodhidharma] coming from the west?"[27]

The teacher Dōgen said: Your tongue is my tongue.

Zhaozhou said, "The cypress tree in the garden."

The teacher Dōgen said: It is difficult to directly reveal the function of going beyond to his face, but [Zhaozhou] offered the ten-thousand-year-old family style for the sake of this person.

The monk said, "Master, do not use objects to guide people."

The teacher Dōgen said: He is forcing his eyes to try to see the North Star [behind his head].

Zhaozhou said, "I am not using objects to guide people."

The teacher Dōgen said: Without any sounds in the branches, the breeze carries the spring color.

The monk [again] asked, "What is the meaning of the ancestral teacher coming from the west?"

The teacher Dōgen said: Next year again there will be new branches profusely blooming; the spring wind never rests.

Zhaozhou said, "The cypress tree in the garden."

The teacher Dōgen said: Who can face this, and still catch fish and shrimp?[28]

Now, although it is like this, I, Eihei, have something further to say. Do you want to hear it?

After a pause Dōgen said: In the cold of the year, I can know the meaning of the green pine, and again I plant its spiritual root on the mountain peak.

For a long while the assembly has been standing compassionately. I respectfully hope you will take good care.

---

27 This story is also discussed by Dōgen in Dharma hall discourses 433 and 488, and in kōan case 45 with verse comment in volume 9. See volume 7 (Dharma hall discourse 488), note 35, for other references.

28 Catching fish and shrimp here may imply that the true meaning cannot be captured.

Family Instructions for the End of the Year

10. Informal Meeting at New Year's Eve

This informal meeting is [where are given] the family instructions of all buddhas and ancestors. In our country of Japan, in previous generations the name of this [shōsan] had not been heard, much less had it ever been practiced. Since I, Eihei, first transmitted this, twenty years have already passed.[29] This is fortunate for our country, and joyful for the people. Why is that so? This comes from the ancestral teacher [Bodhidharma] arriving from the west, and the Buddha Dharma entering the land of China. What we call family instructions is not to carry out anything that is not the activity of buddha ancestors, and not to wear anything that is not the Dharma robes of buddha ancestors. What we call activity is, having quickly abandoned fame and profit and forever casting away self-centeredness, without approaching the rulers and ministers of the country and without coveting donors and patrons, to take your own life lightly in seclusion within mountains and valleys and to value Dharma, never departing from the monastery. A great precious jewel is not the [true] treasure, but cherish each moment. Without worrying about myriad affairs, engage the way with single-mindedness. Being like this, you will be the direct heir of the buddha ancestors, and the guiding teacher of humans and heavenly beings.

Truly, having aroused bodhi mind and having practiced and studied with good teachers is a great sign [of buddhahood after practice] throughout three immeasurable kalpas. Great assembly, do you want to see the three immeasurable kalpas?

Dōgen drew a circle with his whisk and then said: People, what do you call this? Can you call this a circle? Can you call this a square? Can you call this original existence? Can you call this present existence? Can you call this the movement of time and the changing of years through spring and autumn, winter and summer? Can you call this vertically permeating the three times and horizontally filling the ten directions? If you call it any

---

29 This twenty years cannot be exact. We do not know the exact dates of these *shōsan* given at Eiheiji, but the first informal meetings by Dōgen in Kyoto were less than twenty years before Dōgen's last teachings in 1252 and his death in 1253. Dōgen founded his first temple, Kōshōji, in 1233, and, as far as we know, he did not give any talks before that. He did not give anything that might have ever been called a *shōsan* until 1235.

of those, you will be completely wrong, and immediately fall into the mistaken views of those outside the way. Therefore, the virtue of these three immeasurable kalpas cannot be assessed with the calculations of humans and heavenly beings. Why is it like this?

Tonight it is the thirtieth day of the twelfth month, and tomorrow is the beginning of a great new year. It is not at all possible to call tomorrow the final day of the last month, and it is not possible to call tonight the beginning of the new year. Since we cannot call this twelfth month the new year, we know that the new year has not truly arrived. We cannot call the new year the twelfth month, so we know that the old year has not actually passed. The old year has not yet passed, and the new year has also not arrived. Coming and going do not intermingle; new and old are beyond dichotomy.

So a monk asked Shimen Huiche, "How is the time when the year is used up?"

Shimen said, "Elder Wang in the eastern village burns money in the night."[30]

Later a monk asked Kaixian Shanxian, "How is the time when the year is used up?"

Kaixian said, "As of old, early spring is still cold."

Tonight, suppose a monk were to ask me, Eihei, "How is the time when the year is used up?"

I would simply say to him: In the snow, one branch of plum blossoms opens.

You have been standing for a while, late into the night. I respectfully hope you will take good care.

For the Love of Buddha's Lively Eyes

11. Informal Meeting for Beginning the Summer Practice Period

Zen Master Cihang [Fapo] was a venerable teacher in the Huanglong lineage. He abided at Tiantong monastery for thirty years, and at an informal meeting on the occasion of the beginning of summer practice period, he said, "Zen practitioners should first have their noses upright,

---

30 It was a Chinese custom to burn some money on New Year's Eve to pacify the spirits. Both this and the next exchange are from the Recorded Sayings of Yuanwu Keqin.

then must have clear, bright eyes. After that they must value arriving at both the essence and its expression."[31]

Great assembly, do you want to understand the meaning of old man Cihang's saying, the nose is upright? If you can understand this, you have drilled through your nostrils.[32] Do you want to understand clear, bright eyes? [Your old eyes] have been replaced with soapberries by a bystander.[33] Do you want to understand arriving at both the essence and its expression? *Dōgen struck his seat once with his whisk and said:* The essence has arrived; the expression has arrived. There is a skillful means for going beyond.

Old man Cihang also said, "The long period of ninety days starts tomorrow. Your practice should not go outside the guidelines." Great assembly, you should know that these are good words.

This evening I, Eihei, will speak for the sake of everyone. Great assembly, do you want to understand practice that does not go outside the guidelines? From tomorrow until the end of practice period, for ninety days throughout three months, from left to right, from east to west, going beyond buddhas and transcending ancestors, drop off body and mind and drill holes through your nose. Entering the monks' hall, entering the Buddha hall, arriving at the kitchen, arriving at the entry gate, all are practice that does not go outside the guidelines. All buddha ancestors and all patch-robed monks together cannot practice outside the guidelines. Even if they wanted to practice outside the guidelines, it is not possible.

Although this is so, tonight I, Eihei, continue the two sayings of Zen Master Cihang for the sake of testimony about [the value of] never leaving for ninety days.

After a pause Dōgen said: The long period of ninety days starts tomorrow, without practice outside the guidelines. Straw sandals and monks' staffs are completely put aside, for simply loving the vital eye of Gautama.

---

31 This is part of the longer quote discussed by Dōgen in informal meeting 8, above, probably at the opening of the previous summer practice period.

32 Drilling through your nose has the meaning of putting in a nose ring so as to be led and trained like an ox; but it also relates to breathing with ease.

33 Soapberries are mentioned by Dōgen as resembling Buddha eyes, and are used for rosary beads. See Dharma hall discourse 143 and volume 2, note 64. Soapberry beads are also mentioned in Dharma hall discourses 178, 317, 389, and 402.

For a long while the assembly has been standing compassionately. I respectfully hope you will take good care.

The Nectar within Forms and Rituals

12. Informal Meeting for the End of the Summer Practice Period

Informal meetings are primarily for exalting the family instructions. However, they are not caught up in the forms and rituals of the three thousand decorous manners, and do not discuss the vain struggles about the eighty thousand minutiae of formal practice.[34] These [family instructions] are simply the sitting cushions and Zen boards of the seven buddhas, and the source of the life root of the ancestors. Therefore, this is not in the realm of the four dhyānas or eight samādhis. How could it be measured in terms of the three wise or ten sacred stages? Every day just sit, dropping off body and mind. Do not be worried with a scene of laughable confusion about [comparisons between] barbarians or the civilized. Do not vainly waste a moment, but always cherish time.

If you ask about the universal and particular within this, the great venerable precious one is apparent and magnificent. At just this very time, how is it? Great assembly, do you want to clearly enact this?

After a pause Dōgen said:

Within the entire bright clear world, nothing is hidden.
Sitting, cutting off Vairocana, cannot be matched.
Geese drinking milk in water can swallow the pure [milk] flavor.
Bees gathering nectar from flowers
    do not mar remaining fragrance.[35]

I respectfully hope you will take good care.

---

34 "Three thousand manners" refers to the 250 monk precepts, multiplied by the four positions (walking, standing, sitting, and lying down) and again multiplied by the three times (past, present, and future), to make three thousand.

35 Vairocana is the *dharmakāya,* or reality body of Buddha, encompassing the entire phenomenal world. Cutting off Vairocana here implies going beyond Buddha, directly meeting the immediate present. "Geese drinking milk and bees gathering nectar" is a traditional image, used, for example, by Hongzhi in his poem "Guidepost of Silent Illumination." See Leighton and Wu, *Cultivating the Empty Field,* p. 68.

Returning to the Source
13. Informal Meeting at Winter Solstice
Elder and younger brothers, where great virtue matures, the first energy of brightness immediately arises.³⁶ The ten thousand things can return and directly see the venerable worthy one [Buddha]. So it is said, "The whole world in ten directions is your own single eye; the whole world in ten directions is your self; the whole world in ten directions is your own radiant light; the whole world in ten directions is this gate of liberation."³⁷ What place is not a place where you attain buddhahood? What time is not a time when you expound the Dharma? Don't you know the saying that even when Protecting Brightness [Bodhisattva] had not descended from the Tuṣita Heaven, the single circle was complete, pervading the ten directions?³⁸

I appreciate these words [from Hongzhi].

Here is a story.³⁹ Zen Master Nanyue [Huairang] Dahui once visited the sixth ancestor [Huineng] at Caoxi. The ancestor asked him, "Where are you from?"

Nanyue said, "I came from the place of National Teacher Songshan [Hui]an."

The ancestor said, "What is this that thus comes?"

Nanyue never put this question aside. After eight years he told the sixth ancestor, "I, Huairang can now understand the question, 'What is this that thus comes?' that you received me with upon my first arriving to see you."

The sixth ancestor asked, "How do you understand it?"

36 "First energy of brightness" is literally "the first *yang*," implying that the days are getting longer and brighter. The passage from "where great virtue matures" down to "the single circle was complete, pervading the ten directions" (including the quotation from Changsha) is a quote from a Winter Solstice *shōsan* by Hongzhi Zhengjue in his Extensive Record, volume 1.

37 This quote is from Changsha Jingcen.

38 "Protecting Brightness" was the name of Śākyamuni Buddha when he was still a bodhisattva in Tuṣita Heaven, waiting to descend to the world and become the next Buddha.

39 This story is also recounted in Dharma hall discourse 374 and as kōan case 59 in volume 9. See volume 5, note 43, for other references.

Nanyue said, "To explain or demonstrate anything would completely miss the mark."

The sixth ancestor said, "Then do you suppose there is practice-realization or not?"

Nanyue said, "It is not that there is no practice-realization, but only that it cannot be defiled."

The sixth ancestor said, "This nondefilement is exactly what the buddhas protect and care for. I am thus, you are thus, and the ancestors in India also are thus."

Caoxi asked his student a good question, and Nanyue exerted his effort well. Although this is so, I want to count the black and white stones of Śāṇavāsin. Because of his veneration for his teacher, [Śāṇavāsin's disciple Upagupta] could feel the radiance from the white hair curl.[40] At just such a time, ultimately, what can be said?

After a pause Dōgen said: The four great elements return to their own natures, just as a child turns to its mother.[41]

Late into the night, the assembly is compassionate. I respectfully hope you will take good care.

The Solid Rock at the Gate

14. Informal Meeting at New Year's Eve

Here is a story. Yaoshan asked [his disciple] Yunyan, "Aside from your staying with Baizhang, where else have you been before coming here?"

Yunyan said, "I have been to Guangnan."

Yaoshan said, "I have heard it said that the round rock outside the east gate of the city of Guangzhou was shifted by the lord of the city. Is that so?"

---

40 There is a story that the third ancestor in India in the Zen lineage, Śāṇavāsin, a disciple of Ānanda, gave his disciple Upagupta black and white stones, and told him to count black stones when bad mind appeared, and white stones when good mind appeared. The white hair curl refers to the curl of hair on a buddha's forehead from whence light is emitted.

41 "The four great elements return to their own natures, just as a child turns to its mother" is from Shitou Xiqian's Harmony of Difference and Sameness (Jap.: Sandōkai). See Leighton, *Cultivating the Empty Field*, pp. 74–75; and Suzuki, *Branching Streams Flow in the Darkness*, pp. 20–23.

Yunyan said, "Not only the lord of the city, but even if all the people in the entire country tried, they could not move it."[42]

Yaoshan and Yunyan have talked like this. How can I, Eihei, avoid speaking? Not only the lord of the city, not only the entire country, but if all the buddhas of the three times and all the ancestral teachers were to use all their strength trying to shift it, it would not budge. Why is that so?

After a pause Dōgen said: Each and every thing as such has no inside or outside; every particle is firm, set in samādhi. How wondrous and amazing![43] The entire body is bright and glittering, beyond the value of jewels.

Transmitting the Jewels of Yaoshan's Words

15. Informal Meeting for Beginning the Summer Practice Period
Here is a story. Yaoshan had not gone up to the hall [to give a talk] for a long time.[44] The director said, "For a while the great assembly has been missing the master's kind instruction."

Yaoshan said, "Strike the bell." The bell was sounded and the assembly gathered. Yaoshan ascended the seat. After a while he simply descended from the seat, and returned to the abbot's quarters.

The director followed after him and said, "Master, you agreed before to expound the Dharma for the assembly. Why didn't you offer us a single word?"

Yaoshan said, "There are sutra teachers for sutras, and commentary teachers for commentaries. Why do you blame this old monk?"

---

42 This story appears in Keitoku Dentōroku (Jingde Transmission of the Lamp), volume 14, the section on Yunyan. Yunyan's "staying with Baizhang" refers to the story about Yunyan being Baizhang's personal attendant for twenty years, but still not understanding. Finally, Yunyan succeeded to Yaoshan, although there were still questions about his understanding. See Cleary, *Transmission of Light,* pp. 160–163; and Cleary, *Book of Serenity,* pp. 206–209, 291–293.

43 Dongshan Liangjie exclaimed, "How strange and wondrous!" upon realizing that nonsentient beings expound the Dharma. He added that "when you listen with your ears you cannot hear it; when you listen with your eyes you can hear it." See Powell, *Record of Tung-shan,* pp. 23–26; and Wu, *Mind of Chinese Ch'an,* p. 99.

44 This story appears in Dharma hall discourse 492 and also in Shōyōroku, case 7. See Cleary, *Book of Serenity,* pp. 28–31.

Great assembly, do you want to understand the meaning of Yaoshan speaking like this? The clouds in the blue sky; Baofu [Congzhan] points to the boat. The water in the bottle; [Luohan] Dizang [Guichen] plants the fields.[45] A mute person's dream is realized by a mute person; an old woman expounds old woman Zen. Unpolished jewels within the mountain peaks vigorously produce clouds; the lotus flowers within our hands open toward the sun. Although I have spoken like this, I, Kichijō [the mountain name for Eiheiji], tonight yet again would like to proclaim this meaning, expressing it in verse.

After a pause Dōgen said:

What children of the house attain are the true gold coins.
A good horse does not even wait for the shadow of the whip.
Who can comprehend Yaoshan without these words?
Still, ancients and moderns compete to transmit and spread
[his truth].

You have been standing for a while, late into the night. Take good care.

Renewing Laughter

16. Informal Meeting for the End of the Summer Practice Period
Dōgen drew a circle and said: This is the great immeasurable, primary affair. All buddhas in the three times verify this single great matter, and for the sake of all living beings emit light and expound the Dharma.[46] Ancestral teachers in all generations practice this primary matter, and offer

---

45 "The clouds in the blue sky; the water in the bottle" is a saying by Yaoshan in response to the official Li Ao's question, "What is the way?" in Keitoku Dentōroku, volume 14. See Wu, *Mind of Chinese Ch'an,* p. 82. Baofu's pointing to the boat might perhaps refer to Hekiganroku, case 23, in which Baofu, walking in the mountains, pointed and said, "Right here is the summit of the mystic peak." See Cleary and Cleary, *Blue Cliff Record,* pp. 154–158. Dizang's planting the fields refers to his response to a teacher who had come from the south, where he said that there was extensive discussion among Buddhists. Dizang asked how that could compare to him just planting fields and growing rice to eat. See Dharma hall discourse 425 and Shōyōroku, case 12; and Cleary, *Book of Serenity,* pp. 51–55.

46 "This single great matter" (translated here also as "primary affair or matter") is a reference to the Lotus Sutra, chap. 2, which describes the single great cause for buddhas' appearing in the world: to lead suffering beings into the path of awakening. See Katō, Tamura, and Miyasaka, *Threefold Lotus Sutra,* pp. 59–60.

their hands to bestow their marrow. Bodhisattvas who study prajñā transmit this primary matter and make it their face and eyebrows. Sitting for ninety days in the summer, we transcend the three times, completely fulfill awakening, and transform and free all beings.

I can remember, Zhaozhou asked Daci [Huanzhong], "What is the body of prajñā?"[47]

Daci said, "What is the body of prajñā?"

Zhaozhou gave a hearty laugh.

The next day, when Zhaozhou was sweeping the ground, Daci asked, "What is the body of prajñā?"

Zhaozhou threw down his broom and roared with laughter.

In one meeting of these two ancient buddhas, Daci and Zhaozhou, they could not prevent this marvelous wonder. How can we assess it? Yesterday, we had rice in our bowls; this morning we had five-flavored gruel. This is the ordinary livelihood within the house of patch-robed monks. How is it when going beyond the buddha ancestors? Great assembly, do you want to clearly understand this?

After a pause Dōgen said: Daci's "What is the body of prajñā?" refreshes Zhaozhou's laughter yet again.

For a long while the assembly has been standing compassionately. I respectfully hope you will take good care.

Clouds and Waters Meet Equally with Clouds and Waters
17. Informal Meeting for Winter Solstice

When clouds and waters are sufficient, they arrive whether it is from near or far.[48] When gruel and rice are sufficient, right at this time we have our life. The clouds flow through the mountains; the waters are boundless in the ocean. Everywhere monks enter this essential teaching, how could

47 Dōgen also tells this story in Dharma hall discourse 159. See Green, *Recorded Sayings of Zen Master Joshu,* p. 162.

48 There are several puns in this first sentence, which carry through the entire passage. The subject is "clouds and waters," both literally and figuratively—monks are commonly referred to as clouds and waters. "Sufficient" *(soku)* also means legs, so the sentence might also be read as "Monks arrive [at Eiheiji] using their legs, whether from near of far," or, literally, "whether short or long."

there be a different Dharma for each of them? Right at this time, can you all clearly understand? Students with eyes wide open throughout their bodies encounter me, Kichijō [the mountain name for Eiheiji], a person of clouds and waters.

I can remember, the sixth ancestor [Dajian Huineng] asked Master [Nanyue Huai]rang, "Where are you from?"[49]

Nanyue said, "I came from the place of National Teacher Songshan [Hui]an."

The ancestor said, "What is this that thus comes?"

After eight years had passed, Nanyue commented to the sixth ancestor, "To explain or demonstrate anything would completely miss the mark."

The sixth ancestor said, "Then do you suppose there is practice-realization or not?"

Nanyue said, "It is not that there is no practice-realization, but only that it cannot be defiled."

Again, [Nanyue's response came after] eight years had passed.

Tonight, I, Eihei, borrow [Nanyue's] mouth to express it completely, and take his hand to practice together. Again, do you want to clearly understand the point of this story?

After a pause Dōgen said: I want to clarify the person whose head is three feet long, and discuss prajñā with him as an equal.[50]

You have been standing for a while, late into the night. I respectfully hope you will take good care.

---

49 This dialogue is given in slightly expanded form in informal meeting 13, as well as in Dharma hall discourse 374 and as kōan case 59 in volume 9. See volume 5, note 43, for other references.

50 "The person whose head is three feet long" is cited in Xuedou's verse comment to case 59 in the Hekiganroku. See Cleary and Cleary, *Blue Cliff Record,* pp. 387–388. Here, the person with a three-foot-long head seems to be Dōgen's way of referring to the one "that thus comes." "Discuss prajñā with him as an equal" is from the poem about the windbell by Dōgen's teacher, Tiantong Rujing. It is Dōgen's kōan case 58 in volume 9 and is cited by Dōgen in a slightly different version in his Shōbōgenzō Māhāprajñāpāramitā. See Cleary, *Shōbōgenzō: Zen Essays,* p. 26. The poem is also discussed by Dōgen in Hōkyōki, his journals of practice in China. See Kodera, *Dōgen's Formative Years in China,* pp. 135, 191; and Tanahashi, *Enlightenment Unfolds,* p. 23.

Kind Hearts in Deep Snow

18. Informal Meeting at New Year's Eve

Yaoshan asked [his disciple] Yunyan, "Aside from your staying with Baizhang, where else have you been before coming here?"[51]

Yunyan said, "I have been to Guangnan."

Yaoshan said, "I have heard it said that the round rock outside the east gate of the city of Guangzhou was shifted by the lord of the city. Is that so?"

Yunyan said, "Not only the lord of the city, but even if all the people in the entire country tried, they could not budge it."

Yaoshan and Yunyan met each other like this. I, Eihei, am their distant descendant, so how can I avoid studying this?

After a pause Dōgen said: From ancient to modern times, deep snow fills [the Chinese capital] Chang'an.[52] When [Dazu Huike] attained the marrow and [Bodhidharma] transmitted the robe, the cold pierced to the bone. The entire body is bright and glittering. How could its preciousness be evaluated? The kindly minds of old women are not deceived.

Sitting Upright like Bamboo

19. Informal Meeting for the Beginning of the Summer Practice Period

Zen Master Huanglong [Huinan] Puxue instructed his assembly in a Dharma hall discourse, saying, "It is good for monks to dwell in the mountains; abandoning desires in tranquillity is the Dharma of srāmaṇa [monks]. Sutras are there, so you should open and read them. There are various teachers you should visit and question. In that manner, there was a monk who inquired of great teacher Yunju [Daoying] Hongjue, 'Ultimately, how is a monk?'[53]

"[Yunju Hong]jue said, 'Abiding well in the mountains.'"

---

51 This story also appears in informal meeting 14. In his comments in this informal meeting 18, Dōgen seems particularly to be supporting Yunyan's understanding.

52 Chang'an, literally "long peace," was the name of the Chinese capital, sometimes used to symbolize fulfillment of peace and nirvāṇa. Since Eiheiji, the name of Dōgen's temple, also means "eternal peace," Dōgen's use of "Chang'an" here implies that Eiheiji was then covered in deep mid-winter snow, and that Dōgen himself was covered in the peace of deep samādhi.

53 This story was also cited in informal meeting 2.

"The monk did a prostration and arose.

"[Yunju Hong]jue said, 'How do you understand?'

"The monk, said, 'Within the realms of good and bad, life and death, or favor and adversity, a monk's mind ultimately is immovable like a mountain.'

"[Yunju Hong]jue immediately hit [the monk] once with his staff and said, 'You have betrayed the former sages and destroyed my descendants.'

"[Yunju Hong]jue then asked the monk standing next to the first monk, 'How do you understand this?'

"That monk made a prostration, stood up, and said, 'A monk ultimately abides in the mountains, his eyes not seeing the colors black and yellow [of sky and earth], his ears not hearing the music of bamboo and strings.'

"[Yunju Hong]jue said, 'You have betrayed the former sages and destroyed my descendants.'"

[Then in comment] Huanglong said, "What kind of phrase will you say in order not to betray the former sages and not to destroy your descendants? If you can utter it, wherever you go the blue mountains will be no other than the site of enlightenment.[54] If you cannot speak, cold and heat will crush your life-span, and spirits and demons will be jealous of your well-being."

Then Huanglong struck his seat with his whisk and descended.

The teacher Dōgen said: Yunju and Huanglong have spoken this way, how can I, Eihei, their distant descendant, avoid speaking? Do you clearly understand their meaning? Suppose someone were to ask you, "Ultimately, how is a monk?" and someone were to answer, "Abiding well in the mountains." Tell me, what is the meaning of this "abiding well in the mountains"?

After a pause Dōgen said: Encountering conditions is exactly the essence, engage [each] place to fully penetrate it. With the rhymings of pines by the window at dawn, with the heart of the moon in the autumn waters, nurturing the crane I finally cherish its purity. Seeing clouds, we harmonize together without haste. In accord with time and season, the sighing of the breeze is soothing and fragrant. Myriad peaks and valleys are dark

54 "Site of enlightenment" here is *dōjō,* a practice place, used for the bodhi maṇḍala, where a buddha awakens.

and hazy with sprinkles and downpours. Right at such a time, how is it?

Sitting upright with moss thick and boulders slippery, the wind is strong in [Hangzhou] Duofu's bamboo thicket.[55]

Great assembly, you have been standing a while. I respectfully hope you will take good care.

The Village Songs of Mahākāśyapa and Mañjuśrī

20. Informal Meeting for the End of the Summer Practice Period

For ninety days of non-action, the whole assembly has been peaceful and calm. Nevertheless, we have been protected by the buddha ancestors, which is truly the fortune and happiness of the great assembly. Tonight I, Eihei, will hold an informal meeting, as usual [at the end of a practice period]. What we call informal meeting is [an occasion to give] the family instructions. Although there are many family instructions, now I will offer one or two. The ancestral teachers of former generations are all noble people with the mind of the way [bodhicitta]. Without the mind of the way, the myriad practices are mere vain arrangements. Therefore, monks who study and practice must first arouse bodhi mind. Arousing bodhi mind is [arousing] the mind that saves all living beings. First, you must have the mind of the way. Next you must become endowed with yearning for the ancients. Then you must seek what is genuine. These three kinds are what should be studied by both beginners and latecomers. The family instructions of Eihei are simply like this.

I can remember, once long ago during the time of the World-Honored One, on the day of confession, Mañjuśrī had spent the summer at three places.[56] Mahākāśyapa wanted to expel Mañjuśrī, but when he started to approach the sounding block to make the announcement, he

---

55 The bamboo thicket of Hangzhou Duofu, a disciple of Zhaozhou, also mentioned in Dharma hall discourse 520, refers to the following dialogue, recorded in the Gotō Egen collection "Five Lamps Merged into the Source" (Ch.: Wudeng Huiyuan). A monk asked, "How is Duofu's bamboo grove?" Duofu replied, "One or two stalks are leaning." When the monk said he didn't understand, Duofu said, "Three or four stalks are bent over." In this informal meeting by Dōgen, in the context of a true monk's upright sitting, "the wind is strong" may refer to being bent over and flexible like bamboo, without being unseated. "Wind" here also implies strong "style" or "dignity." "Moss thick and boulders slippery" implies remaining settled for a long time.

56 "Day of confession" (Jap.: jishi; Skt.: pravāraṇa) was a day at the end of the practice

suddenly saw hundreds of thousands of myriad millions of Mañjuśrīs. Mahākāśyapa used all of his divine powers, but could not lift the sounding block. The World-Honored One finally asked Mahākāśyapa, "Which Mañjuśrī do you want to expel?" Mahākāśyapa did not respond.

Great assembly, do you want to fully inquire into this occurrence? First, you must deeply trust that spending the summer in practice period is the one great matter in the house of buddha ancestors. Do not take it lightly. Tell me, at that time, did Mahākāśyapa expel Mañjuśrī or not? If you say he had expelled Mañjuśrī, why is it that he could not raise the sounding block with all of his divine powers? If you say he had not expelled Mañjuśrī, since [Mahākāśyapa's] action was completely in accord with regulations, his effort should not be discredited. Great assembly, you should know that if Mahākāśyapa wanted to expel śrāvakas, pratyeka buddhas, beginners, latecomers, or even those of the stages of the ten sages and three wise ones, Mahākāśyapa certainly could have raised the sounding block. Now, if [Mahākāśyapa] wants to expel the hundreds of thousands of myriad millions of Mañjuśrīs, Mahākāśyapa uses a sounding block that cannot be raised. How can this be? Don't you see that a thousand-pound stone bow cannot be used to shoot a small mouse. How could a thousand-ton ship sail, following the ruts of an oxcart? Although it is like this, without intervening in a matter of such realms [of comparisons], is there something more to say that goes beyond?

After a pause Dōgen said:

In a peaceful age the ruler's activity is to govern without signs.
The family style of old peasants seems to be most pristine.
Just concerned with village songs and festival drinking,
How would they know of the virtues of Shun
or the benevolence of Yao?[57]

---

period when monks confessed and reflected upon their misdeeds. The three places where Mañjuśrī had spent the summer were at King Prasenajit's harem, playing with children at an elementary school, and at a bordello, staying a month at each. This story is quoted from Hongzhi's Extensive Record, volume 3, and was also recorded in Yuanwu's Recorded Sayings. Dōgen also cites it in Shōbōgenzō Ango. See Tanahashi, *Beyond Thinking*, pp. 139–40; and Nishijima and Cross, *Master Dogen's Shobogenzo*, book 4, pp. 85–86.

57 These four lines after the pause are quoted, with only minor variations for the sake of

Great assembly, you have been standing a while. I respectfully hope you will take good care.

⁓

Hōgo

Awakening in the Marketplace
1. Dharma Words

In this floating life, fame and profit exist only for a moment. Why should we wait long kalpas for the causes and conditions for nirvāṇa?[58] Therefore, sages who have attained the way and verified the result [of practice] quickly abandon fame for the mountains and wild lands. Wise ones who have reached the other shore and entered the [ultimate] rank rapidly take themselves to forests and streams. Doesn't this seem better for fully grasping the matter of mind and objects? Because of this, they erase the traces of the way within their lifetimes. The true person beyond study does not postpone [abandonment of worldly pursuits].[59]

However, I do not yearn for mountains and forests, and do not depart from the neighborhoods of people. Lotus flowers blossom within the red furnace; above the blue sky there is a white elm. There are actually no clouds in the sky and no mist in the mountains, so the moon advancing toward suchness is high and clear. There may be bamboo fences and flowery hedges, but the wind that follows conditions does not obstruct the echoes [of the Dharma]. Why should I necessarily stay in lofty halls or great temples, and be bound up in the snares and nets of right and wrong?

---

poetic meter, from Hongzhi's verse comment to case 5 of the Shōyōroku. Shun and Yao are ancient wise emperors of Chinese legend. See Cleary, *Book of Serenity,* p. 21.

58 The word translated here as "nirvāṇa" is *jakumetsu,* which means tranquillity and cessation of worldly attachments. These *hōgo,* or "Dharma words," were probably written down for individual students, and not usually presented as talks. They date from before Dōgen moved to Echizen and established Eiheiji, when he was still teaching at Kōshō Hōrinji temple, where the Dharma hall discourses in volume 1 of Eihei Kōroku were given.

59 "Beyond study" refers to those who have completed their study.

It is better to play within the streets and marketplace, and go beyond the threshold of names and forms. Who would cherish this stinking skin-bag and consider it precious? Who would consider it desirable to reject these trivial, complicated dwellings?

Furthermore, the transformative presence [of Śākyamuni Buddha] in the world for eighty years is as unreal as the moon in the water. The helpful methods for twenty-eight generations after his death are empty like reflections in the mirror. Those who seek Buddha and listen to Dharma are still hanging around in the realm of Buddha view and Dharma view. Those who teach people and expound sutras fall into the pitfall of human clinging and ego attachment. When you seek Buddha outside mind, Buddha changes into a demon. Similarly, if you are delighted with pleasures, pleasures will transform into pain. Pure lands and corrupted, unclean lands are both merely coming and going within a dream; how could they be yearned for by awakened ones? Good and bad karma are the order and disorder among drunks, not practiced by sober people. How pitiful are those who dislike delusion with their delusions, as if cleaning mud with more mud. How foolish are those who seek Buddha while already embracing Buddha, just like searching for water in the middle of water.

We should know that truth and falsehood depend on completeness or incompleteness of realization; bondage and liberation are up to the thoroughness or lack of thoroughness of one's verification. Who can transcend discriminating mind and rest in the realm of buddhas? Do not place a heavy load on your shoulders; a light step does not injure your legs. Don't you see that the morning marketplace and the battlefield are the original place of awakening for complete penetration of freedom?[60] Why aren't taverns and houses of prostitution the classrooms of naturally real tathāgatas? This is exactly the significance of the ancient wise one [Śākyamuni] departing from Bodhgaya, and previous worthies traveling to Chang'an.[61]

---

60 "Battlefield" is *sajō*, which also means "desert." Both translations are problematic here, although as an example of places usually thought of as worldly, "battlefield" seems to fit better.

61 Śākyamuni got up from his seat of awakening at Bodhgaya to go and teach. Teachers such as Songshan Hui'an and Nanyue Huairang went to the busy capital of Chang'an and became teachers of emperors. Although the dates of the Dharma words in this volume are not clearly known, we might reasonably speculate that this first one, with its promotion

Without question, at the place of discussion, silence, and walking meditation, the adornments of the lotus treasure naturally follow. While waking up, sleeping, advancing, or halting, the fulfillment of complete perfect enlightenment never ceases. This is already an unconventional model. How is it opposed to the style of home-leavers? I only regret that I have few companions [in this practice].

Traveling through the Great Way
2. Dharma Words
The great way originally has no names or words. Recognizing this principle, still we are compelled to call it the great way. Buddhas and ancestors appear one after another. The wooden man and iron bull follow on each other's heels, ascending and descending.[62] However, they leave no traces to appear before us. But assuredly [the great way] does not depart from this very place, but is always deep and calm. We should know that when we seek we cannot see it.

A long time ago, a monk asked Zen Master Guizong [Zhichang], "What is the way?"

Guizong answered, "You are it."

Also a monk asked Mazu [Guizong's teacher], "What is the way?"

Mazu said, "Ordinary mind is the way."

Also there was a monk who asked an [unknown] ancient worthy, "What is the way?"

The person said, "What you have been going through is it."

Are these three venerable masters' sayings ultimately the same or different? If you say they are the same, ten are just five pairs. If you say they are different, eight ounces are half a pound. Ha!

---

of practice within the world, was given by Dōgen fairly early, while still living in the Japanese capital, Kyoto.

62 The wooden man is a reference to practitioners free from discriminating mind, used, for example, in Dongshan Liangjie's Song of the Precious Mirror Samādhi: "When the wooden man begins to sing the stone woman gets up to dance." See Leighton, *Cultivating the Empty Field*, pp. 76–77. The iron bull represents unshakable determination. The phrase is used, for example, by Yaoshan, who said, "When I was studying with Shitou it was like a mosquito trying to bite an iron bull." See Tanahashi, *Moon in a Dewdrop*, p. 81. It is also featured in Hekiganroku, case 38, "Feng Hsueh's Workings of the Iron Ox." See Cleary and Cleary, *Blue Cliff Record*, pp. 279–287.

How about the words "you are the way"? Among such as the five skand-has, six faculties, and four great elements, where is the way and which things are the way?

Long ago a monk asked Zen Master Fayan [Wenyi], "What is the eternal dharmakāya?"

Fayan said, "Four great elements and five skandhas."

The monk said, "These can still be dispersed. Which is the eternal dharmakāya?"

Fayan said, "Four great elements and five skandhas."

If we look closely at this kōan, within this very body the great way will clearly manifest.

Mazu said, "Ordinary mind is the way." What is this ordinary mind? You should know that this ordinary mind is visiting teachers and inquiring about the way, seeking Dharma and asking about Zen, putting on robes and eating rice, continuing and ceasing activities, chanting Buddha's name and reciting sutras, speaking and silence, waking and sleeping, holding attachments and releasing them—all of these are nothing other than ordinary mind. However, how can we arbitrarily abstract [some ordinary mind] from these?

The ancient worthy said, "What you have been going through is the way." What we have been going through—how is it? It goes on through-out ten thousand kalpas and a thousand lives, when putting on fur and growing horns, arriving and disappearing, turning the head and over-turning the body, facing Buddha and saving beings, climbing mountains and sailing oceans, all through the long days and deep months You should know that this is what we have been going through. If we do not go through this, where could we dwell among the ten thousand miles of white clouds? Having already gone through this, it is right under our feet, so how could we carelessly wish to go beyond our capacity? This is the family style coming from buddha ancestors.

Don't you see that long ago old man Śākyamuni looked to the west and saw the east, climbed to the heavens and descended to earth, took seven steps in the ten directions, and said, "Only I alone am the honored one." This is because he had been going through the way. Moreover, he had departed his palace and plunged into the mountains, sat at the seat of awakening, and proceeded to the Deer Park also because he had reached the way. Later he repaired to Vulture Peak in Rājagṛha, and eventually went to Crane Forest in Kuśinagara.[63] Without the way, how could he have gone through this? We should know that from birth to death we think of eating and drinking, we avoid cold and love warmth; from infancy to adulthood we are either angry or joyful as we leave and return through gain and loss. All of these are not obstructions thanks to the one great way.

Visiting here is the reverend monk Enchi, who is resident monk at Iwamuroji [Stone Room Temple] in Totomi on the Tōkaido Road [between Kyoto and Kamakura]. He has come to see me three times to inquire about the great way. However, this mountain monk [Dōgen], cherishing the intention to nurture the way, has not yet been able to speak freely. This single kōan [about the way] after thirty years [of practice] will certainly be completely settled.[64]

Don't you see that Zen Master Xiangyan Zhixian first visited the great Zen Master Guishan Lingyou. Guishan said, "It is not that it cannot be explained, but if I explain it I'm afraid I will destroy your way." Later [Xiangyan] Zhixian realized the way because of the sound of [a pebble] hitting bamboo, then offered incense and made prostrations toward great Guishan far in the distance, and said, "My great teacher, great Guishan, great Zen master, if you had explained before, how could I experience this affair today?"

Furthermore, great teacher Linji visited Huangbo three times, asking, "What exactly is the great meaning of Buddha Dharma?" Huangbo gave him twenty blows of his staff. With twenty each time, he altogether

63 This passage refers to celebrated events in Śākyamuni's life, from his declaration shortly after his birth that "I alone am the World-Honored One" to his awakening at Bodhgaya, his first teaching at the Deer Park, his preaching at Vulture Peak (including the Lotus Sutra), and his passing away into parinirvāṇa at Kuśinagara.

64 Nothing more is known about Enchi. Totomi is the old name for Shizuoka Prefecture. Presumably this *hōgo* was written for Enchi. Probably this was early in Dōgen's teaching career, perhaps even before he moved to his temple Kōshōji south of Kyoto. According to the scholar Shūken Itō, who has researched the dates of the teachings in Eihei Kōroku, this Dharma word section was given in 1231, because this passage about nurturing the way is very similar to the phrases at the end of Bendōwa, also written in 1231. See Itō, *Dōgen Zen Kenkyū*, p. 384; and Okumura and Leighton, *The Wholehearted Way*, p. 20.

As to the ensuing stories, that of Xiangyan and Guishan appears in Dharma hall discourse 457 and kōan 62 in volume 9. The story of Linji and Huangbo is kōan 51.

received sixty blows. Later he visited Zen Master [Gao'an] Dayu. Dayu said, "Brother [Linji] Yixuan, why did you come here?"

Linji said, "I came seeking the Dharma."

[Gao'an] Dayu said, "Why didn't you ask Huangbo?"

Linji said, "I asked him about the great meaning of Buddha Dharma three times, but only received sixty blows of his staff."

[Gao'an] Dayu said, "That old man has such kindness, like an old woman." Right then [Linji] Yixuan was greatly enlightened.

You should know that the great Guishan was truly a good teacher, and Huangbo also was a great teacher for human and heavenly beings.

Zen person [En]chi, please hang this on your brow all through the long months and deep days, and add frost onto the snow within the way of the buddha ancestors. If you do not dwell in this kind of effort, you will furthermore add flowers onto the golden brocade. Truly the way is without obstacles. Noble and humble, venerable and lowly, old and young, foolish and dull all come and go together. Purple and golden, the lofty venerable [Buddha statue] in the hall attained and arrived through the way. Devadatta, who committed the five grave misdeeds, also had his portion.[65]

You should know that going out and entering are both the way; attempting to move forward and taking a backward step are each the way. It simply exists right here; why would one struggle, either throwing up your hands or clasping them formally (in shashu), inquiring and seeking from other people? The mind that seeks the way is also the mind in accord with the great way of the ancient buddha ancestors. Because of this, [Xuefeng] three times climbed the mountain to see Touzi [Datong], and nine times arrived to see Dongshan [Liangjie]. In ancient times there were such people; why not at present? Seeking the way and visiting teachers is [now] common in this world. You should know that truly this is a time and occasion to spread the Buddha Dharma widely. To give kind instructions is the standard and model for good teachers. Especially teachers who transmit the

---

65 Devadatta was Śākyamuni's cousin who attempted to take over the Buddha's order, and even to have the Buddha killed. But in the Lotus Sutra chapter on Devadatta, the Buddha said that even Devadatta, thanks to his long practice traversing the way in past lives, would eventually become a buddha, i.e., he had his own portion of the way. See Katō, Tamura, and Miyasaka, *Threefold Lotus Sutra,* pp. 207–210.

Dharma must not forget this. You cannot dare to give a phrase that meets people unless you are one who transmits the Buddha mind seal. What is the means for meeting people? That is letting go at once of the mind that seeks the way. This letting go is truly the occasion for penetrating the great way.

Didn't an ancient person say, "The way exists right before your eyes"?[66] What do these words mean? Ultimately what is the way? The sword is gone for a long time [when we ask such questions]. As I cannot avoid such matters, I will express it in verse.

> We must know that the great way exists before our eyes.
> Who would turn and gaze around over mountains and rivers?
> If someone asks about this,
> Traverse the sky that has been above your head
> from the beginning.

The Function of Half-Turning

3. Dharma Words

Turning the self we have not yet departed from here and there. Within the principle of having been turned, there is difficult and easy. What is difficult is half-turning the self. Half-turning the self is both demons and good spirits. What is easy is completely turning the self. Completely turning the self is simply [what is done by] buddhas and ancestors.

Long ago, a monk asked the sixth ancestor [Huineng], "Who attained the essential point of Huangmei [the fifth ancestor]?"

The [sixth] ancestor said, "The people who understand Buddha Dharma attained it."

The monk said, "Master, did you attain it?"

The ancestor said, "I did not attain it."

The monk asked, "Master, why didn't you attain it?"

The ancestor said, "I do not understand Buddha Dharma."[67]

---

66 "The way exists right before your eyes" is a saying from Zhuangzi, chap. 21. See Watson, *Complete Works of Chuang Tzu*, p. 223.

67 This story is recounted in Shūmon Tōyōshū (Collection of the Essence of the Lineage of the Zen School), volume 1, published in 1133.

This previous story presents the principle of half-turning the self. What is half-turning the self? If he had not half turned the self, the sixth ancestor would have understood Buddha Dharma. When he turned, if he could not attain half a portion, then nobody could have turned the essential meaning of Huangmei. Already being a person who understands Buddha Dharma, turning includes half and full [turning]. With full turning there is half; with half-turning there is full. Therefore, complete and half both turn each other ceaselessly. Demons and good spirits make this their activity, never stopping up to the present. The way of other buddha ancestors is not like this. They could turn themselves completely with no traces remaining, so that we could never meet anyone who has seen their traces. In my teaching tradition we turn halfway in the style of practice of demons and good spirits.[68]

In ancient times, Master Nanquan was working in the mountains. A monk passed by and asked, "Where is the path to Nanquan?"

Nanquan said, "I bought this sickle for thirty coins."

The monk said, "I didn't ask how much you paid for your sickle, but where the path is to Nanquan."

Nanquan said, "Even now it still works well."[69]

Was Nanquan able to turn the nature and life of this monk or not? This monk did not understand the meaning of buying a sickle. Why did he say he did not ask about paying thirty coins? He abandoned buying a sickle, yet asked for the path to Nanquan. If the monk had taken one step he would have immediately become manifest as a demon and spirit. Putting aside this monk for a while, although Nanquan understood how to repay the merit of buying a sickle with thirty coins, who would teach the monk the way to use it? Even when he knows how and uses it, how will he understand whether or not it works well? Even when already understanding how to use it well, ultimately it is half used and half not used. How will that monk express the rest of the point?

68 Dōgen advocates half-turning to make the teaching available to others. Half-turning goes beyond full turning when going beyond buddhas.

69 The story of Nanquan's sickle is kōan case 81 in volume 9, and appears in Wudeng Huiyuan (Jap.: Gotō Egen; Five Lamps Merged in the Source), volume 3. See Nelson Foster and Jack Shoemaker, eds., *The Roaring Stream: A New Zen Reader* (Hopewell, N.J.: Ecco Press, 1996), p. 71.

The Inexpressible Dharma

4. Dharma Words

In the teaching schools it is said, "This Dharma cannot be demonstrated; the form of words is quiescent."[70] What is the form of words? What is quiescence? I would say that this Dharma itself is the form of words and the form of quiescence. Commentary that goes beyond can only be truly seen when the eye on the headtop opens.

Long ago Venerable Ānanda visited Mahākāśyapa and asked, "Elder brother, aside from the golden brocade Dharma robe of the Tathāgata, what else were you transmitted?"

Mahākāśyapa called out, "Ānanda."

Ānanda responded.

Mahākāśyapa said, "Take down the banner in front of the gate." Immediately upon hearing this, Ānanda was greatly enlightened.[71]

This single kōan gives a good hand for leisurely realization. Ultimately what is this Dharma? Why can't it be demonstrated? Simply because the form of words is quiescent, it cannot be demonstrated. What is the vital activity within the house [of Dharma] that cannot be demonstrated? This is spoken of as the inexhaustible Dharma gate in which the cypress tree in the garden and bits of clouds on the mountain peaks follow the wind according to the season.

Old man Śākyamuni and great teacher Bodhidharma side by side practice together the matter that is under their feet. One has already left his palace and the other has finally come to the eastern land, and the truth that they have simply transmitted and directly indicated is exactly this Dharma. Whether it can be demonstrated or not, either way it is this Dharma. Seeing and holding it, turning the head and stepping back, and proceeding forward and turning the body over are all nothing other than this Dharma.

70 This quote is from the Lotus Sutra, chap. 2, "Skillful Means." See Hurvitz, *Scripture of the Lotus Blossom of the Fine Dharma*, p. 23.

71 Dōgen also discusses this story in Dharma hall discourse 252 and refers to it in Dharma hall discourse 11.

Wayfarer Ryōnen, you have the seeds of prajñā from early on [in life], intently aspiring to the great way of buddha ancestors.[72] You are a woman, but have strong, robust aspiration. Without begrudging any effort in nurturing the way, for you I will demonstrate the precise meaning coming from the west. That is, if you do not hold on to a single phrase or half a verse, a bit of talk or a small expression, in this lump of red flesh you will have some accord with the clear, cool ground. If you hold on to a single word or half a phrase of the buddha ancestors' sayings or of the kōans from the ancestral gate, they will become dangerous poisons. If you want to understand this mountain monk's activity, do not remember these comments. Truly avoid being caught up in thinking.

The Active Verification of Play in Samādhi
5. Dharma Words
Yongjia [Xuanjie] said, "I traveled over rivers and oceans and crossed mountains and streams, visiting teachers and inquiring about the way to study Zen."[73] This is the manner in which we home-leavers study Zen. Worthy, noble gentlemen do not necessarily [practice] this way.[74] And yet, those who appear as home-leavers but do not have the strong aspiration of home-leavers are not truly home-leavers. Those with the appearance of worthy gentlemen [as lay practitioners], but who act as home-leavers, are superior to home-leavers. An ancient elder called such a person a tiger with horns.

Gentleman Yakō from the Dazaifu [in Kyushu] is a scholar of Confucianism.[75] He has kept his mind on the ancestral way [of Zen] for a long

---

72 Ryōnen was a nun disciple of Dōgen's. Dharma words 4, 9, and 12, all with her name in them, were apparently written for her. A surviving manuscript of Dharma word 12 in Dōgen's own hand at Kasuisai temple in Shizuoka Prefecture indicates that Dharma word 12 was written in 1231, so presumably Ryōnen was an early disciple of Dōgen.

73 This quote by Yongjia is from the Song of Enlightenment. See Suzuki, *Manual of Zen Buddhism*, p. 93; and Sheng-yen, *Poetry of Enlightenment*, p. 52.

74 "Worthy, noble gentlemen" is *shidaijōbu*, which implies upper-class, educated gentlemen, often government officials. This Dharma word selection is addressed to Yakō Daifu (the latter is short for *shidaijōbu*), a lay student of Dōgen's.

75 The Dazaifu was the imperial court office in the southern island of Kyushu that coordinated communication with China. Scholars have speculated about this Yakō and the layperson for whom Dōgen's Genjokōan was written. Genjokōan is dedicated to

time through many years. On his own he has been performing the practice of different kinds.[76] In the winter of the year of the wooden horse [1234], we first met. In the summer of the year of the wooden sheep [1235], he again entered the room [to visit and study with me]. Guest and host conversed, and ultimate and phenomenal mutually interacted. For more than a month between summer and autumn, he asked for guidance about the ancient teaching stories, but I held up and showed him the present situation.[77]

The true Dharma eye treasury, wondrous mind of nirvāṇa of Śākyamuni Buddha, was transmitted only to Mahākāśyapa and did not enter any other hands. In India it was entrusted person to person for twenty-eight generations until it reached great teacher Bodhidharma. The master arrived in China, and for nine years sat facing a wall without creating any other notice. At the end of his life he only entrusted [Dazu] Huike. Six generations conferred it one to another; then the five houses transmitted and maintained it.

Although this is the case, how could they have left different tracks, since they only accepted those who accord with enlightenment? As for this accord with enlightenment, only those who are authenticated have sealed this samādhi up until the present age. At this time of accord with verification, the water of Caoxi [Dajian Huineng, the sixth ancestor] flowed backward, and the wind of Shaolin [Bodhidharma] returned to the west, which is called self-verification.[78] How true this is. Each and every thing verifies the person, and every person verifies the phenomena. From beginning to end, nothing is lacking. An ancient said, "The bright

---

another gentleman, Yō Kōshū, who also worked at the Daizaifu. Perhaps Dōgen met them on his way to and from China. Poem 62 in volume 10 of Eihei Kōroku is also addressed to Yakō Daifu.

76 The "practice of different kinds" is recommended by Nanquan, referring to practice within the distinctions of the world. See Cleary, *Book of Serenity*, case 69, pp. 291–292.

77 According to the scholar Shūken Itō, this Dharma word was given in 1235, because of the dates referred to in this passage. See Itō, *Dōgen Zen Kenkyū*, p. 384.

78 In this paragraph and those following, we are translating the same word, *shō*, as "enlightenment," "authentication," or "verification," according to context. One essay in Shōbōgenzō is called "Samādhi of Self Verification," in which Dōgen says, "When you follow teachers or sutras, you simply follow the self. Sutras are the sutra of the self; teachers are the teacher of the self. Therefore, widely visiting teachers is widely visiting the self." See Nishijima and Cross, *Master Dogen's Shobogenzo*, book 4, pp. 31–42.

clarity of the ancestral teachers' mind is the bright clarity of the hundred grass-tips," which is the same meaning.[79]

Right now, Yakō, your mind of joyfully seeking the ancestral way through your aspiration to visit teachers is activated by verification, and verifies this [practice] activity. Both activity and verification are completely like the waves in the water, and themselves give life and take life. Buddha ancestors call this attaining thoroughness. Finally, we clarify the oneness beneath our feet, and attain the many examples beyond our bounds, and this is called unsurpassed awakening.

This is exactly what Mazu meant when he said, "Since I left confusion behind thirty years ago, I have never lacked for salt or sauce to eat."[80] Other than this, what causes and conditions for ancient people entering the way, and what kōans by which ancient worthies accorded with verification could there be? Why would persons long ago, such as [Jinhua] Juzhi with his single finger, Heshan beating the drum, Linji shouting, or Deshan using his staff, have had many techniques?[81] They all had a single way for matching enlightenment. Sticking his eye on the staff, or attaching his hand onto his shout, they did not take anything else, or see anything else. Naturally the wind blows and grasses sway, and seeing wind we use our sails, so how could there be anything ultimate [beyond this]? When we experience some new particular situation, naturally our affirming mind will not stagnate. This is not done by personal force, but is simply the expression of the way.

Furthermore, within Dharma joy, naturally there is vastness. At the top of a steep cliff, we can casually stroll. We truly know that the way is not false, and directly understand that realization is significant. At this time, using a monk's staff we strike and scatter the explanations about

79 This is a saying by the great layman Pangyun. See Dharma hall discourses 9 and 329.

80 For this quote from Mazu, see Dharma hall discourse 11.

81 Juzhi is famous for always holding up one finger as a response. See Dharma hall discourse 211 and volume 3, note 37, for details. Heshan's response to "What is true going beyond?" was "Knowing how to beat the drum." See Cleary and Cleary, *Blue Cliff Record*, case 44, pp. 312–317. Linji was famous for his shouts, and Deshan for beating students with his staff, all to foster awakening. Dōgen here implies that they all only needed one technique for teaching.

the profound and wondrous, so that there is not the slightest trace of delusion. Holding up a bamboo staff, we strike and destroy explanations about nature and mind, so how could the old ruts remain?[82] Raising a single stalk of grass, we make a sixteen-foot golden body, which radiates light and expounds the Dharma, so that from the beginning nothing is deficient. We use a sixteen-foot golden body to make a single stalk of grass, so the bud blossoming as a flower is not a matter of quick or slow. How can the great work of buddhas not be the play of samādhi?

The Devoted Effort of a Work Leader
6. Dharma Words

Work Leader E'un started his position in the metal mouse year of the En'ō era [1240].[83] He was appointed on New Year's Eve last winter, and now he serves the assembly. On the twenty-fifth day of the fifth month, the rainy season downpour had continued for several days, and the grass roofs were leaking. When this mountain monk [Dōgen] entered the hall to do zazen, in the place where the roofs meet between the monks' hall and the illuminated hall [the passageway to the washrooms behind the monks' hall], waves poured in all over floor. Monks of the pure ocean assembly when coming or going were caught at a standstill there. When the work leader was informed, he removed his robes and, without a rain hat, together with the carpenters climbed up to the roof and took care of the leak. Although dense rainfall burst on his head, he did not hesitate.

I quietly had the thought to write him some words in praise. At that time I simply watched him sympathetically. Since then, six months or two hundred days have passed, and although I have not made any effort [to write something], it has been difficult to forget what he did. In the midst of summer heat I did not write; arriving in the cold, I now use my ink.

This [work leader's example] is exactly the bones and marrow of previous buddhas, without being stopped by concern for self.[84] Since my dis-

82 "Bamboo staff" is *shippei,* a ceremonial staff now used by head monks during the ceremony of questioning the head monk at the end of a practice period. Formerly these were used as teaching staffs.

83 Nothing more is known about E'un than what is in this *hōgo.*

84 This sentence might well be interpreted instead, as it is by Genryū Kagamishima, as "This [custom of not writing in the summer] is exactly the bones and marrow of previous buddhas, so I did not stick to my own preference [of writing sooner]."

ciple was appointed to this position, almost one year has passed. Gradually several temple buildings have been erected, which is the auspicious completed conditions and ripened fruit of his practice efforts. Some come from the north and see that being unburdened is great; others face each other and offer the profound function.[85] Such is this respected disciple's diligent power, which delights many.

Moreover, this temple is on a far distant road that cannot be reached by people who are not serious. Only lofty people, shouldering the heavy baggage [of sincere aspiration], arrive one at a time, strong and determined heroes, departing from conventions and entering the grasses [of Dharma inquiry]. Their minds delighting in what they hear, they all grasp for the unsettled deeds, seeking to compete for the ancestral fields. Sometimes manifesting the form of asuras, sometimes endowed with a thousand hands and eyes, they transmit Dharma and succeed to the ancestors.

Who would say [that this work leader E'un] does not have the ability of a capable person? Although there are phrases about serving the assembly and exerting power, what phrase could I give to him?

When he stirs, he definitely hits a hundred percent. When he acts, it is completely accomplished.

Enlightenment Refreshed in Work
7. Dharma Words

Zen person Ken'e left his homeland, departing from his parents, and on his own joined the activity of the buddha ancestors from ancient times. How delightful that he should keep and maintain, as well as love and cherish [this practice]. People from the east, south, and north have never matched him, and even in the future, this will still be the case. There are many different kinds of practitioners, one being called practice leader, another called follower in the assembly.[86]

Now I appoint you to be in charge of the toilets for the metal ox year of the Ninji era [1241]. Graciously serve the buddha ancestors from the ten

---

85 "Come from the north and see that being unburdened is great" is a paraphrase of Zhaozhou's saying, "Someone coming from the south I unburden; someone coming from the north I load up." See Green, *Record of Zen Master Joshu*, p. 30.

86 "Practice leader" here is *santō*, literally "practice head," referring to experienced practitioners who can guide new practitioners and may be chiefs of monastic departments.

directions. To be either a practice leader or follower, each time raise it up; each time is fresh. What is raising up is to lose great enlightenment. What is fresh is to suddenly be greatly enlightened.

Tell me, why is this so? Do you clearly understand? When you lose money in the river, you search in the river. When you release your horse at the foot of the mountain, you seek it at the foot of the mountain. [Written by] the founding monk of Kōshō Hōrinji monastery.

A Golden Fish Freed from the Hook
8. Dharma Words

Who easily attains the single great matter of the causal condition for the appearance of all buddha tathāgatas?[87] In recent times, those who genuinely seek the Dharma are rare, much less has anyone realized it. Suppose that you memorize the Dharma preachings at the more than 360 assemblies and in the 5,048 volumes of sutras and commentaries; suppose that your expounding of Dharma is swift as clouds and rising mists, and your eloquence is clear like deep water and flows like rivers; suppose you receive offerings from heavenly beings, and demons and spirits take refuge with you; suppose, moreover, that you have supernatural powers to transform yourself and move the great thousandfold worlds, and you can dry up vast oceans, can fly in the sky like a cloud, can walk on water as if on ground, and your body generates fire and water, wind and clouds, and radiant light. Still, in terms of the great matter described previously [of the causal condition for the appearance of buddhas], you have not seen the ultimate Buddha Dharma, even in a dream. Such [supernatural powers and so forth] as mentioned above are simply the affair in the realms of the two vehicles [of listeners and pratyekabuddhas] and of those outside the way, and this is just the livelihood in the demons' cave. How can such people understand this wondrous Dharma of the unsurpassed awakening of the tathāgatas? Even if as many such people as grains of sand in the Ganges River were thinking and assessing for as many kalpas as grains of

---

87 In the Lotus Sutra, chap. 2, "Skillful Means," the single great matter of the causal condition for the appearance of buddhas is elaborated as to open up, demonstrate, realize and help others to enter the insight of buddhas. See Katō, Tamura, and Miyasaka, *Threefold Lotus Sutra*, pp. 59–60; and Hurvitz, *Scripture of the Lotus Blossom of the Fine Dharma*, p. 30.

sand in the Ganges River, not a single or even half a person among them could attain it. Therefore, it is difficult to find a person who truly practices, and also difficult to encounter a truly good teacher.

If you encounter a genuine master with skillful hands, in the withered tree and dead ash flowers will bloom and sprouts will be nurtured. Then the bottom of your old lacquer bucket suddenly falls out, and you attain the ground of vital spontaneity.[88] Seeing forms, we immediately clarify the mind; hearing sounds, we immediately realize the way. Because of this, each ancestor transmitted it correctly, until it naturally reached China, and the Buddha Dharma has not been cut off even up until now.

Don't you see that Zen Master Jiashan [Shan]hui, when he was abbot of Jingkou, gave a Dharma hall discourse, and a monk asked, "What is the dharmakāya?"

[Jiashan] Shanhui said, "The dharmakāya is without form."

The monk asked, "What is the Dharma eye?"

[Jiashan] Shanhui said, "The Dharma eye is without flaw."

At that time, Daowu [Yuan]zhi was sitting in the assembly, and unintentionally laughed.

Jiashan descended from the seat, and with full decorum made prostrations and inquiry [to Daowu].

Daowu said, "I have a fellow practitioner who dwells on a boat on Huating River and gives instruction. If you go to see him, you will certainly receive something. You must change your robes and appear as a teacher from a scriptural school."

Jiashan immediately followed his instructions, dispersed his assembly, and traveled to Huating.

The boatman, Chuanzi [Decheng] saw him coming and asked, "Teacher, in which temple do you dwell?"

Jiashan said, "I do not dwell in a temple. I have nothing resembling a dwelling."

Chuanzi said, "You said it does not resemble, but what does it resemble?"

Jiashan said, "It is not the Dharma before your eyes."

---

88 The old black lacquer bucket is a traditional Zen image for fundamental ignorance.

Chuanzi said, "Where did you study?"

Jiashan said, "It is not a place where ears or eyes reach."

Chuanzi said, "A saying that meets you head-on becomes a stake for tying up a donkey for ten thousand kalpas. I have let down a thousand-foot line, the mind in a deep pool. Depart from the hook by three inches.[89] Why don't you say something?"

Jiashan tried to open his mouth. Chuanzi pushed Jiashan and he fell into the water. Jiashan stuck his head up, and Chuanzi again said, "Speak. Speak."

Jiashan tried to open his mouth, and Chuanzi again hit him. Jiashan suddenly was greatly enlightened, and nodded his head three times.

Chuanzi said, "The line at the tip of the fishing pole moves at your wish. Without disrupting the clear waves, the mind is naturally profound."

Jiashan said, "You have given up the line and discarded the hook. What is your mind, teacher?"

Chuanzi said, "The line hangs in the green water, the float revealing whether or not there is mind. Speak quickly; speak quickly."

Jiashan said, "Words are endowed with inscrutability, without a path; the tongue converses, but says nothing."

Chuanzi said, "Fishing all over the river waves, one first encounters golden scales."

Jiashan thereupon covered his ears.

Chuanzi said, "It is thus; it is thus." Then he entrusted [Jiashan with the Dharma] and said, "I stayed with Yaoshan for thirty years, and truly clarified this matter. Already now you have it. From now on do not stay in cities or towns, but always keep yourself where you leave no traces, and even where you leave no traces, do not keep yourself. Head toward fields you can cultivate in the deep mountains, train one or even half a person, transmit and continue my lineage, and do not allow it to be extinguished."

Jiashan understood his meaning, made farewell prostrations, and got up

---

89 The last two sentences can be interpreted in several ways. The second sentence might simply describe Jiashan as already "apart from the hook by three inches." The "mind" in a deep pool might be read either as Chuanzi's mind or intention, or more generally as the Buddha mind. The passage might even be read as Jiashan fishing for the mind, in which case his hook is missing by three inches.

on the shore and departed. But he repeatedly turned his head to look back.

Chuanzi again called out, "Your reverence!"

Jiashan looked back. Chuanzi raised an oar and said, "Do you have something else to say?" After saying this he overturned the boat and sank into the misty waves.[90]

Dōgen commented: Later he appeared in the world and resided at Jiashan. He can be called a true lion in the Śākya family. However, [Jiashan] was good at Dharma dialogue even when he lived at Jingkou. He ascended the lion's seat, and for the sake of human and heavenly beings, expounded the Dharma, never missing or being defeated. After he met Chuanzi he had no extraneous Dharma. And yet practitioners who genuinely seek the Dharma should practice like this and continue Buddha's life of wisdom, becoming teachers of humans and heavenly beings. These days if we search for such a person throughout the world, in the end they cannot be found. Ah, what bitterness.

Lofty people who inquire about the way should know you must first establish the determination of an iron man, and with your eyes set where you cannot add or remove a single thread, see the style of Chuanzi freed from the hook. How many people can follow such practice? If you are not like this, trample and disperse the solitary moon in the heart of the waves, so that you can play on the billowing waves within the moon.

The Vital Stream of "Mind Itself Is Buddha"
9. Dharma Words
Riding the iron ox, grab the reins and gallop on the water. Employing the wooden man, put on his shoes and cap and let him play in the fire. Even though you see such a person, do not consider him as [your] equal. Immediately you will attain one or half of a vital stream. Here is a previous example for the enactment of this vital stream.

Long ago, Zen Master Damei [Fa]chang visited Mazu and asked, "What is Buddha?"[91]

90 Small portions of this story are used as cases 10, 22, and 28 among the ninety kōans about which Dōgen comments in volume 9. For another version of the story, see Ferguson, *Zen's Chinese Heritage*, pp. 146–148.

91 This story is also discussed by Dōgen in Dharma hall discourses 8 and 319. See volume

Mazu replied, "Mind itself is Buddha."

Immediately [Damei] entered the peaks of Mount Damei. After thirty years, there was a monk in the assembly of Yanguan [Qi'an] who wanted to select a monk's staff [from the mountain woods] and accidentally came upon [Damei's] hermitage.[92] He asked the teacher, "Master, how long have you been dwelling on this mountain?"

The teacher [Damei] said, "I only see that grasses and trees become green and yellow in spring and autumn, never counting the months and years."

The monk said, "Where does this path lead?"

The teacher [Damei] said, "Go following the stream."

When the monk returned he reported this to Yanguan.

The teacher [Yanguan] said, "Once I saw [such] a monk at Mazu's place, but I do not know his current circumstances. I suppose it is that monk."

Later, Mazu sent a monk to ask the teacher [Damei], "Master, when you met great teacher Mazu, with what expression of enlightenment did you accord, such that it led you to dwell on this mountain?"

The teacher [Damei] said, "Mazu simply said to me, 'Mind itself is Buddha.'"

The monk said, "These days his teaching about Buddha is different."

The teacher [Damei] said, "How is it different?"

The monk said, "Now he says, 'No mind, no Buddha.'"

The teacher [Damei] said, "Despite his 'No mind, no Buddha,' for me it is [still] just 'The mind itself is Buddha.'"

The monk went back and told this to Mazu.

Mazu said, "The plum has ripened."[93]

Later students of the way should learn from Master [Damei] Fachang's instructive standard. Even though there are those who have been verified

---

4, note 122, for other references. Dōgen also discusses this story in Shōbōgenzō Gyōji (Continuous Practice). See Tanahashi, *Enlightenment Unfolds*, pp. 122–124.

92 Yanguan Qian was a fellow disciple of Mazu's.

93 The name Damei means "Great Plum." So Mazu here approves Damei's response.

with "No mind, no Buddha," it is difficult to find someone who understands "This mind itself is Buddha." Student Nen, understand this clearly.[94]

Healing the Whole Body
10. Dharma Words

These days people who engage the way have not yet distinguished between dragons and snakes, and finding those who know [the difference] is profoundly difficult. Why is this so difficult? An ancient said, "Deep snow covers the great earth. Spring comes and there is no cold. Accomplishing buddhahood is easy after all, but expounding Zen is more difficult."[95] The buddha ancestors have not yet been relieved of this sickness. Why have they not yet been relieved? They say that accomplishing buddhahood is easy and expounding Zen is difficult; or that expounding Zen is easy and accomplishing buddhahood is difficult. In this way, we can see the difficulty or ease of the buddha ancestors' speaking of Zen, but ultimately, how do we understand this point?

A monk asked Yunmen, "How is it when trees wither and leaves fall?" Yunmen said, "The body is exposed in the golden wind."[96]

Later, [Zhuo'an De]guang Fazhao said, "As usual, Yunmen treats the temple property with his personal sympathies, but if we investigate, how is it that [he] gets hit three thousand times in the morning and eight hundred times in the evening?[97] In the assembly of Liaoan [Zhuo'an Deguang himself], how is it?" Then [Zhuo'an Deguang] threw down his staff.

---

94 This *hōgo* is written to some student of Dōgen's whose name ended with the character *nen*. Although uncertain, it is highly likely that this was written to the nun Ryōnen, to whom *hōgo* 4 and 12 are also written. See note 72 above.

95 This saying is by Fachang Yiyu, from the Jiatai Record of the Universal Lamp (Jap.: Katai Futōroku), volume 2.

96 This answer from Yunmen is in Hekiganroku, case 27. See Cleary and Cleary, *Blue Cliff Record*, pp. 176–180.

97 "Three thousand times in the morning and eight hundred times in the evening" is from Hekiganroku, case 61. As a comment to Xuedou's question, "Are there any patch-robed monks who will live together and die together?" Yuanwu says, "If you know, I admit that you are independent and free. If you do not know, you get hit three thousand times in the morning and eight hundred times in the evening." See Cleary and Cleary, *Blue Cliff Record*, pp. 395–396.

Old man Śākyamuni appeared in the world and became the great Medicine King, taking pity on living beings sinking into the ocean of suffering. Because of this, compassionately he gave joy and relieved suffering, and with various kinds of skillful means, unfolded his great treasury of teachings.[98] These are all medicine given in response to sickness, with prescriptions that allow all sentient beings to reach the land of great peace and joy.

Since Bodhidharma came from the west, all his descendants used violent poisons, wishing to revive the sick after death. Like the single method [on the island] on the ocean, although it may have many spiritual effects, if we see with the true eye, all of this is like gouging wounds in healthy flesh.[99] This is not the authentic treatment. Not grasping onto diagnostic writings, without [diagnosing by] checking the pulses, your eyes work on the minute details, and change according to the particular time. Even if someone has Buddha sickness or ancestor sickness, do not lightly remove it with a single manipulation, or change their disposition or clean out the intestines to make the spirit pure and energy vigorous.[100] Thus it is said, one pill eliminates all illnesses, so do not depend on many medicines. The old man's whole body is sick, so truly you cannot find the origin [of the disease].[101] Monk official Futō, you already have such functioning.[102] Try to look closely. If you can see thoroughly, then Doctor Bianque of the Lu region will stand beneath you.[103]

98 "Compassionately he gave joy and relieved suffering" is literally "aroused *ji* and carried out *hi.*" *Jihi* as a compound means "compassion," but *ji* alone implies providing happiness, and is used as a translation for the Sanskrit *maitrī,* or loving kindness. *Hi* alone implies empathy and care for those suffering, and is used as a translation for the Sanskrit *karuṇā,* or compassion.

99 "The single method [on the island] on the ocean" refers to the Daoist myth of an island, Hōrai, where there is great healing medicine.

100 This sentence, including "single manipulation (or pinch)" and "change disposition" (literally "change the bones"), uses several Chinese medicine and Daoist healing terms.

101 The "old man" may refer to Śākyamuni or Vimalakīrti, whose sickness is the suffering of all deluded beings.

102 "Monk official" refers to a government position overseeing monasteries. Futō, whose name means "Universal Lamp," was apparently the person to whom Dōgen addressed this *hōgo,* but nothing more is known about him.

103 Bianque was a legendary physician in the Warring States period (403–221 B.C.E.) in China.

Verification, Practice, and Expounding Are One and the Same
11. Dharma Words
With the whole body just as it is, who would get stuck in any place? With the entire body familiar, how could we find our way back to a source? Already beyond the single phrase, how could we be troubled by the three vehicles?[104] When you open your hand it is just right; when your body is activated it immediately appears.

Truly, after [Mahākāśyapa] broke into a smile at Vulture Peak, the twenty-eight [Indian ancestors] could not add even the slightest thread.[105] After [Dazu Huike] penetrated the marrow at Shaolin, how could the six generations [of Chinese ancestors] remove the slightest thread? Without exchanging verbal expressions, simply match enlightenment. This is direct pointing, not stagnating in intellection.[106] Because of this, we still hear at this distance the fame of [Bodhidharma's] nine years of facing the wall at Shaoshi Peak. The beautiful scenery of the transmission of the robe at Huangmei [from Daman Hongren to Dajian Huineng] is clearly revealed. Such examples as [Jinhua] Juzhi's one finger, Huangbo's sixty hits, Baizhang's whisk, Linji's shout, Dongshan [Shouchu]'s three pounds of sesame, and Yunmen's dried shitstick are not caught up in the stages from living beings to Buddha, and they already transcend the boundaries of delusion and enlightenment.[107] How could we compare them with those who wait for enlightenment and verification from others, and who recognize shadows rather then their true self; or with those who abide in intellectual views about their essence, and chase after lumps of dirt, never acting for the sake of others.

104 "The single phrase" refers to an ultimate statement. The three vehicles are bodhisattvas, pratyekabuddhas, and śrāvakas.

105 "Not adding a single thread" implies that nothing could be added to the Dharma passed from Śākyamuni to Mahākāśyapa.

106 "Intellection" here is *nensō*, which separately refers to remembrance and to sensation or imagination, and together refers to mental activity.

107 These all refer to either the famous regular teaching method or a famed particular illuminating saying of noted masters (see the Index and glossary of names). Huangbo's sixty shouts refers to his training of Linji. Baizhang's whisk refers to an encounter with his teacher Mazu, in which Baizhang ended up using his teacher's whisk, and thereupon received a deafening shout from Mazu. See commentary to case 11, in Cleary and Cleary,

Truly, the point of the singular transmission between buddha ancestors, the essential meaning of the direct understanding beyond words, does not adhere to the situations of the kōans of the previous wise ones, or the entryways to enlightenment of the ancient worthies. It does not exist in the commentaries and assessments with words and phrases, in the exchanges of questions and answers, in the understandings with intellectual views, in the mental calculations of thought, in conversations about mysteries and wonders, or in explanations of mind and nature.[108] Only when one releases these handles, without retaining what has been glimpsed, is it perfectly complete right here, and can fill the eyes. Behind the head, the path of genuine intimacy opens wide; in front of the face, not knowing is a good friend.[109]

Great teacher Śākyamuni's true Dharma eye treasury has been entrusted through India and China for a long time. Its limit is not known. What has been entrusted for a long time is this single field.[110] This single field is the field directly beneath us. Ancient people considered this the great way. This long time, mentioned just now, cannot be counted or measured. The matter [of entrusting the true Dharma eye treasury] is old, and the time is distant. But although its limits in the four directions are not clear, when one manages, abides in, and maintains this [single field], it is cared for and upheld afresh each day. With this freshness each day, naturally, limits are cut away.

Blue Cliff Record, pp. 73–74. For Dongshan Shouchu's three pounds of sesame and Yunmen's dried shitstick see volume 1 (Dharma hall discourse 69), note 150.

108 The "singular transmission," which these two sentences refer back to, is *tanden* in Japanese. This refers to Dharma transmission as simple, direct, and complete, with the Dharma as the single matter transmitted.

109 This "not knowing" that Dōgen calls a good friend may refer to Bodhidharma's response to Emperor Wu, who asked Bodhidharma who he was. Bodhidharma replied, "I don't know." See Cleary and Cleary, *Blue Cliff Record*, case 1, pp. 1–9; and Cleary, *Book of Serenity*, case 2, pp. 6–10. "Not knowing" also refers to Fayan Wenyi's response to his teacher's inquiry about the purpose of his going on pilgrimage. When Fayan responded, "I don't know," his teacher said, "Not knowing is most intimate." See Cleary, *Book of Serenity*, case 20, pp. 86–90.

110 "This single field" refers to a story about Xuefeng saying to his assembly, "If you discuss this matter, it is like a single rice field. Completely trust your own sowing and cultivation. There is nobody who does not receive benefit from this." This is from Shūmon Rentō Eyō, volume 21.

Within this there is practice, teaching, and verification. This practice is the effort of zazen. It is customary that such practice is not abandoned, even after reaching buddhahood, so that it is [still] practiced by a buddha. Teaching and verification should be examined in the same way. This zazen was transmitted from Buddha to Buddha, directly pointed out by ancestors, and only [transmitted] by legitimate successors. Even when others hear of its name, it is not the same as the zazen of buddha ancestors. This is because the principle of zazen in other schools is to wait for enlightenment. For example, [their practice] is like having crossed over a great ocean on a raft, thinking that upon crossing the ocean one should discard the raft. The zazen of our buddha ancestors is not like this, but is simply Buddha's practice. We could say that the situation of Buddha's house is the oneness in which the essence, practice, and expounding are one and the same. The essence is verification of enlightenment; expounding is the teaching; and practice is cultivation. Even up to now, these have been studied together.

We should know that practice is the practice of essence and expounding; expounding is to expound the essence and practice; and the essence is the verification of expounding and practice. If practice is not the practice of expounding and is not the practice of verification of enlightenment, how can we say it is the practice of Buddha Dharma? If expounding is not the expounding of practice and is not the expounding of verification, it is difficult to call it the expounding of Buddha Dharma. If verification is not the verification of practice and is not the verification of expounding, how can we name it the verification of the Buddha Dharma? Just know that Buddha Dharma is one in the beginning, middle, and end. It is good in the beginning, middle, and end; it is nothing in the beginning, middle, and end; and it is empty in the beginning, middle, and end.[111] This single matter never comes from the forceful activity of people, but from the beginning is the expression and activity of Dharma. We already know that there is teaching, practice, and verification within Buddha Dharma. A single moment in a cultivated field always includes

---

111 "Nothing" in "nothing in the beginning…" is *mu,* or "nonexistence." "Empty" in "empty in the beginning…" is *kū,* "emptiness" or "space."

many times.[112] We should not grasp after the tree at the center that is commonly valued.[113]

The teaching is already thus, the practice is also thus, and verification is also thus. As such, we cannot control whether or not we ourselves can control the teaching, the practice, and verification. Wherever they have penetrated, how could there not be Buddha Dharma?

Taking the Flavor of the Ancient Buddhas
12. Dharma Words

The great way of all buddhas is profound, wondrous, and cannot be reached by thought or discussion. How can those who practice do so easily? Don't you see the wondrous example of ancient people who gave up body and mind, and abandoned their country and palace? As for other things such as a wife and children, they were seen as like tiles and pebbles. After that, [these ancient ones] passed twenty or thirty years, and even proceeded through waves of kalpas staying in solitude in mountain forests with their bodies and minds like dead trees, until finally they were in accord with the way. Once they had joined somewhat with the way, they could hold up and twirl mountains and oceans to wonderfully make them into words, as well as holding up wind and rain to make them into tongues and lips, thoroughly expressing great space and turning the unsurpassed Dharma wheel. What phenomena could they not turn? What dharmas have they not yet turned? Those who aspire to the way should follow such splendid dedication.

In olden days there was a monk who asked Zen Master Fayan [Wenyi], "What is the ancient Buddha?"

Fayan said, "Right now there is no aversion or doubt."

---

112 "Always includes many times" is stated as a double negative. So it is more literally read as "never does not include many times," or as "never is not without many times." Dōgen is indicating that within each moment of practice, a wide range of time is included.

113 "The tree at the center" refers to a commentary by Xuansha to his teacher Xuefeng's statement about the single field; see note 110 above. Xuansha said, "It is like when a contract is signed to sell a single field. The whole field has been sold except for one tree at the very center, and you still own the tree." This is from the section on Xuefeng in Keitoku Dentōroku.

The monk asked again, "Within the twelve hours [the whole day], how can we conduct our practice?"

Fayan said, "Tread step by step."[114]

Another time Fayan also said, "A person who has left home simply follows time and season. When it's cold, it's just cold; when it's hot, it's just hot. If you want to know the meaning of Buddha nature, you should contemplate time and season, causes and conditions.[115] It is good to simply to take care of your responsibilities and spend your time appropriately."[116]

We should contemplate in detail his meaning. What is following time and season? What is taking care of responsibilities? You should know not to place an understanding of no-form onto form, but also not to create an understanding of form, and further not to pursue this as a dichotomy.[117] Right now, forget aversion and doubt, and abide and practice together with the ancient buddhas.

Although this is so, how can we be like a face and mirror in front of each other? Therefore the old teacher Śākyamuni said, "When entering a village or town, monks should be like bees gathering [nectar] from flowers, only taking the flavor, without destroying the color and fragrance."[118] Wise people who are patch-robed disciples, why don't you follow this admonition? Throughout the twelve hours of the day, meeting all the ten thousand forms, take only their flavor and do not destroy the color and

114 This dialogue appears in the Jingde Transmission of the Lamp (Keitoku Dentōroku); see Chang, *Original Teachings of Ch'an Buddhism,* p. 244. In the traditional Asian system, the day was divided into twelve hours, like our current twenty-four hours.

115 "If you want to know the meaning of Buddha nature, you should contemplate time and season, causes and conditions" is from the Mahāparinirvāṇa Sūtra. This saying is discussed by Dōgen in his essay "Buddha Nature," and was previously cited by Baizhang. See Waddell and Abe, *Heart of Dōgen's Shōbōgenzō,* pp. 65–67.

116 This is quoted by Dōgen from the beginning and end of a Dharma hall discourse by Fayan, included in the Jingde Transmission of the Lamp; see Chang, *Original Teachings of Ch'an Buddhism,* pp. 244–245. "Taking care of responsibilities" is more literally "maintaining one's portion or position."

117 This sentence is a paraphrase of the next-to-last sentence from the just previously quoted Dharma hall discourse by Fayan.

118 This quote is from the Sutra of Buddha's Last Teachings (Busshi Hatsu Nehan Ryakusetsu Kyōkai Kyō is its full name in Japanese). See Hubert Nearman, trans., *Buddhist Writings on Meditation and Daily Practice: The Serene Reflection Meditation Tradition* (Mount Shasta, Calif.: Shasta Abbey Press, 1994), p. 250.

fragrance. What is the meaning of taking only the flavor and not destroying the color and fragrance? I say to you, receiving the seal of those ten thousand objects, and being verified by those ten thousand dharmas, this [entire day] should completely be the occasion of not destroying the color and fragrance. Apart from this, how could there be [practice following the buddhas]?

This mountain monk regards the sincerity of the aspiration for the way of wayfarer Ryōnen, and sees that other people cannot match her.[119] Because I cannot avoid it, therefore I have used this brush to portray the way of the buddha ancestors, but how have I necessarily destroyed others' color and fragrance?[120]

The Young Mind of an Ancient Buddha

13. Dharma Words

For young people to follow a teacher is an excellent model since ancient times. Zen person Gyōgen became a monk when he was thirteen years old. Together with my assembly, in the morning he studied and in the evening asked for instruction. This is because he has had the strength of prajñā for a long time. His age happens to match the time when Nanyue was captivated by the [Buddha] way; and his name matches half of Qingyuan [Xingsi's] Dharma name.[121] This is naturally an auspicious coincidence, and indeed a fortunate example.[122] When he was fourteen,

---

119 Dōgen wrote this *hōgo,* or Dharma word, for the nun Ryōnen, for whom he also wrote Dharma words 4 and 9. A surviving manuscript of Dharma word 12 in Dōgen's own hand, at Kasuisai temple in Shizuoka Prefecture, indicates that Dharma word 12 was written in 1231.

120 This rhetorical question implies Dōgen's hope that he has not caused harm with this writing.

121 Qingyuan Xingsi is Seigen Gyōshi in Japanese, whose Dharma name (Jap.: *hō-i*), traditionally written second, has the same character *gyō* as in Gyōgen, for whom Dōgen wrote this *hōgo.* Nothing else is known about Gyōgen besides this writing. Nanyue and Qingyuan were the two great masters of their generation, both disciples of the sixth ancestor, Dajian Huineng. Gyōgen's age is given literally as fourteen and fifteen in the traditional East Asian way of counting age, starting at one at birth; but by the modern way of counting, he was thirteen when he was ordained and fourteen at the time of these Dharma words.

122 "This is naturally an auspicious coincidence" is literally "this is the *nen* of *jinen* (naturally)." Dōgen is playing with the characters here, as in the second part of the sentence

Nanyue abandoned the doctrinal teaching schools to study the way [in practice]. You are also fourteen years old, and are studying the way in accord with the Dharma. The two have become one, attaining thoroughly and thoroughly attained.[123] You should not be called a young person; you are simply an ancient buddha. Studying the way of the ancient buddhas, you must directly embody the body and mind of the ancient buddhas, which is exactly the dignified manner of this [way of the ancient buddhas]. The way is ancient, study is ancient, Buddha is ancient—everything is ancient. Even if you have a thousand or ten thousand, this is no other than a thousand ancients and ten thousand ancients. The ancient is not new.

A monk asked the national teacher [Nanyang Hui]zhong, "What is the mind of the ancient buddhas?"

The teacher said, "Fences, walls, tiles, and pebbles."[124]

Also a monk asked Nanyuan [Daoming], "What is the mind of the ancient buddhas?"

The teacher [Nanyuan Daoming] said, "Mountains, rivers, and the great earth."

Suppose someone asked me, Kōshō, "What is the mind of the ancient buddhas?"[125] I would say to him, "The four great elements and the five skandhas."[126]

These three exchanges are good models. You should know that for eight thousand or a hundred thousand [miles], the ancient buddhas are sepa-

---

when he literally says that this is the *rei* (example) of *karei* (fortunate example).

123 "The two have become one," literally, "Two and one," is another example of Dōgen playing with words, here probably indicating, as suggested by Genryū Kagamishima, that the two ancestors Nanyue and Qingyuan have become one in Gyōgen.

124 This dialogue, in which the national teacher Nanyang responded with "Fences, walls, tiles, and pebbles," is discussed by Dōgen in Shōbōgenzō Kobusshin (Mind of the Ancient Buddhas). See Nishijima and Cross, *Master Dogen's Shobogenzo*, book 3, pp. 25–27. It is also discussed, including a much longer version of this dialogue, in the Recorded Sayings of Dongshan Liangjie; see Powell, *Record of Tung-shan*, pp. 23–24.

125 Kōshō here refers to Dōgen's temple Kōshōji, where this Dharma word was written before he left Kyoto in 1243.

126 "The four great elements and the five skandhas" is also Zhaozhou's response to a monk's question, "What is this indestructible nature?" See Dharma hall discourse 140.

rate from self and land, and are separate from body and mind; they are the entire realm of self and land, and are the entire realm of body and mind.[127] Although this is so, [the ancient buddhas] are never hidden. Disciple [Gyō]nen, having the fortune to study thoroughly in this way, you will finally have realization.

Good Teachers for Lay Practitioners

14. Dharma Words

For ministers and generals studying the way it is most important to visit a teacher.[128] Depending on whether the teacher is false or genuine, the students' understanding will naturally become erroneous or correct. Therefore, declining the selection process for officials, one person went to the place for selecting buddhas.[129] There he was able to pass the examination for the mind of emptiness.[130] Inquiring about directly going beyond, but attaining the understanding of what was directly beneath his feet, he would never be a companion of the ten thousand things.[131] Before having

127 This is like Zhaozhou's response about the indestructible nature, which is the same as the mind of the ancient buddhas. The ancient Buddha is not the five skandhas or the land, but the ancient buddhas are revealed and manifested through the entire world, including the land, self, body, and mind.

128 Although he is not mentioned by name, it is likely that this *hōgo* was written for Dōgen's main patron, Hatano Yoshishige (d. 1258), who was an official on a level comparable to "ministers and generals." Yoshishige, a nobleman with land in Echizen, later provided the land for Dōgen's monastery, Eiheiji.

129 "The place for selecting buddhas" (Jap.: *senbutsujō*) is another name for the monks' hall. This refers to a story about Danxia Tianran, who was on his way to the examinations for officials until a monk suggested he go instead to the "place for selecting buddhas" at Mazu's temple. He later studied with and was eventually considered a successor of Shitou Xiqian. He also is famous for burning a buddha statue to keep warm during his travels to visit teachers.

130 "Passing the examination for the mind of emptiness" is a description by Hongzhi Zhengjue for what happens at the "place for selecting buddhas," or monks' hall.

131 This refers to the first anecdote in Layman Pangyun's recorded sayings, his question to Shitou Xiqian, "Who will never be a companion of the ten thousand things?" Shitou immediately put his hand over Pangyun's mouth, and the latter had a realization. See Sasaki, Iriya, and Fraser, *Recorded Sayings of Layman P'ang*, pp. 45–46.

experienced three calls, someone had broken through the single point.[132] These are exactly the kindly power of the inducement of true teachers.

If you become intimate with a bad teacher, you can never be like this. You will guard a stump, waiting for a rabbit, or grip a stone, thinking it is a jewel.[133] You will fall into the demons' cave and flow down to the pit of malevolent spirits as a result of the confusion from the blind eyes of bad teachers. If you meet a true teacher and establish the aspiration to inquire and practice, you will resolve the great matter of life and death and be liberated from long being stuck in your old nest. Who says there is no support for your effort? And yet it is difficult to happen upon and pay visits to a genuine teacher who has clear eyes. Nevertheless, even if you can meet one, it is most difficult to recognize [whether or not they are a true teacher]. You may hear their words, but still not maintain their practice. Even seeing their practice, I am afraid you will neglect their enlightenment. Without the merit of practice and of serving for a long time, how can you thoroughly become able to transcend the material and go beyond conventional patterns? Moreover, those who clarify the Buddha Dharma are rare even in China, so how could it be easily attained in this remote region? Even in days gone by there were few, so how could there be many now?

There is a good reason why even those who reach the mountain of [the triple] treasure cannot distinguish between jewels and rocks. They have affinity [with the teaching] through causes and conditions, but vainly run around seeking outside, and do not yet understand the backward step of turning the head [away from externals and dualities]. Facing this side they ask about oneness, but have not yet clarified breaking through duality. Facing that side, they ask about duality, but how would they know they

132 "Before experiencing three calls one broke through the single point" refers to a story about the national teacher Nanyang Huizhong calling his attendant three times. Each time the attendant responded, and then the national teacher said, "I thought I betrayed you, but originally you betrayed me." See Ogata, *Transmission of the Lamp*, p. 179; or Mumonkan, case 17, in Shibayama, *Gateless Barrier*, pp. 128–133; Aitken, *Gateless Barrier*, pp. 113–119; or Cleary, *Unlocking the Zen Kōan*, pp. 85–88. Dōgen implies here that the attendant understood before the first call, thanks to the national teacher.

133 "Guarding a stump waiting for a rabbit" refers to a story by Zhuangzi about a farmer who caught a rabbit that was stunned after hitting its head on a stump. Thereafter the farmer abandoned his farm work and waited by the stump for another such rabbit.

have fallen into three [or myriad manifestations]?[134] They are mistaken on both sides, vainly wasting their whole life. Truly we must pity them.

Benevolent people, distinguish between bad teachers who are idly arrogant from one-sided prejudice and true teachers who always cut through discriminations based on material concerns. Good gentlemen, if you earnestly aspire to study the way and visit a genuine master, do not be precipitous.[135] You should transmit the family style of Yangyi Wen[gong]. Why are there no fruits from stable master Li [Zunxu]?[136] Minister Pei[xiu] threw himself into [study with] Guifeng [Zongmi], and further crumbled the lump of mud by responding to Huangbo's call.[137] Yudi went up to Mount Ziyu [and met Ziyu Daotong], and [this example] was further clarified as a radiant flower by Yaoshan's skillfulness with the complete way.[138]

134 "How would they know they have fallen into three?" might also be read as "How could they know how to fall into three?" or as "How would they know about falling into three?" "Three" represents multiplicity and the myriad phenomena. It is not clear whether Dōgen here means, negatively, falling into attachment to things, or, positively, manifesting practice amid the world of phenomena. Furthermore, "this side" usually refers to the world of concrete phenomena, so while asking about oneness, these people are still stuck in dualities. "That side" usually refers to the ultimate nondual reality, and so asking about the duality they may be creating, they are separating themselves into a third element.

135 "Good gentlemen" (Jap.: *shidaijōbu*) traditionally in China referred to those who had passed the examinations and were eligible to be officials.

136 Yangyi, whose honorific name was Wengong (974–1020; Jap.: Yō'oku and Bunkō) was a lay practitioner and official who was also a noted poet. He was the editor of and wrote the preface for the Jingde Transmission of the Lamp (Keitoku Dentōroku), which was originally compiled by the monk Daoyuan (a second-generation successor of Fayan Wenyi). Yangyi was a disciple of a successor to Shoushan Xingnian in the Linji lineage. For his preface, see Ogata, *Transmission of the Lamp*, pp. xxi–xxiv. Stable master Li Zunxu (988–1038; Jap.: Ri Junkyoku) was also a co-editor of the Jingde Transmission of the Lamp, according to the above-mentioned preface. He was a lay disciple of a different successor of Shoushan Xingnian. Li Zunxu edited Tiansheng Guangdeng Yulu (Jap.: Tenshō Kōtōroku), one of the five main lamp transmission texts included in the Wudeng Huiyuan (Five Lamps Merged in the Source). In one of his poems Li Zunxu may have been the first to use the phrase "iron man," saying, "A practitioner of Zen should be an iron man."

137 Minister Peixiu responding to Huangbo's call refers to their first meeting, when Huangbo called his name and Peixiu responded immediately. Then Huangbo asked, "Where are you?" Later Peixiu became the compiler of Huangbo's Recorded Sayings. See Blofeld, *Zen Teaching of Huang Po*, pp. 100–101.

138 Yudi (d. 818; Jap.: Uteki) was prime minister and a lay practitioner, but he is unknown further except for his study with Ziyu Daotong, a successor of Mazu. When he first met

As for the power of Layman Pang clarifying the [difference between] mirror and tile with his polishing at Shitou and Kiangsi [where Mazu taught], and the example of Emperor Suzong distinguishing between a jewel and a rock through his inquiries at Guangzhai [the temple of National Teacher Nanyang Huizhong] and at Danyuan [the mountain of Danyuan Yingzhen]—although these are both the practice of previous wise people, they can further be illuminating for later wayfarers.[139]

Good gentleman, when you meet a teacher, first ask for one case of a [kōan] story, and just keep it in mind and study it diligently.[140] If you climb to the top of the mountain and dry up the oceans, you will not fail to complete [this study]. [Dazu Huike] standing in the snow to attain the Dharma and engaging the way for eight years was not in vain. The eighth-month effort of [Dajian Huineng] pounding rice had the power for [receiving] transmission of the robe. If someone sees wise people and thinks of being their equal, how could they not become a person who rises high above the herd? Already knowing the difficult and lofty, you will never hesitate to advance. Now I see worldly people who visit and practice with teachers, and before clarifying one question, assertively enjoy bringing up other stories. They withdraw from the discussion as if they understand, but are close-mouthed and cannot speak. They have not yet explained one-third of the story, so how will we see a complete saying? Someone says that the Buddha Dharma is difficult to understand. Another

Ziyu, Yudi asked about the section near the beginning of the Lotus Sutra, chap. 25, about Kannon saving those who were blown to the land of man-eating demons. When Yudi asked the meaning of this, Ziyu scolded him, "What's the use of asking that?" When Yudi paled in shame, Ziyu said, "This is falling into the land of man-eating demons." Later Yudi asked, "What is Buddha?" Ziyu called Yudi's name, and when Yudi responded, Ziyu said, "Don't seek apart from this." Later, Yaoshan Weiyan commented that he would have instead responded to Yudi's acknowledgment by saying, "What is this?" Yaoshan's "further clarification" does not involve pointing to self or other, inside or outside. See Ogata, *Transmission of the Lamp*, pp. 205–207; and Hurvitz, *Scripture of the Lotus Blossom of the Fine Dharma*, pp. 311–312.

139 Emperor Suzong reigned from 756 to 762. The story of his dialogue with the national teacher is in Hekiganroku, case 99, with a longer version in the Jingde Transmission of the Lamp. See Cleary and Cleary, *Blue Cliff Record*, pp. 628–635; and Ogata, *Transmission of the Lamp*, p. 182.

140 "Case" is *soku*, used in kōan literature in the term *kosoku*, "ancient cases." "Story" is *inen*, literally "causes and conditions," but used to indicate some particular circumstance.

says that they are not a vessel. They end up wandering on mistaken paths and vainly stumble around the great way. How can we help but pity them?

Even in the mundane world, there was the respectful invitation to Kongtong [Mountains] and the inquiry to the border guard of Hua— adorned with expressions about following the wind or about riding on the clouds [respectively]—both of which have been broadcast for a hundred generations.[141] How could a buddha be without direct pointing that is before words and outside of things, and not have the virtue to change iron into gold? He transforms all the many beings.

Do not be hesitant or disrespectful. Examine for a while the strength of snow and frost, and you will know the faithfulness of pines and cedars. Take another step and you will surmount the imposing barrier. Do you trust this yet?

When even a little word emerges, ten thousand meanings will be apparent. Furthermore, the genuine masters of the great Dharma of all buddhas have endless bounds of skillful means. Who can fathom this? If disciples accumulate diligent effort at purification, their genuine teachers will never neglect the energetic aspiration to [cut through even] a blown hair.[142] Therefore, once at Shaolin there was an ancestral teacher [Dazu Huike] who cut off his arm and attained the marrow, and also we have heard that [Jinhua] Juzhi cut off the boy's finger and saw blood.[143] Blown in the mys-

---

141 The invitation to Kongtong Mountains refers to the legendary Yellow Emperor inviting the hermit sage Guangchengzi, secluded there, to take over his kingdom, an invitation that was refused with criticism for the emperor's materialism. This is from Zhuangzi, chap. 11. See Watson, *Complete Works of Chuang Tzu*, pp. 118–120; and Hamill and Seaton, *Essential Chuang Tzu*, pp. 75–76. The inquiry to the border guard of Hua was from the legendary Emperor Yao, described in Zhuangzi, chap. 12. When the guard wished good fortune to the emperor, the latter declined this wish, saying that fortune brings trouble. Thereupon the guard rebuked the emperor for not accepting fortune like a sage, and then refused the emperor's further inquiry. See Watson, *Complete Works of Chuang Tzu*, pp. 130–131.

142 A "blown hair" implies constant attention to the slightest detail, with reference to the image of a fine sword that can cut through a hair blowing in the wind. This image is expressed in Hekiganroku, case 100, in which a monk asks, "What is the Blown Hair Sword?" and the teacher responds, "Each branch of coral supports the moon." See Cleary and Cleary, *Blue Cliff Record*, pp. 636–640.

143 For the story about Juzhi cutting off the boy's finger, see Dharma hall discourse 211 and volume 3, note 37.

terious wind of Shaolin, we should awaken from the crazy sleep of the long night. Penetrating the blood vein of Juzhi, we should cut through the diseased root of doubt and delusion.

So it is said, as for inquiring about the Dharma, there is asking with the mouth and answering with the mouth, asking with the body and answering with the body, and asking with the mind and answering with the mind. Not knowing this, how would you dare ask about the Dharma? If a monk does not know this, how can he become a teacher? Those who vainly become guiding teachers of humans and heavenly beings only by memorizing phrases written in sutras are great thieves who destroy the wealth of Dharma. Never get close to such people. Recognizing them as teachers will be of no benefit. Oh good people who study, if you meet teachers of the way with the right view, I sincerely suggest that you serve at their side for three to five years; carefully and respectfully inquire with body, speech, and mind; and understand in detail their responses in body, speech, and mind. First clarify the withered tree and dead ashes, then use a bamboo stick and monks' staff.[144] For many months and long days, become integrated, beautifully functioning without cease. Then how could you not become a genuine lion of the Śākya family?

Don't you see, Huangting Jian studied and served under Zen Master Huitang [Zuxin] Baojue. The teacher [Huitang] said, "Do not use your thinking to make calculations. I do not hide anything from you. How is it?"

[Huangting] Jian started to speak.

The teacher [Huitang] said, "Even a little involvement with discrimination immediately becomes extraneous Dharma."

[Huangting Jian] continued to investigate like this for two years, but still had not entered. One day [Hui]tang and [Huang]ting Jian were walking together by the pond. [Hui]tang said, "The lotus flowers in the pond are fragrant."

[Huangting] Jian responded, "The flowering lotuses are fragrant."

[Hui]tang said, "Not hiding anything from you, how is it?"

[Huangting] Jian was suddenly enlightened.

---

144 Clarifying withered trees and dead ashes refers to finding one's own inner vitality through determined study. "Bamboo staff" is *shippei*; see note 82 above. Here using the stick and staff refers to using practice implements, or tools of Dharma.

Truly, this is the power of sustained study and investigation. Ah, who could understand false and genuine if they were lazy in their continuing labors?

~◦

Fukanzazengi

Universally Recommended Instructions for Zazen

Written by monk Dōgen at Kannon Dōri Kōshō Hōrinji[145]

The way is originally perfect and all-pervading; how could it be contingent on practice and realization? The true vehicle is self-sufficient; what need is there for special effort? Indeed, the whole body is free from dust; who could believe in a means to brush it clean? It is never apart from this very place; what is the use of traveling around to practice? And yet, if there is a hairsbreadth deviation, it is like the gap between heaven and earth; if the least like or dislike arises, the mind is lost in confusion. Suppose you are confident in your understanding and rich in enlightenment, gaining the wisdom that glimpses the ground [of buddhahood], attaining the way and clarifying the mind, arousing an aspiration to reach for the heavens. You are playing in the entranceway, but you still are short of the vital path of emancipation.

Consider [Śākyamuni at] Jetavana; although he was wise at birth, the traces of his six years of upright sitting can yet be seen. As for [Bodhidharma at] Shaolin, although he had transmitted the mind-seal, his nine years of facing a wall is celebrated still. If even the ancient sages were like

145 Kannon Dōri Kōshō Hōrinji, Kōshōji for short, was the temple where Dōgen taught in Fukakusa, south of Kyoto, before leaving for Echizen in 1243, where he later established Eiheiji. Fukanzazengi, in its earliest version, was Dōgen's first writing upon returning from China in 1227. That version is no longer extant. There are two later versions, one written in 1233, called the Tempuku bon (from the Tempuku era), and the final version, which is included here in Eihei Kōroku, written perhaps around 1242, called the Rufubon, or popular version. Although Fukanzazengi is written in Chinese, and not part of Shōbōgenzō, a shorter version written in Japanese in 1243, Zazengi, is part of Shōbōgenzō. For a full discussion of Fukanzazengi, its different versions, and its Chinese sources, see Bielefeldt, *Dōgen's Manuals of Zen Meditation*.

this, how can we today dispense with wholehearted practice?

Therefore, put aside the intellectual practice of investigating words and chasing phrases, and learn to take the backward step that turns the light and shines it inward. Body and mind of themselves will drop away, and your original face will manifest. If you want to attain suchness, practice suchness immediately.[146]

For practicing Zen, a quiet room is suitable. Eat and drink moderately. Put aside all involvements and suspend all affairs. Do not think in terms of good or bad. Do not judge true or false. Give up the operations of mind, intellect, and consciousness; stop measuring with thoughts, ideas, and views. Have no designs on becoming a buddha. How could that be limited to sitting or lying down?

At your sitting place, spread out a thick mat and put a cushion on it. Sit either in the full lotus or half lotus position. In the full lotus position, first place your right foot on your left thigh, then your left foot on your right thigh. In the half lotus, simply place your left foot on your right thigh. Tie your robes loosely and arrange them neatly. Then place your right hand on your left leg and your left hand on your right palm, thumbtips lightly touching. Straighten your body and sit upright, leaning neither left nor right, neither forward nor backward. Align your ears with your shoulders and your nose with your navel. Rest the tip of your tongue against the front of the roof of your mouth, with teeth and lips together. Always keep your eyes open, and breathe softly through your nose.

Once you have adjusted your posture, take a breath and exhale fully, rock your body right and left, and settle into steady, immovable sitting. Think of not thinking. How do you think of not thinking? Beyond-thinking.[147] This is the essential art of zazen.

---

146 "If you want to attain suchness, practice suchness immediately" is a paraphrase of a saying by Yunju Daoying, "If you want to attain the matter of suchness, you should be a person of suchness. Already being a person of suchness, why worry about such a matter?" This is from Jingde Transmission of the Lamp, also discussed by Dōgen in Shōbōgenzō Immo (Suchness). See Cleary, *Shōbōgenzō Zen Essays*, pp. 47–56.

147 These three sentences—"Think of not thinking. How do you think of not thinking? Beyond-thinking"—are from a dialogue in which Yaoshan was questioned about his sitting by a monk. See Dharma hall discourse 373. "Beyond-thinking," sometimes translated as "non-thinking," refers to awareness that includes both thinking and not thinking, and is not caught by either.

The zazen I speak of is not meditation practice. It is simply the Dharma gate of peace and bliss, the practice-realization of totally culminated awakening. It is the kōan realized; traps and snares can never reach it. If you grasp the point, you are like a dragon gaining the water, like a tiger taking to the mountains. For you must know that the true Dharma appears of itself, so that from the start dullness and distraction are struck aside.

When you arise from sitting, move slowly and quietly, calmly and deliberately. Do not rise suddenly or abruptly. In surveying the past, we find that transcendence of both mundane and sacred, and dying while either sitting or standing, have all depended entirely on the power of zazen.[148]

In addition, using the opportunity provided by a finger, a banner, a needle, or a mallet, and meeting realization with a whisk, a fist, a staff, or a shout—these cannot be understood by discriminative thinking, much less can they be known through the practice of supernatural power.[149] They must represent dignified conduct beyond seeing and hearing. Are they not a standard prior to knowledge and views?

This being the case, intelligence or lack of it is not an issue; make no distinction between the dull and the sharp witted. If you concentrate your effort single-mindedly, that in itself is wholeheartedly engaging the way. Practice-realization is naturally undefiled.[150] Going forward is, after all, an everyday affair.

In general, in our world and others, in both India and China, all equally hold the Buddha-seal. While each lineage expresses its own style, they are all simply devoted to sitting, fully blocked in the resolute stability of zazen.

---

148 Dying while standing is a reference to the passing away of the Chinese third ancestor, Jianzhi Sengcan. See Ogata, *Transmission of the Lamp*, p. 81.

149 Finger, banner, needle, and mallet all refer to specific stories of awakening. The finger refers to the story of Jinhua Juzhi holding up, and cutting off, a finger. See Dharma hall discourse 211 and volume 3, note 37. The banner refers to Mahākāśyapa's asking Ānanda to take down the banner at the monastery gate. See Dharma hall discourse 252. The needle refers to Nāgārjuna's presenting his disciple Kānadeva with a bowl of water, into which Kānadeva dropped a needle. See Dharma hall discourse 531 and volume 7, note 136. The mallet refers to the story of Mañjuśrī announcing the teaching of suchness of Śākyamuni. See Cleary, *Book of Serenity*, case 1, pp. 3–5.

150 "Practice-realization is naturally undefiled" is a reference to Nanyue Huairang's response to the sixth ancestor, Dajian Huineng. See Dharma hall discourses 374 and 490 and case 59 in the kōan collection with Dōgen's verse comments in volume 9.

Although they say that there are ten thousand distinctions and a thousand variations, they just wholeheartedly engage the way in zazen. Why leave behind the seat in your own home to wander in vain through the dusty realms of other lands?[151] If you make one misstep, you stumble past what is directly in front of you.

You have gained the pivotal opportunity of human form. Do not pass your days and nights in vain. You are taking care of the essential workings of the Buddha way. Who would take wasteful delight in the spark from a flintstone? Besides, form and substance are like the dew on the grass, the fortunes of life like a dart of lightning, emptied in an instant, vanished in a flash.

Please, honored followers of Zen, long accustomed to groping for the elephant, do not be suspicious of the true dragon.[152] Devote your energies to the way that points directly to the real thing. Revere the one who has gone beyond learning and is free from effort. Accord with the enlightenment of all the buddhas; succeed to the samādhi of all the ancestors. Continue in such a way for a long time, and you will be such a person. The treasure store will open of itself, and you may use it freely.

---

151 "Wandering in vain through the dusty realms" refers to the parable of the prodigal son in the Lotus Sutra, chap. 4. See Katō, Tamura, and Miyasaka, *Threefold Lotus Sutra*, pp. 111–125; or Hurvitz, *Scripture of the Lotus Blossom of the Fine Dharma*, pp. 85–99.

152 "Groping for the elephant" refers to an ancient story, recorded in the Mahāparinirvāṇa Sūtra, in which a group of blind men tried to describe an elephant by touching different parts of it. "Suspicious of the true dragon" refers to an old Chinese story from the Later Han History about someone named Ye Gongzu who was fascinated by dragons and filled his house with images of them. When a dragon heard about this, it kindly came to visit and stuck his head in the window, whereupon Ye Gongzu was shocked with fright.

DŌGEN OSHŌ JUKO[1]

MASTER DŌGEN'S VERSES
PRAISING ANCIENT KŌANS

COLLECTED BY SENNE, ATTENDANT OF DŌGEN ZENJI, AND OTHERS

E K
I Ō
H R
E O
I K
U

THE EXTENSIVE RECORD OF EIHEI DŌGEN, VOLUME NINE

Mahākāśyapa Smiling at Śākyamuni's Flower
1. The World-Honored One, at Vulture Peak before an assembly of a million, held up a flower and blinked his eyes, and Mahākāśyapa's face broke into a smile. The World-Honored One announced to the assembly, "I have the true Dharma eye treasury, wondrous mind of nirvāṇa, which I bequeath to Mahākāśyapa. Spread it through the future, never letting it be cut off." Then he entrusted to Mahākāśyapa his golden embroidered saṃghāṭi robe.[2]

> On a terrace in spring he awakened from a dream
> to discern a fragrant flower.
> Widely shown to humans and heavenly beings,
> only Mahākāśyapa saw.
> The rains on the mountain wash away, becoming snow.

1 *Juko* is "Verses praising ancients" and *ko* or "ancient," also implies *kosoku* kōans, the ancient cases or stories from the classical teachers, but *juko* also implies praise of the ancient masters themselves. Such verses, commonly composed by Chinese masters, became the basis for kōan collections such as the Hekiganroku (Blue Cliff Record), and the Shōyōroku (Book of Serenity), in which were included commentary on the *juko* verses as well as on the cases themselves.

2 A *saṃghāṭi* robe is the largest and heaviest of the three robes Indian monks wore, used for ceremonial occasions or giving lectures, and also during cold. The verse that follows may be two four-line poems, the usual length of Dōgen's verses in this volume. But they might also be one poem. Genryū Kagamishima takes them as two poems.

The clouds on the peak disperse, weaving into frost.
Colors mixed with golden scales, furrow patterns in the waves,
Calls of yellow birds in flight bring confusion and heartbreak.
Guest and host are sad, vainly lifting up their hands.
The ascetic [Mahākāśyapa] enjoys knowing the fragrance.

The Flowering of Mind Only
2. The triple world is mind only.[3]

Even as clouds cover mountains and rivers,
It's vain to count sands of the whole earth of no-mind.
Do not wait for the three levels of waves at the dragon gate.[4]
Leave it to the flower at Vulture Peak.

Bodhitāra Playfully Turning the Jewel
3. Venerable Prajñātāra held a priceless jewel and asked the three princes, "This gem is perfect and bright, can anything match it?"[5] Bodhitāra said, "This is a worldly jewel, not qualified to be unsurpassed. Among the many jewels, the Dharma jewel is supreme. This is worldly radiance, not qualified as unsurpassed. Among radiances, the wisdom radiance is supreme. This is worldly brilliance, not qualified as unsurpassed. Among brilliances, the mind brilliance is supreme. The radiant brilliance of this gem cannot

---

3 The triple world is the phenomenal world of the desire, form, and formless realms. This is a quote from the Avataṃsaka Sūtra and also refers to the Yogācāra idea of the phenomenal world as "Mind Only" (Skt.: Cittamatra), which is also another name for the Yogācāra school.

4 The dragon gate is said to be at the bottom of the ocean. Fish that swim through become dragons.

5 This story is from the Jingde Transmission of the Lamp. See Ogata, *Transmission of the Lamp*, p. 54. Prajñātāra, considered the twenty-seventh Indian ancestor in the Zen lineage, visited a king in southern India who had three sons, tested by Prajñātāra in this story. The third son, Prince Bodhitāra, was later renamed Bodhidharma by Prajñātāra, and thereafter brought the Dharma to China. In this passage Bodhitāra sometimes refers to *ju*, which we are translating as "gem," and sometimes to *hō*, which we are translating as "jewel," and is the character commonly used in Buddhism for the triple jewel of Buddha, Dharma, and Sangha. In common usage there is no definite difference between *ju* and *hō*, although *ju* can also mean "pearl" and *hō* is also used for "treasure." Bodhitāra's statement here is obviously playing with these words.

illuminate itself, but always relying on the wisdom radiance, the radiance discerns this [priceless jewel]. Having already discerned this, immediately one knows this gem. Already knowing this gem, immediately realize this jewel. If you realize this jewel, the jewel is not itself a jewel. If you discern this gem, the gem is not itself a gem. The gem is not itself a gem, but always relying on the wisdom gem, the worldly gem is discerned. The jewel is not itself a jewel, but always relying on the wisdom jewel, realizes the Dharma jewel. Therefore, the teacher having this way, this jewel is immediately manifested; when living beings have the way, the mind jewel also is like this.

> Eyeballs bulging, again he meets his teacher,
> Shaking up colorful radiance in playful encounter.
> Blinding all and turning our heads,
>   [Bodhitāra] is able to pierce the nine-sided jewel,[6]
> Without having circles of [people's] legs leave spiritual footprints.

A Welcome Snake in the Grass

4. The first ancestor [Bodhidharma] faced the wall for nine years.

> At Shaolin one sitting was hardly enough to pass the years.
> Raising his eyes with no companions, geese crying in the sky,
> People, do not laugh at him, brushing away weeds
>   to look up at the wind.
> An astonished snake emerges who may be his match.[7]

The Third Ancestor's Cure

5. Great Teacher Second Ancestor [Dazu Huike] once had a layperson [the future third ancestor, Jianzhi Sengcan] ask him, "This disciple's body is bound up in illness. Master, please help me repent for my sins."

The ancestor said, "Bring me your sins, and I will repent them [for you]."

---

6 The nine-sided jewel refers to a story about Confucius being taught by a young girl how to pierce a nine-faceted jewel. The last line of the verse is difficult. But it seems to refer to Bodhitāra's practice as solitary, without attracting crowds or leaving traces, perhaps an ironic line considering his long-term impact later on as Bodhidharma.

7 The snake refers to Bodhidharma's successor, Dazu Huike.

After a pause the layperson said, "Looking for my sins, they are ungraspable."

The ancestor said, "I have finished repenting sins for you. You should live in reliance on Buddha, Dharma, and Sangha."[8]

> Our sins and crimes fill the skies, yet cannot be found anywhere.
> The sins and crimes filling the skies are fine and beneficial.
> Suddenly right here, another encounter,
> The clear wind of the single way blows freely.

A Freely Turning Dragon

6. [At the place of] Great Teacher Third Ancestor [Jianzhi Sengcan], once the novice [Dayi] Daoxin at age fourteen made prostrations to the ancestor and said, "I entreat the master with your compassion to give me the Dharma gate of release and liberation."

The ancestor said, "Who has bound you?"

The novice Daoxin said, "Nobody bound me."

The ancestor said, "Then why are you seeking for liberation?" Daoxin hearing these words had great realization, and worked as a follower there for nine years.[9]

> A phoenix chick is born from a phoenix,
>   but they are not the same.
> A dragon gives birth to a dragon child, but they are not separate.[10]
> If you want to know the meaning of a wheel freely spinning,
> Only someone turning somersaults can show you.

The Rice-Pounder's Response

7. Zen Master Daman [Hongren] at midnight secretly visited the rice-

---

8 This story is from the Jingde Transmission of the Lamp; see Ogata, *Transmission of the Lamp*, p. 75. The third ancestor, Jianzhi Sengcan, is said to have been a leper who was cured by his meeting with Dazu Huike.

9 This story is in the Jingde Transmission of the Lamp; see Ogata, *Transmission of the Lamp*, p. 81.

10 "They are not separate" is, literally, "It [the child] is not additional," in the sense of being extra or superfluous.

pounding hut and asked layman [Hui]neng, "Is the rice refined yet or not?"

Huineng said, "It is refined, but not yet sifted." Daman tapped the mortar three times with his staff. Huineng shook the rice winnow three times and entered the [teacher's] room.[11]

> In the deep night with eyes vivid they saw each other
> As old monk Buddha in India.
> With divine dignity the lion helps [the younger] bounce it back.
> Where the elephant king treads, fox tracks are erased.

The Body, Wind, and Flag Moving with the Sixth Ancestor's Mind

8. The sixth ancestor [Dajian Huineng] arrived at Faxing [Dharma Nature] temple, and stayed [overnight] on a walkway under the temple eaves. In the evening, the wind was blowing the temple banner. He heard two monks arguing. One said the banner was moving; the other said the wind was moving. They bantered back and forth, never reaching the truth. The [sixth] ancestor said, "Would you permit this layperson to join your lofty discussion? Neither the wind nor banner move, but simply your own minds are moving."[12]

> Where the wind and banner move,
>   in their eyes new flowers bloom.
> Each expounding different sides, such movement is familiar.
> This ancient Buddha yet forgot these fellows [fully] move,
> [Saying] these persons' minds moved without turning their bodies.

11 Dōgen also discusses this story in Dharma hall discourse 126. See volume 1, note 243, for other references.

12 This famous story of the sixth ancestor, which recounts his emergence in the world, appears in the Platform Sutra; see Yampolsky, *Platform Sutra of the Sixth Patriarch*, p. 73; Cleary, *Sutra of Hui-neng*, pp. 13–15; and Wong, *Sutra of Hui Neng*, pp. 22–24. It is also in the Gateless Gate, case 29; see Shibayama, *Gateless Barrier*, pp. 209–213; Cleary, *Unlocking the Zen Kōan*, pp. 141–143; and Aitken, *Gateless Barrier*, pp. 184–188. It is also case 146 in some versions of Dōgen's Mana Shōbōgenzō.

Caring for the Myriad Grass-Tips

9. An ancient said, "The bright clear hundreds of grass-tips are the bright clear mind of the ancestral teachers."[13]

> Although wanting it all tied up, for tens of thousands of miles
>   nothing holds.
> Staying within the gate, do not wait for the brightness of others.[14]
> Without your caring, it is easy to lose the path of active practice.
> Even those hard of hearing are moved by the sound
>   of evening rain.

The Boatman's Traceless Activity

10. Following the rhyme scheme of a verse by brother [Sō]kai, here is a story.[15] Master Chuanzi [Decheng] entrusted Jiashan, saying, "After this keep yourself where you leave no traces, and even where you leave no traces, do not keep yourself. I stayed with Yaoshan for thirty years, and truly clarified this matter."[16]

13 This is a saying cited by the famed eighth-century Chan adept Layman Pang to his daughter Lingzhao, herself an adept. The "ancestral teacher" here refers to Bodhidharma. See Sasaki, Iriya, and Fraser, *Recorded Sayings of Layman P'ang*, p. 75; and Chang, *Original Teachings of Ch'an Buddhism*, pp. 145–146. This quotation is cited previously in Dharma hall discourse 9 and is also in Dōgen's Mana Shōbōgenzō, case 88; see Nishijima, *Master Dogen's Shinji Shobogenzo*, p. 116.

14 The first two lines of this poem echo the saying by Dongshan to his monks leaving the monastery at the end of a practice period: "Go where there's not an inch of grass for ten thousand miles." Dayang Qingxuan later added, "Even not going out the gate, still the grass is boundless." See Cleary, *Book of Serenity*, case 89, p. 382.

15 According to Genryū Kagamishima, "Following the rhyme scheme of a verse by brother Sōkai" may be an addition by Senne, the compiler of this volume of Eihei Kōroku. Sōkai was a close disciple of Dōgen who died young in 1242. See Dharma hall discourses 111 and 112. This supports the view that this volume 9 with its kōans was written by Dōgen at Kōshōji.

16 This saying by Chuanzi to Jiashan is the end of a much longer story, given in full in Dharma word 8 in volume 8.

Two poems:[17]

Letting the knife's play disperse the ox, who has such a method?[18]
His thirty-four-foot [line] is exceptional.[19]
This pure deep pool is like a mirror where no fish comes.
The two of them are like the sky, a bird flying alone.

Unexpectedly meeting poison, his whole body died,
Pitiful, not a single hair left on the eyebrows.
With no self nor anyone else, time is not remembered.
Suddenly he forgot all that he had done.

The Ox Returns Home in Evening Brightness
11. Zen Master [Changqing] Da'an asked Baizhang, "This student yearns to understand Buddha. What is it?"

Baizhang said, "You are much like one searching for the ox while riding the ox."

Da'an said, "How is it after understanding?"

Baizhang said, "It is like a person returning home riding the ox."

Da'an said, "I am not clear. How can I protect and care for it from beginning to end?"

Baizhang said, "It is like an oxherd holding up a staff to watch that [the ox] does not disturb people's seedlings."

From then on Da'an grasped the meaning.[20]

---

17 "Two poems" is probably an insertion by the editor Senne, although in other cases in this volume, such as in case 1, multiple poems may be given without such notice.

18 "The knife's play disperses the ox" refers to Zhuangzi's story about a butcher cutting up an ox by allowing his knife to flow through the spaces between the flesh. See Hamill and Seaton, *Essential Chuang Tzu*, pp. 19–20; and Watson, *Complete Works of Chuang Tzu*, pp. 50–51.

19 The thirty-four-foot line refers to Chuanzi's fishing line, mentioned in the story in Dharma word 8, in which Chuanzi says, "The line at the tip of the fishing pole moves at your wish. Without disrupting the clear waves, the mind is naturally profound."

20 This story appears in the Jingde Transmission of the Lamp; see Ogata, *Transmission of the Lamp*, p. 315.

Even with morning mist thin, his robe gets damp.
Where the evening sun sets, birds fly on distant mountains.
In this painting, an oxherd returns home amid evening radiance,
Singing of plum blossoms and the moon above the snow.

Yunyan Sweeps the Moon

12. [Yun]yan was sweeping the ground, and Guishan said, "Too busy."
Yunyan said, "You should know there is one who is not busy."
Guishan said, "If so, then there is a second moon."
Yunyan held up the broom and said, "Which moon is this?"[21]

Who sweeps the ground and also sees the moon?
Holding up the moon, his sweeping truly is not in vain.
Within tens of thousands of moons is placed this moon.
Although called the second, how could there be a first?

Zhaozhou's Jewels amid Poverty

13. Zhaozhou said to the assembly, "If you do not leave the monastery for
your whole life, for five or ten years sitting immovably without saying
anything, nobody can call you mute."[22]

Hundreds of students struggle together in extreme poverty.
In this life, they live again and strive in practice.
How many times have you come here;
    how many years have passed?
Jade and stone are widely arrayed,
    but down in the depths is a jewel.

21 Dōgen refers to this story about Yunyan and the second moon elsewhere in Eihei Kōroku;
see volume 4, note 33, and Dharma hall discourses 344 and 521. This story is case 21 of the
Shōyōroku, except that in that version the questioner is Yunyan's brother Daowu (rather than
Guishan), a fellow student of theirs under Baizhang. See Cleary, *Book of Serenity*, pp. 91–94.
In the Jingde Transmission of the Lamp (Keitoku Dentōroku), in the section on Yunyan,
the questioner is given as Guishan. In Mana Shōbōgenzō, Dōgen cites this as case 83, using
Daowu as the questioner. See Nishijima, *Master Dogen's Shinji Shobogenzo*, p. 111.

22 This story appears in the Recorded Sayings of Zhaozhou; see Green, *Recorded Sayings
of Zen Master Joshu*, p. 20. Dōgen also discusses this quote in the Shōbōgenzō essays Gyōji
(Continuous Practice) and Dōtoku (Complete Expression). See Cook, *How to Raise an Ox*,
pp. 137–138; or Tanahashi, *Enlightenment Unfolds*, pp. 121–122; and Nishijima and Cross,
Master Dogen's Shobogenzo, book 2, p. 271, respectively.

A Worm in the Rice

14. Zen Master Shishuang Qingzhu became rice manager under the great Guishan. One day Shishuang was in the rice storehouse sifting rice. Guishan said, "Food from donors should not be scattered around."

Shishuang said, "It is not scattered around."

Guishan picked up one grain from the floor and said, "You say it's not scattered around, but where does this come from?"

Shishuang did not reply. Guishan again said, "Do not disdain even this single grain. A hundred thousand grains can be born from this single grain."

Shishuang said, "A hundred thousand grains can be born from this single grain. But it is not yet clear; where did this single grain come from?"

Guishan laughed loudly, "Ha! Ha!" and returned to the abbot's quarters. Later in the evening he went to give a Dharma hall discourse and said, "Oh great assembly, there's a worm in the rice."[23]

> Where did he get this single grain?
> Without being told anything, a great talent was realized.
> Hundreds of millions of grains cannot be found,
> As this worm has eaten them up.

The Demon on Tortoise Mountain

15. Xuefeng and Yantou arrived together at Aoshan [Tortoise Mountain] and were snowed in. Xuefeng asked Yantou, "What shall I do?"[24]

---

23 This story is also mentioned by Dōgen in his Eihei Shingi. See Leighton and Okumura, *Dōgen's Pure Standards for the Zen Community*, p. 144.

24 This is a much shortened version of a story that appears in the commentary to Hekiganroku (Blue Cliff Record), case 22, and is also given in its entirety by Dōgen in Mana Shōbōgenzō, case 218; see Nishijima, *Master Dogen's Shinji Shobogenzo*, pp. 279–280. In the longer story Xuefeng, while snowed in for days, continued rigorous sitting day and night, while Yantou slept most of the time. Yantou finally chided Xuefeng, saying he was meaninglessly sitting like an earth guardian deity. Xuefeng complained that his mind was not yet at peace. When Yantou then questioned him about his understanding, Xuefeng brought up his insights about various stories of previous masters. Yantou finally shouted at him and said, "Haven't you heard that what comes in through the gate is not the jewels of the family?" Thereupon Xuefeng asked the question, "What shall I do?" as given in the text of this case, with what ensues. See Cleary and Cleary, *Blue Cliff Record*, pp. 145–146.

Yantou said, "Later on, if you want to disseminate the great teaching, let it flow out from your own breast bit by bit, using yourself to cover heaven and earth." With these words, Xuefeng was greatly enlightened. He made prostrations, then stood and cried out repeatedly, "Today finally Tortoise Mountain has fulfilled the way. Today finally Tortoise Mountain has fulfilled the way."[25]

> In the night he mistakenly practiced [sitting steady]
>   as an earth deity,
> A monstrous rock or strange boulder with many resentments.
> Today Tortoise Mountain fulfills the way.
> One demon died, [making] another demon.[26]

Deep Intimacy Beyond Knowing

16. Zen Master Fayan [Wenyi] once visited Zen Master [Luohan Dizang Gui]chen. Guichen asked, "Elder, where are you going?"

Fayan said, "I am wandering around on pilgrimage."

Guichen asked, "What is the point of your pilgrimage?"

Fayan said, "I don't know."

Guichen said, "Not knowing is most intimate."

Fayan widely opened up realization.[27]

> Cavorting freely all is clear, and again he freely romps.[28]
> How can pilgrimage be bound by straight or twisting ropes?

25 This might also be read as "Today finally on Tortoise Mountain I have fulfilled the way."

26 Although the sentence simply indicates "another demon" after a demon dies, we interpret this as Dōgen criticizing Xuefeng for turning this attainment into a new demon.

27 After this event, Fayan remained and studied with Dizang Guichen. This story appears in Jingde Transmission of the Lamp; see Chang, *Original Teachings of Ch'an Buddhism*, pp. 238–239. It is also case 20 in the Shōyōroku; see Cleary, *Book of Serenity*, pp. 86–90. Dōgen also cites this story in Dharma hall discourse 59 and in Mana Shōbōgenzō, case 171; see Nishijima, *Master Dogen's Shinji Shobogenzo*, p. 223.

28 "Cavorting Freely" Tengteng (Jap.: Tōtō) is a nickname for Fuxian Renjian (a disciple of Songshan Hui'an in the Northern school), who was known for his endless pilgrimage. Called before Empress Wu, he refused to speak but gave her nineteen poems, and then refused her gifts and offerings in return. See Ogata, *Transmission of the Lamp*, pp. 120–121. Only one of the poems, "Clarifying the Source," survives, from which he received his nickname. It ends with the lines "Today I entrust all to destiny, cavorting freely.

If we lack great achievement by one square inch,
This knowing becomes increasingly small, two or three quarts.[29]

The Moon Always Full

17. A monk once asked Touzi [Datong], "How is the moon before it is full?"

Touzi [Datong] said, "It swallows two or three."
The monk asked, "How about after it is full?"
Touzi said, "It vomits up seven or eight."[30]

Two poems:

Polishing a tile, polishing a mirror, polishing the Milky Way,
Cutting through chains of mist and haze, the way is not yet full.
I honestly think there is no moon in autumn.
From the beginning, mid-autumn is in the moon.[31]

Although after full and before full resemble the moon,
They can never be compared to the bright pearl in the night.
Two or three and seven or eight
    I leave to swallowing and vomiting.
How can the radiance of scenery of fullness
    be likened to fire in a furnace?

Qingyuan Holds Up a Whisk

18. Qingyuan [Xingsi] asked Shitou [Xiqian], "Where are you from?"
Shitou said, "I came from Caoxi."

Tomorrow I cavort freely entrusting all to destiny. In the mind I clearly know everything. For a while I have become a dull fool."

29 Dōgen here seems to extol true knowing, rather than some attachment to not knowing.

30 Dōgen cites a slightly different version of this story in Shōbōgenzō Tsuki (The Moon); see Tanahashi, *Moon in a Dewdrop*, p. 131. It is also cited in Mana Shōbōgenzō, case 13. See Nishijima, *Master Dogen's Shinji Shobogenzo*, p. 21.

31 "Mid-autumn" implies fullness, as the full moon of mid-autumn is most cherished in East Asia.

Qingyuan held up his whisk and asked, "Does this exist at Caoxi?"

Shitou said, "Not only does it not exist at Caoxi, but it does not exist even in India."

Qingyuan asked, "Have you ever been to India?"

Shitou said, "If I had been there, so would this be."

Qingyuan said, "That's not enough, speak further."

Shitou said, "Master, you should speak one half. Do not completely rely on Xiqian [myself]."

Qingyuan said, "I do not evade speaking to you, but I am afraid that later nobody would accept it."[32]

Two poems:

At a crossroads, within and without they commented,
Before departing the lattice window, already the bright window.
The sky is dry, the water aged, and the wind formless.
I think the stone man saw the great country.[33]

He only knew that holding up [the whisk] did not yet hit the mark.
He'd not yet understood letting go,
    not seen the family style.
Speaking half completely relied on their single bones.
They did not allow us to penetrate two elders' bits of words.

Qingyuan's Wind Breaking Apart Stages
19. Qingyuan asked the sixth ancestor [Dajian Huineng], "What activity does not fall into classifications?"

---

32 Dōgen also refers to this story in Dharma hall discourse 212 and in Mana Shōbōgenzō, case 1. See Nishijima, *Master Dogen's Shinji Shobogenzo*, p. 3. It also appears in Keizan's Denkōroku; see Cleary, *Transmission of Light*, pp. 150–151; and Cook, *Record of Transmitting the Light*, pp. 178–182. Caoxi is the place where the sixth ancestor [Huineng] taught.

33 The "stone man" refers to Shitou, whose name means "Stone Head." The subject of this last line might also be Qingyuan, as in, "[Qingyuan] thought the stone man saw the great country."

The [sixth] ancestor said, "What have you been doing?"

Qingyuan said, "I do not carry out even the sacred truths."

The ancestor said, "What class do you fall into?"

Qingyuan said, "I do not carry out even the sacred truths; what classification could there be?" The ancestor deeply [appreciated him] as a vessel.[34]

> He raised and rotated the earth's axis,
>   and opened the gateway to heaven.
> Spring come to the cold valley, he plays in peach paradise.[35]
> Mountain bamboo stuck in deep snow,
>   breaks at the joints from the wind.
> He directly pervades the clear waves, leaving a trace on the water.

Yunyan Shakes a Poison Hand

20. Yaoshan asked Yunyan, "What Dharma does brother [Baizhang Huai]hai expound?"

Yunyan said, "Once when he arrived to give a Dharma hall discourse, just as the assembly gathered, he pounded his staff and called the assembly. When the monks turned their heads, Baizhang said, 'What is this?'"

Yaoshan said, "Why didn't you say this earlier?"

With that Yunyan was greatly enlightened.[36]

> I mistakenly followed Yaoshan, another poison hand.[37]
> Rubbing my body in distress, I hated the clouds and wind.

34 This story is in Mana Shōbōgenzō, case 237; see Nishijima, *Master Dogen's Shinji Shobogenzo,* p. 306; and Jingde Transmission of the Lamp, vol. 5.

35 "Peach paradise," literally "source of peaches," refers to a Daoist myth about a lost person who found a utopian land full of peaches, returned home, and then could not find that land again.

36 The longer story appears in Keizan's Denkōroku. This happened after Yunyan, who had been Baizhang Huaihai's attendant for twenty years without realization, had unsuccessfully tried to describe many instances of Baizhang's teachings to Yaoshan. In the full story, Yaoshan said, "Why didn't you say this earlier? Now I can finally see brother Huaihai." See Cleary, *Transmission of Light,* pp. 160–163; and Cook, *Record of Transmitting the Light,* pp. 188–192.

37 "Poison hand" plays on Yaoshan's name, which means "Medicine Mountain." Like Yunyan's practice with Baizhang, for a long time it had seemed futile.

Though my flesh was a thousand pounds,
   my wisdom was barely an inch.
Resenting you before, now I'm filled with gratitude.

The Gates to Zhaozhou

21. A monk asked Zhaozhou, "What is Zhaozhou?"
   Zhaozhou said, "East gate, south gate, west gate, north gate."
   The monk said, "That is not what I asked."
   Zhaozhou said, "Didn't you ask about Zhaozhou?"[38]

Zhaozhou once received a monk's inquiry,
And for him mentioned east, west, south, north gates.
The four points lined up seem to make Zhaozhou.
The great doubt; where can we find the original source?

The Boatman's Profound Music

22. The boatman master of Huating River [Chuanzi Decheng] said, "I have let down a thousand-foot line, the mind in a deep pool. Depart from the hook by three inches. Speak quickly! Speak quickly!" Jiashan tried to open his mouth. The master [Chuanzi] immediately pushed him into the water with his oar. Thereupon [Jiashan] was greatly enlightened.[39]

In Jingkou he was well respected and knew his nose was straight.[40]
At Huating River the waves were wild, stopping his speech.
The river waves calmed down and the golden-scaled fish leaped.
With music so profound, he nodded his head three times.[41]

---

38 Zhaozhou was the name of a town, as well as of this great Zen master. His response might appear to be about the town. This story appears in Green, *Recorded Sayings of Zen Master Joshu*, p. 42. Another version of this story about Zhaozhou is case 9 in the Hekiganroku; see Cleary and Cleary, *Blue Cliff Record*, pp. 59–64. Dōgen also cites it as case 46 of Mana Shōbōgenzō; see Nishijima, *Master Dogen's Shinji Shobogenzo*, p. 65.

39 This case is a small part of the full story given by Dōgen in Dharma word 8 in volume 8. Another small portion also appears as case 10 in this volume. The whole story also appears in Mana Shōbōgenzō, case 90; see Nishijima, *Master Dogen's Shinji Shobogenzo*, pp. 118–120.

40 Jingkou was where Jiashan had been abbot before going in search of the boatman.

41 After being pushed into the water and having a great realization, Jiashan had nodded his head three times.

Xuansha's Bloody Toe
23. Xuansha tried to leave a peak to reach a peak.[42] He injured his toe and blood flowed, whereupon he had insight. Then he returned to Xuefeng, and never went to study elsewhere.

With hands busy but feet clumsy, he banged his toe.
Drops of blood flew, and the great earth was crimson.
Vainly groping around, water is scarce and clouds dissipate,[43]
Following after Elephant Bone [Mountain],
he did not go west or east.[44]

A True Dragon Appears in the Dark
24. One evening, Deshan silently sat outside the [teacher's] room. Longtan [Chongxin] asked, "Why don't you go back to your room?"
Deshan replied, "It's dark." Longtan lit a paper torch and gave it to Deshan. As Deshan grasped it, Longtan immediately blew it out. Deshan was greatly enlightened and made prostrations. Longtan said, "What have you seen?"
Deshan said, "From now on and henceforth, I will never under the heavens doubt the tongue of my old master."[45]

Although your efforts to engage the way should be put to rest,
With a grandmotherly [mind, Longtan] spoke on and on for you.

42 Xuansha was leaving the peak, or temple, of his teacher Xuefeng, heading to Feiyuan (Flying Monkey) Peak, intending to wander around visiting teachers. The story as it follows is also discussed by Dōgen in Shōbōgenzō Ikka no Myōju (One Bright Pearl). See Waddell and Abe, *Heart of Dōgen's Shōbōgenzō*, pp. 31–37; and Cleary, *Shōbōgenzō: Zen Essays by Dōgen*, pp. 58–62. It appears in Jingde Transmission of the Lamp.

43 "Water" and "clouds" in this line may refer to cloud and water *(unsui)* monks, wasting their efforts when vainly seeking.

44 Elephant Bone Mountain is another name for the peak where Xuefeng taught. When Xuansha returned, Xuefeng asked why he was not traveling. Xuansha proclaimed that "Bodhidharma did not come to the eastern land [China]; the second ancestor [Dazu Huike] did not go to the Western Heaven [India]."

45 This story is in Jingde Transmission of the Lamp and also appears in Mumonkan, case 28. See Shibayama, *Gateless Barrier*, pp. 201–208; Aitken, *Gateless Barrier*, pp. 177–183; or Cleary, *Unlocking the Zen Kōan*, pp. 132–134.

Loving the true dragon, the true dragon appeared
In a single scene of blowing out a lantern.

Loving Mountains Beyond Senses and Objects

25. Zen Master Hongzhi said in a verse,

"With coming and going, a person in the mountains
Understands that blue mountains are his body.
The blue mountains are the body, and the body is the self,
So where can one place the senses and their objects?"[46]

The teacher Dōgen followed his rhyme scheme.[47]

A person in the mountains should love the mountains.
With going and coming, the mountains are his body.
The mountains are the body, but the body is not the self
So where can one find any senses or their objects?

Nanquan Taming His Water Buffalo

26. Nanquan said to his assembly, "Since I was young, I, old Master Wang
[Nanquan], have been tending a water buffalo. Trying to tame it in the
east of the valley, I cannot prevent it from eating the marsh grasses of the
ruler. And trying to tame it in the west of the valley, I cannot prevent it

---

46 In Hongzhi's poem, and in Dōgen's verse comment, the word we are translating as
"body" is *shin*, which can also mean "self"; and the word translated as "self" is *ware*, which
also means "myself," or "me." Both Hongzhi's and Dōgen's verses echo poems by the
great Song dynasty poet and Zen practitioner Su Dongpo, also known as Su Shi. A famous
verse of his says, "The true face of Mount Lu cannot be known, / Because the one looking at it is standing in its midst." See Beata Grant, *Mount Lu Revisited: Buddhism in the
Life and Writings of Su Shih* (Honolulu: University of Hawai'i Press, 1994), p. 1. In his
Shōbōgenzō essay Keisei Sanshoku (The Sound of the Valley Streams, the Form of the
Mountains), Dōgen discusses the enlightenment poem of Su Dongpo, which includes
the line "The color of the mountain is the pure body [of Buddha]." See Cook, *How to Raise
an Ox*, pp. 60–71; or Tanahashi, *Enlightenment Unfolds*, pp. 59–60.

47 "The teacher [Dōgen] followed his rhyme scheme" is inserted by the compiler of these
kōans, Senne.

from eating the marsh grasses of the ruler. I must follow after and pay my small portion of compensation, as this is somewhat visible.[48]

> Its nose drifts like a boat in the realm of mountains and waters,
> A donkey in front with a horse behind, not yet plowing the field.[49]
> Directly binding up grasses, against the grain
> of [usual] human will,
> For a while I enter the tens of thousands of peaks.[50]

Wild Fox Powers

27. Tripitaka Master Da'er arrived from India to the capital and said, "I have attained the wisdom eye that sees others' minds." The Emperor Daizong ordered National Teacher [Nanyang] Huizhong to examine him. As soon as the tripitika master saw the teacher, he made a prostration and stood to his right.[51]

The national teacher asked, "Have you attained the divine power to read others' minds?"

He replied, "I wouldn't presume [to say so]."

The national teacher said, "You tell me, where is this old monk right now?"

[Da'er] said, "Master, you are the teacher of a nation, how could you go to Western River to watch the boat races?"

The national teacher again asked, "Tell me, and where is this old monk right now?"

<hr>

48 This story is from Shūmon Rentō Eyō (Collection of the Essence of the Continuous Dharma Lamp), vol. 4, the section on Nanquan.

49 For "a donkey in front with a horse behind," see Dharma hall discourse 4 and volume 1, note 8. The water buffalo's nose above the water might indicate the presence of Buddha nature, though immature.

50 "Binding up grasses" indicates building a hut, or practice place, to deepen and establish practice.

51 Dōgen refers to this story frequently, for example, in Dharma hall discourse 17 (see volume 1, note 45), and also discusses the later commentaries on the story (see Dharma hall discourse 196). It is further discussed in Shōbōgenzō Tashintzu (Penetration of Others' Minds) and in Shōbōgenzō Shinfukatoku (Mind Is Ungraspable), part 2. See Nishijima and Cross, *Master Dogen's Shobogenzo*, book 4, pp. 89–99; book 1, pp. 231–238;

[Da'er] said, "Master, you are the teacher of a nation, how could you watch the monkeys playing on the Tianjin Bridge?"

The national teacher inquired a third time with the same words as before. The tripitika master paused, but did not know where he was.

The national teacher scolded him saying, "This wild-fox spirit; where is your penetration into others' minds?"

The tripitika master had no reply.

> Baiya regrets that Ziqi has not yet come.[52]
> At dawn virtuous clouds gather within this.[53]
> The ten thousand valleys are not other, beyond the paths of mind.
> How pitiful, Buddha taken as wild-fox powers.

The Boatman's Crescent Hook

28. Master Chuanzi [the Boatman] asked Jiashan, "I have let down a thousand-foot line, with mind in a deep pool. Depart from the hook by three inches. Why don't you speak?"[54]

> Who cast out a thousand-foot line?
> He followed and chased the waves for whatever remained.
> A length was offered, but how could it be measured?
> Both curved and straight hooks were used.
> A crescent moon unhidden by clouds,
>   the dragon palace is luminous.

---

52 Baiya was a master zither player. His friend Ziqi was such a great appreciator of music that after Ziqi died, Baiya cut the strings of his instrument and never played again. This story is from the Chinese Daoist classic Liezi, from about 400 B.C.E.

53 "Virtuous clouds" may refer to Meghaśrī, the first of the fifty-two teachers encountered on his pilgrimage by the youth Sudhana in the Gaṇḍavyūha Sūtra, the last chapter of the Avataṃsaka (Flower Ornament) Sūtra. Sudhana could not at first see this teacher for seven days, at which time he found him doing walking meditation on a mountain peak. See Thomas Cleary, trans., *The Flower Ornament Scripture* (Boston: Shambhala, 1993), pp. 1180–1182; see also Thomas Cleary, trans., *Entry into the Realm of Reality, the Guide: A Commentary on the "Gandhavyuha" by Li Tongxuan* (Boston: Shambhala, 1989), pp. 23–24.

54 This is from the lengthy story fully recounted in Dharma word 8, also referred to in kōans 10 and 22. Dōgen's verse comment that follows might be intended as either one long poem or two four-line poems.

The old bow floating on water, the Yang house is in shadows.[55]
Clearly observe the mind that hooks the golden-scaled fish.
Waves calm, wind quiet, speech is at rest.

Rolling Up the Curtain after Thirty Years

29. Changqing [Huiling] asked Lingyun [Zhiqin], "What is the essential meaning of Buddha Dharma?"

Lingyun said, "Before the affairs of the donkey have left, the affair of the horse has arrived."

[Chang]qing went back and forth between Xuefeng and Xuansha for thirty years without clarifying this affair. One day as he was rolling up the curtain, he was greatly enlightened.[56]

What youth would polish their face, already like a jewel?
When returning in old age, his beard is like frost.
Rolling up the curtain, he freely seized the moonlight.
"My official's cap should be washed in the Canglang River."[57]

Just Sitting As Mount Lu Walks

30. A monk asked Yantou, "What is the mind of the ancestral teacher [Bodhidharma]?"

[Yan]tou said, "If you move Mount Lu, I'll tell you."[58]

---

55 Yang was a legendary skilled archer who could hit a willow leaf at a hundred paces. He is also referred to, with another of his names, in the Song of the Precious Mirror Samādhi by Dongshan Liangjie. See Leighton, *Cultivating the Empty Field*, p. 77; and Powell, *Record of Tung-shan*, p. 65. His story is originally recorded in the Book of History by Sima Qian (145–86 B.C.E.)

56 For some of Dōgen's many other references to donkeys and horses, see kōan case 26; Dharma hall discourses 4 and 403; and volume 1, note 8; volume 2 (Dharma hall discourse 128), note 15; volume 4 (Dharma hall discourse 276), note 32. This story about Changqing is in Mana Shōbōgenzō, case 156; see Nishijima, *Master Dogen's Shinji Shobogenzo*, p. 206. It appears in Dahui's collection of six hundred kōans, also entitled Shōbōgenzō.

57 The last line is from a poem by Quyuan (343–277 B.C.E.), who was exiled to the Canglang River for offending fellow officials with his extreme honesty and criticisms. In exile he wrote, "When the water in the Canglang River is clear, I wash my official's cap. When it is muddy, I wash my feet." Washing the feet is a common expression for being rid of something, as in "washing my hands of it." Quyuan died by throwing himself in this river.

58 A longer version of this story appears in Dōgen's Mana Shōbōgenzō, case 75. In that

Two poems:

> Like the face as a bit of mind, refreshed in accord with the season,
> A body with horns on its head demonstrates the same stature.
> Blue mountains are walking beyond human powers.
> Do not say they approach pulled by us.

> Mount Lu moves, and then arrives.
> Who knows that in these previous words, he opened half his mouth?
> It's not yet clear how Yantou will just sit,
> As [Mount Lu] is not the same as rocky peaks of the triple world.

One Saying from Birth to Old Age

31. Zen Master Wuxie Lingmo visited Shitou [Xiqian]. First he thought to himself, "If one of his sayings really fits me, I will stay. Otherwise I will just leave."

Shitou knew [Wuxie Lingmo] was a vessel of Dharma, and gave him instructions. Lingmo did not realize the meaning, and took his leave and departed. When he reached the gate, Shitou called out, "Elder." Wuxie looked back and Shitou said, "From birth to old age, it is just this person. Do not seek anything else." Hearing this, [Wuxie] Lingmo was greatly enlightened.[59]

> Regrettably, this one saying has no handle.
> Leaving or staying is up to him to consider for a while.

---

version the monk first asks, "When the triple world arises ceaselessly, how is it?" Yantou answered, "Just sit." Then, eliciting the response about Mount Lu, the monk asked what Yantou's intention was, although in the version here in Eihei Kōroku, case 30, it is clearly the ancestral teacher's mind or intention, implying Bodhidharma. The triple world here represents the conditioned world of samsāra. See Nishijima, *Master Dogen's Shinji Shobogenzo*, p. 103.

59 A variant version of this story appears in the Jingde Transmission of the Lamp. See Ogata, *The Transmission of the Lamp*, p. 238. There it says that after this incident, Wuxie Lingmo remained for twenty years as Shitou's attendant, although he is considered a successor of Mazu. Dōgen gives this story as case 294, or in some versions case 300, of Mana Shōbōgenzō; see Nishijima, *Master Dogen's Shinji Shobogenzo*, p. 374.

Unless one clearly understands [our life] from birth to old age,
Turning the head and shifting the brain,
  they do not engage each other.[60]

Overcoming Resistance and Accepting Nourishment

32. Zen Master Guanzhi [Zhixian], after becoming abbot, said in a Dharma hall discourse, "I was at father Linji's where I got half a dipper and at mother Moshan's where I got half a dipper. Together they made one full dipper that I drank completely, so that even until now I am satisfied through and through."[61]

Meeting a poison hand, his whole body was pain.
Counting eyebrows, how many are there?
Resenting self and other without yet hating,
Lulian's single arrow carried much feeling.[62]

Shooting Stars Beyond Speaking or Not Speaking

33. Master Touzi [Yi]qing served Dayang [Qingxuan] for three years.[63] One day Dayang inquired of the teacher [Touzi Yiqing] saying, "One

---

60 "They do not engage each other" probably refers to "this person" and "great enlightenment" not connecting without an understanding of the everyday reality of life over time (from birth to old age). It might possibly also refer to Wuxie and Shitou not truly engaging without such a long-term understanding.

61 This story appears in Dōgen's Eihei Shingi and in his Shōbōgenzō Raihai Tokuzui (Paying Homage and Acquiring the Marrow), used to convey his strong disapproval of prejudice against women teachers and practitioners. This statement is at the end of a longer story about Guanzhi, already a successor of the great Linji, visiting the nun and teacher Moshan. He challenged her in Dharma combat unsuccessfully, finally accepting her authority and remaining in her assembly for years. See Leighton and Okumura, *Dōgen's Pure Standards for the Zen Community*, pp. 145–146; and Cook, *How to Raise an Ox*, pp. 99–101.

62 Lulian was a general from Zi in the Warring States period (431–222 B.C.E.) who overcame the country of Yan with one arrow. The arrow here seems to be referring to Moshan shooting down Guanzhi's resistance.

63 This story appears in Record of the Universal Lamp of the Jiatai era (Jap.: Katai Futōroku), one of the five main lamp transmission texts in the Wudeng Huiyuan, but with Fushan Fayuan rather than Dayang as the teacher in the dialogue. It also appears that way in Keizan's Denkōroku; see Cook, *Record of Transmitting the Light*, pp. 221–228.

outside the way asked the Buddha, 'I don't ask you about speaking or not speaking.' The World-Honored One paused for a while. What about this?"[64] [Touzi Yi]qing tried to respond, but [Da]yang covered Yiqing's mouth. Yiqing clearly had an opening to enlightenment, and immediately made prostrations.

Dayang said, "Did you subtly realize the mysterious function?"

Yiqing said, "If I had, I should have vomited it out."

At the time, attendant Zi was standing by them and said, "[Yi]qing Huayan today seems like he is sick in a sweat."

Yiqing looked back at him and said, "Shut your mouth, dog."

> Even though his mouth was covered, what about his nose?
> Since he had not swallowed, why take the trouble to vomit?
> Creating a disciple on behalf of his teacher,
>   the school's branch extends far.
> In the blue sky thunder stops, shooting stars abundant.[65]

Guiding the Person with Three Disabilities

34. Xuansha once gave a talk and said, "Old teachers in various regions all speak about guiding and benefiting beings. Now I ask you, how will you guide a person with the three handicaps of being blind, deaf, and

---

Historically we know that Touzi Yiqing never met Dayang Qingxuan, even though their names are linked together in the standard Sōtō lineage. Dayang asked his friend, the Linji lineage teacher Fushan Fayuan, to pass along his lineage to an able student, which Fushan later did with Touzi Yiqing. In the original versions, this story in case 33 is between Touzi Yiqing and Fushan Fayuan, but apparently this text was changed by an editor, after Dōgen's time, to insert the more orthodox name Dayang Qingxuan. Dōgen himself acknowledged that Touzi Yiqing had never personally met Dayang but had received the Dharma through Fushan Fayuan, as indicated in the third line of his verse. The name Yiqing Huayan is used later in the dialogue, as Touzi Yiqing is known historically for incorporating Huayan teachings in the Sōtō lineage, including using them to supplement and develop the Sōtō five ranks teaching.

64 The story about an outsider questioning the Buddha appears in Hekiganroku, case 65. See Cleary and Cleary, *Blue Cliff Record*, pp. 412–417.

65 "In the blue sky" might refer to Yiqing directly, as the *qing* in his name means blue. So this line might be read as, "In Touzi Yiqing's heaven, thunder stops, shooting stars abundant."

mute? If you hold up a mallet or raise a whisk their eyes will not see it. If you speak to them, their ears will not hear it. Their mouth is also mute. If you cannot help them, the Buddha Dharma provides no spiritual fulfillment at all."[66]

> Depending on the person, they have not merely two or three
> different [diseases].
> Everyone expresses their symptoms with no turning away
> or grasping.
> Despite tens of thousands of medical methods,
> Those who throw up their hands never put out a shingle.[67]

Partridges Singing Beyond Earshot

35. Jiashan said, "Before my eyes there is no Dharma, [just] mind exists. This is not the Dharma before my eyes. It is not reached by ears or eyes."[68]

> Pulling out the eyes of the ten thousand things,
> Shadows flying south and north, he goes beyond sense bindings.
> One morning they completely fall away,
>   and again he arouses attention.
> Filling the trees, partridges sing through the day.

The Meaning Seen in Long and Short

36. Qingping [Lingzun] asked [his teacher] Cuiwei [Mugaku], "What is the essential meaning of [Bodhidharma] coming from the west?"

---

66 This statement, with an additional section, is case 88 of the Hekiganroku; see Cleary and Cleary, *Blue Cliff Record*, pp. 564–570.

67 According to Genryū Kagamishima, "Those who throw up their hands" is a positive statement for letting go as the ultimate medicine. This refers to Yuanwu's comment in the Hekiganroku (Blue Cliff Record) to the last sentence of Xuansha's statement: "How true these words are. This mountain monk holds up my hands in surrender, and thereby has already completed the guidance."

68 The last two sentences are excerpts from the beginning of the dialogue between Jiashan and the boatman in the long story in Dharma word 8, already cited in kōan cases 10, 22, and 28. The first two phrases (including one line from his dialogue with Chuanzi), are from a later Dharma hall discourse by Jiashan in his section of Jingde Transmission of the Lamp.

Cuiwei said, "Wait until nobody is here, and I will tell you."

After a pause Qingping said, "There is nobody; please teacher, tell me."

Cuiwei got down from his seat and led Qingping into a bamboo garden. Qingping again said, "Nobody's here; please master, tell me."

Cuiwei pointed to the bamboo and said, "This bamboo has such shortness; this bamboo has such length."[69]

Two poems:

> Nobody can say the meaning of coming from the west.
> The bamboo expounded it for his sake.
> Arriving, still there is the measure of long and short.
> Who knows hermit Pan riding his donkey backward?[70]

> Ice piling up and water rising, both have no beginning.
> The time as day, month, and year is just a leftover.
> The fennel by the roadside, how does it taste?
> The monkshood of Western River has no mind of its own.[71]

Entrusting the True Human Body

37. Wolong [Huiqiu] asked Director Liao, "My late teacher [Xuansha] said that the entire universe in ten directions is the true human body. Do you see the monks' hall?"

Director Liao said, "Master, do not [create] flowers in the eyes."

[Wo]long said, "Although my late teacher passed away, his flesh is still warm."[72]

---

69 This story is in Mana Shōbōgenzō, case 71. See Nishijima, *Master Dogen's Shinji Shobogenzo*, p. 99. It is also in Jingde Transmission of the Lamp, section 15, on Qingping.

70 Panlang was a tenth-century poet who left his position as a government official and retired to the mountains. When he came to town he would ride backward on his donkey so that he could still see the mountains. Such backwardness is like Cuiwei using discrimination to point to the ultimate beyond.

71 "Western River" is Xichuan (Jap.: Shisen), an area in Sichuan Province in China. Monkshood, or wolfsbane, is a yellow-flowered plant that can be either highly poisonous or medicinal, depending on the amount used.

72 This story is from Jingde Transmission of the Lamp, section 21, on Wolong. It is cited by Dōgen in Mana Shōbōgenzō, case 131; see Nishijima, *Master Dogen's Shinji Shobogenzo*,

Within a flower before spring, an eye opens with fragrance.
Within the eye appears a body, not two or three.
Cold and warmth are entrusted to others as frost and dew.
Intimacy and estrangement are hard to tell apart,
    like water and a deep pool.

Polishing a Mirror

38. Nanyue asked Mazu, "Great worthy, what is your intention in seated meditation (zazen)?"[73]

Mazu said, "I intend to become a buddha."

Nanyue picked up a tile and, in front of Mazu's hermitage, began to polish it with a rock.

Mazu asked, "What are you doing, teacher?"

Nanyue said, "I am polishing it to make a mirror."

Mazu said, "How can you make a mirror by polishing a tile?"

Nanyue said, "How can you become a buddha through zazen?"

Mazu said. "What shall I do?"

Nanyue said, "Like someone riding a cart that won't go, which is right, to hit the cart or to hit the ox?"

Mazu did not reply. [Nanyue] further gave instruction saying, "Do you study sitting meditation, or study sitting Buddha? If you study sitting meditation, meditation has nothing to do with sitting or lying down. If you study sitting Buddha, Buddha has no fixed form. Within the Dharma of non-abiding, you should not pick and choose. If you do sitting Buddha, this is simply killing Buddha. If you cling to the form of sitting, you will never reach the truth."

For Mazu, hearing this admonition was like drinking delicious cream.

---

p. 180. This statement by Xuansha is one of several about "the entire universe in ten directions" that Dōgen discusses, including Xuansha's "the entire universe in ten directions is one bright pearl." See case 41.

73 Dōgen refers frequently to this story about Nanyue polishing a tile to make a mirror for Mazu. It is discussed in Shōbōgenzō in Zazenshin (The Acupuncture Needle of Zazen), and Kokyō (The Ancient Mirror). See, respectively, Bielefeldt, *Dōgen's Manuals of Zen Meditation,* pp. 188–205; and Nishijima and Cross, *Master Dogen's Shobogenzo,* book 1, pp. 239–259. It is in Mana Shōbōgenzō, case 8; see Nishijima, *Master Dogen's Shinji Shobogenzo,* p. 12. Dōgen usually twists the conventional understanding of this story, recommending that students polish a tile to make a mirror.

Two poems:

Polishing a tile to make a mirror is effort in practice.
How can people plan to take a mirror and make it a tile?
The point of deceiving each other is completed within clarity.
Square and circle mold their forms, using themselves as models.

Even when called the iron man, how can you be a tile or mirror?
Even before killing Buddha is born, the sitting Buddha descends.[74]
Sitting, lying, and walking meditation are all just right.
Clouds arise south of the mountain; rain falls on the western river.[75]

No Buddha Nature
39. Guishan said, "All living beings are no Buddha nature."[76]

Crystalline, it keeps turning on its own.
Though opening the matter by tossing it back and forth
     seems too late,
When a person dies the mind vanishes, with birth they have a face.
How many times do spirits and demons foolishly mistrust?

Yangshan's All at Once
40. Yangshan asked the great Gui[shan]. "When the hundreds of thousands of objects come all at once, how is it?"

74 "Buddha descends" implies a buddha's descending from the Tuṣita Heaven to take birth in the world.

75 In Zazenshin, Dōgen says, "Both carved dragons and true dragons have the capacity to cause clouds and make rain." See Bielefeldt, *Dōgen's Manuals of Zen Meditation*, p. 191.

76 This saying is discussed in Shōbōgenzō Busshō (Buddha Nature); see Waddell and Abe, *Heart of Dōgen's Shōbōgenzō*, pp. 86–88. Dōgen's understanding is "All living beings are no Buddha nature," but it might also be read that all beings have no Buddha nature. Toward the end of that section of Busshō, Dōgen addresses this question to Guishan, "Even though you articulated that all sentient beings have no Buddha-nature, you did not say all Buddha-natures have no sentient being, or that all Buddha-natures have no Buddha-nature. Still less could you have seen, even in your dreams, that all buddhas have no Buddha-nature" (Ibid., p. 88). This saying by Guishan is also in Dōgen's Mana Shōbō-genzō, case 115; see Nishijima, *Master Dogen's Shinji Shobogenzo*, p. 160.

Guishan said, "Blue is not yellow; long is not short. All dharmas abide in their own positions, and have nothing to do with my affairs."

Yangshan immediately made prostrations.[77]

Speak about the matter before the Awesome Sound.[78]
In ten thousand mountains, bamboos crack and cuckoos cry.
The high-flying sparrow makes a mud nest on the beams.
When buying a hat, it's the same as the head size.

One Bright Pearl

41. A monk once asked Xuansha, "Master you have said, 'The entire universe in ten directions is one bright pearl.' How can a student understand this?"[79]

Xuansha said, "The entire universe in ten directions is one bright pearl. What is the use of understanding?"

Xuansha the next day asked that monk, "The entire universe in ten directions is one bright pearl. How do you understand this?"

He replied, "The entire universe in ten directions is one bright pearl. What is the use of understanding?"

Xuansha said, "Now I know that you are making your livelihood in the black mountain demons' cave."[80]

---

77 This story is case 14 in Mana Shōbōgenzō; see Nishijima, *Master Dogen's Shinji Shobogenzo*, p. 22.

78 The Buddha Awesome Sound is described in the Lotus Sutra, chap. 20, on the Bodhisattva Never Disparaging, who was born into this Buddha's Buddha field after his parinirvāṇa. See Hurvitz, *Scripture of the Lotus Blossom of the Fine Dharma*, pp. 279–285; and Katō, Tamura, and Miyasaka, *Threefold Lotus Sutra*, pp. 289–295. This line more generally refers to a time before creation, in the kalpa of nonexistence.

79 The word translated as "pearl" might also be translated as "jewel." More accurately, it is the wish-fulfilling gem widely referred to in Mahāyāna Buddhism. It is round like a pearl but also transparent, taking on the colors of the light around it. This story is discussed by Dōgen in Dharma hall discourse 107 and also in Shōbōgenzō Ikka no Myōju (One Bright Pearl). See Waddell and Abe, *Heart of Dōgen's Shōbōgenzō*, pp. 31–37; and Cleary, *Shōbōgenzō: Zen Essays by Dōgen*, pp. 57–62.

80 The "black mountain demons' cave" refers to the trap of attachment to emptiness.

Though illuminating the present, it also illuminates the past.
We should question this matter [of the world] with no roots.
Square or circle, long or short, it has no boundary;
Inside, outside, and in between are no barrier.[81]

The Self Returns to Mountains and Rivers

42. A monk once asked Changsha, "How can we turn the mountains, rivers, and great earth to return them to the self?"

Changsha said, "How can we turn the self to return it to the mountains, rivers, and great earth?"[82]

Mountains and rivers intimately transmit the power
    of mountains and rivers.[83]
From the outset the self has not had much ability.
Who cannot grasp which of these sides returns?
After fully questioning once, question it again.[84]

A White Cloud Flies Straight Ahead

43. Master Zhaozhou instructed the assembly saying, "With the slightest right and wrong, the mind is lost in confusion. Can you respond to this or not?"[85]

---

81 The word "barrier" in this last line means, literally, cliff or precipice. Manzan added the negative, which we are using here. Thus the Monkaku version says they are "each a single barrier."

82 This saying is in the Jingde Transmission of the Lamp. See Ogata, *Transmission of the Lamp,* p. 341. It is discussed by Dōgen in Shōbōgenzō Keisei Sanshoku (The Sound of the Valley Streams, the Form of the Mountains). See Cook, *How to Raise an Ox,* p. 73. It is case 16 in Mana Shōbōgenzō. See Nishijima, *Master Dogen's Shinji Shobogenzo,* p. 24.

83 In his version, Manzan changed the character for "transmit" to "turn," the word in the monk's original question to Changsha, to have this line read, "Mountains and rivers intimately turn the power of mountains and rivers."

84 "Which of these sides returns" refers to the self returning to the mountains, rivers, and earth, or alternatively, to the mountains, rivers, and earth returning to the self. This has clear implications for our relationship with our environment. The last line indicates that even though we may see how we are part of the environment, rather than it belonging to us, we still need to reexamine this connection, as attachment to self is subtle and recurring.

85 "With the slightest right and wrong, the mind is lost in confusion," is a quote by

A monk came forth, slapped the attendant once, and said, "Why don't you reply to the master?"

Zhaozhou returned to the abbot's quarters.

Later the attendant asked for Zhaozhou's guidance, "Did that monk understand or not?"

Zhaozhou said, "The one sitting sees the one standing. The one standing sees the one sitting."[86]

> Without asking about stages on the path, he goes straight ahead.
> Following along in the blue sky, white clouds fly.
> Why don't you know the penetrating power
>   to turn round the heavens?
> The stolid stones nod their heads; sitting or standing, [just] return.

How to Transmit the Warmth

44. Huangbo once asked Baizhang, "How shall I instruct people about the essential vehicle from the ancients?" Baizhang sat still.

Huangbo asked, "What will our descendants in later generations transmit?"

Baizhang said, "I had thought you were that person." Then he returned to the abbot's quarters.[87]

Zhaozhou from the poem "Faith in Mind," attributed to the third ancestor, Jianzhi Sengcan. See Sheng-yen, *Poetry of Enlightenment*, pp. 25–29; or Suzuki, *Manual of Zen Buddhism*, pp. 76–89.

86 This story appears in Mana Shōbōgenzō, case 11. See Nishijima, *Master Dogen's Shinji Shobogenzo*, p. 18. A different version of this story appears in the Recorded Sayings of Zhaozhou. See Green, *Recorded Sayings of Zen Master Joshu*, p. 110. In this version the monk strikes the attendant and leaves without speaking. As to the one sitting and the one standing, presumably the original dialogue is in the setting of a formal *jōdō*, or Dharma hall discourse, in which the teacher, Zhaozhou, is sitting, and the monks are all standing.

87 This story is discussed in Dharma hall discourses 131 and 423. It is also case 2 in Mana Shōbōgenzō. See Nishijima, *Master Dogen's Shinji Shobogenzo*, p. 5.

Having been verified and transmitted by the previous ancestors,
How could the practice of a whole lifetime be in vain?
Long ago, his face broke into a smile on Vulture Peak.[88]
Warmth arrived, and he attained the marrow at Shaoshi.[89]

The Stump of Zhaozhou's Cypress Tree

45. A monk once asked Zhaozhou, "What is the meaning of the ancestral teacher [Bodhidharma] coming from the west?"

Zhaozhou said, "The cypress tree in the garden."

The monk said, "Master, do not use objects to guide people."

Zhaozhou said, "I am not using objects to guide people."

The monk [again] asked, "What is the meaning of the ancestral teacher coming from the west?"

Zhaozhou said, "The cypress tree here in the garden."[90]

Three poems:

The cypress tree without roots hangs in the empty sky.
Is the ancestor's intention in coming from the west before or after?
The ancient Buddha protects the stump
    when branches and leaves have fallen.
On his behalf this saying naturally appeared.

With what plan did he sit immovably as the years passed by?
Through snow and frost, a single bone is here in the garden.
Zhaozhou does not speak the meaning of coming from the west.
How could his ability in the ancient gnarl be on his own?

A monk once asked old Zhaozhou about the way.
He only spoke of the cypress tree in the garden.

---

88 "His face broke into a smile on Vulture Peak" refers to the second Indian ancestor, Mahākāśyapa.

89 "Attaining the marrow at Shaoshi" refers to the second Chinese ancestor, Dazu Huike.

90 This story is also discussed above in Dharma hall discourses 433 and 488 and in *shōsan* 9. See the notes to these Dharma hall discourses for other references.

Although his precise words are marvelous,
Still I regret the delay in arrival of the ancestral teacher's mind.[91]

Fundamental Purity in Time and Season
46. A monk asked Langye [Huijue], "How does fundamental purity suddenly give rise to mountains, rivers, and the great earth?"

Langye said, "How does fundamental purity suddenly give rise to mountains, rivers, and the great earth?"[92]

Spring pine, autumn chrysanthemum follow time and season.
Covering earth and sky, the mirror manifests emptiness.
The bamboo shadow swept away, dust piles high.
The moon pierces the deep pool dissolving together.

Mistake after Mistake Beyond Duality
47. [Jingzhao] Mihu had a monk ask [his Dharma brother] Yangshan, "Do people of today still need enlightenment or not?"

Yangshan said, "It is not that there is no enlightenment; but how do you not let it fall into duality?"

The monk returned and reported this to Mihu, who deeply affirmed it.[93]

We easily discern true and partial in the enlightenment
of people today.[94]
These are traces of the self before the empty kalpa.

---

91 The implication of "the delay in arrival of the ancestral teacher's mind" is that nobody before Zhaozhou expressed Bodhidharma's meaning.

92 This story is the final case 100 in the Shōyōroku; see Cleary, *Book of Serenity*, pp. 428–430. It appears in the commentary to case 35 of the Hekiganroku; see Cleary and Cleary, *Blue Cliff Record*, p. 219. It is also case 6 in Mana Shōbōgenzō; see Nishijima, *Master Dogen's Shinji Shobogenzo*, p. 10.

93 This story is in the Shōyōroku, case 62. See Cleary, *Book of Serenity*, pp. 259–263. Dōgen also cites it in Shōbōgenzō Daigo (Great Enlightenment). See Cleary, *Rational Zen*, pp. 114–115.

94 "True and partial" are *shō* and *hen*, referring to the fundamental dialectic elaborated in the five ranks teaching, also described as being between ultimate and phenomenal, universal and particular, or upright and inclined.

Although carelessly making mistake after mistake,
In the intimate entrustment from west to east they fully meet.[95]

Portrait of a Quiet Plum Blossom

48. Huangbo abandoned the assembly and entered Da'an monastery, mingling with the laborers to clean the temple halls. Once National Minister Peixiu entered the temple and offered incense. Then he asked Huangbo, "The portrait can be seen; where is the high priest?"

In a loud voice Huangbo said, "Where is it?"

The minister immediately had an insight.[96]

> The wall faces the person and the person faces the wall.
> Both said, "Where is it?" wanting to know each other.
> However they only opened their mouths and laughed.
> Breaking through snow, a plum blossoms quietly on a branch.[97]

Coming and Going in Suchness

49. Once a monk asked Master Qingyuan [Xingsi], "What is the meaning of the ancestral teacher [Bodhidharma] coming from the west?"

Qingyuan said, "He has also gone in such a way."[98]

> Coming in such a way and also going as such,
> Clearly remember without foolish doubts.
> Exposed, he turned and approached to inquire.
> For your sake, [Qingyuan] hit the nail on the head.

---

95 "They fully meet" (or meet each other) may refer either to teacher and student or to the integration of true and partial realities.

96 This story is in the Jingde Transmission of the Lamp, the section on Peixiu in volume 12. A longer version of the story is also case 9 of Dōgen's Mana Shōbōgenzō; see Nishijima, *Master Dogen's Shinji Shobogenzo*, p. 15.

97 "Quietly" in this last line is *mitsu*, which usually means esoteric, hidden, or intimate. Here it could also imply subtle or mysterious, like the fragile distinction of the white blossom against the snow.

98 This is the beginning of case 10 in Dōgen's Mana Shōbōgenzō collection. In that version, after Qingyuan's first response the monk asked for more explanation. Qingyuan asked him to approach, and when he did so, Qingyuan told him to remember this clearly. See Nishijima, *Master Dogen's Shinji Shobogenzo*, p. 17.

Hearing When Not Speaking

50. Dongshan [Liangjie] instructed the assembly saying, "Experiencing the matter of going beyond buddhas, finally capable, you can speak a little."

A monk immediately asked, "What is speaking?"

Dongshan said, "At the time of speaking, you do not hear."

The monk said, "Master, do you hear or not?"

Dongshan said, "Just when I do not speak, then I hear."[99]

> Seeing words we know the person like seeing his face.
> Three direct pointers are tongue, sharp wit, and writing.
> Fulfilling the way, wings naturally appear on the body.
> Since meeting myself, I deeply respect him.[100]

Huangbo's Grandmotherly Mind

51. Linji had been in the assembly of Huangbo for three years, his practice and conduct pure and single-minded. The head monk encouraged him to ask [Huangbo] about the essential meaning of Buddha Dharma. Three times he inquired, and three times he was hit with the staff. He went to [Gao'an] Dayu and asked whether he had been at fault or not. Dayu said, "Huangbo was like a grandmother, extremely kind for your sake. Still you come here and ask whether you were at fault or not."

Hearing these words, Linji was greatly awakened and said, "Fundamentally there is not much to Huangbo's Buddha Dharma."

Dayu grabbed him and said, "Such a bed-wetting kid! Just before, you asked if you had any fault or not. Now you say there is not much to Huangbo's Buddha Dharma. What truth have you seen? Speak quickly! speak quickly!" Linji punched Dayu in the side three times.

---

99 This story appears in Jingde Transmission of the Lamp; see Chang, *Original Teachings of Ch'an Buddhism*, p. 65. It is also case 12 in Dōgen's Mana Shōbōgenzō; see Nishijima, *Master Dogen's Shinji Shobogenzo*, p. 20.

100 The pronouns in this line, "Since meeting myself, I deeply respect him," refer to the line in Dongshan's awakening verse, which can be read, "He is actually me, but I am not him" or "It is actually me, but I am not it." The same pronoun can be read as either "him" or "it." See Powell, *Record of Tung-shan*, pp. 27–28; and Chang, *Original Teachings of Ch'an Buddhism*, p. 60.

Dayu released him and said, "Your teacher is Huangbo. It's not my business."

Linji left [Gao'an] Dayu and returned to Huangbo.[101]

The clear eye on the tip of the staff forced a meeting.
Out of pity [Dayu] grabbed his sides, the lump of mud not yet
    dissolved.
For your sake, grandmotherly mind was intense.
This raving maniac; how far upstream the water has flowed.[102]

Hearing Spring with Dharma Eyes

52. Dongshan [Liangjie] visited Yunyan and asked, "Who can hear nonsentient beings expounding the Dharma?"

Yunyan said, "Nonsentient beings can hear nonsentient beings expound the Dharma."

Dongshan said, "Master, can you hear them?"

Yunyan said, "If I could hear them, you would not hear my expounding the Dharma."

Dongshan said, "If so, then I do not hear the master expounding the Dharma."

Yunyan said, "You still do not hear me expound the Dharma; how could you expect to hear nonsentient beings expound the Dharma?"

Dongshan thereupon composed a verse and presented it to Yunyan, saying,

"How marvelous; How marvelous!
Nonsentient beings inconceivably expound Dharma.

101 This story is referred to in Dharma hall discourses 160 and 493 and in Dharma word 2. It appears in the Record of Linji; see Watson, *Zen Teachings of Master Lin-chi*, pp. 104–107. It is also case 86 in the Shōyōroku; see Cleary, *Book of Serenity*, pp. 367–371. Dōgen also cites it in case 27 of Mana Shōbōgenzō; see Nishijima, *Master Dogen's Shinji Shobogenzo*, pp. 39–40.

102 "Raving maniac " is a translation of what Huangbo called Linji after Linji returned and thereupon slapped Huangbo. The full story is in the Recorded Sayings of Linji; see Watson, *Zen Teachings of Master Lin-chi*, pp. 104–107.

Listening with your ears, no sound.
Hearing with your eyes, you directly understand."[103]

The Dharma expounded by nonsentient beings
   the nonsentient understand.
Fences and walls do not create spring for the grass and trees.[104]
Nor is the business of sentient beings, whether common or sage,
Mountains and rivers; sun, moon, or stars.

Fully Grasping Space

53. Shigong [Huizang] asked Xitang [Zhizang], "Do you understand how
to grasp space?"
   Xitang said, "Yes, I understand."
   Shigong said, "How do you grasp it?"
   Xitang grabbed at the air with his hand.
   Shigong said, "You do not understand how to grasp space."
   Xitang said, "Elder brother, how do you grasp it?"
   Shigong grabbed Xitang's nose and pulled.
   Xitang screamed in pain and yelled, "You thug. You're pulling my
nose off!"
   Shigong said, "Now, in this way, you can finally grasp it."[105]

---

103 This story is also fully recounted, with a slight variation in the third line of Dongshan's
verse, in Dharma hall discourse 452. Dōgen also discusses this story at length in Shōbōgenzō Mujō Seppō (Nonsentient Beings Expound the Dharma); see Tanahashi, *Enlightenment Unfolds*, pp. 185–195. It appears also in Dōgen's Mana Shōbōgenzō, case 148; see
Nishijima, *Master Dogen's Shinji Shobogenzo*, p. 197. This story is recounted, much as
Dōgen gives it here, in the Jingde Transmission of the Lamp; see Chang, *Original Teachings of Ch'an Buddhism*, p. 59. A somewhat amplified version of the same story is given in
the Recorded Sayings of Dongshan; see Powell, *Record of Tung-shan*, pp. 25–26.

104 "Fences and walls" might refer to the mind of wall-gazing, or zazen. But also, in the
longer version of this story in the Recorded Sayings of Dongshan, Dongshan had cited the
national teacher Nanyang Huizhong as telling a monk that the mind of the ancient buddhas is fences and walls. See Powell, *Record of Tung-shan*, p. 24.

105 This story is discussed by Dōgen in Shōbōgenzō Kokū (Space); see Tanahashi,
Enlightenment Unfolds, pp. 201–204. It is also case 248, or in some versions case 249, in
Mana Shōbōgenzō; see Nishijima, *Master Dogen's Shinji Shobogenzo*, p. 318.

Who owns the tree at the very center
Of south, north, east, and west; inside, outside, and in between?
Brothers meet together and discuss their father's business.
One hauls the earth, the other hauls the sky.

The Distance between Ancients and Now

54. A monk once asked Touzi [Datong], "What is the Guiding Director of Beings among the ten aspects [of Buddha]?"[106]

Touzi got down from his seat and stood in shashu.

The monk asked, "What is the distance between ordinary beings and sages?"

Touzi [again] got down from his seat and stood in shashu.[107]

Nurture a child until it grows to become a thief in the house,
Ancient records and new events, how many oceans and mountains [distant]?
Spring trees and autumn fur are stirred a little.
Dragon head and snake tail naturally have no markings.

Dragons in Everyday Life

55. Zen Master Longtan [Chongxin] made rice cakes for a living. Then he made prostrations to Master Tianhuang [Daowu] and left home.[108] Tianhuang said, "If you serve me, later I will expound the Dharma gate of the mind essence for you."

---

106 Guiding Director of Beings is one of the ten standard epithets for buddhas. See Kōgen Mizuno, *Essentials of Buddhism: Basic Terminology and Concepts of Buddhist Philosophy and Practice* (Tokyo: Kōsei Publishing, 1996), pp. 64–68. The question asks, literally, What is this epithet among the ten "selves," or "bodies," [of Buddha]? This might imply looking for the arranging and harmonizing function for the ten bodies.

107 This story is case 35 in Mana Shōbōgenzō; see Nishijima, *Master Dogen's Shinji Shobogenzo*, p. 52. *Shashu* is the formal mudrā, or hand position, with hands held against the chest when standing or walking in Zen monasteries, including during walking meditation. The right hand covers the left, which is closed in a fist with thumb inside, although in Dōgen's time and before both hands were sometimes held flat.

108 Longtan had made offerings of ten rice cakes to Tianhuang at his temple every day for many years before receiving ordination. Tianhuang would always return one rice cake. When asked about this, Tianhuang said the cakes were given to him, so they were his to give back. See Ferguson, *Zen's Chinese Heritage,* p. 152.

After about a year passed, Longtan said, "When I arrived [to live here], the master promised to expound the Dharma gate of the mind essence. Up to now I have not received any instructions."

Tianhuang said, "I have been expounding it for you for a long time."

Longtan asked, "When has the master expounded it for me?"

Tianhuang said, "When you greet me, I immediately bow [in gasshō]. When I sit, you stand by to serve. When you bring tea, I receive it for you."

Longtan paused for a while.

Tianhuang said, "When seeing, just see; when deliberating, you go astray."

Longtan immediately had great realization.[109]

This is who; and who am I?
Like coming and going, or bubbles in water,
Over a thousand years, a field has eight hundred owners.
The mind essence of teacher and disciple is flying dragon with
    water dragon.[110]

Cool Moonlight in the Hells

56. A monk once asked Caoshan, "When it is this hot, where can I go to escape?"

Caoshan said, "Escape to a boiling cauldron or coals in the furnace [as in hell]."[111]

The monk said, "Within boiling water or hot coals, how can I escape?"

Caoshan said, "All the suffering cannot reach it."

---

109 This story appears in section 14 of the Jingde Transmission of the Lamp, the section on Longtan. For a slightly longer version, see Ferguson, *Zen's Chinese Heritage*, p. 153.

110 "Flying dragon and water dragon" are simply two different characters for dragons, *ryū* and *kō* in Sino-Japanese. Dragons are awesome beings that represent Dharma guardians or enlightened beings. Perhaps the two words represent two different phases in the dragon's life cycle.

111 A boiling cauldron and coals in the furnace both refer to the sufferings of particular Buddhist hell realms.

Autumn approaches with moonlight cool.
Many fireflies take wing, searching for the fire star,[112]
Toward the red furnace again, seeking another go round.
Clouds reach the peaks, water in the jar.[113]

The Music of Everyday Tea and Rice

57. Master Furong [Dao]kai visited Touzi [Yiqing] and asked, "The words and phrases of the buddha ancestors are like the ordinary rice and tea of our house. Aside from this, are there any other special phrases to benefit people?"

Touzi [Yiqing] said, "Tell me, when the emperor gives orders within his domain, does he require Yao, Shun, Yu, or Tang?"[114]

[Furong Dao]kai wanted to speak, but Touzi brushed Daokai's mouth with his whisk and said, "As soon as you give rise to thoughts, you receive thirty blows."

[Dao]kai thereupon opened enlightenment, again made prostrations, and departed.

Touzi said, "Come back, elder."

Daokai did not look back.

Touzi asked, "Have you reached the ground beyond doubt?"

Daokai covered his ears with his hands.[115]

In the house of buddha ancestors, everyday tea and rice is coarse.
Knowing courtesy to benefit people,
    simply play the cold reed flute.[116]

---

112 "Fire star" is a common term for the planet Mars.

113 "Clouds reach the peaks, water in the jar" is a paraphrase of a saying by Yaoshan, "Clouds in the blue sky, water in the bottle," given by Yaoshan in response to the official Li Ao's question, "What is the way?" in Keitoku Dentōroku, vol. 14. See Wu, *Mind of Chinese Ch'an*, p. 82. Dōgen also refers to this in informal meeting 15; also see volume 8, note 45.

114 Yao, Shun, Yu, and Tang are legendary ancient emperors of China, famed for their virtue and authority. The implication is that within his own domain, the emperor already has his own authority.

115 Dōgen discusses this story in Shōbōgenzō Kajō (Everyday Life); see Cook, *How to Raise an Ox*, pp. 153–154. This is also case 143 in some versions of Mana Shōbōgenzō.

116 According to Genryū Kagamishima, "The Cold Reed Flute" may have been the name of a song.

Covering your ears, don't try to open your mouth.
[Even] with fret glued down, tune the strings
　and play more music.[117]

The Windbell's Ding-Dong-a-Ling

58. Master Tiantong [Rujing] said,

"The whole body is like a mouth hanging in empty space.[118]
Not questioning the winds from east, west, south, or north,
Equally with all of them, speaking of prajñā:
Ding-dong-a-ling ding-dong."

The whole body is just a mouth defining empty space,[119]
Ever arousing the winds from east, west, south, or north,
Equally crystalline, speaking your own words:
Ding-dong-a-ling ding-dong.

Refined Gold Thus Come

59. Zen Master Nanyue [Huairang] once visited the sixth ancestor [Dajian Huineng]. The ancestor asked him, "Where are you from?"

[Nanyue Huai]rang said, "I came from the place of National Teacher Songshan [Hui]an."

---

117 "Tuning the strings by gluing down the fret" is an expression Dōgen mentions in Dharma hall discourse 154. "Gluing down the fret" refers to the movable object that is placed up or down the length of a koto (a traditional Japanese zither) underneath the strings to tune them. This indicates that one cannot change the tuning of a string when this is glued down, and implies that one needs to be flexible to tune one's life. Dōgen's previous response (Dharma hall discourse 154), "Do you fully understand tuning the string by gluing down the fret?" might indicate the value of staying still, as in zazen, for spiritual attunement. Here, Dōgen further indicates that even with fret glued down, one should tune up and play music, i.e., express the Dharma.

118 This poem by Rujing, often discussed by Dōgen, is titled "Windbell." Dōgen discusses it with Rujing in his student journal, Hōkyōki. See Kodera, *Dōgen's Formative Years in China*, pp. 135, 191; and Tanahashi, *Enlightenment Unfolds*, p. 23. The poem is about the emptiness, or wisdom *(prajñā)*, of the whole body (or the whole universe, reality itself, or just Rujing), as symbolized by a windbell. The last line is simply mimicking a bell sound.

119 The word translated as "defining" also has the meanings of judging, clarifying, assessing, and dividing. Dōgen's commentarial version of this poem is more concrete and personal, emphasizing each being's unique expression.

The ancestor said, "What is this that thus comes?"

Nanyue never put this question aside. He served there for eight years and clarified that previous saying. Then he told the [sixth] ancestor, "I, Huairang can now understand the question, 'What is this that thus comes?' that you received me with upon my first arriving to see you."

The sixth ancestor said, "How do you understand it?"

Nanyue said, "To explain or demonstrate anything would completely miss the mark."

The sixth ancestor said, "Then do you suppose there is practice-realization or not?"

Nanyue said, "It is not that there is no practice-realization, but only that it cannot be defiled."

The sixth ancestor said, "This nondefilement is exactly what the buddhas protect and care for. I am thus, you are thus, and the ancestors in India also are thus."[120]

> Having fully cooked all his stuff, this Nanyue
> Played with blowing wind and saw arising clouds,
> Tasted the tiger's scream, and loved the dragon's howl.[121]
> Single-mindedly striving,
> For eight years refining gold,
> Dropping body, dropping body,
> Did he clearly get it or not?
> What is this thus come and thus appeared?
> The mind before your father and mother were born.
> Although directly attaining the wonder right now,
> Vipaśyin Buddha maintained this mind before.[122]

---

120 This story also appears in Dharma hall discourses 374 and 490, and informal meeting 13. See volume 5, note 43, for other references. It also appears in Mana Shōbōgenzō, case 101; see Nishijima, *Master Dogen's Shinji Shobogenzo*, p. 137.

121 As a common East Asian expression, when wind blows, tigers scream; and when clouds arise, dragons howl. Tigers represent yin, or the receptive, and dragons yang, or the creative.

122 Vipaśyin Buddha is the first of the six legendary primordial buddhas who preceded Śākyamuni.

Pointing the Way Upstream

60. Longya asked Dongshan, "What is the mind of the ancestral teacher [Bodhidharma]?"

Dongshan said, "Wait until the Dong Creek flows backward; then I'll tell you."

Thereupon, Longya for the first time realized its meaning.[123]

> A weather vane transcends the limits of clouds and water.[124]
> Throughout earth and sky, use the wind in the sails,
> Loyal advice is harsh to the ear, often redeeming the other.[125]
> Do not begrudge the old fellow's extraordinary words.

Yaoshan's Backache

61. Daowu [Yuanzhi] and Yunyan were attending to Yaoshan, and Yaoshan said, "Never speak of where wisdom doesn't reach. If you speak of it, horns will grow on your head. Practitioner [Daowu Yuan]zhi, what about this?"

[Dao]wu immediately left.

Yunyan asked Yaoshan, "Why did Elder Brother [Yuan]zhi not respond to the master?"

Yaoshan said, "My back hurts today. He understands; go and ask him."

Then Yunyan went and asked Daowu, "Elder brother, why didn't you respond to the master before?"

Daowu said, "You should go ask the master."

When Yunyan was about to pass away, he sent someone with a letter of farewell [to Daowu]. Daowu read the letter and said, "Yunyan did not know it is. I regret I didn't tell him back then. Although this is so, actually, he was nonetheless a successor of Yaoshan."[126]

---

123 This story appears in Dongshan's Recorded Sayings; see Powell, *Record of Tung-shan*, p. 44.

124 "Weather vane" is *goryō*, a feather used on masts as a guide to track the direction of the wind.

125 "Loyal advice is harsh to the ear" is a proverb, akin in meaning to "a bitter pill to swallow."

126 This story is the last part of a longer story about Yunyan and Daowu that appears in the commentary of case 69 of the Shōyōroku; see Cleary, *Book of Serenity*, pp. 291–292. A

Speaking clearly the eyebrows fall out;[127]
Going among different kinds, your upper robe smells of falcon.[128]
In the sunlight, a single lamp loses its brightness.
The sun and moon in a jar are never complete.

A Song of an Empty Mind

62. Once Guishan asked Xiangyan, "When you were born and were still a baby, you did not discriminate east and west, north and south. Right at this time, expound for me [beyond discrimination], and I will check it."

Xiangyan spoke further expounding principles, but nothing he said truly fit.

Then he [gave up, and] entered Mount Wudang and built a hut at the site where National Teacher Nanyang Huizhong used to have a hermitage. One day he was cleaning the path, and a pebble he swept up hit some bamboo, resounding. At that time suddenly he was greatly enlightened.[129]

All day waiting with empty mind for the phoenix to arrive,
A village monk and the single way become neighbors.
Hear the dragon howl and phoenix song without clapping.
Tiles and pebbles transmit the word to a dead tree person.

---

different version of this longer story is case 57 of Mana Shōbōgenzō; see Nishijima, *Master Dogen's Shinji Shobogenzo*, pp. 80–82.

127 "Eyebrows falling out" is the result of lying, in the common expression used elsewhere by Dōgen as well. In this case, "speaking clearly" is not the truth.

128 "Going among different kinds" refers to an earlier part of this story. Before they came to Yaoshan, Yunyan and Daowu went through the same dialogue with Nanquan, who first made the statement later repeated by Yaoshan, "Never speak of where wisdom doesn't reach. If you speak of it, horns will grow on your head." When asked by Yunyan why Daowu had left without speaking, Nanquan had said, "He is acting within different kinds." Nanquan repeated the statement "Never speak of where wisdom doesn't reach. If you speak of it, horns will grow on your head," and then suggested to Yunyan that he should act within different kinds. This "acting within different kinds" refers to being in the world of concrete phenomena and particularities, rather than being attached to emptiness or abstractions. When they went to Yaoshan, Yunyan related this story, which then got reenacted. See Cleary, *Book of Serenity*, pp. 291–292.

129 A longer, full version of this story appears in Dharma hall discourse 457. For other references, see volume 6, notes 97 and 98. It is also in Mana Shōbōgenzō case 17; see Nishijima, *Master Dogen's Shinji Shobogenzo*, p. 25.

Extraordinary Nanquan Seen by the Earth Spirits

63. Nanquan once visited some fields. At that time the field manager had prepared in advance to welcome him.

Nanquan said, "This old monk usually comes and goes without anyone knowing. How could you know in advance to make such arrangements as this?"

The field manager said, "Last night the earth spirit informed me."

Nanquan said, "Old Master Wang [Nanquan] lacks strength of practice, and so was seen by the earth spirit."

His attendant then asked, "You are a great teacher, how could you be seen by the spirit?"

Nanquan said, "Offer another bowl of rice in front of the earth spirit."[130]

> Unknown by others, he has his own lot,
> But all the spirits recognize him.
> Without using practice power it has come to this.
> His ordinary coming and going is truly uncommon.

A Deaf Person Speaks

64. One time Changqing [Huiling] said, "Even if we state that arhats have three poisons, do not state that tathāgatas have two kinds of speech. I do not say the Tathāgata is speechless, but only that he does not have two kinds of speech."

Baofu [Congzhan] asked, "What is the Tathāgata's speech?"

Changqing said, "How can a deaf person hear it?"

Baofu said, "Now I clearly know that you are speaking from the second kind."[131]

---

130 This story appears in the Jingde Transmission of the Lamp; see Chang, *Original Teachings of Ch'an Buddhism*, pp. 154–155. Dōgen also cites this story in his collection of three hundred kōans. See Nishijima, *Master Dogen's Shinji Shobogenzo*, case 18, p. 27. Dōgen recommends that the monastic field manager make offerings to the earth spirit in his Pure Standards for Temple Administrators; see Leighton and Okumura, *Dōgen's Pure Standards for the Zen Community*, pp. 146, 190 n. 61.

131 "Speaking from the second kind" might imply speaking from secondhand knowledge, not personal experience. But primarily it refers to the two levels of speech and of truth, the ultimate and conventional. Baofu expresses that both kinds are included in the Tathāgata's speech.

Changqing asked, "What is the Tathāgata's speech?"
Baofu said, "Have a cup of tea."[132]

Do not state that the Worthy's voice has two or three kinds.
A wooden man is always a wooden man's descendant.
The Tathāgata's speech is Tathāgata's speech,
But further, here's a deaf person writing his own words.

Two Pieces of Buddha Nature

65. High Official Zhu once asked Changsha, "An earthworm is cut into two pieces, and both wriggle. I wonder, which one has the Buddha nature?"

Changsha said, "Don't hold delusive perceptions."

The official said, "What about their movement?"

Changsha said, "Just understand that the wind and fire have not yet dispersed."

The official did not respond. Changsha called out, "High Official!" The official answered.

Changsha said, "That is not your true life."

The official said, "Apart from this response, there should not be a second master."

Changsha said, "The high official should not be called the present emperor."

The official said, "If so, and I were not to respond at all to the teacher, would that be this disciple's [inner] master?

Changsha said, "Not only when you respond or do not respond to this old monk, but from beginningless kalpas, this is the origin of life and death."[133]

Then Changsha gave this verse:

---

132 This story is case 95 in the Hekiganroku; see Cleary and Cleary, *Blue Cliff Record*, pp. 601–605. It is also case 298, or in some versions case 299, in Dōgen's Mana Shōbōgenzō; see Nishijima, *Master Dogen's Shinji Shobogenzo*, p. 373.

133 "This" in "this is the origin of life and death" refers to the wind and fire of the conditioned, conscious mind.

"Students of the way do not know the truth.
Only recognizing conscious mind,
The origin of life and death from beginningless kalpas,
These ignorant people call this the original self."[134]

Wishing to comment on Buddha nature, two heads move.
When wind and fire disperse, the whole body is cool.
Life and death never have a fixed master,
Do not carelessly discuss these terms.

One Seedling, High and Low

66. One day Yangshan followed Guishan to open the ground for a rice paddy. Yangshan inquired, "This place is so low; that one is so high."

Guishan said, "Water makes things level; just level it with water."

Yangshan said, "Water is not reliable, teacher. High places are simply high level; low places low level."

Guishan agreed.[135]

Before the mountains, an ownerless wildland,[136]
Up and down, high and low are left to forage.
Wishing to judge square and circle, or figure bent and straight,
From east, west, south, and north, a single green seedling.

---

134 This dialogue is featured in Dharma hall discourse 509. Dōgen also discusses this story in some detail, although he quotes only the first two exchanges up to "wind and fire have not yet dispersed" in the Shōbōgenzō essay Buddha Nature. See Waddell and Abe, *Heart of Dōgen's Shōbōgenzō*, pp. 94–96. This is also case 20 in Mana Shōbōgenzō; see Nishijima, *Master Dogen's Shinji Shobogenzo*, p. 30.

135 This story appears in Jingde Transmission of the Lamp. See Chang, *Original Teachings of Ch'an Buddhism*, p. 210. Dōgen refers to the principle in this story in his Tenzokyōkun (Instructions for the Cook) and in Pure Standards for the Temple Administrators; see Leighton and Okumura, *Dōgen's Pure Standards for the Zen Community*, pp. 36, 176. It is also case 23 in Dōgen's Mana Shōbōgenzō; see Nishijima, *Master Dogen's Shinji Shobogenzo*, p. 34.

136 "An ownerless wildland" is *kandenchi*, which might perhaps also be read as "leisure in the fields." This line is from a poem by Wuzu Fayan.

Which Is Not a Good Piece?

67. Once Panshan [Baoji] was walking through the marketplace and saw a customer buying pork. [Panshan heard the customer] say to the butcher, "Cut me one good piece."

The butcher put the knife down, stood with hands folded (in shashu), and said, "Sir, which is not a good piece?"

Upon hearing these words, Panshan had insight.[137]

Two verses:

Right at the crossroads, he lost his legs,[138]
Unexpectedly seeing the red face in the light of day.[139]
Stained with dust, his spirit was also in disarray.
From the outset, [realizing] Buddha Dharma is not careless.

At the crossroads a person buys meat;
One with courage asks for a good piece.
The blood and marrow enters the hands of the spring spirit.
With Panshan's seeing, the flowers are naturally red.[140]

Buddha with Nothing Remaining

68. A monk asked Dongshan [Shouchu], "What is Buddha?"
Dongshan [Shouchu] said, "Three pounds of sesame."[141]

---

137 This story is from Shūmon Tōyōshū (Collection of the Essence of the Tradition in the Essential Gate). Dōgen cites this as case 21 in the Mana Shōbōgenzō; see Nishijima, *Master Dogen's Shinji Shobogenzo*, p. 32.

138 "Lost his legs" is an expression for falling down. Sometimes it also refers to "losing face," or losing one's place. Here it might refer to dropping off body and mind.

139 "Red face" implies a youthful, healthy, or lively face, here perhaps implying the original face of Buddha nature.

140 "With Panshan's seeing" more literally means "when the spring spirit or deity sees Panshan." But also, in Genryū Kagamishima's interpretation, Dōgen may be punning on Panshan's name, "Flat Top Mountain," which in the Japanese, Banzan, sounds like the word for "ten thousand mountains." Thus this line might be read, "See that the ten thousand mountains (i.e., the entire world) are naturally covered with red flowers."

141 This reply, three *kin* of *ma*, is often translated as "three pounds of flax (or hemp)," but Dōgen often cites it in the context of Dongshan Shouchu's work as *tenzo*, for example in

Dongshan's Buddha is three pounds of sesame.
When debt of gratitude is deep, enmity also deepens.
Wishing to see the ocean dried all the way down to the bottom,
One finally knows that a dead person has no mind remaining.

Guishan Evades a Name

69. The great Guishan [Lingyou] instructed the assembly saying, "A hundred years from now, this old monk will go to the foot of the mountain and become a water buffalo. On my left side will be written five characters saying, "Monk Guishan Lingyou." At that time, if you call it Monk Guishan, it is also the water buffalo. But if you call it a water buffalo, it is also me, Monk Guishan. Please say, how will you call me?"

Yangshan came forward, made a prostration, and left.[142]

Great Guishan plowed the way at the foot of the mountain.
Calling him either buffalo or monk is not correct.
Please say, what is his right place?
In vain, disciple Yangshan forced a name on him.

Reentry after Leaping Free

70. Two monks named [Fengxian Dao]shen and [Chingliang Zhi]ming once arrived at the Huai River and saw people pulling a fishing net.[143] A carp escaped through the net. [Fengxian Dao]shen said, "Brother Ming, how fleet, just like a patch-robed monk."

---

the Instructions for the Tenzo. In that context, this *ma* is probably sesame, or *goma*, rather than flax or hemp. See Leighton and Okumura, *Dōgen's Pure Standards for the Zen Community*, p. 56 n. 46. This story is frequently cited by Dōgen, also appearing as Mana Shōbōgenzō, case 172; see Nishijima, *Master Dogen's Shinji Shobogenzo*, p. 224. It appears in Hekiganroku, case 12; see Cleary and Cleary, *Blue Cliff Record*, pp. 81–87; and Mumonkan, case 18. See Shibayama, *Gateless Barrier*, pp. 134–139; Cleary, *Unlocking the Zen Kōan*, pp. 89–93; and Aitken, *Gateless Barrier*, pp. 120–125.

142 This story is in the Jingde Transmission of the Lamp; see Chang, *Original Teachings of Ch'an Buddhism*, p. 208. Dōgen refers to it frequently in Eihei Kōroku; and also as case 209 in Mana Shōbōgenzō; see Nishijima, *Master Dogen's Shinji Shobogenzo*, p. 270. It also appears in Hekiganroku, case 24; see Cleary and Cleary, *Blue Cliff Record*, p. 160.

143 These monks, Fengxian Daoshen and Chingliang Ming, were both successors of Yunmen. The characters from their names given here mean "deep" and "bright."

Ming said, "Although that is so, how can it compare to not pushing into the net in the first place?"

[Dao]shen said, "Brother Ming, you lack realization."

Later, in the middle of the night, Ming finally had some insight.[144]

> The flowing waters of the Huai River reach Deep and Bright.[145]
> Leaping free, the primal life of the golden-scaled fish is vivid.
> If this life does not return to the river depths,
> Sadly, it never sees the great wave rolling.

A Ladle's Long Handle and a Stringless Lute

71. On the edge of Mount Xuefeng a monk built a hermitage. For many years he did not shave his head. He made a wooden ladle and went to the rim of a ravine to scoop his drinking water. Once a monk asked him, "What is the meaning of the ancestral teacher [Bodhidharma] coming from the west?"

The hermit said, "As the ravine is deep, the ladle handle is long."

The monk returned and told Xuefeng. Xuefeng said, "This is very rare and wondrous. Nevertheless, this old monk should go and check him to be sure."

One day Xuefeng visited the hermit together with an attendant with a razor. As soon as they met, Xuefeng asked, "If you can say something I will not shave your head."

The hermit thereupon washed his head with water. Xuefeng then shaved his head.[146]

---

144 This story is from Shūmon Tōyōshū (Collection of the Essence of the Tradition in the Essential Gate). Dōgen also cites it in case 124 of Mana Shōbōgenzō; see Nishijima, *Master Dogen's Shinji Shobogenzo*, p. 173.

145 The characters *shen* and *ming* in these monks' names (Fengxian Daoshen and Chingliang Zhiming) mean "deep" and "bright," respectively. Dōgen uses the meanings of these names in the first line of his verse.

146 The hermit was preparing his head to be shaved. This story is from Shūmon Rentō Eyō, chap. 21. Dōgen discusses it in Shōbōgenzō Dōtoku (Full Expression); see Nishijima and Cross, *Master Dogen's Shobogenzo*, book 2, pp. 272–274. It is also case 183 in Dōgen's Mana Shōbōgenzō; see Nishijima, *Master Dogen's Shinji Shobogenzo*, p. 238.

Someone asked the meaning of coming from the west.
The wooden ladle's handle long, the ravine is just as deep.
If you want to know this boundless meaning,
The wind in the pines plays a stringless lute.

Peach Blossom Beyond Doubt

72. Lingyun [Zhiqin] once saw peach blossoms and realized the way. He composed this verse,

"Over thirty years I have been seeking a swordsman;
How many years have the leaves fallen and branches grown anew?
Since having once seen the peach blossoms,
Without wavering, up to the present I have never doubted."

He showed this to Guishan, and Guishan said, "People who enter through causal conditions never regress. Protect and maintain this well."

Xuansha heard it and said, "This really, truly hits the mark. But I dare say that the elder brother has not yet fully penetrated it."[147]

Two verses:

In ancient times a visitor accidentally entered peach paradise.[148]
Both eyes spied flowers on a moving branch.
Proceeding further, he completely forgot the things of that place.
How could he respond to the doubts
    of the great teacher [Xuansha]?

---

147 This story about Lingyun is in Dharma hall discourse 457 (but without the comments from Guishan and Xuansha) and is referred to in many other Dharma hall discourses. The full story appears in the Jingde Transmission of the Lamp, vol. 11, the section on Lingyun. Dōgen discusses it in Shōbōgenzō Keisei Sanshoku (The Sounds of the Valley Streams, the Colors of the Mountains). See Cook, *How to Raise an Ox,* pp. 72–73; and Thomas Cleary, trans., *Rational Zen: The Mind of Dōgen Zenji,* pp. 119–120. Dōgen also uses this story for case 155 of Mana Shōbōgenzō; see Nishijima, *Master Dogen's Shinji Shobogenzo,* p. 205.

148 "Peach paradise," literally "source of peaches," refers to a Daoist myth about a lost person who found a utopian land full of peaches, returned home, and then could not find that land again. The phrase is also used in the verse to kōan case 19.

In flowering of spring, peaches and plums, indigo and vermilion,
For hundreds of ages of springtime [bloom] on the same original
    branch.
Not foolishly despising what's near, value the distant.
Do not take lightly the eye, stressing the ear from ignorant doubt.

The Whole Body of a Dog

73. A monk once asked Zhaozhou, "Does a dog have Buddha nature or
not?"
Zhaozhou said, "Yes."
The monk said, "Since it has, why does it enter into this skin-bag?"
Zhaozhou said, "Because he knows yet deliberately transgresses."
Another monk asked, "Does a dog have Buddha nature or not?"
Zhaozhou said, "No."
The monk said, "All living beings have Buddha nature; why does a dog
not?"
Zhaozhou said, "Because it has karmic consciousness."[149]

The whole body is a dog, the whole body is Buddha.
Is this difficult to discuss or not?
Selling them equally, you must buy them yourself.
Do not grieve for losses or being one-sided.[150]

---

149 This story is frequently cited by Dōgen, for example in Dharma hall discourses
226 and 42; as well as in the Shōbōgenzō essay Buddha Nature. See Waddell and Abe,
Heart of Dōgen's Shōbōgenzō, pp. 91–94. This story appears in the Shōyōroku as it is
given here, and the "no" response is case 1 in Mumonkan. See Cleary, *Book of Serenity*,
case 18, pp. 76–80; and for Mumonkan see Shibayama, *Gateless Barrier*, pp. 19–31;
Aitken, *Gateless Barrier*, pp. 7–18; and Cleary, *Unlocking the Zen Kōan*, pp. 1–8. This
story is also case 114 in Dōgen's Mana Shōbōgenzō; see Nishijima, *Master Dogen's Shinji
Shobogenzo*, p. 159. In Zhaozhou's Recorded Sayings, only the "no" response is given,
with Zhaozhou's explanation. In another dialogue in that Recorded Sayings, Zhaozhou
responds to the same question about a dog having Buddha nature with "The door of
every house leads to the capital." See Green, *Recorded Sayings of Zen Master Joshu*, pp.
53, 116. According to Genryū Kagamishima, the "yes" part of the dialogue does not
appear anywhere before Hongzhi Zhengjue included it in his collection that became the
Shōyōroku (Book of Serenity). So perhaps the "yes" response, also used by Dōgen here,
dates back only to Hongzhi.

150 "Being one-sided" is *henko*, partial or inclined and withered. This might refer to taking only one side, but according to Menzan it may also mean that one side of the body is

Yes and no are two Buddha natures,
Not reaching the vitality of living beings.
Although they resemble kumiss and cheese,[151]
This is really like samādhi without thought.[152]

Peace within Hot and Cold

74. A monk once asked Dongshan [Liangjie], "This season is so hot. Where can I escape it?"

Donghshan said, "Escape to the place where hot and cold do not reach."

The monk said, "What is the place where hot and cold do not reach?"

Donghshan said, "When it is cold, the cold kills you. When it is hot the heat kills you."[153]

When hot and cold comes, let go and proceed.
Eyebrows totally fallen out, your empty name is killed.[154]

---

not working, as in a stroke victim. See Shunkō Itō, *Eihei Kōroku Chūkai Zenshō* (Tokyo: Kōmeisha, 1962), p. 453.

151 Kumiss is a drink from fermented mare's milk, used by Asian nomads.

152 "Samādhi without thought," or "samādhi of complete cessation," is the Chinese translation used for *nirodha samāpati*, the high stage of dhyānic meditation in which consciousness and perception are not present. Although still a worldly state, this is the most elevated form of karmic consciousness. For Dōgen this perhaps represents turning away and evasion of care for the concrete reality of the everyday phenomenal world. Here Dōgen may be referring to concern with the duality of yes and no as futile. "Samādhi without thought" might also refer especially to the "no," or *mu*, practice that had evolved from this story, already in China when Dōgen had visited. But he may also be using this "samādhi without thought" to simply indicate that both sides are empty.

153 This story appears in Dongshan's Recorded Sayings; see Powell, *Record of Tung-shan*, p. 49. It is case 43 in the Hekiganroku; see Cleary and Cleary, *Blue Cliff Record*, pp. 306–311. Dōgen uses it as case 225 in Mana Shōbōgenzō; see Nishijima, *Master Dogen's Shinji Shobogenzo*, p. 291. Dōgen also refers to it in the Shōbōgenzō essay Spring and Autumn; see Tanahashi, *Moon in a Dewdrop*, pp. 108–113.

154 Eyebrows falling out usually connotes lying. Here it may be that they have fallen out from concern to escape hot and cold, and thereafter, with no eyebrows, it is impossible to lie anymore.

Great peace is basically caused by generals,
But don't allow the generals to see great peace.[155]

The Cool Wind of Buddha
75. Mazu said, "This very mind itself is Buddha."[156]

Suddenly, while walking alone, he forgot the path.
Turning to look, how could he have gotten stuck here?
How many times did he sell, and have to buy himself?
So lovely, the mountain bamboo rousing cool wind.[157]

The Cat Cut through Silence
76. One day at Nanquan, the monks from the eastern and western halls were fighting over a cat. Seeing this, Nanquan finally held up the cat and said, "If you can speak, I will not cut the cat." The assembly did not respond. Nanquan cut the cat in two.

Nanquan later related and asked about this event to Zhaozhou. Zhaozhou immediately removed his straw sandals, put them on his head, and left.

Nanquan said, "If you had been there, you would have saved the cat."[158]

---

155 "Great peace" here refers to nirvāṇa, as opposed to the hot and cold of samsāra. "Generals," or warriors, refers to the bodhisattvas and their practice remaining in the world, and here may indicate Dongshan.

156 This saying is in Jingde Transmission of the Lamp; see Chang, *Original Teachings of Ch'an Buddhism*, pp. 149–150. It appears in Mumonkan, case 30; see Shibayama, *Gateless Barrier*, pp. 214–222; Cleary, *Unlocking the Zen Kōan*, pp. 144–145; and Aitken, *Gateless Barrier*, pp. 189–194. Dōgen previously discussed this story in Dharma hall discourses 8, 319, and 370. It is also the subject of Dōgen's essay Sokushin Zebutsu in Shōbōgenzō; see Nishijima and Cross, *Master Dogen's Shobogenzo*, book 1, pp. 49–54.

157 The last two lines of this poem are from the ending of a poem by Wuzu Fayan, the first line of which was used by Dōgen in his verse to case 66. However, Dōgen changed Wuzu's "pines and bamboo" here to "mountain bamboo."

158 This famous story appears in the Recorded Sayings of Zhaozhou. See Green, *Recorded Sayings of Zen Master Joshu*, p. 13. It is cases 63 and 64 in Hekiganroku (see Cleary and Cleary, *Blue Cliff Record*, pp. 406–411), case 9 in Shōyōroku (see Cleary, *Book of Serenity*, pp. 37–41), and case 14 in Mumonkan (see Shibayama, *Gateless Barrier*, pp. 107–113; Cleary, *Unlocking the Zen Kōan*, pp. 66–70; and Aitken, *Gateless Barrier*, pp. 94–99). Dōgen uses it as case 181 in Mana Shōbōgenzō; see Nishijima, *Master Dogen's Shinji Shobogenzo*, p. 235.

Two verses:

Nanquan repeatedly called for a saying.
His monks were refined, with voices like thunder.[159]
How sad, the cat's life like so much dew;
With cold sword, sentimental doubts were cut through.

Chiyang [Nanquan] held up the cat and said,
"If you can speak, the cat will live, otherwise it dies."[160]
Tell me whether Nanquan heard
The monks in both halls with voice like thunder.

A Fox Awakened to Causality

77. On the occasions of Baizhang meeting with the assembly, there was always an old man who followed the assembly to hear the Dharma. When the assembly departed, so did the old man. Unexpectedly, one day he did not leave. Baizhang then asked, "Who is the person standing before me?"

The old man said, "I am not a human being, but at the time of Kaśyāpa

---

Discussing it in Shōbōgenzō Zuimonki, Dōgen suggests that it would be better to cut the cat "into one with one stroke." Dōgen adds, "If I had been [Nanquan], when the students could not answer, I would have released the cat saying that the students had already spoken." See Okumura, "Shōbōgenzō Zuimonki," Sayings of Eihei Dōgen Zenji, pp. 28–30. As to Zhaozhou's action, along with various other traditional interpretations, putting sandals on one's head is a sign of mourning in ancient China.

159 "Voices like thunder" ironically recalls the eloquent silence, compared to thunder, of the great enlightened layman Vimalakīrti in the sutra named after him. See Thurman, The Holy Teachings of Vimalakīrti, pp. 73–77; and Watson, Vimalakirti Sutra, pp. 104–111.

160 According to the furigana (the traditional Japanese notes alongside the Chinese characters giving guidance about how to read the Chinese), which were in the original Monkaku version of Eihei Kōroku, it is "the cat who said, 'If you can speak, the cat will live, otherwise it dies.'" In that case the third line is asking whether Nanquan heard the cat say this or not. Therefore, in Genryū Kagamishima's interpretation, the monks' silence was because they heard this statement of pleading in the cat's voice. Kagamishima suggests that Manzan eliminated the furigana marks, changing the reading of this poem by Dōgen in his later edition to have Nanquan himself make the statement, similar to what he says in the case itself. The fanciful reading of the poem according to the furigana is not necessary in reading the Chinese characters themselves.

Buddha in a previous age, I resided on this mountain.[161] Once a student asked me whether or not a person of great practice falls into cause and effect. I answered him that such a person does not fall into cause and effect. After that for five hundred lives I descended into a wild-fox body. Now I ask the master to give a turning phrase on my behalf, so that I may be released from a wild-fox body." Then he asked, "Does a person of great practice fall into cause and effect or not?"

Baizhang said, "Such a person is not blind to cause and effect."

With these words, the old man was greatly enlightened, made prostrations, and said, "I have been released from the wild-fox body."[162]

Two verses:

[Saying one of great] practice does not fall
    into this cause and effect,
The cave of demons appears, yet he is not [merely] an old fox.
Within the demon's cave, with one turning [phrase],
Suddenly mountains and rivers transform
    and verify his future path.

Pity that [in the age of] Kaśyāpa, an honored Buddha
Sank as a wild fox for five hundred lives.[163]

161 "Resided on this mountain" implies that he was the abbot in residence, in fact the former Baizhang.

162 This famous story appears in many places. For Shōyōroku, case 8, see Cleary, *Book of Serenity*, pp. 32–36. For Mumonkan, case 2, see Shibayama, *Gateless Barrier*, pp. 32–41; Cleary, *Unlocking the Zen Kōan*, pp. 9–17; and Aitken, *Gateless Barrier*, pp. 19–27. Dōgen refers to this story regularly in Eihei Kōroku, for example in Dharma hall discourses 62, 94, 205, and 510. In Dharma hall discourse 205 he calls it "this wild-fox monster." Dōgen discusses the case at length in Shōbōgenzō Daishugyō (Great Practice) and Jinshin Inga (Deep Faith in Cause and Effect). For Daishugyō see Nishijima and Cross, *Master Dogen's Shobogenzo*, book 4, pp. 43–52. For Jinshin Inga see Tanahashi, *Enlightenment Unfolds*, pp. 263–269; Cook, *How to Raise an Ox*, pp. 117–124; or Yokoi and Victoria, *Zen Master Dōgen*, pp. 136–140. Dōgen also uses the fox kōan as case 102 in the Mana Shōbōgenzō; see Nishijima, *Master Dogen's Shinji Shobogenzo*, pp. 139–140. For a book-length treatment of this kōan, including Dōgen's shifting interpretation of it, see Heine, *Shifting Shape, Shaping Text*.

163 Here Dōgen seems to be referring to the former Baizhang, the old man turned fox, as an honored Buddha in the ancient age of Kaśyāpa.

His ears upset hear a lion's roar.
A tongue matured cuts through the reckless crying.[164]

Too Tired to Understand

78. A monk once asked Mazu, "Apart from the four propositions and beyond the hundred negations, I ask the teacher to directly indicate to me the meaning of [Bodhidharma's] coming from the west."[165]

The great teacher [Mazu] said, "I am tired today, and cannot explain it for you. Go ask [Xitang] Zhizang."

The monk asked [Zhi]zang, and [Zhi]zang said, "Why don't you ask the teacher?"

The monk said, "The teacher had me come ask you."

[Zhi]zang said, "Today I have a headache, and cannot explain it for you. Go ask brother [Baizhang Huai]hai."

The monk asked [Baizhang Huai]hai, and [Huai]hai said, "When I reach here, after all I do not understand."

The monk related this to the great teacher [Mazu], and Mazu said, "[Zhi]zang's head is white, and [Huai]hai's head is black."[166]

Apart from the four propositions
  and beyond the hundred negations,
A monk inquired of the master with refined subtlety.
If not fellows from a site for selecting buddhas,
Who would see that Hai and Zang directly pointed it out?[167]

---

164 We are reading "matured" (or "long" or "developed") tongue as a reference to the enlightening speech of buddhas, and in this case to the turning words of the present Baizhang. This phrase might perhaps instead be interpreted as referring to the fox's long tongue, and then be read, "With his long [drooling] tongue he is cut off from reckless crying."

165 The four propositions and hundred negations are logical categories from Nāgārjuna. The four propositions are: it is; it is not; it both is and is not; and it neither is nor is not.

166 For this story in Mazu's recorded sayings, see Cheng Chien, *Sun Face Buddha,* pp. 72–73. This story is in Hekiganroku, case 73; see Cleary and Cleary, *Blue Cliff Record,* pp. 483–488. It appears in Shōyōroku, case 6; see Cleary, *Book of Serenity,* pp. 23–27. Dōgen uses it for case 108 in Mana Shōbōgenzō; see Nishijima, *Master Dogen's Shinji Shobogenzo,* p. 151.

167 "Site for selecting buddhas" is *senbutsujō,* another name for a monks' hall. These "fellows" might be Huaihai and Zhizang themselves, Mazu and the monk, or Dōgen's audience.

Facing the Wall Is My Teacher

79. Whenever Zen Master Luzu Baoyun saw a monk coming, he would immediately face the wall.[168]

Alone my teacher walked the path of turning the self,
Beyond difference and sameness when seeing monks arrive.[169]
Even wishing he could tell half for you,
Instead he faced the wall and lost his merit.

The Play of Sun and Moon

80. When Mazu was not well, a monk asked, "Teacher, these days how is your venerable health?"
    Mazu said, "Sun Face Buddha; Moon Face Buddha."[170]

There used to be a buddha in Kiangsi
Who made the sun and moon his face.[171]
With what was he not endowed?
Surrounded in Go, he met a foe.[172]

---

168 This story, with Nanquan's commentary, is in Jingde Transmission of the Lamp; see Ogata, *Transmission of the Lamp*, p. 222. It appears in Shōyōroku, case 23; see Cleary, *Book of Serenity*, pp. 100–103. Dōgen uses a longer version of the story as case 87 in Mana Shōbōgenzō; see Nishijima, *Master Dogen's Shinji Shobogenzo*, p. 115.

169 Here Dōgen calls Luzu "my teacher"—extraordinary, unique praise from Dōgen for anyone but Buddha or his personal teachers Tiantong Rujing and Butsuju Myōzen. "Beyond difference and sameness," a phrase for nondiscrimination that recalls the dialectic of Shitou's Harmony of Difference and Sameness (Sandōkai) and the Sōtō five ranks teaching, is here used as a laudatory description of Luzu's nondual zazen facing the wall.

170 Mazu's being unwell means that he was on his deathbed. According to the Wisdom Kalpa Sutra, one of the sutras of the Names of Buddhas, Sun Face Buddha turned the wheel for eighteen hundred years, Moon Face Buddha for one day and night. This story appears in Mazu's recorded sayings; see Cheng Chien, *Sun Face Buddha*, p. 61. It is case 3 in Hekiganroku, see Cleary and Cleary, *Blue Cliff Record*, pp. 18–21; and case 36 in Shōyōroku, see Cleary, *Book of Serenity*, pp. 160–162. Dōgen refers frequently in passing to this story, and to "sun face, moon face" in the Dharma hall discourses in Eihei Kōroku.

171 Kiangsi was a name of Mazu, from the place where he taught.

172 Go is an ancient East Asian game, still played, in which black and white stones are placed in turn on intersections of a grid on a board in order to establish territory, sometimes by surrounding and removing the opponent's stones. It is very simple in terms of rules and play, but extremely subtle. Here Go is used as a metaphor for the play of life and death.

Nanquan's Sickle Still Works Well

81. One day Nanquan was working on the mountain. A passing monk asked, "Where is the path to Nanquan?"

Nanquan held up his sickle and said, "I bought this sickle for thirty coins."

The monk said, "I did not ask about your buying the sickle for thirty coins. Where is the path to Nanquan?"

Nanquan said, "Even now it still works well."[173]

A newly arrived clouds and water monk went up to Nanquan.
Not waiting to reach the mountaintop, he saw a good prospect.
Among the grasses, he got wind of the story of a sickle.
Although he was deaf, its fortune survives a thousand years.

Mazu's Shout Poisoned with Kindness

82. Baizhang met again with Mazu. Mazu held up his whisk.

Baizhang said, "Do you identify with this function or separate from this function?"

Mazu hung the whisk in its place.

[Baizhang] stood waiting for a little while.

Mazu said, "Later when you are flapping your lips, how will you be of help to people?"

Baizhang took the whisk and held it up.

Mazu said, "Do you identify with this function or separate from this function?"

Baizhang hung the whisk back in its place.

Mazu immediately shouted.

Later on, Baizhang said to Huangbo, "At that time, when Mazu shouted at me, I was deaf for three days."[174]

---

173 This story of Nanquan's sickle is discussed by Dōgen at the end of Dharma word 3 in volume 8. It appears in Wudeng Huiyuan (Jap.: Gotō Egen; Five Lamps Merged in the Source), vol. 3. See Foster and Shoemaker, *Roaring Stream*, p. 71.

174 Dōgen also comments on this story in Dharma hall discourse 50. A version of this story including an earlier part appears in the Jingde Transmission of the Lamp; see Ogata, *Transmission of the Lamp*, p. 210. It is in the commentary to Hekiganroku, case 11; see Cleary and Cleary, *Blue Cliff Record*, pp. 73–74. Dōgen uses it as Mana Shōbōgenzō, case 54; see Nishijima, *Master Dogen's Shinji Shobogenzo*, p. 76.

Once [Baizhang] was awakened by him, and saw no self.
Who could understand that everything he held was new?
Mistakenly entering Mazu's house, he was given poison wine.
With furrowed brows still he yearned
    for the kindness of former days.

All Going Together

83. Once a monk asked Dazui [Fazhen], "In the boundless fire at the end
of the kalpa, the great thousands of worlds will all be destroyed. I wonder
if this will also be destroyed?"[175]

Dazui said, "Destroyed."

The monk said, "If so, will it follow along with others?"

Dazui said, "It follows along with others."[176]

Wearing hair and sprouting horns, go together with others.
In the boundless kalpa-ending fire, do not turn your head.
Even withered trees and dead ash are scorched completely.
What face do you have that begrudges these conditions?

Springtime for a Buddha

84. [Guizong] Huichao asked Fayan [Wenyi], "What is Buddha?"
Fayan said, "You are Huichao."[177]

Calling on Huichao, spring on New Year's Eve,[178]
Huichao turned his head, no dust on the mirror.
How splendid, Fayan held the function.
Before a word was over, Buddha changed to a spirit.

---

175 Here the "this" about which the monk asks could refer to suchness or Buddha nature.

176 This story appears in Hekiganroku, case 29; see Cleary and Cleary, *Blue Cliff Record*, pp. 187–190. It is case 30 in Shōyōroku; see Cleary, *Book of Serenity*, pp. 131–136. Dōgen cites it as case 24 in Mana Shōbōgenzō; see Nishijima, *Master Dogen's Shinji Shobogenzo*, p. 35.

177 This story is Hekiganroku, case 7; see Cleary and Cleary, *Blue Cliff Record*, pp. 46–51. It is also cited by Dōgen in case 252, or in some versions case 253, of Mana Shōbōgenzō; see Nishijima, *Master Dogen's Shinji Shobogenzo*, p. 322.

178 In the East Asian calendar, New Year's Day occurs at the beginning of spring. See also Dharma hall discourse 302 for the motif of year's end and spring.

Just Sitting Takes Wing

85. Master Tiantong [Rujing] said, "In my place, do not employ offering incense, prostrations, nembutsu, repentance, or reading sutras, but simply engage in just sitting."[179]

> A turtle hides his hands and head, but still holds on.[180]
> In, or, on, of are merely gain and loss.[181]
> Dragons and snakes mixed together
>   still look like dragons and snakes.
> Sitting with whole body coiled, from the outset take wing.

Playing with Dropped Off Body and Mind

86. Master Tiantong [Rujing] said, "Practicing Zen (sanzen) is dropping off body and mind."

> Playing with this wooden ladle, wind and waves arise.
> With benefaction great and virtue deep, rewards also deepen.
> Even when seeing the ocean dried up, cold down to the bottom,
> Do not allow body to die, nor abandon the mind.[182]

179 Dōgen also quotes this statement by Tiantong Rujing in Hōkyōki, his journal of his study in China. See Kodera, *Dōgen's Formative Years in China*, p. 124; and Tanahashi, *Enlightenment Unfolds*, p. 10. He also mentions it in Bendowa (Talk on Wholehearted Practice of the Way), see Okumura and Leighton, *Wholehearted Way*, pp. 21–22. Although Dōgen quotes Tiantong Rujing's instruction not to use these other practices but "simply engage in just sitting," he himself continued to do all these practices. Our interpretation of the point here is to use such practices not as instruments for spiritual advancement, but simply to perform all activities in the spirit of just sitting.

180 Dōgen may imply here that Tiantong Rujing, and he himself, continue to hold to these practices, but without clinging.

181 "In," "or," "on," and "of" are used to mimic the four Chinese characters, each a meaningless prepositional or exclamatory particle by themselves, which are used by Dōgen to begin this line.

182 The third line of Dōgen's verse depicts *shinjin datsuraku*, dropping off or letting go of body and mind. The last line indicates to just continue using body and mind in practice thereafter.

An Urgent Question on Top of a Cliff

87. One day Xiangyan spoke to his assembly, saying, "It is like someone on a thousand-foot-high cliff, hanging to a branch of a tree by his teeth, his feet with no foothold and hands with nothing to grasp. Suppose someone asks, 'What is the meaning of [Bodhidharma] coming from the west?' If he opens his mouth to answer he will lose his body and life. If he does not answer, he is abandoning the questioner. At this very time, what would you do?"

Then Elder Zhao came forward and said, "I don't ask about the time of being up in the tree, but what about before climbing the tree?"

Xiangyan just laughed.[183]

> He lost his body and life, but lives on in death,
> Still cherishing the lips born from his mother.
> Wishing to try and answer, words fill his mouth.
> The questioner too hangs to a branch by his teeth.

The Punishment for Losing Money in the River

88. When Zen Master Hongzhi [Zhengjue] first visited Danxia [Zichun], Danxia asked, "What is your self before the empty kalpa?"

Hongzhi said, "A toad at the bottom of a well swallows up the moon. At midnight it does not borrow a shining curtain for illumination."[184]

Danxia said, "Not yet, say more."

Hongzhi tried to speak, but Danxia hit him with his whisk and said, "Do you still say you don't borrow?"

Hongzhi suddenly was enlightened and made prostrations.

---

183 This story appears in Jingde Transmission of the Lamp; see Chang, *Original Teachings of Ch'an Buddhism*, p. 223. It is also case 5 in Mumonkan; see Shibayama, *Gateless Barrier*, pp. 53–57; Cleary, *Unlocking the Zen Kōan*, pp. 28–32; and Aitken, *Gateless Barrier*, pp. 38–45. Dōgen discusses this story in Shōbōgenzō Sōshi Seirai no I (The Meaning of the Ancestral Teacher Coming from the West). See Nishijima and Cross, *Master Dogen's Shobogenzo*, book 3, pp. 241–245. Dōgen also uses this story as case 243, or in some versions case 244, in Mana Shōbōgenzō; see Nishijima, *Master Dogen's Shinji Shobogenzo*, p. 313.

184 This "shining curtain," according to Kagamishima, is bejeweled and reflects light. It represents looking for light outside, but also personal rather than universal illumination. "Midnight" here is literally the third watch, roughly between 11 P.M. and 1 A.M.

Danxia asked, "Why don't you make some statement?"
Hongzhi said, "Today I lost money and received punishment."
Danxia said, "I have no time to spare to hit you. Go for now."[185]

> He planned to sell the flow of teaching to a buyer.[186]
> The night moon rose above the mountain,
>   and reached the window.
> When money's lost in the river, seek it in the river.
> One crying in the river stops and rests in the river.

Nothing to Pacify

89. The second ancestral great teacher [Dazu Huike] asked the first ancestor [Bodhidharma], "My mind is not yet calm. Would the teacher pacify it?"
  The [first] ancestor said, "Bring your mind, and I will pacify you."
  [Dazu Huike] said, "Seeking my mind I cannot grasp it."
  The [first] ancestor said, "I have finished pacifying your mind."[187]

> When all is totally clear, nothing need be cleared.
> Where all is hidden and dark, is utter confusion.
> Seeking a teacher by the side of the path,
>   he accidentally met himself.
> Enticed by calm water, he walked a bit in the clouds.[188]

185 This story is from Hongzhi's biography and volume 9 of Hongzhi's Extensive Record. See Leighton, *Cultivating the Empty Field,* pp. 4–5.

186 "Flow of teaching" is *fūryū,* literally "flowing wind," here referring back to the original self before the empty kalpa. As a compound this ordinarily means elegance, refinement, gracefulness, or artistry.

187 This story appears in Jingde Transmission of the Lamp; see Ogata, *Transmission of the Lamp,* p. 69. See also Foster and Shoemaker, *Roaring Stream,* p. 7. This story is also case 41 of the Mumonkan; see Aitken, *Gateless Barrier,* pp. 248–254; and Cleary, *Unlocking the Zen Kōan,* pp. 181–184.

188 Water here also refers to the water of Dharma nature.

A Horse within a Begging Bowl

90. Zen Master Zhenxie [Qingliao] visited Danxia [Zichun] and entered the room. Danxia asked, "What is your self during the empty kalpa?"

Zhenxie tried to respond. Danxia said, "You are disturbed. Leave for a while."

One day Zhenxie climbed Begging Bowl Peak and clearly integrated with realization.[189] He returned to see Danxia. While Zhenxie stood waiting, Danxia slapped him and said, "I really had thought you knew."

Zhenxie joyfully made a prostration.[190]

> When they connected, a bad smell afflicted the empty sky.
> Shading the earth and covering the heavens,
>   he wanted to break through.
> Again climbing up to the barrier, together they built a support.
> From the outset, [Danxia] ran the horse around
>   inside the begging bowl.

189 Begging Bowl, or Boyu Peak, is located in the Danxia Mountains, after which Danxia Zichun is named.

190 This story is from the section on Zhenxie in the Jiatai Record of the Universal Lamps (Jap.: Katai Futōroku), published in 1204.

DŌGEN OSHŌ SHINSAN, JISAN, AND GEJU

MASTER DŌGEN'S VERSES OF PRAISE ON PORTRAITS, VERSES OF
PRAISE ON PORTRAITS OF HIMSELF, AND ASSORTED VERSES [1]

COLLECTED BY SENNE, ATTENDANT OF DŌGEN ZENJI, AND OTHERS

E K
I Ō
H R   THE EXTENSIVE RECORD OF EIHEI DŌGEN, VOLUME TEN
E O
I K
   U

Verses of Praise on Portraits

Depictions of Śākyamuni Coming Down from the Mountains

1. A sack of flowing wind tied around his waist,
    He stole the wind in the pines to insert or bring forth.[2]
    Then twirling a branch of winter plum blossoms to sell,[3]
    He came and went under the heavens, planning to find a buyer.

2. After six years of bitter ascetic practice,
    He attained awakening in one sitting.

---

1 Volume 10 consists of various verses by Dōgen in Chinese, in traditional forms. *Shin-san* are verses (and sometimes prose) in praise of portraits of Buddhist teachers, calligraphed on the portraits themselves. Five such verses are included in this volume. *Jisan* are similar verses but inscribed on one's own portrait, usually with self-praise that is ironic and self-deprecating in tone. Twenty such verses to be added to portraits of Dōgen himself are included here. Most of volume 10 consists of one hundred twenty-five *geju*, or verses on various topics. *Geju* is used to translate the Sanskrit *gāthā*, verses memorized and chanted by monks, including verse portions of sutras and verses to maintain mindfulness in daily activity. In this volume all of the headings that appear before some of these verses, or sometimes before groups of the verses, are by Dōgen himself (or perhaps the compiler), unlike the headings in previous volumes by the present translators.

2 Wind here is an image for the teachings, so the meaning is that he freely emptied out his bag of teachings.

3 Here Dōgen imagines that it was a plum blossom that Śākyamuni held up at Vulture Peak.

Glimpsing the ground and arising, how laughable!
What is this broken wooden ladle?

Bodhidharma

3. The twenty-eighth ancestor, venerable Bodhidharma, was the
third child of the great king of Fragrant Arrival, a country in
southern India. Bodhidharma did prostrations to venerable
Prajñātāra, who became his Dharma transmission teacher.
Bodhidharma received the foolish person who cut off his arm
[Dazu Huike] and recognized him as his disciple. At Shaolin
temple he sat upright for nine years. People of the time called
him the great being of wall gazing.[4] When his work was finished
he returned to India. This early morning, why is he eating rice at
a layperson's house?[5]

Ānanda

4. He overturned the banner before the gate.[6]
Sitting on the river, he considered others in allotting his body.
Within a dream, Ānanda broke through the great barrier.[7]
Before, he'd protected the Tathāgata during and after his life.[8]

---

4 "Great being" translates the Sanskrit *mahāsattva*, an epithet for bodhisattvas. What
Dōgen says about Bodhidharma is standard in his legendary story. See Ogata, *Transmission of the Lamp*, pp. 57–74.

5 Manzan suggested that the person eating rice was Dōgen himself on the occasion of
inscribing this painting.

6 Ānanda toppling the banner at the gate refers to his asking Mahākaśyāpa what he
received from the Buddha. Mahākaśyāpa told Ānanda to take down the banner at the
monastery gate, representing debate over the teaching. This story is given with brief comment in Dharma hall discourse 252. See also Mumonkan, case 22; Shibayama, *Gateless
Barrier*, pp. 158–163; Cleary, *Unlocking the Zen Kōan*, pp. 106–109; and Aitken, *Gateless
Barrier*, pp. 142–146.

7 "Allotting his body" refers to the story about Ānanda's passing, confronting the "great
barrier" of life and death, as related in the Jingde Transmission of the Lamp. Two neighboring kings who venerated Ānanda both coveted his relics. So Ānanda chose to sit and
die on a ferryboat on the Ganges River, the border of the two kingdoms, so that his relics
would be divided equally. See Ogata, *Transmission of the Lamp*, pp. 9–10.

8 Ānanda was Śākyamuni Buddha's personal attendant. After the Buddha's parinirvāṇa,
Ānanda preserved his teachings by reciting all of his talks, which Ānanda could remember

Caution![9]
Don't keep your eyes on this painting.
With sincere mind make prostrations and give homage.

Master Butsuju [Myōzen]

5. His everyday practice of the way was thorough and intimate.
   When he passed into nirvāṇa his face was fresh.
   Tell me, what is his affair today?
   Since the vajra flame, he manifests his true body.[10]

[Dōgen's] Verses of Praise on Portraits of Himself

1. Old plum tree, old plum tree,
   A long time nurturing spring in every branch and leaf,
   The function of the immovable ground is clear in each detail;
   The samādhi of adornment is in each and every dust.
   On top of the staff are no knots at all;
   On his sitting cushion is the body in ten directions.[11]
   Playing with a phoenix feather,
   He grasped Tiantong [Rujing]'s nose.
   Entering a tiger's cave,
   He laughed at words from the lips of Daxiu [Tiantong
   Zongjue].[12]

---

perfectly. These became the sutras, all beginning with Ānanda's comment "Thus have I heard."

9 "Caution!" is *totsu,* a shout of alarm.

10 "Vajra flame" refers to the fires of cremation.

11 "Knots" indicates both knots or knobs of branches and also sections, segments, categories, stages, junctions, or junctures. The staff without knots indicates the oneness beyond discrimination or stages of Dōgen's teaching. The "body in ten directions" is short for "The entire world in ten directions is the true human body." This is a saying by Changsha Jingcen, discussed by Dōgen in Shōbōgenzō in, for example, Shinjin Gakudō (Body and Mind Study of the Way); see Tanahashi, *Moon in a Dewdrop,* pp. 92–94.

12 Tiantong Rujing was Dōgen's Dharma teacher at Tiantong monastery in China. Daxiu Zongjue, also known as Tiantong Zongjue, was the teacher of Tiantong Rujing's teacher. Daxiu was a noted poet who had been abbot of this same Tiantong monastery from

A stubborn rock dwelling in the mountains,
He's a senile old fool in the monastery.

2. Not abandoning his sitting cushion until the year of the donkey,[13]
    When asked about the way, he merely raises a fist.
    Ultimately, how can he be comprehended?
    With body and mind lazy, he doesn't practice Zen.

3. Autumn is spirited and refreshing as this mountain ages.[14]
    A donkey observes the sky in the well, white moon floating.[15]
    One [the moon] is not dependent;
        one [the sky] does not contain.[16]
    Letting go, vigorous with plenty of gruel and rice,

1059 until his death in 1062. He had succeeded Tiantong Hongzhi, frequently mentioned by Dōgen in Eihei Kōroku, who had previously been abbot of Tiantong until 1057. Daxiu, or Tiantong Zongjue, had served as head monk under Hongzhi.

13 Among the twelve animal zodiac signs in Chinese astrology, there is no year of the donkey.

14 This verse was written in the eighth month of 1249. The portrait was probably painted not so long before. This painting is in the front of this book, now in the possession of Hōkyōji monastery near Eiheiji. It is the only extant painting of Dōgen done during his life. "Mountain" here presumably refers to Dōgen himself, as a "mountain monk."

15 This line is difficult. Read as we indicate in the text, Dōgen may be referring to himself metaphorically as a donkey, just after referring to himself as a mountain. However, the character for "donkey" on the picture is questionable, as it looks like it might have been appended after the rest of the text, and perhaps should be ignored, as Genryū Kagamishima does in his reading. In that case, the line could be read, "He observes the sky in the well, white moon floating." Manzan changed this line in his edition to read, "The well and donkey observe each other; at dawn a frog floats." In that reading the frog refers to the common East Asian image of the frog in the moon. This reading would refer to the story about Caoshan, discussed in Dharma hall discourse 403, in which Caoshan asked, "A buddha's true Dharma body is like empty space, manifesting forms in response to beings like the moon in water. How do you express the truth of this response?" His disciple responded, "Like a donkey looking in a well," which Caoshan amended to "Like the well looking at the donkey."

16 This line indicates that the moon does not rely on the water and its reflection, while the sky, as reflected in the well, does not contain or encompass the moon.

Flapping with vitality, right from head to tail,[17]
Above and below the heavens, clouds and water are free.[18]

4. The transmission in order,
    Skin, flesh, bones, and marrow understood,
    How do headtop, eyebrows, and nostrils
    Expound the pure ancient marvel?
    His daily activity is lazy like Niutou [Fayong],
    Sitting and lying down as foolish as Budai,
    Hair white as snow in spring mountains,
    Eyes deep as clear autumn water with nothing of value.[19]
    All dharmas transform to the power of dhāraṇīs;[20]
    All objects escape hindrance in samādhi.
    Do you call him ordinary or sage?
    Who says he buys and sells himself?
    The entire world in ten directions appears in part
        as half his body.
    The buddhas of the three times make three full bows
        at their places.
    An old pine, like a dragon coiled at the bottom
        of a mountain stream,
    After eating relaxes and enjoys a nap.[21]

---

17 "Flapping" is *kappapatsu* in Japanese, referring to the flapping of a fish out of water.

18 "Clouds and water" usually refers to an *unsui*, or monk in training, but here it apparently refers to Dōgen himself. This poem includes a complex set of paired images, including sky reflected in the well, sky and moon, and donkey and well seeing each other.

19 Niutou, disciple of the fourth ancestor, was the founder of the "Ox-head school," but bore the nickname "Lazy." For Niutou see also Dharma hall discourses 207 and 313. Budai is the legendary fat laughing Buddha, based on a historical Chinese monk, Hotei in Japanese. The word "foolish" here also implies innocent and straightforward as well as silly. "Eyes deep" refers to wisdom. "Nothing of value," or "without valuables," is literally "with no shellfish," carrying the image of a clear stream.

20 Dhāraṇī are incantations chanted to evoke or develop helpful power in Buddhism. The word used here is *sōji* in Japanese, literally "holding everything," a translation of the literal meaning of dhāraṇī in Sanskrit.

21 "After eating I relax and enjoy a nap" is from Song of the Grass Hut (Jap.: Sōanka) by Shitou Xiqian. See Leighton, *Cultivating the Empty Field*, pp. 72–73.

5. Himself holding up a pine branch,[22]
    A flower opens with five petals.
    Himself holding up a monk's staff,
    Bent and straight are one.[23]
    Right at this time,
    A thunderclap roars,
    In heavens above and among people, Dharma rains abundant.
    For your sake, the old woman is delighted with the spring wind.[24]

6. Having eaten the old fist of Taibai,
    Bulging eyes see both North Star and cowherd.[25]
    Myself is deceived by myself, with nowhere to search.
    For your sake, the old woman still moves gently.

7. Sun face and moon face are the way;[26]
    Buddha face and ancestral face are also the way.
    Face-to-face meeting is expressing the way;
    Expressing the way is face-to-face meeting.
    Right here, directly confronting reality, is the crown of creation.[27]
    The way is completed with the same red clay,
    Verifying the unique realization in the dawn sky.

22 The pine branch here could be an image for the teacher's whisk.

23 The first four lines offer two images, a flower encompassing five petals and the unity of the bent and straight (or good and bad). Both represent the interweaving of the one and many or ultimate and phenomenal, the dialectic of the Sōtō five ranks teaching.

24 "Old woman" refers to Dōgen's grandmotherly or nurturing mind.

25 Taibai is the name of the mountain of Tiantong monastery. So this refers to Dōgen's having absorbed the Dharma (or fist) of his teacher Tiantong Rujing. The cowherd star, Altair, is in the southern sky, so seeing both that and the North Star indicates wide seeing.

26 "Sun face, moon face" are the words of Mazu when asked about his failing health. See kōan 80 in volume 9.

27 "Right here, directly confronting reality" is not in the Monkaku version of the text, which we are usually following, but is added by Manzan in his version. "Directly confronting reality" is literally "hitting yang," indicating the ultimate, but as an expression it also means "facing south," referring to the emperor, who alone faced the south in the Chinese court. "The crown of creation," or "the headtop from the beginning," might refer to Dōgen facing his portrait, or his portrait facing him.

Who speaks of the great round mind?
Simply say, just this is it.[28]

8. Expressing the way, this body appears as the crown
    of a thousand sages.
The total function meeting my face is fresh
    in the ten thousand times.
Some other time, if you want to understand this mountain elder,
Entrusting the bones and entrusting the marrow
    are equally intimate.[29]

9. If you call him not knowing, not understanding,
That's exactly just right.
If you don't call him not knowing, not understanding,
That's not really incorrect.
Tell me, what do you call him?
For now, call him that child of Tiantong [Rujing].

10. Recognizing this as true [portrait],
    How can this be reality?
Upholding this [portrait], how can we wait for the reality?
If you can see it like this,
What is this body hanging in emptiness?
Fences and walls are not the complete mind.[30]

28 "Just this is it" was Yunyan's response when asked by his disciple Dongshan Liangjie how to directly portray his teacher and his teacher's Dharma. See Dharma hall discourse 494 and volume 7, note 51, which relates to this story.

29 "If you want to understand this mountain elder" refers again to Yunyan's response to Dongshan, alluded to in the last line of the previous verse. "Entrusting the bones and entrusting the marrow are equal" echoes Dōgen's teaching in Shōbōgenzō Kattō (Twining Vines). In that essay, Dōgen refers to the story of Bodhidharma's disciples being bequeathed his skins, flesh, bones, and marrow, respectively. Dōgen insists that one is no deeper or superior than the other. Here Dōgen is reaffirming this as his own essential teaching. For Dōgen's "Twining Vines" see Tanahashi, *Moon in a Dewdrop*, pp. 168–174.

30 This refers to Nanyang Huizhong's response about the mind of the ancient buddhas being "fences, walls, tiles, and pebbles." See *hōgo* 13 in volume 8 and its note 124. This poem is inscribed on the portrait of Dōgen now at Eiheiji and reproduced in the front of this book.

11. This time meeting my face, how could I wait to nod [in
     recognition]?
     If you call this a painting of a village monk,
     You are able to play with the gracefulness of going beyond.
     This is the ancestral source of buddha ancestors;
     This is the descendant of buddha ancestors.

12. In my confusion, I plan to cook with salt and sauce.[31]
     Satisfied eating gruel and rice, I wash my eating bowls.
     Although it is like this, do not say,
     "Heaven and earth is one finger,
     The ten thousand things one horse."[32]
     After all, what is this?
     The whole eye is a fist
     Smashing the empty sky into drops and drops of blood.
     The whole fist is an eye
     Seeing through the round earth with every bit of muscle.[33]

13. His humble capacity is lower than monkeys,
     His vulgarity surpassing even monks from Sichuan.
     Nevertheless,
     He walks barefoot, but in Chinese style.[34]

31 This refers to a saying by Mazu, mentioned in Dharma hall discourse 11, "Since I left confusion behind thirty years ago, I have never lacked for salt or sauce to eat." See also Cheng Chien, *Sun Face Buddha,* p. 61.

32 "Heaven and earth is one finger, the ten thousand things one horse" is a quote from Zhuangzi. The passage preceding this reads, "To use a finger to make the point that a finger is not a finger is not as good as using a nonfinger to make the same point. To use a horse to prove that a horse is not a horse is not as good as to use a nonhorse to prove that a horse is not a horse." See Hamill and Seaton, *Essential Chuang Tzu,* p. 12; and Watson, *Complete Works of Chuang Tzu,* p. 40. Watson's translation has "attribute" instead of "finger." Dōgen also quotes this phrase in Dharma hall discourse 401. He seems to be criticizing attachment to the oneness of all things, without its function in different kinds.

33 The eye represents wisdom; fist represents its function.

34 Walking in Chinese style here probably refers to Dōgen following the ways of his Chinese teacher, Tiantong Rujing.

14.   Direct pointing to the human mind
      [Is apparent in his] fist and headtop;
      Seeing the nature and becoming Buddha
      In his nostrils and eyes.
      Attaining the skin and attaining the marrow,
          two or three layers.[35]
      Holding up the flower and smiling opens the five petals.

15.   Bamboo splints and ox skins used for counting
      Total more than eleven hundred.[36]
      Before, I placed this smelly skin-bag on the drumhead,
      On the mountain of ignorance beating thunderclouds.[37]

16.   His nostrils are high on the mountain;
      Eyes bright as the ocean;
      Head flat like a fan;
      Legs spindly as a donkey.
      When students enter the room, he loves to raise his smelly fist.
      Ascending the seat in the hall, he borrows power
          from a monk's staff.
      Meeting someone thirsty for water, he points up to the sky.[38]
      Meeting someone asking for rice, he points to a cold pot.
      Because in the past he maintained the precepts
          of chickens and dogs,
      Today he can steal the cotton robe of buddha ancestors.[39]

---

35 "Two or three layers" probably implies lack of significant difference between skin and marrow.

36 Genryū Kagamishima suggests that Dōgen had then been at Eiheiji more than eleven hundred days. If so, this verse is from 1248.

37 Dōgen's complicated image here is to use his own skin as a drumhead to drum up the Dharma, which roars like thunder. But also implied are the clouds, or monks, being trained, or pounded out, at Eiheiji, sometimes a mountain of ignorance.

38 The word for sky used here is *tenjō*, the characters for which are literally "sky" and "well," giving the ironic overtone of water in the sky

39 "Cotton robe" is the compound for the blue-black monk's robe said to have been transmitted by Bodhidharma.

Although this is so,
Above and below the heavens,
Laughter roars at this rice bag person.

17. Instantly emancipated, at its pinnacle a blind donkey
Roams widely under heaven, becoming a horse or ox.
A thunderclap in great space transcends subject and object.
Even though called a village monk,
Truly, you are the genuine vitality of the capital.

18. For ten thousand fathoms the cold lake is soaked in sky color.
In the quiet night a golden-scaled fish swims along the bottom.
From center to edge, the fishing poles are broken,[40]
On expansive water surface, bright moonlight.

19. Vainly sitting upright, passing spring and winter.
Old tears like ceaseless rain, how they fill my breast.
Who knows the sound of thunder echoing beyond the heavens?
Don't let them rush to strike the bell in the jeweled tower.[41]

20. Sowing the fields and making rice balls
is Dizang's spring farming.[42]
Planting pines in the deep mountains is Linji's bones and flesh.[43]
Although this is so,
With the monk's robe of Yunyan and Yunju,
With the faces of Xuefeng and Xuedou,[44]

---

40 "Center and edge" is *shahan* and *nahō,* literally "this and that," or "here and there," referring to ultimate and phenomenal, or all other dualities.

41 "Don't let them rush to strike the bell" may refer to a bell to end his zazen, and perhaps to go give a Dharma hall discourse. But in the silence is already thunder.

42 [Luohan] Dizang [Guichen]'s farming refers to a story related in Dharma hall discourse 425. See also *Shōyōroku,* case 12, in Cleary, *Book of Serenity,* pp. 51–55.

43 Linji planted pines in the remote mountains to inspire future generations and beautify the mountain gate. See Leighton and Okumura, *Dōgen's Pure Standards for the Zen Community,* pp. 149–150.

44 Dōgen's mention of Yunyan, Yunju, Xuefeng, and Xuedou honors his respect and

He plays with Subhūti's vain talk,
And also laughs at Vimalakīrti's soothing silence.[45]
Confused people hold, "This very mind is Buddha."
Damei ripens with "No mind, no Buddha."[46]

---

use of their teachings. But here he is just playing poetically with their names, the "clouds" *(yun)* of Yunyan and Yunju, and the "snow" *(xue)* of Xuefeng and Xuedou.

45 Here the vain or empty talk of Buddha's disciple Subhūti is a play on his discourses about emptiness, the teaching on which Subhūti was most expert. The "thunderous" silence of the enlightened layman Vimalakīrti is the climax of the sutra about him, but here Dōgen ironically calls his silence "soothing" and laughs at him. In Dharma hall discourse 134, Dōgen discusses the confrontation in which Vimalakīrti critiques and overcomes Subhūti in the sutra. Dōgen rereads the text to support Subhūti and critique Vimalakīrti.

46 These last two lines are open to many interpretations. The story about Damei accepting his teacher Mazu's "This very mind is Buddha" is cited and discussed in Dharma hall discourses 8 and 319 and in Dharma word 9. In the traditional story, Damei accepted Mazu's teaching of "This very mind is Buddha" and went to reside on Mount Damei. Hearing about it later, Damei rejected Mazu's subsequent teaching of "no mind, no Buddha," saying that Mazu was confusing people. Mazu approved this and said that Damei (whose name means Great Plum) was ripe. Here, however, Dōgen seems to be playing with this story. In Manzan's version of Eihei Kōroku, he divides this *jisan* into two and adds two lines: "Life is pure and refined and the teaching of the house is broken. / Right here from the beginning not a single thing exists." Perhaps Dōgen is saying that Damei, not Mazu, has confused people by advocating "This very mind is Buddha." However, Dōgen himself often expounds that saying. Here perhaps Dōgen sees himself in the picture as Damei ripened into "No mind, no Buddha." Or Dōgen may simply be saying that Damei ripened, according to Mazu, after hearing "No mind, no Buddha," even though he stayed with "This very mind." At times Dōgen recommends one or the other of these teachings. Both are full expressions of the truth with which to play. Another possible way of interpreting these two lines, which is more in accord with the traditional story, might be: "[Damei thought that Mazu was] confusing people, [as Damei held to] 'This very mind is Buddha.' [Mazu accepted that] Damei was ripe, [although Mazu was teaching] 'No mind, no Buddha.'" Another interpretation is that Dōgen is saying that he himself confuses students with "This very mind is Buddha," and when they mature tells them, "No mind, no Buddha."

Assorted Verses

Master Dōgen, in the second year of the Baoqing [Hōkyō] era of Song China [1226, wrote the following while] residing at Tiantong Jingde Zen temple on renowned Taibai Mountain in Qingyuan Province.[47]

Following the Rhyme of Supplementary Official Wang[48]

1. Below the mountain I vainly raised a lazy water buffalo.
   In the evening playing freely at his whim,
   Late at night he walks alone, trampling others' seedlings,
   At dawn he returns without excuse.
   In violent wind and rain, he stops longing for a calf.
   With snow and frost deep, his seeking mind's at rest.
   With nose torn, he has no rope [to lead him].
   Head and tail both fallen, only poison energy remains.

Six Verses Following the Rhyme of Examination Graduate Wenben

2. Aroused aspiration inspires poetic phrases.
   Words and meaning fully combined is most wondrous and rare,
   Extensively illuminating countless sands throughout the world.[49]
   Where can you be outside to ask about nirvāṇa?[50]

3. A withered tree below the cliff has a confused path.
   Receive a horse from someone and return an ox.
   Not greedy to cultivate wildlands,
   Let go of human realms and face the distant mountains.

---

47 This is a note by the compiler, Senne. The remainder of volume 8 consists of 125 verses on different topics. The first fifty verses, as indicated by this note, were written while Dōgen was in China at Tiantong monastery. Verses 51–76 were written after his return to Japan but before the departure to Echizen. Verse 77 was written during his visit to Kamakura in 1248. And verses 78–125 were written in Echizen.

48 Nothing is known of this official, but presumably he was a layperson who visited Tiantong temple when Dōgen was there. All other officials or persons mentioned in Dōgen's subsequent poems from Mount Tiantong are also unknown, unless otherwise noted.

49 "Countless sands" is an expression for the innumerable grains of sand of innumerable Ganges Rivers that are frequently elaborated in the sutras.

50 "Nirvāṇa" is our interpretation here, literally given as "the unconditioned."

4. The iron face of a silver mountain is completely shattered.
   Arriving here, who can use their eyes to carefully see?
   Both demon face and spirit head, the whole body is awesome.
   Wearing fur and sprouting horns, how can we say it's difficult?

5. When one object breaks open, we see numerous sutras.
   The benefit of turning the great Dharma wheel
       is completely genuine.
   Popping out of a donkey's womb, born from a horse's belly,
   Each time it's held up it's always fresh.

6. The three teachings' idle names were originally unspoken.[51]
   With one word slightly mistaken all aspects are contrary.
   Clearly know both people and objects are without self.
   Traversing the mysterious barrier arrive at your own home.

7. Compassion responds to the world,
       together with dusts and receptive.
   Awakened before birth with enlightened spirit knowledge,
   The lord's virtue is abundant as three auspicious stars appear.[52]
   The bright sun scales the sky, not waiting for a teacher.

Continuing the Rhyme of Assistant Minister Pu

8. On the nose is an eye that discerns fragrance and stench.
   The Dharma sound universally spreads to all senses.
   All who hear clarify the genuine truth.
   An enlightened person is widely awakened to the mind that
       breaks through emptiness.
   After many years of visiting numerous Dharma seats,
   In a hundred million kalpas difficult to fathom depths of the
       ocean floor,

51 The three teachings here refers to Buddhism, Daoism, and Confucianism.

52 These three stars are a traditional Chinese symbol of guardians of the emperor, represented by the North Star. The "lord" here may refer to Graduate Wenben, for whom these last six verses were written, who presumably was preparing to become an official. But it may also refer to Śākyamuni Buddha, who was in some sense awakened even before birth.

Finally today, thanks to you I fully understand
The intimate function that casts off the jade of old classics.

Following the Rhyme of Official Wenben

9. The great way has continuously pervaded.
   How can Peng and Ying be found outside?[53]
   Strolling along with a staff, chanting in loud voice,
   This lump of red flesh arouses the ancient wind.

Two Verses Following a Rhyme from [Assistant Minister] Pu

10. From his very birth a superior person,
    Already grounded in no mind, how could he be angry?
    He directly removed personal ego and forgot false views.
    Transcending the weary world, he bestows justice and charity.

11. A true person who has reached awakening
        wipes out gain and loss.
    A great being who has clarified mind casts off emptiness.
    Like the spirit tortoise hiding six parts without confusion,
    There is nothing to remove from his skin and bones.[54]

Two Verses Following the Rhyme of Li Ji Chengzhong

12. Coming and going continuous on the familiar path
    Is cut in two with one stroke, forever nothing remaining.
    If you want to know the vast ocean, dried up and exhausted,
    People die with nothing left, mind simply empty.

13. From the beginning, buddha ancestors clarify the mind ground.
    Right at the time of insight, steal their eyes.

---

53 Peng and Ying are legendary Daoist regions populated by *sennin*, wise hermits and sages.

54 The spirit tortoise is one of the Chinese guardian animals of the four directions, along with dragon, phoenix, and tiger. "Hiding six parts" refers to the way a tortoise withdraws its legs, head, and tail into its shell. But here it refers to the six senses, which do not confuse a true person.

The golden lion tries to proceed and steps back.
Iron-spiked spheres spring, and the wooden horse is startled.[55]

Given to the Mother of Ru Qianyi [56]

14. Beautiful and pure, you have opened and clarified the mind.
Face filled with spiritual radiance, you naturally shine.
Do not say that when your merit was completed the way was
attained.
Touching the path, right away you are awesome.

Given to Commissioner of Laws Nan

15. Sneeze sound dissolves great empty space.
Right away, the self is clearly discerned.[57]
All previous buddha ancestors are swallowed completely.
Not following others, total penetrating [of the way] is verified.

Two Verses Following the Rhyme of Official Wang

16. Karmic consciousness rushes to fill the self with the poisons,
Coming and going everywhere, no truth remaining.
This morning he stamped out the red furnace.
His whole body is at ease, a barefoot person.

17. When one flower opens, all forms are fresh,
Equally knowing the spring wind for ten thousand miles.
Falling from trees, red flowers flutter in confused disarray.
Trying to proceed but sliding back,
how many times lost at the crossroads?

---

55 Iron-spiked spheres are caltrops, a weapon used in both medieval Asia and Europe.
These spiked iron balls were scattered on the ground like land mines to obstruct cavalry.
As to the wooden horse, this may refer to Yunmen's wooden horse; see Dharma hall discourses 296 and 345; Chang, *Original Teachings of Ch'an Buddhism,* p. 293; and App, *Master Yunmen,* p. 102.

56 Ru Qianyi may be Examination Graduate Ru, who receives verse 18 below, and perhaps the older brother of Examination Graduate Ru Qianer, who receives verse 47 below.

57 The "self" in this line was added by Manzan, and accepted by Genryū Kagamishima,
in substitution for a compound in the Monkaku version that has no meaning, and

Given to Examination Graduate Ru

18. Natural wondrous wisdom itself is true suchness.
     Why should we employ Confucian discourse or Buddhist texts?
     Rely on sitting at ease at your place,
         and hang your mouth on the wall.
     Friends arrive here and are released from emptiness.

Five Verses Following the Rhyme of Miaopu[58]

19. When I observe Chinese laypeople and monks,
     Those who can light the lamp within the room are few.[59]
     And yet the transmitted flame is not concealed.
     When blood keeps dripping the great earth is frozen.

20. You came here and deeply matched clear understanding.
     Your entire body nakedly exposes the sound of the intimate
         function.
     Your joyous aspiration pierces the heavens
         and dissolves male and female.
     Practice with hands held together does not ask after names.[60]

21. Every bit of your sincere heart pervades the heavens.
     You've directly awakened at once from a thousand dreams.
     But unless you clarify three, eight, nine with your whole body,
     After one doubt will come another.[61]

---

probably was a miscopy. The sneeze would seem to refer to some specific event, and a consequent realization.

58 According to Menzan, Miaopu was a nun who visited Dōgen at Tiantong and gave him poems.

59 "Within the room" refers to meeting face to face with the teacher. Lighting the lamp might be an image of Dharma transmission, or simply of thorough practice.

60 This poem, assuming Menzan is right that Miaopu was a woman, might be read as suggestive. But the focus on dissolving the difference between male and female recalls Shōbō-genzō Raihai Tokuzui (Making Prostrations and Attaining the Marrow), in which Dōgen strongly espouses the equality of men and women in practice. See Cook, *How to Raise an Ox,* pp. 97–110.

61 "Three, eight, nine" may just refer to the multiplicity of different kinds.

22. The passing world is like a dream; stop seeking its traces.
     When the cuckoo sings, it lowers its head,
     But who would retreat on the path returning home?[62]
     People of the whole wide earth, do not ask how long the journey.

23. The original mind ground is fundamentally peaceful,
     With nothing to inquire about, naturally spiritual.
     Study this thoroughly, forgetting to call it ordinary or sacred.
     Why did Yellow Face trouble to see the bright star?[63]

Two Verses Responding to the Rhyme of Inspector Wang

24. The means for cutting off the various streams are many.
     Seeing this, who would not return home to the ancestral shrine?
     The voice of streams and color of mountains
          display the bright function.
     Quickly awaken when spring arrives among people.

25. Words and silence are completely the same,
          pervading the deep wonder.
     The previously offered good prescription
     Pierces the heavens and embraces the earth without bounds.
     The steep lofty ground is filled with spiritual radiance.

Two Verses Seeing the Death Statement of [Kaku]nen

26. Vast emptiness, nothing holy is as hard as iron.[64]
     But placing [him] into the red furnace, he melts like snow.

---

62 Cuckoo is a common translation for the *hototogisu* bird in Japanese, whose song is said to sound like the Chinese words for "never return." These two lines might also be read, "When the cuckoo sings, I lower my head, / Who would have me retreat from the path and return home?"

63 Yellow Face is a name for the Buddha, Siddhartha Gautama, who was raised in Kapilavastu, which means "yellow castle."

64 It is speculated by modern scholars such as Dōshū Ōkubo that the person named Nen in the heading for these two verses refers to Kakunen, a Kenninji monk who was one of four from Kenninji who went to China, including Dōgen, his teacher Myōzen, and a monk named Kōshō. Presumably Kakunen died in China like Myōzen, although there are no records of this. This identification is a reasonable speculation because "Kakunen" means

And now I ask, to where have you returned?
With the green waves deep, what moon do you see?

27. He's melted like a piece of iron,
     Gone we don't know where, like snowflakes.
     The jade rabbit in the sky is not down in the pool's depths.
     Why not cease your finger pointing, and see the real moon?[65]

Continuing the Previous Rhyme from Mount Potalaka[66]

28. The ocean waves crash like thunder below the cliff.
     I strain my ears and see the face of Kanjizai.[67]
     Upholding this, who could measure the ocean of merit?[68]
     Just turn your eyes and see the blue mountain.

Given to Zen Person, Monk Miaozhen of Song China

29. Appearing before my eyes is wondrous suchness.[69]
     Outside of this reality, why trouble dividing true from false?

"vast emptiness." See Kodera, *Dōgen's Formative Years in China*, pp. 33–35. "Vast empti-ness" is also the famous legendary reply that Bodhidharma gave in response to Emperor Wu's question about the highest meaning of the holy truth. See Cleary and Cleary, *Blue Cliff Record*, case 1, pp. 1–9. But in this verse Dōgen seems to be noting how Kakunen, a person hard as iron, melted like snow during his cremation.

65 This refers to the old Zen saying, not to confuse the finger pointing to the moon with the moon itself.

66 Mount Potalaka (Ch.: Butuolujie; Jap.: Hōdaraka) is the legendary sacred place of the bodhisattva of compassion Avalokiteśvara (Ch.: Guanyin; Jap.: Kannon), associated in China with an island off the coast of Ningbo. Apparently Dōgen visited this island. In his version, Manzan places this poem 28 after number 45 below, also written there, presum-ably the "previous rhyme."

67 Kanjizai (Ch.: Guanzizai) is one name for this bodhisattva of compassion, meaning "one who sees freely."

68 "Ocean of merit" refers to the closing lines of the closing verse of the Sutra Invoking Avalokiteśvara, chapter 25 in the Lotus Sutra: "Eyes of compassion, beholding sentient beings, assemble a boundless ocean of merit." See Hurvitz, *Scripture of the Lotus Blossom of the Fine Dharma*, p. 319; or Watson, *Lotus Sutra*, p. 305.

69 "Wondrous suchness" *(myō shinnyō)* is a play on the name of this monk, Wondrous Truth (Ch.: Miaozhen; Jap.: Myōshin).

Seeing colors, hearing sounds, both fully verify it.

Stepping forward and turning within both softly cry out the way.

Two Verses Given to Chengzhong[70]

30. After the mist of chaos breaks, the three forces appear,[71]

Complete as this very person's original nature.

People and things thoroughly merge, not separate as two.

Do not let the stone woman worship the three stars.[72]

31. From the beginning the great way has no set tracks.

East, west, south, and north are all the home of sages.

Even when barefoot, [the way is] hard to find.

Those with empty belly are wary of gruel and tea.[73]

Visiting Zen Person Quan, Who Lost His Child

32. When you raise open eyes, your child appears.

Viewed with dry eyes, the teardrops start to flow.

A good occasion has come to turn yourself around.

Do not carelessly let old Yama know.[74]

---

70 Chengzhong was also recipient of verses 12 and 13.

71 The traditional Chinese three forces, or aspects of the world, are heaven, earth, and humans.

72 The three stars, or heavenly guardians, appeared in verse 7. The stone woman, originally meaning a barren woman, is an image used in Zen from Dongshan Liangjie's Song of the Precious Mirror Samādhi, in the line "When the wooden man gets up to sing, the stone woman starts to dance." See Leighton, *Cultivating the Empty Field,* p. 77. Dōgen often used this image; see, for example, Dharma hall discourses 187, 235, and 341. Both stone woman and wooden man are images of stillness springing to life. Here the meaning seems to be that the stone woman has never been at all separate from the three stars, or three forces, and therefore need not worship them.

73 This implies that the great way surrounds us, but we may be too afraid or needy to enjoy it.

74 Yama is the fierce king of the underworld, who judges the next destination of those who die. This verse is unclear, particularly the import of the last line. Manzan's version changes significantly the first two lines to read, "With traces of tears, drop by drop your child appears. / Like existence and nonexistence, the phantom vision ceases."

In Honor of the Realization of the Way at Requiting Compassion Hermitage[75]

33. Penetrating with one reading of the
    Complete Enlightenment and Śūraṅgama,[76]
    Within Requiting Compassion hermitage,
      he met the ancient person.
    The whole body through the ages became totally sincere,[77]
    The spring flowers gust and rise without waiting for wind.

Given to Baocian [Requiting Compassion Hermitage]

34. Once illuminated, he's complete without host or guest.[78]
    Turning the light within, the self is humble.
    From the beginning there's not a single thing before or after.
    Right here in his hometown tears of regret do not cease.[79]

Five Verses Given to Assistant Minister Wang[80]

35. When seeking and inquiring ends,
      you understand the ups and downs.
    From the beginning it is clear and bright, nothing to polish.

75 "Requiting Compassion Hermitage" is the translation of the name of a person, Baocian, but also refers to his hermitage.

76 Both the Complete Enlightenment Sutra and the Śūraṅgama Sūtra were popular in China. But Dōgen elsewhere questions their authenticity, as they seemed to him to have been written in China rather than India. In Hōkyōki, Tiantong Rujing agrees with Dōgen, as do modern historical scholars now. See Kodera, *Dōgen's Formative Years in China*, pp. 121, 176; and Shōbōgenzō Tenbōrin (Turning the Dharma Wheel), in Tanahashi, *Enlightenment Unfolds*, pp. 197–198. For the Complete Enlightenment Sutra see Muller, *Sutra of Perfect Enlightenment*. The Śūraṅgama Sūtra is different from the Śūraṃgama Samādhi Sūtra, which is an authentically Indian, early Yogācāra sutra. For part of the Śūraṅgama Sūtra, see Lu K'uan Yu, *The Secrets of Chinese Meditation* (New York: Samuel Weiser, 1964), pp. 15–42. For the Śūraṃgama Samādhi Sūtra, see Étienne Lamotte, *Śūraṃgamasamādhisūtra: The Concentration of Heroic Progress: An Early Mahāyāna Buddhist Scripture*, trans. Sara Boin-Webb (Richmond, Surrey: Curzon Press, 1998).

77 The word we translate as "sincere" literally means red, and here is probably short for *seksihin* (red heart), which implies sincere or loyal heart or mind.

78 Without host or guest here implies no subject/object separation.

79 The regret would have been for having searched elsewhere.

80 This might perhaps be the same person to whom verses 16, 17, 24, and 25 were written.

Returning to the original source, still stuck on the path,
If you roam vainly along the way, many people will laugh.

36. Tearing apart the great flower,
        transcending delusion and enlightenment,
     Before your eyes there are no things to equalize.
     The turning function is hasty, and peacefully transforming.
     Viewing the sky in deep night, the Big Dipper is low.

37. The wonder's been expounded and the mystery discussed,
        but who can reach them?
     Forgetting words and quietly sitting,
        the mouth is straight as a wire.[81]
     A good teacher penetrates both essence and expression.
     On the hundred grass-tips, the radiance glistens.

38. The three paths and six realms tower high and steep.[82]
     The restless wind of their coming and going pierces the heart.
     When we observe with true eyes, an occasion is realized
     For third sons of Chang or fourth of Li, even in old age.[83]

39. In the world all endlessly waxes and wanes.
     Arriving here, who understands without confusion?
     The iron ox chains up the waters in the rivers and sky,
     From the crown of Vairocana, all the way down to his feet.[84]

---

81 A more literal translation of the line ending is "the mouth is like an awl." This probably means that the mouth is straight and shut, i.e. "straight as a wire" (rather than penetrating, the more common metaphorical use of the awl). Manzan also found the original problematic, and changed his version to "the mouth like a mallet," i.e., closed and solid. Manzan altered this verse extensively.

82 The six realms of transmigration within the karmic world are heavenly beings, angry deities (asuras), humans, animals, hungry ghosts, and hell-dwellers. The three paths are just the last three lower realms, merely a repetition in this line.

83 "Third son of Chang" and "fourth son of Li" are references to common people (like Smith and Jones). The point seems to be that even common people find an opportunity for release when seeing truly.

84 The iron ox is sometimes used in Zen as an image for someone with complete

Following the Rhyme of Provincial Supervisor Li

40.   The spiritual light leaves no trace.
      Who would bind it to remain in the condition
          of common or sage?
      Let us wait until the next life to meet again.
      Stop seeking to vainly lift up the ship of this life.
      The winds of compassion pervade universally,
      The waters of virtue flow out, extending beyond the heavens.
      I will always remember your lofty brilliance pulling me forward.
      Why shall we labor and strive to make a new carriage?[85]

Following the Rhyme of Official Wang Haopu

41.   Aside from just this, why seek a place of truth?
      When spiritual function starts, past karma is lost.
      Arriving here, who's released from binds of emptiness?
      Without a body, don't ask to discuss sickness.

Given to My Countryman, Elder [Ryū]zen[86]

42.   You laid down your monk's staff, crystal clear without budging.
      Your effort engaging the way is naturally perfect.
      Many days passed since turning your eyes to reverse the light.
      Years piled up since taking the backward step
          and transforming yourself.

---

practice. It also refers to a legendary statue of an ox supposedly built by the founding emperor of the Xia dynasty, around 2,200 B.C.E., which was supposed to keep the waters of the Yellow River from flooding. "Rivers and sky" is also used as the name for the Milky Way, and might also be referring to that here. Vairocana is the reality body Buddha, whose body is one with the whole universe.

85 Genryū Kagamishima speculates that Dōgen was politely refusing an invitation to come visit this person, who may have been departing from Mount Tiantong to his distant home.

86 Since he is called a countryman, the "Elder Zen" referred to in this heading is probably Ryūzen, a disciple of Eisai. Ryūzen had gone to China at least eight years before Dōgen, and practiced with him at Mount Tiantong. See Tanahashi, *Moon in a Dewdrop,* p. 191; Kodera, *Dōgen's Formative Years in China,* pp. 42, 120, 175 n. 24. After Ryūzen returned to Japan, he became the second abbot of Kongō Zammai-In temple on Mount Kōya. The founder of that temple, Gyōyū (1163–1241), was a successor of Eisai and became the abbot of Kenninji after Eisai.

You pierced the nostrils of the water buffalo
And opened the buddha ancestors' iron barrier of Zen.
In this life you leaped the bounds of common and sage,
No need to be born a mushroom in the next life.[87]

Replying to Inspector Zhenpeng

43. Bound by karma of causes and conditions,
    a mountain body is made.
    Where the mind remains with illusions, disease is hard to cure.
    The entire body cast away into the red furnace,
    Becoming dead ash, who has regret or doubt?[88]

Responding to the Rhyme Given by Head Monk Si

44. Not truly knowing what is the great way,
    Even releasing the skeleton, you still remain self-centered.[89]
    Wandering here and there, mistaken while coming and going,
    Once you turn back the light and watch, these traces are gone.

Written on the Occasion of Visiting Mount Potalaka in Changguo District[90]

45. [Guanyin is found] amid hearing, considering, practicing,
    and truly verifying the mind,
    Why seek appearances of her sacred face within a cave?
    I proclaim that pilgrims must themselves awaken.
    Guanyin does not abide on Potalaka Mountain.

---

87 "Born a mushroom" refers to a story from the Jingde Transmission of the Lamp, the section on Kānadeva. A monk who had received alms without clarifying the way was reborn as a mushroom that kept regenerating to continue feeding his past donors, a father and son. The son became the successor of Kānadeva. See Ogata, *Transmission of the Lamp*, pp. 29–30.

88 The red furnace is an image of wholehearted practice. Becoming dead ash refers to completely dropped off karmic body and mind.

89 "Releasing the skeleton" here seems to be an image of feeling free from karmic conditions but still harboring self-attachments.

90 See verse 28. Mount Potalaka is the sacred mountain where the Bodhisattva of Compassion Avalokiteśvara (Ch.: Guanyin; Jap.: Kannon) is said to sit, enshrined in a cave-like grotto.

Following the Rhyme of Official Wang

46.　The wondrous way is perfect,
　　　　universally pervading mountains and oceans.
　　　Having treaded over Vairocana's crown,
　　　The whole body is brilliant and clear without bounds.
　　　The simple elegance of this state is rather familiar.

Given to Examination Graduate Ru Qianer[91]

47.　Know that Buddha Dharma is arriving at the mind of emptiness.
　　　It cannot be fully expressed with human words.
　　　When both hearing sounds and seeing colors are dropped off,
　　　It naturally flows through East, West, South, and North.

Two Verses in Response to Military Commander Li of Great Song China[92]

48.　Once I see your brilliant, majestic splendor,
　　　How can I forget beholding your esteemed form?
　　　In the pure wind and bright moon your appearance remains.
　　　The hearts of ten thousand ancients fill this remembrance of you.

49.　Extraordinary and magnanimous, you move people's hearts.
　　　Your mind is an ocean rushing in torrents, surface waves calm,
　　　Perfectly pervading court and commoners without distinctions.
　　　When spring wind arrives, their voices are unified.

Responding to the Rhyme of Assistant Secretary Zhen

50.　We must cherish this time, as our paths will soon part.
　　　For many months, the days and nights have quickly passed.
　　　The spring wind stirs, and clouds come and go.
　　　A thousand showers of evening rain fill the lake.

---

91 Perhaps Ru Qianer's mother and brother are recipients of verses 14 and 18. See also note 56 above.

92 Though not clear, this eminent person's title (Ch.: *shumi;* Jap.: *sūmitsu*) is identified as Head of the Privy Council in dictionaries, but this entailed either a high military position or supervising of the military.

From here on these were written in Japan.[93]

Given to a Student Asking for a Verse

51. Killing and giving life right here has been intimate.[94]
    Who reaches this without turning over the self?
    Moving forward and stepping back, refinement is severed.
    Whatever meets the eye is none other than the truth.

Given to Zen Person Nin from Mount Kōya[95]

52. Polishing a tile to make a mirror depends on effort.
    We should know this is still stuck halfway along the path.
    If you ask the true meaning of coming from the west,
    On the ground gushing forth, shut your mouth and sit.[96]

Eight Verses Given to a Zen Person

53. I strain my ears, raise my head, and wait for the dawn breeze.
    How many times, dreamily herding an ox in the spring rain?
    Who realizes that this intention pierces the heavens?
    Just remain with raising eyebrows and blinking eyes.[97]

---

93 This is a note from the compiler of this volume, Senne. The previous verses were written in China in 1226 and perhaps 1227. The following were written in Kyoto or his temple Kōshōji in nearby Fukakusa after Dōgen's return.

94 "Killing and giving life" is an image of the workings of instruction.

95 Mount Kōya, or Kōyasan, is the headquarters temple complex of the Japanese Shingon (Vajrayana) school. There was a connection between Mount Kōya and Kenninji, where Dōgen resided before and just after his trip to China. See note 86 above.

96 "Gushing forth" is an expression for an experience of great realization.

97 "Raising eyebrows and blinking eyes" is from a statement made by Mazu Daoyi to Yaoshan Weiyan, which Dōgen discusses in Shōbōgenzō Uji (Being-Time). Mazu said, "Sometimes I let him raise his eyebrows and blink his eyes. Sometimes I do not let him raise his eyebrows and blink his eyes. Sometimes letting him raise his eyebrows and blink his eyes is right. Sometimes letting him raise his eyebrows and blink his eyes is not right." Hearing this, Yaoshan had a great realization. See Tanahashi, *Moon in a Dewdrop*, p. 80–83; Waddell and Abe, *Heart of Dōgen's Shōbōgenzō*, pp. 55–58; and Cleary, *Shōbōgenzō: Zen Essays*, p. 108–109.

54. With buddha ancestors always right before our eyes
       from the outset,
    As autumn deepens it's hard to remember the ancient bulwarks.
    In cold of night, lines of flying geese easily break.
    Left and right, only mist fills the sky.

55. Essence and expression are penetrating,
       before we glimpse the ground.[98]
    Arriving at this, who can be at peace?
    Too bad the echo of wind in the pines doesn't reach a deaf ear.
    Dew from bamboo is repeatedly dropping in front of the moon.

56. When the great function turns, the entire sky moves,
    With not a single trace along the pathway.
    Chanting alone up in the tower, moistened with mist,
    Only the moon color dyes the clouds in the autumn rain.

57. Who hates ignorance, which is simply the autumn dew?
    From the beginning, true form is actually within this.
    Its remains are hard to see at the bottom of rushing waters.
    Bound up it's easy to transform the self we receive.

58. Wind in the pines loudly echoes in the summer evening.
    The rustling bamboo raising a clamor, at dawn tears flow.
    Just touching the path, the whole body moves.
    Who would forget the ancient road and lament?

59. Clouds disappearing in the blue sky, a crane's mind at ease;
    Waves constant on the ancient shore, a fish swims slowly.
    Who can focus their eyes on this vague edge?[99]
    From the hundred-foot pole, take another step.

---

98 "Essence and expression are penetrating, before we glimpse the ground" can be read as implying that the essence and expression of the way are already present in zazen before any particular experience, or glimpsing.

99 The edge or boundary here is between the ocean and sky, but also between oneness and multiplicity.

60. The jade person's dream shatters, with dawn clouds excited.
The night's moon vanishes in mist, the remaining dew empty.
Awakening alone on the cold platform
    resembles waiting for mind.
The wind and light do not recollect seeking mind.

Continuing a Rhyme from a Zen Practitioner

61. How much light rain falls from these evening clouds?
Using frost robes and dew pillows, I'm afraid of sunbeams.
How wonderful that sky and waters do not disturb each other.
With whom can I share my wish for this simple elegance?[100]

Given to Ya Jokō Returning to Dazaifu[101]

62. When the entire body turns, see that nothing is outside.
In front and back, three by three,
    the steps have never stopped.[102]
Further, in the ancestral gate there's a special excellent matter.[103]
In the vast sky a single pattern, the moon moves west.[104]

---

100 For this last line we have adapted Manzan's reading, as the meaning of the Monkaku version is very unclear.

101 Ya Jokō, or Yakō, is the official from Kyushu for whom Dōgen wrote Dharma word 5; see volume 8, note 75. That Dharma word was written in 1235, and this verse may be from the same time. See the section on Dōgen's other disciples in the introduction.

102 "In front and back, three by three" is from a story recorded in case 35 of the Hekiganroku. In the story, Wuzhuo Wenxi visits Mañjuśrī on Mount Wutai. Mañjuśrī asks about Buddhism in the south of China. When Wuzhuo asks about practice in the north, where Wutai is located, Mañjuśrī says, "Ordinary and sage dwell together." When asked about the size of the assemblies, Mañjuśrī says, "In front three by three, in back three by three," indicating they are numberless. See Cleary and Cleary, *Blue Cliff Record,* case 35, pp. 216–220. "Steps never stopped" may refer to Ya Jokō having walked from Kyushu in the south to Kyoto for this visit.

103 When asked what was the "special excellent matter," Baizhang said, "sitting alone on Great Hero Peak." See Dharma hall discourse 147.

104 The moon moving west may allude to Ya Jokō's return to Kyushu.

Given to a Zen Person Asking for a Verse

63. This mind itself is Buddha;
    Practice is difficult, expounding is easy.
    No mind, no Buddha;
    Expounding is difficult, practice is easy.[105]

Given to a Zen Person Asking for a Verse

64. Visiting teachers to ask about the way is practicing Zen.
    This state of fine simplicity is transmitted from the ancients.
    Who would begrudge [crossing] many thousands
        of rivers and mountains?
    Returning home, the ground beneath your feet is always good.

Six Verses at the Time of Leisurely Seclusion[106]

65. Though settled, no longer picking up or discarding,[107]
    At the same time before me myriad things appear.
    [Within] Buddha Dharma, from now on
        [seeking] mind's abandoned.
    After this my activity will just follow conditions.

66. Last night the wooden man broke from his roots and left.[108]
    How the pillars and lanterns yearn for his kindness.

---

105 "This mind itself is Buddha" and "No mind no Buddha" are famous sayings of Mazu, frequently discussed by Dōgen. See kōan case 75 and volume 9, note 156, for references. See also Dharma hall discourses 8 and 319 and Dharma word 9. See also note 46 above to verse 20 in Dōgen's verses on portraits of himself. This comment in verse 63 is one of Dōgen's most concise—very clear and helpful.

106 "Leisurely seclusion," or idle living, goes back to a saying by Confucius, and in Buddhism refers to seclusion while not established in residence at a temple. Here it probably refers to the years 1230–33 when Dōgen dwelled at Anyō-In temple at Fukakusa after leaving Kenninji but before establishing Kōshōji.

107 "No longer picking up or discarding" refers to not choosing in practice, even between enlightenment and delusion. Manzan changes the first line to "Forgetting both picking up and discarding, my thoughts are settled."

108 "Wooden man" is literally "wooden person." But this might likely be a reference to the wooden man and stone woman of Dongshan Liangjie's Song of the Precious Mirror Samādhi. See Dharma hall discourse 187 and volume 3, note 5. "Roots" might refer to

Those who share the same way know going beyond the world.
Do not allow this movement to overturn heaven and earth.

67. Encountering whatever meets the eye, all is intimate.
    In sitting, lying, or walking meditation,
        the body is completely real.
    When someone asks the meaning of this,
    A speck of dust [appears] within the Dharma eye treasury.[109]

68. The great function manifests and hits our eyes afresh.
    And yet, how can we present this truth?
    A sad person should not speak to sad people.
    Talking to sad people, sadness will kill them.[110]

69. In birth and death we sympathize with ceasing then arising.
    Both deluded and awakened paths proceed within a dream.
    And yet there's something difficult to forget,
    In leisurely seclusion at Fukakusa, sound of evening rain.[111]

70. Cool wind just blew through, awakening echoes of autumn.
    The weather, refreshing and clear, bears new fruit.
    Bearing new fruit, fragrance fills the world.
    Where we cannot escape, we intimately hear.

---

sense faculties, attachment to which he is getting free from, but also the image here might refer to a wooden person, like a tree, leaving its roots, like home-leaver monks.

109 The last two lines might also be read, "If someone asks the meaning of this: / Within the Dharma eye treasury is a speck of dust." This might imply that all phenomena, or dusts, are included in the intimacy of the Dharma eye treasury.

110 The last two lines appear as an added saying in Hekiganroku, case 3, and Shōyōroku, case 30. See Cleary and Cleary, *Blue Cliff Record,* p. 20; and Cleary, *Book of Serenity,* p. 135.

111 The sound of rain is pleasant, but it recalls the tears of sadness of birth and death, which Dōgen will not forget, even in peaceful seclusion. Although we do not agree with their interpretation, a few people have read this verse as expressing Dōgen's fond memory of the sound of rain in Fukakusa after moving to Eiheiji.

Snowy Night in Spring

71. Peach and plum blossoms under snow and frost
    are not what I love.
In green pines and emerald bamboo, so much cloudy mist.
Even though not yet stained with chicken skin and crane hair,[112]
For some decades I have abandoned fame and gain.

72. Snow piles up like at Shaolin, resembling ancient times.
The entire sky, entire earth, entire spring is new.
Robe transmitted and marrow attained,
    one becomes an ancestor.
Who would cherish the body, while standing in snow all night?[113]

Great Teacher Śākyamuni dwelled in the world for eighty years, stayed in the womb for eighty years, had a True Dharma Age of eighty years, had a Semblance Dharma Age of eighty years, had a decayed Final Dharma Age of eighty years, and expounded the Dharma for eighty years. Although this is so, none lacking the eight points, all buddhas practice together. Today is his birthday, and I congratulate all his descendants.[114]

73. Late at night a crow's head is covered with snow.
At dawn a deaf person ladles water and calls it a spring.[115]

---

112 "Chicken skin and crane hair," wrinkled and white, are images of old age.

113 This poem refers to the second ancestor, Dazu Huike, who stood all night in the snow at Shaolin to receive teaching from Bodhidharma, and later attained his marrow.

114 The True Dharma Age, Semblance Dharma Age, and Final Dharma Age are stages of the teachings described for all buddhas. The Final Dharma Age, thought to have arrived, was a major concern for many of Dōgen's contemporaries, who lamented the decay of their times. Dōgen here mocks this concern by equating all three ages with Śākyamuni's life-span of eighty years. The eight points of all buddhas are the passages in the life of a buddha: descending from Tuṣita Heaven, entering the womb, being born, leaving home, conquering Māra, accomplishing the way, turning the Dharma wheel, and passing away into nirvāṇa.

115 A black crow covered with snow, and a deaf person, might represent awareness before differentiation, either of black and white, or of sounds.

This family's food different from that of other countries,
Ten feet of pond heart is ten feet of lotus.[116]

The fifteenth night [full moon] of the eighth month, facing the moon each person [in the assembly] composed a verse about the moon. This moon is not the moon of the heart, not the moon in the sky, not yesterday's moon, not the night moon, not the round moon, and not the crescent moon. I suppose it is the autumn moon. How is it?

74.   Although golden waves are not calm,
          [the moon] lodges in the river.
      In refreshing air it shines on high, and all the ground is autumn.
      Reed flowers on the Wei River, snow on Song Peak,[117]
      Who would resent the endlessness of the long night?

Speaking of Aspirations with Brother Monks on the Ninth Day of the Ninth Month

75.   Last year on the ninth month, leaving this place.
      This year on the ninth month, coming from this place.[118]
      Stop dwelling on passing days, months, and years.
      Look with delight in the undergrowth
          where chrysanthemums bloom.[119]

116 This image seems to be of a lotus blossom as wide as the pond, in this case one *jō,* or about ten feet.

117 Dazu Huike lived by the Wei River. Song Peak was the site of Bodhidharma's temple at Shaolin.

118 "This place" refers to the ultimate reality, not separate from this concrete reality, as expressed in everyday mind. Dōgen uses a similar expression in Shōbōgenzō Shinjingakudō (Body-and-Mind Study of the Way). See Tanahashi, *Moon in a Dewdrop,* p. 91.

119 "Undergrowth" is *sō,* or shrubbery, also referring to the monastery, *sōrin.*

Seeing the Brother Monks Speaking of Their Aspirations
on the Winter [Solstice] Night, the Teacher Dōgen Joined In

76.   Over more than twenty-one hundred years,
        In India and China so much has passed, yet Dharma remains.[120]
        Although the robe transmitted by buddha ancestors
            is all pervading,
        I sympathize with clouds and water monks
            in bitter cold wintry night.

Composed Once While Staying at Kamakura in Sagami Province
in the Time of Hearing Exciting Insects[121]

77.   For half a year I've eaten rice in a white-robed person's house.[122]
        On an old tree, plums blossom amid snow and frost.
        Exciting insects, a thunderbolt crashes and roars.
        Spring colors of the emperor's country, red peach blossoms.[123]

120 "Twenty-one hundred years" is the time that was thought to have passed by Dōgen's contemporaries since Śākyamuni's passing away into nirvāṇa. By modern historical reckoning it had only been sixteen or seventeen hundred years.

121 "Exciting Insects" refers to insects awakening underground from hibernation, and is the name for one of the traditional East Asian twenty-four seasons of the year, roughly the first two weeks during the second lunar month. Dōgen was in Kamakura from the eighth month of 1247 to the third month of 1248. See Dharma hall discourse 251. So this poem was written during the second month of 1248.

122 White robes are the garb of Buddhist laypeople according to a tradition going back to India and China.

123 This poem is patterned after a poem by Dōgen's teacher Tiantong Rujing, especially the last line, which in Rujing's version reads, "Spring colors of the emperor's country, red apricot blossoms." The spring "colors" include the insects and thunder. The "emperor's country" might refer to the capital, which Kamakura had become only a little while before Dōgen's birth. However, it might also refer to the ancient capital, Kyoto, where the emperor still lived, or to Eiheiji, for which Dōgen was perhaps longing.

From Here On, All Verses Were Composed in Echizen

Memorial Day for Tenman Tenjin; Following His Original Verse on Seeing Plum Blossoms on a Moonlit Night[124]

78. How would spring pines fear snow of severe winters?
    On an old tree, plum blossoms fly like stars.
    Heavenly beings and people are all within the three realms.[125]
    Eyeballs and nostrils see the mysterious fragrance.

Presented to the Assembly in the Middle [Full Moon Day]
of the Sixth Month

79. Pull yourself by your own nose.[126]
    Summer practice period is for painting a scroll.
    From now on, only thirty days remain.
    Directly make diligent effort to save your head from fire.

124 Tenman Tenjin, literally "Heavenly Spirit Filling Heaven," is the spirit name given to Sugawara Michizane when he became a Shinto deity after his death. Michizane (845–903) was a famous poet, scholar, calligrapher, and high government minister who was banished from the capital, Kyoto, to Kyushu by jealous government rivals. After he died in exile, storms, fires, disease, and other disasters hit the capital, until Michizane was designated a Shinto *kami,* or deity, and offerings were made to soothe his angry spirit. Many shrines to him still remain. In the text of Eihei Kōroku, after this heading is a note by the compiler, presumably Senne. It reads, "In the second year of Saikō [855], Tenjin was ten years old, and saw plum blossoms in a moonlit night. For the first time he stated his mind in verse. His verse read, 'The moon glitters like clear snow. / The plum blossoms are like shining stars. / How moving is the turning of golden mirror [moon], / In the garden, fragrant jeweled clusters.'" According to Kenzeiki, the first biography of Dōgen, compiled in the fifteenth century, there was a Tenmangu shrine to Tenjin in the same village as Yoshiminedera temple, where Dōgen stayed in Echizen before Eiheiji was built. On the memorial day for Tenjin, the twenty-fifth day of the second month, in 1244, Dōgen is said to have visited this shrine and seen this poem by Michizane. Then Dōgen composed the following verse 78.

125 "Heavenly beings" here refers to Tenjin, who became a heavenly deity or spirit by decree. But that is still within the karmic realms.

126 "Pull yourself by your own nose" is an expression for self-reliant practice. See Dharma hall discourses 131 and 238 and volume 2, note 23.

Fifteenth Night of the Eighth Month

80. Echizen moon over Echizen mountains, how bright!
     In the whole cloudless sky its spreading radiance is clear.
     Traces are ended of recognizing reflections but missing the real.
     Late at night, the higher it gets, the brighter.

When Master Tiantong Rujing dwelled at Qingliang temple, in mid-autumn he spoke to the assembly and said, "Clouds disperse in the autumn sky. This very mind watches the moon." He raised his whisk and said, "Look!"[127] *The teacher Dōgen together with his brother monks, divided the three parts [of this Dharma hall discourse from Rujing], and gave appreciation for them over three nights.*

The Night of the Fifteenth;
Verse on "Clouds disperse in the autumn sky."

81. Morning clouds reach the peaks and finally night ends.
     All mountains and the whole ocean are within the round moon.
     Do not let direct pointing [at the moon]
          symbolize heaven and earth.
     A horse in the single sky of autumn is empty.[128]

The Night of the Sixteenth;
Verse on "This very mind watches the moon."

82. We hold up this kōan on the sixteenth night.
     Wishing for fullness of the moon's body,
          you miss moon of mind.

---

127 Tiantong Rujing resided at Qingliang for some period beginning in 1210. He was abbot at three other temples before coming to Mount Tiantong in 1225, soon before meeting Dōgen. The following sentence, and the one in the text following note 131, were inserted by the compiler.

128 This last line is unclear. The character *kū,* which appears twice, can be read as meaning sky or emptiness. Perhaps even a horse appearing in the sky would vanish like the clouds. Although how exactly this is so is unclear to us, these last two lines may well refer to a quote by Zhuangzi, cited in Dharma hall discourse 401 and in Verse on Portraits of Himself *jisan* 12; see note 32 above. The quote is "Heaven and earth is one finger, the ten thousand things one horse." See Hamill and Seaton, *Essential Chuang Tzu,* p. 12; and Watson, *Complete Works of Chuang Tzu,* p. 40.

Seeing the moon somewhat clearly, just then moon is born.
How can we grasp the moon in mid-autumn?

The Night of the Seventeenth;
Verse on Raising His Whisk and Saying, "Look!"
83.   With no fog or mist, and no green waves,
      There is toad or rabbit [of the moon], cold to the bone.[129]
      People cherish [the moon], even hidden by mountains,
            reflected in waters.
      He raised [his whisk] and fooled the heavens; look carefully.[130]

When Master Tiantong Rujing dwelled at Qingliang temple, in mid-autumn he spoke to the assembly and said, "Before the gates of each house, the moon shines bright. Practitioners in each place share the bright moon. Riding on a whale, they grasp the moon."[131] *The teacher Dōgen together with his brother monks, divided the three parts [of this Dharma hall discourse from Rujing], and gave appreciation for them over three nights.*

129 As has been mentioned, in East Asia it is said that a toad or rabbit is in the moon, like our man in the moon. The Monkaku version ends, "with cold hair." We are following Manzan, who added "bones," similar to the English expression we use. In Dōgen's Shōbō-genzō Sokushin Zebutsu (This Very Mind Is Buddha), Dōgen says, "Mind as mountains, rivers, and earth is nothing other than mountains, rivers, and earth, with no additional fog or mist. Mind as sun, moon, and stars is nothing other than sun, moon, and stars, with no additional fog or mist." See Nishijima and Cross, *Master Dogen's Shobogenzo*, book 1, pp. 53–54.

130 This fooling (or blinding) the heavens refers to the moon appearing on the end of Rujing's whisk.

131 This quote from Tiantong Rujing follows immediately the quote cited before verse 81, as part of the same Dharma hall discourse by Tiantong Rujing at Qingliang temple. Presumably Dōgen's verses 84, 85, and 86 were given on the same dates as the verses given in verses 81, 82, and 83, but on the mid-autumn moon in the subsequent year (or perhaps some years thereafter). This Dharma hall discourse of Tiantong Rujing's cited here concludes, after this quote before verse 84, with lines referred to below by Dōgen: "Poling the boat that stores the moon, / Suddenly the moon falls in the quiet night. / How laughable; the barbarian monk with front teeth broken." This last line refers to Bodhidharma, who, according to legend, near the end of his life in China was attacked by jealous monks who broke his front teeth and eventually poisoned him.

The Night of the Fifteenth;
Verse on "Before the gates of each house, the moon shines bright."
84. Eyelids cut off, also his front teeth broken,[132]
    He aimed his eyes high to clearly see the moon.
    The toad in the sky's brightness reaches even the black
        mountain.
    Nevertheless, the jade rabbit falls into the demons' cave.[133]

The Night of the Sixteenth;
Verse on "Practitioners in each place share the bright moon."
85. Without discussing south and north or east and west,
    For fifty years I have been riding this moon.[134]
    How regrettable, the silver laurel branch of the heavens
    Is mistakenly called a dried shitstick by people.[135]

The Night of the Seventeenth;
Verse on "Riding on a whale they grasp the moon."
86. Wearing dragon scales, rabbit horns, and turtle hair,
    With falling rain and rising clouds, we see the path is slippery.

132 Among the legends about Bodhidharma, along with his front teeth being broken, it is said that he had cut off his own eyelids and threw them on the ground to prevent himself from falling asleep. Therefore he is sometimes depicted with round bulging eyes. These eyelids are further said to have sprouted and created tea, which helps monks stay awake.

133 The demon cave in the black mountain is from Buddhist mythology, a place where sun and moonlight do not reach. In Zen it is an image of attachment to emptiness. Here Dōgen is describing the moon, and by implication Bodhidharma, shining into the cave of illusion even while also falling into it, an image of bodhisattva practice.

134 If Dōgen meant that he was exactly fifty years old, by Asian reckoning that would have been in 1249. The mid-autumn Dharma hall discourse for that year is number 344, in which Dōgen also uses the image of laurel for the moon. If indeed verses 84, 85, and 86 were from 1249 (only a speculation), then verses 81, 82, and 83 might have been in 1248, the mid-autumn Dharma hall discourse for which is number 277.

135 Silver laurel is a standard image for the moon in East Asia, like the rabbit or the toad. The dried shitstick is Yunmen's answer to "What is Buddha?" This phrase from Yunmen is referred to frequently by Dōgen. See Dharma hall discourses 69 and 88 and volume 1, notes 150 and 185. Dōgen also implies here that the laurel branch of the moon, or Buddha mind, has been misused in this way by people.

Gouging out the empty sky, seeking has not ceased.
Tonight, finally, I grasp the moon in the water.

Six Verses on Snow

87.   Deepening dusk in early winter, dense snow keeps falling.
      On mountains in all directions, [we see] no cypress or pines.
      Stop discussing snow depths, and the sinking gloom.
      I want this to be like Caoxi Peak on Mount Song.[136]

88.   The five-petal flower opens; a sixth [snowflake] petal's added.
      Though daytime with blue sky, it's as if there were no light.
      If someone asks what color I see,
      These are Gautama's old eyes.[137]

89.   With frosting on the snow, it's difficult to say more.
      December plum blossoms gradually covering,
          the ground becomes spotless.
      Although there are three kinds of conduct for patch-robed
          monks,
      In my assembly we all avoid falling into the black mountain.[138]

90.   In our lifetime, false and true, good and bad are confused.
      While playing with the moon, scorning winds,
          and listening to birds,

---

136 Caoxi Peak on Mount Song is where Bodhidharma sat in the cave for years and Dazu Huike stood all night in the snow.

137 "The five-petal flower" refers to the white plum blossom, which opens in winter while there's still snow. The "sixth petal" could imply additional snowfall on the blossoms, and perhaps new awareness. In Shōbōgenzō Baika (Plum Blossoms), Dōgen quotes a poem by Tiantong Rujing that says, "When Gautama's eyeball vanishes, plum blossoms in snow." Later Dōgen adds, "We correctly transmit and accept that plum blossoms in snow are truly the Tathāgata's eyeball." See Tanahashi, *Moon in a Dewdrop*, pp. 115, 116.

138 The three kinds of conduct of monks refers to a saying by Dahui: superior monks practice zazen in the monks' hall; middling monks compose verses about snow; and inferior monks sit around the fire and talk about food. "We all avoid falling into the black mountain" implies that there are no "inferior monks," although Dōgen himself is middling, composing poems about snow.

For many years I merely saw that mountains had snow.

This winter, suddenly I realize that snow completes mountains.[139]

91.   How can the three realms and ten directions be all one color?

Who would discuss the difference

between human and heavenly beings?

Do not convey talk of birds suffering in the cold.[140]

The lake with no heat of anxiety is on the snowy mountain.[141]

92.   An udumbara flower naturally opens on an old tree.[142]

Early plum blossoms erect a sanctuary,

a bright tower in the night.

A silvery pearl net hangs over the entire world.

The ground becomes pure as lapis lazuli.[143]

Two Verses on Winter Solstice

93.   Yesterday was short; today is longer.

Though without edge or corners,

[the solstice] is good to examine.

I encourage you to look closely.

Stop asking for the sun in the sky.

94.   Everywhere you meet him, completing your face.

139 "Mountains had snow" could also be read as "There is snow on the mountains." "Snow completes mountains" might also be read that snow fulfills or creates the mountains.

140 "Birds suffering in the cold" refers to a kind of Himalayan bird that does not build nests and so is particularly cold. This line refers to complaining.

141 "Lake with no heat of anxiety" is a translation from the Sanskrit of "Lake Anavatapta." In traditional Buddhist cosmology, this lake exists in the northern continent, the source of the four great rivers of India. It represents the coolness of liberation. See Akira Sadakata, *Buddhist Cosmology: Philosophy and Origins* (Tokyo: Kōsei Publishing Co., 1997), pp. 31–32.

142 The udumbara flower blooms every three thousand years, on the occasion of a *cakravartin*, or wheel-turning king, being born.

143 "The ground becomes pure as lapis lazuli" is a line from the Lotus Sutra, chap. 6. See Watson, *Lotus Sutra*, p. 108.

Turn your body and head to pervade the heavens.
In this transition, though borrowing the strength
    of the [teacher's] fist,
From the beginning, the effort of your nostrils
    has been to exhale.

Following the Rhyme of a Song from Yue[144]

95. My marrow is sixty liters, and bright as snow.[145]
    I have a thousand eyes, shining like jewels;
    A dragon's activities and a tiger's great roar.
    How could a rabbit or deer survive at a lion's dwelling?

Buddha Completed the Way

96. Catching the morning star, the world glowed red.
    His eyes thundered and broke through empty space.
    He further upheld completion of the way in the Sahā world.[146]
    Everywhere the wind of a wooden ladle blows toward spring.[147]

On a Year with Two Beginnings of Spring[148]

97. The severe winter has not yet ended, but early spring arrives.[149]
    What's the use of stretching out my legs?

144 Yue was a feudal state in what is now Zhejiang, the province of Mount Tiantong.

145 Sixty liters is an approximate equivalent of a hundred *shō*, a traditional East Asian measurement.

146 Upholding completion of the way in the Sahā world, or world of suffering, refers to Buddha's willingness to teach.

147 Dōgen sometimes uses the image of a wooden ladle as a useful implement to represent Buddha; see Dharma hall discourse 320. The wind is an image for Buddha's teaching.

148 Certain years in one of the Chinese lunar calendar systems have two days designated as the beginning of spring. The usual beginning of spring occurs after the regular New Year's Day, and the occasional second beginning falls in the month before New Year's Day. According to Genryū Kagamishima, at the ends of 1248 and 1251 there were second beginnings of spring. He speculates that the year referred to in verse 97 is 1251, in other words, during the twelfth month of 1251. See also Dharma hall discourse 302 from 1248.

149 Here winter could represent practice, and spring awakening. This calendar event can symbolize how these interpenetrate each other.

Leaping from their own natures,
    [winter and spring] merge together;
Within one year, two springs.

While sick on a snowy night, moved by Scribe Gijun's twenty-eight-character [verse], I allowed him to calligraph [my following verse in response].[150]

98.   He climbed high, inquiring about the way
        on a deep snowy night.
    How poignant; his body covered, buried to the waist.[151]
    Though severing heads or arms is depraved,
    A true teacher leaps free from tangles and snakes.

Fifteen Verses on Dwelling in the Mountains

99.   How delightful, mountain dwelling so solitary and tranquil.
    Because of this I always read the Lotus Blossom Sutra.
    With wholehearted vigor under trees, what is there to love or
        hate?[152]
    How enviable; sound of evening rains in deep autumn.

100.   The ancestral way come from the west I transmit east.
    Polishing the moon, cultivating clouds,
        I long for the ancient wind.
    How could red dusts from the mundane world fly up to here?
    Snowy night in the deep mountains in my grass hut.

---

150 Scribe (Jap.: Shoki) Gijun was the former Daruma school monk who had requested Dharma hall discourse 507 as a memorial for Kakuzen Ekan. The "twenty-eight characters" is four lines of seven characters, also the standard form for most of Dōgen's verses here in volume 10.

151 The first line might also refer to Gijun coming to see Dōgen in the snow. But the second and third lines clearly refer to Dazu Huike, standing in the snow waiting for Bodhidharma, then cutting off his own arm.

152 "With wholehearted vigor under trees" is a quote from the Lotus Sutra, chap. 19, "The Merits of Dharma Teachers": "At the foot of trees in a forest, with single-minded vigor sitting in dhyāna." See Hurvitz, *Scripture of the Lotus Blossom of the Fine Dharma*, p. 272.

101. Sitting as the night gets late, sleep not yet arrived,
Ever more I realize engaging the way is best
        in mountain forests.
Sound of valley streams enters my ears;
        moonlight pierces my eyes.
Other than this, not a thought's in my mind.

102. When I love mountains, mountains love their master.
For rocks big and small, how can the way cease?[153]
White clouds and yellow leaves await their time and season.
Already discarded are the nine mundane streams.[154]

103. Grasping source of clouds and passing through water barriers,
[My] face opens in reverence as the [mountain] face displays
        flowers.[155]
Clearly realizing the promise from beginningless kalpas,
Mountains love the master, and I enter the mountains.

104. Staying in mountains, I gradually awaken
        to mountain sounds and colors.
Fruit growing and flowers open,
        I question release from [this] emptiness.
For a while I've wondered, what is the original color?
Blue, yellow, red, and white are all in the painting.

105. For a long while I've abandoned human realms,
        beyond attachments,
Writing with brush and inkstone already discarded.

153 A monk asked Guizong Daoquan, "What is the Buddha Dharma in Nine Peak Mountain?" Daoquan answered, "In this mountain big rocks are big, small rocks are small." See Dharma hall discourses 194 and 502.

154 "The nine mundane streams" refer to nine worldly philosophies including Confucianism, Daoism, Yin-yang, and Legalists.

155 "Displaying flowers" are also the characters for Śākyamuni's "holding up the flower" at Vulture Peak.

Seeing flowers and hearing birdsong brings little attraction.
Though dwelling in mountains, I'm still ashamed
    at my lack of talent.[156]

106. How sad, my faded picture of a figure.
Although over time my eyes and ears have blurred,
There is something difficult to let go and easy to soak in.
At night in my grass hut, sound of autumn rain
    and valley streams.

107. At dusk in late autumn, the weather becomes cool.
Chirping insects under crescent moon bring many feelings.
Late in the quiet night, I gaze up at the Big Dipper.
As dawn approaches, it slides toward the east.

108. A six-meter-square thatched hut is filled with coolness;[157]
Fragrant autumn chrysanthemums can hardly deceive my nose.
How could iron eyes and brass pupils be decayed?[158]
In Echizen I've seen the double yang nine times.[159]

109. Towers in front and pavilions behind stand splendid.
On the peak is a stupa of five or six levels.
Under the moon in cool autumn wind, a crane sleeps standing.
The robe is transmitted at midnight to a monk in zazen.

---

156 Manzan changed this poem. His first line reads, "For a long while I've abided in human realms, beyond attachments." Manzan's fourth line is very different, reading, "I don't mind if people of this time laugh at my lack of talent." This eliminates the irony implied by the Monkaku version, ostensibly Dōgen's original, in which he is ashamed of something he claims to have abandoned.

157 Six meters is literally three *ken*, one *ken* being a little less than two meters.

158 Iron eyes and brass pupils are images of keen, perceptive seeing.

159 "Double yang" refers to the festival on the ninth month of the ninth day, which features viewing chrysanthemums. See also verse 75. Since Dōgen says he has been in Echizen for nine years, this verse is from the ninth month of 1252, and thus one of Dōgen's latest writings.

110. The evening bell rings in moonlight and lanterns are raised.
Training monks sit in the hall and quietly observe emptiness.
Having fortunately attained the three robes,
   now they plant seeds.[160]
How heartwarming, their ripening liberation in the one mind.

111. Grasshopper thinking and insect chirping; how earnest.
Soft breeze and hazy moon are both calm.
Clouds envelop pines and cedars round the old hall by the pond.
By the mountain temple autumn raindrops fall
   on the empress tree.[161]

112. Setting up a lamp and holding a brush, I wish to speak my heart.
From a distance I yearn for India,
   and traces of the founding ancestor.
Our Buddha's transmission of the robe
   commenced this cold valley,
Solitary, not only in winter at Mount Song's Shaolin temple.[162]

113. In a grass hut in the deep mountains and valleys,
Contemplation and zazen cannot be exhausted.
Add even a speck of dust to the high peak of merit.[163]
The Tathāgata's disciples wish for divine power.[164]

---

160 The three monks' robes, literally "rice paddy robes," were traditionally received at ordination. The three had five, seven, and nine strips.

161 The "empress tree" is a paulownia, a common Japanese tree with violet or blue blossoms in spring and beautiful soft wood, said to be the only tree upon which a phoenix will rest.

162 The founding ancestor here refers to Śākyamuni Buddha's disciple Mahākāśyapa. The sense here is that carrying this transmission always can feel like being alone in a cold valley, for Dōgen and those in each generation, as well as for Bodhidharma sitting amid the snows at Shaolin.

163 Adding a speck of dust echoes a line from Dōgen's Instructions for the Tenzo, where it is said not just in the context of measuring ingredients, but also referring to increasing the merit and virtue of practice. See Leighton and Okumura, *Dōgen's Pure Standards for the Zen Community*, p. 35.

164 In Shōbōgenzō Jinzu (Divine Power), Dōgen talks about divine or supernatural power

Verses for the Twelve Hours[165]

Midnight; Hour of the Rat [about 11 P.M.–1 A.M.]
114.   The barbarian knows he has not yet arrived,
            but still has understanding,
        Don't wonder about the robe transmitted before midnight.
        Sit cutting off the apparent within,
            together with reality arriving.[166]
        Turning this over, make your bed and sleep.

Rooster Crows; Hour of the Ox [about 1–3 A.M.]
115.   The entire body resembles the self, and is the entire body.
        How can you make the entire body renew a solitary dream?
        Buddha belly and ancestor womb are both vigorous.
        Covered with hair and crowned with horns,
            we see distant and intimate.[167]

---

in terms of the virtue of everyday activity. See Tanahashi, *Enlightenment Unfolds*, pp. 104–115.

165 In the Chinese system, there were twelve hours of the day, corresponding to the twelve animals of the Chinese zodiac. Dōgen here offers verses on the activities of the monastic schedule throughout the day. A number of Chinese masters wrote similar collections of verses on the twelve hours before Dōgen. For example, see Zhaozhou's amusing verses in Green, *Recorded Sayings of Zen Master Joshu*, pp. 171–174.

166 "The apparent within, together with reality arriving" is an abbreviated reference to the five ranks teaching of Dongshan, founder of the Chinese Sōtō school. These are five interrelationships between the real and apparent (also describable as the ultimate and phenomenal, or universal and particular) aspects of our life and practice. These five have been described in various ways, one list being: the apparent within the real, the real within the apparent, coming from within the real, going within both apparent and real, and arriving within both together. See Leighton, *Cultivating the Empty Field*, pp. 8–11, 62, 76–77; Alfonso Verdu, *Dialectical Aspects in Buddhist Thought: Studies in Sino-Japanese Mahāyāna Idealism* (Lawrence: Center for East Asian Studies, University of Kansas, 1974); and Powell, *Record of Tung-shan*, pp. 61–62.

167 The last line given in the text is the version from the Chinese characters in the Monkaku version, and is adopted by Manzan. If read from the *furigana* (additional markings) in the Monkaku version, which might be from Dōgen himself, it would read, "When covered with hair and crowned with horns, how can you see distant and intimate?" The latter version, as a question, emphasizes no duality or distinction between distant and intimate for all the monks sleeping in the monks' hall at this hour. The version given in the text implies that both the Buddha body and the karmic body coexist.

Before Dawn; Hour of the Tiger [about 3–5 A.M.]

116. Right now the self cannot be deceived.
      Six ears, seven holes, eight cavities—Listen![168]
      Without a mouth the iron hammer simply exhales.
      Still you all exclaim about enlightenment
          with the morning star.[169]

Sun Up; Hour of the Rabbit [about 5–7 A.M.]

117. Trading in your eyeballs, we see each other.
      Drilling your own nostrils, how many thousand times?
      Waiting for daylight in the snowy night, wasn't the valley cold?[170]
      The sun being born is the womb of sunlight.

Breakfast Time; Hour of the Dragon [about 7–9 A.M.]

118. Eat up the monk's hall; swallow the Buddha hall.
      Lofty mind, empty stomach loves the clouds and mist.
      Setting out the bowl in India, wetting it in Korea,
      Without visiting Zhaozhou, filled with rice and tea.

Midmorning; Hour of the Snake [about 9–11 A.M.]

119. Going beyond, nodding the head, the dragon reaches water.
      Body and mind speak together; grass meets with spring.
      Contesting and encountering, there is no other face.
      Striking down length and width, not a bit of dust.

168 The six ears refer to the six sense organs, including the mind faculty that observes thought objects. The seven holes refer to the body's orifices. So altogether this implies the whole body.

169 The end of the third line might be read as "the iron hammer emitting energy." The subject of the last line might be read as "the great person" rather than "all you monks in the assembly." In that case it would refer more directly to Śākyamuni's needing to proclaim his awakening at this hour. Either way, the implication might be that speaking about the realization is superfluous.

170 Manzan changes the third line to "East of the ocean [in Japan] in the snowy dawn, the valley is not cold." Presumably it is not cold because of knowing of impending dawn.

Sun in the South; Hour of the Horse [about 11 A.M.–1 P.M.]

120. This sun at this point is both bright and dark.
      Glistening water and colors of spring shine and saturate the sky.
      Although I have been selling, I also buy.
      At the market there's no stealing, no talk of merit.

Sun Reflected; Hour of the Sheep [about 1–3 P.M.]

121. Within the eye of the sun face is a round moon face.[171]
      Getting a sutra to put over your eyes, your eyes become a sutra.[172]
      With study and mastery, ultimately nothing's outside;
      Clouds in the blue sky, water in a jar.[173]

Afternoon; Hour of the Monkey [about 3–5 P.M.]

122. A foot kicks over oceans and mountains.
      A seamless fist arouses black clouds.
      Suddenly a thunderstorm roars and crashes.
      Reflection while just sitting plays with inner spirit.[174]

171 "Sun face Buddha, moon face Buddha," is the response of Mazu, frequently referred to by Dōgen in Eihei Kōroku, when Mazu was asked about his failing health. See kōan 80 in volume 9.

172 A monk asked Yaoshan why he was reading a sutra, although he had not allowed the monks to do so. Yaoshan said that he was only covering his eyes. This appears in Keitoku Dentōroku, vol. 14. See Wu, *Mind of Chinese Ch'an*, p. 82. The early afternoon period referred to in this verse by Dōgen was when monks read sutras in the study hall.

173 "Clouds in the blue sky, water in a jar" is a saying by Yaoshan in response to the official Li Ao's question, "What is the way?" in Keitoku Dentōroku, vol. 14. See Wu, *Mind of Chinese Ch'an*, p. 82. Dōgen refers to it previously in *shōsan* 15 (see volume 8, note 45) and in his comment to kōan 56 in volume 9.

174 "Reflection while just sitting" refers to this hour in the afternoon, which is spent in zazen in the meditation hall.

Sunset; Hour of the Rooster [about 5–7 P.M.]

123. How stupid to consider your son a thief.[175]
    One arousing aspiration to reach the heavens is hearty.[176]
    If you want to study the exact meaning,
    Gourd vine is entangled with gourd vine.[177]

Twilight; Hour of the Dog [about 7–9 P.M.]

124. How could a dog not have dog nature?
    A frog's whole body is like a frog.
    A barefoot Chinaman learns Chinese walking;
    Persians from the southern ocean offer ivory.[178]

People Settle In; Hour of the Boar [about 9–11 P.M.]

125. Accepting phrases [of teaching] afterward
        is not truly astonishing.
    Presenting something before it functions is knowing with ease.
    People with high spirits have an eye on the tip of their tongue.
    A lion cub returns again to defeat his enemy.[179]

175 This paraphrases a line from the Song of Enlightenment by Yongjia Xuanjie, "To mistake a thief for his own son." See Sheng-yen, *Poems of Enlightenment,* p. 54; and Suzuki, *Manual of Zen Buddhism,* p. 96.

176 "Arousing aspiration to reach the heavens" is also in the first paragraph of Dōgen's Fukanzazengi (Universally Recommended Instructions for Zazen); see the end of volume 8.

177 The image of "gourd vine entangled with gourd vine" is the motif of Dōgen's essay Kattō (Twining Vines). See Tanahashi, *Moon in a Dewdrop,* pp. 168–174.

178 Ivory from elephant tusks arrived from India, but all foreigners in China were called "Persians." This might be a reference to the arrival of Bodhidharma from India.

179 "For people with high spirits, a lion cub returns again to defeat his enemy" is a saying by Nantang Daoxing from the Shūmon Tōyōshū kōan collection. The last line might instead be read as "A lion cub defeats his enemy and returns it to another," referring to getting the teaching and passing it along to others.

CHRONOLOGICAL INDEX OF DHARMA HALL DISCOURSES WITH DATES

THE DHARMA HALL DISCOURSES for which dates are identified (or otherwise known), in volumes 1–7, are listed chronologically by their numbers. These are usually significant, commemorated dates in the monastic or Buddhist calendar. Years are given by their Western calendar equivalent. The month, then day, is given according to the traditional East Asian lunar calendar, in which the full moon is on the 15th day. The first month in this system begins roughly in late January to early March by the Western calendar reckoning.

YEAR AND DISCOURSE #		MONTH/DAY	OCCASION
Volume 1			
1236	1	10/3	
1240	13	8/15	Mid-autumn full moon
	14	10/1	Opening fireplace
	18	10/15	
	25	11/1	Winter solstice
1241	32	1/1	New Year
	42	4/8	Buddha's birthday
	44	4/15	Opening summer practice period
	77	8/15	Mid-autumn full moon
	88	12/8	Enlightenment day

1242	90	1/1	New Year
	98	4/8	Buddha's birthday
	102	7/15	Closing summer practice period
	104	8/1	"Mid-Heaven" festival
	105	8/6	Arrival of Tiantong Rujing Recorded Sayings
	106	8/15	Mid-autumn full moon
	109	10/1	Opening fireplace
	115	11/22	Winter solstice
1243	116	1/1	New Year
	121	2/15	Buddha's parinirvāṇa
	122	3/1	Closing fireplace
	75	4/8	Buddha's birthday [out of order in text]
	118	4/15	Opening summer practice period [out of order in text]
	126	7/?	
		7/18	Departed Kyoto with community, three days after closing the summer practice period

Volume 2

1245	127	4/15	Opening summer practice period
	130	7/15	Closing summer practice period
	135	11/25	Winter solstice
	136	12/8	Enlightenment day
1246	142	1/1	New Year
	146	2/15	Buddha's parinirvāṇa
	152	3/20	

	256	4/8	Buddha's birthday
	257	4/15	Opening summer practice period

Volume 4

	259	4/25	
	261	5/5	
	274	7/17	Memorial for Tiantong Rujing
	277	8/15	Mid-autumn full moon
	279	9/1	Traditional renewed meditation schedule
	288	10/1	Opening fireplace
	296	11/29	Winter solstice
	297	12/8	Enlightenment day
	302	12/25	"Leap year" beginning of spring
1249	303	1/1	New Year
	305	1/10	
	311	2/15	Buddha's parinirvāṇa
	320	4/8	Buddha's birthday
	322	4/15	Opening summer practice period
	324	4/25	
	325	5/1	
	326	5/5	
	341	7/15	Closing summer practice period
	342	7/17	Memorial for Tiantong Rujing
	344	8/15	Mid-autumn full moon

Volume 5

	347	9/1	Traditional renewed meditation schedule

	363	9/2	Memorial for Dōgen's father [out of order in text]
	353	10/1	Opening fireplace
	360	12/8	Enlightenment day
1250	367	2/15	Buddha's parinirvāṇa
	379	6/10	Ceremony to stop rain
	384	7/17	Memorial for Tiantong Rujing
	413	8/15	Mid-autumn full moon [out of order in text]
	389	9/1	Traditional renewed meditation schedule
	396	10/1	Opening fireplace
	406	12/8	Enlightenment day
	392	12/10	Memorial for Dazu Huike's arm [out of order in text]
	409	12/17–19?	Memorial for Dōgen's mother
1251	412	1/15	

Volume 6

	418	2/15	Buddha's parinirvāṇa
	427	4/8	Buddha's birthday
	435	5/27	Memorial for Myōzen
	441	7/5	Memorial for Eisai
	442	7/15	Closing summer practice period
	276	7/17	Memorial for Tiantong Rujing [out of order in text]
	448	8/15	Mid-autumn full moon
	451	9/1	Traditional renewed meditation schedule
	462	10/1	Opening fireplace

Volume 7

	475	12/8	Enlightenment day
	478	12/17–19?	Memorial for Dōgen's mother
1252	481	1/15	
	486	2/15	Buddha's parinirvāṇa
	489	3/1	Closing fireplace
	495	4/8	Buddha's birthday
	504	5/27	Memorial for Myōzen
	505	6/1	Traditional relaxed meditation schedule
	512	7/5	Memorial for Eisai
	514	7/15	Closing summer practice period
	515	7/17	Memorial for Tiantong Rujing
	521	8/15	Mid-autumn full moon
	524	9/2	Memorial for Dōgen's father
	528	10/1	Opening fireplace
	506	12/8	Enlightenment day [out of order in text]

INDEX AND GLOSSARY OF NAMES

NAMES OF PERSONS in *Dōgen's Extensive Record* are given in alphabetical order. Chinese people are listed by their Chinese pinyin transliteration, followed by dates, alternate Wade-Giles Chinese transliteration in brackets, and Japanese pronunciation. Japanese and Indian persons are listed alphabetically by their Japanese and Sanskrit names without Chinese pronunciation. The Japanese version of an Indian name is given when it varies significantly from a direct transliteration. The names and dates are followed by brief biographical identifications and the volume and item numbers where they appear in the text or notes. Notes are designated by *n* plus the note number. For volume 8, items are listed either as IM (informal meetings for the *shosan*), DW (Dharma words for the *hōgo*), or FKZG for Fukanzazengi. Volume 10 items are listed either for *shinsan* verses or *jisan* verses, or just by number for the other verses. Chinese characters for names are given at the end of the glossary in a separate listing for Chinese and Japanese persons, listed alphabetically, for Chinese names in pinyin, and in transliterated Japanese for Japanese persons.

Ajātaśatru [Sanskrit; Japanese: Ajase] (6th cent. B.C.E.). Son of King Bimbisāra, he killed his father but then repented and became Buddha's student. He sponsored the first council after Buddha's death. 6.437.

Ājñātakauṇḍinya [Skt.; Jap.: Anyakyōchinnyo] (6th cent. B.C.E.). He was one of Śākyamuni Buddha's first five disciples, who had accompanied him in his ascetic practices before his awakening. 5.374.

Ānanda [Skt.] (6th cent. B.C.E.). Śākyamuni Buddha's cousin, close disciple, and personal attendant, Ānanda was known for his perfect recall, and the sutras were all dictated by him after Śākyamuni's passing into parinirvāṇa, each with Ānanda's opening, "Thus have I heard..." Ānanda did not awaken until after Buddha's death, when he became the second ancestor after Mahākāśyapa in the Zen lineage. 1.11.n24; 1.46; 3.252; 4.278; 5.384.n72; 5.412.n147; 6.435; 6.444; 7.480; 8.DW4; 8.FKZG.n149; 10.Shinsan4.

Aṅgulimālya [Skt.; Jap.: Ōkutsumara] (6th cent. B.C.E.). A disciple of the Buddha who became an arhat, before his conversion by Śākyamuni he had been a serial killer, and was dissuaded from making the Buddha his hundredth victim. 5.381.

Aniruddha [Skt.; Jap.: Anaritsu] (6th cent. B.C.E.). He was a blind disciple of Śākyamuni. After falling asleep once during a discourse by Śākyamuni, he vowed never to sleep again. Fulfilling this vow, he ruined his eyesight, but also developed the heavenly eye with the supernatural power to see past and future. 5.381.

Asaṅga [Skt.; Jap.: Mujaku] (5th cent.). He was a great Indian teacher and scholar monk, who was a master of Yogācāra teaching and wrote many great Mahāyāna commentaries. Asaṅga is said to have been inspired by the bodhisattva Maitreya, and studied with Maitreya in the Tuṣita Heaven, where Maitreya waits to become the next future Buddha. Asaṅga converted his brother Vasubandhu to the Mahāyāna. 2.180; 5.390.n91; 6.464.n113.

Aśoka [Skt.; Jap.: Aiku] (d. ca. 232 B.C.E.). He was a powerful warrior king who unified India and then became a devout patron of Buddhism, building many temples. 7.530.n131.

Aśvaghoṣa [Skt.; Jap.: Memyō] (1st–2nd cent.?). Buddhist poet and teacher, he is considered the twelfth Indian ancestor in the Zen tradition, two generations before Nāgārjuna. Among texts traditionally though uncertainly attributed to him are the early Mahāyāna classics The Awakening of Faith and The Dharma of Serving Your Teacher. 7.480; 7.525.

Aśvajit [Skt.; Pali: Assaji; Jap.: Asetsuji] (6th cent. B.C.E.). He was one of Śākyamuni Buddha's first five disciples, who had accompanied him in his ascetic practices before his awakening, and later became an arhat. 4.315; 5.381.

Baizhang Huaihai (749–814) [Pai-chang Huai-hai] Hyakujō Ekai. A Dharma successor of Mazu, he was said to have compiled the first regulations for a Zen community, and to have insisted, "A day of no work is a day of no food." Teacher of Huangbo and Guishan, he was also famous for giving a monk's funeral to a fox. 1.6.n11; 1.10.n20; 1.13;

10.Jisan8.n29; 10.26.n64; 10.72.n113; 10.74.n117; 10.84.n131–33; 10.87.n136; 10.98.n.151; 10.112.n162; 10.124.n178.

Bucchi Kakuan (n.d.). He was a Dharma heir of Dainichi Nōnin in the Daruma school, and teacher of Kakuzen Ekan, who became a disciple of Dōgen. 3.185.n1; 5.391.n94; 7.507.n80.

Budai (d. 916) [Pu-tai] Hotei. Legendary as a Chinese incarnation of Maitreya, by which name he is commonly referred to, this is the famous fat jolly Buddha of Chinese temples and restaurants. An historical monk, he wandered the streets with a large sack. 10.Jisan4.

Buddhabhadra [Skt.] (359–429). He was an Indian teacher considered another successor to Bodhidharma's teacher Prajñatāra. Buddhabhadra is said to have come to China and have given transmission to Sengzhao. 7.482.

Buddhamitra [Skt.; Jap.: Fudamitta] (n.d.). He is the ninth Indian ancestor in the Zen tradition. 6.426.n25.

Buddhānandi [Skt.; Jap.: Butsudanandai] (n.d.). He is the eighth Indian ancestor after Śākyamuni in the Zen tradition. 6.426.n25.

Butsuju Myōzen [Jap.] (1184–1225). A Dharma successor of Eisai, he was Dōgen's Japanese teacher and friend, who accompanied Dōgen to China and died there while staying at the Tiantong monastery. Dōgen praised him highly. 6.435; 6.441; 7.504; 9.79.n169; 10.Shinsan5; 10.26.n64.

Caoshan Benji (840–901) [Ts'ao-shan Pên-chi] Sōzan Honjaku. A Dharma heir of Dongshan Liangjie, and sometimes considered the co-founder of the Caodong (Sōtō) school, he developed the five ranks philosophical teachings. 3.217; 4.345.n169; 5.403; 7.531.n132; 9.56; 10.Jisan3.n15.

Changlu Qingliao. See Zhenxie Qingliao.

Changqing Da'an (793–883) [Ch'ang-ch'ing Ta-an] Chōkei Daian. A successor of Baizhang's, Changqing became the second abbot of Guishan. 1.99.n200; 9.11.

Changqing Huiling (854–932) [Ch'ang-ch'ing Hui-ling] Chōkei Eryō. He was a successor of Xuefeng. 9.29; 9.64.

Changsha Jingcen (d. 768) [Ch'ang-sha Ching-ts'ên] Chōsa Keishin. Changsha, a successor of Nanquan and Dharma brother of Zhaozhou, encouraged students to take one step from the top of a hundred-foot pole. 1.12.n30; 1.74; 4.328; 7.504.n77; 7.509; 8.IM13.n.36, n37; 9.42; 9.65; 10.Jisan1.n11.

Changzi Kuang (n.d.) [Ch'ang-szu K'uang] Chōshi Kō. He was a successor of Shitou Xiqian. 7.531n133.

Chengtian Huiyun (n.d.) [Ch'êng-t'ien Hui-yun] Shōten E'un. He was a successor of Xuedou. 1.63.n138.

Chingliang Zhiming (n.d.) [Ch'ing-liang Chih-ming] Seiryō Chimei. He was a successor of Yunmen. 9.70.

Chuanzi Decheng (n.d.) [Ch'uan-tzu Tê-ch'êng] Sensu Tokujō. A Dharma heir of Yaoshan and nicknamed "the boatman," he lived in the world as a ferryman after the persecution of Buddhism in 842. After transmitting the Dharma to Jiashan Shanhui, he overturned his boat and disappeared into the water. 4.277; 4.304; 8.DW8; 9.10; 9.22; 9.28; 9.35.n68.

Cihang Fapo (n.d.) [Si-hang Fa-p'o] Jikō Ryōboku. He was a successor five generations after Huanglong Huinan. 8.IM8; 8.IM11.

Ciming [Shishuang] Quyuan (986–1039) [Tz'u-ming Shih-shuang Ch'ü-yüan] Jimyō [Sekisō] Soen. Student of Fenyang Shanzhao, and teacher of both Yangqi and Huanglong, founders of the two main branches of Linji/Rinzai Zen, Ciming taught at Shishuang Mountain, the temple established by Shishuang Qingzhu. 1.6.n14; 2.128; 4.300.n88.

Cuiwei Wuxue (n.d.) [Ts'ui-wei Wu-hsueh] Suibi Mugaku. He was a successor of Danxia Tianran. 9.35.

Daci Huanzhong (780–862) [Ta-tz'u Huan-chung] Daiji Kanchū. Daci was a successor of Baizhang Huaihai. 1.10; 2.159; 7.498; 8.IM16.

Dahui Zonggao (1089–1163) [Ta-hui Tsung-kao] Daie Sōkō. A Dharma successor of Yuanwu Keqin, famous as a proponent of intent kōan-introspection and huatou kōan practice, and critic of silent illumination meditation, he is a key figure in the Linji/Rinzai lineage. In some writings Dōgen strongly criticized him. Intro; 8.IM7.n24; 9.29.n56; 10.89.n138.

Dainichi Nōnin [Jap.] (n.d.). He founded the Daruma school, an early Japanese Zen movement before Dōgen. Many of the monks in his school later became important disciples of Dōgen. Intro; 3.185.n1.

Dajian Huineng (638–713) [Ta-chien Hui-nêng] Daikan Enō. The famous sixth ancestor of Chan (five generations after the founder Bodhidharma), whose biography and teachings were expounded in the

Platform Sutra of the Sixth Ancestor. The sixth ancestor is a primary
example in Zen of a humble, illiterate person who realizes complete
awakening. He is also referred to as Caoxi (Sōkei in Japanese), the
name of the mountain where he taught. 1.3.n6; 1.53.n127; 1.126;
2.136.n49; 3.198.n21; 3.212; 4.260; 4.298.n84; 4.301.n92; 4.304;
4.320.n126; 5.369; 5.374; 5.383; 5.387; 6.430; 6.431; 6.454.n90;
6.457.n100; 6.470; 7.486; 7.490; 7.491; 7.497.n61; 7.525.n119;
7.526.n120; 8.IM2; 8.IM13; 8.IM17; 8.DW3; 8.DW5; 8.DW11;
8.DW13.n121; 8.DW14; 8.FKZG.n150; 9.7; 9.8; 9.18.n32; 9.19; 9.59.

Daman Hongren (602–675) [Ta-man Hung-jen] Daiman Kōnin. The
fifth Chinese ancestor, he was also known as Huangmei after the name
of his mountain. 1.55; 1.126; 3.212.n40; 3.244; 4.260; 5.369; 6.430; 6.431;
6.454.n90; 7.483; 7.497; 7.525; 8.IM2; 8.DW3; 8.DW11; 9.7.

Damei Fachang (752–839) [Ta-mei Fa-ch'ang] Daibai Hōjō. He was a
Dharma successor of Mazu Daoyi. 1.8; 4.319; 8.DW9; 10.Jisan20.

Danxia Tianran (739–824) [Tan-hsia T'ien-jan] Tanka Tennen. A student of Shitou, Danxia is famous for burning a buddha statue to warm
himself. His second generation successor was Touzi Datong. 3.199;
6.462; 8.DW14.n129.

Danxia Zichun (1064–1117) [Tan-hsia Tzu-ch'un] Tanka Shijun. A successor of Furong Daokai in the Caodong/Sōtō lineage, he was
Hongzhi's teacher. 2.128; 3.256; 9.88; 9.90.

Danyuan Yingzhen (n.d.) [Tan-yüan Ying-chên] Tangen Ōshin. He was
Dharma heir of National Teacher Nanyang Huizhong. 1.1.n3;
8.DW14.

Daofu (n.d.) [Tao-fu] Dōfuku. He was one of the four main disciples of
Bodhidharma. 1.46.

Daosheng (ca. 360–434) [Tao-sheng] Dōshō. A disciple of the great Central Asian translator Kumārajīva, Daosheng was a brilliant scholar
responsible for many early Chinese commentaries on Mahāyāna sutras,
including the Māhāprajñāpāramitā and the Lotus. He was expelled
from his temple late in life as a purported heretic for declaring that all
beings have Buddha nature, but he was reinstated soon thereafter
when the Mahāparinirvāṇa Sūtra was translated into Chinese and
affirmed his viewpoint. 3.194.n16.

Daowu Yuanzhi (769–835) [Tao-wu Yüan-chih] Dōgo Enchi. Daowu
was a student of Baizhang, then became a Dharma heir of Yaoshan

Weiyen, along with Daowu's biological and Dharma brother Yunyan. A number of dialogues between Daowu and Yunyan remain as kōans, which are especially significant to Dōgen since Yunyan was teacher of the Caodong/Sōtō founder Dongshan Liangjie. 2.161; 3.200.n27; 4.258.n3; 4.277.n33; 4.277.n34; 4.304; 4.305.n101; 4.321.n127; 4.344.n167; 7.521.n106; 8.DW8; 9.12.n21; 9.61.

Daoyu (n.d.) [Tao-yu] Dōiku. He was one of the four main disciples of Bodhidharma. 1.46.

Daxiu Zhengjue. See Tiantong Zhengjue.

Dayang Qingxuan (d. 1027) [Ta-yang Ch'ing-hsüan] Taiyō Kyōgen. Friend of Fushan Fayuan, who transmitted Dayang's Caodong lineage to his own student Touzi on Dayang's behalf, after Dayang's death. 9.9.n14; 9.33.

Dayi Daoxin (580–651) [Ta-yi Tao-hsin] Dai-I Dōshin. He is the fourth Chinese ancestor. 1.55; 4.313; 9.6.

Dazu Huike (487–593) [Ta-su Hui-ke] Taiso Eka. The second Chinese ancestor, according to apocryphal legend he is said to have cut off his arm to prove his sincerity to the Chan founder Bodhidharma. Later he inherited Bodhidharma's "marrow" after making prostrations to demonstrate his understanding. Before meeting Bodhidharma his name was Shenguang (Shinkō in Japanese). 1.41.n99; 1.43; 1.80.n174; 2.146.n73; 3.188; 3.241; 4.258; 4.300; 5.349; 5.392; 5.400; 6.445.n72; 6.451.n82; 6.459.n105; 7.482; 7.486; 7.491; 8.IM18; 8.DW5; 8.DW11; 8.DW14; 9.4.n7; 9.5; 9.23.n44; 9.44.n89; 9.89; 10.Shinsan3; 10.72.n113; 10.74.n117; 10.87.n136; 10.98.n.151.

Dazui Fazhen (834–919) [Ta-sui Fa-chen] Daizui Hōshin. He was a successor of Changqing Daan. 9.83.

Deng Yinfeng (n.d.) [Teng Yin-feng] Tō Inbō. A Dharma successor of Mazu, he was very eccentric, famous for dying while standing on his head. 1.31.

Deshan Xuanjian (780–865) [Tê-shan Hsüan-chien] Tokusan Senkan. Teacher of Xuefeng, he is famous for his animated style of teaching by shouts and striking his students. 1.15.n43; 1.84.n179; 1.113.n224; 2.128; 3.233; 4.271; 4.291; 8.DW5; 9.24.

Devadatta [Skt.; Jap.: Daibadatta] (6th cent. B.C.E.). Śākyamuni Buddha's cousin, who after joining his order tried to become his rival, and even tried to have the Buddha killed. 6.437; 8.DW2.

Dignāga [Skt.; Jap.: Jinna] (420–500). An Indian Buddhist logician, he was a disciple of Vasubandhu in the Yogācāra school. 5.402.

Dizang Guichen. See Luohan Dizang Guichen.

Dōgen. See Eihei Dōgen.

Dongan Changcha (n.d.) [Tung-an Ch'ang-ch'a] Dōan Josatsu. He was Dharma heir of a successor of Shishuang Qingzhu. 1.65.n145; 8.IM2.

Dongshan Liangjie (807–869) [Tung-shan Liang-chieh] Tōzan Ryōkai. He was founder of the Caodong/Sōtō lineage, one of the five houses of Chan later transmitted by Dōgen to Japan. Author of the Song of the Precious Mirror Samadhi (Ch.: Baojing Sanmeike; Jap.: Hōkyō Zammaika), the text that established the teaching of the five ranks or degrees as a dialectical underpinning to Caodong practice, Dongshan was Dharma successor of Yunyan, although he also studied with Nanquan and Guishan. His posthumous title was Wupen, "Realizing the Origin." 1.10; 1.61; 1.84.n179; 2.128.n14; 2.130.n21; 3.187.n5; 3.221; 3.224; 3.235.n76; 4.269.n22; 4.273.n26; 4.274.n28; 4.276; 4.279.n40; 4.315; 4.341.n164; 4.345.n170; 5.351; 5.401.n114; 6.452; 6.457.n101; 7.494; 7.498; 8.IM1.n3; 8.IM2; 8.IM6; 8.IM14.n43; 8.DW2; 8.DW2.n62; 8.DW13.n124; 9.9.n14; 9.28.n55; 9.50; 9.52; 9.60; 9.74; 10.Jisan7.n28; 10.Jisan8.n29; 10.30.n72; 10.66.n108; 10.114.n166.

Dongshan Shouchu (910–990) [Tung-shan Shou-ch'u] Tōzan Shusho. He was a successor of Yunmen cited by Dōgen as a model *tenzo*. 1.69.n150; 4.291.n62; 5.405.n126; 7.499.n67; 8.DW11; 9.68.

Dongsi Ruhui (744–823) [Tung-tzu Ju-hui] Tōji Nyo-e. He was a successor of Mazu. Mazu had so many disciples that by the time Ruhui entered, when he took his seat in the monks' hall the sitting platform collapsed. So he was called "Platform-Breaker Hui." 2.162; 4.323.

Ehu Dayi (745–818) [E-hu Ta-I] Gako Daigi. He was a Dharma successor of Mazu. 7.511.

Ehu Zhifu (n.d.) [E-hu Chi-fu] Gako Chifu. He was a successor of Xuefeng. 6.454.

Eihei Dōgen [Jap.] (1200–1253). Founder of the Japanese Sōtō Zen lineage, and of Eiheiji monastery, he was author of Shōbōgenzō, Eihei Shingi, and Eihei Kōroku.

Eihei Gien. See Gien.

Eisai. See Myōan Eisai.

Ejō. See Koun Ejō.

Ekan. See Kakuzen Ekan.

Enni Ben'en [Jap.] (1201–1280). First abbot of the Rinzai monastery Tōfukuji in southwest Kyoto, built near Dōgen's temple Kōshiji, he had studied in China from 1235 to 1241. Intro.

Fachang Yiyu (1005–1081) [Fa-ch'ang Yi-yu] Hōshō Igu. He was a teacher in the Yunmen lineage. 8.DW10.n95.

Fayan Wenyi (885–958) [Fa-yen Wên-yi] Hōgen Mon'eki. Three generations after Xuefeng, the student of Luohan Guichen, Fayan is considered the founder of the Fayan lineage, one of the five houses of classical Chan. 1.15; 1.52; 1.59; 1.101.n202; 3.186; 4.287.n54; 8.DW2; 8.DW11.n109; 8.DW12; 8.DW14.n136; 9.16; 9.84.

Fengxian Daoshen (n.d.) [Fêng-hsien Tao-shên] Hōsen Dōshin. He was a successor of Yunmen. 9.70.

Fengxue Yanzhao (896–973) [Fêng-hsüeh Yen-chao] Fuketsu Enshō. Three generations after Linji, he was a successor of Nanyuan Huiyong. The subsequent Rinzai tradition descends from his lineage, as Yangshan supposedly predicted. He was teacher of Shoushan Xingnian. 1.73.n155; 5.358.n16; 8.DW2.n62.

Fenyang Shanzhao (947–1024) [Fên-yang Shan-chao] Funyō Zenshō. Teacher of Ciming Quyuan, and thus ancestor of all surviving Linji lineages, Fenyang was the first master to add verse commentaries to the old stories or kōans. A student of the Caodong/Sōtō lineage before receiving the Linji/Rinzai transmission from his teacher Shoushan Xingnian, Fenyang introduced the Sōtō five ranks teaching into the Linji tradition. 1.12.n33; 2.128.

Foyan Qingyuan (1067–1120) [Fo-yen Ch'ing-yüan] Butsugen Seion. He was a successor of Wuzu Fayan. 8.IM2.

Fu Dashi (497–569) [Fu Ta-shi] Fu Daishi. Mahāsattva (Great Being) Fu was a legendary lay teacher, said to have met Bodhidharma. 4.325.n139.

Furong [Dayang] Daokai (1043–1118) [Fu-jung Tao-k'ai] Fuyo [Taiyō] Dōkai. Dayang and, later, Furong are both places he taught; although Dōgen refers to him as Dayang, he is more commonly known by the name Furong. The Dharma heir of Touzi Yiqing, Furong was particularly known for revitalizing the monastic standards of the Caodong/Sōtō lineage. He is particularly praised by Dōgen for adamantly refusing the offer of imperial honors and fancy robes. 1.23.n55; 2.128.n14; 2.145.n71; 3.256; 8.IM2; 9.57.

Fushan Fayuan (991–1067) [Fu-shan Fa-yüan] Fusan Hōen. He was Dharma heir of Shexian Guisheng, despite having been previously expelled from Guisheng's assembly. Fushan also saved the Caodong/Sōtō lineage from extinction when Dayang Qingxuan was going to die without a Dharma heir. Fushan was in complete Dharma accord with Dayang, but was unwilling to take on the responsibility of publicly proclaiming the Sōtō style in addition to his Rinzai lineage from Guisheng. However, he was able later to transmit the Sōtō lineage from Dayang to his own student, Touzi Yiqing. 9.33.n63.

Fuxian Renjian (n.d.) [Fu-hsien Jên-chien] Fukusen Ninken. A disciple of Songshan Hui'an in the Northern school, after leaving his teacher he wandered widely, thus receiving the nickname Tengteng, or "Cavorting Freely." 9.16.n28.

Fuxing Fatai (n.d.) [Fo-hsing Fa-t'ai] Busshō Hōtai. He was a successor of Yuanwu. 2.179.

Gao (n.d.) [Kao] Kō. A close disciple of Yaoshan Weiyan, known as Novice (Śāmi) Gao. He received novice precepts, but declined full ordination. Tiantong Rujing referred to Novice Gao when Dōgen inquired about receiving the full vinaya. 6.455.

Gao'an Dayu (n.d.) [Kao-an Ta-yü] Kō'an Daigu. A successor of Guizong Zhichang, two generations after Mazu Dao-I, Gao'an was teacher of the nun Moshan, and also was one of Linji's teachers. 2.160; 7.493; 8.DW2; 9.51.

Gautama. See Śākyamuni.

Gayaśāta [Skt.; Jap.: Kayashata] (1st cent. B.C.E.). Considered the eighteenth Indian ancestor in the Zen lineage, he was successor of Sanghānandi. 4.283.n45.

Gien [Jap.] (d. 1314). One of Dōgen's main disciples, he later received Dharma transmission from Koun Ejō. He compiled volumes 4–6 of Eihei Kōroku, and became the fourth abbot of Eiheiji after Tettsū Gikai. He is also known as Eihei Gien. Intro; 3.185.n1; 5.358.n14; 5.383.n68; 5.406.n128; 5.408.n131; 6.441.n63; 7.475.n8,n10.

Giin. See Kangan Giin.

Gijun [Jap.] (n.d.). Originally a disciple of Kakuzen Ekan, he became a disciple of Dōgen, and later a Dharma successor of Koun Ejō. He stayed for some time to take care of Kōshōji after Dōgen moved to Echizen, and later joined him at Eiheiji. 7.507; 10.98.

Gikai. See Tettsū Gikai.

Guangzhou Zhidao (n.d.) [Kuang-chou Chih-tao] Kōshū Shidō. He was a disciple of the sixth ancestor. Before meeting Huineng he had studied the Mahāparinirvāṇa Sūtra for ten years. 7.486.

Guanzhi Zhixian (d. 895) [Kuan-chih Chih-Hsien] Kankei Shikan. Considered a Dharma heir of Linji, Guanzhi also studied under, and venerated, the nun Moshan Laoran. 9.32.

Guifeng Zongmi (780–841) [Kuei-fêng Tsung-mi] Keihō Shumitsu. He was the fifth ancestor of the Huayan school in China, developed from the Avataṃsaka (Flower Ornament) Sūtra, which they held as the foremost sutra. But Zongmi was also a Chan/Zen lineage holder five generations after the sixth ancestor, and wrote many important sutra commentaries. 3.236.n78; 6.447; 8.DW14.

Guishan Lingyou (771–853) [Kuei-shan Ling-yü] Isan Reiyū. A Dharma heir of Baizhang Huaihai, Guishan was the founder, along with his successor Yangshan Huiji, of one of the five lineages of classical Chinese Zen Buddhism, the Guiyang (Jap.: Igyō) house. Guishan's *Admonitions* is an early warning against laxity in the Zen community. He predicted that in the next life he would become a water buffalo at the foot of the mountain. He is praised frequently by Dōgen. 1.15.n42; 1.17.n48; 1.30; 2.138; 2.159; 2.160; 2.162; 2.164; 3.234; 4.273.n25; 4.274; 4.288.n57; 4.295.n71; 4.296; 4.306.n103; 4.326; 4.340; 5.352; 5.394.n100; 5.401.n114; 5.401.n116; 6.457; 7.528.n126; 8.DW2; 9.12; 9.14; 9.39; 9.40; 9.62; 9.66; 9.69; 9.72.

Guizong Danquan (n.d.) [Kuei-tsang Tan-ch'üan] Kisu Tangon. He was a successor of Dongshan's Dharma heir, Yunju Daoying. 3.224.

Guizong Daoquan (930–985) [Kuei-tsang Tao-ch'üan] Kisū Dōsen. Not much is known of him, although one of his responses was quoted by Tiantong Rujing. 3.194; 7.502; 10.102.n153.

Guizong Huichao (n.d.) [Kuei-tsung Hui-ch'ao] Kisū Echō. He was a successor of Fayan, also known as Cezhen (Jap.: Sakushin). 9.84.

Guizong Zhichang (n. d.) [Kuei-tsung Chi-ch'ang] Kisū Chijō. He was a successor of Mazu and teacher of Gao'an Dayu. 2.163.n112; 4.325.n138; 8.DW2.

Gyōyū [Jap.] (1163–1241). A successor of Eisai and second abbot of Kenninji, he also founded a temple on Mount Koya. 10.42.n86.

Haihui [Baiyun] Shouduan (1025–1072) [Hai-hui Pai-yün Shou-tuan] Kai'e [Haku'un] Shutan. He was primary successor of Yangqi Fanghui and teacher of Wuzu Fayan. 1.17.n45; 1.17.n46; 3.196.

Hangzhou Duofu (n.d.) [Hang-chou To-fu] Kōshū Tafuku. He was a Dharma successor of Zhaozhou. 7.520; 8.IM19.

Hangzhou Tianlong (9th cent.) [Hang-chou Tien-lung] Kōshu Tenryū. He was teacher of Jinhua Juzhi, and began the one-finger technique. 3.211.

Hanshan (8th cent.) [Han-shan] Kanzan. Legendary and beloved Chan poet and "fool," his name means "Cold Mountain," as his poems often describe the hardships of mountain recluse life. Hanshan is said to have lived on Mount Tiantai, although he may have been a layperson. He has often been translated, and is frequently depicted in Zen paintings with his friend Shide. 4.259; 4.324.

Hatano Yoshishige [Jap.] (d. 1258). Dōgen's primary patron, he was a feudal lord who resided in Kamakura and Kyoto but also owned land in Echizen, some of which he donated to build Eiheiji. Dōgen's Shōbōgenzō essay Zenki (Total Dynamic Activity) was presented as a talk at Yoshishige's residence in Kyoto, as he was apparently also a lay student of Dōgen. Yoshishige may have been involved in Dōgen's trip to Kamakura in 1247–48, described in Dharma discourse 251. 5.361; 5.362; 5.366.n29; 8.DW14.n128.

Heshan Wuyin (884–960) [Ho-shan Wu-yin] Kasan Muin. He was two generations after Shishuang Qingzhu in Yaoshan's lineage. 8.DW5.

Hongzhi Zhengjue (1091–1157) [Hung-chih Chêng-chüeh] Wanshi Shōgaku. Hongzhi was successor of Danxia Zichun. He was also called Tiantong Hongzhi, having been abbot at the Tiantong monastery where Dōgen's master Tiantong Rujing later taught. Hongzhi was the most influential Chinese Caodong/Sōtō teacher in the century before Dōgen, and a great influence on Dōgen, who quotes Hongzhi frequently in Eihei Kōroku. A prolific writer, Hongzhi poetically articulated the Sōtō tradition's meditation praxis, known as silent or serene illumination, and he also selected the cases and wrote the verse commentaries that were later compiled into the important kōan collection called the Book of Serenity (Ch.: Congronglu, Jap.: Shōyōroku). Intro; 1.6.n14; 1.10.n20; 1.25.n58; 1.52.n125; 2.128.n15; 2.135; 2.142; 2.145.n71; 2.180.n139; 2.183.n146; 3.186.n3; 3.187.n5; 3.203; 3.206; 3.216; 3.220.n50; 3.222.n56; 3.223.n59; 3.226.n63; 3.227.n64; 3.227.n65; 3.236;

3.242; 3.246; 3.247.n95; 3.256; 3.257; 4.261; 4.264.n11; 4.269; 4.285.n48; 4.296; 4.303; 4.309.n107; 4.320; 4.322; 4.326; 4.337.n158; 4.340.n162; 4.341; 4.344; 5.400.n109; 5.403.n124; 6.418.n8; 6.465.n115; 6.468.n119; 7.481.n21; 7.498; 7.514.n94; 8.IM2; 8.IM3.n9; 8.IM12.n35: 8.IM13.n36; 8.IM20.n56; 8.IM20.n57; 8.DW14.n130; 9.25; 9.73.n149; 9.88.

Hongzhou Shuiliao (n.d.) [Hung-chou Shui-liao] Kōshū Suirō. A successor of Mazu, he awakened and laughed after Mazu kicked him in the chest. Shuiliao laughed ever after. 8.IM6.

Huangbo Xiyun (d. 850) [Huang-po Hsi-yün] Ōbaku Kiun. Dharma heir of Baizhang and teacher of Linji, Huangbo was a tall, imposing figure, known for dynamic teaching, including beating students with a stick. 1.12; 1.50.n120; 1.58; 1.62.n137; 1.125; 2.129; 2.131; 2.160; 3.212.n42; 3.223; 4.291; 4.295.n71; 4.296.n78; 4.304; 4.334; 4.345.n168; 6.423; 6.468; 7.493; 7.497; 7.525; 8.IM6; 8.IM8; 8.DW2; 8.DW11; 8.DW14; 9.44; 9.48; 9.51; 9.82.

Huanglong Huinan (1002–1069) [Huang-lung Hui-nan] Ōryu E'nan. Dharma heir of Ciming Quyuan and teacher of Huitang Zuxin, Huanglong is considered founder of one of the main branches of Rinzai Zen, from which Dōgen's first Zen teacher Myōzen was descended. His posthumous name given by the emperor is Zen Master Pujue, or "Universal Awakening." 1.70.n153; 3.233; 6.414; 6.420; 6.453.n87; 6.470; 8.IM6.n16; 8.IM19.

[Huanglong] Huitang Zuxin (1025–1100) [Hui-t'ang Tsu-hsin] [Ōryu] Maidō Sōshin. Dharma heir of Huanglong Huinan, Huitang taught by raising a fist and saying, "If you call this a fist you've said too much. If you say it's not a fist you do not hit the mark." His honorific name from the emperor is Baojue, or "Jeweled Awakening." 8.DW14.

[Huanglong] Sixin Wuxin (1044–1115) [Ssu-hsin Wu-hsin] [Ōryu] Shishin Goshin. He was Dharma heir of Huanglong Huitang. 6.447.

Huangmei. See Daman Hongren.

Huangting Jian (1045–1105) [Shan-k'u Huang-t'ing Chien] Kōtei Ken. A noted poet, and a government official, who was a lay disciple of Huitang Zuxin, his name as a poet was Shanku, or "Mountain Valley." 8.DW14.

Huguo Shoucheng Jingguo (n.d.) [Hu-kuo Shou-ch'eng Ching-kuo] Gokoku Shuchō Jōka. He was a successor of one of Dongshan

Liangjie's successors, Shushan Kuangren. Jingguo, "Pure Fruit," was an honorific posthumous name given by the emperor. 3.246.

Huineng. See Dajian Huineng.

Huitang Zuxin. See Huanglong Huitang.

Huizhao. See Linji Yixuan. Huizhao, a posthumous name, is Eshō in Japanese.

Jakuen. See Jiyuan.

Jayata [Skt.; Jap.: Shayata]. He is considered twentieth ancestor in the Indian Zen lineage. 7.485; 7.517.

Jianyuan Zhongxing (n.d.) [Chien-yüan Chung-hsing] Zengen Chūkō. He is considered a Dharma heir of Daowu Yuanzhi. 2.161.

Jianzhi Sengcan (d. 606) [Chien-shih Sêng-ts'an] Kanchi Sōsan. The third ancestor of Chan, a leper who was later cured, is said to have died standing up. The still popular long teaching poem "Inscription on Faith in Mind" (Ch.: Hsinhsinming; Jap.: Shinjinmei) is attributed to him. 4.334.n153; 5.371; 6.470; 7.472; 8.FKZG.n148; 9.5; 9.6; 9.43.n85.

Jiashan Shanhui (805–881) [Chia-shan Shan-hui] Kassan Zenne. He was Dharma heir of "the boatman," Chuanzi Dechung, who, after transmitting the Dharma to Jiashan, capsized his boat and disappeared in the water. 1.10.n23; 2.138; 3.222; 4.277.n34; 8.DW8; 9.10; 9.22; 9.28; 9.35.

Jingqi Zhanran (711–782) [Ching-ch'i Chan-jan] Keikei Tan'en. The sixth ancestor of the Chinese Tiantai school, he was the first teacher to say that grasses and trees can become buddhas. 2.151.n86; 5.402.n117.

Jingqing Daofu (868–937) [Ching-ch'ing Tao-fu] Kyōsei Dōfu. He was a successor of Xuefeng. 1.32; 1.39; 1.88.n187; 2.132.

Jingshan Daoqin (714–792) [Ching-shan Tao-ch'in] Kinzan Dōkin. He was a successor in the sixth generation of the Oxhead school, founded by Niutou Farong, a disciple of the fourth ancestor. Jingshan was given the posthumous title Great Awakened Zen Master by the emperor. 3.237.

Jingzhao Mihu (n.d.) [Ching-chao Mi-hu] Keichō Beiko. He was a successor of Guishan. 9.48.

Jinhua Juzhi (n.d.) [Chin-hua Chu-chi] Kinka Gutei. A successor two generations after Damei, he was famous for responding to questions by holding up one finger. 3.211; 8.DW5; 8.DW11; 8.DW14; 8.FKZG.n149.

2.127.n1; 2.135.n44; 2.177.n134; 2.182.n144; 2.184.n148; 3.185.n1; 3.216.n46; 4.261.n8; 4.296.n72; 4.303.n95; 4.320.n125; 4.322.n128; 4.324.n136; 4.326.n141; 5.391.n94; 7.509.n83.

Kumārajīva [Skt.; Jap.: Kumarajū] (344–413). He was the great Central Asian translator of sutras into Chinese, including the Lotus Sutra and Vimalakīrti Sūtra. 2.147.n80; 2.182.n141; 3.194.n16; 5.366.n28; 5.372.n38; 5.408.n132.

Kumārata [Skt.; Jap.: Kumorata] (n.d.). He is considered nineteenth ancestor in the Indian Zen lineage. 7.485; 7.517.

Kyōgō [Jap.] (n.d.). A student of Dōgen who became a successor of Senne, Kyōgō wrote important commentaries on Shōbōgenzō. Intro.

Langye Huijue (n.d.) [Lang-yeh Hui-chüeh] Rōya Ekaku. Langye was a successor of Fenyang Shanzhao in the Linji lineage. 1.12; 4.278; 9.46.

Laozi (6th cent. B.C.E.) [Lao-tzu] Rōshi. Legendary founder of Daoism; he was author of the great philosophical and spiritual classic, the Dao De Qing. 1.25.n58; 2.168.n124; 5.383; 5.401.n112; 6.419.n10.

Lingyun Zhiqin (n.d.) [Ling-yun Chi-ch'in] Reiun Shigon. A successor of Guishan, he is famous for awakening upon viewing peach blossoms. 1.36; 4.308; 4.317; 6.421; 6.457; 9.29; 9.72.

Lingzhao (n.d.) [Ling-chao] Reishō. Daughter of the famed eighth-century Chan adept Layman Pang, she is herself noted as an adept. 1.9.n17; 4.329.n145; 9.9.n13.

Linji Yixuan (d. 867) [Lin-chi Yi-hsüan] Rinzai Gigen. A successor to Huangbo, he is the great, dynamic founder of the Linji/Rinzai branch of Zen. Intro; 1.52.n122; 1.58; 1.102; 1.108.n215; 2.160; 2.166.n121; 3.199; 3.221; 3.233; 4.271; 4.278.n37; 4.291; 4.304; 4.317; 4.334.n154; 4.345.n169; 6.468; 7.493; 7.497.n61; 8.DW2; 8.DW5; 8.DW11; 9.32; 9.51; 10.Jisan20.

Longji Shaoxiu (d. 954) [Lung-chi Shao-hsiu] Ryūsai Shōshu. He was a successor of Luohan Guichen and Dharma brother of Fayan Wenyi. 1.56; 1.101; 6.425.

Longshan (n.d.) [Lung-shan] Ryūzan. A disciple of Mazu who lived as a hermit, he was visited by Dongshan Liangjie. 4.345.n170.

Longtan Chongxin (9th cent.) [Lung-t'an Ch'ung-hsin] Ryōtan Sōshin. Longtan was Deshan's teacher. 1.15.n43; 1.113.n224; 4.291; 9.24; 9.55.

Longya Judun (835–923) [Lung-ye Ru-tun] Ryūge Koton. A successor of Dongshan Liangjie praised by Dōgen as a founding ancestor of the Sōtō lineage. 5.355; 9.60.

Luohan Dizang Guichen (867–928) [Lo-han Te-tsang Kuei-ch'ên] Rakan Jizō Keichin. A successor of Xuansha, he was the teacher of Fayan Wenyi, founder of the Fayan lineage of Chan. Dōgen praises Luohan for his saying "The *tenzo* enters the kitchen." Luohan was also named after his temple, Dizang-yuan, which was named after the great archetypal bodhisattva Dizang (Jap.: Jizō; Earth Storehouse). 1.59; 1.101.n202; 6.415; 6.425; 8.IM15; 9.16; 10.Jisan20.

Luopu Yuanan (834–898) [Lo-p'u Yüan-an] Rakuho Gen'an. Luopu was a successor of Jiashan Shanhui. 1.10; 2.152.n91; 7.498.

Luzu Baoyun (n.d.) [Lu-tsu Pao-yun] Roso Hōun. Luzu was a successor of Mazu. 9.79.

Mahākāśyapa [Skt.; Jap.: Makakashō] (6th cent. B.C.E.). The disciple of Śākyamuni considered to be the first Indian ancestor of Zen, he is said to have received transmission of the true Dharma eye treasury when he smiled at Śākyamuni's twirling of a flower before the assembly at Vulture Peak. He was known as foremost among the disciples in ascetic practice, and legend holds that he is waiting in a Himalayan cave to transmit Śākyamuni's robe to the future Buddha Maitreya. 1.11.n24; 1.27; 1.41.n99; 1.80.n173; 1.99.n199; 2.135; 2.141; 3.188; 3.242; 3.252; 4.278; 4.334; 5.349; 5.381; 5.383; 5.397.n105; 5.400; 6.428; 6.435; 6.441.n65; 6.445.n72; 6.446; 7.483; 7.486; 7.494; 8.IM2; 8.IM20; 8.DW4; 8.DW5; 8.DW11; 8.FKZG.n149; 9.1; 9.44.n88; 10.112.n162.

Manzan Dōhaku [Jap.] (1636–1715). He compiled a version of Eihei Kōroku in 1672. (This version, although consulted, is not the one translated here.) In 1700 Manzan led a reform in Sōtō Zen to return to transmission lineages based on personal connection with teachers, rather than temple lineages. Intro; 1.5.n10; 1.11.n27; 1.17.n46; 1.41.n102; 1.43.n107; 1.48.n116; 1.67.n147; 1.108.n215; 2.137.n52; 2.143.n63; 2.184.n148; 3.218.n49; 5.381.n63; 6.459.n105; 9.41.n81; 9.42.n83; 9.76.n160; 10.Shinsan3.n5; 10.Jisan3.n15; 10.Jisan7.n27; 10.15.n57; 10.28.n66; 10.32.n74; 10.37.n81; 10.61.n100; 10.65.n107; 10.83.n129; 10.105.n156; 10.115.n167; 10.117.n170.

Maudgalyāyana [Skt.; Jap.: Mokuren] (6th cent. B.C.E.). One of Śākyamuni's ten great disciples, he was foremost in the manifestation of supernatural powers. He was *inō* (monks' supervisor) at Venuvana vihāra, the monastery donated by King Bimbisāra. 1.17.n48; 4.271; 5.381.

Māyā [Skt.]. Śākyamuni Buddha's mother, who died in giving birth to him. 4.320; 6.427; 7.495.

Mazu Daoyi (709–788) [Ma-tsu Tao-i] Baso Dōitsu. A successor two generations after the sixth ancestor, Huineng, he was the great master of his time along with Shitou, and had 139 awakened disciples, including Baizhang and Nanquan. An instigator of dynamic, animated Chan style, he is also known as Kiangsi (Jap.: Kōsei), after the province where he taught. He was given the posthumous title, Zen Master Daji (Great Tranquillity). 1.5.n9; 1.8; 1.11; 1.13; 1.31; 1.50; 2.135.n40; 3.199.n23; 3.223.n58; 3.237; 3.241.n80; 4.258.n2; 4.270.n23; 4.277.n33; 4.277.n35; 4.292; 4.301.n92; 4.319; 4.323; 4.334.n154; 4.345.n168; 5.354; 5.370; 5.376; 6.424.n19; 6.451.n84; 6.453.n86; 6.453.n88; 7.491; 7.497.n60; 7.511.n86; 7.521.n105; 7.525; 8.IM6.n20; 8.DW2; 8.DW5; 8.DW9; 8.DW11.n107; 8.DW14; 9.31.n59; 9.38; 9.75; 9.78; 9.80; 9.82; 10.Jisan7.n26; 10.Jisan12.n31; 10.Jisan20.n46; 10.53.n97; 10.63.n105; 10.121.n171.

Menzan Zuihō [Jap.] (1683–1769). An important scholar in Sōtō Zen history, he wrote many books, including commentaries on Shōbōgenzō and a revision of Dōgen's biography, Kenzeiki. He also published editions of some of Dōgen's works, although contemporary Sōtō scholars consider that he added his own revisions to them. Intro; 5.363.n26; 9.73.n150; 10.19.n58; 10.21.n60.

Mingjiao Zhimen Shikuan (n.d.) [Ming-chiao Chi-men Shi-k'uan]. Meikyō Chimon Shikan. A successor of Yunmen, he was given the honorific name Mingjiao (Bright Teacher) by an emperor. 1.32.

Mingzhao Deqian (n.d.) [Ming-chao Te-ch'ien] Myoshō Tokken. He was a successor two generations after Yantou. 3.215.

Moshan Laoran (n.d.) [Mo-shan Lao-jan] Massan Ryōnen. A nun who was Dharma heir of Gao'an Dayu, one of Linji's teachers, she was a teacher of Linji's disciple Guanzhi Zhixian. 9.32.

Muzhou Daoming (780–877) [Mu-chou Tao-ming] Bokushū Dōmyō. A Dharma successor of Huangbo, he was head student when Linji arrived, and he encouraged Linji to persist in questioning Huangbo. 2.133; 3.208.

Myōan [Yōjō] **Eisai** [Jap.] (1141–1215). He traveled to China and became a successor in the Huanglong (Ōryu) branch of Rinzai Zen, which he introduced to Japan. He founded the Kenninji temple in Kyoto, where Dōgen practiced before, and just after, going to China. Dōgen, who as a young monk may have met Eisai, later spoke of him with great respect. His posthumous name from the emperor was Senkō (Thousand Lights). 6.441; 7.512; 10.42.n86.

Myōzen. See Butsuju Myōzen.

Nāgārjuna [Skt.; Jap.: Ryūju] (2nd–3rd cent.). A great early exponent of Mahāyāna Buddhism in India and especially of the Mādhyamika teaching, he minutely analyzed the implications of the śūnyatā (relativity or emptiness) doctrine. Nāgārjuna's teaching is so universally acclaimed that virtually all later Mahāyāna movements claim him as an ancestor; he is considered the fourteenth ancestor in the Zen lineage. 1.75.n158; 1.99.n199; 2.182.n141; 3.221.n55; 4.311.n112; 5.354.n9; 5.372.n38; 5.381.n59; 5.390.n88; 6.432.n40–41; 6.435.n48; 6.455.n93; 7.479.n17; 7.498; 7.516; 7.521.n107; 7.531; 8.FKZG.n149; 9.78.n165.

Nanda [Skt.] (6th cent. B.C.E.). Nanda was the half-brother of Śākyamuni (both were sons of King Śuddhodana). After Śākyamuni left home Nanda became the heir to the throne, but he later joined the Buddha's order and became an awakened arhat. 2.139.

Nanquan Puyuan (748–835) [Nan-ch'üan P'u-yüan] Nansen Fugan. A Dharma heir of Mazu and a teacher of the great Zhaozhou, Nanquan is featured in many kōans. He is known for his sickle, his love of cows, and for killing a cat. 1.12.n30; 1.13; 1.33.n82; 1.61; 1.74; 1.83.n177; 2.129; 2.148.n81; 2.156.n101; 2.161.n111; 2.170; 2.175; 4.267; 4.292; 4.309.n108; 4.340; 5.370; 5.376; 5.381.n65; 6.422; 6.438; 7.521.n105; 7.529; 8.DW3; 8.DW5.n76; 9.26; 9.61.n128; 9.63; 9.76; 9.79.n168; 9.81.

Nantang Daoxing (1065–1135) [Nan-t'ang Tao-hsing] Nandō Dōkō. He was a successor of Wuzu Fayan. 10.125.n179.

Nanyang Huizhong (d. 776) [Nan-yüan Hui-chung] Nan'yō Echū. A Dharma heir of the sixth ancestor who was designated national teacher, he received the posthumous title Dazheng (Great Realization). 1.1.n3; 1.17; 3.196; 3.237; 4.269; 4.302.n94; 4.314; 5.376; 6.452; 6.457; 8.DW13; 8.DW14.n132; 8.DW14; 9.27; 9.52.n104; 9.62; 10.Jisan10.n30.

Nanyuan Daoming (n.d.) [Nan-yüan Tao-ming] Nangen Dōmyō. A successor of Mazu. 8.DW13.

Nanyue Huairang (677–744) [Nan-yüeh Huai-jang] Nangaku Ejō. Nanyue was a successor of Huineng, the sixth ancestor, and the teacher of Mazu. He received the posthumous title Dahui (Great Wisdom). 1.3.n6; 1.11; 1.41.n101; 3.198; 3.200.n26; 3.207; 4.270.n23; 4.301.n92; 4.304; 4.345.n168; 5.374; 5.383; 5.411; 6.426.n26; 6.453.n86; 6.453.n88; 6.454.n90; 6.457.n100; 7.490; 7.491; 7.497; 7.499.n68; 8.IM2; 8.IM13; 8.IM17; 8.DW1.n61; 8.DW13; 8.FKZG.n150; 9.38; 9.59.

Niutou Fayong (594–657) [Niu-T'ou Fa-yung] Gozu Hōyū. A disciple of the fourth ancestor, Dayi Daoxin, Niutou was founder of the Oxhead school, which was popular in northern China for several generations. He was nicknamed "Lazy Fayong." 3.207; 4.313; 10.Jisan4.

Pangyun (d. 808) [P'ang-yün] Hō-on. This famous lay adept, known as Layman Pang, was a student of Mazu, Shitou, and Yaoshan, among others. His whole family were practitioners, and his daughter Lingzhao also is especially noted as an adept. 1.9.n17; 4.296.n79; 4.297.n81; 4.301.n92; 4.329.n145; 8.DW5.n79; 8.DW14.n131; 8.DW14; 9.9.n13.

Panshan Baoji (720–814) [P'an-shan Pao-chi] Banzan Hōshaku. He was a successor of Mazu and teacher of Puhua. 9.67.

Peixiu (797–870) [P'ei-hsiu] Haikyū. Prime minister and governor of several provinces, he was also a lay Chan adept who studied with many masters, including Guishan and Huangbo. Peixiu compiled Huangbo's Record, and arranged the building of Huangbo's temple. 8.DW14; 9.48.

Piṇḍola Bhāradvājā [Skt.; Jap.: Pinzuru] (n.d.). A disciple of Śākyamuni, and one of the sixteen arhats, he is depicted with long eyebrows. 7.530.

Prajñātāra. [Skt.; Jap.: Hannyatara] (n.d.). He is considered the twenty-seventh Indian ancestor in the Chan lineage, and the teacher of Bodhidharma. 1.20; 1.36.n90; 4.300.n89; 6.458.n102; 9.3; 10.Shinsan3.

Prasenajit [Skt.; Jap.: Hashinoku] (n.d.). King of Kosala and a patron of Śākyamuni, Prasenajit was killed by his son Virudhaka, who also conquered Śākyamuni's homeland, Kapilavastu. King Prasenajit's daughter became Queen Śrimālā, a Buddhist devotee about whom there is an important sutra. 7.530; 8.IM20.n56.

Puhua (9th cent.) [P'u-hua] Fuke. A disciple of Panshan Baoji and friend of Linji, Puhua was noted for eccentric behavior. He helped Linji establish his temple, but Linji's Recorded Sayings include many stories in which Puhua acts like a trickster, for example, knocking over the table at feasts provided by donors. The Japanese Fuke school, which includes playing shakuhachi music with meditation practice, is named for Puhua. 1.52.n122; 2.166.n121; 4.278.n37.

Punyayaśas [Skt.; Jap.: Funayasha] (n.d.). He is considered the eleventh Indian ancestor in the Zen lineage. 7.480.

Qingfeng Zhuanchu (9th cent.) [Ch'ing-fêng Chuan-ch'u] Seihō Denso. A successor of Yaopu Yuan'an, he was probably the teacher of Bao'en Xuanze before Fayan. 1.15.

Qingping Lingzun (845–919) [Ch'ing-p'ing Ling-tsun] Seihei Reijun. He was a successor of Cuiwei Wuxue. 9.36.

Qingqi Hongjin (n.d.) [Ch'ing-ch'i Hungchin] Seikei Koshin. He was a successor of Luohan Guichen and Dharma brother of Fayan Wenyi. 1.101.

Qingyuan Xingsi (d. 740) [Ch'ing-yüan Hsing-ssu] Seigen Gyōshi. One of the two main successors of the sixth ancestor along with Nanyue Huairang, Qingyuan was the teacher of Shitou. He received from the emperor the posthumous name Hongji (Broadly Saving). 2.148.n81; 2.166; 3.207; 3.212.n39; 3.241.n81; 3.244; 4.301.n92; 4.334; 5.383; 5.400.n110; 6.422.n15; 6.465; 6.468; 7.491; 7.497; 7.527.n121; 7.531; 8.IM2; 8.DW13; 9.18; 9.19; 9.49.

Ruhui. See Dongsi Ruhui.

Ryōnen [Jap.] (n.d.). She was a nun and early disciple of Dōgen at Kōshōji. Intro; 8.DW4; 8.DW9; 8.DW12.

Ryūzen [Jap.] (n.d.). A disciple of Eisai, he had been practicing in China when Dōgen arrived. Later he founded a temple on Mount Kōya. 10.42.

Śākyamuni [Skt.] (6th cent. B.C.E.). Śākyamuni, whose name means "Sage of the Śākya Clan," was the northern Indian prince Siddhārtha Gautama, who awakened and became the historical Buddha. He was the founder of Buddhism and the Buddhist order, and speaker of the sutras, or scriptures of Buddhism. Often referred to as the World-Honored One, he is considered to be the seventh Buddha of this age and world. 1.17.n48; 1.29; 1.30; 1.35; 1.37; 1.38.n96; 1.41.n99; 1.42; 1.44.n109; 1.46.n113; 1.52.n123; 1.61.n134; 1.64.n139; 1.75.n158; 1.79.n169; 1.81.n173; 1.88; 1.91.n191; 1.98; 1.99.n198,199; 1.102; 1.110.n220; 1.119.n229; 1.121; 2.132.n26,28; 2.135; 2.136; 2.138.n55; 2.139.n58; 2.143; 2.146; 2.149; 2.150; 2.151; 2.155; 2.163.n112; 2.165; 2.168; 2.171; 2.182;

2.183; 3.188.n6; 3.189.n8; 3.190.n11; 3.197; 3.198.n21; 3.204.n31; 3.207;
3.210; 3.213; 3.218; 3.225; 3.233; 3.236; 3.239; 3.240; 3.246.n94; 3.254;
3.256; 3.257; 4.262; 4.268.n20; 4.275; 4.278; 4.285; 4.289; 4.294.n67;
4.295; 4.310; 4.311; 4.315; 4.317.n120; 4.320; 4.334.n154; 5.349; 5.351.n5;
5.360; 5.367.n31; 5.372; 5.379; 5.381; 5.383; 5.386; 5.394; 5.397.n105; 5.399;
5.404; 5.406; 5.412; 6.414; 6.418; 6.427; 6.428; 6.430; 6.432; 6.437;
6.441.n65; 6.444; 6.445.n72; 6.446; 6.449; 6.451.n82; 6.470.n123;
7.471.n2; 7.472.n5; 7.473; 7.475; 7.477; 7.478; 7.479; 7.480; 7.482;
7.485; 7.486; 7.491; 7.494.n52; 7.495; 7.503; 7.506; 7.521; 7.524;
7.527.n121; 7.530; 8.IM2; 8.IM11; 8.IM13.n38; 8.IM20; 8.DW1; 8.DW2;
8.DW4; 8.DW5; 8.DW10; 8.DW11.n105; 8.DW11; 8.DW12; 8.FKZG;
9.1; 9.33; 10.Shinsan1; 10.Shinsan2; 10.7.n52; 10.23; 10.73; 10.76.n120;
10.88; 10.96; 10.103.n155; 10.112; 10.116.n169.

Śāṇavāsin [Skt.; Jap.: Shōnawashu] (n.d.). A disciple of Ānanda, he is considered the third Indian ancestor in the Zen tradition. He is said to have been born wearing a monk's robe. 4.278; 4.287; 5.380; 8.IM13.

Sanghānandi [Skt.; Jap.: Sōgyanandai] (d. 74 B.C.E.). A prince who abandoned kingship to become a monk, he is recognized as the seventeenth Indian ancestor in the Zen lineage. 4.283.n45; 5.386.n75.

Sanping Yizhong (781–872) [San-p'ing I-chung] Sanpei Gichū. A monk who faced Shigong Huizang's arrow, Sanping later became the Dharma heir of a successor of Shitou Xiqian. 4.277.n35; 8.IM3.n9.

Sansheng Huiran (n.d.) [San-sheng Hui-jan] Sanshō Enen. He was a successor of Linji. 3.220.n50.

Śāriputra [Skt.; Jap.: Sharishi] (6th cent. B.C.E.). One of the ten great disciples of Śākyamuni, he was especially noted for wisdom. 1.17.n48; 2.151; 4.271; 4.315; 5.381.

Sengzhao (374 or 385?–414) [Seng-chao] Sōjō. An eminent disciple of the great translator Kumārajīva, Sengzhao wrote important treatises on Mahāyāna teachings. His writings influenced Shitou and many other Chan teachers. 2.148; 7.482; 7.484; 7.501.n69.

Senne. See Yōkō Senne.

Shanglan Shun (n.d.) [Shang-lan Shun] Jōran Jun. He was a successor of Huanglong Huinan. 1.5.n9; 1.70.n153.

Shanku Huang. See Huangting Jian.

ied with him before meeting the sixth ancestor Huineng. 3.198; 5.374; 7.490; 8.IM13; 8.IM17; 8.DW1.n61; 9.16.n28; 9.59.

Śrivati [Skt.; Jap.: Fukuzō] (6th cent. B.C.E.). He was a wealthy student of Śākyamuni who became a monk when over a hundred years of age. Also known as Punyavadharna. 5.381.

Subhūti [Skt.; Jap.: Shubodai] (6th cent. B.C.E.). He was one of the ten great disciples of the Buddha, known especially for his understanding of emptiness. 2.134; 2.165; 10.Jisan20.

Su Dongpo (1037–1101) [Su Tong-p'o] Sotōba. Also known as Su Shih (Jap.: Soshoku), he was a famed poet who was also a high official and an adept Zen lay practitioner. 9.25.n46.

Sunita [Skt.] 6th cent. B.C.E.) A low-caste carrier of night soil, he became an adept disciple of Śākyamuni Buddha. 5.381.

Tenkei Denson [Jap.] (1648–1735). A brilliant medieval Sōtō commentator on Dōgen's writings, he criticized and corrected Dōgen's writings to accord with his own use of kōans directed toward *kenshō*, and with his nonsectarian approach to Zen. Intro.

Tettsū Gikai [Jap.] (1219–1309) A student of Dōgen, he later became a Dharma heir of Koun Ejō and the third abbot of Eiheiji. He traveled to China to study Chinese monastic architecture and forms and was the teacher of Keizan Jōkin. Intro; 1.91.n192; 1.111.n222; 3.185.n1.

Tianhuang Daowu (748–807) [T'ien-huang Tao-wu] Tennō Dōgo. He was a successor of Shitou and the teacher of Deshan, from whom the Yunmen and Fayan lineages descend. 1.22; 9.55.

Tiantai Zhiyi (538–597) [T'ien-t'ai Chih-I] Tendai Chigi. Author of the Great Treatise on Śamatha and Vipaśyanā Meditation (Ch.: Mohe Zhiguan; Jap.: Maha Shikan), he was founder of the Chinese Tiantai school, with its comprehensive synthesis of all Buddhist teachings. The Lotus Sutra was its foremost scripture. 2.151.n86; 4.274.n27; 4.322.n133; 5.390.n88; 5.402.n117; 5.412.n143; 6.446.n75; 6.446.n79; 7.479.n17.

Tiantong Hongzhi. See Hongzhi Zhengjue.

Tiantong Rujing (1163–1228) [T'ien-t'ung Ju-ching] Tendō Nyojō. He was Dōgen's teacher, with whom he practiced for three years at Mt. Tiantong in China, and from whom he received the Caodong/Sōtō lineage. Intro; 1.25.n58; 1.33.n81; 1.48; 1.105; 1.125.n241; 2.128; 2.135; 2.136; 2.145.n71-72; 2.147; 2.179; 2.184; 3.194; 3.247.n95; 3.249; 4.258.n4;

4.274; 4.276; 4.318; 4.319; 4.333.n152; 4.342; 5.348; 5.360.n21; 5.379; 5.383.n68; 5.384; 5.390; 5.394.n101; 5.401.n113: 5.412.n148; 6.424; 6.432; 6.437; 6.438; 6.469; 7.471.n1; 7.478.n16; 7.491.n43; 7.498.n63; 7.502; 7.503; 7.509.n83; 7.515; 7.522; 7.530.n131; 8.IM2; 8.IM17.n50; 9.58; 9.79.n169; 9.85; 9.86; 10.Jisan1; 10.Jisan6.n25; 10.Jisan9; 10.Jisan13.n34; 10.33.n76; 10.77.n123; 10.81; 10.83; 10.84; 10.88.n137.

Tiantong Zongjue (1091–1162) [T'ien-t'ung Chung-chüeh] Tendō Sogaku. Also known as Daxiu Zongjue (Jap.: Daikyū Sogaku), he was a noted poet and a successor of Zhenxie Qingliao, who was Dharma brother of Hongzhi Zhengjue. Tiantong Zongjue was head monk under Hongzhi, and in 1159, two years after Hongzhi died, succeeded to Hongzhi as abbot of Tiantong monastery (where Dōgen later trained). Tiantong Zongjue was in the lineage two generations before Dōgen's own teacher Tiantong Rujing. 10.Jisan1.

Tongan Daopi (n.d.) [T'ung-an Tao-p'i] Doan Dōhi. He was a successor of Dongshan Liangjie's successor Yunju Daoying. 2.145.

Touzi Datong (819–914) [T'ou-tzu Ta-t'ung] Tōsu Daidō. Touzi was a lineage successor two generations after Danxia Tianran, the student of Shitou who was famous for burning a buddha statue to warm himself. 3.191; 4.305; 4.313; 5.361; 6.426.n27; 8.DW2; 9.17; 9.54.

Touzi Yiqing (1032–1083) [T'ou-tzu Yi-ch'ing] Tōsu Gisei. Touzi Yiqing, a student of Fushan Fayuan who received from him the Sōtō lineage of Dayang, maintained that tradition while incorporating his prior Huayan studies. He was the teacher of Furong Daokai. 2.145.n71; 3.222.n57; 9.33; 9.57.

Upagupta [Skt.; Jap.: Ubakikuta] (ca. 3rd cent. B.C.E.). He was the fourth ancestor in the Indian lineage accepted in Zen. Upagupta was teacher of the great Buddhist ruler and patron Aśoka. 3.207; 4.287; 8.IM13.

Upāli [Skt.; Jap.: Upari] (6th cent. B.C.E.). One of Śākyamuni's ten great disciples, he was foremost in discipline, having remembered and recited the vinaya, 5.381.

Vasubandhu [Skt.; Jap.: Seshin] (5th cent.). A great Indian teacher and scholar monk, considered an ancestor in the Zen lineage, he wrote the Abhidharma Kośa commentary on early Buddhist psychology, or Abhidharma, and then was converted by his brother Asaṅga to Yogācāra teaching. Vasubandhu wrote many great Mahāyāna commentaries. 2.180; 3.243.n87; 4.321.n127; 4.322.n132; 5.372.n39; 5.390.n89; 5.412.n145.

Wansong Xingxiu (1166–1246) [Wan-sung Hsing-hsiu] Banshō Gyōshū. A Caodong/Sōtō lineage master, seven generations after Furong (his teacher was named Xueyuan), Wansong took Hongzhi's two collections of one hundred kōans, one with verse and one with Hongzhi's prose comments, and expanded them to form the Book of Serenity (Shōyōroku) and the Record of Further Inquiries anthologies, respectively. After serving as abbot of several monasteries by imperial appointment, he retired to Serenity hermitage, where he wrote the Book of Serenity. Intro; 1.52.n125.

Wolong Huiqiu (d. 913) [Woo-lung Hui-ch'iu] Garyū Ekyū. He was a successor of Xuansha. 9.37.

Wufeng Changguan (n.d.) [Wu-feng Ch'ang-kuan] Gohō Jōkan. He was a successor of Baizhang Huaihai. 2.164.

Wuwai Yiyuan (n.d.) [Wu-wei I-yüan] Mugai Gion. A disciple of Dōgen's teacher Tiantong Rujing, Wuwai Yiyuan sent Tiantong's Recorded Sayings to Dōgen, and he edited the Eihei Dōgen Zenji Goroku, an abridged selection from Eihei Kōroku, which had been brought to China by Kangan Giin. Intro; 1.48.n116.

Wuxie Lingmo (747–818) [Wu-hsieh Ling-mo] Gosetsu Reimoku. He was a successor of Mazu and also an early teacher of Dongshan Liangjie. 9.31.

Wuzhuo Wenxi (821–900) [Wu-cho Wên-hsi] Mujaku Bunki. He was a Dharma heir of Yangshan, known for his conversations with Mañjuśrī, the bodhisattva of wisdom. 2.138; 5.401.n115; 10.62.n102.

Wuzu Fayan (1024–1104) [Wu-tsu Fa-yen] Goso Hōen. Named for his temple site on Wuzu [Fifth Ancestor] Mountain where the fifth ancestor had taught, Wuzu was a successor of Haihui Shouduan, who was a successor of Yangqi. Known for his straightforward style, Wuzu was the teacher of Yuanwu Keqin (the compiler of the Blue Cliff Record) and of Foyan Qingyuan. 2.132; 2.167; 2.179; 6.469; 8.IM2; 9.66.n136; 9.75.n157.

Xiangyan Zhixian (d. 988) [Hsiang-yan Chih-hsien] Kyōgen Chikan. Xiangyan, a successor of Guishan, is famous for awakening with the sound of stone hitting bamboo while he was sweeping around the tomb of the national teacher Nanyang Huizhong. 1.17.n48; 4.285.n50; 5.352; 5.394.n100: 6.426.n24; 6.457; 8.DW2; 9.62; 9.87.

Xinghua Cunjiang (830–888) [Hsing-hua Ts'un-chiang] Kōke Sonshō. The Dharma heir of Linji from whom all the surviving Linji lineage derives, he compiled the Recorded Sayings of Linji. 3.234.n73.

Xitang Zhizang (735–814) [Hsi-t'ang Chih-tsang] Seidō Chizō. Xitang was a Dharma successor of Mazu. 1.13; 4.258; 7.521.n105; 9.53; 9.78.

Xuan Huaichang (12th cent.) [Hsu-an Huai-ch'ang] Koan Eshō. He was a successor in the Huanglong branch of Linji Chan and a teacher of Myōan Eisai, founder of Japanese Rinzai Zen. This connection to Xuan Huaichang may likely be the reason why Dōgen went to Tiantong monastery when he visited China, as Xuan had been an abbot of Tiantong monastery between Hongzhi Zhengjue and Dōgen's teacher Tiantong Rujing. 6.441.

Xuansha Shibei (835–908) [Hsüan-sha Shih-pei] Gensha Shibi. A successor of Xuefeng, Xuansha is celebrated by Dōgen for his statement "The entire universe is one bright pearl." 1.11.n25; 1.17; 1.17n45; 1.91.n191; 1.107; 2.132; 2.142.n62; 3.196; 3.199.n24; 3.216.n48; 3.223; 3.230; 3.241.n82; 4.289; 4.303.n95; 6.415; 6.458.n104; 7.521; 7.528.n125; 8.DW11.n113; 9.23; 9.29; 9.34; 9.37; 9.41; 9.72.

Xuedou Chongxian (980–1052) [Hsüeh-tou Ch'ung-hsien] Setchō Jūken. A master in the Yunmen lineage and a noted poet, his selection of one hundred cases with verse commentaries were the basis for the famous Blue Cliff Record (Ch.: Biyanlu; Jap.: Hekiganroku) kōan anthology. Intro; 1.17.n46; 3.196; 3.254; 5.394.n99; 8.IM2; 8.IM17.n50; 8.DW10.n97; 10.Jisan20.

Xuefeng Yicun (822–908) [Hsüeh-fêng I-tsun] Seppō Gison. After serving as *tenzo* at many temples, he finally became the heir of Deshan Xuanjian. Xuefeng was the teacher of Yunmen and was the third-generation ancestor of Fayan, founders of two of the five classical Chan lineages. 1.84; 2.135; 2.138; 2.159; 2.167; 3.199; 3.206; 3.220; 3.228.n66; 4.293.n66; 4.295; 5.401.n114; 5.408; 6.454; 6.469; 7.528; 8.DW2; 8.DW11.n110,n113; 9.15; 9.23; 9.29; 9.71; 10.Jisan20.

Yangqi Fanghui (992–1049) [Yang-ch'i Fang-hui] Yōgi Hōe. Yangqi was the founder of one of the two main branches of Linji (Rinzai) Zen; all modern Japanese Rinzai Zen derives from his lineage. He was a successor of Ciming [or Shishuang] Quyuan. 4.300.n88.

Yangshan Huiji (807–883) [Yang-shan Hui-chi] Gyōsan Ejaku. Student of Guishan, he is considered a co-founder of the Guiyang (Igyō) lineage, one of the classical five houses of Chan. Yangshan is sometimes said to have had prophetic talents, and he also used symbolic diagrams in his teaching. He was nicknamed "Little Śākyamuni." 1.17; 1.17.n45, 48; 1.30; 2.160; 2.162; 3.196; 4.273.n25; 5.394.n100; 9.40; 9.47; 9.66; 9.69.

Yanguan Qi'an (750–842) [Yen-kuan Ch'i-an] Enkan Seian. A successor of Mazu, he was given the title of national teacher. 5.358; 8.DW9.

Yantou Quanhuo (828–887) [Yen-t'ou Ch'üan-hue] Gantō Zenkatsu. A Dharma brother of Xuefeng and student of Deshan who became an accomplished master with six Dharma heirs, Yantou is known for an amazingly loud shout, heard for many miles, that he gave when he was killed by bandits. 3.192; 9.15; 9.30.

Yaoshan Weiyan (745–828) [Yao-shan Wei-yen] Yakusan Igen. A Dharma heir of Shitou, he also studied with Mazu. He was the teacher of Dongshan Liangjie's teacher Yunyan. His description of zazen as "beyond-thinking" *(hishiryō)* is much quoted by Dōgen. 2.128; 4.261.n9; 4.270.n23; 4.304; 5.373; 5.389.n87; 6.424.n18; 6.451.n84; 6.455; 6.465; 7.491; 7.492; 7.514.n93; 7.524; 8.IM2; 8.IM14; 8.IM15; 8.IM18; 8.DW2.n62; 8.DW8; 8.DW14; 8.FKZG.n147; 9.10; 9.20; 9.56.n113; 9.61; 10.53.n97; 10.121.n171,172.

Yinzong (627–713) [Yin-tsung] Inshū. He lectured on the Mahāparinirvāṇa Sūtra and also studied with the fifth ancestor, Daman Hongren. Later he gave ordination to the sixth ancestor, Dajian Huineng, and became one of his Dharma successors. 6.430.

Yōjō. See Myōan Eisai.

Yōkō Senne [Jap.] (n.d.). Early Sōtō writings state that Senne, one of Dōgen's main disciples, received Dharma transmission, as did Koun Ejō and Sōkai. Senne was the compiler of volume 1, most of volumes 9 and 10, and part of volume 8 of Eihei Kōroku. Senne's commentaries on Shōbōgenzō, written together with his own successor Kyōgō (who also had studied with Dōgen), remain important sources for understanding Dōgen's teachings. Intro; 1.88.n183; 1.105.n211; 1.111.n222; 2.127.n1; 9.10.n15,17; 9.25.n47; 10.1.n47; 10.51.n93; 10.78.n124.

Yongjia Xuanjie (675–713) [Yung-chia Hsüan-chieh] Yōka Genkaku. He was famous for becoming a successor to the sixth ancestor, Huineng, after spending only one night at his temple. Yongjia's Song of Enlightenment [or Verification] of the Way (Ch.: Zhengdaoke; Jap.: Shōdōka) remains a popular Zen text. 1.17; 1.17n45; 3.257.n117; 4.322.n130; 7.518.n101; 8.DW5; 10.123.n175.

Yongming Yanshou (904–975) [Yung-ming Yen-shou] Yōmyō Enju. A second-generation successor in the house of Fayan Wenyi, he is known for the True Mirror Source Collection (Ch.: Zongjinglu; Jap.: Sugyōroku), a voluminous collection of writings from a variety of sutras and Buddhist stories with his own commentaries. He was one of the first teachers to combine Zen and Pure Land practice. 5.386.n77.

Yuanwu Keqin (1063–1135) [Yüan-wu Kê-ch'in] Engo Kokugon. He was a Dharma heir of Wuzu Fayan and compiler of the Blue Cliff Record (Ch.: Biyanlu; Jap.: Hekiganroku) kōan collection based on Xuedou's verse comments. He was the teacher of Dahui. Intro; 1.74; 1.102.n209; 1.119.n230; 2.167; 2.179; 3.236.n77; 3.247.n98; 4.259; 4.324; 5.388; 5.408.n134; 6.469; 8.IM10.N30; 8.IM20.n56; 8.DW10.n97; 9.34.n67.

Yunfeng Wenyue (998–1062) [Yun-feng Wen-yüeh] Unpō Mon'etsu. He was a second-generation successor after Fenyang Shanzhao in the Linji lineage. 6.417.n6.

Yunju Daoying (d. 902) [Yün-chü Tao-ying] Ungo Dōyō. Yunju was the successor of Dongshan Liangjie whose lineage was transmitted to Dōgen. His posthumous name was Hongjue (Vast Awakening). 1.10; 1.21; 1.33; 1.38.n95; 1.61; 1.84; 4.273; 5.408; 7.497; 7.498; 8.IM2; 8.IM19; 8.FKZG.n146; 10.Jisan20.

Yunmen Wenyan (864–949) [Yun-mên Wên-yen] Unmon Bun'en. A Dharma successor of Xuefeng and founder of one of the five houses of Chan, he is famous for pithy responses to questions and is featured in many of the classical kōans. Intro; 1.32.n78; 1.69.n150; 1.88.n185; 1.89 1.108.n215; 1.123.n237; 2.133; 2.135; 2.138; 2.143; 2.159.n106; 2.165; 2.181; 3.189; 3.206; 3.207; 3.209; 3.217; 3.229.n69; 3.236; 3.252.n105; 4.259.n5; 4.262; 4.264.n12; 4.293.n66; 4.295.n70; 4.296; 4.310.n110; 4.345.n170; 5.401.n113; 6.416; 6.448; 7.495.n57; 7.503; 8.IM3.n9; 8.IM4.n10; 8.IM6; 8.DW10; 8.DW11; 10.13.n55; 10.85.n135.

Yunyan Tansheng (781–841) [Yün-yen T'an-shêng] Ungan Donjō. He was a Dharma heir of Yaoshan after serving twenty years as Baizhang's attendant without having realization, unlike his older biological brother, Daowu. Yunyan and Daowu both also studied with Baizhang and Yaoshan. Yunyan later was the teacher of Dongshan Liangjie, who honored Yunyan as his master before other, more famous teachers only because Yunyan "never directly explained anything" to Dongshan. 2.164; 3.200.n27; 4.258.n3; 4.277.n33; 4.279.n40; 4.304; 4.305.n101; 4.321.n127; 4.344; 6.452; 6.465.n117; 7.494; 7.497; 7.521; 8.IM1.n3; 8.IM2; 8.IM14; 8.IM18; 9.12; 9.20; 9.52; 9.61; 9.70.n143; 10.Jisan7.n28; 10.Jisan8.n29; 10.Jisan20.

Zhaozhou Congshen (778–897) [Chao-chou Ts'ung-shên] Jōshu Jūshin. A Dharma successor of Nanquan Puyuan, Zhaozhou is considered one of the all-time great Zen masters, and is source of many of the classic kōans, such as his responses to the question "Does a dog have Buddha nature?" His Dharma was so strong that no students were capable of matching and succeeding him, and his own lineage did not long survive. But he is revered in all subsequent Zen lineages. 1.5.n9; 1.12.n30; 1.17; 1.33; 1.64.n144; 1.70.n153; 1.74; 1.77.n161; 1.81.n175; 1.112; 2.128; 2.140; 2.144; 2.148.n81; 2.154; 2.159; 2.163.n114; 2.175; 3.196; 3.212.n41; 3.226; 3.231.n71; 3.245; 3.250; 4.295; 4.313.n114; 4.314; 4.330; 4.331; 4.339; 5.370; 5.377; 5.380; 5.391.n95; 5.400.n110; 5.410; 6.417; 6.426.n27; 6.428; 6.429; 6.433; 6.436; 6.438; 6.455; 7.477; 7.488; 7.499; 7.520; 7.522; 7.529; 8.IM5; 8.IM7; 8.IM9; 8.IM16; 8IM19.n55; 8.DW6.n85; 8.DW13.n126–127; 9.13; 9.21; 9.43; 9.45; 9.73; 9.76; 10.114.n165; 10.118.

Zhenxie Qingliao (1089–1151) [Chen-hsieh Ching-liao] Shinketsu Seiryō. The successor of Danxia Zichun from whom Dōgen's lineage descends, he was also known by his mountain name Changlu (Jap.: Chōrō). Zhenxie Qingliao was an older Dharma brother of Hongzhi Zhengjue, and Hongzhi served as head monk under Zhenxie. 3.256.n113; 9.90.

Zhimen Guangzuo (n.d.) [Chi-mon Kuang-chuo] Chimon Kōso. A successor in the Yunmen lineage, he was the teacher of Xuedou. 3.254.

Zhiyi. See Tiantai Zhiyi.

Zhuangzi (4th cent. B.C.E.) [Chuang-tzu] Soji. Highly venerated early Daoist philosopher and writer, he was known for his wit, colorful parables, and deep insight. 2.184.n147; 3.239.n79; 4.266.n14; 5.372.n40; 5.401.n111; 8.IM2.n4; 8.DW2.n66; 8.DW14.n133,141; 9.10.n18; 10.Jisan12.n32; 10.81.n128.

Zhuo'an Deguang (1121–1203) [Cho-an Tê-kuang] Setsuan Tokkō. A successor of Dahui Zonggao, he was an abbot of Ayuwang monastery. He was given the title Zen Master Fazhao (Buddha Illumination) by the emperor. Dainichi Nōnin, founder of the Japanese Daruma school prior to Dōgen, received transmission from him through emissaries. 8.DW10.

Zihu Lizong (800–880) [Tzu-hu Li-tsung] Shiko Rishō. A successor of Nanquan, he is known for challenging visitors to look at his dog. 4.293.

Ziyu Daotong (731–813) [Tzu-yu Tao-T'ung] Shigyoku Dōtsū. He was a successor of Mazu. 8.DW14.

Zongchi (n.d.) [Tsung-chi] Sōji. A nun who was one of the four main legendary disciples of Bodhidharma, Zongchi is described in some apocryphal legends as the daughter of Emperor Wu, whom Bodhidharma had encountered and departed from when he first came to China. 1.46; 5.384.n72.

NAMES OF CHINESE AND JAPANESE PERSONS in *Dōgen's Extensive Record* are given in alphabetical order, by their Chinese pinyin transliteration [in small capitals] and Japanese pronunciation for Chinese people, or just with Japanese transliteration for Japanese people, followed by Chinese characters for all names.

BAIZHANG HUAIHAI	Hyakujō Ekai	百丈懷海
BAIZHAO ZHIYUAN	Hakuchō Shien	白兆志圓
BAJIAO HUIQING	Bashō Esei	芭蕉慧清
BAO'EN XUANZE	Hōon Gensoku	報恩玄則
BAOFU CONGZHAN	Hofuku Jūten	保福從展
BAOJI [HUAYAN] XIUJING	Hōji [Kegon] Kyūjō	寶智[華厳]休静
BAOMING RENYONG	Honei Ninyū	保寧仁勇
	Bucchi Kakuan	佛地覺晏
BUDAI	Hotei	布袋
	Butsuju Myōzen	佛樹明全
CAOSHAN BENJI	Sōzan Honjaku	曹山本寂
CHANGQING DA'AN	Chōkei Daian	長慶大安
CHANGQING HUILING	Chōkei Eryō	長慶慧稜
CHANGSHA JINGCEN	Chōsa Keishin	長沙景岑
CHANGZI KUANG	Chōshi Kō	長髭曠
CHENGTIAN HUIYUN	Shōten E'un	承天慧運
CHINGLIANG ZHIMING	Seiryō Chimei	清涼智明
CHUANZI DECHENG	Sensu Tokujō	船子德誠
CIHANG FAPO	Jikō Ryōboku	慈航了朴
CIMING [SHISHUANG] QUYUAN	Jimyō [Sekisō] Soen	慈明[石霜]楚圓
CUIWEI WUXUE	Suibi Mugaku	翠微無學
DACI HUANZHONG	Daiji Kanchū	大慈寰中
DAHUI ZONGGAO	Daie Sōkō	大慧宗杲

	Dainichi Nōnin	大日能忍
DAJIAN HUINENG	Daikan Enō	大鑑慧能
DAMAN HONGREN	Daiman Kōnin	大満弘忍
DAMEI FACHANG	Daibai Hōjō	大梅法常
DANXIA TIANRAN	Tanka Tennen	丹霞天然
DANXIA ZICHUN	Tanka Shijun	丹霞子淳
DANYUAN YINGZHEN	Tangen Ōshin	耽源應真
DAOFU	Dōfuku	道副
DAOSHENG	Dōshō	道生
DAOWU YUANZHI	Dōgo Enchi	道吾圓智
DAOYU	Dōiku	道育
DAYANG QINGXUAN	Taiyō Kyōgen	太陽警玄
DAYI DAOXIN	Dai-I Dōshin	大医道信
DAZU HUIKE	Taiso Eka	太祖慧可
DAZUI FAZHEN	Daizui Hōshin	大随法真
DENG YINFENG	Tō Inbō	鄧隱峰
DESHAN XUANJIAN	Tokusan Senkan	徳山宣鑑
DONGAN CHANGCHA	Dōan Jōsatsu	同安常察
DONGSHAN LIANGJIE	Tōzan Ryōkai	洞山良价
DONGSHAN SHOUCHU	Tōzan Shusho	洞山守初
DONGSI RUHUI	Tōji Nyo-e	東寺如會
EHU DAYI	Gako Daigi	鷲湖大義
EHU ZHIFU	Gako Chifu	鷲湖智孚
	Eihei Dōgen	永平道元
	Enni Ben'en	圓爾辨圓
FACHANG YIYU	Hōshō Igu	法昌倚遇
FAYAN WENYI	Hōgen Mon'eki	法眼文益
FENGXIAN DAOSHEN	Hōsen Dōshin	奉先道深
FENGXUE YANZHAO	Fūketsu Enshō	風穴延昭
FENYANG SHANZHAO	Funyō Zenshō	汾陽善昭
FOYAN QINGYUAN	Butsugen Seion	佛眼清遠
FU DASHI	Fu Daishi	傅大士
FURONG [DAYANG] DAOKAI	Fuyo [Taiyō] Dōkai	芙蓉[太陽]道楷
FUSHAN FAYUAN	Fusan Hōen	浮山法遠
FUXIAN RENJIAN	Fukusen Ninken	福先仁俭
FUXING FATAI	Busshō Hōtai	仏性法泰
GAO	Kō	高

Gao'an Dayu	Kō'an Daigu	高安大愚
	Gien	義演
	Gijun	義準
Guangzhou Zhidao	Kōshū Shidō	広州志道
Guanzhi Zhixian	Kankei Shikan	灌渓志閑
Guifeng Zongmi	Keihō Shūmitsu	圭峰宗密
Guishan Lingyou	Isan Reiyū	潙山霊祐
Guizong Danquan	Kisū Tangon	歸宗澹権
Guizong Daoquan	Kisū Dōsen	歸宗道詮
Guizong Huichao	Kisū Echō	歸宗慧超
Guizong Zhichang	Kisū Chijō	歸宗智常
	Gyōyū	行勇
Haihui [Baiyun] Shouduan	Kai'e [Haku'un] Shutan	海會[白雲]守端
Hangzhou Duofu	Kōshū Tafuku	杭州多福
Hangzhou Tianlong	Kōshu Tenryū	杭州天龍
Hanshan	Kanzan	寒山
	Hatano Yoshishige	波多野義重
Heshan Wuyin	Kasan Muin	禾山無殷
Hongzhi Zhengjue	Wanshi Shōgaku	宏智正覺
Hongzhou Shuiliao	Kōshū Suirō	洪州水潦
Huangbo Xiyun	Ōbaku Kiun	黄檗希運
Huanglong Huinan	Ōryu E'nan	黄龍慧南
[Huanglong] Huitang Zuxin	[Ōryu] Maidō Soshin	[黄龍]晦堂祖心
[Huanglong] Sixin Wuxin	[Ōryu] Shishin Goshin	[黄龍]死心悟新
Huangting Jian	Kōtei Ken	黄庭堅
Huguo Shoucheng Jingguo	Gokoku Shuchō Jōka	護国守澄浄果
Jianyuan Zhongxing	Zengen Chūkō	漸源仲興
Jianzhi Sengcan	Kanchi Sōsan	鑑智僧璨
Jiashan Shanhui	Kassan Zenne	夾山善會
Jingqi Zhanran	Keikei Tan'en	荊渓湛然
Jingqing Daofu	Kyōsei Dōfu	鏡清道
Jingshan Daoqin	Kinzan Dōkin	径山道欣
Jingzhao Mihu	Keichō Beiko	京兆米胡
Jinhua Juzhi	Kinka Gutei	金華倶胝
Jiyuan	Jakuen	寂圓
Juefan Huihong	Kakuhan Ekō	覺範慧洪
Kaixian Shanxian	Kaisen Zensen	開先善暹

	Kakuzen Ekan	覺禅懐鑑
	Kangan Giin	寒巖義尹
	Keizan Jōkin	瑩山紹瑾
	Koun Ejō	孤雲懐奘
	Kyōgō	経豪
LANGYE HUIJUE	Rōya Ekaku	瑯瑘慧覺
LAOZI	Rōshi	老子
LINGYUN ZHIQIN	Reiun Shigon	靈雲志勤
LINGZHAO	Reishō	靈照
LINJI YIXUAN	Rinzai Gigen	臨済義玄
LONGJI SHAOXIU	Ryūsai Shōshu	龍済紹修
LONGSHAN	Ryūzan	龍山
LONGTAN CHONGXIN	Ryōtan Sōshin	龍潭崇信
LONGYA JUDUN	Ryūge Koton	龍牙居遁
LUOHAN DIZANG GUICHEN	Rakan Jizō Keichin	羅漢[地蔵]桂琛
LUOPU YUANAN	Rakuho Gen'an	洛浦元安
LUZU BAOYUN	Roso Hōun	魯祖寶雲
	Manzan Dōhaku	卍山道白
MAZU DAOYI	Baso Dōitsu	馬祖道一
	Menzan Zuihō	面山瑞方
MINGJIAO ZHIMEN SHIKUAN	Meikyō Chimon Shika	明教[智門]師寛
MINGZHAO DEQIAN	Myoshō Tokken	明招徳謙
MOSHAN LAORAN	Massan Ryōnen	末山了然
MUZHOU DAOMING	Bokushū Dōmyō	睦州道明
	Myōan [Yōjō] Eisai	明庵[葉上]栄西
NANQUAN PUYUAN	Nansen Fugan	南泉普願
NANTANG DAOXING	Nandō Dōkō	南堂道興
NANYANG HUIZHONG	Nan'yō Echū	南陽慧忠
NANYUAN DAOMING	Nangen Dōmyō	南源道明
NANYUE HUAIRANG	Nangaku Ejō	南嶽懐讓
NIUTOU FAYONG	Gozu Hōyū	牛頭法融
PANGYUN	Hō-on	龐薀
PANSHAN BAOJI	Banzan Hōshaku	盤山寶積
PEIXIU	Haikyū	裴休
PUHUA	Fuke	普化
QINGFENG ZHUANCHU	Seihō Denso	青峰伝楚
QINGPING LINGZUN	Seihei Reijun	清平令遵

Qingqi Hongjin	Seikei Kōshin	清溪洪進
Qingyuan Xingsi	Seigen Gyōshi	青原行思
	Ryonen	了然
	Ryūzen	隆禅
Sanping Yizhong	Sanpei Gichū	三平義忠
Sansheng Huiran	Sanshō Enen	三聖慧然
Sengzhao	Sōjō	僧肇
Shanglan Shun	Jōran Jun	上藍順
Shexian Guisheng	Sekken Kishō or Kissei	葉県歸省
Shigong Huizang	Sekkyō Ezō	石鞏慧蔵
Shimen Huiche	Sekimon Etetsu	石門慧徹
Shishuang Qingzhu	Sekisō Keisho	石霜慶諸
Shitou Xiqian	Sekitō Kisen	石頭希遷
Shoushan Xingnian	Shusan Shōnen	首山省念
Sikung Benjing	Shikū Honjō	司空本浄
	Sōkai	僧海
Songshan Hui'an	Sūzan E'an	嵩山慧安
Su Dongpo	Sotōba	蘇東坡
	Tenkei Denson	天桂伝尊
	Tettsū Gikai	徹通義介
Tianhuang Daowu	Tennō Dōgo	天皇道悟
Tiantai Zhiyi	Tendai Chigi	天台智顗
Tiantong Rujing	Tendō Nyojō	天童如浄
Tiantong Zongjue	Tendō Sogaku	天童宗珏
Tongan Daopi	Doan Dōhi	同安道丕
Touzi Datong	Tōsu Daidō	投子大同
Touzi Yiqing	Tōsu Gisei	投子義青
Wansong Xingxiu	Banshō Gyōshū	万松行秀
Wolong Huiqiu	Garyū Ekyū	臥龍慧球
Wufeng Changguan	Gohō Jōkan	五峰常観
Wuwai Yiyuan	Mugai Gion	無外義遠
Wuxie Lingmo	Gosetsu Reimoku	五洩霊黙
Wuzhuo Wenxi	Mujaku Bunki	無著聞喜
Wuzu Fayan	Goso Hōen	五祖法演
Xiangyan Zhixian	Kyōgen Chikan	香厳智閑
Xinghua Cunjiang	Kōke Sonshō	興化存奨
Xitang Zhizang	Seidō Chizō	西堂智堂

Xuan Huaichang	Koan Eshō	虛庵懷敞
Xuansha Shibei	Gensha Shibi	玄沙師備
Xuedou Chongxian	Setchō Jūken	雪竇重顯
Xuefeng Yicun	Seppō Gison	雪峰義存
Yangqi Fanghui	Yōgi Hōe	楊岐方會
Yangshan Huiji	Gyōsan Ejaku	仰山慧寂
Yanguan Qian	Enkan Seian	塩官斎安
Yantou Quanhuo	Gantō Zenkatsu	巌頭全豁
Yaoshan Weiyan	Yakusan Igen	薬山惟儼
Yinzong	Inshū	印宗
	Yōkō Senne	永興詮慧
Yongjia Xuanjie	Yōka Genkaku	永嘉玄覺
Yongming Yanshou	Yōmyō Enju	永明延壽
Yuanwu Keqin	Engo Kokugon	圓悟克勤
Yunfeng Wenyue	Unpō Mon'etsu	雲峰文悦
Yunju Daoying	Ungo Dōyō	雲居道膺
Yunmen Wenyan	Unmon Bun'en	雲門文偃
Yunyan Tansheng	Ungan Donjō	雲巌曇晟
Zhaozhou Congshen	Jōshu Jūshin	趙州從諗
Zhenxie Qingliao	Shinketsu Seiryō	真歇清了
Zhimen Guangzuo	Chimon Kōso	智門光祚
Zhuangzi	Soji	莊子
Zhuo'an Deguang	Setsuan Tokkō	拙庵德光
Zihu Lizong	Shiko Rishō	子湖利蹤
Ziyu Daotong	Shigyoku Dōtsū	紫玉道通
Zongchi	Sōji	總持

INDEX OF TRANSLATORS' NAMES
OF DHARMA HALL DISCOURSES

Works in Chinese

Dachuan Puji, ed. *Wu Deng Hui Yuan* (Five Lamps Merged in the Source; Jap.: Gotō Egen). 1252. Taipei: Guang Wen Bookstore, 1971.

Daoyuan, ed. *Jingde Chuandeng Lu* (Jingde Transmission of the Lamp; Jap.: Keitoku Dentōroku). 1004. In *Taishō Shinshū Daizōkyō*, vol. 51, pp. 196–467. Tokyo: Taishō Issaikyō Kankokai, 1924–33.

Hongzhi Chan Shi Guang Lu (Extensive Record of Chan Master Hongzhi). In *Taishō Shinshū Daizōkyō*, no. 2001, vol. 48, pp. 73–78, 98–100. Tokyo: Taishō Issaikyō Kankokai, 1924–33.

Lao-Tzu: "My Words Are Very Easy to Understand": Lectures on the "Tao Teh Ching" by Man-jan Cheng. Original Chinese with translation by Tam C. Gibbs. Richmond, Calif.: North Atlantic Books, 1981.

Yuan Chi, ed. *Xu Chuan Deng Lu* (Later Record of the Transmission of the Lamp). 14th century. In *Taishō Shinshū Daizōkyō*, no. 2077, vol. 51, p. 579. Tokyo: Taishō Issaikyō Kankokai, 1924–33.

Works in Japanese and Chinese

Ishii Seijun. "Dōgen Zenji no Sōdan ni Taisuru Ishiki ni Tsuite; Setsuji no Haikei to Shite." In Ishii Shūdō et al., eds., *Dōgen Shisō Taikei*, vol. 4. Kyoto: Dōhōsha Shuppan, 1995.

———, ed. "Shōbōgenzō Zuimonki, Eihei Kōroku to Dōgen Zen." In Ishii Shūdō et al., eds.,*Dōgen Shisō Taikei*, vol. 10. Kyoto: Dōhōsha Shuppan, 1995.

Itō Shūken. *Dōgen Zen Kenkyū*. Tokyo: Daizō Shuppan, 1998.

Itō Shunkō. *Eihei Kōroku Chūkai Zenshō*. 4 vols. Tokyo: Kōmeisha, 1962.

Kagamishima Genryū. *Dōgen Zenji Goroku.* Tokyo: Kōdansha, 1990.

———. *Genbun-taishō Gendaigoyaku Dōgen Zenji Zenshū.* Vols. 10–13. Tokyo: Shunjūsha, 1999.

Kasuga Yūhō. *Shinshaku Eihei Kōroku.* Tokyo: Perikansha, 1998.

Kikuchi Ryōichi. *Dōgen no Kanshi Eihei Kōroku Shishō.* Ashikaga: Ashikaga Kōgyō Daigaku, 2000.

Ōkubo Dōshū. *Dōgen Zenji Zenshū.* Vol. 2. Tokyo: Chikuma Shobō, 1970.

Ōtani Tetsuo. *Dōgen Zenji Oriori no Hōwa—Eihei Kōroku ni Manabu.* Tokyo: Sōtō Shū Shūmuchō, 1999.

———. *Manzanbon Eihei Kōroku Sozanbon-taikō.* Tokyo: Ichihosha, 1991.

Sawaki Kōdō. *Dōgen Zen Sankyū.* Tokyo: Chikuma Shobō, 1976.

Shinohara Hisao. *Eihei Kōroku.* Tokyo: Daitō Shuppansha, 1993.

Terada Tōru. *Nihon-no-Zengoroku.* Vol. 2, *Dōgen.* Tokyo: Kōdansha, 1981.

Watanabe Kenshū and Ōtani Tetsuo. *Sozanbon Eihei Kōroku Kōchū-shūsei.* 2 vols. Tokyo: Ichihosha, 1992.

Yokoi Yūhō. *Gendaigoyaku Eihei Kōroku.* Tokyo: Sankibō Busshorin, 1978.

Zengaku Daijiten Hensansho. *Zengaku Daijiten.* Tokyo: Daishūkan Shoten, 1978.

Works in English

Abe, Masao. *A Study of Dōgen: His Philosophy and Religion.* Albany: State University of New York Press, 1992.

Abé, Ryūichi. *The Weaving of Mantra: Kūkai and the Construction of Esoteric Buddhist Discourse.* New York: Columbia University Press, 1999.

Abé, Ryūichi, and Peter Haskell, trans. *Great Fool: Zen Master Ryōkan: Poems, Letters and Other Writings.* Honolulu: University of Hawai'i Press, 1996.

Adolphson, Mikael. *The Gates of Power: Monks, Courtiers, and Warriors in Premodern Japan.* Honolulu: University of Hawai'i Press, 2000.

Aitken, Robert, trans. *The Gateless Barrier: The Wu-men Kuan (Mumonkan).* Berkeley: North Point Press, 1990.

Anacker, Stefan. *Seven Works of Vasubandhu: The Buddhist Psychological Doctor.* Delhi: Motilal Banarsidass, 1984.

Anderson, Reb. *Being Upright: Zen Meditation and the Bodhisattva Precepts.* Berkeley: Rodmell Press, 2001.

———. *Warm Smiles from Cold Mountains: Dharma Talks on Zen Meditation.* Berkeley: Rodmell Press, 1999.

App, Urs. *Master Yunmen: From the Record of the Chan Teacher "Gate of the Clouds."* New York: Kodansha International, 1994.

Bielefeldt, Carl. *Dōgen's Manuals of Zen Meditation.* Berkeley: University of California Press, 1988.

Birnbaum, Raoul. *The Healing Buddha.* Rev. ed. Boston: Shambhala, 1989.

Blofeld, John. *The Zen Teaching of Huang Po: On the Transmission of Mind.* New York: Grove Press, 1958.

Bodiford, William M. *Sōtō Zen in Medieval Japan.* Honolulu: Kuroda Institute, University of Hawai'i Press, 1993.

Buddhist Text Translation Society. *Buddha Speaks the Brahma Net Sutra: The Ten Major and Forty-eight Minor Bodhisattva Precepts.* Trans. Bhikshuni Heng Tao. Talmage, Calif.: Dharma Realm Buddhist University, 1982.

Chang Chung-Yuan, trans. *Original Teachings of Ch'an Buddhism: Selected from "Transmission from the Lamp."* New York: Vintage Books, 1968.

Chang, Garma C. C. *The Buddhist Teaching of Totality: The Philosophy of Hwa Yen Buddhism.* University Park: Pennsylvania State University Press, 1971.

———. *The Practice of Zen.* New York: Perennial Library, 1959.

———, ed. *A Treasury of Mahāyāna Sūtras: Selections from the Mahāratnakūta Sūtra.* University Park: Pennsylvania State University Press, 1983.

Chien, Cheng Bhikshu, trans. *Manifestation of the Tathāgata: Buddhahood According to the Avataṃsaka Sūtra.* Boston: Wisdom Publications, 1993.

———. *Sun Face Buddha: The Teachings of Ma-tsu and the Hung-chou School of Ch'an.* Berkeley: Asian Humanities Press, 1992.

Chih-hsu Ou-I. *The Buddhist I Ching.* Trans. Thomas Cleary. Boston: Shambhala, 1987.

Cleary, J. C., trans. *Swampland Flowers: The Letters and Lectures of Zen Master Ta Hui.* New York: Grove Press, 1977.

———, trans. and ed. *Zen Dawn: Early Zen Texts from Tun Huang.* Boston: Shambhala, 1986.

Cleary, J. C., and Thomas Cleary, trans. *Zen Letters: Teachings of Yuanwu.* Boston: Shambhala, 1994.

Cleary, Thomas, trans. *The Book of Serenity.* Hudson, N.Y.: Lindisfarne Press, 1990; Boston: Shambhala, 1998.

———. *Buddhist Yoga: A Comprehensive Course.* Boston: Shambhala, 1995.

———. *Entry into the Inconceivable: An Introduction to Hua Yen Buddhism.* Honolulu: University of Hawai'i Press, 1983.

———. *Entry into the Realm of Reality: A Translation of the Gandavyuha, the Final Book of the Avatamsaka Sutra.* Boston: Shambhala, 1987.

———. *Entry into the Realm of Reality, the Guide: A Commentary on the "Gandhavyuha" by Li Tongxuan.* Boston: Shambhala, 1989.

———. *The Five Houses of Zen.* Boston: Shambhala, 1997.

———. *The Flower Ornament Scripture: A Translation of the Avatamsaka Sutra.* Boston: Shambhala, 1984.

———. *Minding Mind: A Course in Basic Meditation.* Boston: Shambhala, 1995.

———. *The Original Face: An Anthology of Rinzai Zen.* New York: Grove Press, 1978.

———. *Rational Zen: The Mind of Dōgen Zenji.* Boston: Shambhala, 1993.

———. *Record of Things Heard: The "Shōbōgenzō Zuimonki," Talks of Zen Master Dōgen as Recorded by Zen Master Ejō.* Boulder, Colo.: Prajñā Press, 1980.

———. *Sayings and Doings of Pai-chang: Ch'an Master of Great Wisdom.* Los Angeles: Center Publications, 1978.

———. *Secrets of the Blue Cliff Record: Zen Comments by Hakuin and Tenkei.* Boston: Shambhala, 2000.

———. *Shōbōgenzō: Zen Essays by Dōgen.* Honolulu: University of Hawai'i Press, 1986.

———. *Stopping and Seeing: A Comprehensive Course in Buddhist Meditation by Chih-I.* Boston: Shambhala, 1997.

———. *The Sutra of Hui-neng: With Hui-neng's Commentary on the Diamond Sutra.* Boston: Shambhala, 1998.

———. *Timeless Spring: A Sōtō Zen Anthology.* Tokyo: Weatherhill, 1980.

————. *Transmission of Light: Zen in the Art of Enlightenment by Zen Master Keizan.* San Francisco: North Point Press, 1990.

————. *Unlocking the Zen Kōan, A New Translation of the Wumenguan.* Berkeley: North Atlantic Books, 1997. (Originally published as *No Barrier: Unlocking the Zen Kōan, A New Translation of the Wumenguan.* New York: Bantam Books, 1993.)

Cleary, Thomas, and J. C. Cleary, trans. *The Blue Cliff Record.* Boulder: Prajñā Press, 1978. [Page citations in the notes are from this first edition in one volume, which has the same pagination as the Shambhala 1977 edition in 3 volumes. A later one-volume edition from Shambhala, 1992, differs in pagination. Case numbers in the citations do not vary between editions.]

Collcutt, Martin. *Five Mountains: The Rinzai Zen Monastic Institution in Medieval Japan.* Cambridge: Council on East Asian Studies, Harvard University Press, 1981.

Conze, Edward, trans. *The Perfection of Wisdom in Eight Thousand Lines and Its Verse Summary.* Bolinas, Calif.: Four Seasons Foundation, 1973.

Cook, Francis. *How to Raise an Ox: Zen Practice As Taught in Zen Master Dōgen's "Shōbōgenzō."* Boston: Wisdom Publications, 2002.

————, trans. *The Record of Transmitting the Light: Zen Master Keizan's Denkōroku.* Boston: Wisdom Publications, 2003.

————. *Sounds of Valley Streams: Enlightenment in Dōgen's Zen.* Albany: State University of New York Press, 1989.

Donner, Neal, and Daniel Stevenson. *The Great Calming and Contemplation: A Study and Annotated Translation of the First Chapter of Chih-I's Mo-Ho Chih-Kuan.* Honolulu: Kuroda Institute, University of Hawai'i Press, 1993.

Dumoulin, Heinrich. *Zen Buddhism: A History.* Trans. James W. Heisig and Paul Knitter. 2 vols. New York: Macmillan, 1990.

Ebrey, Patricia Buckley, and Peter N. Gregory, eds. *Religion and Society in T'ang and Sung China.* Honolulu: University of Hawai'i Press, 1993.

Eidmann, Phillip Karl, trans., *The Sutra of the Teaching Left by Buddha.* Osaka: Koyata Yamamoto, 1952.

Faure, Bernard. "The Daruma-shu, Dōgen, and Sōtō Zen" *Monumenta Nipponica* 42, no. 1 (spring 1987).

————. *Visions of Power: Imagining Medieval Japanese Buddhism.* Princeton: Princeton University Press, 1996.

Ferguson, Andy. *Zen's Chinese Heritage: The Masters and Their Teachings.* Boston: Wisdom Publications, 2000.

Foster, Nelson, and Jack Shoemaker, eds. *The Roaring Stream: A New Zen Reader.* Hopewell, N.J.: Ecco Press, 1996.

Gimello, Robert M., and Peter N. Gregory, eds. *Studies in Ch'an and Hua Yen.* Honolulu: Kuroda Institute, University of Hawai'i Press, 1983.

Grant, Beata. *Mount Lu Revisited: Buddhism in the Life and Writings of Su Shih.* Honolulu: University of Hawai'i Press, 1994.

Green, James, trans. *The Recorded Sayings of Zen Master Joshu.* Boston: Shambhala, 1998.

Gregory, Peter. *Tsung-mi and the Sinification of Buddhism.* Honolulu: Kuroda Institute, University of Hawai'i Press, 2002.

————, ed. *Traditions of Meditation in Chinese Buddhism.* Honolulu: Kuroda Institute, University of Hawai'i Press, 1986.

Gregory, Peter, and Daniel Getz, Jr., eds. *Buddhism in the Sung.* Honolulu: Kuroda Institute, University of Hawai'i Press, 1999.

Groner, Paul. *Saichō: The Establishment of the Japanese Tendai School.* Berkeley: Berkeley Buddhist Study Series, 1984.

Hakeda, Yoshito S., trans. *The Awakening of Faith; Attributed to Aśvaghosha.* New York: Columbia University Press, 1967.

————. *Kūkai: Major Works.* New York: Columbia University Press, 1972.

Hamill, Sam, and J. P. Seaton, trans. *The Essential Chuang Tzu.* Boston: Shambhala, 1999.

Heine, Steven. *A Blade of Grass: Japanese Poetry and Aesthetics in Dōgen Zen.* New York: Peter Lang, 1989.

————. *Dōgen and the Kōan Tradition: A Tale of Two "Shōbōgenzō" Texts.* Albany: State University of New York Press, 1994.

————. "The Dōgen Canon: Dōgen's Pre-Shōbōgenzō Writings and the Question of Change in His Later Works." *Japanese Journal of Religious Studies* 24, nos. 1–2 (spring 1997).

————. "Dōgen Casts Off 'What': An Analysis of Shinjin Datsuraku." *Journal of the International Association of Buddhist Studies* 9, no. 1 (1986).

————. *Existential and Ontological Dimensions of Time in Heidegger and Dōgen.* Albany: State University of New York Press, 1985.

————. "Kōans in the Dōgen Tradition: How Dōgen Does What He Does with Kōans." *Philosophy East and West* 52, no. 2 (2004).

————. *Shifting Shape, Shaping Text: Philosophy and Folklore in the Fox Kōan.* Honolulu: University of Hawai'i Press, 1999.

————. *The Zen Poetry of Dōgen: Verses from the Mountain of Eternal Peace.* Boston: Tuttle, 1997.

Heine, Steven, and Dale Wright, eds. *The Kōan: Texts and Contexts in Zen Buddhism.* Oxford: Oxford University Press, 2000.

Hirakawa Akira. *A History of Indian Buddhism: From Śakyamuni to Early Mahāyāna.* Trans. and ed. Paul Groner. Honolulu: University of Hawai'i Press, 1990.

Hori, Victor. "Kōan and Kenshō in the Rinzai Zen Curriculum." In Steven Heine and Dale Wright, eds., *The Kōan: Texts and Contexts in Zen Buddhism.* Oxford: Oxford University Press, 2000.

Hurvitz, Leon, trans. *Scripture of the Lotus Blossom of the Fine Dharma.* New York: Columbia University Press, 1976.

Ishigami, Zenno, ed. *Disciples of the Buddha.* Trans. by Richard Gage and Paul McCarthy. Tokyo: Kōsei, 1989.

Jaffe, Paul, trans. *Flowers of Emptiness: Dōgen's Genjōkōan with Commentary by Yasutani Roshi.* Boston: Shambhala, 1997.

Kalupahana, David. *The Principles of Buddhist Psychology.* Albany: State University of New York Press, 1987.

Kasahara, Kazuo, ed. *A History of Japanese Religion.* Trans. Paul McCarthy and Gaynor Sekkimori. Tokyo: Kōsei, 2001.

Kashiwahara, Yūsen, and Kōyū Sonoda, eds. *Shapers of Japanese Buddhism.* Trans. Gaynor Sekimori. Tokyo: Kōsei, 1994.

Kasulis, Thomas P. *Zen Action / Zen Person.* Honolulu: University of Hawai'i Press, 1981.

Katagiri, Dainin. *Returning to Silence, Zen Practice in Daily Life*. Boston: Shambhala, 1988.

Katō, Bunnō, Yoshirō Tamura, and Kōjirō Miyasaka, trans. *The Threefold Lotus Sutra: Innumerable Meanings, The Lotus Flower of the Wonderful Law, and Meditation on the Bodhisattva Universal Virtue*. New York: Weatherhill, 1975.

Kato, Kazumitsu. *Lin-chi and the Record of His Sayings*. Nagoya: Nagoya University of Foreign Studies, 1994.

Khoroche, Peter, trans. *Once the Buddha Was a Monkey: Ārya Śūra's Jātakamala*. Chicago: University of Chicago Press, 1989.

Kim, Hee Jin. *Eihei Dōgen: Mystical Realist*. Boston: Wisdom Publicatons, 2004. (Originally published as *Dōgen Kigen—Mystical Realist*. Tucson: University of Arizona Press, 1975.)

————, trans. *Flowers of Emptiness: Selections from Dōgen's "Shōbōgenzō."* Lewiston, N.Y.: Edwin Mellen Press, 1985.

King, Sallie B. *Buddha Nature*. Albany: State University of New York Press, 1991.

Kōdera, Takashi James. *Dōgen's Formative Years in China: An Historical Study and Annotated Translation of the "Hōkyō-ki."* Boulder: Prajñā Press, 1980.

————. "Ta Hui Tsung-Kao (1089–1163) and His 'Introspecting the Kung-An Ch'an (Kōan Zen).'" *Ohio Journal of Religious Studies* 6, no. 1 (1978).

Kubo, Tsugunari, and Akira Yuyama. *The Lotus Sutra*. Berkeley: Numata Center for Buddhist Translation and Research, 1993.

LaFleur, William, ed. *Dōgen Studies*. Honolulu: Kuroda Institute, University of Hawai'i Press, 1985.

————. *The Karma of Words: Buddhism and the Literary Arts in Medieval Japan*. Berkeley: University of California Press, 1983.

Lamotte, Étienne. *Śūraṃgamasamādhisūtra: The Concentration of Heroic Progress: An Early Mahāyāna Buddhist Scripture*. Trans. Sara Boin-Webb. Richmond, England: Curzon Press, 1998.

La Vallee Poussin, Louis de, trans. *Abhidharmakośabhāṣyam*. Trans. Leo M. Pruden. 4 vols. Berkeley: Asian Humanities Press, 1988.

Leighton, Taigen Dan. "Being Time through Deep Time." *Kyoto Journal*, no. 20 (1992).

————. *Faces of Compassion: Classic Bodhisattva Archetypes and Their Modern Expressions*. Rev. ed. Boston: Wisdom Publications, 2003. (Originally published as *Bodhisattva Archetypes: Classic Buddhist Guides to Awakening and Their Modern Expressions*. New York: Penguin Arkana, 1998.)

————. "Sacred Fools and Monastic Rules: Zen Rule-Bending and the Training for Pure Hearts." In Bruno Barnhart and Joseph Wong, eds., *Purity of Heart and Contemplation: A Monastic Dialogue between Christian and Asian Traditions*. New York: Continuum, 2001.

Leighton, Taigen Daniel, and Shohaku Okumura, trans. *Dōgen's Pure Standards for the Zen Community: A Translation of Eihei Shingi*. Albany: State University of New York Press, 1996.

Leighton, Taigen Daniel, with Yi Wu, trans. *Cultivating the Empty Field: The Silent Illumination of Zen Master Hongzhi*. Rev. ed. Boston: Tuttle, 2000.

Liebenthal, Walter. *Chao Lun: The Treatises of Seng-chao*. Hong Kong: Hong Kong University Press, 1968.

Loori, John Daido, ed. *The Art of Just Sitting: Essential Writings on the Zen Practice of Shikantaza*. Boston: Wisdom Publications, 2002.

————. *Two Arrows Meeting in Mid-Air: The Zen Koan*. Boston: Tuttle, 1994.

Lopez, Donald, ed. *Buddhist Hermeneutics*. Honolulu: University of Hawai'i Press, 1988.

Lu K'uan Yu. *The Secrets of Chinese Meditation*. New York: Samuel Weiser, 1964.

Masunaga, Reihō. *A Primer of Sōtō Zen: A Translation of Dōgen's Shōbōgenzō Zuimonki*. Honolulu: University of Hawai'i Press, 1978.

Matsunaga, Alicia. *The Buddhist Philosophy of Assimilation: The Historical Development of the Honji-Suijaku Theory*. Tokyo: Tuttle, 1969.

Matsunaga, Daigan, and Alicia Matsunaga. *Foundation of Japanese Buddhism*. 2 vols. Los Angeles: Buddhist Books International, 1976.

McGreal, Ian, ed. *Great Thinkers of the Eastern World*. New York: HarperCollins, 1995.

McMahan, David. *Empty Vision: Metaphor and Visionary Imagery in Mahāyāna Buddhism*. London: RoutledgeCurzon, 2002.

Miura, Isshu, and Ruth Fuller Sasaki. *Zen Dust: The History of the Kōan and Kōan Study in Rinzai (Lin-chi) Zen*. New York: Harcourt, Brace, and World, 1966.

(Later republished, although without the voluminously comprehensive and invaluable footnotes, as *The Zen Kōan: Its History and Use in Rinzai Zen.*)

Mizuno, Kōgen. *Buddhist Sutras: Origin, Development, Transmission.* Tokyo: Kōsei, 1982.

———. *Essentials of Buddhism: Basic Terminology and Concepts of Buddhist Philosophy and Practice.* Tokyo: Kōsei, 1996.

Morrell, Robert. *Early Kamakura Buddhism: A Minority Report.* Berkeley: Asian Humanities Press, 1987.

Muller, Charles, trans. *The Sutra of Perfect Enlightenment.* Albany: State University of New York Press, 1999.

Nagao, Gadjin. *Mādhyamika and Yogācāra.* Trans. Leslie Kawamura. Albany: State University of New York Press, 1989.

Ñāṇamoli, Bhikku, and Bhikku Bodhi, trans. *The Middle Length Discourses of the Buddha: A Translation of the Majjhima Nikāya.* Rev. ed. Boston: Wisdom Publications, 2001.

Nearman, Hubert, trans. *Buddhist Writings on Meditation and Daily Practice: The Serene Reflection Meditation Tradition.* Mount Shasta, Calif.: Shasta Abbey Press, 1994.

Nhat Hanh, Thich. *Breathe! You Are Alive: Sutra on the Full Awareness of Breathing.* Berkeley: Parallax Press, 1996.

Nishijima, Gudo. *Master Dogen's Shinji Shobogenzo.* Woods Hole, Mass.: Windbell Publications, 2003.

Nishijima, Gudo Wafu, and Chodo Cross. *Master Dogen's Shobogenzo.* 4 vols. Woods Hole, Mass.: Windbell Publications, 1994–99.

Nyanaponika Thera and Helmuth Hecker. *Great Disciples of the Buddha: Their Lives, Their Works, Their Legacy.* Boston: Wisdom Publications, 1997.

Ogata, Sohaku, trans. *The Transmission of the Lamp, Early Masters: Compiled by Tao Yuan, a Ch'an Monk of the Sung Dynasty.* Durango, Colo.: Longwood Academic, 1990.

Okumura, Shohaku, trans. and ed. *Dōgen Zen.* Kyoto: Kyoto Sōtō Zen Center, 1988.

———, ed. *Dōgen Zen and Its Relevance for Our Times: An International Symposium Held in Celebration of the 800th Anniversary of the Birth of Dōgen Zenji.* San Francisco: Sōtō Zen Buddhism International Center, 2003.

———. *Shikantaza: An Introduction to Zazen.* Kyoto: Kyoto Sōtō Zen Center, 1985.

———, trans. *"Shōbōgenzō-Zuimonki," Sayings of Eihei Dōgen Zenji Recorded by Koun Ejō.* Kyoto: Kyoto Sōtō Zen Center, 1987.

———. *Sōtō Zen: An Introduction to Zazen.* Tokyo: Sōtō Shū Shūmuchō, 2002.

Okumura, Shohaku, and Taigen Daniel Leighton, trans. *The Wholehearted Way: A Translation of Eihei Dōgen's Bendōwa with Commentary by Kōshō Uchiyama Roshi.* Boston: Tuttle, 1997.

Okumura, Shohaku, and Thomas Wright, trans. *Opening the Hand of Thought.* New York: Arkana; Viking Penguin, 1994.

Payne, Richard, ed. *Re-Visioning Kamakura Buddhism.* Honolulu: University of Hawai'i Press, 1998.

Powell, William F., trans. *The Record of Tung Shan.* Honolulu: Kuroda Institute, University of Hawai'i Press, 1986.

Powers, John, trans. *Wisdom of Buddha: The Saṁdhinirmocana Mahāyāna Sūtra.* Berkeley: Dharma Publishing, 1995.

Price, A. F., and Wong Mou-Lam, trans. *The Diamond Sutra and The Sutra of Hui Neng.* Berkeley: Shambhala, 1969.

Red Pine, trans. *The Zen Teaching of Bodhidharma.* San Francisco: North Point Press, 1989.

Reeves, Gene, ed. *A Buddhist Kaleidoscope: Essays on the Lotus Sutra.* Tokyo: Kōsei, 2002.

Reps, Paul, and Nyogen Senzaki. *Zen Flesh Zen Bones: A Collection of Zen and Pre-Zen Writings.* Garden City, N.Y.: Doubleday Anchor Books.

Robinson, Richard. *Early Mādhyamika in India and China.* Madison: University of Wisconsin Press, 1967.

Sadakata, Akira. *Buddhist Cosmology: Philosophy and Origins.* Tokyo: Kōsei, 1997.

Sangharakshita. *The Eternal Legacy: An Introduction to the Canonical Literature of Buddhism.* London: Tharpa Publications, 1985.

Sasaki, Ruth Fuller, Yoshitaka Iriya, and Dana R. Fraser, trans. *The Recorded Sayings of Layman P'ang: A Ninth-Century Zen Classic.* New York: Weatherhill, 1971.

Saso, Michael. *Zen Is for Everyone: The Xiao Zhi Guan Text by Zhi Yi.* Carmel, Calif.: New Life Center, 2000.

Sato, Shunmyo. *Two Moons: Short Zen Stories.* Trans. Rev. and Mrs. Shugen Komagata and Daniel Itto Bailey. Honolulu: Hawaii Hochi, 1981.

Saunders, Dale. *Mudrā: A Study of Symbolic Gestures in Japanese Buddhist Sculpture.* Princeton: Princeton University Press, 1960.

Schloegl, Irmgard, trans. *The Zen Teaching of Rinzai.* Berkeley: Shambhala, 1976.

Sheng-Yen, trans. and ed. *Complete Enlightenment: Translation and Commentary on the Sutra of Complete Enlightenment.* Boston: Shambhala, 1999.

———, trans. and ed. *The Poetry of Enlightenment: Poems by Ancient Ch'an Masters.* Elmhurst, N.Y.: Dharma Drum Publications, 1987.

Shibayama, Zenkei. *The Gateless Barrier: Zen Comments on the Mumonkan.* Boston: Shambhala, 2000.

Snyder, Gary. *Mountains and Rivers without End.* Washington, D.C.: Counterpoint, 1996.

———. *The Practice of the Wild.* New York: North Point Press, 1990.

Stambaugh, Joan. *Impermanence Is Buddha-Nature: Dōgen's Understanding of Temporality.* Honolulu: University of Hawai'i Press, 1990.

Stevens, John. *Three Zen Masters: Ikkyū, Hakuin, Ryōkan.* Tokyo: Kodansha International, 1993.

Stevenson, Dan. "Silent Illumination Ch'an." *Ch'an Magazine* 2, no. 5 (1981).

Stone, Jacqueline. *Original Enlightenment and the Transformation of Medieval Japanese Buddhism.* Honolulu: University of Hawai'i Press, 1999.

Suzuki, D. T., trans. *The Laṅkāvatāra Sūtra: A Mahāyāna Text.* London: Routledge & Kegan Paul, 1932.

———. *Manual of Zen Buddhism.* New York: Grove Press, 1960.

Suzuki, Shunryu. *Branching Streams Flow in the Dark: Zen Talks on Sandokai.* Berkeley: University of California Press, 1999.

———. *Not Always So: Practicing the True Spirit of Zen.* New York: HarperCollins, 2002.

———. *Zen Mind, Beginner's Mind.* New York: Weatherhill, 1970.

Swanson, Paul. *Foundations of T'ien-T'ai Philosophy.* Berkeley: Asian Humanities Press, 1989.

Tanabe, George J., Jr. *Myōe the Dreamkeeper: Fantasy and Knowledge in Early Kamakura Buddhism.* Cambridge: Harvard University Press, 1992.

———, ed. *Religions of Japan in Practice.* Princeton: Princeton University Press, 1999.

Tanabe, George J., Jr. and Willa Tanabe. *The Lotus Sutra in Japanese Culture.* Honolulu: University of Hawai'i Press, 1989.

Tanahashi, Kazuaki, ed. and trans. *Beyond Thinking: Meditation Guide by Zen Master Dōgen.* Boston: Shambhala, 2004.

———. *Enlightenment Unfolds: Life and Work of Zen Master Dōgen.* Boston: Shambhala, 1998.

———, ed. and trans. *Moon in a Dewdrop: Writings of Zen Master Dōgen.* San Francisco: North Point Press, 1985.

Tanahashi, Kazuaki, and Tensho David Schneider, eds. *Essential Zen.* San Francisco: Harper, 1994.

Thurman, Robert A. F., trans. *The Holy Teachings of Vimalakīrti: A Mahāyāna Scripture.* University Park: Pennsylvania State University Press, 1976.

———, trans. *The Tibetan Book of the Dead.* New York: Bantam Books, 1994.

Verdu, Alfonso. *Dialectical Aspects in Buddhist Thought: Studies in Sino-Japanese Mahāyāna Idealism.* Lawrence: Center for East Asian Studies, University of Kansas, 1974.

Waddell, Norman, and Masao Abe, trans. *The Heart of Dōgen's Shōbōgenzō.* Albany: State University of New York Press, 2002.

Walshe, Maurice, trans. *Thus Have I Heard: The Long Discourses of the Buddha; Dīgha Nikāya.* London: Wisdom Publications, 1987.

Warner, Jisho, Shohaku Okumura, John McRae, and Taigen Dan Leighton, eds. *Nothing Is Hidden: Essays on Zen Master Dōgen's Instructions for the Cook.* New York: Weatherhill, 2001.

Warren, Henry C., trans. *Buddhism in Translation.* Cambridge: Harvard University Press, 1922. (Originally published 1896.)

Watson, Burton, trans. *The Complete Works of Chuang Tzu.* New York: Columbia University Press, 1968.

———. *Han Fei Tzu: Basic Writings.* New York: Columbia University Press, 1969.

———. *The Lotus Sutra.* New York: Columbia University Press, 1993.

————. *Ryōkan: Zen Monk-Poet of Japan.* New York: Columbia University Press, 1977.

————. *Su Tung-p'o: Selections from a Sung Dynasty Poet.* New York: Columbia University Press, 1965

————. *The Vimalakirti Sutra.* New York: Columbia University Press, 1997.

————. *The Zen Teachings of Master Lin-Chi.* Boston: Shambhala, 1993.

Wayman, Alex, and Hideko Wayman, trans. *The Lion's Roar of Queen Śrīmālā.* New York: Columbia University Press, 1974.

Wilhelm, Richard, trans., *The I Ching or Book of Changes.* Rendered into English by Cary Baynes. Princeton: Princeton University Press, 1967.

Williams, Paul. *Mahāyāna Buddhism: The Doctrinal Foundations.* London: Routledge, 1989.

Willis, Janice Dean. *On Knowing Reality: The* Tattvārtha *Chapter of Asaṅga's* Bodhisattvabhūmi. New York: Columbia University Press, 1979.

Wright, Thomas, trans. *Refining Your Life: From Zen Kitchen to Enlightenment, by Zen Master Dōgen and Kōshō Uchiyama.* New York: Weatherhill, 1983.

Wu, John C. H. *The Golden Age of Zen.* Taipei: United Publishing Center, 1975.

Wu, Yi, trans. *The Book of Lao Tzu.* San Francisco: Great Learning Publishing, 1989.

————. *Chinese Philosophical Terms.* Lanham, Md.: University Press of America, 1986.

————. *The Mind of Chinese Ch'an (Zen): The Ch'an School Masters and Their Kung-ans.* San Francisco: Great Learning Publishing, 1989.

Yamada, Kōun, trans. *Gateless Gate.* Los Angeles: Center Publications, 1979.

Yampolsky, Philip B., trans. *The Platform Sutra of the Sixth Patriarch.* New York: Columbia University Press, 1967.

Yifa. *The Origins of Buddhist Monastic Codes in China: An Annotated Translation and Study of the Chanyuan Qinggui.* Honolulu: University of Hawai'i Press, 2002.

Yokoi, Yūhō, trans. *The Eihei Kōroku.* Tokyo: Sankibo Buddhist Bookstore, 1987.

Yokoi, Yūhō, and Daizen Victoria, trans. *Zen Master Dōgen: An Introduction with Selected Writings.* Tokyo: Weatherhill, 1976.

ABOUT THE TRANSLATORS

TAIGEN DAN LEIGHTON is a Sōtō Zen priest and Dharma successor in the lineage of Shunryu Suzuki Roshi and the San Francisco Zen Center. Leighton began formal Sōtō practice and everyday zazen in 1975 at the New York Zen Center with Kando Nakajima Roshi, and graduated in East Asian Studies from Columbia College. Leighton was ordained in 1986 and received Dharma Transmission in 2000 from Reb Anderson Roshi. Leighton also practiced for two years in Japan, and he is currently Dharma Teacher of the Mountain Source Sangha meditation groups, based in the San Francisco Bay Area. He is author of *Faces of Compassion: Classic Bodhisattva Archetypes and Their Modern Expression,* and is co-translator and editor of several Zen texts, including *Cultivating the Empty Field: The Silent Illumination of Zen Master Hongzhi,* as well as *The Wholehearted Way: A Translation of Eihei Dōgen's Bendōwa with Commentary by Kōshō Uchiyama Roshi* and *Dōgen's Pure Standards for the Zen Community: A Translation of Eihei Shingi,* both translated together with Shohaku Okumura. Leighton is also a co-translator of collections of Dōgen's writings: *Moon in a Dewdrop, Enlightenment Unfolds* and *Beyond Thinking.* He teaches at the Institute of Buddhist Studies of the Berkeley Graduate Theological Union, and has taught at several other universities.

SHOHAKU OKUMURA is an ordained priest and Dharma successor of Kōshō Uchiyama Roshi in the lineage of Kōdō Sawaki Roshi. He is a graduate of Komazawa University and has practiced at Antaiji, Zuioji, and the Kyoto Sōtō Zen Center in Japan, and the Pioneer Valley Zendo in Massachusetts. More recently Okumura was the head teacher of the Minnesota Zen Meditation Center, and then Director of the Sōtō Zen Buddhism International Center in San Francisco. His previously published books of translation include *Shikan Taza: An Introduction to Zazen; "Shōbōgenzō Zuimonki": Sayings of Eihei Dōgen Zenji; Dōgen Zen; Zen Teachings of 'Homeless' Kōdō; Opening the Hands of Thought; The Wholehearted Way: A Translation of Eihei Dōgen's Bendōwa with Commentary by Kōshō Uchiyama Roshi;* and *Dōgen's Pure Standards for the Zen Community: A*

Translation of Eihei Shingi. Okumura is also editor of *Dōgen Zen and Its Relevance for Our Time;* and *Sōtō Zen: An Introduction to Zazen.* He is the founding teacher of the Sanshin Zen Community, based in Bloomington, Indiana, where he lives with his family.

WISDOM PUBLICATIONS, a nonprofit publisher, is dedicated to making available authentic Buddhist works for the benefit of all. We publish translations of the sutras and tantras, commentaries and teachings of past and contemporary Buddhist masters, and original works by the world's leading Buddhist scholars. We publish our titles with the appreciation of Buddhism as a living philosophy and with the special commitment to preserve and transmit important works from all the major Buddhist traditions.

To learn more about Wisdom, or to browse books online, visit our website at wisdompubs.org.

You may request a copy of our mail-order catalog online or by writing to:

Wisdom Publications
199 Elm Street
Somerville, Massachusetts 02144 USA
Telephone: (617) 776-7416
Fax: (617) 776-7841
Email: info@wisdompubs.org
www.wisdompubs.org

THE WISDOM TRUST

As a nonprofit publisher, Wisdom is dedicated to the publication of fine Dharma books for the benefit of all sentient beings and dependent upon the kindness and generosity of sponsors in order to do so. If you would like to make a donation to Wisdom, please do so through our Somerville office. If you would like to sponsor the publication of a book, please write or email us at the address above.

Thank you.

Wisdom is a nonprofit, charitable 501(c)(3) organization affiliated with the Foundation for the Preservation of the Mahayana Tradition (FPMT).